KINGDOM NEW TESTAMENT

A CONTEMPORARY TRANSLATION

N. T. Wright

HarperOne

An Imprint of HarperCollinsPublishers

HarperOne

HarperCollins books may be purchased for educational, business, or sales promotional use. For information, please e-mail the Special Markets Department at SPsales@harpercollins.com.

HarperCollins website: http://www.harpercollins.com
HarperCollins®, 📚®, and HarperOne™ are trademarks of HarperCollins Publishers.

Maps by Pantek Arts Ltd., Maidstone, Kent, UK.

FIRST HARPERCOLLINS PAPERBACK EDITION PUBLISHED IN 2012

Library of Congress Cataloging-in-Publication Data
    Bible. N. T. English. Wright. 2011.
      The Kingdom New Testament : a contemporary translation /
    by N. T. Wright. — 1st ed.
      p. cm.
      Translated from the original Greek text.
      ISBN 978-0-06-206492-9
      I. Wright, N. T. (Nicholas Thomas)   II. Title.
    BS2095.W68   2011
    225.5'209—dc23   2011017199

17 18 19 RRD(H) 10 9 8 7 6 5

For

Maggie

and

Julian, Rosamund, Harriet, and Oliver

Contents

List of Maps   ix
Preface   xi

Matthew   1
Mark   66
Luke   106
John   171
The Acts of the Apostles   225
Romans   311
1 Corinthians   339
2 Corinthians   365
Galatians   382
Ephesians   391
Philippians   401
Colossians   408
1 Thessalonians   415
2 Thessalonians   421
1 Timothy   425
2 Timothy   432
Titus   437
Philemon   440
Hebrews   442
James   463
1 Peter   470
2 Peter   478
1 John   483
2 John   490
3 John   492
Judah   494
The Revelation of John   497

Maps

Galilee, Samaria, and Judaea in the
    First Century AD   xviii
The Eastern Mediterranean in the
    First Century AD   224
Acts 1:6–8   226
Acts 2:5–13   228
Acts 3:1–16   232
Acts 6:9   239
Acts 8:4–25   244
Acts 8:26–40   246
Acts 9:1–9   247
Acts 9:19–26, 30   249
Acts 9:32, 35, 36   250
Acts 10:1–16   251
Acts 11:19–30   256
Acts 12:20–25   258
Acts 13:1–6   259
Acts 13:13–25   260
Acts 13:51   263
Acts 14:1–7   264
Acts 14:21–28   266
Acts 15:1–11   267
Acts 15:39–41   269
Acts 16:1–10   270
Acts 16:11–12   271
Acts 17:1   274
Acts 17:10–21   274
Acts 18:1   277
Acts 18:18–28   279
Acts 19:1–10   281

Acts 20:1–12   284
Acts 20:13–27   285
Acts 21:1–14   287
Acts 21:15–17   289
Acts 23:23–35   295
Acts 27:1–12   302
Acts 27:13–32   304
Acts 28:11–22   307
The Destinations of Paul's Letters   310
1 Peter 1:1   471
The Seven Churches of Asia   499

Preface

The first thing that happened in the life of the church was *translation*. On the day of Pentecost, God's powerful wind swept through Jesus's followers, filling them, like the sails of a great oceangoing sailing ship, so that they could take God's good news to the ends of the earth. And they found themselves speaking other languages, so that everyone in the crowd could understand.

Part of the point of Jesus's message, after all, is that it's about God coming to people where they are, not sitting back sternly and waiting for them to come to him. Not for nothing does John call Jesus "the *word* of God." There's no point speaking a word that nobody can understand.

So, right from the start, they translated. Sometimes it happened, as at Pentecost, by the direct action of the holy spirit. Mostly, though, it was through people eagerly turning the message into other languages. Much of the time, Jesus himself spoke Aramaic, an updated dialect of Hebrew, but the gospels were written in Greek. Greek was everybody's second language at the time, a bit like English in many parts of our world today. So, since the message was designed to be good news for everyone, not just native speakers of one language, it was important to translate it. Once begun, the process continued.

It took fifteen hundred years for the whole Bible to appear in English, but once that had happened—particularly through the work of one of my lifelong heroes, William Tyndale (d. 1536)—the idea caught on quickly. Several translations appeared during the sixteenth century, culminating in the King James ("Authorized") Version at the start of the seventeenth.

And in the twentieth century, too, there have been several new
English versions. Some have been quite strict translations, almost word for word; others have been paraphrases, trying to
convey the message in a looser, less formal way.

Two questions, then. Is this new version really a translation, or a paraphrase? And why do we need yet another one?

It's a translation, not a paraphrase. I have tried to stick
closely to the original. But, as with all translations, even
within closely related modern European languages, there are
always going to be places where you simply can't do it word by
word. To do so would be "correct" at one level and deeply in-
correct at another. There is no "safe" option: all translation is
risky, but it's a risk we have to take.

This is particularly so when the language in question is, in
the technical sense, "dead." Nobody today speaks first-century
Greek, so we can't simply phone a native speaker and ask what
is meant by a particular phrase. Even if we could do so, there's
no guarantee that the person we called would necessarily understand all that a New Testament writer has put into a word,
phrase, or sentence. The New Testament, after all, is telling a
story which is deeply rooted in the ancient scriptures of Israel. Often its key technical terms mean something more like
their equivalents in Hebrew than their regular usage in secu-
lar, non-Christian Greek.

Greek often goes quite easily into English, but not always.
A couple of examples may help, one about little words and one
about big ones.

Greek often uses little words to join sentences together;
English often makes do with punctuation. (That last sentence
is a good example: I could have written "*but* English often
makes do with punctuation," but the semicolon does the job
more elegantly.) St. Paul, in particular, uses the little word *gar*
a great deal to connect his sentences, and English versions
often translate it as "for" in the sense of "because." But people
today don't often use the word "for" in that way. It sounds formal and stilted, especially if you repeat it over and over as Paul
does. People don't say it much in conversation, and a lot of the
New Testament is more like conversation than like a great lit-
erary work. So, on various occasions, I have done it differently.

"If by the Spirit you put to death the deeds of the body, you will live," writes Paul in Romans 8:13–14 in the New Revised Standard Version translation, "*for* all who are led by the Spirit of God are children of God." I decided, instead of that "for," to put in the colloquial English "you see": "all who are led by the spirit of God, *you see,* are God's children." Or, sometimes, I have linked the two points by asking a question and answering it: "There is no condemnation for those who are in the Messiah, Jesus! *Why not? Because* the law of the spirit of life in the Messiah, Jesus, released you from the law of sin and death" (Romans 8:1–2). That "Why not? Because . . ." is how I'd say it, if I were Paul giving a lecture.

Or take the bigger words. Some of the great New Testament words are like ships loaded with several different kinds of cargo, and we simply haven't got words that can carry all that freight today. Thus, for instance, the English word "righteousness" has been a technical term in theology for many years, and has often been used to translate the Greek *dikaiosyne.* But for many English speakers today it means *self-*righteousness: it's become a proud, "churchy" sort of word. So what are the alternatives? We simply haven't got them. We want a word that can pack "justice," "covenant faithfulness," and "right standing or relationship" all into the same hold, and can set off, with this cargo safely on board, to sail around the world. There isn't such a word. So I have done my best to bring out the different flavor which *dikaiosyne* seems to carry in this or that passage. I have done the same with *Christos:* most translations simply say "Christ," but most modern English speakers assume that that word is simply a proper name (as though "Jesus" were Jesus's "Christian" name and "Christ" were his "surname"). For all sorts of reasons, I disagree; so I have experimented not only with "Messiah" (which is what the word literally means) but sometimes, too, with "King." These experiments are risky. But they also present a glorious opportunity.

It's an opportunity (here is the answer to the second question, why yet another translation?) because translating the New Testament is something that, in fact, each generation ought to be doing. This is a special, peculiar, and exciting point about the very nature of Christian faith. Just as Jesus taught us to pray for our *daily* bread, our bread for each day, we can never simply live on yesterday's bread, on the interpretations and translations of previous generations. To be sure, we can and must learn from those who have gone before us in the faith. But they themselves would tell us that living faith requires that we do business with God for ourselves. Inherited spiritual capital may help to get you started, but you need to do fresh work for yourself, to think things through, to struggle and pray and ponder and try things out. And a new translation, as carefully faithful as it ought to be but also as open to new possibilities as it needs to be, is a key tool for that larger task.

There are two ways to use a tool like this. First, it's good to read right through chapters, sections, and entire books at a single sitting. The "books" which make up the New Testament weren't written to be read in ten-verse sections at a time; imagine what would happen if you tried to listen to a symphony that way, or to read a novel at the rate of a single page once a week. I hope this present translation will make it easier for people to do this, to feel the flow and pull, the energy and power, of large chunks at a time.

But, second, it's always worth sitting down with a short passage and studying it intensely, trying to work out precisely what is meant by each sentence, each phrase, each word. And for that (even if you know Greek itself, but especially if you don't) you should always have at least two English translations open in front of you. No one translation—certainly not this one—will be able to give you everything that was there in the Greek. But I hope this one will take its place as one of the two or three that will help the next generation to do its own homework, to acquire its own firsthand, rather than secondhand, understanding of what the New Testament said in its own world, and what it urgently wants to say in ours.

That sense of urgency, indeed, has pushed me into a less formal and academic, and a more deliberately energetic, style. Most of the New Testament isn't "great literature" in terms of the high standards of the day. Mark's gospel is more like a revolutionary tract; Paul's letters, though capable of poetic brilliance, often seem to reflect the kind of animated discussion you might have after a lecture in a crowded room. Again, it has seemed to me more important to convey that sense of excitement than to imitate the more formal, somewhat stately English prose we know from the traditions of the King James or Revised Standard Versions, good in their way though they have been.

This has affected all kinds of decisions: for instance, how to reproduce Jesus's discussions and debates. We simply don't say, in today's English, "Jesus answered and said to them, 'Go and tell John what you have seen and heard.'" As with a novel, we'd be much more likely to say, "'Go and tell John,' replied Jesus, 'what you've seen and heard.'" So that's how I've done it. I think it makes quite a difference as to how we hear, and feel, the whole story.

In particular, this translation was made originally to accompany a series of "guides" or popular commentaries on the New Testament. This series (Matthew for Everyone and the rest) was itself designed for people who would never normally read a "biblical commentary," but who just wanted some help to get into the text for themselves. People like that might well have been confused if I'd always been saying, "Well, the RSV says this, the NIV says that, but I'm telling you something different." I wanted to comment on a text without having to make that kind of remark all the time. Equally, as with all translations ever made, I have taken a particular view on point after point of interpretation, and my understanding of the many controversial passages in the New Testament shows up, naturally enough, in the translation as well.

A couple of final comments. First, all translations of the New Testament depend on other people's work in producing editions of the Greek New Testament from the literally thousands of manuscripts that have survived from the first few centuries. From time to time, I have had to make tricky decisions about which text to follow, but in a work of this sort I haven't wanted to distract the reader by inserting notes saying, "Other ancient authorities say . . ." For that you will have to look elsewhere. In the same way, sometimes whole verses were added to biblical manuscripts, often by scribes who remembered (say) the equivalent passage in Mark to the one they were transcribing from Matthew, or vice versa. Thus, for instance, Matthew 6:15 has crept into some manuscripts of Mark 11, creating an extra verse (26). Modern editions leave these "extra" verses out, because they aren't there in the best and earliest manuscripts. But occasionally this means that the verse-numbering has to skip, since the numbering was done several centuries ago, before these much better manuscripts turned up. Again, translations which include footnotes will make this clear. There are two extra "endings" for Mark's gospel. They are not found in the best manuscripts. Most likely the original version was damaged; this often happened to scrolls. (Some think Mark intended to stop with 16:8, but I consider this less likely.) Then, some time later, two copyists decided to add "endings" to round the story off, and these found their way into the manuscript tradition. The shorter of the two endings (printed in double square brackets) doesn't have a verse number. The second is known as Mark 16:9–20.

Finally, I have tried to use gender-neutral language throughout when referring to human beings. Sometimes this has been, to put it mildly, quite difficult. I have often had to use what some people regard as an ugly and ungrammatical form, saying "they" rather than "he or she." This is a classic example of what happens when a language is going through a time of change. That can't be helped. Indeed, it is because languages are constantly changing that we regularly need fresh translations.

My hope and prayer for this book is that many people will discover through it just how exciting and relevant the New Testament really is. If it helps the church as a whole, and individuals within it, to be refreshed in their faith and reinvigorated to take forward God's mission in tomorrow's world, I will be delighted. I have had the amazing privilege of spending the best years of my life studying and teaching the New Testament in both church circles and academic settings, and I hope that this translation will enable that work to reach a wider audience.

I am extremely grateful to my friends and publishers at SPCK in London, especially Simon Kingston and Joanna Moriarty, who commissioned the For Everyone series in the first place and have provided constant encouragement all the way through. And I am very grateful to HarperOne in San Francisco, especially Mickey Maudlin and Mark Tauber, for publishing this translation in the United States. If only all working relationships could be as happy. I owe a special, enormous debt of gratitude to Dr. Michael Lakey of Ripon College Cuddesdon, who, in the last stages before publication, worked through the whole text with a meticulous eye, a theologian's heart, and a grammarian's delight in the precise nuance of language. He has not only rescued me from a few howlers but gently suggested numerous excellent emendations. The mistakes that remain are my own, some of them the result of my not taking his advice.

Finally, in connection with my constant attempt to write clear, brisk English, I should also mention my beloved wife and children. They have regularly stopped me from using long, fuzzy words where short, sharp ones would do instead. This book is dedicated to them in gratitude and love.

Tom Wright
St. Andrews, Scotland

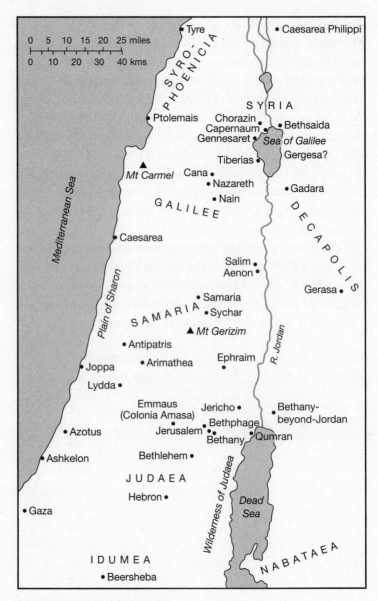

Galilee, Samaria, and Judaea in the First Century AD

The Gospel According to
Matthew

1 The book of the family tree of Jesus the Messiah, the son of David, the son of Abraham.

[2]Abraham became the father of Isaac, Isaac of Jacob, Jacob of Judah and his brothers, [3]Judah of Peres and Zara (by Tamar), Peres of Esrom, Esrom of Aram, [4]Aram of Aminadab, Aminadab of Naason, Naason of Salmon, [5]Salmon of Boaz (by Rahab), Boaz of Obed (by Ruth), Obed of Jesse, [6]and Jesse of David the king.

David was the father of Solomon (by the wife of Uriah), [7]Solomon of Rehoboam, Rehoboam of Abijah, Abijah of Asaph, [8]Asaph of Jehosaphat, Jehosaphat of Joram, Joram of Uzziah, [9]Uzziah of Joatham, Joatham of Ahaz, Ahaz of Hezekiah, [10]Hezekiah of Manasseh, Manasseh of Amoz, Amoz of Josiah, [11]Josiah of Jeconiah and his brothers, at the time of the exile in Babylon.

[12]After the Babylonian exile, Jeconiah became the father of Salathiel, Salathiel of Zerubbabel, [13]Zerubbabel of Abioud, Abioud of Eliakim, Eliakim of Azor, [14]Azor of Sadok, Sadok of Achim, Achim of Elioud, [15]Elioud of Eleazar, Eleazar of Matthan, Matthan of Jacob, [16]and Jacob of Joseph the husband of Mary, from whom was born Jesus, who is called "Messiah."

[17]So all the generations from Abraham to David add up to fourteen; from David to the Babylonian exile, fourteen generations; and from the Babylonian exile to the Messiah, fourteen generations.

[18]This was how the birth of Jesus the Messiah took place. His mother, Mary, was engaged to Joseph; but before they

came together she turned out to be pregnant—by the holy spirit. ¹⁹Joseph, her husband-to-be, was an upright man. He didn't want to make a public example of her. So he decided to set the marriage aside privately. ²⁰But, while he was considering this, an angel of the Lord suddenly appeared to him in a dream.

"Joseph, son of David," the angel said, "Don't be afraid to get married to Mary. The child she is carrying is from the holy spirit. ²¹She is going to have a son. You are to give him the name Jesus; he is the one who will save his people from their sins."

²²All this happened so that what the Lord said through the prophet might be fulfilled: ²³"Look: the virgin is pregnant, and will have a son, and they shall give him the name Emmanuel"—which means, in translation, "God with us."

²⁴When Joseph woke up from his sleep he did what the Lord's angel had told him to. He married his wife, ²⁵but he didn't have sexual relations with her until after the birth of her son. And he gave him the name Jesus.

The Magi Visit Jesus

2 When Jesus was born, in Bethlehem of Judaea, at the time when Herod was king, some wise and learned men came to Jerusalem from the east.

²"Where is the one," they asked, "who has been born to be king of the Jews? We have seen his star rising in the east, and we have come to worship him."

³When King Herod heard this, he was very disturbed, and the whole of Jerusalem was as well. ⁴He called together all the chief priests and scribes of the people, and inquired from them where the Messiah was to be born.

⁵"In Bethlehem of Judaea," they replied. "That's what it says in the prophet:

⁶'You, Bethlehem, in Judah's land
Are not the least of Judah's princes;
From out of you will come the ruler
Who will shepherd Israel my people.'"

⁷Then Herod called the wise men to him in secret. He found out from them precisely when the star had appeared. ⁸Then he sent them to Bethlehem.

"Off you go," he said, "and make a thorough search for the child. When you find him, report back to me, so that I can come and worship him too."

9When they heard what the king said, they set off. There was the star, the one they had seen rising in the east, going ahead of them! It went and stood still over the place where the child was. 10When they saw the star, they were beside themselves with joy and excitement. 11They went into the house and saw the child, with Mary his mother, and they fell down and worshipped him. They opened their treasure-chests and gave him presents: gold, frankincense, and myrrh.

12They were warned in a dream not to go back to Herod. So they returned to their own country by a different route.

13After the Magi had gone, suddenly an angel of the Lord appeared to Joseph in a dream.   **Travels to Egypt**

"Get up," he said, "and take the child, and his mother, and hurry off to Egypt. Stay there until I tell you. Herod is going to hunt for the child, to kill him."

14So he got up and took the child and his mother by night, and went off to Egypt. 15He stayed there until the death of Herod. This happened to fulfill what the Lord said through the prophet:

> *Out of Egypt I called my son.*

16When Herod saw that he had been tricked by the Magi, he flew into a towering rage. He dispatched people to kill all the boys in Bethlehem, and in all its surrounding districts, from two years old and under, according to the time the Magi had told him. 17That was when the word that came through Jeremiah the prophet was fulfilled:

> 18*There was heard a voice in Rama,*
> *Crying and loud lamentation.*
> *Rachel is weeping for her children,*
> *And will not let anyone comfort her,*
> *Because they are no more.*

19After the death of Herod, suddenly an angel of the Lord appeared in a dream to Joseph in Egypt.

20"Get up," he said, "and take the child and his mother and go to the land of Israel. Those who wanted to kill the child are dead."

21So he got up, took the child and his mother, and went to the land of Israel.

22But when he heard that Archelaus was ruling Judaea instead of his father Herod, he was afraid to go back there. After being advised in a dream, he went off to the region of Galilee. 23When he got there, he settled in a town called Nazareth. This was to fulfill what the prophet had spoken:

He shall be called a Nazorean.

The Preaching of John the Baptist

3 In those days John the Baptist appeared. He was preaching in the Judaean wilderness.

2"Repent!" he was saying. "The kingdom of heaven is coming!"

3John, you see, is the person spoken of by Isaiah the prophet, when he said,

The voice of someone shouting in the desert:
"Prepare the route that the Lord will take,
Straighten out his paths!"

4John himself had clothing made from camel's hair, and a leather belt around his waist. His food was locusts and wild honey. 5Jerusalem, and all Judaea, and the whole area around the Jordan, were going off to him. 6They were being baptized by him in the river Jordan, confessing their sins.

7He saw several Pharisees and Sadducees coming to be baptized by him.

"You brood of vipers!" he said to them. "Who warned you to escape from the coming wrath? 8You'd better prove your repentance by bearing the right sort of fruit! 9And you needn't start thinking to yourselves, 'We have Abraham as our father.' Let me tell you, God is quite capable of raising up children for Abraham from these stones! 10The axe is already taking aim at the root of the tree. Every tree that doesn't produce good fruit is to be cut down and thrown into the fire.

¹¹"I am baptizing you with water, for repentance," John continued. "But the one who is coming behind me is more powerful than me! I'm not even worthy to carry his sandals. He will baptize you with the holy spirit and fire! ¹²He's got his shovel in his hand, ready to clear out his barn, and gather all his corn into the granary. But he'll burn up the chaff with a fire that will never go out."

¹³Then Jesus arrived at the Jordan from Galilee, and came to John to be baptized by him.

¹⁴John tried to stop him.

"I ought to be baptized by you," he said, "And are you going to come to me?"

¹⁵"This is how it's got to be right now," said Jesus. "This is the right way for us to complete God's whole saving plan."

So John consented, ¹⁶and Jesus was baptized. All at once, as he came up out of the water, suddenly the heavens were opened, and he saw God's spirit coming down like a dove and landing on him.

¹⁷Then there came a voice out of the heavens.

"This is my son, my beloved one," said the voice. "I am delighted with him."

4 Then Jesus was led out into the wilderness by the spirit to be tested by the devil. ²He fasted for forty days and forty nights, and at the end of it was famished. ³Then the tempter approached him.

"If you really are God's son," he said, "tell these stones to become bread!"

⁴"The Bible says," replied Jesus, "that it takes more than bread to keep you alive. You actually live on every word that comes out of God's mouth."

⁵Then the devil took him off to the holy city and stood him on a pinnacle of the Temple.

⁶"If you really are God's son," he said, "throw yourself down. The Bible does say, after all, that 'God will give his angels a command about you'; and 'they will carry you in their hands, so that you won't hurt your foot against a stone.'"

⁷"But the Bible also says," replied Jesus, "that you mustn't put the Lord your God to the test!"

8Then the devil took him off again, this time to a very high mountain. There he showed him all the magnificent kingdoms of the world.

9"I'll give the whole lot to you," he said, "if you will fall down and worship me."

10"Get out of here, you satan!" replied Jesus. "The Bible says, 'Worship the Lord your God, and serve him alone!'"

11Then the devil left him, and angels came and looked after him.

Announcing the Kingdom

12When Jesus heard that John had been arrested, he went off to Galilee. 13He left Nazareth and went to live at Capernaum, a small town by the sea in the region of Zebulon and Naphtali. 14This happened so that the word spoken through Isaiah the prophet might come true:

> 15*The land of Zebulon and the land of Naphtali,*
> *The road by the sea, beyond the Jordan,*
> *Galilee, land of the nations:*
> 16*The people who sat in the dark saw a great light;*
> *Light dawned on those who sat in the shadowy land*
> *of death.*

17From that time on Jesus began to make his proclamation. "Repent!" he would say. "The kingdom of heaven is arriving!"

Jesus Calls the Disciples

18As Jesus was walking beside the Sea of Galilee he saw two brothers, Simon (also called Peter) and Andrew his brother. They were fishermen, and were casting nets into the sea.

19"Follow me!" said Jesus. "I'll make you fish for people!"

20Straightaway they abandoned their nets and followed him.

21He went on further, and saw two other brothers, James the son of Zebedee and John his brother. They were in the boat, mending their nets, with Zebedee their father. He called them. 22At once they left the boat, and their father, and followed him.

23He went on through the whole of Galilee, teaching in their synagogues and proclaiming the good news of the kingdom, healing every disease and every illness among the people.

24Word about him went out around the whole of Syria. They brought to him all the people tormented with various kinds of diseases and ailments, demon-possessed people, epileptics, and paralytics, and he healed them. 25Large crowds followed him from Galilee, the Ten Towns, Jerusalem, Judaea, and beyond the Jordan.

5 When Jesus saw the crowds, he went up the hillside and sat down. His disciples came to him. 2He took a deep breath, and began his teaching:

The Beatitudes

3"Blessings on the poor in spirit! The kingdom of heaven is yours.

4"Blessings on the mourners! You're going to be comforted.

5"Blessings on the meek! You're going to inherit the earth.

6"Blessings on people who hunger and thirst for God's justice! You're going to be satisfied.

7"Blessings on the merciful! You'll receive mercy yourselves.

8"Blessings on the pure in heart! You will see God.

9"Blessings on the peacemakers! You'll be called God's children.

10"Blessings on people who are persecuted because of God's way! The kingdom of heaven belongs to you.

11"Blessings on you, when people slander you and persecute you, and say all kinds of wicked things about you falsely because of me! 12Celebrate and rejoice: there's a great reward for you in heaven. That's how they persecuted the prophets who went before you.

13"You're the salt of the earth! But if the salt becomes tasteless, how is it going to get salty again? It's no good for anything. You might as well throw it out and walk all over it.

Fulfilling the Law

14"You're the light of the world! A city can't be hidden if it's on top of a hill. 15People don't light a lamp and put it under a bucket; they put it on a lampstand. Then it gives light to everybody in the house. 16That's how you must shine your light in front of people! Then they will see what wonderful things you do, and they'll give glory to your father in heaven.

17"Don't suppose that I came to destroy the law or the prophets. I didn't come to destroy them; I came to fulfill them! 18I'm telling you the truth: until heaven and earth disappear, not one stroke, not one dot, is going to disappear from the law until it's all come true. 19So anyone who relaxes a single one of these commandments, even the little ones, and teaches that to people, will be called least in the kingdom of heaven. But anyone who does them and teaches them will be called great in the kingdom of heaven.

[20]"Yes, let me tell you: unless your covenant behavior is far superior to that of the scribes and Pharisees, you will never get in to the kingdom of heaven."

On Murder and Reconciliation

[21]"You heard that it was said to the ancient people, 'You shall not murder'; and anyone who commits murder shall be liable to judgment. [22]But I say to you that everyone who is angry with his brother shall be liable to judgment; anyone who uses foul and abusive language will be liable to the lawcourt; and anyone who says, 'You fool,' will be liable to the fires of Gehenna.

[23]"So, if you are coming to the altar with your gift, and there you remember that your brother has a grievance against you, [24]leave your gift right there in front of the altar, and go first and be reconciled to your brother. Then come back and offer your gift. [25]Make friends with your opponent quickly, while you are with him in the street, in case your opponent hands you over to the judge, and the judge to the officer, and you find yourself being thrown into jail. [26]I'm telling you the truth: you won't get out until you've paid every last copper coin.

On Adultery and Oaths

[27]"You heard," Jesus continued, "that it was said, 'You shall not commit adultery.' [28]But I say to you: everyone who gazes at a woman in order to lust after her has already committed adultery with her in his heart. [29]If your right eye trips you up, tear it out and throw it away. Yes: it's better for you to have one part of your body destroyed than for the whole body to be thrown into Gehenna. [30]And if your right hand trips you up, cut it off and throw it away. Yes: it's better for you to have one part of your body destroyed than for your whole body to go into Gehenna.

[31]"It was also said, 'If someone divorces his wife, he should give her a legal document to prove it.' [32]But I say to you: everyone who divorces his wife, unless it's in connection with immorality, makes her commit adultery; and anyone who marries a divorced woman commits adultery.

[33]"Again, you heard that it was said to the people long ago: 'You shall not swear falsely, but you shall give to the Lord what you promised under oath.' [34]But I say to you: don't swear at

all! Don't swear by heaven (it's God's throne!); 35don't swear by the earth (it's God's footstool!); don't swear by Jerusalem (it's the city of the great king!); 36don't swear by your head (you can't make one hair of it turn white or black!). 37When you're talking, say yes when you mean yes, and no when you mean no. Anything more than that comes from the evil one.

38"You heard that it was said, 'An eye for an eye, and a tooth for a tooth.' 39But I say to you: don't use violence to resist evil! Instead, when someone hits you on the right cheek, turn the other one toward him. 40When someone wants to sue you and take your shirt, let him have your cloak, too. 41And when someone forces you to go one mile, go a second one with him. 42Give to anyone who asks you, and don't refuse someone who wants to borrow from you.

Loving Your Enemies

43"You heard that it was said, 'Love your neighbor and hate your enemy.' 44But I tell you: love your enemies! Pray for people who persecute you! 45That way, you'll be children of your father in heaven! After all, he makes his sun rise on bad and good alike, and sends rain both on the upright and on the unjust. 46Look at it like this: if you love those who love you, do you expect a special reward? Even tax-collectors do that, don't they? 47And if you only greet your own family, what's so special about that? Even Gentiles do that, don't they? 48Well then: you must be perfect, just as your heavenly father is perfect.

Piety in Secret

6 "When you are practicing your piety, mind you don't do it with an eye on the audience! Otherwise, you won't have any reward from your father in heaven.

2"So when you give money to the poor, don't sound a trumpet in front of you. That's what people do when they're just play-acting, in the synagogues and the streets. They do it so that people will be impressed by them. I'm telling you the truth: they've received their reward in full. 3No: when you give money, don't let your left hand have any idea what your right hand is up to. 4That way, your giving will be in secret. And your father, who sees in secret, will repay you.

5"When you pray, you mustn't be like the play-actors. They love to pray standing in the synagogues and on street corners, so that people will notice them. I'm telling you the truth: they have received their reward in full. 6No: when you pray, go into your own room, shut the door, and pray to your father who is there in secret. And your father, who sees in secret, will repay you.

The Lord's Prayer

7"When you pray, don't pile up a jumbled heap of words! That's what the Gentiles do. They reckon that the more they say, the more likely they are to be heard. 8So don't be like them. You see, your father knows what you need before you ask him.

9"So this is how you should pray:

> 'Our father in heaven,
> May your name be honored,
> 10May your kingdom come,
> May your will be done
> As in heaven, so on earth.
> 11Give us today the bread we need now;
> 12And forgive us the things we owe,
> As we too have forgiven what was owed to us.
> 13Don't bring us into the great trial,
> But rescue us from evil.'

14"Yes: if you forgive people the wrong they have done, your heavenly father will forgive you as well. 15But if you don't forgive people, neither will your heavenly father forgive you what you have done wrong.

On Fasting and Lasting Treasure

16"When you fast, don't be gloomy like the play-actors. They make their faces quite unrecognizable, so that everyone can see they're fasting. I'm telling you the truth: they have received their reward in full. 17No: when you fast, tidy your hair and beard the way you normally do, and wash your face, 18so that others won't notice you're fasting—except your father, privately. Then your father, who sees in private, will repay you.

19"Don't store up treasure on earth. Moths and rust will eat it away, and robbers will break in and steal it. 20No: store up for yourselves treasure in heaven! Moths and rust don't eat it away there, and no robbers break in and steal it. 21Show me your treasure, and I'll show you where your heart is.

22"The eye is the lamp of the body. So if your eye is honest and clear, your whole body will be full of light. 23But if your eye is evil, your whole body is in the dark. So, if the light within you turns out to be darkness, darkness doesn't come any darker than that.

²⁴"Nobody can serve two masters. Otherwise, they will either hate the first and love the second, or be devoted to the first and despise the second. You can't serve both God and wealth.

²⁵"So let me tell you: don't worry about your life—what to eat, what to drink; don't worry about your body—what to wear. There's more to life than food! There's more to the body than a suit of clothes! ²⁶Have a good look at the birds in the sky. They don't plant seeds, they don't bring in the harvest, they don't store things in barns—and your father in heaven feeds them! Think how different you are from them! ²⁷Can any of you add fifteen inches to your height just by worrying about it?

Do Not Worry

²⁸"And why worry about what to wear? Take a tip from the lilies in the countryside. They don't work; they don't weave; ²⁹but, let me tell you, not even Solomon in all his finery was dressed as well as one of these. ³⁰So if God gives that sort of clothing even to the grass in the field, which is here today and on the bonfire tomorrow, isn't he far more likely to clothe you too, you little-faith lot?

³¹"So don't worry away with your 'What'll we eat?' and 'What'll we drink?' and 'What'll we wear?' ³²Those are all the kinds of things the Gentiles fuss about, and your heavenly father knows you need them all. ³³Instead, make your top priority God's kingdom and his way of life, and all these things will be given to you as well.

³⁴"So don't worry about tomorrow. Tomorrow can worry about itself. One day's trouble at a time is quite enough.

7 "Don't judge people, and you won't be judged yourself. ²You'll be judged, you see, by the judgment you use to judge others! You'll be measured by the measuring-rod you use to measure others! ³Why do you stare at the splinter in your neighbor's eye, but ignore the plank in your own? ⁴How can you say to your neighbor, 'Here—let me get that splinter out of your eye,' when you've got the plank in your own? ⁵You're just play-acting! First take the plank out of your own eye, and then you'll see clearly enough to take the splinter out of your neighbor's eye.

On Judging Others

⁶"Don't give holy things to dogs. Don't throw your pearls to pigs. If you do, they will trample them under their feet—and then turn around and attack you!"

On Prayer

⁷"Ask and it will be given to you! Search and you will find! Knock and the door will be opened for you! ⁸Everyone who asks receives; everyone who searches finds; everyone who knocks will have the door opened. ⁹Don't you see? Supposing your son asks you for bread—which of you is going to give him a stone? ¹⁰Or if he asks for a fish—which of you is going to give him a serpent? ¹¹Well then: if you know how to give good gifts to your children, evil as you are, how much more will your father in heaven give good things to those who ask him!

¹²"So whatever you want people to do to you, do just that to them. Yes: this is what the law and the prophets are all about.

The Two Ways

¹³"Go in by the narrow gate. The gate that leads to destruction, you see, is nice and wide, and the road going there has plenty of room. Lots of people go that way. ¹⁴But the gate leading to life is narrow, and the road going there is a tight squeeze. Not many people find their way through.

¹⁵"Watch out for false prophets. They will come to you dressed like sheep, but inside they are hungry wolves. ¹⁶You'll be able to tell them by the fruit they bear: you don't find grapes growing on thorn-bushes, do you, or figs on thistles? ¹⁷Well, in the same way, good trees produce good fruit, and bad trees produce bad fruit. ¹⁸Actually, good trees *can't* produce bad fruit, nor can bad ones produce good fruit! ¹⁹Every tree that doesn't produce good fruit is cut down and thrown on the fire. ²⁰So: you must recognize them by their fruits.

²¹"Not everyone who says to me, 'Master, Master,' will enter the kingdom of heaven; only people who do the will of my father in heaven. ²²On that day lots of people will say to me, 'Master, Master—we prophesied in your name, didn't we? We cast out demons in your name! We performed lots of powerful deeds in your name!'

²³"Then I will have to say to them, 'I never knew you! You're a bunch of evildoers—go away from me!'

True Obedience

²⁴"So, then, everyone who hears these words of mine and does them will be like a wise man who built his house on the rock. ²⁵Heavy rain fell; floods rose up; the winds blew and beat

on that house. It didn't fall, because it was founded on the rock.
26And everyone who hears these words of mine and doesn't do
them—they will be like a foolish man who built his house on
sand. 27Heavy rain fell; floods rose up; the winds blew and battered the house—and down it fell! It fell with a great crash."

28And so it was, when Jesus finished these words, that the
crowds were astonished at his teaching. 29He was teaching
them, you see, on his own authority, not like their scribes used
to do.

8 When Jesus came down from the hillside, large crowds
followed him. 2Suddenly someone with a virulent skin
disease approached, and knelt down in front of him.

Two Healings

"Master," he said, "if you want, you can make me clean!"

3Jesus stretched out his hand and touched him.

"I do want to," he said. "Be clean!"

At once his disease was cured.

4"Take care," Jesus said to him, "that you don't say anything to anyone. Instead, go and show yourself to the priest,
and make the offering which Moses commanded. That will be
a proof to them."

5Jesus went into Capernaum. A centurion came up and
pleaded with him.

6"Master," he said, "my servant is lying at home, paralyzed.
He's in a very bad state."

7"I'll come and make him better," said Jesus.

8"Master," replied the centurion, "I don't deserve to have
you come under my roof! Just say the word, and my servant
will be healed. 9I know what authority's all about, you know—
I've got soldiers answering to me, and I can say to one of them,
'Go!' and he goes, and to another one, 'Come here!' and he
comes, and I can say, 'Do this,' to my slave, and he does it."

10Jesus was fair amazed when he heard this.

"I'm telling you the truth," he said to the people who were
following. "I haven't found faith like this—not even in Israel!
11Let me tell you this: lots of people will come from east and
west and join the great party of celebration with Abraham,
Isaac, and Jacob in the kingdom of heaven. 12But the children
of the kingdom will be thrown into outer darkness, where
people will weep and gnash their teeth."

13Then he turned to the centurion.

"Go home," he said. "Let it be for you as you believed."

And his servant was healed at that very moment.

On Following Jesus 14Jesus went into Peter's house. There he saw Peter's mother-in-law laid low with a fever. 15He touched her hand. The fever left her, and she got up and waited on him.

16When evening came, they brought to him many people who were possessed by demons. He cast out the spirits with a word of command, and healed everyone who was sick. 17This happened so that the word spoken by Isaiah the prophet might come true:

> He himself took our weaknesses
> And bore our diseases.

18When Jesus saw the crowd all around him, he told them to go across to the other side of the lake. 19A scribe came up and spoke to him.

"Teacher," he said, "I will follow you wherever you go!"

20"Foxes have their dens," replied Jesus, "and the birds in the sky have their nests. But the son of man has nowhere he can lay his head."

21"Master," said another of his disciples, "let me first go and see to my father's funeral."

22"Follow me!" replied Jesus. "And leave the dead to bury their own dead."

The Calming of the Storm 23So Jesus got into the boat, and his disciples followed him. 24All of a sudden a great storm blew up on the sea, so that the boat was being swamped by the waves. Jesus, however, was asleep. 25They came and woke him up.

"Help! Master! Rescue us!" they shouted. "We're done for!"

26"Why are you so scared, you little-faith lot?" he replied.

Then he got up and told the wind and the sea to behave themselves, and there was a great calm. 27They were all astonished.

"What sort of man is this," they said, "that the winds and the sea do what he says?"

The Healing of the Demoniacs 28So he went across to the other side, to the region of the Gadarenes. Two demon-possessed men met him, coming out of the tombs. They were very violent and made it impossible for anyone to go along that road.

²⁹"What is it with us and you, son of God?" they yelled. "Have you come here to torture us ahead of the time?"

³⁰Some way off from where they were there was a large herd of pigs feeding.

³¹"If you cast us out," the demons begged Jesus, "send us into the herd of pigs!"

³²"Off you go, then!" said Jesus.

So the demons went out of the men and into the pigs. Then and there the entire herd rushed down the steep slope into the lake, and were drowned in the water.

³³The herdsmen took to their heels. They went off to the town and told the whole tale, including the bit about the demon-possessed men. ³⁴So the whole town came out to see Jesus for themselves. When they saw him, they begged him to leave their district.

9 Jesus got into the boat and crossed back over to his own town.

²Some people brought to him a paralyzed man lying on a bed. When Jesus saw their faith, he said to the paralyzed man, "Cheer up, my son! Your sins are forgiven!"

³"This fellow's blaspheming!" said some of the scribes to themselves.

⁴Jesus read their thoughts. "Why let all this wickedness fester in your hearts?" he said. ⁵"Which is easier: to say, 'Your sins are forgiven,' or to say, 'Get up and walk'? ⁶But, to let you know that the son of man has authority on earth to forgive sins"—he spoke to the paralyzed man—"Get up, pick up your bed, and go home!"

⁷And he got up, and went away to his home. ⁸When the crowds saw it they were frightened, and praised God for giving authority like this to humans.

⁹As Jesus was walking along, he saw a man called Matthew sitting at the tax-office.

"Follow me!" he said to him. And he rose up and followed him.

¹⁰When he was at home, sitting down to a meal, there were lots of tax-collectors and sinners there who had come to have dinner with Jesus and his disciples. ¹¹When the Pharisees saw it, they said to his disciples, "Why does your teacher eat with tax-collectors and sinners?"

The Healing of the Paralytic

The Call of Matthew

¹²Jesus heard them.

"It isn't the healthy who need a doctor," he said; "it's the sick. ¹³Go and learn what this saying means: 'It's mercy I want, not sacrifice.' My job isn't to call upright people, but sinners."

¹⁴Then John's disciples came to him with a question.

"How come," they asked, "we and the Pharisees fast a good deal, but your disciples don't fast at all?"

¹⁵"Wedding guests can't fast, can they," replied Jesus, "as long as the bridegroom is with them? But sooner or later the bridegroom will be taken away from them. They'll fast then all right.

¹⁶"No one," he went on, "sews a patch of unshrunk cloth onto an old coat. The patch will simply pull away from the coat, and you'll have a worse hole than you started with. ¹⁷People don't put new wine into old wineskins, otherwise the skins will split; then the wine will be lost, and the skins will be ruined. They put new wine into new skins, and then both are fine."

The Raising of the Little Girl

¹⁸As Jesus was saying this, suddenly an official came up and knelt down in front of him.

"It's my daughter!" he said. "She's just died! But—if you'll come and lay your hand on her, she'll come back to life."

¹⁹Jesus got up and followed him. So did his disciples.

²⁰Just then a woman appeared. She had suffered from internal bleeding for twelve years. She came up behind Jesus and touched the hem of his coat.

²¹"If I can only touch his coat," she said to herself, "I'll be rescued."

²²Jesus turned around and saw her.

"Cheer up, my daughter!" he said. "Your faith has rescued you."

And the woman was healed from that moment.

²³Jesus went into the official's house. There he saw the flute-players, and everybody in a great state of agitation.

²⁴"Go away!" he said. "The little girl isn't dead. She's asleep!" And they laughed at him.

²⁵So when the crowd had been put out, he went in and took hold of her hand, and she got up. ²⁶The report of this went out around the whole of that region.

27As Jesus was leaving the area, two blind men followed him, shouting, "Have pity on us, son of David!" at the tops of their voices.

28Jesus went into the house, and the blind men came to him.

"Do you believe that I can do this?" asked Jesus.

"Yes, Master," they replied.

29Then Jesus touched their eyes. "As you have believed, so let it happen," he said. 30And their eyes were opened.

Then Jesus gave them a stern warning. "Take good care," he said, "that nobody gets to know about this." 31But they went out and spread the news in the whole of that region.

32After they had left, people brought to Jesus a demon-possessed man who couldn't speak. 33Jesus cast out the demon, and the man spoke. The crowds were amazed. "Nothing like this ever happened in Israel," they said. 34But the Pharisees said, "He casts out demons by the prince of demons."

35Jesus went around all the towns and villages, teaching in their synagogues, announcing the good news of the kingdom, and healing every disease and every sickness. 36When he saw the crowds, he felt deeply sorry for them, because they were distressed and dejected, like sheep without a shepherd. 37Then he said to his disciples, "There's plenty of harvest to be had, but not many workers! 38So pray the master of the harvest to send more workers to harvest his fields!"

10 Jesus called his twelve disciples to him, and gave them authority over unclean spirits, to cast them out and to heal every disease and every sickness.

2These are the names of the twelve apostles. First, Simon, who is called Peter ("the rock"), and Andrew his brother; James the son of Zebedee, and John his brother; 3Philip and Bartholomew, Thomas and Matthew the tax-collector, James son of Alphaeus, and Thaddaeus; 4Simon the Cananaean; and Judas Iscariot (who betrayed him).

5Jesus sent these Twelve off with these instructions.

"Don't go into Gentile territory," he said, "and don't go into a Samaritan town. 6Go instead to the lost sheep of the house of Israel. 7As you go, declare publicly that the kingdom of heaven has arrived. 8Heal the sick, raise the dead, cleanse people with skin diseases, cast out demons.

"It was all free when you got it; make sure it's free when you give it. 9Don't take any gold or silver or copper in your belts; 10no bag for the road, no second cloak, no sandals, no stick. Workers deserve their pay.

11"When you go into a town or village, make careful inquiry for someone who is good and trustworthy, and stay there until you leave. 12When you go into the house, give a solemn greeting. 13If the house is trustworthy, let your blessing of peace rest upon it, but if not, let it return to you. 14If anyone won't welcome you or listen to your message, go out of the house or the town and shake the dust off your feet. 15I'm telling you the truth: it will be more bearable for Sodom and Gomorrah on the day of judgment than for that town.

Sheep Among Wolves

16"See here," Jesus continued, "I'm sending you out like sheep surrounded by wolves. So be as shrewd as snakes and as innocent as doves.

17"Watch out for danger from people around you. They will hand you over to councils, and flog you in their synagogues. 18You will be dragged before governors and kings because of me, as evidence to them and to the nations. 19But when they hand you over, don't worry how to speak or what to say. What you have to say will be given to you at that moment. 20It won't be you speaking, you see; it will be the spirit of your father speaking in you.

21"One brother will betray another to death; fathers will betray children, and children will rebel against their parents and have them put to death. 22You will be hated by everyone because of my name. But the one who holds out to the end will be delivered.

23"When they persecute you in one town, run off to the next one. I'm telling you the truth: you won't have gone through all the towns of Israel before the son of man comes.

Warnings and Encouragements

24"The disciple isn't greater than the teacher; the slave isn't greater than the master. 25It's quite enough for the disciple to be like the teacher, and the slave to be like the master. If they called the master of the house 'Beelzebul,' think what they're going to call his family!

²⁶"Don't be afraid of them. Nothing is hidden, you see, that won't come to light; nothing is secret that won't be made known. ²⁷What I tell you in the dark, speak in the light, and what you hear whispered in your ears, announce from the roofs of the houses.

²⁸"Don't be afraid of people who can kill the body, but can't kill the soul. The one you should be afraid of is the one who can destroy both body and soul in Gehenna. ²⁹How much would you get for a couple of sparrows? A single copper coin if you're lucky? And not one of them falls to the ground without your father knowing about it. ³⁰When it comes to you—why, every hair on your head is counted. ³¹So don't be afraid! You're worth much more than a great many sparrows.

³²"So: everyone who owns up in front of others to being on my side, I will own them before my father in heaven. ³³But anyone who disowns me in front of others, I will disown that person before my father in heaven.

Jesus Causes Division

³⁴"Don't think it's my job to bring peace on the earth. I didn't come to bring peace—I came to bring a sword! ³⁵I came to divide a man from his father, a daughter from her mother, and a daughter-in-law from her mother-in-law. ³⁶Yes, you'll find your enemies inside your own front door.

³⁷"If you love your father or mother more than me, you don't deserve me. If you love your son or daughter more than me, you don't deserve me. ³⁸Anyone who doesn't pick up their cross and follow after me doesn't deserve me. ³⁹If you find your life you'll lose it, and if you lose your life because of me you'll find it.

⁴⁰"Anyone who welcomes you, welcomes me; and anyone who welcomes me, welcomes the one who sent me. ⁴¹Anyone who welcomes a prophet in the name of a prophet will receive a prophet's reward; and anyone who receives an upright person in the name of an upright person will receive an upright person's reward. ⁴²Anyone who gives even a cup of cold water to one of these little ones, in the name of a disciple—I'm telling you the truth, they won't go short of their reward!"

11 So when Jesus had finished giving instructions to the twelve disciples, he moved on from there to teach and preach in their towns.

Jesus and John the Baptist

²Meanwhile, John, who was in prison, heard about these messianic goings-on. He sent word through his followers.

³"Are you the one who is coming?" he asked. "Or should we be looking for someone else?"

⁴"Go and tell John," replied Jesus, "what you've seen and heard. ⁵Blind people are seeing! Lame people are walking! People with virulent skin diseases are being cleansed! Deaf people can hear again! The dead are being raised to life! And—the poor are hearing the good news! ⁶And God bless you if you're not upset by what I'm doing."

The Identity of John the Baptist

⁷As the messengers were going away, Jesus began to speak to the crowds about John.

"What were you expecting to see," he asked, "when you went out into the desert? A reed wobbling in the wind? ⁸No? Well, then, what were you expecting to see? Someone dressed in silks and satins? If you want to see people like that you'd have to go to somebody's royal palace. ⁹All right, so what *were* you expecting to see? A prophet? Ah, now we're getting there: yes indeed, and much more than a prophet! ¹⁰This is the one the Bible was talking about when it says,

> *'See, I'm sending my messenger ahead of you*
> *And he will clear your path before you.'*

¹¹"I'm telling you the truth: John the Baptist is the greatest mother's son there ever was. But even the least significant person in heaven's kingdom is greater than he is. ¹²From the time of John the Baptist until now the kingdom of heaven has been forcing its way in—and the men of force are trying to grab it! ¹³All the prophets and the law, you see, made their prophecies up to the time of John. ¹⁴In fact, if you'll believe it, he is Elijah, the one who was to come. ¹⁵If you've got ears, then listen!

Jesus Condemns the Cities

¹⁶"What picture shall I give you for this generation?" asked Jesus. "It's like a bunch of children sitting in the town square, and singing songs to each other. ¹⁷This is how it goes:

> *'You didn't dance when we played the flute;*
> *You didn't cry when we sang the dirge!'*

¹⁸"What do I mean? When John appeared, he didn't have any normal food or drink—and people said 'What's gotten

into him, then? Some demon?' [19]Then along comes the son of man, eating and drinking normally, and people say, 'Ooh, look at him—guzzling and boozing, hanging around with tax-collectors and other riffraff.' But, you know, wisdom is as wisdom does—and wisdom will be vindicated!"

[20]Then he began to berate the towns where he'd done most of his powerful deeds, because they hadn't repented.

[21]"A curse on you, Chorazin!" he said. "A curse on you, Bethsaida! If Tyre and Sidon had seen the kind of powerful things you saw, they would have repented long ago with hair-shirts and ashes. [22]But I can tell you this: on the day of judgment Tyre and Sidon will have a better time of it than you will. [23]And what about you, Capernaum? You think you're going to be exalted to heaven, do you? No—you'll be sent down to Hades! If the powerful works that happened in you had happened in Sodom, it would still be standing today. [24]But I can tell you this: on the day of judgment the land of Sodom will have a better time of it than you will!"

[25]At that time Jesus turned to God with this prayer: "I give you my praise, Father, Lord of heaven and earth! You hid these things from the wise and intelligent and revealed them to children! [26]Yes, Father, that's the way you decided to do it!" [27]My father gave me everything: nobody knows the son except the father, and nobody knows the father except the son—and anyone the son wants to reveal him to.

Jesus's Invitation

[28]"Are you having a real struggle? Come to me! Are you carrying a big load on your back? Come to me—I'll give you a rest! [29]Pick up my yoke and put it on; take lessons from me! My heart is gentle, not arrogant. You'll find the rest you deeply need. [30]My yoke is easy to wear; my load is easy to bear."

12 At that time Jesus went through the cornfields on the sabbath. His disciples were hungry, and they began to pluck ears of corn and eat them. [2]When the Pharisees observed this they said to him, "Look here! Your disciples are doing something that's not permitted on the sabbath!"

Lord of the Sabbath

[3]"Did you never read what David did?" replied Jesus. "When he and his men were hungry, [4]they went into God's house and ate the holy bread which neither he nor his men were allowed

to eat—only the priests had that right. ⁵Or didn't you read in the law that the priests in the Temple do things on the sabbath which are against sabbath law—and they aren't guilty? ⁶Let me tell you this: something greater than the Temple is here. ⁷If you'd known what this saying means—'Mercy, not sacrifice, is what I really want'—you wouldn't have passed judgment on blameless people. ⁸Yes, you see: the son of man is master of the sabbath, too."

⁹He left the place and went into their synagogue, ¹⁰where there was a man with a withered hand.

They put the question to him: "Is it lawful to heal on the sabbath?"

(They asked this so that they could frame a charge against him.)

¹¹"Supposing one of you has just one sheep," replied Jesus, "and it falls into a ditch on the sabbath. You'll grab it and haul it out, won't you? ¹²Well then, think how much more important a human being is than a sheep! So, you see, it is permitted to do good on the sabbath."

¹³Then he said to the man, "Stretch your hand out." He stretched it out, and it was restored to health, just like the other one. ¹⁴But the Pharisees went off and plotted against him, with the intention of doing away with him.

The Servant ¹⁵Jesus discovered the plots against him, and left the district. Large crowds followed him, and he healed them all, ¹⁶giving them strict instructions not to tell people about him. ¹⁷This was so that what was spoken through Isaiah the prophet might come true:

> ¹⁸*Look! Here's my servant, whom I chose;*
> *My beloved one, my heart's delight.*
> *My spirit I will place on him,*
> *And he'll announce true judgment*
> *To the whole wide world.*
> ¹⁹*He will not argue, nor will he*
> *Lift up his voice and shout aloud;*
> *Nobody in the streets will hear*
> *His voice.* ²⁰*He will not break the damaged*

Reed, or snuff the guttering lamp,
Until his judgment wins the day.
21The world will hope upon his name.

22They brought to Jesus a man who was possessed by a demon that made him unable to see or speak. Jesus healed him, so that the sick man was able to talk and see. 23All the crowds were astonished.

"He can't be David's son, can he?" they said.

24The Pharisees heard this.

"The only reason this fellow can cast out demons," they said, "is because he's in league with Beelzebul, the prince of demons!"

25Jesus knew their thoughts.

"Suppose a kingdom is split down the middle," he said to them. "It'll go to rack and ruin! If a city or a household is split down the middle, it's doomed! 26And if the satan drives out the satan, he's split down the middle—so how can his kingdom stay standing?

27"What's more, if I cast out demons by Beelzebul, whose power are your people in league with when they cast them out? Yes, they'll tell you what's what! 28But if I'm casting out demons because I'm in league with God's spirit—well, then, God's kingdom has arrived on your doorstep!

29"Look at it like this. Suppose you want to break into a strong man's house and steal his belongings. How are you going to do that unless you first tie up the strong man? Then you can plunder his house to your heart's content. 30If you're not with me, you're against me. Unless you're gathering the flock with me, you're scattering it.

31"So let me tell you this: people will be forgiven for every sin and blasphemy; but blasphemy against the spirit will not be forgiven. 32If anyone speaks a word against the son of man, it will be forgiven. But if anyone speaks a word against the holy spirit, it won't be forgiven, either in the present age or in the age to come.

33"You must make up your mind between two possibilities," Jesus went on. "Either the tree is good, in which case its

The Sign
of Jonah

fruit is good; or the tree is bad, in which case its fruit is bad. You can tell the tree by its fruits, after all.

34"You're a family of snakes! How can you say good things when you're bad inside? What the mouth speaks is what fills the heart. 35A good person produces good things from a good storeroom; an evil person produces evil things from an evil storeroom. 36Let me tell you this: on judgment day people will have to own up to every trivial word they say. 37Yes: you will be vindicated by your own words—and you will be condemned by your own words."

38"Teacher," responded some of the scribes and Pharisees, "we would like to see a sign from you."

39"This wicked and immoral generation is looking for a sign," replied Jesus. "But no sign will be given to it—except the sign of Jonah. 40Jonah, you see, was in the stomach of the sea monster for three days and three nights—and in the same way the son of man will be in the heart of the earth for three days and three nights. 41The men of Nineveh will rise up at the judgment along with this generation and will condemn it. They, after all, repented when they heard Jonah's warnings! And, in case you hadn't noticed, something greater than Jonah is here. 42The Queen of the South will be raised at the judgment with this generation and will condemn it. She, after all, came from the ends of the earth to hear the wisdom of Solomon! And, in case you hadn't noticed, something greater than Solomon is here.

Jesus's True Family

43"When the unclean spirit goes out of a person," Jesus continued, "it goes wandering through waterless places looking for somewhere to rest, and doesn't find anywhere. 44Then it says, 'I'll go back to my house, the one I left.' When it gets there it finds it standing empty, clean and tidy. 45Then it goes out and collects seven other spirits to join it, spirits worse than itself. They go in and take up residence there. The poor person ends up worse off than they were to start with! And that's what will happen with this wicked generation."

46Suddenly, while he was speaking to the crowds, his mother and his brothers came and stood outside, hoping for a chance to speak to him.

⁴⁷"Look," someone said to him, "your mother and your brothers are standing outside wanting to speak to you."

⁴⁸"Who is my mother?" said Jesus to the person who had spoken to him. "Who are my brothers?"

⁴⁹Then he stretched out his hand toward his disciples.

"Look!" he said. "Here are my mother and my brothers. ⁵⁰Yes: anyone who does what my heavenly father wants is my brother, and my sister, and my mother."

13 That very day Jesus went out of the house and sat down beside the sea. ²Large crowds gathered around him, so he got into a boat and sat down. The whole crowd was standing on the shore.

The Parable of the Sower

³He had much to say to them, and he said it all in parables.

"Listen!" he said. "Once there was a sower who went out to sow. ⁴As he sowed, some seed fell beside the path, and the birds came and ate it up. ⁵Some seed fell on rocky soil, where it didn't have much earth. It sprang up at once because it didn't have depth of soil. ⁶But when the sun was high it got scorched, and it withered because it didn't have any root. ⁷Other seed fell in among thorns, and the thorns grew up and choked it. ⁸And other seed fell into good soil, and produced a crop, some a hundred times over, some sixty, and some thirty times over. ⁹If you've got ears, then listen!"

¹⁰His disciples came to him.

"Why are you speaking to them in parables?" they asked.

The Reason for Parables

¹¹"You've been given the gift of knowing the secrets of the kingdom of heaven," he replied, "but they haven't been given it. ¹²Anyone who already has something will be given more, and they will have plenty. But anyone who has nothing—even what they have will be taken away! ¹³That's why I speak to them in parables, so that they may look but not see, and hear but not understand or take it in. ¹⁴Isaiah's prophecy is coming true in them:

'You will listen and listen but won't understand,
You will look and look but not see.
¹⁵This people's heart has gone flabby and fat,
Their ears are muffled and dull,

> *Their eyes are darkened and shut;*
> *In order that they won't see with their eyes*
> *Or hear with their ears, or know in their heart,*
> *Or turn back again for me to restore them.'*

[16]"But there's great news for *your* eyes: they can see! And for *your* ears: they can hear! [17]I'm telling you the truth: many prophets and holy people longed to see what you see and didn't see it, and to hear what you hear and didn't hear it.

The Parable of the Sower Explained

[18]"All right, then," Jesus continued, "this is what the sower story is all about. [19]When someone hears the word of the kingdom and doesn't understand it, the evil one comes and snatches away what was sown in their heart. This corresponds to what was sown beside the path. [20]What was sown on rocky ground is the person who hears the word and immediately receives it with delight, [21]but doesn't have any root of their own. Someone like that only lasts a short time; as soon as there's any trouble or persecution because of the word, they trip up at once. [22]The one sown among thorns is the one who hears the word, but the world's worries and the seduction of wealth choke the word and it doesn't bear fruit. [23]But the one sown on good soil is the one who hears the word and understands it. Someone like that will bear fruit: one will produce a hundred times over, another sixty, and another thirty times over."

The Parable of the Weeds

[24]He put another parable to them.

"The kingdom of heaven," he said, "is like this. Once upon a time a man sowed good seed in his field. [25]While the workers were asleep, his enemy came and sowed weeds in among the wheat, and went away. [26]When the crop came up and produced wheat, then the weeds appeared as well.

[27]"So the farmer's servants came to him.

"'Master,' they said, 'didn't you sow good seed in your field? Where have the weeds come from?'

[28]"'This is the work of an enemy,' he replied.

"'So,' the servants said to him, 'do you want us to go and pull them up?'

[29]"'No,' he replied. 'If you do that you'll probably pull up the wheat as well, while you're collecting the weeds. [30]Let them both grow together until the harvest. Then, when it's time for

harvest, I will give the reapers this instruction: First gather
the weeds and tie them up in bundles to burn them, but gather
the wheat into my barn.'"

³¹He put another parable to them.

"The kingdom of heaven," he said, "is like a grain of mustard seed, which someone took and sowed in his field. ³²It's
the smallest of all the seeds, but when it grows it turns into the
biggest of the shrubs. It becomes a tree, and the birds in the
sky can then come and nest in its branches."

³³He told them another parable.

"The kingdom of heaven is like leaven," he said, "which a
woman took and hid inside three measures of flour, until the
whole thing was leavened."

³⁴Jesus said all these things to the crowds in parables. He
didn't speak to them without a parable. ³⁵This was to fulfill
what was spoken by the prophet:

> I will open my mouth in parables,
> I will tell the things that were hidden
> Since the very foundation of the world.

³⁶Then Jesus left the crowds and went into the house. His
disciples came and joined him.

"Explain to us," they said, "the parable of the weeds in the
field."

The Parable of the Weeds Explained

³⁷"The one who sows the good seed," said Jesus, "is the son
of man. ³⁸The field is the world; the good seed are the children
of the kingdom. The weeds are the children of the evil one;
³⁹the enemy who sowed them is the devil. The harvest is the
close of the age, and the reapers are angels.

⁴⁰"So: when the weeds are gathered and burned in the fire,
that's what it will be like at the close of the age. ⁴¹The son of
man will send out his angels, and they will collect together
out of his kingdom everything that causes offense, and everyone who acts wickedly. ⁴²They will throw them into the fiery
furnace, where there will be weeping and gnashing of teeth.
⁴³Then the righteous will shine like the sun in the kingdom of
their father. If you have ears, then hear!

⁴⁴"The kingdom of heaven," Jesus continued, "is like treasure hidden in a field. Someone found it and hid it, and in great

Other Parables

delight went off and sold everything he possessed, and bought that field.

⁴⁵"Again, the kingdom of heaven is like a trader who was looking for fine pearls, ⁴⁶and who found one that was spectacularly valuable. He went off and sold everything he possessed, and bought it.

⁴⁷"Again, the kingdom of heaven is like a net that was thrown into the sea, and collected every type of fish. ⁴⁸When it was full, the fishermen brought it to shore. They sat down and selected the good ones, which they put into a bucket; but they threw out the bad ones. ⁴⁹That's what it will be like at the close of the age. The angels will go off and separate the wicked from the righteous, ⁵⁰and they will throw them into the fiery furnace, where there will be weeping and gnashing of teeth.

⁵¹"Have you understood all this?" asked Jesus.

"Yes," they answered.

⁵²"Well, then," he said to them, "every scribe who has been trained for the kingdom of heaven is like a householder who brings out of his storeroom some new things and some old things."

⁵³When Jesus had finished these parables, he went away from there.

Opposition in Nazareth

⁵⁴Jesus came to the town where he had been brought up. He taught them in their synagogue, and they were astonished.

"Where did this fellow get this wisdom, and these powers?" they said.

⁵⁵"Isn't he the carpenter's son? Isn't his mother called Mary, and his brothers James, Joseph, Simon, and Judah? ⁵⁶And aren't all his sisters here with us? So where does he get it all from?" ⁵⁷They were offended by him.

So Jesus said to them, "No prophet lacks respect—except in his own town and his own house!"

⁵⁸And he didn't perform many mighty works there, because they didn't believe.

The Death of John the Baptist

14 At that time Herod the tetrarch heard reports about Jesus.

²"This fellow must be John the Baptist," he said to his servants. "He's been raised from the dead! That's why these powers are at work in him."

³This is what had happened. Herod had seized John, tied him up, and put him in prison because of Herodias, the wife of his brother Philip. ⁴John had been telling him that it wasn't right for him to have her. ⁵Herod wanted to kill him, but he was afraid of the crowd, because they reckoned that John was a prophet.

⁶When Herod's birthday came around, the daughter of Herodias danced for the assembled company, and delighted Herod. ⁷So he swore a great oath that he would give her whatever she requested. ⁸Prompted by her mother, she said, "Give me—here, on a platter—the head of John the Baptizer!" ⁹The king was sorry; but because of his oaths, and his guests, he gave orders for it to be given to her. ¹⁰He sent to the prison and had John beheaded. ¹¹His head was brought on a platter and given to the girl, and she passed it on to her mother. ¹²His disciples came and took away the body and buried it. Then they went and told Jesus.

¹³When Jesus heard it, he went away from there in a boat to a deserted spot by himself. The crowds heard it, and followed him on foot from the towns. ¹⁴When he came out and saw the large crowd, he was sorry for them. He healed their sick.

The Feeding of the Five Thousand

¹⁵When it was evening, the disciples came to him.

"This is a deserted spot," they said, "and it's already getting late. Send the crowds away so that they can go into the villages and buy food for themselves."

¹⁶"They don't need to go away," said Jesus. "You give them something to eat."

¹⁷"All we have here," they said, "is five loaves of bread and two fish."

¹⁸"Bring them here to me," he said.

¹⁹He told the crowds to sit down on the grass. Then he took the five loaves and the two fish and looked up to heaven. He blessed the loaves, broke them, and gave them to the disciples, and the disciples gave them to the crowds. ²⁰Everybody ate and was satisfied, and they picked up twelve baskets full of broken pieces. ²¹There were about five thousand men who had eaten, besides women and children.

²²Jesus at once made the disciples get into the boat and go on ahead of him to the opposite shore, while he dismissed the crowds.

Jesus Walks on Water

23After he had sent the crowds away, Jesus went up the mountain by himself to pray. When evening came he was there by himself. 24The boat had already gone some distance from the shore and was being smashed around by the waves, since the wind was against it.

25At the very dead of night he came toward them, walking on the water. 26The disciples saw him walking on the sea and panicked. "It's a ghost!" they said, and they screamed in terror. 27But Jesus at once spoke to them.

"Cheer up," he said, "it's me! Don't be frightened!"

28"If it's really you, Master," said Peter in reply, "give me the word to come to you on the water."

29"Come along, then," said Jesus.

Peter got out of the boat and walked on the water and came toward Jesus. 30But when he saw the strong wind he was afraid, and began to sink.

"Master," he yelled, "rescue me!"

31Jesus at once reached out his hand and caught him.

"A fine lot of faith you've got!" he said. "Why did you doubt?"

32They got into the boat, and the wind died down. 33The people in the boat worshipped him.

"You really are God's son!" they said.

34So they crossed over to the land called Gennesaret. 35The men of that region recognized him and sent word to all the surrounding district. They brought all their sick people to him, 36and begged him to be allowed simply to touch the hem of his clothes. And everyone who touched it was cured.

Discussions of Clean and Unclean

15 At that time some Pharisees and scribes came from Jerusalem to Jesus. They had a question for him.

2"Why," they said, "do your disciples go against the tradition of the elders? They don't wash their hands when they eat their food!"

3"Why," Jesus replied, "do *you* go against the command of God because of your tradition? 4What God said was 'Honor your father and mother' and 'If anyone speaks evil of father or mother, they must certainly die.' 5But you say, 'If anyone says to father or mother, "What you might have gained from me is given to God," 6they don't need to honor their father anymore.'

As a result, you make God's word null and void because of your tradition.

7"You play-actors! Isaiah had the right words for you in his prophecy:

> 8'*This people gives me honor with their lips;*
> *Their heart, however, holds me at arm's length.*
> 9*The worship which they offer me is vain,*
> *Because they teach, as law, mere human precepts.'*"

10Then Jesus called the crowd, and said to them, "Listen and understand. 11What makes someone unclean isn't what goes into the mouth. It's what comes out of the mouth that makes someone unclean."

The Parable of Clean and Unclean

12Then the disciples came to Jesus.

"Do you know," they said, "that the Pharisees were horrified when they heard what you said?"

13"Every plant that my heavenly father hasn't planted," replied Jesus, "will be plucked up by the roots. 14Let them be. They are blind guides. But if one blind person guides another, both of them will fall into a pit."

15Peter spoke up. "Explain the riddle to us," he said.

16"Are you still slow on the uptake as well?" replied Jesus. 17"Don't you understand that whatever goes into the mouth travels on into the stomach and goes out into the toilet? 18But what comes out of the mouth begins in the heart, and that's what makes someone unclean. 19Out of the heart, you see, come evil plots, murder, adultery, fornication, theft, false witness, and blasphemy. 20These are the things that make someone unclean. But eating with unwashed hands doesn't make a person unclean."

21Jesus left that place and went off to the district of Tyre and Sidon. 22A Canaanite woman from those parts came out and shouted, "Have pity on me, Lord, son of David! My daughter is demon-possessed! She's in a bad way!" 23Jesus, however, said nothing at all to her.

The Canaanite Woman

His disciples came up.

"Please send her away!" they asked. "She's shouting after us."

²⁴"I was only sent," replied Jesus, "to the lost sheep of the house of Israel."

²⁵The woman, however, came and threw herself down at his feet.

"Master," she said, "please help me!"

²⁶"It isn't right," replied Jesus, "to take the children's bread and throw it to the dogs."

²⁷"I know, Master. But even the dogs eat the scraps that fall from their master's table."

²⁸"You've got great faith, haven't you, my friend!" replied Jesus. "All right; let it be as you wish."

And her daughter was healed from that moment.

The Feeding of the Four Thousand

²⁹Jesus went away from there and arrived beside the Sea of Galilee. He went up the mountain and sat down. ³⁰Large crowds came to him, with their lame, blind, crippled, mute, and many others. They laid them at his feet, and he healed them. ³¹When the crowd saw the mute speaking, the crippled made whole, the lame walking, and the blind seeing, they were astonished, and they gave praise to the God of Israel.

³²Jesus called his disciples, and said, "I am really sorry for the crowd. They've been around me now for three days and they haven't got anything to eat. I don't want to send them away hungry; they might faint on the way home."

³³The disciples said to him, "Where could we get enough bread to feed a crowd this size, out in the country like this?"

³⁴"How many loaves have you got?" asked Jesus.

"Seven," they replied, "and a few fish."

³⁵Jesus told the crowd to sit down on the ground. ³⁶Then he took the seven loaves and the fish, gave thanks, broke them, and gave them to the disciples, and the disciples gave them to the crowds. ³⁷They all ate and were satisfied. And they picked up seven baskets full of what was left of the broken pieces. ³⁸There were four thousand men who had eaten, besides the women and children.

³⁹Jesus sent the crowds away. Then he got into the boat and went over to the Magadan coast.

The Leaven of the Pharisees

16 The Pharisees and Sadducees came to Jesus and tried to catch him out by asking him to show them a sign from heaven.

2This was his reply to them: "When it's evening you say, 'Sky looks like wine, it's going to be fine.' 3And in the morning you say, 'Red in the sky, rain by and by.' Well then: you know how to work out the look of the sky, so why can't you work out the signs of the times? 4The generation that wants a sign is wicked and corrupt! No sign will be given to it, except the sign of Jonah."

With that, he left them and went away.

5When the disciples crossed over the lake, they forgot to bring any bread. 6"Watch out," said Jesus to them, "and beware of the leaven of the Pharisees and Sadducees."

7They discussed it with each other. "It's because we didn't bring any bread," they said.

8But Jesus knew what they were thinking.

"You really are a little-faith lot!" he said. "Why are you discussing with each other that you haven't got any bread? 9Don't you understand, even now? Don't you remember the five loaves and the five thousand, and how many basketfuls you picked up afterward? 10Or the seven loaves and the four thousand, and how many baskets you picked up? 11Why can't you see that I wasn't talking about bread? Watch out for the leaven of the Pharisees and Sadducees!"

12Then they understood that he wasn't telling them to beware of the leaven you get in bread, but of the teaching of the Pharisees and Sadducees.

13Jesus came to Caesarea Philippi. There he put this question to his disciples: "Who do people say that the son of man is?"

14"John the Baptist," they replied. "Others say Elijah. Others say Jeremiah, or one of the prophets."

15"What about you?" he asked them. "Who do you say I am?"

16Simon Peter answered.

"You're the Messiah," he said. "You're the son of the living God!"

17"God's blessing on you, Simon, son of John!" answered Jesus. "Flesh and blood didn't reveal that to you; it was my father in heaven. 18And I've got something to tell you, too: you are Peter, the rock, and on this rock I will build my church, and the gates of hell won't overpower it. 19I will give you the keys of the kingdom of heaven. Whatever you tie up on earth

Peter's Declaration of Jesus's Messiahship

will have been tied up in heaven, and whatever you untie on earth will have been untied in heaven."

20Then he sternly ordered the disciples not to tell anyone that he was the Messiah.

Jesus Predicts His Death

21From then on Jesus began to explain to his disciples that he would have to go to Jerusalem, and suffer many things from the elders, chief priests, and scribes, and be killed, and be raised on the third day.

22Peter took him and began to tell him off. "That's the last thing God would want, Master!" he said. "That's never, ever going to happen to you!"

23Jesus turned on Peter. "Get behind me, Satan!" he said. "You're trying to trip me up! You're not looking at things like God does! You're looking at things like a mere mortal!"

24Then Jesus said to his disciples, "If anyone wants to come after me, they must give themselves up, and pick up their cross, and follow me. 25Yes: if someone wants to save their life, they must lose it; and if anyone loses their life for my sake they will find it. 26What use will it be, otherwise, if you win the whole world but forfeit your true life? What will you give to get your life back? 27You see, the son of man is going to 'come in the glory of his father with his angels,' and then 'he will reward everyone for the work they have done.' 28I'm telling you the truth: some of those standing here will not taste death until they see 'the son of man coming in his kingdom.'"

The Transfiguration

17 After six days Jesus took Peter, James, and James's brother John, and led them off up a high mountain by themselves. 2There he was transformed in front of them. His face shone like the sun, and his clothes became as white as light. 3Then, astonishingly, Moses and Elijah appeared to them. They were talking with Jesus.

4Peter just had to say something. "Master," he said to Jesus, "it's wonderful for us to be here! If you want, I'll make three shelters here—one for you, one for Moses, and one for Elijah!"

5While he was still speaking, a bright cloud overshadowed them. Then there came a voice out of the cloud. "This is my dear son," said the voice, "and I'm delighted with him. Pay attention to him."

6When the disciples heard this, they fell on their faces and were scared out of their wits. 7Jesus came up and touched them.

"Get up," he said, "and don't be afraid."

8When they raised their eyes, they saw nobody except Jesus, all by himself.

9As they were coming down the mountain, Jesus gave them strict instructions. "Don't tell anyone about the vision," he said, "until the son of man has been raised from the dead."

The Question About Elijah

10"So why," asked the disciples, "do the scribes say that 'Elijah must come first'?"

11"Elijah does indeed come," replied Jesus, "and 'he will restore everything.' 12But let me tell you this: Elijah has already come, and they didn't recognize him! They did to him whatever they wanted. That's how the son of man, too, will suffer at their hands."

13Then the disciples realized that he was talking to them about John the Baptist.

14When they came near the crowd, a man approached and knelt in front of him.

Faith That Moves Mountains

15"Master," he said, "take pity on my son! He suffers from awful fits which are frightful for him. He often falls into the fire, and often into the water. 16I brought him to your disciples, but they couldn't cure him."

17"You unbelieving and twisted generation!" responded Jesus. "How much longer must I be with you? How much longer must I put up with you? Bring him here to me."

18Then Jesus rebuked the demon and it came out of him. The boy was cured from that moment.

19The disciples came to Jesus in private. "Why couldn't we cast it out?" they asked.

20"Because of your lack of faith," Jesus replied. "I'm telling you the truth: if you have faith like a grain of mustard seed, you will say to this mountain, 'Move from here to there,' and it will move. Nothing will be impossible for you."

22As they regathered in Galilee, Jesus said to them, "The son of man is going to be given over into human hands. 23They will kill him, and on the third day he will be raised." And they were very sad.

The Temple Tax

²⁴They came to Capernaum, where the officials who collected the Temple tax approached Peter.

"Your teacher pays the Temple tax, doesn't he?" they asked. ²⁵"Yes," he replied.

When he came into the house, Jesus spoke first, "What d'you think, Simon? When the kings of the world collect taxes or duties, who do they collect them from? From their own families, or from outsiders?"

²⁶"From outsiders," he replied.

"Well then," said Jesus, "that means the families are free. ²⁷But we don't want to give them offense, do we? So why don't you go down to the sea and cast out a hook? The first fish you catch, open its mouth and you'll find a coin. Take that and give it to them for the two of us."

Humility and Danger

18 At that time the disciples came to Jesus.

"So, then," they said, "who is the greatest in the kingdom of heaven?"

²Jesus called a child and stood her in the middle of them.

³"I'm telling you the truth," he said. "Unless you turn inside out and become like children, you will never, ever, get into the kingdom of heaven. ⁴So if any of you make yourselves humble like this child, you will be great in the kingdom of heaven. ⁵And if anyone welcomes one such child in my name, they welcome me.

⁶"Whoever causes one of these little ones who believe in me to trip up," he went on, "it would be better for them to have a huge millstone hung around their neck and be drowned far out in the deep sea. ⁷It's a terrible thing for the world that people will be made to stumble. Obstacles are bound to appear and trip people up, but it will be terrible for the person who makes them come.

More About the "Little Ones"

⁸"But if your hand or your foot causes you to trip up," Jesus continued, "cut it off and throw it away. It's better to enter into life crippled or lame than to go into eternal fire with both hands and both feet! ⁹And if your eye causes you to trip up, pull it out and throw it away. Going into life with one eye is better than going into hell with two!

¹⁰"Take care not to despise one of these little ones. I tell you this: in heaven, their angels are always gazing on the face of my father who lives there.

¹²"How does it seem to you? If someone has a hundred sheep and one of them wanders off and goes missing, what will he do? He'll leave the ninety-nine on the hillside and go off after the one that's missing, won't he? ¹³And when, eventually, he finds it, I'll tell you the truth: he will celebrate over that one more than over the ninety-nine that didn't go missing! ¹⁴It's the same with your father in heaven. The last thing he wants is for a single one of these little ones to be lost.

¹⁵"If another disciple sins against you," Jesus continued, "go and have it out, just between the two of you alone. If they listen to you, you've won back a brother or sister. ¹⁶But if they won't listen, you should take with you one or two others, so that 'everything may be established from the mouth of two or three witnesses.' ¹⁷If they won't listen to them, tell it to the assembly. And if they won't listen to the assembly, you should treat such a person like you would a Gentile or a tax-collector. ¹⁸I'm telling you the truth: whatever you tie up on earth will have been tied up in heaven; and whatever you untie on earth will have been untied in heaven.

Reconciliation and Prayer in the Community

¹⁹"Again, let me tell you the truth: if two of you come to an agreement on earth about any matter that you want to ask, it will be done for you by my father in heaven. ²⁰Yes: where two or three come together in my name, I'll be there in the midst of them."

²¹Then Peter came to Jesus.

The Challenge of Forgiveness

"Master," he said, "how many times must I forgive my brother when he sins against me? As many as seven times?"

²²"I wouldn't say seven times," replied Jesus. "Why not— seventy times seven?

²³"So, you see," he went on, "the kingdom of heaven is like a king who wanted to settle up accounts with his servants. ²⁴As he was beginning to sort it all out, one man was brought before him who owed ten thousand talents. ²⁵He had no means of paying it back, so the master ordered him to be sold, with his wife and children and everything he possessed, and payment to be made.

²⁶"So the servant fell down and prostrated himself before the master.

"'Be patient with me,' he said, 'and I'll pay you everything!'

27"The master was very sorry for the servant, and let him off. He forgave him the loan.

28"But that servant went out and found one of his fellow servants, who owed him a hundred dinars. He seized him and began to throttle him. 'Pay me back what you owe me!' he said.

29"The colleague fell down and begged him, 'Be patient with me, and I'll pay you!'

30"But he refused, and went and threw him into prison until he could pay the debt.

31"So when his fellow servants saw what had happened, they were very upset. They went and informed their master about the whole affair. 32Then his master summoned him.

"'You're a scoundrel of a servant!' he said to him. 'I let you off the whole debt, because you begged me to. 33Shouldn't you have taken pity on your colleague, like I took pity on you?'

34"His master was angry, and handed him over to the torturers, until he had paid the whole debt. 35And that's what my heavenly father will do to you, unless each of you forgives your brother or sister from your heart."

The Question About Divorce

19 So this is what happened next. When Jesus had finished saying all this, he went away from Galilee and came to the region of Judaea across the Jordan. 2Large crowds followed him, and he healed them there.

3Some Pharisees approached him with a trick question.

"Is it lawful," they asked, "for a man to divorce his wife for any reason at all?"

4"Haven't you read," he replied, "that the creator from the beginning 'made them male and female'? 5And this is what he said: 'For this reason a man shall leave his father and mother and be joined to his wife, and the two shall become one flesh.' 6As a result, they are no longer two, but one flesh. So humans shouldn't split up what God has joined together."

7"So, then," they asked, "why did Moses give the regulation that one should give the woman a certificate of divorce and make the separation legal?"

8"Moses gave you this instruction about how to divorce your wives," replied Jesus, "because your hearts were hard. But that's not how it was at the beginning. 9Let me tell you

this: anyone who divorces his wife, except for immorality, and
marries another woman, commits adultery."

¹⁰The disciples said to Jesus, "If that's the situation of a man
with his wife, it would be better not to marry!"

¹¹"Not everyone can accept this word," replied Jesus; "only
the people it's given to. ¹²You see, there are some eunuchs who
are that way from birth. There are some who have been made
eunuchs by others. And there are some who have made themselves eunuchs for the sake of the kingdom of heaven. If anyone can receive this, let them do so."

Marriage, Celibacy, and Children

¹³Then children were brought to Jesus for him to lay his
hands on them and pray. The disciples spoke sternly to them.
¹⁴But Jesus said, "Let the children come to me! Don't stop
them! They are the sort the kingdom of heaven belongs to!"
¹⁵And he laid his hands on them.

Then he moved on elsewhere.

¹⁶Suddenly a man came up to Jesus. "Teacher," he asked,
"what good thing must I do if I'm to possess the life of the age
to come?"

The Rich Young Man

¹⁷"Why come to me with questions about what's good?" re-
torted Jesus. "There is One who is good! If you want to enter
into life, keep the commandments."

¹⁸"Which ones?" he asked.

"These ones," Jesus answered: "'don't murder, don't com-
mit adultery, don't steal, don't tell lies under oath, ¹⁹respect
your father and mother,' and 'love your neighbor as yourself.'"

²⁰"I've kept the lot," said the young man. "What am I still
short of?"

²¹"If you want to complete the set," Jesus replied, "go and
sell everything you own and give it to the poor. That way you'll
have treasure in heaven! Then come and follow me."

²²When the young man heard him say that, he went away
very sad. He had many possessions.

²³Jesus said to his disciples, "I'm telling you the truth:
it's very hard for a rich person to get into the kingdom of
heaven. ²⁴Let me say it again: it's easier for a camel to go
through the eye of a needle than for a rich person to enter
God's kingdom."

The First and the Last

25The disciples were completely flabbergasted when they heard that. "So who then can be saved?" they asked.

26Jesus looked around at them. "Humanly speaking," he replied, "it's impossible. But everything's possible with God."

27Then Peter spoke up. "Look here," he said, "we've left everything behind and followed you. What can we expect?"

28"I'm telling you the truth," Jesus replied. "In God's great new world, when the son of man sits on his glorious throne, those of you who have followed me will sit on twelve thrones— yes, you!—and rule over the twelve tribes of Israel. 29And anyone who's left houses or brothers or sisters or father or mother or children or estates because of my name will get back a hundred times over, and will inherit the life of that new age. 30But many at the front will find themselves at the back, and the back ones at the front.

The Workers in the Vineyard

20 "So you see," Jesus continued, "the kingdom of heaven is like a landowner who went out early in the morning to hire workers for his vineyard. 2He agreed with the workers to give them a dinar a day, and sent them off to his vineyard.

3"He went out again in the middle of the morning, and saw some others standing in the marketplace with nothing to do.

4" 'You too can go to the vineyard,' he said, 'and I'll give you what's right.' 5So off they went.

"He went out again about midday, and then in the middle of the afternoon, and did the same. 6Then, with only an hour of the day left, he went out and found other people standing there.

" 'Why are you standing here all day with nothing to do?' he asked them.

7" 'Because no one has hired us,' they replied.

" 'Well,' he said, 'you too can go into the vineyard.'

8"When evening came, the vineyard-owner said to his servant, 'Call the workers and give them their pay. Start with the last, and go on to the first.'

9"So the ones who had worked for one hour came, and each of them received a dinar. 10When the first ones came, they thought they would get something more; but they, too, each received a dinar.

¹¹"When they had been given it, they grumbled against the landowner. ¹²'This lot who came in last,' they said, 'have only worked for one hour—and they've been put on a level with us! And we did all the hard work, all day, and in the heat as well!'

¹³" 'My friend,' he said to one of them, 'I'm not doing you any wrong. You agreed with me on one dinar, didn't you? ¹⁴Take it! It's yours! And be on your way. I want to give this fellow who came at the end the same as you. ¹⁵Or are you suggesting that I'm not allowed to do what I like with my own money? Or are you giving me the evil eye because I'm good?'

¹⁶"So those at the back will be at the front, and the front ones at the back."

¹⁷Jesus was on his way up to Jerusalem. He took the twelve disciples aside in private, while they were on the road, and said to them, ¹⁸"Look here. We're going up to Jerusalem. The son of man will be handed over to the chief priests and the scribes, and they're going to condemn him to death. ¹⁹They will hand him over to the pagans, and they're going to mock him, flog him, and crucify him. And on the third day he will be raised."

The Cup He Had to Drink

²⁰Then the mother of Zebedee's sons came up, with her sons, to Jesus. She bowed low in front of him and indicated that she had a special request to make.

²¹"What do you want?" he asked her.

"It's about these two sons of mine," she said to him. "Please say that, when you're king, they may sit, one at your right hand and one at your left."

²²"You don't know what you're asking for," said Jesus. "Can you two drink the cup I'm going to drink?"

"Yes, we can," they replied.

²³"Well," said Jesus, "so you will drink my cup, then! But sitting at my right and left is not something I can grant. That's up to my father to give to whoever he has in mind."

²⁴When the other ten heard this they were annoyed with the two brothers. ²⁵But Jesus called them together.

"You know how it is with pagan rulers," he said. "They lord it over their subjects. They get all high and mighty and let everybody know it. ²⁶But that's not how it's to be with you. If any of you wants to be great, he must be your servant. ²⁷If any of you wants to be first, he must be the slave of all. ²⁸That's how it is with the son of man: he didn't come to have servants obey him, but to *be* a servant—and to give his life as 'a ransom for many.'"

The Healing of Two Blind Men

29As they were going out of Jericho, a large crowd was following Jesus. 30Just then two blind men were sitting by the wayside, and heard that Jesus was going by. "Have pity on us, Master, son of David!" they shouted.

31The crowd scolded them and told them to be silent. But they shouted out all the more, "Have pity on us, Master, son of David!"

32Jesus came to a stop. He called them.

"What do you want me to do for you?" he asked.

33"Master," they replied, "we want you to open our eyes."

34Jesus was very moved. He touched their eyes. At once they could see again, and they followed him.

Jesus Rides into Jerusalem

21 When they came near to Jerusalem, and arrived at Bethphage on the Mount of Olives, Jesus sent two of the disciples on ahead.

2"Go into the village over there," he said, "and at once you'll find a donkey tied up, and a foal beside it. Untie them and bring them to me. 3And if anyone says anything to you, say, 'The master needs them, and he'll send them back straightaway.'"

He sent them off at once.

4This happened so that the prophet's words might be fulfilled:

> 5*Tell this to Zion's daughter:*
> *Look now! Here comes your king;*
> *He's humble, mounted on an ass,*
> *Yes, on a foal, its young.*

6So the disciples went off and did as Jesus had told them. 7They brought the donkey and its foal, and put their cloaks on them, and Jesus sat on them.

8The huge crowd spread their cloaks on the road. Others cut branches from the trees and scattered them on the road. 9The crowds who went on ahead of him, and those who were following behind, shouted out,

"Hosanna now to David's Son!
God's blessing on the coming one—
The one who comes in the Lord's own name!
Hosanna in the highest!"

¹⁰When they came into Jerusalem, the whole city was gripped with excitement.

"Who is this?" they were saying.

¹¹"This is the prophet, Jesus," replied the crowds, "from Nazareth in Galilee!"

¹²Jesus went into the Temple and threw out all the people who were buying and selling in the Temple. He upturned the tables of the money-changers and the seats of the dove-sellers.

The Temple and the Fig Tree

¹³"This is what the Bible says," he said to them,

'My house will be called a house of prayer—
But you have made it a brigands' lair!'"

¹⁴The blind and the lame came to him in the Temple, and he healed them. ¹⁵But when the chief priests and the scribes saw the remarkable things he was doing, and the children shouting out "Hosanna to David's son!" in the Temple, they were very cross.

¹⁶"Do you hear what they're saying?" they asked Jesus.

"Yes," said Jesus. "Did you never read what it says,

'You called forth praise to rise to you
From newborn babes and infants too!'"

¹⁷Then he left them, and went out of the city to Bethany, where he stayed the night.

¹⁸Early the next morning Jesus went back to the city. He was hungry. ¹⁹He saw a single fig tree beside the road, but when he came up to it he found nothing on it except leaves.

"May you never bear fruit, ever again!" he said to it. Instantly the fig tree withered up.

²⁰The disciples saw it and were astonished.

"Look how quickly the fig tree has withered up!" they said.

²¹"I'm telling you the truth," replied Jesus. "If you have faith, and don't doubt, you will not only be able to do this to

a fig tree, but if you say to this mountain, 'Be lifted up and thrown into the sea,' it will happen. 22Whatever you ask in prayer, you'll get it, if you believe."

The Question
About John

23Jesus went into the Temple. As he was teaching, the chief priests and the elders of the people came up to him.

"By what right are you doing these things?" they asked him. "Who gave you this right?"

24"I'm going to ask you one question, too," replied Jesus, "and if you tell me the answer then I'll tell you by what right I'm doing these things. 25Where did John's baptism come from? Was it from heaven, or from this world?"

They debated this among themselves. "If we say 'from heaven,'" they said, "he's going to say to us, 'So why didn't you believe him?' 26But if we say 'from this world,' we'll have to watch out for the crowd, because they all reckon that John was a prophet."

27So they answered Jesus, "We don't know."

"Well, then," said Jesus, "nor will I tell you by what right I'm doing these things."

28"What d'you think?" he went on. "Once upon a time there was a man who had two sons.

"He went to the first one and said, 'Now then, my boy, off you go and do a day's work in the vineyard.'

29"'Don't want to,' replied the son; but afterward he thought better of it and went.

30"He went to the other son and said the same thing.

"'Certainly, Master,' he said; but he didn't go.

31"So which of the two did what his father wanted?"

"The first," they answered.

"I'm telling you the truth," Jesus said to them. "The tax-collectors and prostitutes are going into God's kingdom ahead of you! 32Yes: John came to you, in accordance with God's righteous covenant plan, and you didn't believe him—but the tax-collectors and prostitutes believed him. But when you saw it, you didn't think better of it afterward and believe him.

The Parable of
the Tenants

33"Listen to another parable," Jesus went on. "Once upon a time there was a householder who planted a vineyard, built a wall for it, dug out a winepress in it, and built a tower. Then he rented it out to tenant farmers and went away on a journey.

³⁴"When harvest time arrived, he sent his slaves to the farmers to collect his produce. ³⁵The farmers seized his slaves; they beat one, killed another, and stoned another. ³⁶Again he sent other slaves, more than before, and they treated them in the same way. ³⁷Finally he sent his son to them.

" 'They'll respect my son,' he said.

³⁸"But the farmers saw the son.

" 'This fellow's the heir!' they said among themselves. 'Come on, let's kill him, and then we can take over the property!'

³⁹"So they seized him, threw him out of the vineyard, and killed him.

⁴⁰"Now then: when the vineyard-owner returns, what will he do to those farmers?"

⁴¹"He'll kill them brutally, the wretches!" they said. "And he'll lease the vineyard to other farmers who'll give him the produce at the right time."

⁴²"Did you never read what the Bible says?" said Jesus to them:

> " 'The stone the builders threw away
> Is now atop the corner;
> It's from the Lord, all this, they say
> And we looked on in wonder.'

⁴³"So then let me tell you this: God's kingdom is going to be taken away from you and given to a nation that will produce the goods. ⁴⁴Anyone who falls on this stone will be smashed to pieces, and anyone it falls on will be crushed."

⁴⁵When the chief priests and the Pharisees heard his parables, they knew he was talking about them. ⁴⁶They tried to arrest him, but they were afraid of the crowds, who regarded him as a prophet.

The Parable of the Wedding Feast

22 Jesus spoke to them once again in parables.

²"The kingdom of heaven," he said, "is like a king who made a wedding feast for his son. ³He sent his slaves to call the invited guests to the wedding, and they didn't want to come.

⁴"Again he sent other slaves, with these instructions: 'Say to the guests, Look! I've got my dinner ready; my bulls and fatted

calves have been killed; everything is prepared. Come to the wedding!'

5"But they didn't take any notice. They went off, one to his own farm, another to see to his business. 6The others laid hands on his slaves, abused them, and killed them. 7(The king was angry, and sent his soldiers to destroy those murderers and burn down their city.) 8Then he said to his slaves, 'The wedding is ready, but the guests didn't deserve it. 9So go to the roads leading out of town, and invite everyone you find to the wedding.' 10The slaves went off into the streets and rounded up everyone they found, bad and good alike. And the wedding was filled with partygoers.

11"But when the king came in to look at the guests, he saw there a man who wasn't wearing a wedding suit.

12" 'My friend,' he said to him, 'how did you get in here without a wedding suit?' And he was speechless. 13Then the king said to the servants, 'Tie him up, hands and feet, and throw him into the darkness outside, where people weep and grind their teeth.'

14"Many are called, you see, but few are chosen."

Paying Taxes to Caesar 15Then the Pharisees went and plotted how they might trap him into saying the wrong thing. 16They sent their followers to him, with the Herodians.

"Teacher," they said, "we know that you are truthful, and that you teach God's way truthfully. You don't care what anyone thinks about you, because you don't try to flatter people or favor them. 17So tell us what you think. Is it lawful to pay tribute to Caesar, or not?"

18Jesus knew their evil intentions.

"Why are you trying to trick me, you hypocrites?" he said. 19"Show me the tribute coin." They brought him a dinar.

20"This . . . image," said Jesus, "and this . . . inscription. Who do they belong to?"

21"Caesar," they said.

"Well then," said Jesus, "you'd better give Caesar back what belongs to Caesar! And—give God back what belongs to God!"

22When they heard that they were astonished. They left him and went away.

²³The same day some Sadducees came to him. (The Saddu-cees deny the resurrection.) Their question was this.

The Question of the Resurrection

²⁴"Teacher," they began, "Moses said, 'If a man dies with-out children, his brother should marry his widow and raise up seed for his brother.' ²⁵Well now, there were seven brothers liv-ing among us. The first got married, and then died, and since he didn't have children he left his wife to his brother. ²⁶The same thing happened with the second and the third, and so on with all seven. ²⁷Last of all the woman died. ²⁸So: in the resur-rection, whose wife will she be, of all the seven? All of them had married her, after all."

²⁹This was Jesus's answer to them: "You are quite mis-taken," he said, "because you don't know your Bibles or God's power. ³⁰In the resurrection, you see, people don't marry or get married off; they are like angels in heaven. ³¹But as for the resurrection of the dead, did you never read what was said to you by God, in these words: ³²'I am the God of Abraham, and the God of Isaac, and the God of Jacob'? He isn't God of the dead, but of the living."

³³The crowds heard this, and they were astonished at his teaching.

³⁴When the Pharisees heard that Jesus had silenced the Sadducees, they got together in a group. ³⁵One of them, a law-yer, put him on the spot with this question.

The Great Commandment and David's Master

³⁶"Teacher," he said, "which is the most important com-mandment in the law?"

³⁷"You must love the Lord your God," replied Jesus, "with all your heart, with all your life, and with all your mind. ³⁸This is the first commandment, and it's the one that really matters. ³⁹The second is similar, and it's this: you must love your neigh-bor as yourself. ⁴⁰The entire law hangs on these two com-mandments—and that goes for the prophets, too."

⁴¹While the Pharisees were gathered there, Jesus asked them, ⁴²"What's your view of the Messiah? Whose son is he?"

"David's," they said to him.

⁴³"Why then," said Jesus, "does David (speaking by the spirit) call him 'Master,' when he says,

44'The Master says to my master,
Sit here at my right hand,
Until I place your enemies
Down beneath your feet.'

45"If David calls him 'Master,' how can he be his son?"

46Nobody was able to answer him a single word. From that day on nobody dared ask him anything anymore.

Warnings Against Scribes and Pharisees

23 Then Jesus spoke to the crowds and to his disciples: 2"The scribes and Pharisees," he said, "sit on the seat of Moses. 3So you must do whatever they tell you, and keep it, but don't do the things they do. You see, they talk but they don't do. 4They tie up heavy bundles which are difficult to carry, and they dump them on people's shoulders—but they themselves aren't prepared to lift a little finger to move them!

5"Everything they do is for show, to be seen by people. Yes, they make their prayer-boxes large and their prayer-tassels long, 6and they love the chief places at dinners, the main seats in the synagogues, 7the greetings in the marketplaces, and having people call them 'Rabbi.'

8"You mustn't be called 'Rabbi.' You have one teacher, and you are all one family. 9And you shouldn't call anyone 'Father' on earth, because you have one father, in heaven. 10Nor should you be called 'Teacher,' because you have one teacher, the Messiah.

11"The greatest among you should be your servant. 12People who make themselves great will be humbled; and people who humble themselves will become great.

Condemnation of Scribes and Pharisees (1)

13"Woe betide you, scribes and Pharisees, you hypocrites!" Jesus continued. "You lock up the kingdom of heaven in front of people's faces. You don't go in yourselves, and when other people try to enter, you stop them.

15"Woe betide you, scribes and Pharisees, you hypocrites! You cross sea and land to make one single Gentile take up Judaism, and when that happens you make the convert twice as much a child of Gehenna as you are yourselves.

16"Woe betide you, you blind guides! This is what you say: 'If anyone swears by the Temple, it's nothing; but if anyone

swears by the gold in the Temple, the oath is valid.' ¹⁷How
crazy and blind can you get! Which is greater, the gold, or the
Temple that makes the gold sacred? ¹⁸And you say, 'If anyone swears by the altar, it's nothing; but if anyone swears by
the gift on it, the oath is valid.' ¹⁹How blind you are! Which is
greater, the gift, or the altar that makes the gift sacred? ²⁰So
whoever swears by the altar swears by it and by everything on
it. ²¹And whoever swears by the Temple swears by it and by the
one who lives in it. ²²And whoever swears by heaven swears by
the throne of God and by the one who sits on it.

²³"Woe betide you, scribes and Pharisees, you hypocrites!"
Jesus went on. "You tithe mint and dill and cumin, and you
omit the serious matters of the law like justice, mercy, and
loyalty. You should have done these, without neglecting the
others. ²⁴You're blind guides! You filter out a gnat, but you gulp
down a camel!

Condemnation of Scribes and Pharisees (2)

²⁵"Woe betide you, scribes and Pharisees, you hypocrites!
You scrub the outside of the cup and the dish, but the inside
is full of extortion and moral flabbiness. ²⁶You blind Pharisee,
first make the inside of the cup clean, and then the outside will
be clean as well.

²⁷"Woe betide you, scribes and Pharisees, you hypocrites!
You're like whitewashed graves, which look very fine on the
outside, but inside they are full of the bones of the dead and
uncleanness of every kind. ²⁸That's like you: on the outside
you appear to be virtuous and law-abiding, but inside you are
full of hypocrisy and lawlessness.

²⁹"Woe betide you, scribes and Pharisees, you hypocrites!
You build the tombs of the prophets, and you decorate the
memorials of the righteous, ³⁰and you say, 'If we'd lived in
the days of our ancestors, we wouldn't have gone along with
them in killing the prophets.' ³¹So you testify against yourselves that you are the children of the people who murdered
the prophets! ³²Well then, go ahead: complete the work your
ancestors began! ³³You snakes, you nest of vipers, how can you
escape the judgment of Gehenna?

³⁴"Because of all this," Jesus concluded, "I'm sending you
prophets, wise men, and scribes. Some of them you will kill
and crucify. Some of them you will whip in your synagogues.

Judgment on Jerusalem and Its Leaders

You'll chase them from town to town. ³⁵That's how all the righteous blood that's been shed on earth, from the blood of righteous Abel to the blood of Zechariah son of Barachiah—you murdered him between sanctuary and altar—will come upon you. ³⁶I'm telling you the solemn truth: it will all come on this generation.

³⁷"Jerusalem, Jerusalem, killing the prophets and stoning those who are sent to you! How often have I longed to gather up your children, the way a hen gathers up her brood under her wings, and you didn't want me to! ³⁸Now, see here: your house has been abandoned by God; it's a ruin. ³⁹Yes, I tell you: you won't see me again from now on until you say, 'God's blessing on the coming one, the one who comes in the Lord's own name!'"

The Beginning of the Birth Pangs

24 Jesus left the Temple and went away. As he did so, his disciples came and pointed out the Temple buildings to him. ²"Yes," he said, "and you see all these things? I'm telling you the truth: not one stone will be left standing upon another. All of them will be thrown down."

³As he was sitting on the Mount of Olives, his disciples came to him privately.

"Tell us," they said, "when will these things happen? And what will be the sign that you are going to appear as king, and that the end of the age is upon us?"

⁴"Watch out," replied Jesus. "Don't let anyone deceive you. ⁵You see, there will be several who will come along, using my name, telling you 'I'm the Messiah!' They will fool lots of people. ⁶You're going to hear about wars, actual wars and rumored ones; make sure you don't get alarmed. This has got to happen, but it doesn't mean the end is coming yet. ⁷Nations will rise against one another, and kingdoms against each other. There will be famines and earthquakes here and there. ⁸All this is just the start of the birth pangs.

⁹"Then they will hand you over to be tortured, and they will kill you. You will be hated by all nations because of my name. ¹⁰Then many will find the going too hard, and they will betray each other and hate each other. ¹¹Many false prophets will arise, and they will deceive plenty of people. ¹²And because lawlessness will be on the increase, many will find their love

growing cold. ¹³But the one who lasts out to the end will be delivered. ¹⁴And this gospel of the kingdom must be announced
to the whole world, as a witness to all the nations. Then the
end will come.

¹⁵"So when you see 'the sacrilege that desolates,' as Daniel
the prophet put it, 'standing in the holy place' (the reader
should understand), ¹⁶then those who are in Judaea should
take to their heels and run to the mountains. ¹⁷If you're up on
your roof, don't go down into the house to get things out. ¹⁸If
you're in the fields, don't go back to pick up your cloak. ¹⁹It's
going to be terrible for pregnant and nursing women during
those days. ²⁰Pray that it won't be winter when you have to
run away, or for that matter a sabbath. ²¹Yes: there's going to
be such great suffering then as has never been since the start
of the world until now—no, and won't ever be again. ²²And if
those days had not been shortened, nobody at all would have
been rescued. But for the sake of God's chosen ones those days
will be shortened.

²³"Then if anyone says to you, 'Look! Here is the Messiah!'
or 'Look! There he is!' don't believe them. ²⁴False messiahs
will arise, you see, and false prophets too. They will provide
great signs and portents, so as to deceive even God's chosen
ones, if that were possible. ²⁵Remember, I'm telling you this
beforehand!

²⁶"So if someone says to you, 'Look! He's out in the wilderness,' don't go out. If they say, 'Look, he's in the inner room,'
don't believe them. ²⁷You see, the royal appearing of the son
of man will be like the lightning that comes from the east and
flashes across to the west. ²⁸Where the carcass is, there the
vultures will gather.

²⁹"Straightaway," Jesus continued, "after the suffering that
those days will bring,

> 'The sun will turn to darkness,
> And the moon won't give its light;
> The stars will fall from heaven,
> And the powers of heaven will shake.'

³⁰"And then the sign of the son of man will appear in heaven;
then all the tribes of the earth will mourn. They will see 'the

The Desolating Sacrilege

The Coming of the Son of Man

son of man coming on the clouds of heaven' with power and great glory. 31He will send off his messengers with a great trumpet-blast, and they will collect his chosen ones from the four winds, from one end of heaven to the other.

32"Learn the hidden meaning from the fig tree. When its branch begins to sprout, and to push out its leaves, then you know that summer is nearly there. 33So with you: when you see all these things, you will know that it is near, at the very gates. 34I'm telling you the truth: this generation won't be gone before all these things happen. 35Heaven and earth will disappear, but my words will never, ever disappear.

The Unexpected Coming

36"Nobody knows what day or time this will happen," Jesus went on. "The angels in heaven don't know it, and nor does the son; only the father knows. 37You see, the royal appearing of the son of man will be like the days of Noah.

38"What does that mean? Well, in those days, before the flood, they were eating and drinking, they were getting married and giving children in marriage, right up to the day when Noah went into the ark. 39They didn't know about it until the flood came and swept them all away. That's what it'll be like at the royal appearing of the son of man.

40"On that day there will be two people working in the field. One will be taken; the other will be left. 41There will be two women grinding corn in the mill. One will be taken; the other will be left.

42"So keep alert! You don't know what day your master will come. 43But bear this in mind: if the householder had known what time of night the burglar was going to come, he would have stayed awake and wouldn't have let his house get broken into. 44So you too must be ready! The son of man is coming at a time you don't expect.

The Wise and Wicked Slaves

45"So," Jesus went on, "who then is the trustworthy and sensible slave, the one the master will set over his household, so that he will give them their meals at the right time? 46Blessings on the servant whom the master, when he comes, finds doing just that. 47I'm telling you the truth: he'll promote him to be over all his belongings. 48But if the wicked slave says in his heart, 'My master's taking his time,' 49and starts to beat the other slaves, and to feast and drink with the drunkards,

50the master of that slave will come on a day he doesn't expect, and at a time he doesn't know. 51He will cut him in two, and put him along with the hypocrites, where people will weep and grind their teeth.

25 "Then," continued Jesus, "the kingdom of heaven will be like ten girls who each took their own torches and went out to meet the bridegroom. 2Five of them were silly, and five were sensible. 3The silly ones took their torches, but didn't take oil with them. 4The sensible ones took oil, in flasks, along with their torches.

5"The bridegroom took his time coming, and they all nodded off and went to sleep. 6In the middle of the night a shout went up: 'Here's the bridegroom! Come on and meet him!' 7Then all the girls got up and trimmed the wicks of their torches.

8"The silly ones said to the sensible ones, 'Give us some of your oil! Our torches are going out!'

9"But the sensible ones answered, 'No! If we do that, there won't be enough for all of us together! You'd better go to the dealers and buy some for yourselves.'

10"So off they went to buy oil. But, while they were gone, the bridegroom arrived. The ones who were ready went in with him to the wedding party, and the door was shut.

11"Later on the other girls came back. 'Master, Master!' they said, 'open the door for us!'

12" 'I'm telling you the truth,' he said, 'I don't know you.'

13"So keep awake! You don't know the day or the hour.

14"This is what it will be like," Jesus went on. "It will be like a man who was going off on a journey. He summoned his slaves, and handed over control of his property to them. 15He gave five talents to the first, two to the next, and one to the last—each according to his ability. Then he left.

"Straightaway 16the man who had been given the five talents went out and traded with them, and made five more. 17Similarly, the one who had received two talents went and made another two. 18But the one who received a single talent went and dug a hole in the ground, and hid his master's money.

19"After a long time, the master of those slaves came back and settled accounts with them. 20The man who had received five talents came forward and gave him the other five talents. 'Master,' he said, 'you gave me five talents. Look: I've made another five!' 21'Well done indeed,' said his master. 'You're an excellent slave, and loyal too! You've been trustworthy with small things, and now I'm going to put you in charge of bigger ones. Come and join your master's celebration!'

22"Then the man who'd had the two talents came forward. 'Master,' he said, 'you gave me two talents. Look: I've made another two!' 23'Well done indeed,' said his master. 'You're an excellent slave, and loyal too! You've been trustworthy with small things, and now I'm going to put you in charge of bigger ones. Come and join your master's celebration!'

24"Then the man who'd had the one talent came forward. 'Master,' he said, 'I knew that you were a hard man. You reap where you didn't sow, and you profit from things you never invested in. 25So I was scared! I went and hid your talent in the ground. Here it is: it's yours; you can have it back.'

26" 'You're a wicked and lazy slave!' answered his master. 'So! You knew that I reap where I didn't sow, and profit from investments I never made? 27Then you should have put my money with the bankers, and when I returned I would have received back what I had with interest!

28" 'So take the talent from him,' he went on, 'and give it to the man who has ten talents.' 29(If someone already has something, you see, they will be given more, and they'll have plenty. But if someone has nothing, even what they have will be taken away from them.) 30'But as for this useless slave, throw him outside in the dark, where people weep and grind their teeth.'

The Sheep and the Goats

31"When the son of man comes in his glory," Jesus went on, "and all the angels with him, then he will sit on his glorious throne. 32All the nations will be assembled in front of him, and he will separate them from one another, like a shepherd separates the sheep from the goats. 33He will stand the sheep at his right hand, and the goats at his left.

34"Then the king will say to those on his right, 'Come here, you people who my father has blessed. Inherit the kingdom prepared for you from the foundation of the world! 35Why? Because I was hungry and you gave me something to eat. I was thirsty and you gave me something to drink. I was a stranger

and you made me welcome. ³⁶I was naked and you clothed me;
I was sick and you looked after me; I was in prison and you
came to me.'

³⁷"Then the righteous will answer him, 'Master, when did
we see you hungry and feed you, or thirsty and give you a
drink? ³⁸When did we see you a stranger and welcome you, or
naked and clothe you? ³⁹When did we see you sick or in prison
and come to see you?'

⁴⁰"Then the king will answer them, 'I'm telling you the
truth: when you did it to one of the least significant of my
brothers and sisters here, you did it to me.'

⁴¹"Then he will say to those on his left hand, 'Get away from
me! You're accursed! Go to the everlasting fire prepared for
the devil and his angels! ⁴²Why? Because I was hungry and you
gave me nothing to eat! I was thirsty and you gave me nothing
to drink! ⁴³I was a stranger and you didn't welcome me; I was
naked and you didn't clothe me; I was sick and in prison and
you didn't look after me!'

⁴⁴"Then they too will answer, 'Master, when did we see you
hungry or thirsty, or a stranger, or naked, or sick, or in prison,
and didn't do anything for you?'

⁴⁵"Then he will answer them, 'I'm telling you the truth:
when you didn't do it for one of the least significant of my
brothers and sisters here, you didn't do it for me.'

⁴⁶"And they will go away into everlasting punishment, but
the righteous will go into everlasting life."

26 So this is how it finally happened.
When Jesus had finished all these sayings, he
said to his disciples, ²"In two days' time, as you
know, it'll be Passover! That's when the son of man will be
handed over to be crucified."

³Then the chief priests got together with the elders of the
people, in the official residence of the high priest, who was
called Caiaphas. ⁴They plotted how to capture Jesus by some
trick, and kill him.

⁵"We'd better not try anything at the feast," they said. "We
don't want the people to riot."

⁶While Jesus was at Bethany, in the house of Simon (known
as "the Leper"), ⁷a woman came to him who had an alabaster

Preparations for Jesus's Death

vase of extremely valuable ointment. She poured it on his head as he was reclining at the table.

8When the disciples saw it, they were furious.

"What's the point of all this waste?" they said. 9"This could have been sold for a fortune, and the money could have been given to the poor!"

10Jesus knew what they were thinking.

"Why make life difficult for the woman?" he said. "It's a lovely thing, what she's done for me. 11You always have the poor with you, don't you? But you won't always have me. 12When she poured this ointment on my body, you see, she did it to prepare me for my burial. 13I'm telling you the truth: wherever this gospel is announced in all the world, what she has just done will be told, and people will remember her."

Passover and Betrayal

14Then one of the Twelve, called Judas Iscariot, went to the chief priests.

15"What will you give me," he said, "to hand him over to you?"

They settled the deal with him at thirty pieces of silver. 16From that moment on, he was watching for an opportunity to hand him over.

17On the first day of the Feast of Unleavened Bread, the disciples said to Jesus, "Where do you want us to get the Passover ready for you to eat it?"

18"Go into the city," he said, "to a certain man, and say to him, 'The Teacher says, My time is very close. I'm going to keep the Passover at your house with my disciples.'"

19So the disciples did as Jesus had told them, and got the Passover ready.

20When evening came, he settled down with the Twelve. 21As they were eating, he said, "I'm telling you the truth: one of you will betray me." 22They were extremely upset, and began to say one by one, "It's not me, is it, Master?"

23"It's one who's dipped his hand with me in the dish," Jesus replied. "That's the one who will betray me. 24The son of man is on his way, as the Bible said it would happen, but it's misery for the man who hands him over. It would be better for that man if he'd never been born."

²⁵At this, Judas, who was planning to betray him, said, "It isn't me, is it, Teacher?"

"You've just said so," he replied.

²⁶As they were eating, Jesus took some bread, blessed it, broke it, and gave it to the disciples.

The Last Supper

"Take it and eat it," he said; "this is my body."

²⁷Then he took a cup; and, after giving thanks, he gave it to them.

"Drink this, all of you," he said. ²⁸"This is my blood of the covenant, which is poured out for many for the forgiveness of sins. ²⁹But let me tell you this: I will not drink any more from this fruit of the vine, until that day when I drink it new with you in the kingdom of my father."

³⁰They sang a hymn, and went out to the Mount of Olives.

³¹Then Jesus said to them, "You are all going to stumble and fall tonight because of me. This is what the Bible says, you see:

'I shall strike the shepherd,
  And the sheep of the flock will be scattered.'

³²"But after I am raised up, I shall go on ahead of you to Galilee."

³³"Even if everyone else trips and falls," said Peter in reply to him, "I'm never going to do that!"

³⁴"I'm telling you the truth," said Jesus to him, "this very night, before the cock has crowed, you will deny me three times."

³⁵"Even if I have to die with you," said Peter to him, "I won't ever deny you!"

And all the disciples said the same.

³⁶So Jesus went with them to the place called Gethsemane.

Gethsemane

"You sit here," he said to the disciples, "while I go over there and pray."

³⁷He took Peter and the two sons of Zebedee with him, and began to be very upset and distressed.

³⁸"My soul is overwhelmed with grief," he said, "even to death. Stay here and keep watch with me."

³⁹Then, going a little further on, he fell on his face and prayed.

"My father," he said, "if it's possible—please, please let this cup go away from me! But . . . not what I want, but what you want."

40He came back to the disciples and found them asleep.

"So," he said to Peter, "couldn't you keep watch with me for a single hour? 41Watch and pray so that you don't get pulled down into the time of testing. The spirit is eager, but the body is weak."

42Again, for the second time, he went off and said, "My father, if it's not possible for this to pass unless I drink it, let your will be done."

43Again he came and found them asleep; their eyes were heavy. 44Once more he left them and went away. He prayed for the third time, using the same words once again. 45Then he came back to the disciples.

"You can sleep now," he said, "and have a good rest! Look— the time has come, and the son of man is given over into the hands of wicked people! 46Get up and let's be going. Look! Here comes the one who's going to betray me!"

Jesus Is Arrested

47While Jesus was still speaking, there was Judas, one of the Twelve. He had come with a large crowd, with swords and clubs, from the chief priests and the elders of the people. 48The one who was intending to betray him gave them a sign: "The one I kiss—that's him! Grab hold of him!"

49So he went up at once to Jesus and said "Greetings, Teacher!" and kissed him.

50"My friend," said Jesus, "what have you come to do?"

Then they came and laid hands on Jesus, and arrested him.

51At that, one of the men with Jesus reached out his hand, drew his sword, and hit the high priest's slave, cutting off his ear.

52"Put your sword back where it belongs!" said Jesus to him. "People who use the sword die by the sword! 53Don't you realize that I could call on my father and have him send me more than twelve legions of angels, just like that? 54But how then can the Bible come true when it says this has to happen?"

55At that time Jesus said to the crowds, "Have you really come out with swords and sticks to arrest me, as if I were some kind of brigand? I sat there teaching in the Temple every day,

and you didn't arrest me! ⁵⁶But all this has happened so that
the writings of the prophets would be fulfilled."

Then all the disciples abandoned him and ran away.

⁵⁷The people who had arrested Jesus took him off to Caiaphas
the high priest. The scribes and elders had already gathered at
his house. ⁵⁸Peter, however, followed him at some distance, all
the way to the high priest's residence. He went in and sat with
the servants, to see how things would work out.

⁵⁹The high priest and the whole council tried to produce
false evidence against Jesus, to frame a capital charge and have
him killed. ⁶⁰But even though they brought in plenty of lying
witnesses, they couldn't find the evidence they wanted. Finally
two people came forward ⁶¹and declared: "This fellow said, 'I
can destroy God's Temple and build it again in three days!'"

⁶²Then the high priest stood up.

"Aren't you going to answer?" he said to him. "What are
these people accusing you of?"

⁶³But Jesus remained silent.

Then the high priest said to him, "I put you on oath before
the living God: tell us if you are the Messiah, God's son!"

⁶⁴"You said the words," replied Jesus. "But let me tell you
this: from now on you will see 'the son of man sitting at the
right hand of the Power, and coming on the clouds of heaven.'"

⁶⁵Then the high priest tore his robes.

"He's blasphemed!" he said. "Why do we need any more
witnesses? Look—you've heard his blasphemy, here and now!
⁶⁶What's your verdict?"

"He deserves to die," they answered.

⁶⁷Then they spat in his face and hit him. Some of them
slapped him, ⁶⁸and said, "Prophesy for us, Mr. Messiah! Who
was it who hit you?"

⁶⁹Meanwhile, Peter sat outside in the courtyard.

One of the servant-girls came up to him. "You were with
Jesus the Galilean too, weren't you?" she said.

⁷⁰He denied it in front of everyone.

"I don't know what you're talking about," he said.

⁷¹He went out to the gateway. Another girl saw him, and said
to the people who were there, "This fellow was with Jesus the
Nazarene!"

Jesus Before Caiaphas

Peter's Denial

⁷²Once more he denied it, this time swearing, "I don't know the man!"

⁷³After a little while the people standing around came up and said to Peter, "You really are one of them! Look—the way you talk makes it obvious!"

⁷⁴Then he began to curse and swear, "I don't know the man!" And then, all at once, the cock crowed.

⁷⁵And Peter remembered.

He remembered the words Jesus had spoken to him: "Before the cock crows, you will deny me three times."

And he went outside and cried like a baby.

The Death of Judas

27 When dawn broke, all the chief priests and elders of the people held a council meeting about Jesus, in order to have him put to death. ²They tied him up, took him off, and handed him over to Pilate, the governor.

³Meanwhile Judas, who had betrayed him, saw that he had been condemned, and was filled with remorse. He took the thirty pieces of silver back to the high priests and elders.

⁴"I've sinned!" he said. "I betrayed an innocent man, and now I've got his blood on my hands!"

"See if we care!" they replied. "Deal with it yourself."

⁵And he threw down the money in the Temple, and left, and went and hanged himself.

⁶"Well now," said the chief priests, picking up the money. "According to the law, we can't put it into the Temple treasury. It's the price of someone's blood."

⁷So they had a discussion, and used it to buy the Potter's Field, as a burial place for foreigners. ⁸(That's why that field is called Blood Field, to this day.) ⁹Then the word that was spoken by Jeremiah the prophet came true:

> *They took the thirty pieces of silver,*
> *The price of the one who was valued,*
> *Valued by the children of Israel;*
> *¹⁰And they gave them for the potter's field,*
> *As the Lord instructed me.*

Jesus and Barabbas Before Pilate

¹¹So Jesus stood in front of the governor.

"Are you the king of the Jews?" the governor asked him.

"If you say so," replied Jesus.

¹²The chief priests and elders poured out their accusations against him, but he made no answer.

¹³Then Pilate said to him, "Don't you hear all this evidence they're bringing against you?"

¹⁴He gave him no answer, not even a word, which quite astonished the governor.

¹⁵Now the governor had a custom. At festival-time he used to release one prisoner for the crowd, whoever they chose. ¹⁶Just then they had a famous prisoner, called Jesus Barabbas. ¹⁷So when the people were all gathered there, Pilate said to them, "Who do you want me to release for you? Jesus Barabbas, or Jesus the so-called Messiah?" ¹⁸(He knew that they'd handed him over out of sheer envy.)

¹⁹While he was presiding in the court, his wife sent a message to him.

"Don't have anything to do with that man," she said. "He's innocent! I've had a really bad time today in a dream, all because of him."

²⁰The high priests and the elders persuaded the crowds to ask for Barabbas, and to have Jesus killed. ²¹So when the governor came back to them again, and asked, "Which of the two do you want me to release for you?" they said, "Barabbas!"

²²"So what shall I do with Jesus the so-called Messiah?" asked Pilate.

"Let him be crucified!" they all said.

²³"Why?" asked Pilate. "What's he done wrong?"

But they shouted all the louder, "Let him be crucified!"

²⁴Pilate saw that it was no good. In fact, there was a riot brewing. So he took some water and washed his hands in front of the crowd.

"I'm not guilty of this man's blood," he said. "It's your problem."

²⁵"Let his blood be on us!" answered all the people, "and on our children!"

²⁶Then Pilate released Barabbas for them. He had Jesus flogged, and handed him over to be crucified.

²⁷Then the soldiers of the governor took Jesus into the barracks and gathered the whole regiment together. ²⁸They took off his clothes and dressed him up in a scarlet military

Jesus Mocked and Crucified

cloak. 29They wove a crown out of thorns and stuck it on his head, and put a reed in his right hand. Then they knelt down in front of him.

"Greetings, king of the Jews!" they said, making fun of him.

30They spat on him. Then they took the reed and beat him about the head. 31When they had finished mocking him, they took off the cloak, dressed him in his own clothes again, and led him off to crucify him.

32As they were going out they found a man from Cyrene, called Simon. They forced him to carry Jesus's cross.

33When they came to the place called Golgotha, which means Skull Place, 34they gave him a drink of wine mixed with bitter herbs. When he tasted it, he refused to drink it.

35Then they crucified him. They divided up his clothes by casting lots, 36and they sat down and kept watch over him there. 37And they placed the written charge above his head: "This is Jesus, the king of the Jews."

38Then they crucified two brigands alongside him, one on his right and one on his left.

Jesus Mocked on the Cross
39The people who were going by shouted blasphemies at Jesus. They shook their heads at him.

40"So!" they said. "You were going to destroy the Temple and build it in three days, were you? Save yourself, if you're God's son! Come down from the cross!"

41The chief priests, too, and the scribes and the elders, mocked him.

42"He rescued others," they said, "but he can't rescue himself! All right, so he's the king of Israel!—well, let him come down from the cross right now, and then we'll really believe that he is! 43He trusted in God; let God deliver him now, if he's that keen on him—after all, he did say he was God's son!"

44The brigands who were crucified alongside him heaped insults on him as well.

The Death of God's Son
45From noon until mid-afternoon there was darkness over the whole land. 46About the middle of the afternoon Jesus shouted out in a loud voice, *"Eli, Eli, lema sabachthani!"*—which means, "My God, my God, why did you abandon me?"

47Some of the people who were standing there heard it and said, "This fellow's calling Elijah!"

⁴⁸One of them ran at once and got a sponge. He filled it with vinegar, put it on a reed, and gave him a drink.

⁴⁹The others said, "Wait a bit. Let's see if Elijah is going to come and rescue him!"

⁵⁰But Jesus shouted out loudly one more time, and then breathed his last breath.

⁵¹At that instant the Temple curtain was torn in two, from top to bottom. The earth shook, the rocks were split, ⁵²and the tombs burst open. Many bodies of the sleeping holy ones were raised. ⁵³They came out of the tombs after Jesus's resurrection, and went into the holy city, where they appeared to many people.

⁵⁴When the centurion and the others with him, keeping watch over Jesus, saw the earthquake and the things that happened, they were scared out of their wits.

"He really was God's son!" they said.

⁵⁵There were several women there, watching from a distance. They had followed Jesus from Galilee, helping to look after his needs. ⁵⁶They included Mary Magdalene, Mary the mother of James and Joseph, and the mother of Zebedee's sons.

⁵⁷When evening came, a rich man from Arimathea arrived. **The Burial** He was called Joseph, and he too was a disciple of Jesus. ⁵⁸He **of Jesus** went to Pilate and requested the body of Jesus. Pilate gave the order that it should be given to him.

⁵⁹So Joseph took the body and wrapped it in a clean linen cloth. ⁶⁰He laid it in his own new tomb, which he had carved out of the rock. Then he rolled a large stone across the doorway of the tomb and went away.

⁶¹Mary Magdalene was there, and so was the other Mary. They were sitting opposite the tomb.

⁶²On the next day (that is, the day after Preparation Day), the chief priests and the Pharisees went as a group to Pilate.

⁶³"Sir," they said, "when that deceiver was still alive, we recall that he said, 'After three days, I'll rise again.' ⁶⁴So please give the order for the tomb to be made secure until the third day. Otherwise his disciples might come and steal him away, and then tell the people, 'He's been raised from the dead!' and so the last deception would be worse than the first."

⁶⁵"You may have a guard," said Pilate; "go and make it as secure as you know how." ⁶⁶So they went and made the tomb secure, sealing the stone and putting a guard on watch.

The Resurrection of Jesus

28 Dawn was breaking on the first day of the week; the sabbath was over. Mary Magdalene and the other Mary had come to look at the tomb, ²when suddenly there was a great earthquake. An angel of the Lord came down from heaven. He came to the stone, rolled it away, and sat down on top of it. ³Looking at him was like looking at lightning, and his clothes were white, like snow. ⁴The guards trembled with terror at him, and became like corpses themselves.

⁵"Don't be afraid," said the angel to the women. "I know you're looking for Jesus, who was crucified. ⁶He isn't here! He's been raised, as he said he would be! Come and see the place where he was lying—⁷and then go at once, and tell his disciples that he's been raised from the dead, and that he's going on ahead of you to Galilee. That's where you'll see him. There: I've told you."

⁸The women scurried off quickly away from the tomb, in a mixture of terror and great delight, and went to tell his disciples. ⁹Suddenly, there was Jesus himself. He met them and said, "Greetings!" They came up to him and took hold of his feet, prostrating themselves in front of him.

¹⁰"Don't be afraid," said Jesus to them. "Go and tell my brothers that they should go to Galilee. Tell them they'll see me there."

The Priests and the Guards

¹¹While the women were on their way, some of the soldiers who had been on guard went into the city and told the chief priests everything that had happened. ¹²They called an emergency meeting with the elders, allotted a substantial sum of money, and gave it to the soldiers.

¹³"This," they told them, "is what you are to say: 'His disciples came in the night, while we were asleep, and stole him away.' ¹⁴And if this gets reported to the governor, we'll explain it to him and make sure you stay out of trouble."

¹⁵They took the money and did as they had been instructed. And this story still goes the rounds among the Jews to this day.

¹⁶So the eleven disciples went off to Galilee, to the mountain where Jesus had instructed them to go. ¹⁷There they saw him, and worshipped him, though some hesitated.

¹⁸Jesus came toward them and addressed them.

"All authority in heaven and on earth," he said, "has been given to me! ¹⁹So you must go and make all the nations into disciples. Baptize them in the name of the father, and of the son, and of the holy spirit. ²⁰Teach them to observe everything I have commanded you. And look: I am with you, every single day, to the very end of the age."

The Great Commission

The Gospel According to
Mark

1 This is where the good news starts—the good news of Jesus the Messiah, God's son.

²Isaiah the prophet put it like this ("Look! I am sending my messenger ahead of me; he will clear the way for you!"):

³"A shout goes up in the desert: Make way for the Lord! Clear a straight path for him!"

⁴John the Baptizer appeared in the desert. He was announcing a baptism of repentance, to forgive sins. ⁵The whole of Judaea, and everyone who lived in Jerusalem, went out to him; they confessed their sins and were baptized by him in the river Jordan. ⁶John wore camel-hair clothes, with a leather belt around his waist. He used to eat locusts and wild honey.

⁷"Someone a lot stronger than me is coming close behind," John used to tell them. "I don't deserve to squat down and undo his sandals. ⁸I've plunged you in the water; he's going to plunge you in the holy spirit."

⁹This is how it happened. Around that time, Jesus came from Nazareth in Galilee, and was baptized by John in the river Jordan. ¹⁰That very moment, as he was getting out of the water, he saw the heavens open, and the spirit coming down like a dove onto him. ¹¹Then there came a voice, out of the heavens: "You are my son! You are the one I love! You make me very glad."

¹²All at once the spirit pushed him out into the desert. ¹³He was in the desert forty days, and the satan tested him there. He was with the wild beasts, and angels waited on him.

¹⁴After John's arrest, Jesus came into Galilee, announcing God's good news.

The Calling of the Disciples

¹⁵"The time is fulfilled!" he said; "God's kingdom is arriving! Turn back, and believe the good news!"

¹⁶As he went along beside the Sea of Galilee he saw Simon and his brother Andrew. They were fishermen, and were casting nets into the sea.

¹⁷"Follow me!" said Jesus to them. "I'll have you fishing for people!"

¹⁸Straightaway they left their nets and followed him. ¹⁹He went on a bit, and saw James, Zebedee's son, and John his brother. They were in the boat mending their nets, ²⁰and he called them then and there. They left their father Zebedee in the boat with the hired servants, and went off after him.

²¹They went to Capernaum. At once, on the sabbath, Jesus went into the synagogue and taught. ²²They were astonished at his teaching. He wasn't like the legal teachers; he said things on his own authority.

Exorcism and Healings

²³All at once, in their synagogue, there was a man with an unclean spirit.

²⁴"What business have you got with us, Jesus of Nazareth?" he yelled. "Have you come to destroy us? I know who you are: you're God's Holy One!"

²⁵"Be quiet!" ordered Jesus. "And come out of him!"

²⁶The unclean spirit convulsed the man, gave a great shout, and came out of him. ²⁷Everyone was astonished.

"What's this?" they started to say to each other. "New teaching—with real authority! He even tells the unclean spirits what to do, and they do it!"

²⁸Word about Jesus spread at once, all over the surrounding district of Galilee.

²⁹They came out of the synagogue, and went at once (with James and John) into Simon and Andrew's house. ³⁰Simon's mother-in-law was in bed with a fever, and they told Jesus about her right away. ³¹He went in, took her by the hand, and raised her up. The fever left her, and she waited on them.

³²When the sun went down and evening came, they brought to Jesus everyone who was ill, all who were demon-possessed.

³³The whole town was gathered around the door. ³⁴Jesus healed many people suffering from all kinds of diseases, and cast out many demons. He didn't allow the demons to speak, because they knew him.

The Healing of a Man with a Skin Disease

³⁵Very early—in the middle of the night, actually—Jesus got up and went out, off to a lonely place, and prayed. ³⁶Simon, and those with him, followed. ³⁷When they found him, they said, "Everyone is looking for you!"

³⁸"Let's go off to the other towns around here," Jesus replied, "so that I can tell the news to people there too. That's why I came out."

³⁹So he went into their synagogues, throughout the whole of Galilee, telling the news and casting out demons.

⁴⁰A man with a virulent skin disease came up to him. He knelt down and begged him, "If you want to, you can make me clean!"

⁴¹Jesus was deeply moved. He reached out his hand and touched him, and said to him, "I do want to: be clean!" ⁴²The disease left him at once, and he was clean.

⁴³Jesus sent him away at once, with this stern warning: ⁴⁴"Mind you don't say anything to anyone! Just go and show yourself to the priest, and make the offering Moses commanded, to purify yourself and to give them a sign."

⁴⁵But the man went out and began to tell the news widely. He spread the tale so effectively that Jesus couldn't any longer go publicly into a town. He stayed out in the open country, and people came to him from all around.

The Healing of the Paralytic

2 Jesus went back again to Capernaum, where, after a few days, word got around that he was at home. ²A crowd gathered, with the result that people couldn't even get near the door as he was telling them the message.

³A party arrived: four people carrying a paralyzed man, bringing him to Jesus. ⁴They couldn't get through to him because of the crowd, so they opened up the roof above where he was. When they had dug through it, they used ropes to let down the stretcher the paralyzed man was lying on.

⁵Jesus saw their faith, and said to the paralyzed man, "Child, your sins are forgiven!"

6"How dare the fellow speak like this?" grumbled some of the legal experts among themselves. 7"It's blasphemy! Who can forgive sins except God?"

8Jesus knew at once, in his spirit, that thoughts like this were in the air. "Why do your hearts tell you to think that?" he asked. 9"Answer me this," he went on. "Is it easier to say to this cripple, 'Your sins are forgiven,' or to say, 'Get up, pick up your stretcher, and walk'?

10"You want to know that the son of man has authority on earth to forgive sins?" He turned to the paralytic. 11"I tell you," he said, "Get up, take your stretcher, and go home." 12He got up, picked up the stretcher in a flash, and went out before them all.

Everyone was astonished, and they praised God. "We've never seen anything like this!" they said.

13Once more Jesus went out beside the sea. All the crowd came to him, and he taught them.

The Calling of Levi

14As he went along he saw Levi, son of Alphaeus, sitting at the tollbooth. "Follow me!" he said. And he got up and followed him.

15That's how Jesus came to be sitting at home with lots of tax-collectors and sinners. There they were, plenty of them, sitting with Jesus and his disciples; they had become his followers.

16When the legal experts from the Pharisees saw him eating with tax-collectors and sinners, they said to his disciples, "Why does he eat with tax-collectors and sinners?"

17When Jesus heard it, he said to them, "It's sick people who need the doctor, not healthy ones. I came to call the bad people, not the good ones."

Questions About Fasting

18John's disciples, and the Pharisees' disciples, were fasting. People came and said to Jesus, "Look here: John's disciples are fasting, and so are the Pharisees' disciples; why aren't yours?"

19"How can the wedding guests fast," Jesus replied, "if the bridegroom is there with them? As long as they've got the bridegroom with them, they can't fast.

20"Mind you, the time is coming when the bridegroom will be taken away from them. They'll fast then all right.

21"No one sews unshrunk cloth onto an old cloak. If they do, the new patch will tear the old cloth, and they'll end up with a worse hole. 22Nor does anyone put new wine into old wineskins. If they do, the wine will burst the skins, and they'll lose the wine and the skins together. New wine needs new skins."

Teachings on the Sabbath

23One sabbath, Jesus was walking through the cornfields. His disciples made their way along, plucking corn as they went.

24"Look here," said the Pharisees to him, "why are they doing something illegal on the sabbath?"

25"Haven't you ever read what David did," replied Jesus, "when he was in difficulties, and he and his men got hungry? 26He went into God's house (this was when Abiathar was high priest), and ate the 'bread of the presence,' which only the priests were allowed to eat—and he gave it to the people with him.

27"The sabbath was made for humans," he said, "not humans for the sabbath; 28so the son of man is master even of the sabbath."

Healing of the Man with the Withered Hand

3 Once more Jesus went to the synagogue. There was a man there with a withered hand. 2People were watching to see if Jesus would heal him on the sabbath, so that they could frame a charge against him.

3"Stand up," said Jesus to the man with the withered hand, "and come out here." And he said to them, 4"Is it lawful to do good on the sabbath, or to do evil? To save life or to kill?" They stayed quiet.

5He was deeply upset at their hard-heartedness, and looked around at them angrily. Then he said to the man, "Stretch out your hand." He stretched it out—and his hand was restored. 6The Pharisees went out right away and began to plot with the Herodians against Jesus, trying to find a way to destroy him.

The Twelve Are Appointed

7Jesus went off toward the sea with his disciples, and a large crowd from Galilee followed him. A great company, too, from Judaea, 8Jerusalem, Idumaea, Transjordan, and the region of Tyre and Sidon, heard what he was doing and came to him.

9There was a real danger that he might be crushed by the crowd, so he told his disciples to get a boat ready for him. 10He healed large numbers, and sick people were pushing toward him to touch him. 11Whenever unclean spirits saw him, they fell down in front of him and yelled out, "You are the son of God!" 12He gave them strict orders not to reveal his identity.

13Jesus went up the mountain and summoned the people he wanted, and they came to him. 14He appointed twelve (naming them "apostles") to be with him and to be sent out as heralds, 15and to have authority to cast out demons. 16In appointing the Twelve, he named Simon "Peter"; 17James, son of Zebedee, and his brother John, he named "Boanerges," which means "sons of thunder." The others were 18Andrew, Philip, Bartholomew, Matthew, Thomas, James son of Alphaeus, Thaddaeus, Simon the Cananaean, 19and Judas Iscariot (the one who handed him over).

20He went into the house. A crowd gathered again, so they couldn't even have a meal. 21When his family heard it, they came to restrain him. "He's out of his mind," they said.

Jesus and Beelzebul

22Experts who had come from Jerusalem were saying, "He is possessed by Beelzebul! He casts out demons by the prince of demons!"

23Jesus summoned them and spoke to them in pictures. "How can the Accuser cast out the Accuser? 24If a kingdom splits into two factions, it can't last; 25if a household splits into two factions, it can't last. 26So if the Accuser revolts against himself and splits into two, he can't last—his time is up! 27But remember: no one can get into a strong man's house and steal his property unless first they tie up the strong man; then they can plunder his house.

28"I'm telling you the truth: people will be forgiven all sins, and all blasphemies of whatever sort. 29But people who blaspheme the holy spirit will never find forgiveness. They will be guilty of an eternal sin." 30That was his response to their claim that he had an unclean spirit.

Jesus's Family

31Jesus's mother and brothers appeared. They waited outside the house, and sent in a message, asking for him.

32"Look!" said the crowd sitting around Jesus. "Your mother, your brothers, and your sisters are outside! They're searching for you!"

33"Who is my mother?" replied Jesus. "Who are my brothers?"

34He looked around him at the people sitting there in a ring. "Here is my mother!" he said. "Here are my brothers!

35Anybody who does God's will is my brother! And my sister! And my mother!"

The Parable of
the Sower

4 Once again Jesus began to teach beside the sea. A huge crowd gathered; so he got into a boat and stationed himself on the sea, with all the crowd on the shore looking out to sea. 2He taught them lots of things in parables. This is how his teaching went.

3"Listen!" he said. "Once upon a time there was a sower who went out sowing. 4As he was sowing, some seed fell beside the path, and the birds came and ate it up. 5Other seed fell on the rock, where it didn't have much soil. There was no depth to the ground, so it shot up at once; 6but when the sun came up it was scorched, and withered away, because it hadn't got any root. 7Other seed fell in among thorns; the thorns grew up and choked it, and it didn't give any crop. 8And other seeds fell into good soil, and gave a harvest, which grew up and increased, and bore a yield, in some cases thirtyfold, in some sixtyfold, and in some a hundredfold."

9And he added, "If you've got ears, then listen!"

10When they were alone, the people who were around Jesus, with the Twelve, asked him about the parables.

11"The mystery of God's kingdom is given to you," he replied, "but for the people outside it's all in parables, 12so that 'they may look and look but never see, and hear and hear but never understand; otherwise they would turn and be forgiven.'

13"Don't you understand the parable?" he said to them. "How are you going to understand all the parables?

14"The sower sows the word. 15The ones by the path are people who hear the word, but immediately the Accuser comes and takes away the word that has been sown in them. 16The ones sown on the rock are those who hear the word and accept it with excitement, 17but don't have any root in themselves. They are short-term enthusiasts. When the word brings them trouble or hostility, they quickly become disillusioned. 18The others—the ones sown among thorns—are those who hear the word, 19and the worries of the present age, and the deceit of riches, and desires for other kinds of things, come in and choke the word, so that it produces no fruit. 20But the ones sown on good soil are the people who hear the word and receive it, and produce fruit, some thirtyfold, some sixtyfold, some a hundredfold."

²¹Jesus said to them, "When you bring a lamp into a room, do you put it under a bucket, or under a bed? Of course not! It goes on a lampstand. ²²No: nothing is secret except what's meant to be revealed, and nothing is covered up except what's meant to be uncovered. ²³If you have ears, then listen!

A Lamp on Its Stand

²⁴"Be careful with what you hear," he went on. "The scales you use will be used for you, and more so. ²⁵If you have something, you'll be given more; but if you have nothing, even what you have will be taken away.

²⁶"This is what God's kingdom is like," said Jesus. "Once upon a time a man sowed seed on the ground. ²⁷Every night he went to bed; every day he got up; and the seed sprouted and grew without him knowing how it did it. ²⁸The ground produces crops by itself: first the stalk, then the ear, then the complete corn in the ear. ²⁹But when the crop is ready, in goes the sickle at once, because harvest has arrived.

More Seed Parables

³⁰"What shall we say God's kingdom is like?" he said. "What picture shall we give of it? ³¹It's like a grain of mustard seed. When it's sown on the ground, it's the smallest of all the seeds of the earth. ³²But when it's sown, it springs up and becomes the biggest of all shrubs. It grows large branches, so that 'the birds of the air make their nests' within its shade."

³³He used to tell them a lot of parables like this, speaking the word as much as they were able to hear. ³⁴He never spoke except using parables. But he explained everything to his own disciples in private.

³⁵That day, when it was evening, Jesus said to them, "Let's go over to the other side."

Jesus Calms the Storm

³⁶They left the crowd, and took him with them in the boat he'd been in. There were other boats with him too.

³⁷A big windstorm blew up. The waves beat on the boat, and it quickly began to fill. ³⁸Jesus, however, was asleep on a cushion in the stern. They woke him up.

"Teacher!" they said to him, "We're going down! Don't you care?"

³⁹He got up, scolded the wind, and said to the sea, "Silence! Shut up!"

The wind died, and there was a flat calm. ⁴⁰Then he said to them, "Why are you scared? Don't you believe yet?"

⁴¹Great fear stole over them. "Who *is* this?" they said to each other. "Even the wind and the sea do what he says!"

The Healing of the Demoniac

5 So they came over the sea to the land of the Gerasenes. ²When they got out of the boat, they were suddenly confronted by a man with an unclean spirit. ³He was emerging from a graveyard, which was where he lived. Nobody had been able to tie him up, not even with a chain; ⁴he had often been bound with shackles and chains, but he used to tear up the chains and snap the shackles. No one had the strength to tame him. ⁵On and on, night and day, he used to shout out in the graveyard and on the hillside, and slash himself with stones.

⁶When he saw Jesus a long way away, he ran and threw himself down in front of him.

⁷"Why you and me, Jesus?" he shouted at the top of his voice. "Why you and me, son of the High God? By God, stop torturing me!"—⁸this last, because Jesus was saying to him, "Unclean spirit, come out of him!"

⁹"What's your name?" Jesus asked him.

"Legion," he replied. "That's my name—there are lots of us!" ¹⁰And he implored Jesus not to send them out of the country.

¹¹It so happened that right there, near the hillside, was a sizable herd of pigs. They were grazing.

¹²"Send us to the pigs," begged the spirits, "so that we can enter them."

¹³So Jesus gave them permission. The unclean spirits came out and went into the pigs. The herd rushed down the steep slope into the sea—about two thousand of them!—and were drowned.

¹⁴The herdsmen fled. They told it in the town, they told it in the countryside, and people came to see what had happened. ¹⁵They came to Jesus; and there they saw the man who had been demon-possessed, who had had the "legion," seated, clothed and stone-cold sober. They were afraid. ¹⁶The people who had seen it all told them what had happened to the man— and to the pigs. ¹⁷And they began to beg Jesus to leave their district.

18Jesus was getting back into the boat, when the man asked if he could go with him. 19Jesus wouldn't let him.

"Go back home," he said. "Go to your people and tell them what the Lord has done for you. Tell them how he had pity on you."

20He went off and began to announce in the Ten Towns what Jesus had done for him. Everyone was astonished.

21Jesus crossed over once more in the boat to the other side. There a large crowd gathered around him, and he was by the seashore.

Jairus's Daughter and the Woman with Chronic Bleeding

22One of the synagogue presidents, a man named Jairus, arrived. When he saw Jesus, he fell down at his feet.

23"My daughter's going to die! My daughter's going to die!" he pleaded. "Please come—lay your hands on her—rescue her and let her live!"

24Jesus went off with him. A large crowd followed, and pressed in on him.

25A woman who'd had internal bleeding for twelve years heard about Jesus. 26(She'd had a rough time at the hands of one doctor after another; she'd spent all she had on treatment, and had gotten worse rather than better.) 27She came up in the crowd behind him and touched his clothes. 28"If I can just touch his clothes," she said to herself, "I'll be rescued." 29At once her flow of blood dried up. She knew, in her body, that her illness was cured.

30Jesus knew at once, inside himself, that power had gone out of him. He turned around in the crowd and said, "Who touched my clothes?"

31"You see this crowd crushing you," said the disciples, "and you say 'Who touched me?'"

32He looked around to see who had done it. 33The woman came up; she was afraid and trembling, but she knew what had happened to her. She fell down in front of him and told him the whole truth.

34"My daughter," Jesus said to her, "your faith has rescued you. Go in peace. Be healed from your illness."

35As he said this, some people arrived from the synagogue president's house.

The Raising of Jairus's Daughter

"Your daughter's dead," they said. "Why bother the teacher anymore?"

³⁶Jesus overheard the message. "Don't be afraid!" he said to the synagogue president. "Just believe!"

³⁷He didn't let anyone go with him except Peter, James, and James's brother John. ³⁸They arrived at the synagogue president's house, and saw a commotion, with a lot of weeping and wailing. ³⁹Jesus went inside.

"Why are you making such a fuss?" he said. "Why all this weeping? The child isn't dead; she's asleep." ⁴⁰And they laughed at him.

He put them all out. Then he took the child's father and mother, and his companions, and they went in to where the child was. ⁴¹He took hold of her hand and said to her, *"Talitha koum,"* which means, "Time to get up, little girl!" ⁴²At once the girl got up and walked about. (She was twelve years old.) They were astonished out of their wits. ⁴³Then he commanded them over and over not to let anyone know about it, and told them to give her something to eat.

A Prophet in His Own Town

6 Jesus went away from there, and came to his home region. His disciples followed him. ²On the sabbath, he began to teach in the synagogue. When they heard him, lots of people were astonished.

"Where does he get it all from?" they said. "What's this wisdom he's been given? How does he get this kind of power in his hands? ³Isn't he the handyman, Mary's son? Isn't he the brother of James, Joses, Judah, and Simon? And aren't his sisters here with us?" They took offense at him.

⁴"Prophets have honor everywhere," said Jesus, "except in their own country, their own family, and their own home."

⁵He couldn't do anything remarkable there, except that he laid hands on a few sick people and cured them. ⁶Their unbelief dumbfounded him.

He went around the villages, teaching.

The Twelve Sent Out

⁷Jesus called the Twelve, and began to send them out in pairs, giving them authority over unclean spirits. ⁸These were his instructions: they were not to take anything for the road, just one staff; no bread, no bag, no cash in the belt; ⁹to wear sandals, and not to wear a second tunic.

¹⁰"Whenever you go into a house," he told them, "stay there until you leave the district. ¹¹If any place doesn't welcome you,

or won't listen to you, go away and wipe the dust from your feet as evidence against them."

¹²They went off and announced that people should repent. ¹³They cast out several demons; and they anointed many sick people with oil, and cured them.

¹⁴Jesus's name became well known, and reached the ears of King Herod.

The Speculations of Herod

"It's John the Baptist," he said, "risen from the dead! That's why these powers are at work in him."

¹⁵Other people said, "It's Elijah!"

Others said, "He's a prophet, like one of the old prophets."

¹⁶"No," said Herod when he heard this. "It's John. I cut off his head, and he's been raised."

¹⁷What had happened was this. Herod had married Herodias, his brother Philip's wife. ¹⁸John regularly told Herod it wasn't right for him to take his brother's wife; so Herod gave the word, arrested him, and tied him up in prison. ¹⁹Herodias kept up a grudge against him and wanted to kill him, but couldn't; ²⁰Herod was afraid of John, knowing that he was a just and holy man. So he protected him, and used to listen to him regularly. What he heard disturbed him greatly, and yet he enjoyed listening to him.

Herod and John the Baptist

²¹And then, one day, the moment came. There was a great party. It was Herod's birthday, and he gave a feast for his leading retainers, militia officers, and the great and good of Galilee. ²²Herodias's daughter came in and danced, and Herod and his guests were delighted.

"Tell me what you'd like," said the king to the girl, "and I'll give it you!"

²³He swore to her, over and over again, "Whatever you ask me, I'll give it you—right up to half my kingdom!"

²⁴She went out and said to her mother, 'What shall I ask for?'

"The head of John the Baptist," she replied.

²⁵So she went back at once to the king, all eager, and made her request: "I want you to give me, right now, on a dish—the head of John the Baptist!"

²⁶The king was distraught. But his oaths on the one hand, and his guests on the other, meant he hadn't the guts to refuse her. ²⁷So he sent a jailer straightaway with orders to

bring John's head. He went and beheaded him in the prison, [28]brought the head on a dish, and gave it to the girl. The girl gave it to her mother.

[29]When John's followers heard about it, they came and took his body, and buried it in a tomb.

The Feeding of the Five Thousand

[30]The apostles came back to Jesus and told him all they had done and taught. [31]"All right," he said, "it's time for a break. Come away, just you, and we'll go somewhere lonely and private." (Crowds of people were coming and going and they didn't even have time to eat.)

[32]So they went off privately in the boat to a deserted spot. [33]And . . . crowds saw them going, realized what was happening, hurried on foot from all the towns, and arrived there first. [34]When Jesus got out of the boat he saw the huge crowd, and was deeply sorry for them, because they were like a flock without a shepherd. So he started to teach them many things.

[35]It was already getting late when his disciples came to him and said, "Look: there's nothing here. It's getting late. [36]Send them away. They need to go off into the countryside and the villages and buy themselves some food."

[37]"Why don't you give them something?" Jesus replied.

"Are you suggesting," they asked, "that we should go and spend two hundred dinars and get food for this lot?"

[38]"Well," said Jesus, "how many loaves have you got? Go and see."

They found out, and said, "Five, and a couple of fish."

[39]Jesus told them to sit everyone down, group by group, on the green grass. [40]So they sat down in companies, by hundreds and by fifties. [41]Then he took the five loaves and the two fish, looked up to heaven, blessed the bread, broke it, and gave it to his disciples to give to the crowd. Then he divided the two fish for them all. [42]Everyone ate, and had plenty. [43]They picked up the leftovers, and there were twelve baskets of broken pieces, and of the fish.

[44]The number of men who had eaten was five thousand.

Jesus Walks on Water

[45]At once Jesus made his disciples get into the boat and set sail across toward Bethsaida, while he dismissed the crowd. [46]He took his leave of them and went off up the mountain to pray.

⁴⁷When evening came, the boat was in the middle of the sea, and he was alone on the shore. ⁴⁸He saw they were having to work hard at rowing, because the wind was against them; and he came to them, about the fourth watch of the night, walking on the sea. He intended to go past them, ⁴⁹but they saw him walking on the sea and thought it was an apparition. They yelled out; ⁵⁰all of them saw him, and they were scared stiff.

At once he spoke to them.

"Cheer up," he said, "it's me. Don't be afraid."

⁵¹He came up to them and got into the boat, and the wind stopped. They were overwhelmed with astonishment; ⁵²they hadn't understood about the loaves, because their hearts were hardened.

⁵³They made landfall at Gennesaret, and tied the boat up. ⁵⁴People recognized Jesus as soon as they got out of the boat, ⁵⁵and they scurried about the whole region to bring sick people on stretchers to wherever they heard that he was. ⁵⁶And wherever he went, in villages, in towns, or in the open country, they placed the sick in the marketplaces and begged him to let them touch even the hem of his garment. And all who touched it were healed.

7 The Pharisees gathered around Jesus, together with some legal experts from Jerusalem. ²They saw that some of his disciples were eating their food with unclean (that is, unwashed) hands.

God's Law and Human Tradition

³(The Pharisees, you see—and indeed all the Jews—don't eat unless they first carefully wash their hands. This is to maintain the tradition of the elders. ⁴When they come in from the market, they never eat without washing. There are many other traditions which they keep: washings of cups, pots, and bronze dishes.)

⁵Anyway, the Pharisees and legal experts asked Jesus, "Why don't your disciples follow the tradition of the elders? Why do they eat their food with unwashed hands?"

⁶"Isaiah summed you up just right," Jesus replied. "Hypocrites, the lot of you! What he said was this:

'With their lips this people honor me,
But with their hearts they turn away from me;

7All in vain they think to worship me;
All they teach is human commands.'

8"You abandon God's commands, and keep human tradition!

9"So," he went on, "you have a fine way of setting aside God's command so as to maintain your tradition. 10Here's an example: Moses said, 'Honor your father and your mother,' and, 'Anyone who slanders father or mother should die.' 11But you say, 'If someone says to their father or mother, "What you might get from me—it's Korban!"' (which means, "given-to-God"), 12you don't let them do anything else for their father or mother! 13The net result is that you invalidate God's word through this tradition which you hand on. And there are lots more things like that which you do."

Clean and Unclean

14Jesus summoned the crowd again.

"Listen to me, all of you," he said, "and get this straight. 15What goes into you from outside can't make you unclean. What makes you unclean is what comes out from inside."

17When they got back into the house, away from the crowd, his disciples asked him about the parable.

18"You didn't get it either?" he asked. "Don't you see that whatever goes into someone from outside can't make them unclean? 19It doesn't go into the heart; it only goes into the stomach, and then carries on, out down the drain." (Result: all foods are clean.)

20"What makes someone unclean," he went on, "is what comes out of them. 21Evil intentions come from inside, out of people's hearts—sexual immorality, theft, murder, 22adultery, greed, wickedness, treachery, debauchery, envy, slander, pride, stupidity. 23These evil things all come from inside. They are what make someone unclean."

The Syrophoenician Woman

24Jesus got up, left that place, and went to the region of Tyre. When he took up residence in a house, he didn't want anyone to know, but it wasn't possible for him to remain hidden. 25On the contrary: news of him at once reached a woman who had a young daughter with an unclean spirit. She came and threw herself down at his feet. 26She was Greek, a Syrophoenician by race; and she asked him to cast the demon out of her daughter.

²⁷"Let the children eat what they want first," Jesus replied. "It's not right to take the children's bread and throw it to the dogs."

²⁸"Well, Master," she said, "even the dogs under the table eat the crumbs that the children drop."

²⁹"Well said!" replied Jesus. "Off you go; the demon has left your daughter."

³⁰So she went home, and found the child lying on the bed and the demon gone.

³¹Jesus went away from the region of Tyre, through Sidon, around toward the Sea of Galilee, and into the region of the Ten Towns. ³²They brought to him a man who was deaf and had a speech impediment, and asked that he would lay his hand on him.

A Deaf and Mute Man Is Healed

³³Jesus took the man off in private, away from the crowd. He put his fingers into his ears, spat, and touched his tongue. ³⁴Then he looked up to heaven, groaned, and said to him, "*Ephphatha*" (that is, "Be opened"). ³⁵Immediately the man's ears were opened, and his tongue was untied, and he spoke clearly.

³⁶Jesus gave them orders not to tell anyone. But the more he ordered them, the more they spread the news. ³⁷They were totally astonished.

"Everything he does is marvelous!" they said. "He even makes the deaf hear and the mute speak!"

8 Once again, about that time, a large crowd gathered with nothing to eat.

Jesus called the disciples.

The Feeding of the Four Thousand

²"I'm really sorry for the people," he said. "They've been with me three days now, and they haven't got anything to eat. ³If I send them home hungry, they'll collapse on the way. Some of them have come from miles off."

⁴"Where could you get food for all this lot, out here in the wilderness?" answered his disciples.

⁵"How many loaves have you got?" he asked.

"Seven," they replied.

⁶He told the crowd to sit down on the ground. Then he took the seven loaves, gave thanks, broke them, and gave them to his disciples to share around, and they gave them to the crowd.

7They had a few small fish, which he also blessed and told them to distribute. 8They ate; they were satisfied; and they took up seven baskets of leftover bits. 9There were about four thousand people. And he sent them away.

10At once Jesus got into the boat with his disciples and went to the region of Dalmanoutha.

The Yeast of the Pharisees and Herod

11The Pharisees came out and began to dispute with Jesus. They were asking him for a sign from heaven, to test him out.

12Jesus groaned deeply in his spirit. "Why is this generation looking for a sign?" he said. "I'm telling you the truth: no sign will be given to this generation." 13He left them again, got into the boat, and crossed over to the other side.

14They had forgotten to get any bread, and had only one loaf with them in the boat.

15"Beware!" said Jesus sternly to them, "Watch out for leaven—the Pharisees' leaven, and Herod's leaven too!"

16"It must be something to do with us not having any bread," they said to each other.

17"Why are you mumbling about not bringing bread?" said Jesus, who knew what they were thinking. "Don't you get it? Don't you understand? Have your hearts gone hard?

18*'Can't you see with your two good eyes?*
Can't you hear with your two good ears?'

—and don't you remember? 19When I broke the five loaves for the five thousand, how many baskets full of broken bits were left over?"

"Twelve," they said.

20"And the seven loaves for the four thousand—how many baskets full of bits were left over?"

"Seven."

21"You still don't get it?"

Peter's Declaration of Jesus's Messiahship

22They arrived at Bethsaida. A blind man was brought to Jesus, and they begged him to touch him. 23He took his hand, led him off outside the village, and put spittle on his eyes. Then he laid his hands on him and asked, "Can you see anything?"

24"I can see people," said the man, peering around, "but they look like trees walking about."

25Then Jesus laid his hands on him once more. This time he looked hard, and his sight came back: he could see everything clearly. 26Jesus sent him back home.

"Don't even go into the village," he said.

27Jesus and his disciples came to the villages of Caesarea Philippi. On the way he asked his disciples, "Who are people saying that I am?"

28"John the Baptist," they said, "or, some say, Elijah. Or, others say, one of the prophets."

29"What about you?" asked Jesus. "Who do you say I am?"

Peter spoke up. "You're the Messiah," he said.

30He gave them strict orders not to tell anyone about him.

31Jesus now began to teach them something new.

Jesus Predicts His Death

"There's big trouble in store for the son of man," he said. "The elders, the chief priests, and the scribes are going to reject him. He will be killed—and after three days he'll be raised." 32He said all this quite explicitly.

At this, Peter took him aside and started to scold him. 33But he turned around, saw the disciples, and scolded Peter.

"Get behind me, Accuser!" he said. "You're thinking human thoughts, not God's thoughts."

34He called the crowd to him, with his disciples. "If any of you want to come the way I'm going," he said, "you must say no to your own selves, pick up your cross, and follow me. 35Yes: if you want to save your life, you'll lose it; but if you lose your life because of me and the message you'll save it. 36After all, what use is it to win the world and lose your life? 37What can you give in exchange for your life? 38If you're ashamed of me and my words in this cheating and sinning generation, the son of man will be ashamed of you when he 'comes in the glory of his father with the holy angels.'

9 "I'm telling you the truth," he said; "some people standing here won't experience death before they see God's kingdom come in power."

2A week later, Jesus took Peter, James, and John away by themselves, and went up a high mountain. There he was transformed before their eyes. 3His clothes shone with a whiteness that no laundry on earth could match. 4Elijah appeared to them, and Moses too, and they were talking with Jesus.

The Transfiguration

⁵"Teacher," said Peter as he saw this, "it's great to be here! I tell you what—we'll make three shelters, one for you, one for Moses, and one for Elijah!" ⁶(He didn't know what to say; they were terrified.)

⁷Then a cloud overshadowed them, and a voice came out of the cloud: "This is my son, the one I love. Listen to him!"

⁸Then, quite suddenly, they looked around and saw nobody there anymore, only Jesus with them.

⁹As they came down the mountain, Jesus instructed them not to talk to anyone about what they had seen, "until," he said, "the son of man has been raised from the dead." ¹⁰They held on to this saying among themselves, puzzling about what this "rising from the dead" might mean.

¹¹"Why then," they asked him, "do the legal experts say 'Elijah must come first'?"

¹²"Elijah does come first," he replied, "and his job is to put everything straight. But what do you think it means that 'the son of man must suffer many things and be treated with contempt'? ¹³Actually, listen to this: Elijah has already come, and they did to him whatever they wanted. That's what scripture said about him."

The Demon-Possessed Boy

¹⁴The four of them made their way back to the other disciples. There they saw a large crowd surrounding them, and legal experts arguing with them. ¹⁵As soon as the crowd saw Jesus they were astounded, and they all ran up to greet him.

¹⁶"What's all the fuss about?" he asked.

¹⁷"Teacher," said someone from the crowd, "I brought my son to you. He's got a spirit that stops him speaking. ¹⁸Whenever it takes hold of him it throws him on the ground; he foams at the mouth, and grinds his teeth, and goes rigid. I spoke to your disciples about casting it out, but they couldn't."

¹⁹"You unbelieving generation!" replied Jesus. "How much longer must I be with you? How much longer must I put up with you? Bring the boy to me."

²⁰They brought him to him. When the spirit saw Jesus, it immediately threw the boy into a convulsion, and he fell on the ground and rolled about, foaming at the mouth.

²¹"How long has it been like this with him?" asked Jesus.

"Since childhood," replied the man. 22"Often it even throws him into fire or water to kill him. But if you can do anything… please, please help us! Have pity on us!"

23"What d'you mean, 'If you can'?" said Jesus. "Everything is possible to someone who believes."

24At this the father gave a great shout. "I do believe!" he roared. "Help me in my unbelief!"

25Jesus saw that the crowd was getting bigger by the minute. He scolded the unclean spirit: "Speechless and deaf spirit," he said, "I command you—come out of him, and never go back again!"

26The spirit yelled, gave the boy a huge convulsion, and came out. The boy seemed to be dead; in fact, several people did say, "He's dead!" 27But Jesus took him by the hand and helped him to his feet, and he stood up.

28"Why couldn't we cast it out?" asked his disciples, once they were back in the house by themselves.

29"This sort," replied Jesus, "can only be cast out by prayer."

30They went away from there and were traveling through Galilee. Jesus didn't want anyone to know, 31because he was teaching his disciples.

True Greatness

"The 'son of man,' he was saying, "is to be given over into human hands. They will kill him; and, when he's been killed, after three days he will rise again."

32They didn't understand the saying, and were afraid to ask him.

33They came to Capernaum. When they got into the house he asked them, "What were you arguing about on the road?"

34They said nothing, because on the road they had been arguing about which of them was the greatest.

35Jesus sat down and called the Twelve.

"If you want to be first," he said, "you must be last of all, and servant of all." 36He took a small child, and stood it in the middle of them. Then he hugged the child, and said to them, 37"If anyone welcomes one child like this in my name, they welcome me. And if anyone welcomes me, it isn't me they welcome, but the one who sent me."

**Warnings
About Sin**

38"Teacher," said John, "we saw someone casting out demons in your name. We stopped him, because he wasn't following us."

39"Don't stop him," said Jesus. "No one who does powerful things by my name will be able to say bad things about me
soon afterward. 40Anyone who's not against us is on our side.
41Anyone who even gives you a cup of water in my name, because you belong to the Messiah—I'm telling you the truth,
that person won't go unrewarded.

42"Think about these little ones who believe in me," he went
on. "If anyone causes one of them to slip up, it would be much
better for that person to have a huge millstone put around
their neck, and be thrown into the sea.

43"And if your hand causes you to slip up, cut it off. It's better for you to go into life maimed than to have two hands and
go into Gehenna, into the fire that never goes out.

45"And if your foot causes you to slip up, cut it off. It's better
for you to go into life lame than to have two feet and be thrown
into Gehenna.

47"And if your eye causes you to slip up, throw it away. It's
better for you to go into the kingdom of God with one eye than
to have two eyes and to be thrown into Gehenna, 48where

> 'Their worm lives on forever
> And the fire can never be quenched.'

49"You see, everyone will be salted with fire. 50Salt is great
stuff; but if salt becomes unsalty, how can you make it salty
again? You need salt among yourselves. Live at peace with
each other."

**Teachings on
Divorce**

10 Jesus left the region, and went to the districts of
Judaea across the Jordan. A large crowd gathered
around him, and once more, as his custom was, he
taught them.

2Some Pharisees approached him with a question. "Is it
permitted," they asked, "for a man to divorce his wife?" They
said this to trap him.

3"Well," answered Jesus, "what did Moses command you?"

4"Moses permitted us," they replied, "to write a notice of
separation and so to complete the divorce."

⁵"He gave you that command," said Jesus, "because you are hard-hearted. ⁶But from the beginning of creation

> 'male and female he made them; ⁷and that's why
> the man must leave his father and his mother
> and cleave unto his wife; ⁸so that the two
> become one flesh.'

"There you are, then: they are no longer two, but one flesh. ⁹What God has joined, humans must not split up."

¹⁰When they were back indoors, the disciples asked him about this.

¹¹"Anyone who divorces his wife," said Jesus, "and marries someone else commits adultery against her. ¹²And if she divorces her husband and marries someone else she commits adultery."

¹³People brought children to Jesus for him to touch them. The disciples reprimanded them. ¹⁴But Jesus was angry when he saw it, and said to them, "Let the children come to me! Don't stop them! The kingdom of God belongs to people like that. ¹⁵I'm telling you the truth: anyone who doesn't receive the kingdom of God like a child will never get into it."

¹⁶And he hugged them, laid his hands on them, and blessed them.

¹⁷As he was setting out on the road, a man ran up and knelt down in front of him.

The Rich Young Ruler

"Good teacher," he asked, "what should I do to inherit the life of the age to come?"

¹⁸"Why call me 'good'?" replied Jesus. "No one is good except God alone. ¹⁹You know the commandments:

> 'Don't kill.
> Don't commit adultery.
> Don't steal.
> Don't swear falsely.
> Don't defraud.
> Honor your father and your mother.'"

²⁰"Teacher," he said, "I've kept all of them since I was little."
²¹Jesus looked hard at him, and loved him.

"One more thing," he said. "Go away, and whatever you possess—sell it, and give it to the poor. You will have treasure in heaven! Then: come and follow me."

22At that, his face fell, and he went off sadly. He was very wealthy.

23Jesus looked slowly around. Then he said to his disciples, "How difficult it is for the wealthy to enter the kingdom of God!"

24The disciples were astonished at what he was saying. So Jesus repeated once more, "Children, it's very hard to enter the kingdom of God! 25It would be easier for a camel to go through the eye of a needle than for a rich man to enter God's kingdom."

26They were totally amazed, and said to each other, "So who then can be saved?"

27"It's impossible for mortals," Jesus said, looking hard at them, "but it's not impossible for God. All things are possible for God."

28"Look here," Peter started up, "we've left everything and followed you."

29"I'll tell you the truth," replied Jesus. "No one who has left a house, or brothers or sisters, or mother or father, or children, or lands because of me and the gospel 30will fail to receive back a hundred times more in the present age: houses, brothers, sisters, mothers, children, and lands—with persecutions!—and finally the life of the age to come. 31But plenty of people at the front will end up at the back, and the back at the front."

The Request of James and John

32They were on the road, going up to Jerusalem. Jesus was walking ahead of them; they were amazed, and the people following were afraid.

Again he took the Twelve aside and began to tell them what was going to happen to him. 33"Look," he said, "we're going up to Jerusalem. The son of man will be handed over to the chief priests and the legal experts, and they will condemn him to death, and hand him over to the pagans. 34They will taunt him and spit at him and flog him and kill him—and after three days he will rise again."

35James and John, Zebedee's sons, came up to him.

"Teacher," they said, "we want you to grant us whatever we ask."

36"What do you want me to do for you?" asked Jesus.

37"Grant us," they said, "that when you're there in all your glory, one of us will sit at your right, and the other at your left."

38"You don't know what you're asking for!" Jesus replied. "Can you drink the cup I'm going to drink? Can you receive the baptism I'm going to receive?"

39"Yes," they said, "we can."

"Well," said Jesus, "you will drink the cup I drink; you will receive the baptism I receive. 40But sitting at my right hand or my left—that's not up to me. It's been assigned already."

41When the other ten disciples heard, they were angry with James and John. 42Jesus called them to him.

"You know how it is in the pagan nations," he said. "Think how their so-called rulers act. They lord it over their subjects. The high and mighty ones boss the rest around. 43But that's not how it's going to be with you. Anyone who wants to be great among you must become your servant. 44Anyone who wants to be first must be everyone's slave. 45Don't you see? The son of man didn't come to be waited on. He came to be the servant, to give his life 'as a ransom for many.'"

46They came to Jericho. As Jesus, his disciples, and a substantial crowd were leaving the town, a blind beggar named Bartimaeus, the son of Timaeus, was sitting by the road. 47When he heard it was Jesus of Nazareth, he began to shout out, "Son of David! Jesus! Take pity on me!"

Jesus Heals a Blind Beggar

48Lots of people told him crossly to be quiet. But he shouted out all the louder, "Son of David—take pity on me!"

49Jesus came to a stop. "Call him," he said.

So they called the blind man.

"Cheer up," they said, "and get up. He's calling you."

50He flung his cloak aside, jumped up, and came to Jesus.

Jesus saw him coming. 51"What do you want me to do for you?" he asked.

"Teacher," the blind man said, "let me see again."

52"Off you go," said Jesus. "Your faith has saved you." And immediately he saw again, and he followed him on the way.

The Triumphal Entry

11 So they approached Jerusalem. They got as far as Bethphage and Bethany, on the Mount of Olives, when Jesus sent two of his disciples on ahead with a specific task.

2"Go to the village over there," he said to them, "and as soon as you enter it you will find a colt tied up—one that nobody has ever ridden before. Untie it and bring it here. 3And if anyone says to you, 'Why are you doing that?' then say, 'The master needs it, and he will return it at once.'"

4They went off and found the colt tied up beside a door, out in the street; and they untied it.

5Some of the bystanders said to them, "Why are you untying the colt?" 6They gave the answer Jesus had told them, and they let them carry on. 7So they brought the colt to Jesus and laid their cloaks on it, and he mounted it. 8Several people spread their cloaks out in the road. Others did the same with foliage that they had cut in the fields. 9Those in front, and those coming behind, shouted out, "Hosanna! Welcome in the Lord's name! 10Welcome to the kingdom of our father David, the kingdom coming right now! Hosanna in the highest!"

11Jesus entered Jerusalem, went into the Temple, and looked all around. It was already getting late, and he returned to Bethany with the Twelve.

Jesus Cleanses the Temple

12The next day, as they were leaving Bethany, Jesus was hungry. 13From some distance away he saw a fig tree covered with leaves, and hoped to find some fruit on it; but when he came up to it he found nothing but leaves. (It wasn't yet the season for figs.)

14He addressed the tree directly. "May no one ever eat fruit from you again," he said. And his disciples heard.

15They came into Jerusalem. Jesus went into the Temple and began to drive out the traders, those who bought and sold in the Temple, and overturned the tables of the money-changers and the seats of the dove-sellers. 16He permitted no one to carry any vessel through the Temple. 17He began to teach: "Isn't this what's written," he said,

'My house shall be called
A house of prayer
For all the world to share'?

"But you've made it a brigands' den!"

[18]The chief priests and the legal experts heard, and looked for a way to get rid of him. But they were afraid of him, because the whole crowd was astonished at his teaching.

[19]When evening came, they went back out of the city.

[20]As they were returning, early in the morning, they saw the fig tree withered from its roots.

[21]"Look, Teacher!" said Peter to Jesus, remembering what had happened before. "The fig tree you cursed has withered."

[22]"Have faith in God," replied Jesus. [23]"I'm telling you the truth: if anyone says to this mountain, 'Be off with you—get yourself thrown into the sea,' if they have no doubt in their heart, but believe that what they say will happen, it will be done for them. [24]That's why I'm telling you, everything that you request in prayer, everything you ask God for, believe that you receive it, and it will happen for you.

[25]"And when you are standing there praying, if you have something against someone else, forgive them—so that your father in heaven may forgive you your trespasses."

[27]Once more they went into Jerusalem. As Jesus was walking in the Temple he was approached by the chief priests, the legal experts, and the elders.

The Authority of Jesus Is Questioned

[28]"By what right do you do these things?" they asked. "Who gave you the right to do them?"

[29]"I have one question for you, too," replied Jesus, "and if you tell me the answer I shall tell you by what right I do these things. [30]Was the baptism of John from heaven, or was it a human invention? What's your answer?"

[31]"Well now," they muttered to each other, "if we say it was from heaven, he will say, Then why didn't you believe him? [32]But if we say it was a human invention . . ." They were afraid of the crowd, because everyone regarded John as a prophet.

[33]"We don't know," they said to Jesus.

"Nor will I tell you," replied Jesus, "by what right I do these things."

12 Jesus began to speak to them with parables.

"Once upon a time," he began, "there was a man who planted a vineyard. He built a fence around it, dug out a winepress, built a watchtower, and then leased it out

The Parable of the Tenants

to tenant farmers. He himself went abroad. ²When the time came, he sent a slave to the farmers to collect from them his portion of the vineyard's produce. ³They seized him, beat him, and sent him away empty-handed.

⁴"So again he sent another slave to them. This one they beat about the head and treated shamefully. ⁵He sent another, and they killed him. He sent several more; they beat some and killed others.

⁶"He had one more to send: his beloved son. He sent him to them last of all, thinking, 'They will respect my son.'

⁷"But the tenant farmers said to themselves, 'This is the heir! Come on—let's kill him, and we'll get the inheritance!' ⁸So they seized him and killed him, and threw him out of the vineyard.

⁹"So what will the vineyard owner do? He will come and destroy those tenants, and give the vineyard to others. ¹⁰Or haven't you read the scripture which says,

> 'There is the stone the builders refused;
> Now it's in place at the top of the corner.
> ¹¹This happened the way the Lord planned it;
> We were astonished to see it.' "

¹²They tried to find a way of arresting him, because they realized he had directed the parable against them. But they were afraid of the crowd. They left him and went away.

On Paying Taxes to Caesar

¹³They sent some Pharisees to Jesus, and some Herodians, to try to trick him into saying the wrong thing.

¹⁴"Teacher," they said, "we know you are a man of integrity; you don't regard anybody as special. You don't bother about the outward show people put up; you teach God's way truly.

"Well then: is it lawful to give tribute to Caesar or not? Should we pay it, or shouldn't we?"

¹⁵He knew the game they were playing. "Why are you trying to trap me?" he said. "Bring me a tribute-coin; let me look at it."

¹⁶They brought one to him.

"This image," he asked, "whose is it? And whose is this superscription?"

"Caesar's," they replied.

¹⁷"Well then," said Jesus, "give Caesar back what belongs to Caesar—and give God back what belongs to God!"

They were astonished at him.

¹⁸Some Sadducees approached Jesus. (Sadducees, by the way, deny the resurrection.)

Marriage and the Resurrection

¹⁹"Teacher," they said, "Moses wrote for us that 'if a man's brother dies, and leaves a wife but no child, the brother should take the wife and raise up descendants for his brother.' ²⁰Well now, there were once seven brothers. The first married a wife, and died without children. ²¹The second married the widow, and died without children. The third did so as well, ²²and so did all seven, still without leaving children. Finally the woman died too. ²³So: when they rise again in the resurrection, whose wife will she be? All seven had her, after all."

²⁴"Where you're going wrong," replied Jesus, "is that you don't know the scriptures, or God's power. ²⁵When people rise from the dead, they don't marry, nor do people give them in marriage. They are like angels in heaven.

²⁶"However, to show that the dead are indeed to be raised, surely you've read in the book of Moses, in the passage about the bush, what God says to Moses? 'I am Abraham's God, Isaac's God, and Jacob's God'? ²⁷He isn't the God of the dead, but of the living. You are completely mistaken."

²⁸One of the legal experts came up and overheard the discussion. Realizing that Jesus had given a splendid answer, he put a question of his own.

The Most Important Commandment

"Which commandment," he asked, "is the first one of all?"

²⁹"The first one," replied Jesus, "is this: 'Listen, Israel: the Lord your God, the Lord is one; ³⁰and you shall love the Lord your God with all your heart, and with all your soul, and with all your understanding, and with all your strength.' ³¹And this is the second one: 'You shall love your neighbor as yourself.' No other commandment is greater than these."

³²"Well said, Teacher," answered the lawyer. "You are right in saying that 'he is one and there is no other beside him,' ³³and that 'to love him with all the heart, and with all the intelligence, and with all the strength' and 'to love one's neighbor as oneself' is worth far more than all burnt offerings and sacrifices."

³⁴Jesus saw that his answer came out of deep under-standing.

"You are not far from God's kingdom," he said to him.

After that, nobody dared put any more questions to him.

David's Son and the Widow's Mite

³⁵By way of response to it all, Jesus began to teach in the Temple.

"Why do the experts say," he asked, "that the Messiah is the son of David? ³⁶David himself, inspired by the holy spirit, said:

> 'The Lord said to my Lord:
> Sit at my right hand,
> Until I place your enemies
> Right underneath your feet.'

³⁷"David himself calls him 'Lord'; how then can he be his son?"

The whole crowd listened to him with delight.

³⁸During his teaching, he said, "Beware of the lawyers! They like to walk about in long robes, and to be greeted in the marketplaces. ³⁹They take the chief seats in the synagogue and the best places at dinner parties. ⁴⁰They devour the property of widows and make long prayers without meaning them. They will receive all the more condemnation."

⁴¹As he sat opposite the Temple treasury, he watched the crowd putting money into the almsboxes. Lots of rich people put in substantial amounts. ⁴²Then there came a single poor widow, who put in two tiny coins, together worth a single penny.

⁴³Jesus called his disciples.

"I'm telling you the truth," he said. "This poor widow just put more into the treasury than everybody else. ⁴⁴You see, all the others were contributing out of their wealth; but she put in everything she had, out of her poverty. It was her whole liveli-hood."

Signs of the End

13 As they were going out of the Temple, one of Jesus's disciples said to him, "Teacher! Look at these huge stones, and these huge buildings!"

²"You see these enormous buildings?" said Jesus. "There will not be one single stone left on top of another. They will all be torn down."

³Peter, James, John, and Andrew approached him privately as he was sitting on the Mount of Olives opposite the Temple.

⁴"Tell us," they asked. "When will these things happen? What will be the sign that these things are about to be completed?"

⁵"Take care that nobody deceives you," Jesus began to say to them. ⁶"Plenty of people will come in my name, saying 'I'm the one!' and they will lead plenty astray. ⁷But whenever you hear about wars, and rumors about wars, don't be disturbed. These things have to happen, but it doesn't mean the end is here. ⁸One nation will rise up against another; one kingdom will rise up against another. There will be earthquakes from place to place, and famines too. These are the first pains of childbirth.

⁹"But watch out for yourselves. They will hand you over to courts, they will beat you in synagogues; you will stand before rulers and kings because of me, as a witness against them. ¹⁰And the message of the kingdom must first be announced to all the nations. ¹¹And when they put you on trial and hand you over, don't work out beforehand what you are going to say, but say whatever is given you at that moment. It won't be you speaking, you see, but the holy spirit.

¹²"One brother will hand over another to death. Fathers will hand over children. Children will rebel against parents and have them put to death. ¹³And you will be hated by everyone because of my name. But the one who is patient through to the end—that one will be saved.

¹⁴"However," Jesus continued, "when you see 'the desolating abomination' set up where it ought not to be" (let the reader understand) "then those who are in Judaea should run away to the mountains. ¹⁵If you're on the housetop, don't go down, and don't go in to get anything from the house. ¹⁶If you're out in the countryside, don't turn back again to pick up your cloak.

Further Signs of the End

¹⁷"It will be a terrible time for pregnant and nursing mothers. ¹⁸Pray that it won't happen in winter. ¹⁹Yes, those days will bring trouble like nothing that's ever happened from the beginning of creation, which God created, until now, or ever will again. ²⁰In fact, if the Lord had not shortened the

days, no one would be rescued. But for the sake of his chosen ones, those whom he appointed, he shortened the days.

21"So at that time, if someone says to you, 'Look—here is the Messiah!' or, 'Look—there he is!' don't believe them; 22because false messiahs and false prophets will arise, and will perform signs and portents to lead astray even God's chosen ones, if that were possible. 23But you must be on your guard. I've told you everything ahead of time.

> 24'But in those days, after that suffering,
> "The sun will be dark as night
> And the moon will not give its light;
> 25The stars will fall from heaven
> And the powers in heaven will shake.'

26"Then they will see 'the son of man coming on clouds with great power and glory.' 27And then he will dispatch his messengers, and will gather in his chosen ones from the four winds, from the ends of earth to the ends of heaven.

Watching for the Son of Man

28"Learn this lesson from the fig tree. When its branch becomes soft and sprouts leaves, you know that summer is near. 29In the same way, when you see these things happen, you should know that it is near, right at the gates. 30I'm telling you the truth: this generation won't disappear until all of this has happened. 31Heaven and earth will disappear, but my words won't disappear.

32"No one knows, though, the day or the hour. The angels in heaven don't know it; nor does the son; only the father.

33"Keep watch, stay awake. You don't know when the moment will arrive. 34It's like a man who goes away from home: he leaves his house, giving each of his slaves authority for their own tasks; and he commands the doorkeeper to keep watch. 35Keep watch, then, because you don't know when the master of the house is going to come. It might be at evening, or at midnight, or at cockcrow, or in the morning! 36You don't want him to come suddenly and find you asleep. 37What I am telling you, I am telling everyone: keep watch!"

Jesus Is Anointed at Bethany

14 Passover—the Feast of Unleavened Bread—was due in two days. The chief priests and the lawyers were plotting how to seize Jesus by a trick, and kill him.

²"We can't do it at the feast," they said. "The people might riot."

³Jesus was in Bethany, at the house of Simon (known as "the Leper"). While he was at table, a woman came up with an alabaster pot containing extremely valuable ointment made of pure spikenard. She broke the pot and poured the ointment on Jesus's head.

⁴Some of the people there grumbled to one another.

"What's the point of wasting the ointment?" they asked. ⁵"That ointment could have been sold for three hundred dinars, and given to the poor."

And they were angry with her.

⁶"Leave her alone," said Jesus. "Why make trouble for her? She has done a wonderful thing for me. ⁷You have the poor with you always; you can help them whenever you want to. But you won't always have me.

⁸"She has played her part. She has anointed my body for its burial, ahead of time. ⁹I'm telling you the truth: wherever the message is announced in all the world, the story of what she has just done will be told. That will be her memorial."

¹⁰Judas Iscariot, one of the Twelve, went to the chief priests, to arrange to hand Jesus over to them. ¹¹They were delighted with his proposal, and made an agreement to pay him. And he began to look for a good moment to hand him over.

¹²On the first day of unleavened bread, when the Passover lambs were sacrificed, Jesus's disciples said to him, "Where would you like us to go and get things ready for you to eat the Passover?"

The Last Supper

¹³He sent off two of his disciples, with these instructions:

"Go into the city, and you will be met by a man carrying a water-pot. Follow him. ¹⁴When he goes indoors, say to the master of the house, 'The teacher says, where is the guest room for me, where I can eat the Passover with my disciples?' ¹⁵He will show you a large upstairs room, set out and ready. Make preparations for us there."

¹⁶The disciples went out, entered the city, and found it exactly as he had said. They prepared the Passover.

¹⁷When it was evening, Jesus came with the Twelve. ¹⁸As they were reclining at table and eating, Jesus said, "I'm telling

you the truth: one of you is going to betray me—one of you that's eating with me."

¹⁹They began to be very upset, and they said to him, one after another, "It isn't me, is it?"

²⁰"It's one of the Twelve," said Jesus, "one who has dipped his bread in the dish with me. ²¹Yes: the son of man is completing his journey, as scripture said he would; but it's bad news for the man who betrays him! It would have been better for that man never to have been born."

²²While they were eating, he took bread, blessed it, broke it, and gave it to them.

"Take it," he said. "This is my body."

²³Then he took the cup, gave thanks, and gave it to them, and they all drank from it.

²⁴"This is my blood of the covenant," he said, "which is poured out for many. ²⁵I'm telling you the truth: I won't ever drink from the fruit of the vine again, until that day—the day when I drink it new in the kingdom of God."

Jesus Is Arrested

²⁶They sang a hymn and went out to the Mount of Olives.

²⁷"You're all going to desert me," said Jesus, "because it's written,

> 'I shall attack the shepherd
> And then the sheep will scatter.'

²⁸"But after I am raised up, I will go ahead of you to Galilee." ²⁹Peter spoke up.

"Everyone else may desert you," he said, "but I won't."

³⁰"I'm telling you the truth," Jesus replied. "Today—this very night, before the cock has crowed twice—you will renounce me three times."

³¹This made Peter all the more vehement.

"Even if I have to die with you," he said, "I will never renounce you."

And all the rest said the same.

³²They came to a place called Gethsemane.

"Stay here," said Jesus to the disciples, "while I pray."

³³He took Peter, James, and John with him, and became quite overcome and deeply distressed.

34"My soul is disturbed within me," he said, "right to the point of death. Stay here and keep watch."

35He went a little further, and fell on the ground and prayed that, if possible, the moment might pass from him.

36"Abba, Father," he said, "all things are possible for you! Take this cup away from me! But—not what I want, but what you want."

37He returned and found them sleeping.

"Are you asleep, Simon?" he said to Peter. "Couldn't you keep watch for a single hour? 38Watch and pray, so that you won't come into the time of trouble. The spirit is eager, but the body is weak."

39Once more he went off and prayed, saying the same words. 40And again, when he returned, he found them asleep, because their eyes were very heavy. They had no words to answer him. 41But the third time he came, he said to them, "All right—sleep as much as you like now. Have a good rest. The job is done, the time has come—and look! The son of man is betrayed into the clutches of sinners. 42Get up; let's be on our way. Here comes the man who's going to betray me."

43At once, while he was still speaking, Judas, one of the Twelve, arrived, accompanied by a crowd with swords and clubs, from the chief priests, the legal experts, and the elders. 44The betrayer had given them a coded sign: "The one I kiss—that's him! Seize him and take him away safely."

45He came up to Jesus at once. "Rabbi!" he said, and kissed him.

46The crowd laid hands on him and seized him. 47One of the bystanders drew a sword and struck the high priest's servant, cutting off his ear. 48Then Jesus spoke to them.

"Anyone would think," he said, "you'd come after a brigand! Fancy needing swords and clubs to arrest me! 49Day after day I've been teaching in the Temple, under your noses, and you never laid a finger on me. But the scriptures must be fulfilled."

50Then they all abandoned him and ran away.

51A young man had followed him, wearing only a linen tunic over his otherwise naked body. 52They seized him, and he left the tunic and ran away naked.

⁵³They took Jesus away to the high priest. All the chief priests and the elders and the legal experts were assembled. ⁵⁴Peter followed him at a distance and came to the courtyard of the high priest's house, where he sat with the servants and warmed himself at the fire.

⁵⁵The chief priests, and all the Sanhedrin, looked for evidence for a capital charge against Jesus, but they didn't find any. ⁵⁶Several people invented fictitious charges against him, but their evidence didn't agree. ⁵⁷Then some stood up with this fabricated charge: ⁵⁸"We heard him say, 'I will destroy this Temple, which human hands have made, and in three days I'll build another, made without human hands.'"

⁵⁹But even so their evidence didn't agree.

⁶⁰Then the high priest got up in front of them all and interrogated Jesus.

"Haven't you got any answer about whatever it is these people are testifying against you?"

⁶¹Jesus remained silent, and didn't answer a word.

Once more the high priest questioned him.

"Are you the Messiah, the Son of the Blessed One?"

⁶²"I am," replied Jesus, "and you will see 'the son of man sitting at the right hand of Power, and coming with the clouds of heaven.'"

⁶³"Why do we need any more evidence?" shouted the high priest, tearing his clothes. ⁶⁴"You heard the blasphemy! What's your verdict?"

They all agreed on their judgment: he deserved to die.

⁶⁵Some of them began to spit at him. They blindfolded him and hit him, and said, "Prophesy!" And the servants took charge of him and beat him.

⁶⁶Peter, meanwhile, was below in the courtyard. One of the high priest's servant-girls came up ⁶⁷and saw him warming himself. She looked closely at him and said, "You were with Jesus the Nazarene too, weren't you?"

⁶⁸"I don't know what on earth you're talking about," replied Peter.

He went outside into the forecourt, and the cock crowed.

⁶⁹The servant-girl saw him, and once more began to say to

the bystanders, "This man is one of them." 70But Peter again denied it.

A little while later the bystanders said again to Peter, "You really are one of them, aren't you? You're a Galilean!"

71At that he began to curse and swear, "I don't know this man you're talking about." 72And immediately the cock crowed for the second time. Then Peter remembered the words that Jesus had said to him: "Before the cock crows twice, you will renounce me three times." And he burst into tears.

15 As soon as morning came, the chief priests held a council meeting with the elders, the legal experts, and the whole Sanhedrin. They bound Jesus, took him off to Pilate, and handed him over.

Jesus Before Pilate

2"Are you the king of the Jews?" asked Pilate.

"You have said it," replied Jesus.

3The chief priests laid many accusations against him.

4Pilate again interrogated him: "Aren't you going to make any reply? Look how many things they're accusing you of!"

5But Jesus gave no reply at all, which astonished Pilate.

6The custom was that at festival time he used to release for them a single prisoner, whoever they would ask for. 7There was a man in prison named Barabbas, one of the revolutionaries who had committed murder during the uprising. 8So the crowd came up and began to ask Pilate to do what he normally did.

9"Do you want me," answered Pilate, "to release for you 'the king of the Jews'?"

10He said this because he knew that the chief priests had handed him over out of envy. 11The chief priests stirred up the crowd to ask for Barabbas instead to be released to them. So Pilate once again asked them, 12"What then do you want me to do with the one you call 'the king of the Jews'?"

13"Crucify him!" they shouted again.

14"Why?" asked Pilate. "What has he done wrong?"

"Crucify him!" they shouted all the louder.

15Pilate wanted to satisfy the crowd; so he released Barabbas for them. He had Jesus flogged, and handed him over to be crucified.

The Crucifixion

¹⁶The soldiers took Jesus into the courtyard—that is, the Praetorium—and called together the whole squad. ¹⁷They dressed Jesus up in purple; then, weaving together a crown of thorns, they stuck it on him. ¹⁸They began to salute him: "Greetings, king of the Jews!" ¹⁹And they hit him over the head with a staff, and spat at him, and knelt down to do him homage. ²⁰Then, when they had mocked him, they took the purple robe off him, and put his own clothes back on.

Then they led him off to crucify him. ²¹They compelled a man called Simon to carry Jesus's cross. He was from Cyrene, and was coming in from out of town. He was the father of Alexander and Rufus.

²²They took Jesus to the place called Golgotha, which in translation means Skull Place. ²³They gave him a mixture of wine and myrrh, but he didn't drink it.

²⁴So they crucified him; they "parted his clothing between them, casting lots" to see who would get what. ²⁵It was about nine o'clock in the morning when they crucified him. ²⁶The inscription, giving the charge, read: "The king of the Jews." ²⁷They also crucified two bandits alongside him, one on his right and one on his left.

²⁹People who were passing by abused him. They shook their heads at him.

"Hah!" they said. "You were going to destroy the Temple, were you? And build it again in three days? ³⁰Why don't you rescue yourself, and come down from the cross?"

³¹The chief priests and the lawyers were mocking him in the same way among themselves.

"He rescued others," they said, "but he can't rescue himself. ³²Messiah, is he? King of Israel, did he say? Well, let's see him come down from the cross! We'll believe him when we see that!"

The two who were crucified alongside him taunted him as well.

The Death of Jesus

³³At midday there was darkness over all the land until three in the afternoon. ³⁴At three o'clock Jesus shouted out in a powerful voice, *"Eloi, Eloi, lema sabachthani?"* Which means, "My God, my God, why did you abandon me?"

³⁵When the bystanders heard it, some of them said, "He's calling for Elijah!"

³⁶One of them ran and filled a sponge with sour wine, put it on a pole, and gave it him to drink.

"Well then," he declared, "let's see if Elijah will come and take him down."

³⁷But Jesus, with another loud shout, breathed his last.

³⁸The Temple veil was torn in two, from top to bottom. ³⁹When the centurion who was standing facing him saw that he died in this way, he said, "This fellow really was God's son."

⁴⁰Some women were watching from a distance. They included Mary Magdalene, Mary the mother of the younger James and of Joses, and Salome. ⁴¹They had followed Jesus in Galilee, and had attended to his needs. There were several other women, too, who had come up with him to Jerusalem.

The Burial of Jesus

⁴²It was already getting toward evening, and it was the day of Preparation, that is, the day before the sabbath. ⁴³Joseph of Arimathea, a reputable member of the council who was himself eagerly awaiting God's kingdom, took his courage in both hands, went to Pilate, and requested the body of Jesus.

⁴⁴Pilate was surprised that he was already dead. He summoned the centurion and asked whether he had been dead for some time. ⁴⁵When he learned the facts from the centurion, he conceded the body to Joseph.

⁴⁶So Joseph bought a linen cloth, took the body down, wrapped it in the cloth, and laid it in a tomb cut out of the rock. He rolled a stone against the door of the tomb. ⁴⁷Mary Magdalene and Mary the mother of Joses saw where he was buried.

16

When the sabbath was over, Mary Magdalene, Mary the mother of James, and Salome bought spices so that they could come and anoint Jesus. ²Then, very early on the first day of the week, they came to the tomb, just at sunrise. ³They were saying to one another, "There's that stone at the door of the tomb—who's going to roll it away for us?"

The Resurrection

⁴Then, when they looked up, they saw that it had been rolled away. (It was extremely large.)

⁵So they went into the tomb, and there they saw a young man sitting on the right-hand side. He was wearing white. They were totally astonished.

⁶"Don't be astonished," he said to them. "You're looking for Jesus the Nazarene, who was crucified. He has been raised! He isn't here! Look—this is the place where they laid him.

⁷"But go and tell his disciples—including Peter—that he is going ahead of you to Galilee. You'll see him there, just like he told you."

⁸They went out, and fled from the tomb. Trembling and panic had seized them. They said nothing to anyone, because they were afraid.

Two Extra Endings*

[They gave a brief account to the people around Peter of what they had been told. After this, Jesus himself sent out from east to west, through their work, the sacred and imperishable proclamation of eternal salvation. Amen.]

⁹[[When Jesus was raised, early on the first day of the week, he appeared first of all to Mary Magdalene, from whom he had cast out seven demons. ¹⁰She went and told the people who had been with him, who were mourning and weeping. ¹¹When they heard that he was alive, and that he had been seen by her, they didn't believe it.

¹²After this he appeared in a different guise to two of them as they were walking into the countryside. ¹³They came back and told the others, but they didn't believe them.

¹⁴Later Jesus appeared to the eleven themselves, as they were at table. He told them off for their unbelief and hardheartedness, for not believing those who had seen him after he had been raised.

¹⁵"Go into all the world," he said to them, "and announce the message to all creation. ¹⁶Anyone who believes and is baptized will be rescued, but people who don't believe will be condemned. ¹⁷And these signs will happen around those who believe: they will drive out demons in my name, they will speak with new tongues, ¹⁸they will pick up serpents in their hands; and if they drink anything poisonous it won't harm

---

*See the Preface, page xvi.

them. They will lay their hands on the sick, and they will get better."

[19]When the Lord Jesus had spoken with them, he was taken up into heaven, and sat down at God's right hand. [20]They went out and announced the message everywhere. The Lord worked with them, validating their message by the signs that accompanied them.]]

The Gospel According to
Luke

1 Many people have undertaken to draw up an orderly account of the events that have been fulfilled in our midst. ²It has been handed down to us by the original eyewitnesses and stewards of the word. ³So, most excellent Theophilus, since I had traced the course of all of it scrupulously from the start, I thought it a good idea to write an orderly account for you, ⁴so that you may have secure knowledge about the matters in which you have been instructed.

⁵In the time when Herod was king of Judaea, there was a priest called Zechariah, of the priestly division of Abijah. His wife, who came from the Aaron family, was called Elizabeth. ⁶Both of them were righteous in God's sight; they followed all the Lord's commandments and ordinances without fault. ⁷They had no children. Elizabeth was barren, and both of them were of an advanced age.

⁸It so happened, when Zechariah was performing his priestly service before God, according to the order of his division, ⁹that the lot fell to him, according to the priestly custom, to go in to the Lord's sanctuary to offer incense. ¹⁰The people were praying outside in a large crowd, at the time of the incense-offering. ¹¹An angel of the Lord appeared to him, standing on the right-hand side of the incense-altar. ¹²Zechariah was troubled and terror-struck when he saw the angel.

¹³But the angel said to him: "Don't be afraid, Zechariah: your prayer has been heard. Your wife Elizabeth will bear you a son, and you shall call his name John. ¹⁴This will bring you joy and celebration, and many will rejoice at his birth. ¹⁵He

will be a great man in God's sight; he will drink no wine or strong drink. He will be filled with the holy spirit from his mother's womb, 16and will turn many of the children of Israel to the Lord their God. 17He will go before him in the spirit and power of Elijah, and he will turn the hearts of fathers to children, and of unbelievers to the wisdom of the righteous. He will get ready for the Lord a prepared people."

18"How can I be sure of this?" said Zechariah to the angel. "I'm an old man! My wife's not as young as she used to be, either!"

19"Look here," replied the angel, "I'm Gabriel. I stand in God's presence. I was sent to speak to you and give you this splendid news. 20Now, listen: you will be silent—you won't be able to speak—until the day when it all happens, because you didn't believe my words. But they will come true at the proper time."

21Meanwhile, the people were waiting for Zechariah, and were surprised that he was taking such a long time in the sanctuary. 22But when he came out he couldn't speak to them, and they understood that he had seen a vision in the sanctuary. He made gestures to them, but remained speechless.

23So, when the days of his priestly service were complete, he went back home. 24After that time, Elizabeth his wife conceived. She stayed in hiding for five months.

25"This is the Lord's doing," she said; "at last he has looked on me, and taken away my public shame."

26In the sixth month, Gabriel the angel was sent from God to a town in Galilee called Nazareth, 27to a virgin engaged to a man called Joseph, from the family of David. The virgin was called Mary.

The Annunciation of the Birth of Jesus

28"Greetings, favored one!" said the angel when he arrived. "May the Lord be with you!"

29She was disturbed at this, and wondered what such a greeting might mean.

30"Don't be afraid, Mary," said the angel to her. "You're in favor with God. 31Listen: you will conceive in your womb and will have a son; and you shall call his name Jesus. 32He will be a great man, and he'll be called the son of the Most High. The Lord God will give him the throne of David his father, 33and he shall reign over the house of Jacob forever. His kingdom will never come to an end."

34"How will this happen?" said Mary to the angel. "I'm still a virgin!"

35"The holy spirit will come upon you," replied the angel, "and the power of the Most High will overshadow you. For that reason the Holy One who is born from you will be called God's son.

36"Let me tell you this, too: your cousin Elizabeth, in her old age, has also conceived a son. This is the sixth month for her, a woman who people used to say was barren. 37With God, you see, nothing is impossible."

38"Here I am," said Mary; "I'm the Lord's servant-girl. Let it happen to me as you've said."

Then the angel left her.

The Magnificat: Mary's Song of Praise

39Mary got up then and there, and went in excitement to the hill country of Judaea. 40She went into Zechariah's house, and greeted Elizabeth. 41When Elizabeth heard Mary's greeting, the baby gave a leap in her womb. Elizabeth was filled with the holy spirit, 42and shouted at the top of her voice: "Of all women, you're the blessed one! And the fruit of your womb—he's blessed, too! 43Why should this happen to me, that the mother of my Lord should come to me? 44Look—when the sound of your greeting came to my ears, the child in my womb gave a great leap for joy! 45A blessing on you, for believing that what the Lord said to you would come true!"

46Mary said,

> *"My soul declares that the Lord is great,*
> *47My spirit exults in my savior, my God.*
> *48He saw his servant-girl in her humility;*
> *From now on, I'll be blessed by all peoples to come.*
> *49The Powerful One, whose name is Holy,*
> *Has done great things for me, for me.*
> *50His mercy extends from father to son,*
> *From mother to daughter for those who fear him.*
> *51Powerful things he has done with his arm:*
> *He routed the arrogant through their own cunning.*
> *52Down from their thrones he hurled the rulers,*

Up from the earth he raised the humble.
53The hungry he filled with the fat of the land,
But the rich he sent off with nothing to eat.
54He has rescued his servant, Israel his child,
Because he remembered his mercy of old,
55Just as he said to our long-ago ancestors –
Abraham and his descendants forever."

56Mary stayed with Elizabeth for three months, and then returned home.

57The time arrived for Elizabeth's child to be born, and she gave birth to a son. 58Her neighbors and relatives heard that the Lord had increased his mercy to her, and they came to celebrate with her.

59Now on the eighth day, when they came to circumcise the child, they were calling him by his father's name, Zechariah. 60But his mother spoke up.

"No," she said, "he is to be called John."

61"None of your relatives," they objected, "is called by that name."

62They made signs to his father, to ask what he wanted him to be called. 63He asked for a writing tablet, and wrote on it, "His name is John."

Everyone was astonished. 64Immediately his mouth and his tongue were unfastened, and he spoke, praising God. 65Fear came over all those who lived in the neighborhood, and all these things were spoken of throughout all the hill country of Judaea. 66Everyone who heard about it turned the matter over in their hearts.

"What then will this child become?" they said. And the Lord's hand was with him.

67John's father, Zechariah, was filled with the holy spirit, and spoke this prophecy:

68"Blessed be the Lord, Israel's God!
He's come to his people and bought them their freedom.
69He's raised up a horn of salvation for us
In David's house, the house of his servant,
70Just as he promised, through the mouths of his prophets,

Zechariah's Song of Praise

The holy ones, speaking from ages of old:
71Salvation from our enemies, rescue from hatred,
72Mercy to our ancestors, keeping his holy covenant.
73He swore an oath to Abraham our father,
74To give us deliverance from fear and from foes,
So we might worship him, 75holy and righteous
Before his face to the end of our days.
76You, child, will be called the prophet of the Highest One.
Go ahead of the Lord, preparing his way,
77Letting his people know of salvation,
Through the forgiveness of all their sins.
78The heart of our God is full of mercy;
That's why his daylight has dawned from on high,
79Bringing light to the dark, as we sat in death's shadow,
Guiding our feet in the path of peace."

80The child grew, and became powerful in the spirit. He lived in the wilderness until the day when he was revealed to Israel.

The Birth of Jesus

2 At that time a decree was issued by Augustus Caesar: a census was to be taken of the whole world. 2(This was the first census, before the one when Quirinius was governor of Syria.) 3So everyone set off to be registered, each to their own town. 4Joseph too, who belonged to the house and family of David, went from the city of Nazareth in Galilee to Bethlehem in Judaea, David's city, 5to be registered with his fiancée, Mary, who was pregnant.

6So that's where they were when the time came for her to give birth; 7and she gave birth to her firstborn, a son. She wrapped him up and put him to rest in a feeding-trough, because there was no room for them in the normal living quarters.

8There were shepherds in that region, out in the open, keeping a night watch around their flock. 9An angel of the Lord stood in front of them. The glory of the Lord shone around them, and they were terrified.

10"Don't be afraid," the angel said to them. "Look: I've got good news for you, news which will make everybody very happy. 11Today a savior has been born for you—the Messiah, the

Lord!—in David's town. 12 This will be the sign for you: you'll
find the baby wrapped up, and lying in a feeding-trough."
13 Suddenly, with the angel, there was a crowd of the heavenly armies. They were praising God, saying,

14 "Glory to God in the highest,
And peace upon earth among those in his favor."

15 So when the angels had gone away again into heaven, the
shepherds said to each other, "Well then; let's go to Bethlehem
and see what it's all about, all this that the Lord has told us."
16 So they hurried off and found Mary and Joseph, and the
child lying in the feeding-trough. 17 When they saw it, they told
them what had been said to them about this child. 18 And all
the people who heard it were amazed at the things the shepherds said to them. 19 But Mary treasured all these things and
mused over them in her heart.
20 The shepherds returned, glorifying and praising God for
all they had heard and seen, as it had been told to them.

Simeon and Anna

21 After eight days, the time came to circumcise the baby. He
was called by the name Jesus, which the angel had given him
before he had been conceived in the womb.
22 When the time came for them to be purified according
to the law of Moses, they took him up to Jerusalem to present
him before the Lord. 23 That's what the law of the Lord says:
"Every firstborn male shall be called holy to the Lord." 24 They
also came to offer sacrifice, according to what it says in the law
of the Lord: "A pair of turtledoves or two young pigeons."
25 Now there was a man in Jerusalem named Simeon. He
was righteous and devout, waiting for God to comfort Israel,
and the holy spirit was upon him. 26 He had been told by the
holy spirit that he would not die until he had seen the Lord's
Messiah. 27 Led by the spirit, he came into the Temple. As
Jesus's parents brought him in, to do for him what the law's
regulations required, 28 he took the baby in his arms and
blessed God with these words:

29 "Now, Master, you are dismissing your servant in peace,
just as you said.

30These eyes of mine have seen your salvation,
31Which you made ready in the presence of all peoples:
32A light for revelation to the nations,
And glory for your people Israel."

33His father and mother were astonished at the things that were said about him. 34Simeon blessed them.

"Listen," he said to Mary his mother, "this child has been placed here to make many in Israel fall and rise again, and as a sign that will be spoken against 35(yes, a sword will go through your own soul as well), so that the thoughts of many hearts may be disclosed."

36There was also a prophetess called Anna, the daughter of Phanuel, of the tribe of Asher. She was of a great age, having been widowed after a seven-year marriage, 37and was now eighty-four. She never left the Temple, but worshipped with fasting and prayer night and day. 38She came up at that moment and gave thanks to God, and spoke about Jesus to everyone who was waiting for the redemption of Jerusalem.

39So when they had finished everything according to the law of the Lord, they returned to Galilee, to their town of Nazareth. 40The child grew and became strong, and was full of wisdom, and God's grace was upon him.

The Boy Jesus   41Jesus's parents used to go to Jerusalem every year for the Passover festival. 42When he was twelve years old, they went up as usual for the festival. 43When the feast days were over, they began the journey back, but the boy Jesus remained in Jerusalem. His parents didn't know; 44they thought he was in the traveling party, and went a day's journey before looking for him among their relatives and friends.

45When they didn't find him, they went back to Jerusalem to look for him. 46And so it happened that after three days they found him in the Temple, sitting among the teachers, listening to them and asking them questions. 47Everyone who heard him was astonished at his understanding and his answers.

48When they saw him they were quite overwhelmed.

"Child," said his mother, "why did you do this to us? Look—your father and I have been in a terrible state looking for you!"

⁴⁹"Why were you looking for me?" he replied. "Didn't you know that I would have to be getting involved with my father's work?"

⁵⁰They didn't understand what he had said to them. ⁵¹He went down with them and came to Nazareth, and lived in obedience to them. And his mother kept all these things in her heart.

⁵²So Jesus became wiser and taller, gaining favor both with God and with the people.

3 It was the fifteenth year of the reign of Tiberius Caesar. Pontius Pilate was governor of Judaea; Herod was Tetrarch of Galilee; his brother Philip was Tetrarch of Ituraea and Trachonitis; Lysanias was Tetrarch of Abilene. ²Annas and Caiaphas were the high priests.

The Preaching of John the Baptist

At that time, the word of God came to John, the son of Zechariah, in the wilderness. ³He went through all the region of the Jordan, announcing a baptism of repentance for the forgiveness of sins. ⁴This is what is written in the book of the words of Isaiah the prophet:

"A voice shouting in the wilderness:
Get ready a path for the Lord,
Make the roads straight for him!
⁵Every valley shall be filled in,
And every mountain and hill shall be flattened;
The twisted paths will be straightened out,
And the rough roads smoothed off,
⁶And all that lives shall see God's rescue."

⁷"You brood of vipers," John used to say to the crowds who came out to be baptized by him. "Who told you to escape from the coming anger? ⁸You'd better prove your repentance by bearing the proper fruit! Don't start saying to yourselves, 'We have Abraham as our father'; let me tell you, God can raise up children for Abraham from these stones! ⁹The axe is already standing by the roots of the tree—so every tree that doesn't produce good fruit will be cut down and thrown into the fire."

¹⁰"What shall we do?" asked the crowds.

¹¹"Anyone who has two cloaks," replied John, "should give one to someone who hasn't got one. The same applies to anyone who has plenty of food."

John the Baptist Confronts the Crowd

¹²Some toll-collectors came to be baptized. "Teacher," they said, "what should we do?"

¹³"Don't collect more than what is laid down," he replied.

¹⁴Some soldiers, too, asked John, "What about us? What should we do?"

"No extortion," replied John, "and no blackmail. Be content with your wages."

¹⁵The people were very excited, and everyone was questioning in their hearts whether John might not be the Messiah. ¹⁶To all of them John responded: "I am baptizing you with water. But someone is coming who is stronger than I am. I don't deserve to untie his sandal-strap. He will baptize you with the holy spirit and with fire. ¹⁷He will have his winnowing-fork to hand, ready to sort out the mess on his threshing floor and gather the corn into his barn. Any rubbish he will burn with a fire that will never go out."

¹⁸John urged his news on the people with many other words. ¹⁹But Herod the Tetrarch—whom John had accused in the matter of his brother's wife Herodias, and for all the evil things which Herod had done—²⁰added this to his list of crimes: he shut John up in prison.

Jesus's Baptism and Genealogy

²¹So it happened that, as all the people were being baptized, Jesus too was baptized, and was praying. The heaven was opened, ²²and the holy spirit descended in a bodily form, like a dove, upon him. There came a voice from heaven: "You are my son, my dear son! I'm delighted with you."

²³Jesus was about thirty years old at the start of his work. He was, as people thought, the son of Joseph, from whom his ancestry proceeds back in the following line: Heli, ²⁴Matthat, Levi, Melchi, Jannai, Joseph, ²⁵Mattathias, Amos, Nahum, Esli, Naggai, ²⁶Maath, Mattathias, Semein, Josech, Joda, ²⁷Johanan, Rhesa, Zerubbabel, Shealtiel, Neri, ²⁸Melchi, Addi, Kosam, Elmadam, Er, ²⁹Joshua, Eliezer, Jorim, Matthat, Levi, ³⁰Simeon, Judah, Joseph, Jonam, Eliakim, ³¹Melea, Menna, Mattatha, Nathan, David, ³²Jesse, Obed, Boaz, Sala, Nahshon, ³³Amminadab, Admin, Arni, Hezron, Perez, Judah, ³⁴Jacob, Isaac, Abraham, Terah, Nahor, ³⁵Serug, Reu, Peleg, Eber, Shela, ³⁶Kainan, Arphachsad, Shem, Noah, Lamech, ³⁷Methuselah, Enoch, Jared, Mahalaleel, Kainan, ³⁸Enosh, Seth, Adam, and God.

4 Jesus returned from the Jordan, filled with the spirit. The spirit took him off into the wilderness ²for forty days, to be tested by the devil. He ate nothing during that time, and at the end of it he was hungry.

³"If you are God's son," said the devil, "tell this stone to become a loaf of bread."

⁴"It is written," replied Jesus, " 'It takes more than bread to keep you alive.' "

⁵The devil then took him up and showed him, in an instant, all the kingdoms of the world.

⁶"I will give you authority over all of this," said the devil, "and all the prestige that goes with it. It's been given to me, you see, and I give it to anyone I like. ⁷So it can all be yours . . . if you will just worship me."

⁸"It is written," replied Jesus, " 'The Lord your God is the one you must worship; he is the only one you must serve.' "

⁹Then the devil took him to Jerusalem and stood him on a pinnacle of the Temple.

"If you are God's son," he said, "throw yourself down from here; ¹⁰it's written, 'He will give his angels a command about you, to look after you'; ¹¹and 'They will carry you in their hands, so that you won't hit your foot against a stone.' "

¹²"It has been said," replied Jesus, " 'You mustn't put the Lord your God to the test.' "

¹³When the devil had finished each temptation, he left him until another opportunity.

¹⁴Jesus returned to Galilee in the power of the spirit. Word about him went out throughout the whole district. ¹⁵He taught in their synagogues, and gained a great reputation all around.

¹⁶He came to Nazareth, where he had been brought up. On the sabbath, as was his regular practice, he went into the synagogue and stood up to read. ¹⁷They gave him the scroll of the prophet Isaiah. He unrolled the scroll and found the place where it was written:

¹⁸*"The spirit of the Lord is upon me*
Because he has anointed me
To tell the poor the good news.
He has sent me to announce release to the prisoners

And sight to the blind,
To set the wounded victims free,
¹⁹*To announce the year of God's special favor."*

²⁰He rolled up the scroll, gave it to the attendant, and sat down. All eyes in the synagogue were fixed on him.

²¹"Today," he began, "this scripture is fulfilled in your own hearing."

²²Everyone remarked at him; they were astonished at the words coming out of his mouth—words of sheer grace.

"Isn't this Joseph's son?" they said.

²³"I know what you're going to say," Jesus said. "You're going to tell me the old riddle: 'Heal yourself, doctor!' 'We heard of great happenings in Capernaum; do things like that here, in your own country!'

²⁴"Let me tell you the truth," he went on. "Prophets never get accepted in their own country. ²⁵This is the solemn truth: there were plenty of widows in Israel in the time of Elijah, when heaven was shut up for three years and six months, and there was a great famine over all the land. ²⁶Elijah was sent to none of them, only to a widow in the Sidonian town of Zarephath.

²⁷"And there were plenty of people with virulent skin diseases in Israel in the time of Elisha the prophet, and none of them was healed—only Naaman, the Syrian."

²⁸When they heard this, everyone in the synagogue flew into a rage. ²⁹They got up and threw him out of town. They took him to the top of the mountain on which their town was built, meaning to fling him off. ³⁰But he slipped through the middle of them and went away.

Jesus's Authoritative Healings

³¹Jesus went down to Capernaum, a town of Galilee. He used to teach them every sabbath. ³²They were astonished at his teaching, because his message was powerful and authoritative.

³³There was a man in the synagogue who had the spirit of an unclean demon.

³⁴"Hey, you!" he yelled out at the top of his voice. "What's going on with you and me, Jesus of Nazareth? Have you come to destroy us? I know who you are—you're God's Holy One!"

[35]"Shut up!" Jesus rebuked him. "Come out of him!"

The demon threw the man down right there in front of them, and came out without harming him. [36]Fear came over them all. "What's all this?" they started to say to one another. "He's got power! He's got authority! He tells the unclean spirits what to do, and they come out!" [37]Word about him went out to the whole surrounding region.

[38]He left the synagogue and went into Simon's house. Simon's mother-in-law was sick with a high fever, and they asked him about her. [39]He stood in front of her, rebuked the fever, and it left her. And straightaway she got up and waited on them.

[40]When the sun went down, everyone who had sick people—all kinds of sicknesses—brought them to him. He laid his hands on each one in turn and healed them. [41]Demons came out of many people, shouting out, "You are the son of God!" He sternly forbade them to speak, because they knew he was the Messiah.

[42]When day dawned he left the town and went off to a deserted place. The crowds hunted for him, and when they caught up with him they begged him not to leave them.

[43]"I must tell the good news of God's kingdom to the other towns," he said. "That's what I was sent for." [44]And he was announcing the message to the synagogues of Judaea.

5 One day, as the crowds were pressing close to him to hear the word of God, Jesus was standing by the lake of Gennesaret. [2]He saw two boats moored by the land; the fishermen had gone ashore and were washing their nets. [3]He got into one of the boats—it was Simon's—and asked him to put out a little way from the land. Then he sat down in the boat and began to teach the crowd.

The Miraculous Catch of Fish

[4]When he had finished speaking, he said to Simon, "Put out into the deeper part, and let down your nets for a catch."

[5]"Master," replied Simon, "we were working hard all night and caught nothing at all. But if you say so, I'll let down the nets."

[6]When they did so, they caught such a huge number of fish that their nets began to break. [7]They signaled to their partners in the other boat to come and help them. So they came, and filled both the boats, and they began to sink.

8When Simon Peter saw it, he fell down at Jesus's knees.

"Go away," he said. "Leave me, Lord! I'm a sinner!" 9He and all his companions were gripped with amazement at the catch of fish they had taken; 10this included James and John, the sons of Zebedee, who were partners with Simon.

"Don't be afraid," said Jesus to Simon. "From now on you'll be catching people."

11They brought the boats in to land. Then they abandoned everything and followed him.

The Healing of the Man with a Virulent Skin Disease

12It so happened that, as Jesus was in one particular town, there was a man whose body was riddled with a virulent skin disease. When he saw Jesus, he fell on his face.

"Lord," he begged, "if you want, you can make me clean."

13Jesus stretched out his hand and touched him.

"I do want to," he said. "Be clean."

And the skin disease disappeared immediately.

14Jesus instructed the man not to tell anyone. "Go and show yourself to the priest," he said, "and make the offering commanded by Moses in connection with your healing, as evidence for them."

15The news about Jesus, though, spread all around, and large crowds came to hear and to be healed from their diseases. 16He used to slip away to remote places and pray.

The Healing of the Paralytic Lowered Through the Roof

17One day, as Jesus was teaching, there were Pharisees and legal experts sitting there who had come from every village of Galilee, and from Judaea and Jerusalem. The power of the Lord was with Jesus, enabling him to heal. 18Just then some men appeared, carrying a paralyzed man on a mattress; they were trying to bring him in and lay him before Jesus. 19The crowd made it impossible for them to get through, so they went up on the roof and let him down through the tiles, mattress and all, so that he landed right in the middle, in front of Jesus.

20Jesus saw what trust they had.

"My friend," he said, "your sins are forgiven."

21The legal experts and Pharisees began to argue. "Who does he think he is?" they said. "He's blaspheming! Nobody can forgive sins—only God can do that!"

22Jesus knew their line of thought.

"Why are you complaining in your hearts?" he replied.
23"Which is easier, to say, 'Your sins are forgiven,' or to say,
'Get up and walk'? 24But if you want to be convinced that the
son of man has authority on earth to forgive sins—" (here he
turned to the paralyzed man) "—I say to you, get up, pick up
your mattress, and go home."

25At once he got up in front of them all, picked up what he'd
been lying on, and went off home, praising God.

26A sense of awe came over everyone. They praised God,
and were filled with fear. "We've seen extraordinary things
today," they said.

27After this Jesus went out and saw a tax-collector called
Levi, sitting at the tax-office. "Follow me," he said. 28And he
abandoned everything, got up, and followed him.

Questions About Table-Company and Fasting

29Levi made a great feast for him in his house, and a large
crowd of tax-collectors and others were there reclining at
table. 30The Pharisees and the legal experts began to grumble
to Jesus's disciples.

"Why do you lot eat and drink," they asked, "with tax-
collectors and sinners?"

31"Healthy people don't need a doctor;" replied Jesus; "it's
sick people who do! 32I haven't come to call the righteous; I'm
calling sinners to repentance."

33"John's disciples often fast and say prayers," they said to
him, "and so do the Pharisees' followers—but your disciples
eat and drink."

34"Can you make the wedding guests fast," replied Jesus,
"while the bridegroom is with them? 35But the time will come
when the bridegroom is taken away from them. That's when
they will fast."

36He added this parable. "Nobody tears a piece of cloth
from a new coat to make a patch on an old one. If they do, they
tear the new, and the patch from it won't fit the old one anyway. 37And nobody puts new wine into old wineskins. If they
do, the new wine will burst the skins: it will go to waste, and
the skins will be ruined too. 38You have to put new wine in new
skins. 39And nobody who drinks old wine wants new. 'I prefer
the old,' they say."

**Teachings on
the Sabbath**

6 One sabbath, Jesus was walking through some cornfields. His disciples were plucking and eating ears of
grain, rubbing them with their hands.

2"Why," asked some Pharisees, "are you doing something
that isn't permitted on the sabbath?"

3"Haven't you read what David did?" replied Jesus. "When
he and his men were hungry, 4he went into God's house
and took the 'bread of the Presence,' which no one but the
priests was allowed to eat. He ate some, and gave it to his
companions.

5"The son of man," he declared, "is Lord of the sabbath."

6On another sabbath he went into the synagogue and was
teaching. A man was there whose right hand was withered.
7The scribes and Pharisees were watching him, to see if he
would heal him on the sabbath, so that they could find an accusation against him.

8He knew what they were thinking.

"Get up," he said to the man with the withered hand, "and
come out here in the middle." He got up and came out.

9"Let me ask you something," Jesus said to them. "Is it lawful to do good on the sabbath or to do evil? To save life or to
destroy it?"

10He looked around at all of them.

"Stretch out your hand," he said to the man.

He did so; and his hand was restored. 11But they were filled
with rage, and discussed with each other what they might do
to Jesus.

The Beatitudes

12It happened around that time that Jesus went up into
the mountain to pray, and he spent all night in prayer to God.
13When day came, he called his disciples, and chose twelve of
them, calling them "apostles": 14Simon, whom he called Peter,
and Andrew his brother, and James and John, and Philip,
Bartholomew, 15Matthew, Thomas, James son of Alphaeus,
Simon who was called "the hothead," 16Judas son of James,
and Judas Iscariot, who turned traitor.

17He went down with them, and took up a position on a level
plain where there was a large crowd of his followers, with a
huge company of people from all Judaea, from Jerusalem,
and from the coastal region of Tyre and Sidon. 18They came

to hear him, and to be cured from their diseases. Those who were troubled by unclean spirits were healed, [19]and the whole crowd tried to touch him, because power was going out from him and healing everybody.

[20]He lifted up his eyes and looked at his disciples, and said:

"Blessings on the poor: God's kingdom belongs to you!

[21]"Blessings on those who are hungry today: you'll have a feast!

"Blessings on those who weep today: you'll be laughing!

[22]"Blessings on you, when people hate you, and shut you out, when they slander you and reject your name as if it was evil, because of the son of man. [23]Celebrate on that day! Jump for joy! Don't you see: in heaven there is a great reward for you! That's what their ancestors did to the prophets.

[24]"But woe betide you rich: you've had your comfort!

[25]"Woe betide you if you're full today: you'll go hungry!

"Woe betide you if you're laughing today: you'll be mourning and weeping!

[26]"Woe betide you when everyone speaks well of you: that's what their ancestors did to the false prophets.

[27]"But this is my word," Jesus continued, "for those of you who are listening: love your enemies! Do good to people who hate you! [28]Bless people who curse you! Pray for people who treat you badly!

Loving Your Enemies

[29]"If someone hits you on the cheek—offer him the other one! If someone takes away your coat—don't stop him taking your shirt! [30]Give to everyone who asks you, and don't ask for things back when people have taken them.

[31]"Whatever you want people to do to you, do that to them. [32]If you love those who love you, what credit is that to you? Think about it: even sinners love people who love them. [33]Or again, if you do good only to people who do good to you, what credit is that to you? Sinners do that too. [34]If you lend only to people you expect to get things back from, what credit is that to you? Even sinners lend to sinners to get paid back. [35]No: love your enemies, do good, and lend without expecting any return. Your reward will be great! You will be children of the Highest! He is generous, you see, to the stingy and wicked. [36]You must be merciful, just as your father is merciful.

37"Don't judge, and you won't be judged. Don't condemn, and you won't be condemned. Forgive, and you'll be forgiven. 38Give, and it will be given to you: a good helping, squashed down, shaken in, and overflowing—that's what will land in your lap. Yes: the ration you give to others is the ration you'll get back for yourself."

Judging Others and True Obedience

39Jesus told them this riddle. "What do you get when one blind man guides another? Both of them falling in a ditch! 40Students can't do better than the teacher; when the course is done, they'll all be just like the teacher.

41"Why look at the speck of dust in your brother's eye, when you haven't noticed the plank in your own eye? 42How can you say to your brother, 'Dear brother, let me take the speck out of your eye,' when you can't see the plank in your own? You're a fraud! First take the plank out of your own eye, and then you'll see clearly to take the speck out of your brother's eye.

43"You see, no good tree bears bad fruit; nor can a bad tree produce good fruit. 44Every tree is known by its fruit. You don't pick figs from thorns; nor do you get grapes from a briar-bush. 45The good person brings good things out of the good treasure of the heart; the evil person brings evil things out of evil. What comes out of the mouth is what's overflowing in the heart.

46"Why do you call me, 'Lord, Lord,' and don't do what I say? 47I'll show you what people are like when they come to me, and hear my words, and do them. 48They are like a wise man building a house: he dug, he went down deep, and he laid a foundation on rock. When a flood came, the river burst its banks all over the house, but it couldn't shake it because it was well built. 49But when people hear but don't obey—that's like a man who built a house on the ground, without a foundation. When the river burst over it, it fell down at once. The ruin of that house was devastating."

The Healing of the Centurion's Servant

7 When Jesus had finished saying all these words in the hearing of the people, he went into Capernaum.

2There was a centurion who had a slave who was particularly precious to him. This slave was ill, at the point of death. 3The centurion heard about Jesus, and sent some

Jewish elders to him, to ask him to come and rescue his slave. ⁴They approached Jesus and begged him eagerly.

"He deserves a favor like this from you," they said. ⁵"He loves our people, and he himself built us our synagogue."

⁶Jesus went with them.

When he was not far off from the house, the centurion sent friends to him with a further message.

"Master," he said, "don't trouble yourself. I don't deserve to have you come under my roof. ⁷That's why I didn't think myself worthy to come to you in person. But—just say the word, and my slave will be healed. ⁸You see, I'm used to living under authority, and I have soldiers reporting to me. I say to this one, 'Go,' and he goes; to another one, 'Come,' and he comes; and to my slave, 'Do this,' and he does it."

⁹When Jesus heard this he was astonished.

"Let me tell you," he said, turning to the crowd that was following him, "I haven't found faith of this kind, even in Israel."

¹⁰The people who had been sent to him went back to the house. There they found the slave in good health.

¹¹Not long afterward, Jesus went to a town called Nain. His disciples went with him, and so did a large crowd. ¹²As he got near to the gate of the city, a young man was being carried out dead. He was the only son of his mother, and she was a widow. There was a substantial crowd of the townspeople with her.

Raising of the Widow's Son

¹³When the master saw her, he was very sorry for her. "Don't cry," he said to her. ¹⁴Then he went up and touched the bier, and the people carrying it stood still.

"Young fellow," he said, "I'm telling you—get up!" ¹⁵The dead man sat up and began to speak, and he gave him to his mother.

¹⁶Terror came over all of them. They praised God.

"A great prophet has risen among us!" they said. "God has visited his people!"

¹⁷This report went out about him in the whole of Judaea and the surrounding countryside.

¹⁸The disciples of John the Baptist told him about all these things. John called two of these followers ¹⁹and sent them to the master with this message: "Are you the Coming One, or should we expect someone else?"

Jesus and John the Baptist

20The men arrived where Jesus was. "John the Baptist," they said, "has sent us to you to say, 'Are you the Coming One, or should we expect someone else?'"

21Then and there Jesus healed several people of diseases, plagues, and possession by unclean spirits; and he gave several blind people back their sight. 22Then he answered them: "Go and tell John what you have seen and heard: the blind see; the lame walk; people with virulent skin diseases are cleansed; the deaf hear; the dead are raised; the poor hear the gospel. 23And a blessing on the person who isn't shocked by me!"

24So off went John's messengers.

Jesus then began to talk to the crowds about John. "Why did you go out into the desert?" he asked. "What were you looking for? A reed swaying in the breeze? 25Well then, what did you go out to see? Someone dressed in silks and satins? See here, if you want to find people who wear fine clothes and live in luxury, you'd better look in royal palaces. 26So what did you go out to see? A prophet? Yes indeed, and more than a prophet. 27This is the one of whom the Bible says, 'Look: I send my messenger before my face; he will get my path ready ahead of me.'

28"Let me tell you this," he went on. "Nobody greater than John has ever been born of woman. But the one who is least in God's kingdom is greater than he is."

29When all the people, and the tax-collectors, heard that, they praised God for his faithfulness; they had been baptized with John's baptism. 30But the Pharisees and the lawyers, who had not been baptized by John, rejected God's plan for them.

31"What picture can I use," Jesus continued, "for the people of this generation? What are they like? 32They're like children sitting in the square and calling this old riddle to each other:

'We piped for you and you didn't dance;
We wailed for you and you didn't cry!'

33"When John the Baptist came, he didn't eat bread or drink wine, and you say, 'He's got a demon!' 34When the son of man came, eating and drinking, you say, 'Look! A glutton and a drunkard, a friend of tax-collectors and sinners!' 35And wisdom is justified by all her children."

³⁶A Pharisee asked Jesus to dine with him, and he went into the Pharisee's house and reclined at table. ³⁷A woman from the town, a known bad character, discovered that he was there at table in the Pharisee's house. She brought an alabaster jar of ointment. ³⁸Then she stood behind Jesus's feet, crying, and began to wet his feet with her tears. She wiped them with her hair, kissed his feet, and anointed them with the ointment.

³⁹The Pharisee who had invited Jesus saw what was going on.

"If this fellow really was a prophet," he said to himself, "he'd know what sort of a woman this is who is touching him! She's a sinner!"

⁴⁰"Simon," replied Jesus, "I have something to say to you."

"Go ahead, Teacher," he replied.

⁴¹"Once upon a time there was a money-lender who had two debtors. The first owed him five hundred dinars; the second a tenth of that. ⁴²Neither of them could pay him, and he let them both off. So which of them will love him more?"

⁴³"The one he let off the more, I suppose," replied Simon.

"Quite right," said Jesus.

⁴⁴Then, turning toward the woman, he said to Simon, "You see this woman? When I came into your house, you didn't give me water to wash my feet—but she has washed my feet with her tears, and wiped them with her hair. ⁴⁵You didn't give me a kiss, but she hasn't stopped kissing my feet from the moment I came in. ⁴⁶You didn't anoint my head with oil, but she has anointed my feet with ointment.

⁴⁷"So the conclusion I draw is this: she must have been forgiven many sins! Her great love proves it! But if someone has been forgiven only a little, they will love only a little."

⁴⁸Then he said to the woman, "Your sins are forgiven."

⁴⁹"Who is this," the other guests began to say among themselves, "who even forgives sins?"

⁵⁰"Your faith has saved you," said Jesus to the woman. "Go in peace."

8 Soon afterward, Jesus went about in person, with the Twelve, through the towns and villages, announcing and telling the good news of God's kingdom. ²They were

Jesus Anointed by a Sinful Woman

The Parable of the Sower

accompanied by various women who had been healed from evil spirits and diseases: Mary who was called Magdalene, from whom seven demons had gone out, ³Joanna the wife of Chouza (Herod's steward), and Susanna, and many others. They looked after the needs of Jesus and his companions out of their own pockets.

⁴A large crowd came together, and people came to him from town after town. He spoke to them in parables: ⁵"A sower went out to sow his seed. As he was sowing, some fell by the road, and was trodden on, and the birds of the air ate it up. ⁶Other seed fell on stony ground, and when it came up it withered, because it didn't have any moisture. ⁷Other seed fell in among thorns, and when the thorns grew up they choked it. ⁸Other seed again fell into good soil, and came up, and gave a hundredfold yield."

As he said this, he called out, "If you've got ears to hear, then hear!"

⁹His disciples asked him what this parable was about.

¹⁰"You are being let in on the secrets of God's kingdom," he said, "but to the rest it happens in parables, so that 'they may see but not perceive, and hear but not understand.'

¹¹"This is the parable: The seed is the word of God. ¹²Those by the roadside are people who hear, but then the devil comes and takes away the word from their hearts, so that they won't believe it and be saved. ¹³Those on the stony ground are those who hear the word and receive it with delight—but they don't have any root, and so they believe only for a time, and then, when a time of testing comes, they draw back. ¹⁴The seed that falls in among thorns represents people who hear, but as they go on their way they are choked by the cares and riches and pleasures of life, and they don't bear proper, ripening fruit. ¹⁵But those in the good soil are the ones who hear the word and hold on to it with an upright and good heart, and who patiently produce fruit.

Jesus Calms the Storm

¹⁶"Nobody lights a lamp," continued Jesus, "and then hides it under a pot or a bed. They put it on a lampstand, so that people who come in can see the light. ¹⁷You see, nothing is hidden which won't become visible; nothing is concealed that won't come to light.

¹⁸"So be careful how you listen. If you've got something, more will be given to you; if you haven't, even what you imagine you have will be taken away from you."

¹⁹His mother and brothers came to him, and couldn't get near him because of the crowd. ²⁰So they sent a message to him: "Your mother and your brothers are standing outside, wanting to see you."

²¹"Mother and brothers, indeed?" replied Jesus. "Here are my mother and brothers—people who hear God's word and do it!"

²²One day he got into a boat with his disciples, and suggested that they cross to the other shore. So they set off. ²³As they were sailing, he fell asleep. A violent wind swept down on the lake, and the boat began to fill dangerously with water.

²⁴"Master, Master!" shouted the disciples, coming and waking him up. "Master, we're lost!"

He got up and scolded the wind and the waves. They stopped, and there was a flat calm.

²⁵"Where's your faith?" he asked them.

They were afraid and astonished. "Who is this, then," they asked one another, "if he can give orders to wind and water, and they obey him?"

²⁶They sailed to the land of the Gerasenes, which is on the other side from Galilee. ²⁷As he got out on land, a demon-possessed man from the town met him. For a long time he had worn no clothes, and he didn't live in a house but among the tombs. ²⁸When he saw Jesus he screamed and fell down in front of him.

The Healing of the Demoniac

"You and me, Jesus—you and me!" he yelled at the top of his voice. "What is it with you and me, you son of the Most High God? Don't torture me—please, please don't torment me!" ²⁹Jesus was commanding the unclean spirit to come out of the man. Many times over it had seized him, and he was kept under guard with chains and manacles; but he used to break the shackles, and the demon would drive him into the desert.

³⁰"What's your name?" Jesus asked him.

"Regiment!" replied the man—for many demons had entered him. ³¹And they begged him not to order them to be sent into the Pit.

³²A sizable herd of pigs was feeding on the hillside, and the demons begged him to allow them to go into them. He gave them permission. ³³The demons went out of the man and entered the pigs, and the herd rushed down the steep slope into the lake and was drowned.

³⁴The herdsmen saw what had happened. They took to their heels and spread the news in town and country, ³⁵and people came out to see what had happened. They came to Jesus, and found the man from whom the demons had gone out sitting there at Jesus's feet, clothed and in his right mind. They were afraid. ³⁶People who had seen how the demoniac had been healed explained it to them. ³⁷The whole crowd, from the surrounding country of the Gerasenes, asked him to go away from them, because great terror had seized them. So he got into the boat and returned.

³⁸The man who had been demon-possessed begged Jesus to let him stay with him. But he sent him away. ³⁹"Go back to your home," he said, "and tell them what God has done for you." And he went off around every town, declaring what Jesus had done for him.

Jairus's Daughter and the Woman with Chronic Bleeding

⁴⁰Jesus returned. A large crowd was waiting for him and welcomed him back. ⁴¹A man named Jairus, a ruler of the synagogue, came and fell down in front of his feet. He pleaded with him to come to his house, ⁴²because he had an only daughter, twelve years old, who was dying. So they set off, and the crowd pressed close in around him.

⁴³There was a woman who'd had an internal hemorrhage for twelve years. She had spent all she had on doctors, but had not been able to find a cure from anyone. ⁴⁴She came up behind Jesus and touched the hem of his robe. Immediately her flow of blood dried up.

⁴⁵"Who touched me?" asked Jesus.

Everybody denied it. "Master," said Peter, "the crowds are crushing you and pressing you!"

⁴⁶"Somebody touched me," said Jesus. "Power went out from me, and I knew it."

⁴⁷When the woman saw that she couldn't remain hidden, she came up, trembling, and fell down in front of him. She told

him, in front of everyone, why she had touched him, and how she had been healed instantly.

⁴⁸"Daughter," said Jesus, "your faith has saved you. Go in peace."

⁴⁹While he was still speaking, someone arrived from the synagogue-ruler's house. "Your daughter's dead," he said. "Don't bother the teacher any longer."

⁵⁰"Don't be afraid," said Jesus when he heard it. "Just believe, and she will be rescued."

⁵¹When they got to the house, he didn't let anyone come in with them except Peter, John, and James, and the child's father and mother. ⁵²Everyone was weeping and wailing for her.

"Don't cry," said Jesus. "She isn't dead; she's asleep." ⁵³They laughed at him, knowing that she was dead.

⁵⁴But he took her by the hand. "Get up, child," he called. ⁵⁵Her spirit returned, and she got up at once. He told them to give her something to eat. ⁵⁶Her parents were astounded, but he told them to tell nobody what had happened.

9 Jesus called together the Twelve, and gave them power and authority over all demons, and to cure diseases. ²He sent them out to announce God's kingdom and cure the sick.

The Twelve Sent Out and the Feeding of the Five Thousand

³"Don't take anything for the journey," he said to them; "no stick, no bag, no bread, no money, no second cloak. ⁴Whenever you go into a house, stay there and leave from there. ⁵If anyone won't receive you, go out of that town and wipe the dust off your feet as evidence against them."

⁶So off they went and traveled through the villages, announcing the good news and healing people everywhere.

⁷Herod the tetrarch heard what was going on, and was very puzzled. Some people were saying that John had been raised from the dead. ⁸Others were saying that Elijah had appeared; still others, that one of the old prophets had arisen.

⁹"I beheaded John," said Herod, "but I keep hearing all these things about this other fellow. Who is he?" And he tried to get to see him.

¹⁰The apostles returned and told Jesus what they had done. He took them off and went away privately to a town called

Bethsaida. ¹¹When the crowds found out, they followed him. He welcomed them and spoke to them about the kingdom of God, and he healed those who needed it.

¹²As the day wore on, the Twelve came to Jesus.

"Send the crowd away," they said, "so that they can go into the villages and countryside nearby, find somewhere to stay, and get something to eat. We're in quite a lonely spot here."

¹³"You give them something to eat," he replied.

"All we've got here," they said, "is five loaves and a couple of fish—unless you mean we should go ourselves and buy food for all these people?" ¹⁴(There were about five thousand men.)

"Get them to sit down," Jesus said to them, "in groups of around fifty each."

¹⁵They did so, and everyone sat down. ¹⁶Then Jesus took the five loaves and the two fish. He looked up to heaven, blessed the food, divided it, and gave it to the disciples to pass around the crowd. ¹⁷Everyone ate and was satisfied. They took up twelve baskets of broken bits left over.

Peter's Declaration of Jesus's Messiahship

¹⁸When Jesus was praying alone, his disciples gathered around him.

"Who do the crowds say I am?" he asked them.

¹⁹"John the Baptist," they responded. "And others say Elijah. Others say that one of the ancient prophets has arisen."

²⁰"What about you?" said Jesus. "Who do you say I am?"

"God's Messiah," answered Peter.

²¹He gave them strict and careful instructions not to tell this to anyone.

²²"The son of man," he said, "must suffer many things, and be rejected by the elders, and the chief priests, and the legal experts. He must be killed, and raised up on the third day."

²³He then spoke to them all. "If any of you want to come after me," he said, "you must say no to yourselves, and pick up your cross every day, and follow me. ²⁴If you want to save your life, you'll lose it; but if you lose your life because of me, you'll save it. ²⁵What good will it do you if you win the entire world, but lose or forfeit your own self? ²⁶If you're ashamed of me and my words, the son of man will be ashamed of you, when he comes in the glory which belongs to him, and to the father, and to the holy angels.

27"Let me tell you," he concluded, "there are some standing here who won't experience death until they see God's kingdom."

28About eight days after this conversation, Jesus took Peter, John, and James and went up a mountain to pray. 29And, as he was praying, the appearance of his face changed, and his clothes became shining white. 30Two men appeared, talking with him: it was Moses and Elijah, 31who appeared in glory and were speaking of his departure, which he was going to fulfill in Jerusalem.

The Transfiguration

32Peter and those who were with him were heavy with sleep, but they managed to stay awake. They saw his glory, and the two men who were standing there with him.

33As they were going away from him, Peter said to Jesus, "Master, it's wonderful for us to be here! Let's make three tents—one for you, one for Moses, and one for Elijah!" He didn't know what he was saying; 34but as the words were coming out of his mouth a cloud appeared and overshadowed them. They were afraid as they entered the cloud. 35And a voice came from the cloud: "This is my son, my chosen one: listen to him." 36As the voice spoke, there was Jesus by himself. They kept silent, and told nobody at that time anything of what they had seen.

37The next day, as they were going down from the mountain, a large crowd met them. 38A man from the crowd shouted out, "Teacher! Please, please have a look at my son! He's my only child, 39and look what's happening to him! A spirit seizes him, and suddenly it shrieks and convulses him, so that he foams at the mouth. It goes on savaging him, and it's almost impossible to get it to leave him. 40I begged your disciples to cast it out, but they couldn't."

41"You faithless and depraved generation!" said Jesus in reply. "How long shall I be with you and have to put up with you? Bring your son here."

42While he was on the way, the demon tore at him and threw him into convulsions. Jesus rebuked the unclean spirit, healed the child, and gave him back to his father. 43Everyone was astonished at the greatness of God.

While they were all still expressing amazement at everything he had done, Jesus said to his disciples, 44"Let these words go right down into your ears: the son of man is to be given over into human hands." ⁴⁵They had no idea what he was talking about. It was hidden from them, so that they wouldn't perceive it, and they were afraid to ask him about what he had said.

The Nature of
Discipleship

⁴⁶A dispute arose among them about which of them was the greatest. ⁴⁷Jesus knew this quarrel was going on in their hearts, so he took a child and stood it beside him.

⁴⁸"If you receive this child in my name," he said, "you receive me. And anyone who receives me, receives the one who sent me. Whoever is the least among you—that's the one who is great."

⁴⁹"Master," commented John, "we saw someone casting out demons in your name. We told him to stop, because he wasn't part of our company."

⁵⁰"Don't stop him," replied Jesus. "Anyone who isn't against you is on your side."

⁵¹As the time came nearer for Jesus to be taken up, he settled it in his mind to go to Jerusalem. ⁵²He sent messengers ahead of him. They came into a Samaritan village to get them ready, ⁵³and they refused to receive him, because his mind was set on going to Jerusalem. ⁵⁴When the disciples James and John saw it, they said, "Master, do you want us to call down fire from heaven and burn them up?" ⁵⁵He turned and rebuked them, ⁵⁶and they went on to another village.

⁵⁷As they were going along the road a man addressed Jesus.

"Wherever you're going," he said, "I'll follow you!"

⁵⁸"Foxes have lairs," Jesus replied, "and the birds in the sky have nests; but the son of man doesn't have anywhere to lay his head."

⁵⁹To another person he said, "Follow me."

"Master," he replied, "let me first go and bury my father."

⁶⁰"Let the dead bury their dead," said Jesus. "You must go and announce God's kingdom."

⁶¹"I will follow you, Master," said another, "but first let me say goodbye to the people at home."

⁶²"Nobody," replied Jesus, "who begins to plow and then looks over his shoulder is fit for God's kingdom."

10

After this the master commissioned seventy others, and sent them ahead of him in pairs to every town and place where he was intending to go.

²"There's a great harvest out there," he said to them, "but there aren't many workers. So plead with the harvest-master to send out workers for the harvest.

³"Off you go now. Remember, I'm sending you out like lambs among wolves. ⁴Take no money-bag, no pack, no sandals—and don't stop to pass the time with anyone on the road. ⁵Whenever you go into a house, first say, 'Peace on this house.' ⁶If a child of peace lives there, your peace will rest on them; but if not, it will return to you.

⁷"Stay in the same house, and eat and drink what they provide. The worker deserves to be paid, you see. Don't go from house to house. ⁸If you go into a town and they welcome you, eat what is provided, ⁹heal the sick who are there, and say to them, 'God's kingdom has come close to you.' ¹⁰But if you go into a town and they don't welcome you, go out into the streets of the town and say, ¹¹'Here is the very dust of your town clinging to our feet—and we're wiping it off in front of your eyes! ¹²But you should know this: God's kingdom has come close to you!' Let me tell you, on that day it will be more tolerable for Sodom than for that town.

¹³"Woe betide you, Chorazin! Woe betide you, Bethsaida! If the powerful deeds done in you had been done in Tyre and Sidon, they would have repented long ago, sitting in sackcloth and ashes. ¹⁴But it will be more tolerable for Tyre and Sidon in the judgment than for you. ¹⁵And you, Capernaum—you want to be lifted up to heaven, do you? No: you'll be sent down to Hades!

¹⁶"Anyone who hears you, hears me; anyone who rejects you, rejects me; and anyone who rejects me, rejects the one who sent me."

¹⁷The seventy came back exhilarated.

"Master," they said, "even the demons obey us in your name!"

¹⁸"I saw the satan fall like lightning from heaven," he replied. ¹⁹"Look: I've given you authority to tread on snakes and scorpions, and over every power of the enemy. Nothing will

ever be able to harm you. 20But—don't celebrate having spirits under your authority. Celebrate this, that your names are written in heaven."

21Then and there Jesus celebrated in the holy spirit.

"I thank you, Father," he said, "Lord of heaven and earth! You hid these things from the wise and intelligent, and revealed them to babies. Yes, Father, that was what you graciously decided. 22Everything has been given me by my father. Nobody knows who the son is except the father, and nobody knows who the father is except the son, and anyone to whom the son wishes to reveal him."

23Jesus then turned to the disciples privately.

"A blessing on the eyes," he said, "which see what you see! 24Let me tell you, many prophets and kings wanted to see what you see, and they didn't see it; and to hear what you hear, and they didn't hear it!"

The Parable of the Good Samaritan

25A lawyer got up and put Jesus on the spot.

"Teacher," he said, "what should I do to inherit the life of the coming age?"

26"Well," replied Jesus, "what is written in the law? What's your interpretation of it?"

27"You shall love the Lord your God," he replied, "with all your heart, all your soul, all your strength, and all your understanding; and your neighbor as yourself."

28"Well said!" replied Jesus. "Do that and you will live."

29"Ah," said the lawyer, wanting to win the point, "but who is my neighbor?"

30Jesus rose to the challenge. "Once upon a time," he said, "a man was going down from Jerusalem to Jericho, and was set upon by brigands. They stripped him and beat him and ran off leaving him half-dead. 31A priest happened to be going down that road, and when he saw him he went past on the opposite side. 32So too a Levite came by the place; he saw him too, and went past on the opposite side.

33"But a traveling Samaritan came to where he was. When he saw him he was filled with pity. 34He came over to him and bound up his wounds, pouring in oil and wine. Then he put him on his own beast, took him to an inn, and looked after him. 35The next morning, as he was going on his way, he gave the innkeeper two dinars. 'Take care of him,' he said, 'and on my way back I'll pay you whatever else you need to spend on him.'

36"Which of these three do you think turned out to be the neighbor of the man who was set upon by the brigands?"

37"The one who showed mercy on him," came the reply.

"Well," Jesus said to him, "you go and do the same."

38On their journey, Jesus came into a village. There was a woman there named Martha, who welcomed him. 39She had a sister named Mary, who sat at the master's feet and listened to his teaching.

Martha and Mary

40Martha was frantic with all the work in the kitchen.

"Master," she said, coming in to where they were, "don't you care that my sister has left me to do the work all by myself? Tell her to give me a hand!"

41"Martha, Martha," he replied, "you are fretting and fussing about so many things. 42Only one thing matters. Mary has chosen the best part, and it's not going to be taken away from her."

11 Once Jesus was praying in a particular place. When he had finished, one of his disciples approached.

"Teach us to pray, Master," he said, "just like John taught his disciples."

The Lord's Prayer

2"When you pray," replied Jesus, "this is what to say:

"Father, may your name be honored; may your kingdom come; 3give us each day our daily bread; 4and forgive us our sins, since we too forgive all our debtors; and don't put us to the test.

5"Suppose one of you has a friend," he said, "and you go to him in the middle of the night and say, 'My dear friend, lend me three loaves of bread! 6A friend of mine is on a journey and has arrived at my house, and I have nothing to put in front of him!' 7He will answer from inside his house, 'Don't make life difficult for me! The door is already shut, and my children and I are all in bed! I can't get up and give you anything.' 8Let me tell you, even if he won't get up and give you anything just because you're his friend, because of your shameless persistence he will get up and give you whatever you need.

9"So this is my word to you: ask and it will be given you; search and you will find; knock and it will be opened to you.

10You see, everyone who asks receives! Everyone who searches finds! Everyone who knocks has the door opened for them! 11If your son asks you for a fish, is there a father among you who will give him a snake? 12Or if he asks for an egg, will you give him a scorpion? 13Face it: you are evil. And yet you know how to give good presents to your children. How much more will your heavenly father give the holy spirit to those who ask him!"

Jesus and Beelzebul

14Jesus was casting out a demon that prevented speech. When the demon had gone out, the man who had been silent spoke, and the crowds were amazed. 15But some of them said, "He casts out demons by Beelzebul, the prince of demons!" 16Others, trying to test him out, asked him to produce a sign from heaven.

17Jesus knew what they were thinking.

"Every kingdom split down the middle goes to ruin," he said. "If a house turns in on itself, it falls. 18Well then: if even the satan is split down the middle, how can his kingdom last? This," he added, "is because you say that I cast out demons by Beelzebul!

19"Now look: supposing I do cast out demons by Beelzebul, whose power are your own people using when they cast them out? Think about it: they will be your judges. 20But if it's by God's finger that I cast out demons, then God's kingdom has come upon you.

21"Imagine a strong man, armed to the teeth, guarding his palace. Everything he owns is safe and sound. 22But supposing someone stronger comes and overpowers him, and takes away the armor he was trusting in—then he can help himself and start giving the booty away! 23If you're not with me, you're against me. If you're not gathering with me, you're scattering.

24"When the unclean spirit goes out of a person, it roams through desert landscapes looking for a place to rest. When it doesn't find anywhere, it says to itself, 'I shall go back to the house I left behind.' 25And it finds the place neat and tidy. 26So it sets off and brings along seven other spirits more evil than itself, and goes back to live there. That person will end up worse off than he began."

27While he was saying these things, a woman from the

crowd raised her voice. "A blessing on the womb that bore you," she shouted, "and the breasts that you sucked!"

28"On the contrary," replied Jesus. "A blessing on those who hear God's word and keep it!"

29The crowds kept increasing. Jesus began to say to them, "This generation is an evil generation! It looks for a sign, and no sign will be given to it except the sign of Jonah.

The Sign of Jonah

30"Jonah was a sign to the people of Nineveh; just so, the son of man will be a sign to this generation. 31The Queen of the South will rise up in the judgment with the men of this generation and will condemn them: she came from the ends of the earth to listen to Solomon's wisdom, and look—something greater than Solomon is here. 32The men of Nineveh will rise up in the judgment with this generation and will condemn it: they repented at Jonah's preaching, and look—something greater than Jonah is here.

33"Nobody lights a lamp in order to hide it or put it under a jug. They put it on a lampstand, so that people who come in can see the light.

34"Your eye is the lamp of your body. If your eye is focused, your whole body is full of light. But if it's evil, your body is in darkness. 35Watch out, then, in case the light inside you turns to darkness. 36If your whole body is illuminated, with no part in darkness, everything will be illuminated, just as you are by a flash of lightning."

37While he was speaking, a Pharisee invited him to have dinner at his house. So he went in and sat down. 38The Pharisee, watching him, was surprised that he didn't first wash before dinner.

39"Now, you Pharisees," said the master to him, "you clean the outside of the plate and cup, but your insides are full of violent robbery and wickedness. 40That's stupid! Didn't the one who made the outside make the inside as well? 41You should give for alms what's inside the bowl, and then everything will be clean for you."

42"But woe betide you Pharisees!" Jesus continued. "You tithe mint and rue and herbs of all kinds; and you have sidestepped justice, mercy, and the love of God. You should have done these, without leaving out the others.

Woes Against the Pharisees

⁴³"Woe betide you Pharisees! You love the chief seats in the synagogues and greetings in the marketplaces.

⁴⁴"Woe betide you! You are like hidden tombs, and people walk over them without knowing it."

⁴⁵At this, one of the legal experts spoke up. "Teacher," he said, "when you say this, you're insulting us too!"

⁴⁶"Woe betide you lawyers, too!" replied Jesus. "You give people heavy loads to carry which they can hardly bear, and you yourselves don't lift a finger to help!

⁴⁷"Woe betide you! You build the tombs of the prophets, and your ancestors killed them. ⁴⁸So you bear witness that you approve of what your ancestors did: they killed them, and you build their tombs.

⁴⁹"For all this, God's Wisdom says, 'I'm sending you prophets and ambassadors; some of them you will kill and persecute,' ⁵⁰so that the blood of all the prophets shed ever since the beginning of the world may be required from this generation—⁵¹from the blood of Abel to the blood of Zacharias, who died between the altar and the sanctuary. Yes, let me tell you, it will all be required from this generation.

⁵²"Woe betide you lawyers! You have taken away the key of knowledge. You didn't go in yourselves, and you stopped the people who were trying to go in."

⁵³He went outside, and the scribes and Pharisees began to be very threatening toward him. They interrogated him about several things, ⁵⁴lying in wait for him to catch him in something he might say.

Further Warnings

12 Crowds were gathering in the thousands, so much so that they were trampling on each other. Jesus began to say to his disciples, "Watch out for the leaven of the Pharisees—I mean, their hypocrisy. This is a matter of first importance.

²"Nothing is concealed that won't be uncovered; nothing is hidden that won't be made known. ³So whatever you say in the darkness will be heard in the light, and whatever you speak indoors into someone's ear will be proclaimed from the housetops.

⁴"So, my friends, I have this to say to you: don't be afraid of those who kill the body, and after that have nothing more they

can do. ⁵I will show you who to fear: fear the one who starts by killing and then has the right to throw people into Gehenna. Yes, let me tell you, that's the one to fear!

⁶"How much do five sparrows cost? Two copper coins? And not one of them is forgotten in God's presence. ⁷But the hairs of your head have all been counted. Don't be afraid! You are worth more than lots of sparrows.

⁸"Let me tell you: if anyone acknowledges me before others, the son of man will acknowledge that person before God's angels. ⁹But if anyone denies me before others, that person will be denied before God's angels.

¹⁰"Everyone who speaks a word against the son of man will have it forgiven; but the one who blasphemes against the holy spirit will not be forgiven.

¹¹"When they bring you before synagogues, rulers, and authorities, don't worry about how to give an answer or what to say. ¹²The holy spirit will teach you what to say at that very moment."

¹³Someone from the crowd said to Jesus, "Teacher, tell my brother to divide the inheritance with me!"

The Parable of the Rich Fool

¹⁴"Tell me, my good man," replied Jesus, "who appointed me as a judge or arbitrator over you?

¹⁵"Watch out," he said to them, "and beware of all greed! Your life doesn't consist of the sum total of your possessions."

¹⁶He told them a parable. "There was a rich man whose land produced a fine harvest. ¹⁷'What shall I do?' he said to himself. 'I don't have enough room to store my crops!

¹⁸"'I know!' he said. 'I'll pull down my barns—and I'll build bigger ones! Then I'll be able to store all the corn and all my belongings there. ¹⁹And I shall say to my soul, Soul, you've got many good things stored up for many years. Take it easy! Eat, drink, have a good time!'

²⁰"But God said to him, 'Fool! This very night your soul will be demanded of you! Now who's going to have all the things you've got ready?' ²¹That's how it is with someone who stores up things for himself and isn't rich before God.

²²"So let me tell you this," he said to the disciples. "Don't be anxious about your life—what you should eat; or about your body—what you should wear. ²³Life is more than food! The

body is more than clothing! ²⁴Think about the ravens: they don't sow seed, they don't gather harvests, they don't have storehouses or barns; and God feeds them. How much more will he feed you! Think of the difference between yourselves and the birds!

²⁵"Which of you by being anxious can add a day to your lifetime? ²⁶So if you can't even do a little thing like that, why worry about anything else? ²⁷Think about the lilies and the way they grow. They don't work hard, they don't weave cloth; but, let me tell you, not even Solomon in all his glory was dressed up like one of them. ²⁸So if that's how God clothes the grass in the field—here today, into the fire tomorrow—how much more will he clothe you, you little-faith lot!

²⁹"So don't you go hunting about for what to eat or what to drink, and don't be anxious. ³⁰The nations of the world go searching for all that stuff, and your father knows you need it. ³¹This is what you should search for: God's kingdom! Then all the rest will be given you as well. ³²Don't be afraid, little flock. Your father is delighted to give you the kingdom.

³³"Sell your possessions and give alms. Make yourselves purses that don't wear out, a treasure in heaven that lasts forever, where the thief doesn't come near and the moth doesn't destroy. ³⁴Yes: where your treasure is, there your heart will be too.

Jesus's Call to Watchfulness ³⁵"Make sure you're dressed and ready with your lamps alight," said Jesus. ³⁶"You need to be like people waiting for their master when he comes back from the wedding-feast, so that when he comes and knocks they will be able to open the door for him at once. ³⁷A blessing on the servants whom the master finds awake when he comes! I'm telling you the truth: he will put on an apron and sit them down and come and wait on them. ³⁸A blessing on them if he comes in the second watch of the night, or even the third, and finds them like that!

³⁹"But you should know this: if the householder had known what time the thief was coming, he wouldn't have let his house be broken into. ⁴⁰You too should be ready, because the son of man is coming at a time you don't expect."

⁴¹"Master," said Peter, "are you telling this parable for us, or for everyone?"

⁴²"Who then is the faithful and wise servant," said Jesus, "whom the master will set over all his household, to give them their allowance of food at the proper time? ⁴³A blessing on the servant that his master, when he comes, finds doing just that! ⁴⁴I'm telling you truly, he will install him as manager over all his possessions. ⁴⁵But if that servant says in his heart, 'My master is taking his time over coming back,' and begins to beat the slaves and slave-girls, to eat and drink and get drunk—⁴⁶then the master of that servant will come on a day he doesn't expect him to, and at a moment he didn't imagine, and he will cut him in two. He will give him the same place as the unbelievers.

⁴⁷"If a servant knew what the master wanted, and didn't get ready or do what was wanted, the punishment will be a severe beating. ⁴⁸If the servant didn't know, and did what deserved a beating, it will be a light beating. Much will be required from one who is given much; if someone is entrusted with much, even more will be expected in return.

⁴⁹"I came to throw fire upon the earth," Jesus continued, "and I wish it were already alight! ⁵⁰I have a baptism to be baptized with, and I am under huge pressure until it's happened!

Reading the Signs of the Times

⁵¹"Do you suppose I've come to give peace to the earth? No, let me tell you, but rather division. ⁵²From now on, you see, families will be split down the middle: three against two in a family of five, and two against three, ⁵³father against son and son against father, mother against daughter and daughter against mother, mother-in-law against daughter-in-law and daughter-in-law against mother-in-law.

⁵⁴"When you see a cloud rising in the west," he said to the crowds, "you say at once, 'It's going to rain,' and rain it does. ⁵⁵When you see the south wind getting up, you say, 'It's going to be very hot,' and that's what happens. ⁵⁶You impostors! You know how to work out what the earth and the sky are telling you; why can't you work out what's going on at this very moment?

⁵⁷"Why don't you judge for yourselves what you ought to do? ⁵⁸When you go with your accuser before a magistrate, do your best to reach a settlement with him. Otherwise he may drag you in front of the judge, and the judge will hand you over

to the officer, and the officer will throw you into jail. [59]Let me tell you, you won't get out from there until you have paid the last coin."

The Parable of the Fig Tree

13 At that moment some people came up and told them the news. Some Galileans had been in the Temple, and Pilate had mixed their blood with that of the sacrifices.

[2]"Do you suppose," said Jesus, "that those Galileans suffered such things because they were greater sinners than all other Galileans? [3]No, let me tell you! Unless you repent, you will all be destroyed in the same way.

[4]"And what about those eighteen who were killed when the tower in Siloam collapsed on top of them? Do you imagine they were more blameworthy than everyone else who lives in Jerusalem? [5]No, let me tell you! Unless you repent, you will all be destroyed in the same way."

[6]He told them this parable. "Once upon a time there was a man who had a fig tree in his vineyard. He came to it looking for fruit, and didn't find any. [7]So he said to the gardener, 'Look here! I've been coming to this fig tree for three years hoping to find some fruit, and I haven't found any! Cut it down! Why should it use up the soil?'

[8]"'I tell you what, Master,' replied the gardener; 'let it alone for just this one year more. I'll dig all around it and put on some manure. [9]Then, if it fruits next year, well and good; and if not, you can cut it down.'"

Jesus Heals a Crippled Woman on the Sabbath

[10]One sabbath, Jesus was teaching in one of the synagogues. [11]There was a woman there who'd had a spirit of weakness for eighteen years. She was bent double, and couldn't stand fully upright. [12]Jesus saw her and called to her.

[13]"Woman," he said, laying his hands on her, "you are freed from your affliction." And at once she stood upright, and praised God.

[14]The synagogue president was angry that Jesus had healed on the sabbath.

"Look here," he said to the crowd, "there are six days for people to work! Come on one of those days and be healed, not on the sabbath day!"

15"You bunch of hypocrites!" replied Jesus. "You would all be quite happy to untie an ox or a donkey from its stall on the sabbath day and lead it out for a drink! 16And isn't it right that this daughter of Abraham, tied up by the satan for these eighteen years, should be untied from her chains on the sabbath day?"

17At that, all the people who had been opposing him were ashamed. The whole crowd was overjoyed at all the splendid things he was doing.

18So Jesus said, "What is God's kingdom like? What shall we compare it with? 19It's like a mustard seed that someone took and placed in his garden. It grew, and became a tree, and the birds of the sky made nests in its branches."

20And again he said, "What shall we say God's kingdom is like? 21It's like leaven that a woman took and hid in three measures of flour, until the whole thing was leavened."

22Jesus went through the towns and villages, teaching as he went, making his way toward Jerusalem.

Entering Through the Narrow Door

23"Master," somebody said to him, "will there be only a few that are saved?"

24"Struggle hard," Jesus replied, "to get in by the narrow gate. Let me tell you: many will try to get in and won't be able to. 25When the householder gets up and shuts the door—at that moment you will begin to stand outside and knock at the door and say, 'Master, open the door for us.' Then he will say in response, 'I don't know where you've come from.' 26Then you will begin to say, 'We ate with you and drank with you, and you taught in our streets!' 27And he will say to you, 'I don't know where you people are from. Be off with you, you wicked lot.'

28"That's where you'll find weeping and gnashing of teeth: when you see Abraham and Isaac and Jacob and all the prophets in God's kingdom, and you yourselves thrown out. 29People will come from east and west, from north and south, and sit down to feast in God's kingdom. 30And, listen to this: some who are last will be first, and some of the first will be last."

31Just then some Pharisees came up and spoke to Jesus.

Jesus Grieves over Jerusalem

"Get away from here," they said, "because Herod wants to kill you."

³²"Go and tell that fox," replied Jesus, " 'Look here: I'm casting out demons today and tomorrow, and completing my healings. I'll be finished by the third day. ³³But I have to continue my travels today, tomorrow, and the day after that! It couldn't happen that a prophet would perish except in Jerusalem.

³⁴"Jerusalem, Jerusalem! You kill the prophets and stone the people sent to you! How many times did I want to collect your children, like a hen gathers her brood under her wings, and you would have none of it! ³⁵Look, your house has been abandoned. Let me tell you this: you will never see me until you are prepared to say, 'A blessing upon you! Welcome in the name of the Lord!' "

Jesus and the Pharisee

14 One sabbath, Jesus went to a meal in the house of a leading Pharisee. They were keeping a close eye on him.

²There was a man there in front of Jesus who suffered from dropsy. ³So Jesus asked the lawyers and Pharisees, "Is it lawful to heal on the sabbath or not?" ⁴They remained silent. He took the man, healed him, and dismissed him.

⁵Then he said to them, "Suppose one of you has a son—or an ox!—that falls into a well. Are you going to tell me you won't pull him out straightaway on the sabbath day?" ⁶They had no answer for that.

⁷He noticed how the guests chose the best seats, and told them this parable.

⁸"When someone invites you to a wedding feast," he said, "don't go and sit in the best seat, in case some other guest more important is invited, ⁹and the person who invited you both comes and says to you, 'Please move down for this man,' and you will go to the end of the line covered with embarrassment. ¹⁰Instead, when someone invites you, go and sit down at the lowest place. Then, when your host arrives, he will say to you, 'My dear fellow! Come on higher up!' Then all your fellow guests will show you respect. ¹¹All who push themselves forward, you see, will be humbled, and all who humble themselves will be honored."

The Parable of the Great Banquet

¹²He then turned to his host. "When you give a lunch or a supper," he said, "don't invite your friends or your family or relatives, or your rich neighbors. They might ask you back

again, and you'd be repaid. ¹³When you give a feast, invite the
poor, the crippled, the lame, and the blind. ¹⁴God will bless
you, because they have no way to repay you! You will be repaid
at the resurrection of the righteous."

¹⁵One of the guests heard this and commented, "A blessing
on those who eat food in God's kingdom!"

¹⁶Jesus said, "Once a man made a great dinner, and invited
lots of guests. ¹⁷When the time for the meal arrived, he sent his
servant to say to the guests, 'Come now—everything's ready!'
¹⁸But the whole pack of them began to make excuses. The first
said, 'I've just bought a field, and I really have to go and see it.
Please accept my apologies.' ¹⁹Another one said, 'I've just bought
five yoke of oxen, and I've got to go and test them out—please
accept my apologies.' ²⁰And another one said, 'I've just gotten
married, so naturally I can't come.' ²¹So the servant went back
and told his master all this. The householder was cross, and said
to his servant, 'Go out quickly into the streets and lanes of the
town and bring in here the poor, the crippled, the lame, and the
blind.' ²²'All right, Master,' said the servant, 'I've done that—but
there's still room.' ²³'Well then,' said the master to the servant,
'go out into the roads and hedgerows and make them come in, so
that my house may be full! ²⁴Let me tell you this: none of those
people who were invited will get to taste my dinner.'"

²⁵A large crowd was gathering around him. Jesus turned to
face them.

²⁶"If any of you come to me," he said to them, "and don't
hate your father and your mother, your wife and your children, your brothers and your sisters—yes, and even your own
life!—you can't be my disciple. ²⁷If you don't pick up your own
cross and come after me, you can't be my disciple.

²⁸"Don't you see? Supposing one of you wants to build a
tower; what will you do? You will first of all sit down and work
out how much it will cost, to see whether you have enough to
finish it. ²⁹Otherwise, when you've laid the foundation and
then can't finish it, everyone who sees it will begin to make
fun of you. ³⁰'Here's a fellow,' they'll say, 'who began to build
but couldn't finish!'

³¹"Or think of a king, on the way to fight a war against another
king. What will he do? He will first sit down and discuss with

**The Cost of
Discipleship**

his advisers whether, with ten thousand troops, he is going to be a match for the other side who are coming with twenty thousand! 32If they decide he isn't, he will send a delegation, while the other one is still a long way away, and sue for peace.

33"In the same way, none of you can be my disciple unless you give up all your possessions.

34"Salt is good; but if even the salt loses its savor, how can it be made salty again? 35It's no good for soil and no good for manure. People throw it away. If you have ears, then listen!"

The Parables of the Lost Sheep and the Lost Coin

15 All the tax-collectors and sinners were coming close to listen to Jesus. 2The Pharisees and the legal experts were grumbling. "This fellow welcomes sinners!" they said. "He even eats with them!"

3So Jesus told them this parable. 4"Supposing one of you has a hundred sheep," he said, "and you lose one of them. What will you do? Why, you'll leave the ninety-nine out in the countryside, and you'll go off looking for the lost one until you find it! 5And when you find it, you'll be so happy—you'll put it on your shoulders 6and go home, and you'll call your friends and neighbors in. 'Come and have a party!' you'll say. 'Celebrate with me! I've found my lost sheep!'

7"Well, let me tell you: that's how glad they will be in heaven over one sinner who repents—more than over ninety-nine righteous people who don't need repentance.

8"Or supposing a woman has ten drachmas and loses one of them. What will she do? Why, she'll light a lamp, and sweep the house, and hunt carefully until she finds it! 9And when she finds it she'll call her friends and neighbors in. 'Come and have a party!' she'll say. 'Celebrate with me! I've found my lost coin!'

10"Well, let me tell you: that's how glad God's angels feel when a single sinner repents."

The Parable of the Prodigal: The Father and the Younger Son

11Jesus went on: "Once there was a man who had two sons. 12The younger son said to the father, 'Father, give me my share in the property.' So he divided up his livelihood between them. 13Not many days later the younger son turned his share into cash, and set off for a country far away, where he spent his share in having a riotous good time.

14"When he had spent it all, a severe famine came on that country, and he found himself destitute. 15So he went and attached himself to one of the citizens of that country, who sent him into the fields to feed his pigs. ¹⁶He longed to satisfy his hunger with the pods that the pigs were eating, and nobody gave him anything.

¹⁷"He came to his senses. 'Just think!' he said to himself. 'There are all my father's hired hands with plenty to eat—and here am I, starving to death! ¹⁸I shall get up and go to my father, and I'll say to him, "Father; I have sinned against heaven and before you; ¹⁹I don't deserve to be called your son any longer. Make me like one of your hired hands."' ²⁰And he got up and went to his father.

"While he was still a long way off, his father saw him and his heart was stirred with love and pity. He ran to him, hugged him tight, and kissed him. ²¹'Father,' the son began, 'I have sinned against heaven and before you; I don't deserve to be called your son any longer.' ²²But the father said to his servants, 'Hurry! Bring the best clothes and put them on him! Put a ring on his hand, and shoes on his feet! ²³And bring the calf that we've fattened up, kill it, and let's eat and have a party! ²⁴This son of mine was dead, and is alive again! He was lost, and now he's found!' And they began to celebrate.

²⁵"The older son was out in the fields. When he came home and got near to the house, he heard music and dancing. ²⁶He called one of the servants and asked what was going on.

²⁷"'Your brother's come home!' he said. 'And your father has thrown a great party—he's killed the fattened calf!—because he's got him back safe and well!'

²⁸"He flew into a rage, and wouldn't go in.

"Then his father came out and pleaded with him. ²⁹'Look here!' he said to his father, 'I've been slaving for you all these years! I've never disobeyed a single commandment of yours. And you never even gave me a young goat so I could have a party with my friends. ³⁰But when this son of yours comes home, once he's finished gobbling up your livelihood with his whores, you kill the fattened calf for him!'

³¹"'My son,' he replied, 'you're always with me. Everything I have belongs to you. ³²But we had to celebrate and be happy! This brother of yours was dead and is alive again! He was lost, and now he's found!'"

The Parable of the Prodigal: The Father and the Older Son

The Parable of the Shrewd Manager

16 Jesus said to his disciples, "Once there was a rich man who had a steward, and charges were laid against him that he was squandering his property. ²So he called him and said to him, 'What's all this I hear about you? Present an account of your stewardship; I'm not going to have you as my steward anymore!'

³"At this, the steward said to himself, 'What shall I do? My master is taking away my stewardship from me! I can't do manual work, and I'd be ashamed to beg...

⁴"'I have an idea what to do!—so that people will welcome me into their households when I am fired from being steward.'

⁵"So he called his master's debtors to him, one by one. 'How much,' he asked the first, 'do you owe my master?'

⁶"'A hundred measures of olive oil,' he replied.

"'Take your bill,' he said to him, 'sit down quickly, and make it fifty.'

⁷"To another he said, 'And how much do you owe?'

"'A hundred measures of wheat,' he replied.

"'Take your bill,' he said, 'and make it eighty.'

⁸"And the master praised the dishonest steward because he had acted wisely. The children of this world, you see, are wiser than the children of light when it comes to dealing with their own generation.

⁹"So let me tell you this: use that dishonest stuff called money to make yourselves friends! Then, when it gives out, they will welcome you into homes that will last.

Teachings on Stewardship

¹⁰"Someone who is faithful in a small matter," Jesus continued, "will also be faithful in a large one. Someone who is dishonest in a small matter will also be dishonest in a large one. ¹¹If you haven't been faithful with that wicked thing called money, who is going to entrust you with true wealth? ¹²And if you haven't been faithful in looking after what belongs to someone else, who is going to give you what is your own?

¹³"Nobody can serve two masters. You will end up hating one and loving the other, or going along with the first and despising the other. You can't serve God and money."

¹⁴The Pharisees, who loved money, heard all this, and mocked Jesus. ¹⁵So he said to them, "You people let everyone

else know that you're in the right—but God knows your hearts. What people call honorable, God calls abominable!

16"The law and the prophets lasted until John. From now on, God's kingdom is announced, and everyone is trying to attack it. 17But it's easier for heaven and earth to pass away than for one dot of an 'i' to drop out of the law.

18"Anyone who divorces his wife and marries another commits adultery, and a person who marries a divorced woman commits adultery.

19"There was once a rich man," said Jesus, "who was dressed in purple and fine linen, and feasted in splendor every day. 20A poor man named Lazarus, who was covered with sores, lay outside his gate. 21He longed to feed himself with the scraps that fell from the rich man's table. Even the dogs came and licked his sores.

The Parable of the Rich Man and Lazarus

22"In due course the poor man died, and was carried by the angels into Abraham's bosom. The rich man also died, and was buried. 23As he was being tormented in Hades, he looked up and saw Abraham far away, and Lazarus in his bosom.

24" 'Father Abraham!' he called out. 'Have pity on me! Send Lazarus to dip the tip of his finger in water and cool my tongue! I'm in agony in this fire!'

25" 'My child,' replied Abraham, 'remember that in your life you received good things, and in the same way Lazarus received evil. Now he is comforted here, and you are tormented. 26Besides that, there is a great chasm standing between us. People who want to cross over from here to you can't do so, nor can anyone get across from the far side to us.'

27" 'Please, then, Father,' he said, 'send him to my father's house. 28I've got five brothers. Let him tell them about it, so that they don't come into this torture-chamber.'

29" 'They've got Moses and the prophets,' replied Abraham. 'Let them listen to them.'

30" 'No, Father Abraham,' he replied, 'but if someone went to them from the dead, they would repent!'

31" 'If they don't listen to Moses and the prophets,' came the reply, 'neither would they be convinced, even if someone rose from the dead.' "

17

Jesus said to his disciples, "There are bound to be things that trip people up; but woe betide the person who brings them about! 2It would be better to have a millstone hung around your neck, and be thrown into the sea, than to trip up one of these little ones. 3So watch out for yourselves.

"If your brother sins against you, rebuke him; and if he apologizes, forgive him. 4Even if he sins against you seven times, and turns around seven times and says sorry to you, you must forgive him."

5The apostles said to the master, "Give us greater faith!"

6"If you had faith," replied the master, "as a grain of mustard seed, you would say to this mulberry tree, 'Be uprooted and be planted in the sea,' and it would obey you.

7"Supposing one of you has a slave plowing or keeping sheep out in the field. When he comes in, what will you say? 'Come here at once, and sit down for a meal'? 8No, you will be far more likely to say, 'Get something ready for me to eat! Get properly dressed, and wait on me while I eat and drink! After that you can have something to eat and drink yourself.' 9Will you thank the slave because he did what you told him?

10"That's how it is with you. When you've done everything you're told, say this: 'We're just ordinary slaves. All we've done is what we we were supposed to do.'"

Ten Men Healed

11As Jesus was on his way to Jerusalem, he passed along the borderlands between Samaria and Galilee. 12As he was going into one particular village he was met by ten men with virulent skin diseases who stayed at some distance from him.

13"Jesus, Master!" they called out loudly. "Have pity on us!"

14When Jesus saw them he said to them, "Go and show yourselves to the priests." And as they went, they were healed.

15One of them, seeing that he had been healed, turned back and gave glory to God at the top of his voice. 16He fell on his face in front of Jesus's feet and thanked him. He was a Samaritan.

17"There were ten of you healed, weren't there?" responded Jesus. "Where are the nine? 18Is it really the case that the only one who had the decency to give God the glory was this foreigner?

19"Get up, and be on your way," he said to him. "Your faith has saved you."

20The Pharisees asked Jesus when the kingdom of God was coming.

"God's kingdom," replied Jesus, "isn't the sort of thing you can watch for and see coming. 21People won't say, 'Look, here it is,' or 'Look, over there!' No: God's kingdom is within your grasp."

22Then Jesus said to the disciples, "The days are coming when you will long to see one of the days of the son of man, and you won't see it. 23They will say to you, 'Look, there!' or 'Look, here!' Don't go off or follow them. 24The son of man in his day will be like lightning that shines from one end of the sky to the other. 25But first he must suffer many things and be rejected by this generation.

26"What will it be like in the days of the son of man? It will be like the days of Noah. 27People were eating and drinking, they were getting married and giving wedding parties, until the day when Noah went into the ark—and that day the flood came and swept them all away. 28And it will be like the days of Lot. They were eating and drinking, they were buying and selling, they were planting and building. 29But on the day when Lot left Sodom, it rained fire and sulphur from the sky and they were all destroyed. 30That's what it will be like on the day when the son of man is revealed.

31"On that day anyone up on the roof, with all their possessions in the house, shouldn't go down to get them. Anyone out in the field shouldn't go back to get anything. 32Remember Lot's wife. 33If you try to save your life you'll lose it, but anyone who loses it will keep it.

34"Let me tell you, in that night there will be two people sleeping side by side: one will be taken, and the other left behind. 35There will be two women working side by side grinding corn: one will be taken, and the other left behind."

37"Where will this be, Master?" they asked him.

"Where the body is," replied Jesus, "there the vultures will gather."

18 Jesus told them a parable about how they should always pray and not give up.

2"There was once a judge in a certain town," he said, "who didn't fear God and didn't have any respect for people. ³There was a widow in that town, and she came to him and said, 'Judge my case! Vindicate me against my enemy!'

⁴"For a long time he refused. But, in the end, he said to himself, 'It's true that I don't fear God and don't have any respect for people. ⁵But because this widow is causing me a lot of trouble, I will put her case right and vindicate her, so that she doesn't end up coming and giving me a black eye.'

⁶"Well," said the master, "did you hear what this unjust judge says? ⁷And don't you think that God will see justice done for his chosen ones, who shout out to him day and night? Do you suppose he is deliberately delaying? ⁸Let me tell you, he will vindicate them very quickly. But—when the son of man comes, will he find faith on the earth?"

⁹He told this next parable against those who trusted in their own righteous standing and despised others.

¹⁰"Two men," he said, "went up to the Temple to pray. One was a Pharisee; the other was a tax-collector. ¹¹The Pharisee stood and prayed in this way to himself: 'God, I thank you that I am not like the other people—greedy, unjust, immoral, or even like this tax-collector. ¹²I fast twice in the week; I give tithes of all that I get.'

¹³"But the tax-collector stood a long way off, and didn't even want to raise his eyes to heaven. He beat his breast and said, 'God, be merciful to me, sinner that I am.' ¹⁴Let me tell you, he was the one who went back to his house vindicated by God, not the other. Don't you see? People who exalt themselves will be humbled, and people who humble themselves will be exalted."

The Rich Young Ruler

¹⁵People were bringing even tiny babies to Jesus for him to touch them. When the disciples saw it, they forbade them sternly. ¹⁶But Jesus called them. "Let the children come to me," he said, "and don't stop them! God's kingdom belongs to the likes of these. ¹⁷I'm telling you the truth: anyone who doesn't receive God's kingdom like a child will never get into it."

¹⁸There was a ruler who asked him, "Good teacher, what must I do to inherit the life of the age to come?"

¹⁹"Why call me 'good'?" said Jesus to him. "No one is good except God alone. ²⁰You know the commandments: don't com-

mit adultery; don't kill; don't steal; don't swear falsely; honor your father and mother."

²¹"I've kept them all," he said, "since I was a boy."

²²When Jesus heard that, he said to him, "There's just one thing you're short of. Sell everything you own, and distribute it to the poor, and you will have treasure in heaven. Then come and follow me."

²³When he heard that he turned very sad; he was extremely wealthy.

²⁴Jesus saw that he had become sad, and said, "How hard it is for those with possessions to enter God's kingdom! ²⁵Yes: it's easier for a camel to go through the eye of a needle than for a rich man to enter God's kingdom."

²⁶The people who heard it said, "So who can be saved?"

²⁷"What's impossible for humans," said Jesus, "is possible for God."

²⁸"Look here," said Peter, "we've left everything and followed you."

²⁹"I'm telling you the truth," said Jesus, "everyone who has left house or wife or brothers or parents or children, because of God's kingdom, ³⁰will receive far more in return in the present time—and in the age to come they will receive the life that belongs to that age."

³¹Jesus took the Twelve aside.

"Look," he said, "we're going up to Jerusalem. Everything that's written in the prophets about the son of man will be fulfilled. ³²Yes: he will be handed over to the pagans; he'll be mocked, abused, and spat upon. ³³They will beat him and kill him; and on the third day he'll be raised."

Jesus Heals a Blind Beggar

³⁴They didn't understand any of this. The word was hidden from them, and they didn't know what he meant.

³⁵As they were getting near Jericho there was a blind man sitting by the road, begging. ³⁶When he heard a crowd passing through the town he asked what was going on.

³⁷"Jesus of Nazareth is coming by," people said to him.

³⁸So he shouted out, "Jesus—David's son! Have pity on me!"

³⁹The people who were at the front of the group firmly told him to be silent. But he yelled out all the more, "David's son! Have pity on me!"

40Jesus stopped, and told them to bring the man to him. When he came up, he asked him, 41"What d'you want me to do for you?"

"Master," he said, "I want to see again."

42"Then see again," said Jesus. "Your faith has saved you."

43At once he received his sight again, and followed him, glorifying God. And when all the people saw it, they gave praise to God.

The Calling of Zacchaeus

19 They went into Jericho and passed through. 2There was a man named Zacchaeus, a chief tax-collector, who was very rich. 3He was trying to see who Jesus was, but, being a small man, he couldn't, because of the crowd. 4So he ran on ahead, along the route Jesus was going to take, and climbed up into a sycamore tree to see him.

5When Jesus came to the place, he looked up.

"Zacchaeus," he said to him, "hurry up and come down. I have to stay at your house today." 6So he hurried up, came down, and welcomed him with joy.

7Everybody began to murmur when they saw it. "He's gone in to spend time with a proper old sinner!" they were saying.

8But Zacchaeus stood there and addressed the master.

"Look, Master," he said, "I'm giving half my property to the poor. And if I have defrauded anyone of anything, I'm giving it back to them four times over."

9"Today," said Jesus, "salvation has come to this house, because he too is a son of Abraham. 10You see, the son of man came to seek and to save the lost."

The King, the Servants, and the Money

11While people were listening to this, Jesus went on to tell a parable. They were, after all, getting close to Jerusalem, and they thought that the kingdom of God was going to appear at once.

12"There was once a nobleman," he said, "who went into a country far away to be given royal authority and then return. 13He summoned ten of his slaves and gave them ten silver coins. 'Do business with these,' he said, 'until I come back.' 14His subjects, though, hated him, and sent a delegation after him to say, 'We don't want this man to be our king.'

15"So it happened that when he received the kingship and came back again, he gave orders to summon these slaves who had received the money, so that he could find out how they had got on with their business efforts. ¹⁶The first came forward and said, 'Master, your money has made ten times its value!'

¹⁷ 'Well done, you splendid servant!' he said. 'You've been trustworthy with something small; now you can take command of ten cities.'

¹⁸"The second came and said, 'Master, your money has made five times its value!'

¹⁹ 'You too—you can take charge of five cities.'

²⁰"The other came and said, 'Master, here is your money. I kept it wrapped in this handkerchief. ²¹You see, I was afraid of you, because you are a hard man: you profit where you made no investment, and you harvest what you didn't sow.'

²²" 'I'll condemn you out of your own mouth, you wicked scoundrel of a servant!' he replied. 'So: you knew that I was a hard man, profiting where I didn't invest and harvesting where I didn't sow? ²³So why didn't you put my money with the bankers? Then I'd have had the interest when I got back!'

²⁴" 'Take the money from him,' he said to the bystanders, 'and give it to the man who's got it ten times over!' ²⁵("Master," they said to him, "he's got ten times that already!")

²⁶"Let me tell you: everyone who has will be given more; but if someone has nothing, even what he has will be taken away from him. ²⁷But as for these enemies of mine, who didn't want me to be king over them—bring them here and slaughter them in front of me."

²⁸With these words, Jesus went on ahead, going up to Jerusalem.

²⁹As they came close, as near as Bethany and Bethphage, at the place called the Mount of Olives, he sent two of the disciples on ahead. ³⁰"Go into the village over there," he said, "and as you arrive you'll find a colt tied up, one that nobody has ever ridden. Untie it and bring it here. ³¹If anyone says to you, 'Why are you untying it?' you should say, 'Because the master needs it.'"

³²The two who were sent went off and found it just as Jesus had said to them. ³³They untied the colt, and its owners said to them, "Why are you untying the colt?"

³⁴"Because the master needs it," they replied.

The Triumphal Entry

³⁵They brought it to Jesus, threw their cloaks on the colt, and mounted Jesus on it. ³⁶As he was going along, people kept spreading their cloaks on the road.

³⁷When he came to the descent of the Mount of Olives, the whole crowd of disciples began to celebrate and praise God at the tops of their voices for all the powerful deeds they had seen.

> ³⁸"Welcome, welcome, welcome with a blessing,"
>   they sang.
> "Welcome to the king in the name of the Lord!
> Peace in heaven, and glory on high!"

³⁹Some of the Pharisees from the crowd said to Jesus, "Teacher, tell your disciples to stop that."

⁴⁰"Let me tell you," replied Jesus, "if they stayed silent, the stones would be shouting out!"

Jesus Cleanses the Temple

⁴¹When he came near and saw the city, he wept over it. ⁴²"If only you'd known," he said, "on this day—even you!—what peace meant. But now it's hidden, and you can't see it. ⁴³Yes, the days are coming upon you when your enemies will build up earthworks all around you, and encircle you, and squeeze you in from every direction. ⁴⁴They will bring you crashing to the ground, you and your children within you. They won't leave one single stone on another, because you didn't know the moment when God was visiting you."

⁴⁵He went into the Temple and began to throw out the traders.

⁴⁶"It's written," he said, "'My house shall be a house of prayer; but you've made it a brigands' cave.'"

⁴⁷He was teaching every day in the Temple. But the chief priests, the scribes, and the leading men of the people were trying to destroy him. ⁴⁸They couldn't find any way to do it, because all the people were hanging on his every word.

The Question About Jesus's Authority

20 On one of those days, while Jesus was teaching the people in the Temple, and announcing the good news, the chief priests and the scribes came up with the elders and said to him, ²"Tell us: by what authority are you doing these things? Or who gave you this authority?"

³"I've got a question for you, too," said Jesus, "so tell me this: ⁴was John's baptism from God, or was it merely human?"

⁵"If we say it was from God," they said among themselves, "he'll say, So why didn't you believe him? ⁶But if we say 'merely human,' all the people will stone us, since they're convinced that John was a prophet."

⁷So they replied that they didn't know where John and his baptism came from.

⁸"Very well, then," said Jesus. "Nor will I tell you by what authority I do these things."

⁹Jesus began to tell the people this parable. "There was a man who planted a vineyard, leased it out to tenant farmers, and went abroad for a long while. ¹⁰When the time came, he sent a slave to the farmers to collect from them some of the produce of the vineyard. But the farmers beat him and sent him away empty-handed. ¹¹He then sent a further slave, and they beat him, abused him, and sent him back empty-handed. ¹²Then he sent yet a third, and they beat him up and threw him out.

The Parable of the Tenants

¹³"So the master of the vineyard said, 'What shall I do? I'll send my beloved son. They will certainly respect him!' ¹⁴But when the farmers saw him they said to each other, 'This is the heir! Let's kill him, and then the inheritance will belong to us!' ¹⁵And they threw him out of the vineyard and killed him.

"So what will the master of the vineyard do? ¹⁶He will come and wipe out those farmers, and give the vineyard to others."

When they heard this, they said, "God forbid!" ¹⁷But Jesus looked around at them and said, "What then does it mean in the Bible when it says,

> 'The very stone the builders refused
> Now for the corner's top is used'?

¹⁸"Everyone who falls on that stone will be smashed to smithereens; but if it falls on anyone, it will crush them."

¹⁹The scribes and the chief priests tried to lay hands on him then and there. But they were afraid of the people, because they knew that Jesus had told this parable against them.

²⁰So the authorities watched Jesus, and sent people to lie in wait for him. They pretended to be upright folk but were

On Paying Taxes to Caesar

trying to trap him in something he said, so that they could hand him over to the rule and authority of the governor. 21So they asked him this question.

"Teacher," they said, "we know that you speak and teach with integrity. You are completely impartial, and you teach God's way and God's truth. 22So: is it right for us to give tribute to Caesar, or not?"

23Jesus knew they were playing a trick.

24"Show me a tribute-coin," he said. "This image . . . and this inscription . . . who do they belong to?"

"Caesar," they said.

25"Well, then," replied Jesus, "you'd better give Caesar back what belongs to him! And give *God* back what belongs to *him*."

26They couldn't catch him in anything he said in front of the people. They were amazed at his answer, and had nothing more to say.

Marriage and the Resurrection

27Some of the Sadducees came to Jesus to put their question. (The Sadducees deny that there is any resurrection.)

28"Teacher," they said, "Moses wrote for us that 'if a man's brother dies, leaving a widow but no children, the man should marry the widow and raise up a family for his brother.' 29Well, now: there were seven brothers; the eldest married a wife, and died without children. 30The second 31and the third married her, and then each of the seven, and they died without children. 32Finally the woman died as well. 33So, in the resurrection, whose wife will the woman be? The seven all had her as their wife."

34"The children of this age," replied Jesus, "marry and are given in marriage. 35But those who are counted worthy of a place in the age to come, and of the resurrection of the dead, don't marry, and they are not given in marriage. 36This is because they can no longer die; they are the equivalent of angels. They are children of God, since they are children of the resurrection.

37"But when it comes to the dead being raised, Moses too declares it, in the passage about the burning bush, where scripture describes the Lord as 'the God of Abraham, the God of Isaac, and the God of Jacob.' 38God is God, not of the dead, but of the living. They are all alive to him."

³⁹"That was well said, Teacher," commented some of the scribes, ⁴⁰since they no longer dared ask him anything else.

⁴¹Jesus said to them, "How can people say that the Messiah is the son of David? ⁴²David himself says, in the book of Psalms,

David's Son and the Widow's Mite

> 'The Lord says to the Lord of mine
> Sit here at my right hand;
> ⁴³Until I place those foes of thine
> Right underneath thy feet.'

⁴⁴"David, you see, calls him 'Lord'; so how can he be his son?"

⁴⁵As all the people listened to him, he said to the disciples, ⁴⁶"Watch out for the scribes who like to go about in long robes, and enjoy being greeted in the marketplace, sitting in the best seats in the synagogues, and taking the top table at dinners. ⁴⁷They devour widows' houses, and make long prayers without meaning them. Their judgment will be all the more severe."

21 He looked up and saw rich people putting their contributions into the Temple treasury. ²He also saw an impoverished widow putting in two tiny copper coins.

³"I'm telling you the truth," he said. "This poor widow has put in more than all of them. ⁴They all contributed into the collection out of their plenty, but she contributed out of her poverty, and gave her whole livelihood."

⁵Some people were talking about the Temple, saying how wonderfully it was decorated, with its beautiful stones and dedicated gifts.

Signs of the End

"Yes," said Jesus; ⁶"but the days will come when everything you see will be torn down. Not one stone will be left standing on another."

⁷"Teacher," they asked him, "when will these things happen? What will be the sign that it's all about to take place?"

⁸"Watch out that nobody deceives you," said Jesus. "Yes: lots of people will come using my name, saying, 'I'm the one!' and 'The time has come!' Don't go following them. ⁹When you hear about wars and rebellions, don't be alarmed. These things have to happen first, but the end won't come at once.

¹⁰"One nation will rise against another," he went on, "and one kingdom against another. ¹¹There will be huge earthquakes,

famines, and plagues in various places, terrifying omens, and great signs from heaven.

12"Before all this happens they will lay hands on you and persecute you. They will hand you over to the synagogues and prisons. They will drag you before kings and governors because of my name. 13That will become an opportunity for you to tell your story. 14So settle it in your hearts not to work out beforehand what tale to tell; 15I'll give you a mouth and wisdom, which none of your opponents will be able to resist or contradict.

16"You will be betrayed by parents, brothers and sisters, relatives, and friends, and they will kill some of you. 17You will be hated by everyone because of my name. 18But no hair of your head will be lost. 19The way to keep your lives is to be patient.

The Distress of Jerusalem Predicted

20"But," continued Jesus, "when you see Jerusalem surrounded by armies, then you will know that her time of desolation has arrived. 21Then people in Judaea should run off to the hills, people in Jerusalem itself should get out as fast as they can, and people in the countryside shouldn't go back into the city. 22Those will be the days of severe judgment, which will fulfill all the biblical warnings. 23Woe betide pregnant women, and nursing mothers, in those days! There is going to be huge distress on the earth, and divine anger against this people. 24The hungry sword will eat them up; they will be taken off as prisoners to every nation; and Jerusalem will be trampled by the pagans, until the times of the pagans are done.

25"There will be signs in the sun, the moon, and the stars. On earth the nations will be in distress and confusion because of the roaring and swelling of the sea and its waves. 26People will faint from fear, and from imagining all that's going to happen to the world. The powers of the heavens will be shaken. 27Then they will see 'the son of man coming on a cloud' with power and great majesty. 28When all these things start to happen, stand up and lift up your heads, because the time has come for you to be redeemed."

29He told them this parable. "Look at the fig tree and all the trees. 30When they are well into leaf, you can see for yourselves and know that summer is upon you. 31In the same way, when you see all these things happening, you will know that

God's kingdom is upon you. 32I'm telling you the truth; this generation won't be gone before all of this happens. 33Heaven and earth may disappear, but these words of mine won't disappear.

34"So watch out for yourselves," said Jesus, "that your hearts may not grow heavy with dissipation and drunkenness and the cares of this life, so that that day comes upon you suddenly, 35like a trap. It will come, you see, on everyone who lives on the face of the earth. 36Keep awake at all times, praying that you may have strength to escape all these things that will happen, and to stand before the son of man."

37Jesus was teaching in the Temple by day, but at night he went out and stayed in the place called the Mount of Olives. 38And from early morning all the people flocked to him in the Temple, to hear him.

22 The time came for the Festival of Unleavened Bread, known as Passover. 2The chief priests and the scribes looked for a way to assassinate Jesus, a difficult task because of the crowds.

3The satan entered into Judas, whose surname was Iscariot, who was one of the company of the Twelve. 4He went and held a meeting with the chief priests and officers, to discuss how he might hand Jesus over. 5They were delighted, and promised to pay him. 6He agreed, and started to look for an opportunity to hand him over to them when the crowds weren't around.

7The day of Unleavened Bread arrived, the day when people had to kill the Passover lamb. 8Jesus dispatched Peter and John.

"Off you go," he said, "and get the Passover ready for us to eat."

9"Where d'you want us to prepare it?" they asked him.

10"Listen carefully," said Jesus. "As you go into the city a man will meet you carrying a jar of water. Follow him, and when he goes into a house, go after him. 11Then say to the householder there, 'The teacher says, "Where is the living-room where I can eat the Passover with my disciples?"' 12And he will show you a large upstairs room, laid out and ready. Make the preparations there."

13So they went and found it as he had said to them, and they prepared the Passover.

14When the time came, Jesus sat down at table, and the apostles with him.

15"I have been so much looking forward to eating this Passover with you before I have to suffer," he said to them. 16"For—let me tell you—I won't eat it again until it's fulfilled in the kingdom of God."

17Then he took a cup, and gave thanks, and said, "Take this and share it among yourselves. 18Let me tell you, from now on I won't drink from the fruit of the vine until the kingdom of God comes."

19Then he took some bread. He gave thanks, broke it, and gave it to them.

"This is my body," he said, "which is given for you. Do this in memory of me."

20So too, after supper, with the cup: "This cup," he said, "is the new covenant, in my blood which is shed for you.

21"But look here! The hand of the one who will betray me is with me at this table. 22The son of man is indeed going, as it is marked out for him; but woe betide that man by whom he is betrayed!"

23They began to ask each other which of them was going to do this.

Prediction of Peter's Denial

24A quarrel began among them: which of them was to be seen as the most important?

25"Pagan kings lord it over their subjects," said Jesus to them, "and people in power get themselves called 'benefactors.' 26That's not how it's to be with you. The most important among you ought to be like the youngest. The leader should be like the servant. 27After all, who is the more important, the one who sits at table or the one who waits on him? The one at table, obviously! But I am with you here like a servant.

28"You are the ones who have stuck it out with me through the trials I've had to endure. 29This is my bequest to you: the kingdom my father bequeathed to me! 30What does this mean? You will eat and drink at my table, in my kingdom, and you will sit on thrones, judging the twelve tribes of Israel.

31"Simon, Simon, listen to this. The satan demanded to have you. He wanted to shake you into bits like wheat. 32But I prayed for you; I prayed that you wouldn't run out of faith.

And, when you turn back again, you must give strength to your brothers."

³³"Master," replied Simon, "I'm ready to go with you to prison—or to death!"

³⁴"Let me tell you, Peter," replied Jesus, "the cock won't crow today before you have three times denied that you know me."

³⁵"When I sent you out," Jesus said to them, "without purse or bag or sandals, were you short of anything?"

"Nothing," they replied.

³⁶"But now," he said, "anyone who has a purse should take it, and the same with a bag. And anyone who doesn't have a sword should sell his cloak and buy one. ³⁷Let me tell you this: when the Bible says, 'He was reckoned with the lawless,' it must find its fulfillment in me. Yes: everything about me must reach its goal."

³⁸"Look, Master," they said, "we've got a couple of swords here."

"That's enough!" he said to them.

³⁹So off they went. Jesus headed, as usual, for the Mount of Olives, and his disciples followed him.

Jesus Is Arrested

⁴⁰When he came to the place, he said to them, "Pray that you won't come into the trial."

⁴¹He then withdrew from them about a stone's throw, and knelt down to pray.

⁴²"Father," he said, "if you wish it—please take this cup away from me! But it must be your will, not mine." ⁴³An angel appeared to him from heaven, strengthening him. ⁴⁴By now he was in agony, and he prayed very fervently. And his sweat became like clots of blood, falling on the ground. ⁴⁵Then he got up from praying, and came to the disciples and found them asleep because of sorrow.

⁴⁶"Why are you sleeping?" he said to them. "Get up and pray, so that you won't come into the trial."

⁴⁷While he was still speaking, a crowd appeared. The man named Judas, one of the Twelve, was leading them. He came toward Jesus to kiss him, ⁴⁸but Jesus said to him, "Judas! Are you going to betray the son of man with a kiss?"

⁴⁹Jesus's followers saw what was about to happen.

"Master!" they said. "Shall we go in with the swords?" ⁵⁰And one of them struck the high priest's servant, and cut off his right ear.

⁵¹"Enough of that!" said Jesus, and healed the ear with a touch.

⁵²Then Jesus spoke to the chief priests, the Temple guardsmen, and the elders who had come after him.

"Anyone would think I was a brigand," he said, "for you to come out with swords and clubs! ⁵³Every day I've been in the Temple with you and you never laid hands on me. But your moment has come at last, and so has the power of darkness."

Peter Denies Jesus

⁵⁴So they arrested Jesus, took him off, and brought him into the high priest's house. Peter followed at a distance. ⁵⁵They lit a fire in the middle of the courtyard and sat around it, and Peter sat in among them.

⁵⁶A servant-girl saw him sitting by the fire. She stared hard at him. "This fellow was with him!" she said.

⁵⁷Peter denied it. "I don't know him, woman," he said.

⁵⁸After a little while another man saw him and said, "You're one of them!"

"No, my friend, I'm not," replied Peter.

⁵⁹After the space of about an hour, another man insisted, "It's true! This man was with him; he's a Galilean too!"

⁶⁰"My good fellow," said Peter, "I don't know what you're talking about." And at once, while he was still speaking, the cock crowed. ⁶¹The master turned and looked at Peter, and Peter called to mind the words the master had spoken to him: "Before the cock crows, this very day, you will deny me three times." ⁶²And he went outside and wept bitterly.

⁶³The men who were holding Jesus began to make fun of him and knock him about. ⁶⁴They blindfolded him.

"Prophesy!" they told him. "Who is it that's hitting you?"

⁶⁵And they said many other scandalous things to him.

⁶⁶When the day broke, the official assembly of the people, the chief priests, and the scribes came together, and they took him off to their council.

⁶⁷"If you are the Messiah," they said, "tell us!"

"If I tell you," he said to them, "you won't believe me. ⁶⁸And if I ask you a question, you won't answer me. ⁶⁹But from now on the son of man will be seated at the right hand of God's power."

70"So you're the son of God, are you?" they said.

"You say that I am," he said to them.

71"Why do we need any more witnesses?" they said. "We've heard it ourselves, from his own mouth!"

23 The whole crowd of them got up and took Jesus to Pilate.

2They began to accuse him. "We found this fellow," they said, "deceiving our nation! He was forbidding people to give tribute to Caesar, and saying that he is the Messiah—a king!"

3So Pilate asked Jesus, "You are the king of the Jews?"

"You said it," replied Jesus.

4"I find no fault in this man," said Pilate to the chief priests and the crowds. 5But they became insistent.

"He's stirring up the people," they said, "teaching them throughout the whole of Judaea. He began in Galilee, and now he's come here."

6When Pilate heard that, he asked if the man was indeed a Galilean. 7When he learned that he was from Herod's jurisdiction he sent him to Herod, who happened also to be in Jerusalem at that time.

8When Herod saw Jesus he was delighted. He had been wanting to see him for quite some time now, since he'd heard about him, and hoped to see him perform some sign or other. 9He questioned him this way and that, but Jesus gave no answer at all. 10The chief priests and the scribes stood by, accusing him vehemently. 11Herod and his soldiers treated Jesus with contempt; they ridiculed him by dressing him up in a splendid robe, and sent him back to Pilate. 12And so it happened, that very day, that Herod and Pilate became friends with each other. Up until then, they had been enemies.

13So Pilate called the chief priests, the rulers, and the people.

14"You brought this man before me," he said to them, "on the grounds that he was leading the people astray. Look here, then: I examined him in your presence and I found no evidence in him of the charges you're bringing against him. 15Nor did Herod; he sent him back to me. Look: there is no sign that he's done anything to deserve death. ¹⁶So I'm going to flog him and let him go."

¹⁸"Take him away!" they shouted out all together. "Release Barabbas for us!" ¹⁹(Barabbas had been thrown into prison because of an uprising that had taken place in the city, and for murder.) ²⁰Pilate spoke to them again, with the intention of letting Jesus go, ²¹but they shouted back, "Crucify him! Crucify him!"

²²"Why?" he said for the third time. "What's he done wrong? I can't find anything he's done that deserves death, so I'm going to beat him and let him go."

²³But they went on shouting out at the tops of their voices, demanding that he be crucified; and eventually their shouts won the day. ²⁴Pilate gave his verdict that their request should be granted. ²⁵He released the man they asked for, the one who'd been thrown into prison because of rebellion and murder, and gave Jesus over to their demands.

²⁶As they led him away, they grabbed a man from Cyrene called Simon, who was coming in to the city from outside, and they forced him to carry the crossbeam behind Jesus.

The Crucifixion

²⁷A great crowd of the people followed Jesus, including women who were mourning and wailing for him. ²⁸Jesus turned and spoke to them.

"Daughters of Jerusalem," he said, "don't cry for me. Cry for yourselves instead! Cry for your children! ²⁹Listen: the time is coming when you will say, 'A blessing on the barren! A blessing on wombs that never bore children, and breasts that never nursed them!' ³⁰At that time people will start to say to the mountains, 'Fall on us,' and to the hills, 'Cover us'! ³¹Yes: if this is what they do with the green tree, what will happen to the dry one?"

³²Two other criminals were taken away with him to be executed. ³³When they came to the place called The Skull, they crucified him there, with the criminals, one on his right and one on his left.

³⁴"Father," said Jesus, "forgive them! They don't know what they're doing!"

They divided his clothes, casting lots for them.

35The people stood around watching. The rulers hurled abuse at him.

"He rescued others," they said; "let him try rescuing himself, if he really is the Messiah, God's chosen one!"

36The soldiers added their taunts, coming up and offering him cheap wine.

37"If you're the king of the Jews," they said, "rescue yourself!"

38The charge was written above him: "This is the King of the Jews."

39One of the bad characters who was hanging there began to insult him. "Aren't you the Messiah?" he said. "Rescue yourself—and us, too!"

40But the other one told him off. "Don't you fear God?" he said. "You're sharing the same fate that he is! 41In our case it's fair enough; we're getting exactly what we asked for. But this fellow hasn't done anything out of order.

42"Jesus," he went on, "remember me when you finally become king."

43"I'm telling you the truth," replied Jesus, "you'll be with me in paradise, this very day."

44By the time of the sixth hour, darkness came over all the land. 45The sunlight vanished until the ninth hour. The veil of the Temple was ripped down the middle. 46Then Jesus shouted out at the top of his voice, "Here's my spirit, Father! You can take care of it now!" And with that he died.

The Death and Burial of Jesus

47The centurion saw what happened, and praised God.

"This fellow," he said, "really was in the right."

48All the crowds who had come together for the spectacle saw what happened, and they went away beating their breasts. 49Those who knew Jesus, including the women who had followed him from Galilee, remained at a distance and watched the scene.

50Now there was a man named Joseph, a member of the council. He was a good and righteous man, 51and had not given his consent to the court's verdict or actions. He was from Arimathea, a town in Judaea, and he was longing for God's kingdom. 52He approached Pilate and asked for Jesus's body. 53He took it down, wrapped it in a shroud, and put it in a tomb hollowed out of the rock, where no one had ever been laid. 54It was the day of Preparation, and the sabbath was beginning.

55The women who had followed Jesus, the ones who had come with him from Galilee, saw the tomb and how the body was laid. 56Then they went back to prepare spices and ointments. On the sabbath they rested, as the commandment specified.

The Resurrection

24 The women went to the tomb in the very early morning of the first day of the week, carrying the spices they had prepared. 2They found the stone rolled away from the tomb, 3and when they went in they didn't find the body of the Lord Jesus.

4As they were at a loss what to make of it all, suddenly two men in shining clothes stood beside them. 5The women were terrified, and bowed their faces toward the ground.

But the men said to them, "Why look for the living with the dead? 6He isn't here—he's been raised! Don't you remember? While you were still in Galilee he told you that 7the son of man must be handed over into the hands of sinners, and be crucified, and rise again on the third day."

8And they remembered his words.

9They went back, away from the tomb, and told all this to the eleven and all the others. 10It was Mary Magdalene, Joanna, and Mary the mother of James, and the others with them. They said this to the apostles; 11and this message seemed to them just stupid, useless talk, and they didn't believe them.

12Peter, though, got up and ran to the tomb. He stooped down and saw only the grave-clothes. He went back home, perplexed at what had happened.

On the Road to Emmaus

13That very day, two of them were going to a village called Emmaus, which lay about seven miles from Jerusalem. 14They were discussing with each other all the various things that had taken place. 15As they were discussing, and arguing with each other, Jesus himself approached and walked with them. 16Their eyes, though, were prevented from recognizing him.

17"You're obviously having a very important discussion on your walk," he said; "what's it all about?"

They stood still, a picture of gloom. 18Then one of them, Cleopas by name, answered him. "You must be the only person around Jerusalem," he said, "who doesn't know what's been going on there these last few days."

19"What things?" he asked.

"To do with Jesus of Nazareth," they said to him. "He was a prophet. He acted with power and he spoke with power, before God and all the people. 20Our chief priests and rulers handed him over to be condemned to death, and they crucified him. 21But we were hoping that he was going to redeem Israel!

"And now, what with all this, it's the third day since it happened. 22But some women from our group have astonished us. They went to his tomb very early this morning, 23and didn't find his body. They came back saying they'd seen a vision of angels, who said he was alive. 24Some of the folk with us went off to the tomb and found it just as the women had said, but they didn't see *him.*"

25"You are so senseless!" he said to them. "So slow in your hearts to believe all the things the prophets said to you! Don't you see? 26This is what *had* to happen: the Messiah had to suffer, and then come into his glory!"

27So he began with Moses, and with all the prophets, and explained to them the things about himself throughout the whole Bible.

28They drew near to the village where they were heading. Jesus gave the impression that he was going further, 29but they urged him strongly not to.

Jesus Revealed at Emmaus

"Stay with us," they said. "It's nearly evening; the day is almost gone." And he went in to stay with them.

30As he was sitting at table with them he took the bread and gave thanks. He broke it and gave it to them. 31Then the eyes of both of them were opened, and they recognized him; and he vanished from their sight.

32Then they said to each other, "Do you remember how our hearts were burning inside us, as he talked to us on the road, as he opened up the Bible for us?"

33And they got up then and there and went back to Jerusalem. There they found the eleven, and the people with them, gathered together.

34They were saying, "The Lord really has been raised! He's appeared to Simon!" 35Then they told what had happened on the road, and how he was known to them in the breaking of the bread.

Jesus's Promise and Ascension

36As they were saying this, Jesus himself stood in the midst of them, and said, "Peace be with you." 37They were terrified and alarmed, and thought they were seeing a ghost.

38"Why are you so disturbed?" he said. "Why do these questionings come up in your hearts? 39Look at my hands and feet; it really is me, myself. Touch me and see! Ghosts don't have flesh and bones like you can see I have."

40With these words, he showed them his hands and feet.

41While they were still in disbelief and amazement from sheer joy, he said to them, "Have you got something here to eat?" 42They gave him a piece of baked fish, 43which he took and ate in front of them.

44Then he said to them, "This is what I was talking to you about when I was still with you. Everything written about me in the law of Moses, and in the prophets and the Psalms, had to be fulfilled." 45Then he opened their minds to understand the Bible.

46"This is what is written," he said. "The Messiah must suffer and rise from the dead on the third day, 47and in his name repentance, for the forgiveness of sins, must be announced to all the nations, beginning from Jerusalem. 48You are the witnesses for all this. 49Now look: I'm sending upon you what my father has promised. But stay in the city until you are clothed with power from on high."

50Then he took them out as far as Bethany, and lifted up his hands and blessed them. 51As he was blessing them, he was separated from them and carried into heaven.

52They worshipped him, and went back to Jerusalem in great joy. 53They spent all their time in the Temple, praising God.

The Gospel According to
John

1 In the beginning was the Word. The Word was close beside God, and the Word was God. ²In the beginning, he was close beside God.

**The Word
Made Flesh**

³All things came into existence through him; not one thing that exists came into existence without him. ⁴Life was in him, and this life was the light of the human race. ⁵The light shines in the darkness, and the darkness did not overcome it.

⁶There was a man called John, who was sent from God. ⁷He came as evidence, to give evidence about the light, so that everyone might believe through him. ⁸He was not himself the light, but he came to give evidence about the light.

⁹The true light, which gives light to every human being, was coming into the world. ¹⁰He was in the world, and the world was made through him, and the world did not know him. ¹¹He came to what was his own, and his own people did not accept him. ¹²But to anyone who did accept him, he gave the right to become God's children; yes, to anyone who believed in his name. ¹³They were not born from blood, or from fleshly desire, or from the intention of a man, but from God.

¹⁴And the Word became flesh, and lived among us. We gazed upon his glory, glory like that of the father's only son, full of grace and truth.

¹⁵John gave evidence about him, loud and clear.

"This is the one," he said, "that I was speaking about when I told you, 'The one who comes after me ranks ahead of me, because he was before me.'"

16Yes: it's out of his fullness that we have all received, grace indeed on top of grace. 17The law, you see, was given through Moses; grace and truth came through Jesus the Messiah. 18Nobody has ever seen God. The only-begotten God, who is intimately close to the father—he has brought him to light.

The Evidence of John

19This is the evidence John gave, when the Judaeans sent priests and Levites from Jerusalem to ask him, "Who are you?"

20He was quite open about it; he didn't try to deny it. He said, quite openly, "I am not the Messiah."

21"What then?" they asked. "Are you Elijah?"

"No, I'm not," he replied.

"Are you the Prophet?"

"No."

22"Well, then, who *are* you?" they said. "We've got to take some kind of answer back to the people who sent us. Who do you claim to be?"

23"I'm 'a voice calling in the desert,'" he said, "'Straighten out the road for the master!'"—just as the prophet Isaiah said.

24The people who had been sent were from the Pharisees. 25They continued to question him.

"So why are you baptizing," they asked, "if you aren't the Messiah, or Elijah, or the prophet?"

26"I'm baptizing with water," John replied. "But there is someone standing among you that you don't know, 27someone who is to come after me. I'm not good enough to undo his sandal-strap."

28This took place in Bethany beyond the Jordan, where John was baptizing.

The Lamb and the Spirit

29The next day, John saw Jesus coming toward him.

"Look!" he said. "There's God's lamb! He's the one who takes away the world's sin! 30He's the one I was speaking about when I said, 'There's a man coming after me who ranks ahead of me, because he was before me!' 31I didn't know who it would be, but this was the reason I came to baptize with water—so that he could be revealed to Israel."

32So John gave this evidence: "I saw the spirit coming down like a dove out of heaven and remaining on him. 33I didn't know who it would be; but the one who sent me to baptize with water said to me, 'When you see the spirit coming down and resting on someone, that's the person who will baptize with the holy spirit.' 34Well, that's what I saw, and I've given you my evidence: he is the son of God."

35The following day John was again standing there, with two of his disciples. 36He saw Jesus walking by, and said, "Look! There goes God's lamb!"

The First Disciples

37The two disciples heard him say this, and they followed Jesus.

38Jesus turned and saw them following him.

"What do you want?" he asked.

"Rabbi," they said (the word means "teacher"), "where are you staying?"

39"Come and see," he replied.

So they came and saw where he was staying, and stayed with him that day. It was late in the afternoon.

40One of the two who heard what John said and followed Jesus was Andrew, Simon Peter's brother. 41The first person he found was his own brother Simon.

"We've found the Messiah!" he said (that means "the anointed one," like our word "Christ"). 42He brought him to Jesus.

Jesus looked at him.

"So," he said, "you're Simon, John's son, are you? We'd better call you Cephas!" (That means "the Rock," like our word "Peter.")

43The next day Jesus decided to go to Galilee, where he found Philip.

Philip and Nathanael

"Follow me," he said to him.

44Philip came from Bethsaida, the town Andrew and Peter hailed from. 45Philip found Nathanael.

"We've found him!" he said. "The one Moses wrote about in the law! And the prophets, too! We've found him! It's Jesus, Joseph's son, from Nazareth!"

46"Really?" replied Nathanael. "Are you telling me that something good can come out of Nazareth?"

"Come and see," replied Philip.

47Jesus saw Nathanael coming toward him.

"Here he comes," he said. "Look at him! He's a real Israelite. Genuine through and through."

48"How did you get to know me?" asked Nathanael.

"Oh," replied Jesus, "I saw you under the fig tree, before Philip spoke to you."

49"Rabbi," replied Nathanael, "you're the son of God! You're the king of Israel!"

50"Wait a minute," said Jesus. "Are you telling me that you believe just because I told you I saw you under the fig tree? You'll see a lot more than that!

51"In fact," he went on, "I'm telling you the solemn truth. You'll see heaven opened, and God's angels ascending and descending on the son of man."

Water into Wine

2 On the third day there was a wedding at Cana in Galilee. Jesus's mother was there, 2and Jesus and his disciples were also invited to the wedding.

3The wine ran out.

Jesus's mother came over to him.

"They haven't got any wine!" she said.

4"Oh, Mother!" replied Jesus. "What's that got do to do with you and me? My time hasn't come yet."

5His mother spoke to the servants. "Do whatever he tells you," she said.

6Six stone water-jars were standing there, ready for use in the Jewish purification rites. Each held about twenty or thirty gallons.

7"Fill the jars with water," said Jesus to the servants. And they filled them, right up to the brim.

8"Now draw some out," he said, "and take it to the chief steward." They did so.

9When the chief steward tasted the water that had turned into wine (he didn't know where it had come from, but the servants who had drawn the water knew), he called the bridegroom.

10"What everybody normally does," he said, "is to serve the good wine first, and then the worse stuff when people have had plenty to drink. But you've kept the good wine till now!"

¹¹This event, in Cana of Galilee, was the first of Jesus's signs. He displayed his glory, and his disciples believed in him.

¹²After this, he went down to Capernaum, with his mother, his brothers, and his disciples. He remained there for a few days.

¹³It was nearly time for the Judaean Passover, and Jesus went up to Jerusalem.

Jesus in the Temple

¹⁴In the Temple he found people selling cows, sheep, and doves, and the money-changers sitting there. ¹⁵He made a whip out of cords and drove them all out of the Temple—sheep, cows, and all. He spilled the money-changers' coins onto the ground, and knocked over their tables.

¹⁶"Take these things away!" he said to the people selling doves. "You mustn't turn my father's house into a market!"

¹⁷His disciples remembered that it was written, "The zeal of your house has eaten me up."

¹⁸The Judaeans had this response for him. "What sign are you going to show us," they said, "to explain why you're doing this?"

¹⁹"Destroy this Temple," replied Jesus, "and I'll raise it up in three days."

²⁰"It's taken forty-six years to build this Temple," responded the Judaeans, "and are you going to raise it up in three days?" ²¹But he was speaking about the "temple" of his body. ²²So when he was raised from the dead, his disciples remembered that he had said this, and they believed the Bible and the word which Jesus had spoken.

²³While he was in Jerusalem during the Passover festival, several people came to trust in his name, because they had seen the signs he did. ²⁴But Jesus didn't entrust himself to them. He knew everything, ²⁵and had no need for anyone to give him information about people. He himself knew what was inside people.

3 There was a man of the Pharisees called Nicodemus, a ruler of the Judaeans. ²He came to Jesus by night.

Jesus and Nicodemus

"Rabbi," he said to him, "we know that you're a teacher who's come from God. Nobody can do these signs that you're doing, unless God is with him."

³"Let me tell you the solemn truth," replied Jesus. "Unless someone has been born from above, they won't be able to see God's kingdom."

⁴"How can someone possibly be born," asked Nicodemus, "when they're old? You're not telling me they can go back a second time into the mother's womb and be born, are you?"

⁵"I'm telling you the solemn truth," replied Jesus. "Unless someone is born from water and spirit, they can't enter God's kingdom. ⁶Flesh is born from flesh, but spirit is born from spirit. ⁷Don't be surprised that I said to you, You must be born from above. ⁸The wind blows where it wants to, and you hear the sound it makes; but you don't know where it's coming from or where it's going to. That's what it's like with someone who is born from the spirit."

⁹"How can this be so?" asked Nicodemus.

¹⁰"Well, well!" replied Jesus. "You're a teacher of Israel, and yet you don't know about all this? ¹¹I'm telling you the solemn truth: we're talking about things we know about. We're giving evidence about things we've seen. But you won't admit our evidence. ¹²If I told you earthly things and you don't believe, how will it be if I tell you heavenly things? Are you going to believe then? ¹³And nobody has gone up into heaven except the one who came down from heaven, the son of man.

The Snake and the Love of God

¹⁴"So, just as Moses lifted up the snake in the desert, in the same way the son of man must be lifted up, ¹⁵so that everyone who believes in him may share in the life of God's new age. ¹⁶This, you see, is how much God loved the world: enough to give his only, special son, so that everyone who believes in him should not be lost but should share in the life of God's new age. ¹⁷After all, God didn't send the son into the world to condemn the world, but so that the world could be saved by him.

¹⁸"Anyone who believes in him is not condemned. But anyone who doesn't believe is condemned already, because they didn't believe in the name of God's only, special son. ¹⁹And this is the condemnation: that light has come into the world, and people loved darkness rather than light, because what they were doing was evil. ²⁰For everyone who does evil hates the light; people like that don't come to the light, in case their deeds get shown up and reproved. ²¹But people who do the

truth come to the light, so that it can become clear that what they have done has been done in God."

22After this, Jesus and his disciples went into the country-side of Judaea, and he stayed there with them and baptized. 23John, too, was baptizing at Aenon, close to Salim. There was plenty of water there, and people came to him and were baptized. 24This, of course, was before John had been put into prison.

The Bridegroom and His Friend

25There was, perhaps inevitably, a dispute between the dis-ciples of John and a Judaean, on the subject of purification. 26They came to John.

"Rabbi," they said, "remember the man who was with you beyond the Jordan, the one you gave evidence about? Well, look! He's baptizing, and everyone's going to him!"

27"Nobody can receive anything unless heaven first gives it," replied John. 28"You yourselves can bear me out that I said I wasn't the Messiah, but that I was sent ahead of him. 29It's the bridegroom who gets the bride. The bridegroom's friend, who stands nearby and hears him, is very, very happy when he hears the bridegroom's voice. So, you see, my joy is now com-plete. 30He must increase, but I must decrease."

31The one who comes from above is over everything. The one who is from the earth has an earthly character, and what he says has "earth" written all over it. The one who comes from heaven is above all. 32He gives evidence about what he has heard and seen, and nobody accepts his evidence. 33The one who does ac-cept his evidence has put his signature to the fact that God is true. 34The one God sent, you see, speaks God's words, because he gives the spirit lavishly. 35The father loves the son and has given everything into his hand. 36Anyone who believes in the son shares in the life of God's new age. Anyone who doesn't be-lieve in the son won't see life, but God's wrath rests on him.

4 So when Jesus knew that the Pharisees had heard that he was making more disciples than John, and was bap-tizing them 2(Jesus himself didn't baptize people; it was his disciples who were doing it), 3he left Judaea and went back to Galilee.

The Woman of Samaria

4He had to go through Samaria, 5and he came to a town in Samaria named Sychar. It was near the place which Jacob gave to his son Joseph. 6Jacob's well was there. So Jesus, tired from the journey, sat down there by the well. It was about midday.

7A Samaritan woman came to draw water, and Jesus spoke to her.

"Give me a drink," he said. 8(The disciples had gone off into the town to buy food.)

9"What!" said the Samaritan woman. "You, a Jew, asking for a drink from me, a woman, and a Samaritan at that?" (Jews, you see, don't have any dealings with Samaritans.)

10"If only you'd known God's gift," replied Jesus, "and who it is that's saying to you, 'Give me a drink,' you'd have asked him, and he would have given you living water."

11"But sir," replied the woman, "you haven't got a bucket! And the well's deep! So how were you thinking of getting living water? 12Are you greater than our father Jacob, who gave us the well, and drank of it himself, with his sons and his animals?"

13"Everyone who drinks this water," Jesus replied, "will get thirsty again. 14But anyone who drinks the water I'll give them won't ever be thirsty again. No: the water I'll give them will become a spring of water welling up to the life of God's new age."

15"Sir," the woman said, "give me this water! Then I won't be thirsty anymore, and I won't have to come here to draw from the well."

Jesus and the Woman 16"Well then," said Jesus to the woman, "go and call your husband and come here."

17"I haven't got a husband," replied the woman.

"You're telling me you haven't got a husband!" replied Jesus. 18"The fact is, you've had five husbands, and the one you've got now isn't your husband. You were speaking the truth!"

19"Well, sir," replied the woman, "I can see you're a prophet . . . 20Our ancestors worshipped on this mountain. And you say that in Jerusalem is the place where people ought to worship."

21"Believe me, woman," replied Jesus, "the time is coming when you won't worship the father on this mountain or in Jerusalem. 22You worship what you don't know. We worship what we do know; salvation, you see, is indeed from the Jews. 23But the time is coming—indeed, it's here already!—when true worshippers will worship the father in spirit and in truth. Yes: that's the kind of worshippers the father is looking for. ²⁴God is spirit, and those who worship him must worship in spirit and in truth."

²⁵"I know that Messiah is coming," said the woman, "the one they call 'the anointed.' When he comes, he'll tell us everything."

²⁶"I'm the one—the one speaking to you right now," said Jesus.

²⁷Just then Jesus's disciples came up. They were astonished that he was talking with a woman; but nobody said, "What did you want?" or "Why were you talking with her?" ²⁸So the woman left her water-jar, went into the town, and spoke to the people.

Sower and Reaper Rejoice Together

²⁹"Come on!" she said. "Come and see a man who told me everything I ever did! You don't think he can be the Messiah, do you?"

³⁰So they left the town and were coming out to him.

³¹Meanwhile, the disciples were nagging him. "Come on, Rabbi!" they were saying. "You must have something to eat!"

³²"I've got food to eat that you know nothing about," he said.

³³"Nobody's brought him anything to eat, have they?" said the disciples to one another.

³⁴"My food," replied Jesus, "is to do the will of the one who sent me, and to finish his work! ³⁵Don't you have a saying, 'Another four months, then comes harvest'? Well, let me tell you, raise your eyes and see! The fields are white! It's harvest time already! ³⁶The reaper earns his pay, and gathers crops for the life of God's coming age, so that sower and reaper can celebrate together. ³⁷This is where that saying comes true, 'One sows, another reaps.' ³⁸I sent you to reap what you didn't work for. Others did the hard work, and you've come into the results."

³⁹Several Samaritans from that town believed in Jesus because of what the woman said in evidence about him: "He told me everything I did." ⁴⁰So when the Samaritans came to him, they asked him to stay with them. And he stayed there two days.

⁴¹Many more believed because of what he said.

⁴²"We believe, too," they said to the woman, "but it's no longer because of what you told us. We've heard him ourselves! We know that he really is the one! He's the savior of the world!"

The Official's Son

⁴³After the two days in Samaria, Jesus went off from there to Galilee. ⁴⁴Jesus himself gave evidence, after all, that a prophet isn't honored in his own country. ⁴⁵So when he came to Galilee, the Galileans welcomed him. They had seen all the things he had done in Jerusalem at the festival, since they had been at the festival too.

⁴⁶So he went once more to Cana in Galilee, where he had turned the water into wine.

There was a royal official in Capernaum whose son was ill. ⁴⁷He heard that Jesus had come from Judaea into Galilee, and he went to him and asked him to come down and heal his son, since he was at the point of death.

⁴⁸"Unless you see signs and miracles," replied Jesus, "you won't ever believe."

⁴⁹"Sir," replied the official, "come down before my child dies!"

⁵⁰"Off you go!" said Jesus. "Your son will live!"

The man believed the word which Jesus had spoken to him, and he set off. ⁵¹But while he was still on his way down to Capernaum, his servants met him with the news that his son was alive and well.

⁵²So he asked them what time he had begun to get better.

"Yesterday afternoon, about one o'clock," they said. "That's when the fever left him."

⁵³So the father knew that it had happened at the very moment when Jesus had said to him, "Your son will live!" He himself believed, and so did all his household.

⁵⁴This was now the second sign Jesus did, when he came out of Judaea into Galilee.

The Healing of the Disabled Man

5 After this there was a Jewish festival, and Jesus went up to Jerusalem.

²In Jerusalem, near the Sheep Gate, there is a pool which is called, in Hebrew, Bethesda. It has five porticoes, ³where there were several sick people lying. They were blind, lame, and paralyzed.

[5]There was a man who had been there, in the same sick state, for thirty-eight years. [6]Jesus saw him lying there, and knew that he had been there a long time already.

"Do you want to get well?" he asked him.

[7]"Well, sir," the sick man replied, "I don't have anyone to put me into the pool when the water gets stirred up. While I'm on my way there, someone else gets down before me."

[8]"Get up," said Jesus, "pick up your mattress and walk!"

[9]At once the man was healed. He picked up his mattress and walked.

The day all this happened was a sabbath. [10]So the Judaeans confronted the man who had been healed.

God's Son Breaks the Sabbath!

"It's the sabbath!" they said. "You shouldn't be carrying your mattress!"

[11]"Well," he replied, "the man who cured me told me to pick up my mattress and walk!"

[12]"Oh, really?" they said. "And who is this man, who told you to pick it up and walk?"

[13]But the man who'd been healed didn't know who it was. Jesus had gone away, and the place was crowded.

[14]After this Jesus found the man in the Temple.

"Look!" he said. "You're better again! Don't sin anymore, or something worse might happen to you!"

[15]The man went off and told the Judaeans that it was Jesus who had healed him. [16]This was why the Judaeans began to persecute Jesus, because he did these things on the sabbath.

[17]This was Jesus's response to them.

"My father," he said, "is going on working, and so am I!"

[18]So for this reason the Judaeans were all the more eager to kill him, because he not only broke the sabbath, but spoke of God as his own father, making himself equal to God.

[19]So Jesus made this response to them.

The Coming Judgment

"I'm telling you the solemn truth," he said. "The son can do nothing by himself. He can only do what he sees the father doing. Whatever the father does, the son does too, and in the same way. [20]The father loves the son, you see, and shows him all the things that he's doing. Yes: he will show him even greater things than these, and that'll amaze you! [21]For, just as the father raises the dead and gives them life, in the same way the son gives life to anyone he chooses.

22"The father doesn't judge anyone, you see; he has handed over all judgment to the son, 23so that everyone should honor the son just as they honor the father. Anyone who doesn't honor the son doesn't honor the father who sent him.

24"I'm telling you the solemn truth: anyone who hears my word, and believes in the one who sent me, has the life of God's coming age. Such a person won't come into judgment; they will have passed out of death into life. 25I'm telling you the solemn truth: the time is coming—in fact, it's here already!—when the dead will hear the voice of God's son, and those who hear it will live. 26You see, just as the father has life in himself, in the same way he has given the son the privilege of having life in himself. 27He has even given him authority to pass judgment, because he is the son of man.

28"Don't be surprised at this. The time is coming, you see, when everyone in the tombs will hear his voice. 29They will come out—those who have done good, to the resurrection of life, and those who have done evil, to the resurrection of judgment.

The Evidence in Support of Jesus

30"I can't do anything on my own authority," Jesus went on. "I judge on the basis of what I hear. And my judgment is just, because I'm not trying to carry out my own wishes, but the wishes of the one who sent me.

31"If I give evidence about myself, my evidence isn't true. 32There is someone else who gives evidence about me, and I know that the evidence which he brings about me is true. 33You sent messengers to John, and he gave evidence about the truth. 34Not that I need evidence from human beings; but I'm saying this so that you may be saved.

35"John was a burning, bright lamp, and you were happy to celebrate in his light for a while. 36But I have greater evidence on my side than that of John. The works which the father has given me to complete—these works, which I'm doing, will provide evidence about me, evidence that the father has sent me. 37And the father who sent me has given evidence about me. You've never heard his voice; you've never seen his form.

38What's more, you haven't got his word abiding in you, because you don't believe in the one he sent.

39"You study the Bible," Jesus continued, "because you suppose that you'll discover the life of God's coming age in it. In fact, it's the Bible which gives evidence about me! 40But you won't come to me so that you can have life.

Jesus and Moses

41"I'm not accepting glory from human beings; 42but I know that you haven't got the love of God within you. 43I have come in the name of my father, and you won't receive me. If someone else comes in his own name, you will receive him! 44How can you believe, when you receive glory from one another, and you're not looking for the glory which comes from the one and only God?

45"Don't think that I'm going to accuse you to the father. There is someone who accuses you: it's Moses, the one you've put your hope in! 46You see, if you'd believed Moses, you would have believed me—because it was me he was writing about. 47But if you don't believe his writings, how are you going to believe my words?"

6 After this Jesus went away to beside the Sea of Galilee—that is, the Sea of Tiberias. 2A large crowd followed him, because they saw the signs he was doing in healing the sick. 3Jesus went up onto the mountain and sat down there with his disciples. 4It was nearly time for the Passover, a Jewish festival.

Feeding the Five Thousand

5Jesus looked up and saw a great crowd coming to him.

"Where are we going to buy bread," he said to Philip, "so that they can have something to eat?" 6(He said this to test him. He himself knew what he intended to do.)

7"Even with six months' pay," replied Philip, "you wouldn't be able to buy enough bread for each of them to have just a little!"

8One of his disciples, Andrew, Simon Peter's brother, joined in.

9"There's a lad here," he said, "who's got five barley loaves and two fish. But what use are they with this many people?"

10"Make the men sit down," said Jesus.

There was a lot of grass where they were, so the men sat down, about five thousand in all. 11So Jesus took the loaves, gave thanks, and gave them to the people sitting down, and then did the same with the fish, as much as they wanted.

¹²When they were satisfied, he called the disciples.

"Collect up the bits and pieces left over," he said, "so that we don't lose anything."

¹³So they collected it up and filled twelve baskets with broken pieces of the five barley loaves left behind by the people who had eaten.

¹⁴When the people saw the sign that Jesus had done, they said, "This really is the Prophet, the one who is to come into the world." ¹⁵So when Jesus realized that they were intending to come and seize him to make him king, he withdrew again, by himself, up the mountain.

Jesus Walking on the Water

¹⁶When it was evening, Jesus's disciples went down to the seashore. ¹⁷They got into a boat and went across the sea toward Capernaum. It was already getting dark, and Jesus had not yet come to them. ¹⁸A strong wind blew up, and the sea began to get rough. ¹⁹They had been rowing for about three or four miles when they saw Jesus walking on the sea, coming toward the boat. They were terrified.

²⁰But he spoke to them. "It's me!" he said. "Don't be afraid!"

²¹Then they were eager to take him into the boat; and at once the boat arrived at the land they had been making for.

²²The next day the crowd that had remained on the far side of the lake saw that there had only been the one boat there. They knew that Jesus hadn't gone with his disciples, but that the disciples had set off by themselves. ²³But other boats came from Tiberias, near the place where they had eaten the bread after the Lord had given thanks. ²⁴When the crowd saw that neither Jesus nor his disciples were there, they themselves got into the boats and came to Capernaum looking for Jesus.

²⁵When they found him beside the sea, they said to him, "Rabbi, when did you come here?"

Bread from Heaven

²⁶This was Jesus's reply.

"I'm telling you the solemn truth," he said. "You aren't looking for me because you saw signs, but because you ate as much bread as you could. ²⁷You shouldn't be working for perishable food, but for food that will last to the life of God's coming age—

the food which the son of man will give you, the person whom God the father has stamped with the seal of his approval."

28"What should we be doing," they asked him, "so that we can be doing the work God wants?"

29"This is the work God wants of you," replied Jesus, "that you believe in the one he sent."

30"Well, then," they said to him, "what sign are you going to do, so that we can see it and believe you? What work are *you* doing? 31Our ancestors ate the manna in the wilderness; it says in the Bible that 'he gave them bread from heaven to eat.'"

32"I'm telling you the solemn truth," Jesus replied. "It wasn't Moses who gave you the bread from heaven. It was my father who gave you the true bread from heaven. 33God's bread, you see, is the one who comes down from heaven and gives life to the world."

34"Master," they said, "give us this bread—give it to us always!"

35"I am the bread of life," replied Jesus. "Anyone who comes to me will never be hungry! Anyone who believes in me will never be thirsty!"

36"But I told you," Jesus continued, "that you have indeed seen me—and still you don't believe! 37All that the father gives me will come to me; and I won't reject anyone who comes to me, 38because I came down from heaven not to do my own will but the will of the one who sent me. 39And this is the will of the one who sent me, that I should lose nothing out of everything that he has given me, but that I should raise it up on the last day. 40This is the will of my father, you see: that all who see the son and believe in him should have the life of God's coming age; and I will raise them up on the last day."

41The Judaeans then grumbled about him because he had said, "I am the bread which came down from heaven."

42"Isn't this Jesus, Joseph's son?" they said. "We know his father and mother, don't we? So how can he say 'I came down from heaven'?"

43"Don't grumble among yourselves," answered Jesus. 44"No one can come to me unless the father who sent me draws them—and I will raise them up on the last day. 45It is written

The Father's Will

in the prophets, 'They shall all be taught by God.' Everyone who listens to what comes from the father and learns from it comes to me. 46Not that anyone has seen the father except the one who is from God; he has seen the father."

Eating and Drinking the Son of Man

47"I'm telling you the solemn truth," Jesus went on. "Anyone who believes in me has the life of God's coming age. 48I am the bread of life. 49Your ancestors in the wilderness ate the manna, and they died. 50This is the bread which comes down from heaven, so that people can eat it and not die. 51I am the living bread which came down from heaven. If anyone eats from this bread, they will live forever. And the bread which I shall give is my flesh, given for the life of the world."

52This caused a squabble among the Judaeans.

"How can this fellow give us his flesh to eat?" they asked.

53"I'm telling you the solemn truth," Jesus replied. "If you don't eat the flesh of the son of man, and drink his blood, you have no life in yourselves. 54Anyone who feasts upon my flesh and drinks my blood has the life of God's coming age, and I will raise them up on the last day. 55My flesh is true food, you see, and my blood is true drink. 56Anyone who eats my flesh and drinks my blood remains in me, and I remain in them. 57Just as the living father sent me, and I live because of the father, so the one who eats me will live because of me. 58This is the bread which came down from heaven; it isn't like the bread which the ancestors ate, and died. The one who eats this bread will share the life of God's new age."

59He said this in the synagogue, while he was teaching in Capernaum.

Division Among Jesus's Followers

60When they heard this, many of Jesus's disciples said, "This is difficult stuff! Who can bear to listen to it?"

61Jesus knew in himself that his disciples were grumbling about what he'd said.

"Does this put you off?" he said. 62"What if you were to see the son of man ascending to where he was before? 63It's the spirit that gives life; the flesh is no help. The words that I have spoken to you—they are spirit, they are life. 64But there are some of you who don't believe."

Jesus knew from the beginning, you see, those who didn't believe, and the one who was going to betray him.

65"That's why I said," he went on, "that no one can come to me unless it is given to them by the father."

66From that time on, several of his disciples drew back, and no longer went about with him.

67Jesus turned to the Twelve.

"You don't want to go away too, do you?" he asked.

68Simon Peter spoke up.

"Master," he said, "who can we go to? You're the one who's got the words of the life of the coming age! 69We've come to believe it—we've come to know it!—that you are God's Holy One."

70"Well," replied Jesus, "I chose you twelve, didn't I? And one of you is an accuser!"

71He was referring to Judas, son of Simon Iscariot. He was one of the Twelve, and he was going to betray him.

7 After this, Jesus went about in Galilee. He didn't want to go about in Judaea, because the Judaeans were after his blood.

Jesus and His Brothers

2The time came for the Jewish Festival of Tabernacles. 3So Jesus's brothers approached him.

"Leave this place," they said, "and go to Judaea! Then your disciples will see the works you're doing. 4Nobody who wants to become well known does things in secret. If you're doing these things, show yourself to the world!"

5Even his brothers, you see, didn't believe in him.

6"My time isn't here yet," replied Jesus, "but your time is always here. 7The world can't hate you, but it hates me, because I am giving evidence against it, showing that its works are evil. 8I tell you what: you go up to the feast. I'm not going up to this feast; my time is not yet complete."

9With these words, he stayed behind in Galilee.

10But when Jesus's brothers had gone up to the festival, then he himself went up, not openly, but, so to speak, in secret. 11The Judaeans were looking for him at the feast.

Disputes About Jesus

"Where is he?" they were saying.

12There was considerable dispute about him among the crowds.

"He's a good man!" some were saying.

"No, he isn't," others would reply. "He's deceiving the people!"

13But nobody dared speak about him openly, for fear of the Judaeans.

14About the middle of the feast, Jesus went up into the Temple and began to teach. 15The Judaeans were astonished.

"Where does this fellow get all his learning from?" they asked. "He's never been trained!"

16"My teaching isn't my own," replied Jesus. "It comes from the one who sent me! 17If anyone wants to do what God wants, they will know whether this teaching is from God, or whether I'm just speaking on my own account. 18Anyone who speaks on his own behalf is trying to establish his own reputation. But if what he's interested in is the reputation of the one who sent him, then he is true, and there is no injustice in him.

Moses and the Messiah

19"Moses gave you the law, didn't he?" Jesus continued. "But none of you obeys the law. Why are you wanting to kill me?"

20The crowd responded to this.

"You must have a demon inside you!" they said. "Who is trying to kill you?"

21"Look here," replied Jesus. "I did one single thing, and you are all amazed. 22Moses commanded you to practice circumcision (not that it starts with Moses, of course; it comes from the patriarchs), and you circumcise a man on the sabbath. 23Well, then, if a man receives circumcision on the sabbath, so that the law of Moses may not be broken, how can you be angry with me if I make an entire man healthy on the sabbath? 24Don't judge by appearances! Judge with proper and right judgment!"

25Some Jerusalem residents commented, "Isn't this the man they're trying to kill? 26Look—he's speaking quite openly, and nobody is saying anything to him. You don't suppose our rulers really know he's the Messiah, do you? 27The thing is, we know where he comes from—but when the Messiah appears, nobody will know where *he* comes from."

28As Jesus was teaching in the Temple, he shouted out, "You know me! You know where I come from! I haven't come on my own behalf—but the one who sent me is true, and you don't know him! 29I know him, because I come from him, and he sent me!"

³⁰So they tried to arrest him. But nobody laid hands on him, because his time had not yet come.

³¹Many people from the crowd believed in Jesus.

"When the Messiah comes," they were saying, "will he do more signs than this man has done?"

³²The Pharisees heard that the crowd was full of this rumor about him, and the chief priests and Pharisees sent servants to arrest him.

³³So Jesus said, "I'm just with you for a little while, and then I'm going to the one who sent me. ³⁴You will look for me and you won't find me, and you can't come where I am."

³⁵"Where does he think he's going," said the Judaeans to one another, "if we won't be able to find him? He's not going to go off abroad, among the Greeks, is he, and teach the Greeks? ³⁶What does he mean when he says, 'You'll look for me and you won't find me,' and 'Where I am, you can't come'?"

³⁷On the last day of the festival, the great final celebration, Jesus stood up and shouted out, "If anybody's thirsty, they should come to me and have a drink! ³⁸Anyone who believes in me will have rivers of living water flowing out of their heart, just like the Bible says!"

³⁹He said this about the spirit, which people who believed in him were to receive. The spirit wasn't available yet, because Jesus was not yet glorified.

⁴⁰When they heard these words, some people in the crowd said, "This man really is 'the prophet'!"

⁴¹"He's the Messiah!" said some others.

But some of them replied, "The Messiah doesn't come from Galilee, does he? ⁴²Doesn't the Bible say that the Messiah is descended from David, and comes from Bethlehem, the city where David was?"

⁴³So there was a division in the crowd because of him. ⁴⁴Some of them wanted to arrest him, but nobody laid hands on him.

⁴⁵So the servants went back to the chief priests and the Pharisees.

"Why didn't you get him?" they asked.

⁴⁶"No man ever spoke like this!" the servants replied.

Rivers of Living Water

Where Does the Messiah Come From?

47"You don't mean to say you've been taken in too?" answered the Pharisees. 48"None of the rulers or the Pharisees have believed in him, have they? 49But this rabble that doesn't know the law—a curse on them!"

50Nicodemus, who went to Jesus earlier, and who was one of their own number, spoke up.

51"Our law doesn't condemn a man, does it, unless first you hear his side of the story and find out what he's doing?"

52"Oh, so you're from Galilee too, are you?" they answered him. "Check it out and see! No prophet ever rises up from Galilee!"

Adultery and Hypocrisy

53They all went off home,

8 and Jesus went to the Mount of Olives. 2In the morning he went back to the Temple. All the people came to him, and he sat down and taught them.

3The scribes and Pharisees brought a woman who had been caught out in adultery. They stood her out in the middle.

4"Teacher," they said to him. "This woman was caught in the very act of adultery. 5In the law, Moses commanded us to stone people like this. What do you say?"

6They said this to test him, so that they could frame a charge against him.

Jesus squatted down and wrote with his finger on the ground. 7When they went on pressing the question, he got up and said to them, "Whichever of you is without sin should throw the first stone at her."

8And once again he squatted down and wrote on the ground.

9When they heard that, they went off one by one, beginning with the oldest. Jesus was left alone, with the woman still standing there.

10Jesus looked up. "Where are they, woman?" he asked. "Hasn't anybody condemned you?"

11"Nobody, sir," she replied.

"Well, then," said Jesus, "I don't condemn you either! Off you go—and from now on don't sin again!"

The Light of the World

12Jesus spoke to them again.

"I am the light of the world," he said. "People who follow me won't go around in the dark; they'll have the light of life!"

[13]"You're giving evidence in your own case!" said the Pharisees. "Your evidence is false!"

[14]"Even if I do give evidence about myself," replied Jesus to them, "my evidence is true, because I know where I came from and where I'm going to. But you don't know where I come from or where I'm going to. [15]You are judging in merely human terms; I don't judge anyone. [16]But even if I do judge, my judgment is true, because I'm not a lone voice; I have on my side the father who sent me. [17]It is written in your law that the evidence of two people is true. [18]I'm giving evidence about myself, and the father who sent me is giving evidence about me."

[19]"Where is your father?" they said to him.

"You don't know me," replied Jesus, "and you don't know my father! If you had known me, you would have known my father as well."

[20]He said all this in the treasury, while he was teaching in the Temple. Nobody arrested him, though, because his time hadn't yet come.

[21]So Jesus spoke to them once more.

"I am going away," he said. "You will look for me, and you will die in your sin. You can't come where I'm going."

From Below or from Above

[22]"Is he going to kill himself?" asked the Judaeans. "Is that what he means when he says we can't come where he's going?"

[23]"You come from below," Jesus said to them, "but I come from above. You are from this world; I am not from this world. [24]I told you that you would die in your sins; you see, that's what will happen to you if you don't believe that I am the one."

[25]"Who are you?" they asked.

"What I've been telling you from the beginning," replied Jesus. [26]"There are plenty of things I could say about you—yes, and against you too! But the one who sent me is true, and I tell the world what I heard from him."

[27]They didn't understand that he was talking about the father.

[28]So Jesus said to them, "When you've lifted up the son of man, then you will know that I'm the one, and that I never act on my own initiative; I say exactly what the father taught me. [29]And the one who sent me is with me. He hasn't left me alone, because I always do what pleases him."

30As Jesus said all this, several people believed in him.

31So Jesus spoke to the Judaeans who had believed in him.

"If you remain in my word," he said, "you will truly be my disciples, 32and you will know the truth, and the truth will make you free."

33"We are Abraham's descendants!" they replied. "We've never been anyone's slaves! How can you say, 'You'll become free'?"

34"I'm telling you the solemn truth," Jesus replied. "Everyone who commits sin is a slave of sin. 35The slave doesn't live in the house forever; the son lives there forever. 36So, you see, if the son makes you free, you will be truly free."

37"I know you're Abraham's descendants," Jesus went on. "But you're trying to kill me, because my word doesn't find a place among you. 38I am speaking of what I have seen with the father; and you, too, are doing what you heard from your father."

39"Abraham is our father!" they replied.

"If you really were Abraham's children," replied Jesus, "you would do what Abraham did! 40But now you're trying to kill me—me, a man who has told you the truth which I heard from God! That's not what Abraham did. 41You're doing the works of *your* father."

"There wasn't anything immoral about the way *we* were born!" they replied. "We've got one father, and that's God!"

42"If God really was your father," replied Jesus, "you would love me, because I came from God, and here I am. I didn't come on my own initiative, you see, but he sent me. 43Why don't you understand what I'm saying? It can only be because you can't hear my word. 44You are from your father—the devil! And you're eager to get on with what he wants. He was a murderer from the beginning, and he's never remained in the truth, because there is no truth in him. When he tells lies, he speaks what comes naturally to him, because he is a liar—in fact, he's the father of lies! 45But because I speak the truth, you don't believe me. 46Which of you can bring a charge of sin against me? If I speak the truth, why don't you believe me? 47The one who is from God speaks God's words. That's why you don't listen, because you're not from God."

Before Abraham,
"I Am"

⁴⁸This was the Judaeans' response to Jesus.

"Haven't we been right all along," they said, "in saying you're a Samaritan, and that you've got a demon inside you?"

⁴⁹"I haven't got a demon!" replied Jesus. "I am honoring my father, and you are dishonoring me. ⁵⁰I'm not looking for my own glory; there is one who is looking after that, and he will be the judge. ⁵¹I'm telling you the solemn truth: anyone who keeps my word will never, ever see death."

⁵²"Now we know that you really *have* got a demon!" replied the Judaeans. "Look here: Abraham died! So did the prophets! And here are you, saying, 'Anyone who keeps my word will never, ever taste death.' ⁵³You're not suggesting, are you, that you're greater than our father Abraham? He died, and so did the prophets! Who are you making yourself out to be?"

⁵⁴"If I do give myself glory," replied Jesus, "my glory is nothing. My father is the one who brings me glory—the one you say is 'our God'; ⁵⁵and you don't know him! I know him, though. If I were to say I didn't know him, I would be a liar like you. But I do know him, and I keep his word. ⁵⁶Your father Abraham celebrated the fact that he would see my day. He saw it and was delighted."

⁵⁷"You're not yet fifty years old!" responded the Judaeans. "Have you seen Abraham?"

⁵⁸"I'm telling you the solemn truth," replied Jesus. "Before Abraham existed, I Am."

⁵⁹So they picked up stones to throw at him. But Jesus hid, and left the Temple.

The Man Born
Blind

9 As Jesus was going along, he saw a man who had been blind from birth.

²"Teacher," his disciples asked him, "whose sin was it that caused this man to be born blind? Did he sin, or did his parents?"

³"He didn't sin," replied Jesus, "nor did his parents. It happened so that God's works could be seen in him. ⁴We must work the works of the one who sent me as long as it's still daytime. The night is coming, and nobody can work then! ⁵As long as I'm in the world, I'm the light of the world."

⁶With these words, he spat on the ground and made some mud out of his spittle. He spread the mud on the man's eyes.

⁷"Off you go," he said to him, "and wash in the pool of Siloam" (which means "sent"). So he went off and washed. When he came back, he could see.

⁸His neighbors, and the people who used to see him begging, remarked on this.

"Isn't this the man," they said, "who used to sit here and beg?"

⁹"Yes, it's him!" said some of them.

"No, it isn't!" said some others. "It's somebody like him."

But the man himself spoke.

"Yes, it's me," he said.

¹⁰"Well, then," they said to him, "how did your eyes get opened?"

¹¹"It was the man called Jesus!" he replied. "He made some mud; then he spread it on my eyes and told me to go to Siloam and wash. So I went, and washed, and I could see!"

¹²"Where is he?" they asked.

"I don't know," he replied.

The Blind Man's Parents

¹³They took the man who had been blind and brought him to the Pharisees. ¹⁴(The day Jesus had made the mud, and opened his eyes, was a sabbath.) ¹⁵So the Pharisees began to ask him again how he had come to see.

"He put some mud on my eyes," he said, "and I washed, and now I can see!"

¹⁶"The man can't be from God," some of the Pharisees began to say. "He doesn't keep the sabbath!"

"Well, but," replied some of the others, "how can a man who is a sinner do signs like these?"

And they were divided.

¹⁷So they spoke to the blind man again.

"What have you got to say about him?" they asked. "He opened your eyes, after all."

"He's a prophet," he replied.

¹⁸The Judaeans didn't believe that he really had been blind and now could see. So they called the parents of the newly sighted man ¹⁹and put the question to them.

"Is this man really your son," they asked, "the one you say was born blind? How is it that he can now see?"

20"Well," replied his parents, "we know that he is indeed our son, and that he was born blind. 21But we don't know how it is that he can now see, and we don't know who it was that opened his eyes. Ask him! He's grown up. He can speak for himself."

22His parents said this because they were afraid of the Judaeans. The Judaeans, you see, had already decided that if anyone declared that Jesus was the Messiah, they should be put out of the synagogue. 23That's why his parents said, "He's grown up, so you should ask him."

24So for the second time they called the man who had been blind.

"Give God the glory!" they said. "We know that this man is a sinner."

25"I don't know whether he's a sinner or not," replied the man. "All I know is this: I used to be blind, and now I can see."

26"What did he do to you?" they asked. "How did he open your eyes?"

27"I told you already," replied the man, "and you didn't listen. Why d'you want to hear it again? You don't want to become his disciples too, do you?"

28"You're his disciple," they scoffed, "but we are Moses's disciples. 29We know that God spoke to Moses, but we don't know where this man comes from."

30"Well, here's a fine thing!" replied the man. "You don't know where he's from, and he opened my eyes! 31We know that God doesn't listen to sinners; but if anyone is devout, and does his will, he listens to them. 32It's never, ever been heard of before that someone should open the eyes of a person born blind. 33If this man wasn't from God, he couldn't do anything."

34"You were born in sin from top to toe," they replied, "and are *you* going to start teaching *us*?" And they threw him out.

35Jesus heard that they had thrown the man out. He found him and spoke to him.

"Do you believe in the son of man?" he asked.

36"Who is he, sir," asked the man, "so that I can believe in him?"

37"You have seen him," replied Jesus. "In fact, it's the person who's talking to you."

Is Jesus from God?

Seeing and Not Seeing

38"Yes, sir," said the man; "I do believe." And he worshipped him.

39"I came into the world for judgment," said Jesus, "so that those who can't see would see, and so that those who can see would become blind."

40Some of the Pharisees were nearby, and they heard this.

"So!" they said. "We're blind too, are we?"

41"If you were blind," replied Jesus, "you wouldn't be guilty of sin. But now, because you say, 'We can see,' your sin remains.

The Good Shepherd

10 "I'm telling you the solemn truth," said Jesus. "Anyone who doesn't come into the sheepfold by the gate, but gets in by some other way, is a thief and a brigand. 2But the one who comes in through the gate is the sheep's own shepherd. 3The doorkeeper will open up for him, and the sheep hear his voice. He calls his own sheep by name, and leads them out. 4When he has brought out all that belong to him, he goes on ahead of them. The sheep follow him, because they know his voice. 5They won't follow a stranger; instead, they will run away from him, because they don't know the stranger's voice."

6Jesus spoke this parable to them, but they didn't understand what it was he was saying to them.

7So he spoke to them again.

"I'm telling you the solemn truth," he said. "I am the gate of the sheep. 8All the people who came before me were thieves and brigands, but the sheep didn't listen to them. 9I am the gate. If anyone comes in by me, they will be safe, and will go in and out and find pasture. 10The thief only comes to steal, and kill, and destroy. I came so that they could have life—yes, and have it full to overflowing.

The Shepherd and the Sheep

11"I am the good shepherd," Jesus continued. "The good shepherd lays down his life for the sheep. 12But supposing there's a hired servant, who isn't himself the shepherd, and who doesn't himself own the sheep. He will see the wolf coming, and leave the sheep, and run away. Then the wolf will snatch the sheep and scatter them. 13He'll run away because he's only a hired servant, and doesn't care about the sheep.

14"I am the good shepherd. I know my own sheep, and my own know me—15just as the father knows me and I know the father. And I lay down my life for the sheep. ¹⁶And I have other sheep, too, which don't belong to this sheepfold. I must bring them, too, and they will hear my voice. Then there will be one flock, and one shepherd.

¹⁷"That's why the father loves me, because I lay down my life so that I can take it up again. ¹⁸Nobody takes it from me; I lay it down of my own accord. I have the right to lay it down, and I have the right to receive it back again. This is the command I received from my father."

¹⁹So there was again a division among the Judaeans because of what Jesus had said.

The Messiah and the Father

²⁰"He's demon-possessed!" some were saying. "He's raving mad! Why listen to him?"

²¹"No," said some others, "that's not how demon-possessed people talk. Anyway, how could a demon open a blind man's eyes?"

²²It was the Feast of the Dedication in Jerusalem. It was winter, ²³and Jesus was walking in the Temple, in Solomon's Porch. ²⁴The Judaeans surrounded him.

"How much longer are you going to keep us in suspense?" they asked. "If you are the Messiah, say so out loud!"

²⁵"I told you," replied Jesus, "and you didn't believe. The works which I'm doing in my father's name give evidence about me. ²⁶But you don't believe, because you don't belong to my sheep.

²⁷"My sheep hear my voice. I know them, and they follow me. ²⁸I give them the life of the coming age. They will never, ever perish, and nobody can snatch them out of my hand. ²⁹My father, who has given them to me, is greater than all, and nobody can snatch them out of my father's hand. ³⁰I and the father are one."

³¹So the Judaeans once more picked up stones to stone him.

Blasphemy!

³²"I've shown you many fine deeds from the father," Jesus replied to them. "Which of these deeds are you stoning me for?"

³³"We're not stoning you for good deeds," replied the Judaeans, "but because of blasphemy! Here you are, a mere man, and you're making yourself into God!"

³⁴"It's written in your law, isn't it," replied Jesus to them, "'I said, you are gods'? ³⁵Well, if the law calls people 'gods,'

people to whom God's word came (and you can't set the Bible aside), ³⁶how can you accuse someone of blasphemy when the father has placed him apart and sent him into the world, and he says, 'I am the son of God'?

³⁷"If I'm not doing the works of my father, don't believe me. ³⁸But if I am doing them, well—even if you don't believe me, believe the works! That way you will know and grasp that the father is in me, and I am in the father."

³⁹So again they tried to arrest him. But Jesus managed to get away from them.

⁴⁰He went off once more across the Jordan, to the place where John had been baptizing at the beginning, and he stayed there. ⁴¹Several people came to him.

"John never did any signs," they said, "but everything that John said about this man was true."

⁴²And many believed in him there.

The Death of Lazarus

11 There was a man in Bethany named Lazarus, and he became ill. Bethany was the village of Mary and her sister, Martha. ²(This was the Mary who anointed the Lord with myrrh, and wiped his feet with her hair; Lazarus, who was ill, was her brother.)

³So the sisters sent messengers to Jesus.

"Master," they said, "the man you love is ill."

⁴When Jesus got the message, he said, "This illness won't lead to death. It's all about the glory of God! The son of God will be glorified through it."

⁵Now Jesus loved Martha, and her sister, and Lazarus. ⁶So when he heard that he was ill, he stayed where he was, to begin with, for two days.

⁷Then, after that, he said to the disciples, "Let's go back to Judaea."

⁸"Teacher," replied the disciples, "the Judaeans were trying to stone you just now! Surely you don't want to go back *there*!"

⁹"There are twelve hours in the day, aren't there?" replied Jesus. "If you walk in the day, you won't trip up, because you'll see the light of this world. ¹⁰But if anyone walks in the night, they will trip up, because there is no light in them."

¹¹When he had said this, Jesus added, "Our friend Lazarus has fallen asleep. But I'm going to wake him up."

¹²"Master," replied the disciples, "if he's asleep, he'll be all right."

¹³(They thought he was referring to ordinary sleep; but Jesus had in fact been speaking of his death.)

¹⁴Then Jesus spoke to them plainly.

"Lazarus," he said, "is dead. ¹⁵Actually, I'm glad I wasn't there, for your sakes; it will help your faith. But let's go to him."

¹⁶Thomas, whose name was the Twin, addressed the other disciples.

"Let's go too," he said. "We may as well die with him."

¹⁷So when Jesus arrived, he found that Lazarus had already been in the tomb for four days. ¹⁸Bethany was near Jerusalem, about two miles away. ¹⁹Many of the Judaeans had come to Martha and Mary to console them about their brother.

The Resurrection and the Life

²⁰When Martha heard that Jesus had arrived, she went to meet him. Mary, meanwhile, stayed sitting at home.

²¹"Master," said Martha to Jesus, "if only you'd been here! Then my brother wouldn't have died! ²²But even now I know that God will give you whatever you ask him for."

²³"Your brother will rise again," replied Jesus.

²⁴"I know he'll rise again," said Martha, "in the resurrection on the last day."

²⁵"I am the resurrection and the life," replied Jesus. "Anyone who believes in me will live, even if they die. ²⁶And anyone who lives and believes in me will never, ever die. Do you believe this?"

²⁷"Yes, Master," she said. "This is what I've come to believe: that you are the Messiah, the son of God, the one who was to come into the world."

²⁸With these words, Martha went back and called her sister, Mary.

Jesus Goes to the Tomb

"The teacher has come," she said to her privately, "and he's asking for you."

²⁹When she heard that, she got up quickly and went to him. ³⁰Jesus hadn't yet gotten to the village. He was still in the place where Martha had met him.

³¹The Judaeans who were in the house with Mary, consoling her, saw her get up quickly and go out. They guessed that she was going to the tomb to weep there, and they followed her.

³²When Mary came to where Jesus was, she saw him and fell down at his feet.

"Master!" she said. "If only you'd been here, my brother wouldn't have died!"

³³When Jesus saw her crying, and the Judaeans who had come with her crying, he was deeply stirred in his spirit, and very troubled.

³⁴"Where have you laid him?" he asked.

"Master," they said, "come and see."

³⁵Jesus burst into tears.

³⁶"Look," said the Judaeans, "see how much he loved him!"

³⁷"Well, yes," some of them said, "but he opened the eyes of a blind man, didn't he? Couldn't he have done something to stop this fellow from dying?"

The Raising of Lazarus

³⁸Jesus was once again deeply troubled within himself. He went to the tomb. It was a cave, and a stone was placed in front of it.

³⁹"Take away the stone," said Jesus.

"But, Master," said Martha, the dead man's sister, "there'll be a smell! It's the fourth day already!"

⁴⁰"Didn't I tell you," said Jesus, "that if you believed you would see God's glory?"

⁴¹So they took the stone away.

Jesus lifted up his eyes.

"Thank you, Father," he said, "for hearing me! ⁴²I know you always hear me, but I've said this because of the crowd standing around, so that they may believe that you sent me."

⁴³With these words, he gave a loud shout: "Lazarus—come out!"

⁴⁴And the dead man came out. He was tied up, hand and foot, with strips of linen, and his face was wrapped in a cloth.

"Untie him," said Jesus, "and let him go."

⁴⁵The result of all this was that several of the Judaeans who had come to Mary, and who had seen what he had done, believed in him. ⁴⁶But some of them went off to the Pharisees and told them what Jesus had done.

The Plan of Caiaphas

⁴⁷So the chief priests and the Pharisees called an assembly.

"What are we going to do?" they asked. "This man is performing lots of signs. ⁴⁸If we let him go on like this, everyone is going to believe in him! Then the Romans will come and take away our holy place, and our nation!"

49But one of them, Caiaphas, the high priest that year, addressed them.

"You know nothing at all!" he said. 50"You haven't worked it out! This is what's best for you: let one man die for the people, rather than the whole nation being wiped out."

51He didn't say this of his own accord. Since he was high priest that year, it was a prophecy. It meant that Jesus would die for the nation; 52and not only for the nation, but to gather into one the scattered children of God. 53So from that day on they plotted how to kill him.

54So Jesus didn't go around openly any longer among the Judaeans. He went away from there to the region by the desert, to a town called Ephraim. He stayed there with the disciples.

55The time came for the Judaeans' Passover. Lots of people went up to Jerusalem from the countryside, before the Passover, to purify themselves. 56They were looking for Jesus. As they stood there in the Temple, they were discussing him with one another.

"What d'you think?" they were saying. "Do you suppose he won't come to the festival?"

57The chief priests and the Pharisees had given the order that if anyone knew where he was, they should tell them, so that they could arrest him.

Mary and Her Ointment

12 Six days before the Passover, Jesus came to Bethany. Lazarus was there, the man he had raised from the dead. 2So they made a dinner for him there. Martha served, and Lazarus was among the company at table with him.

3Then Mary took a pound of very expensive perfume, made of pure nard. She anointed Jesus's feet with it, and wiped his feet with her hair. The house was filled with the smell of the perfume.

4At this, Judas Iscariot, one of his disciples (the one who was going to betray him), spoke up.

5"Why wasn't this ointment sold?" he asked. "It would have fetched a year's wages! You could have given it to the poor!"

6(He didn't say this because he cared for the poor, but because he was a thief. He kept the common purse, and used to help himself to what was in it.)

7"Let her alone," replied Jesus. "She's been keeping it for the day of my burial! 8You always have the poor with you, but you won't always have me."

Jesus Enters Jerusalem

9When the great crowd of Judaeans discovered that Jesus was there, they came to Bethany not just because of Jesus, but to see Lazarus, the one he had raised from the dead. 10So the chief priests planned to kill Lazarus as well, 11because many of the Judaeans were leaving their side on account of him, and were believing in Jesus.

12On the next day, the large crowd that had come up for the festival heard that Jesus had come to Jerusalem. 13They took palm branches and went out to meet him.

"Hosanna!" they shouted. "Welcome in the name of the Lord! Welcome to Israel's king!"

14Jesus found a little donkey and sat on it. As the Bible says,

> 15*Do not fear, daughter of Zion!*
> *Look! Your king is coming now;*
> *Sitting on a donkey's colt.*

16His disciples didn't understand this to begin with. But when Jesus was glorified, they remembered that these things had been written about him, and that these things had been done to him. 17The crowd that was with him when he called Lazarus out of the tomb, and raised him from the dead, told their story. 18That's why the crowd went out to meet him, because they heard that he had done this sign.

19The Pharisees conferred.

"You see?" they said to each other. "It's impossible. There's nothing you can do. Look—the world has gone off after him!"

The Seed Must Die

20Some Greeks had come up with all the others to worship at the festival. 21They went to Philip, who was from Bethsaida in Galilee.

"Sir," they said, "we would like to see Jesus."

22Philip went and told Andrew, and Andrew and Philip went together to tell Jesus.

²³"The time has come," said Jesus in reply. "This is the moment for the son of man to be glorified. ²⁴I'm telling you the solemn truth: unless a grain of wheat falls into the earth and dies, it remains all by itself. If it dies, though, it will produce lots of fruit. ²⁵If you love your life, you'll lose it. If you hate your life in this world, you'll keep it for the life of the coming age.

²⁶"If anyone serves me, they must follow me. Where I am, my servant will be too. If anyone serves me, the father will honor them.

²⁷"Now my heart is troubled," Jesus went on. "What am I going to say? 'Father, save me from this moment'? No! It was because of this that I came to this moment. ²⁸Father, glorify your name!"

The Hour Has Come

"I have glorified it," came a voice from heaven, "and I will glorify it again."

²⁹"That was thunder!" said the crowd, standing there listening.

"No," said others. "It was an angel, talking to him."

³⁰"That voice came for your sake, not mine," replied Jesus. ³¹"Now comes the judgment of this world! Now this world's ruler is going to be thrown out! ³²And when I've been lifted up from the earth, I will draw all people to myself."

³³He said this in order to point to the kind of death he was going to die.

³⁴So the crowd spoke to him again.

"We heard in the law," they said, "that the Messiah will last forever. How can you say that the son of man must be lifted up? Who is this 'son of man'?"

³⁵"The light is among you a little while longer," replied Jesus. "Keep walking while you have the light, in case the darkness overcomes you. People who walk in the dark don't know where they're going. ³⁶While you have the light, believe in the light, so that you may be children of light."

With these words, Jesus went away and was hidden from them.

³⁷They didn't believe in him, even though he had done so many signs in front of their eyes. ³⁸This was so that the word of Isaiah the prophet might be fulfilled:

Glory and Blindness

Lord, who believed the story we told?
Your powerful arm—who saw it unveiled?

39That's why they couldn't believe. As Isaiah again put it,

40*He has caused their eyes to be blind,*
And caused their hearts to be hard;
So they wouldn't see with their eyes,
Or understand with their hearts,
Or turn, so that I could heal them.

41Isaiah said this because he saw his glory, and spoke about him.

42Even so, however, quite a few of the rulers did believe in him. But, because of the Pharisees, they didn't declare their faith, for fear of being put out of the synagogue. 43This was because they loved the praise of other people more than the praise of God.

The Final Challenge

44"Anyone who believes in me," shouted Jesus in a loud voice, "doesn't believe in me, but in the one who sent me! 45Anyone who sees me sees the one who sent me! 46I've come into the world as light, so that everyone who believes in me won't need to stay in the dark.

47"If anyone hears my words and doesn't keep them, I'm not going to judge them. That wasn't why I came. I came to save the world, not to judge it. 48Anyone who rejects me and doesn't hold on to my words has a judge. The word which I have spoken will judge them on the last day.

49"I haven't spoken on my own authority. The father who sent me gave me his own command about what I should say and speak. 50And I know that his command is the life of the coming age. What I speak, then, is what the father has told me to speak."

Washing the Disciples' Feet

13 It was before the Festival of Passover. Jesus knew that his time had come, the time for him to leave this world and go to the father. He had always loved his own people in the world; now he loved them right through to the end.

2It was suppertime. The devil had already put the idea of betraying him into the heart of Judas, son of Simon Iscariot.

³Jesus knew that the father had given everything into his hands, and that he had come from God and was going to God. ⁴So he got up from the supper-table, took off his clothes, and wrapped a towel around himself. ⁵Then he poured water into a bowl and began to wash the disciples' feet, and to wipe them with the towel he was wrapped in.

⁶He came to Simon Peter.

"Master," said Peter, "what's this? You, washing my feet?"

⁷"You don't understand yet what I'm doing," replied Jesus, "but you'll know afterward."

⁸"I'm not going to have you washing my feet!" said Peter. "Never!"

"If I don't wash you," replied Jesus, "you don't belong to me."

⁹"All right then, Master," said Simon Peter, "but not only my feet—wash my hands and my head as well!"

¹⁰"Someone who has washed," said Jesus to him, "doesn't need to wash again, except for their feet. They are clean all over. And you are clean—but not all of you."

¹¹Jesus knew, you see, who was going to betray him. That's why he said, "You are not all clean."

¹²So when he had washed their feet, he put on his clothes and sat down again.

"Do you know what I've done to you?" he asked. ¹³"You call me 'teacher,' and 'master,' and you're right. That's what I am. ¹⁴Well, then: if I, as your master and teacher, washed your feet just now, you should wash each other's feet. ¹⁵I've given you a pattern, so that you can do things in the same way that I did to you.

¹⁶"I'm telling you the solemn truth," he continued. "The slave isn't greater than the master. People who are sent are not greater than the person who sends them. ¹⁷If you know these things, God's blessing on you if you do them.

¹⁸"I'm not talking about all of you," he went on. "I know the ones I have chosen. What the Bible says has to come true: 'The person who ate my bread lifted up his heel against me.' ¹⁹I'm telling you this now, before it happens, so that when it does happen you may believe that I am who I am. ²⁰I'm telling you the solemn truth: anyone who welcomes someone I send,

**Like Master,
Like Servant**

welcomes me, and anyone who welcomes me, welcomes the one who sent me."

Judas Goes Out
21After saying this, Jesus was troubled in spirit. He told them why.

"I'm telling you the solemn truth," he said. "One of you will betray me."

22The disciples looked at each other in shock, wondering who he could be talking about. 23One of the disciples, the one Jesus specially loved, was reclining at table close beside him. 24Simon Peter motioned to him to ask who it was he was talking about. 25So, leaning back against Jesus's chest, he asked him, "Who is it, Master?"

26"It's the one I'm going to give this piece of bread to," said Jesus, "when I've dipped it in the dish."

So he dipped the piece of bread and gave it to Judas, son of Simon Iscariot. 27After the bread, the satan entered into him.

"Do it quickly, won't you?" said Jesus to him.

28None of the others at the table knew what he meant. 29Because Judas kept the common purse, some were thinking that he meant, "Buy what we need for the festival," or that he was to give something to the poor.

30So when Judas had taken the bread, he went out at once. It was night.

Love One Another
31When Judas had gone out, Jesus began to speak.

"Now the son of man is glorified!" he said. "Now God is glorified in him! 32And if God is glorified in him, God will glorify him in himself, and glorify him at once. 33Children, I'm with you only a little longer. You will look for me, and, as I said to the Judaeans that where I was going they couldn't come, so I'm saying the same to you now.

34"I'm giving you a new commandment, and it's this: love one another! Just as I have loved you, so you must love one another. 35This is how everybody will know that you are my disciples, if you have love for each other."

36Simon Peter spoke up.

"Master," he said, "where are you going?"

"Where I'm going," replied Jesus, "you can't follow me just now. You will follow later, though."

38"Will you really lay down your life for me?" smiled Jesus. "I'm telling you the solemn truth: by the time the cock crows you will have disowned me three times.

14 "Don't let your hearts be troubled," Jesus continued. "Trust God—and trust me, too! 2There is plenty of room to live in my father's house. If that wasn't the case, I'd have told you, wouldn't I? I'm going to get a place ready for you! 3And if I do go and get a place ready for you, I will come back and take you to be with me, so that you can be there, where I am. 4And as to where I'm going—you know the way!"

The Way, the Truth, the Life

5"Actually, Master," said Thomas to him, "we don't know where you're going, so how can we know the way?"

6"I am the way," replied Jesus, "and the truth and the life! Nobody comes to the father except through me. 7If you had known me, you would have known my father. From now on you do know him! You have seen him."

8"Just show us the father, then, Master," said Philip to Jesus, "and that'll be good enough for us!"

9"Have I been with you for such a long time, Philip," replied Jesus, "and still you don't know me? Anyone who has seen me has seen the father! How can you say, 'Show us the father'? 10Don't you believe that I am in the father, and the father is in me? The words I'm speaking to you, I'm not speaking on my own initiative. It's the father, who lives within me, who is doing his own works. 11You must trust me that I am in the father and the father is in me. If not, then trust because of all the things you've seen done.

12"I'm telling you the solemn truth," Jesus continued. "Anyone who trusts in me will also do the works that I'm doing. In fact, they will do greater works than these, because I'm going to the father! 13And whatever you ask in my name, I will do it, so that the father may be glorified in the son. 14If you ask anything in my name, I will do it.

Another Helper

15"If you love me," he went on, "you will keep my commands. 16And I will ask the father, and he will give you another helper, to be with you forever. 17This other helper is the spirit of truth.

The world can't receive him, because it doesn't see him or know him. But you know him, because he lives with you, and will be in you.

18"I'm not going to leave you bereft. I am coming to you. 19Not long from now, the world won't see me anymore; but you will see me. Because I live, you will live too. 20On that day you will know that I am in my father, and you in me, and I in you.

21"Anyone who has my commandments and keeps them—that's the person who loves me. Anyone who loves me will be loved by my father, and I will love them and show myself to them."

My Peace I Give to You

22Judas spoke up. (This was the other Judas, not Iscariot.)

"Master," he said, "how will it be that you will show yourself to us and not to the world?"

23"If anyone loves me," Jesus replied, "they will keep my word. My father will love them, and we will come to them and make our home with them. 24Anyone who doesn't love me won't keep my word. And the word which you hear isn't mine. It comes from the father, who sent me.

25"I've said all this to you while I'm here with you. 26But the helper, the holy spirit, the one the father will send in my name, he will teach you everything. He will bring back to your mind everything I've said to you.

27"I'm leaving you peace. I'm giving you my own peace. I don't give gifts in the way the world does. Don't let your hearts be troubled; don't be fearful. 28You heard that I said to you, 'I'm going away, and I'm coming back to you.' If you loved me, you would be happy that I'm going to the father—because the father is greater than me. 29And now I've told you before it happens, so that when it does happen, you may believe.

30"I haven't got much more to say to you. The ruler of the world is coming. He has nothing to do with me. 31But all this is happening so that the world may know that I love the father, and that I'm doing what the father has told me to do.

"Get up. Let's be going.

The True Vine

15 "I am the true vine," said Jesus, "and my father is the gardener. 2He cuts off every branch of mine that doesn't bear fruit; and he prunes every branch that

does bear fruit, so that it can bear more fruit. ³You are already clean. That's because of the word that I've spoken to you.

⁴"Remain in me, and I will remain in you! The branch can't bear fruit by itself, but only if it remains in the vine. In the same way, you can't bear fruit unless you remain in me. ⁵I am the vine; you are the branches. People who remain in me, and I in them, are the ones who bear plenty of fruit. Without me, you see, you can't do anything.

⁶"If people don't remain in me, they are thrown out, like a branch, and they wither. People collect the branches and put them on the fire, and they are burned. ⁷If you remain in me, and my words remain in you, ask for whatever you want and it will happen for you. ⁸My father is glorified in this: that you bear plenty of fruit, and so become my disciples.

⁹"As the father loved me," Jesus continued, "so I loved you. Remain in my love. ¹⁰If you keep my commands, you will remain in my love, just as I have kept my father's commands and remain in his love. ¹¹I've said these things to you so that my joy may be in you, and so that your joy may be full.

Obeying and Loving

¹²"This is my command: love one another, in the same way that I loved you. ¹³No one has a love greater than this, to lay down your life for your friends. ¹⁴You are my friends, if you do what I tell you. ¹⁵I'm not calling you 'servants' any longer; servants don't know what their master is doing. But I've called you 'friends,' because I've let you know everything I heard from my father.

¹⁶"You didn't choose me. I chose you, and I appointed you to go and bear fruit, fruit that will last. Then the father will give you whatever you ask in my name. ¹⁷This is my command to you: love one another.

¹⁸"If the world hates you," Jesus went on, "know that it hated me before it hated you. ¹⁹If you were from the world, the world would be fond of its own. But the world hates you for this reason: that you're not from the world. No: I chose you out of the world.

If the World Hates You

²⁰"Remember the word that I said to you: servants are not greater than their masters. If they persecuted me, they will persecute you too. If they kept my word, they will keep yours too. ²¹But they will do all these things to you because of my name, because they don't know the one who sent me.

²²"If I hadn't come and spoken to them, they wouldn't be guilty of sin. But now they have no excuse for their sin. ²³(Anyone who hates me, hates my father as well!) ²⁴If I hadn't done, there in the middle of them, the works which nobody else did, they wouldn't be guilty of sin. But now they have seen me, and my father—and they've hated us both! ²⁵All this has happened, however, so that the word written in their law might be fulfilled: 'They hated me for no reason.'

²⁶"When the helper comes—the one I shall send you from the father, the spirit of truth who comes from the father—he will give evidence about me. ²⁷And you will give evidence as well, because you have been with me from the start.

The Spirit and the World

16 "I've said these things to you," Jesus went on, "to stop you from being tripped up. ²They will put you out of the synagogues. In fact, the time is coming when anyone who kills you will suppose that they are in that way offering worship to God. ³They will do these things because they haven't known the father, or me. ⁴But I have been talking to you about these things so that, when their time comes, you will remember that I told you about them.

"I didn't say these things to you from the start, because I was with you. ⁵But now I'm going to the one who sent me. None of you asks me, 'Where are you going?' ⁶But because I've said these things to you, sorrow has filled your heart. ⁷However, it's the truth that I'm telling you: it's better for you that I should go away. If I don't go away, you see, the helper won't come to you. But if I go away, I will send him to you.

⁸"When he comes, he will prove the world to be in the wrong on three counts: sin, justice, and judgment. ⁹In relation to sin—because they don't believe in me. ¹⁰In relation to justice—because I'm going to the father, and you won't see me anymore. ¹¹In relation to judgment—because the ruler of this world is judged.

Your Hearts Will Rejoice

¹²"There are many things I still have to say to you," Jesus continued, "but you're not yet strong enough to take them. ¹³When the spirit of truth comes, though, he will guide you in all the truth. He won't speak on his own account, you see, but he will speak whatever he hears. He will announce to you

what's to come. [14]He will glorify me, because he will take what belongs to me and will announce it to you. [15]Everything that the father has is mine. That's why I said that he would take what is mine and announce it to you.

[16]"Not long from now, you won't see me anymore. Then again, not long after that, you will see me!"

[17]"What's he talking about?" some of his disciples asked each other. "What's this business about 'not long from now, you won't see me, and again not long after that you will see me'? And what's this about 'going to the father'?"

[18]They kept on saying it.

"What is this 'not long'?"

"What's it all about?"

"We don't know what he means!"

[19]Jesus knew that they wanted to ask him.

"You're discussing with each other what I meant, aren't you?" he said. "You want to know what I meant by saying, 'Not long from now, you won't see me; and then again, not long after that, you will see me.' That's it, isn't it? [20]Well, I'm going to tell you the solemn truth.

"You will weep and wail, but the world will celebrate. You will be overcome with sorrow, but your sorrow will turn into joy. [21]When a woman is giving birth she is in anguish, because her moment has come. But when the child is born, she no longer remembers the suffering, because of the joy that a human being has been born into the world. [22]In the same way, you have sorrow now. But I shall see you again, and your hearts will celebrate, and nobody will take your joy away from you.

[23]"On that day," Jesus went on, "you won't ask me for anything. I'm telling you the solemn truth: whatever you ask the father in my name, he will give you. [24]Up to now, you haven't asked for anything in my name. Ask, and you will receive, so that your joy may be full!

[25]"I've been saying all this to you in picture-language. The time is coming when I won't speak in pictures anymore. Instead, I'll tell you about the father quite plainly. [26]On that day you will ask in my name. I won't say I will ask the father on your behalf, [27]because the father himself loves you!

Ask, and You Will Receive

That's because you have loved me, and have believed that I came from God. 28I came from the father, and I've come into the world. Now I'm leaving the world and going back to the father."

29"Ah!" said his disciples. "Now you're speaking plainly! You're not talking in pictures. 30Now we know that you know all things, and you don't need to have anybody ask you anything. This makes us trust that you came from God."

31"So you do now believe, do you?" replied Jesus. 32"Look here: the time is coming (in fact, it's now arrived!) when you will be scattered, each of you to his own place. You will leave me alone—though I'm not alone, because the father is with me. 33I've said these things to you so that you can have peace in me. You'll have trouble in the world. But cheer up! I have defeated the world!"

Glorify the Son

17 After Jesus had said this, he lifted up his eyes to heaven.

"Father," he said, "the moment has come. Glorify your son, so that your son may glorify you. 2Do this in the same way as you did when you gave him authority over all flesh, so that he could give the life of God's coming age to everyone you gave him. 3And by 'the life of God's coming age' I mean this: that they should know you, the only true God, and Jesus the Messiah, the one you sent.

4"I glorified you on earth, by completing the work you gave me to do. 5So now, Father, glorify me, alongside yourself, with the glory which I had with you before the world existed.

6"I revealed your name to the people you gave me out of the world. They belonged to you; you gave them to me; and they have kept your word. 7Now they know that everything which you gave me comes from you. 8I have given them the words you gave me, and they have received them. They have come to know, in truth, that I came from you. They have believed that you sent me.

Jesus Prays for His People

9"I'm praying for them. I'm not praying for the world, but for the people you've given me. They belong to you. 10All mine are yours; all yours are mine; and I'm glorified in them.

11"I'm not in the world any longer, but they're still in the world; I'm coming to you. Holy Father, keep them in your name, the name you've given to me, so that they may be one, just as we are one.

12"When I was with them, I kept them in your name, the name you've given me. I guarded them, and none of them has been destroyed (except the son of destruction; that's what the Bible said would happen). 13But now I'm coming to you. I'm speaking these things in the world, so that they can have my joy fulfilled in them.

14"I have given them your word. The world hated them, because they are not from the world, just as I am not from the world. 15I'm not asking that you should take them out of the world, but that you should keep them from the evil one. 16They didn't come from the world, just as I didn't come from the world. 17Set them apart for yourself in the truth; your word is truth. 18Just as you sent me into the world, so I sent them into the world. 19And on their account I set myself apart for you, so that they, too, may be set apart for you in the truth.

20"I'm not praying simply for them. I'm praying, too, for the people who will come to believe in me because of their word. 21I am praying that they may all be one—just as you, Father, are in me, and I in you, that they too may be in us, so that the world may believe that you sent me.

That They May Be One

22"I have given them the glory which you have given to me, so that they may be one, just as we are one. 23I in them, and you in me; yes, they must be completely one, so that the world may know that you sent me, and that you loved them just as you loved me.

24"Father, I want the ones you've given me to be with me where I am. I want them to see my glory, the glory which you've given me, because you loved me before the foundation of the world.

25"Righteous Father, even the world didn't know you. But I have known you, and these ones have known that you sent me. 26I made your name known to them—yes, and I will make it known; so that the love with which you loved me may be in them, and I in them."

18 With these words, Jesus went out with his disciples across the Kidron Valley to a place where there was a garden. He and his disciples went in.

The Arrest of Jesus

²Judas, his betrayer, knew the place, because Jesus often used it as a meeting place with his disciples. ³So Judas took a band of soldiers, with some servants of the chief priests and the Pharisees, and went there with torches, lights, and weapons.

⁴Jesus knew everything that was going to happen to him. He went out to meet them.

"Who are you looking for?" he asked.

⁵"Jesus of Nazareth," they answered.

"I'm the one," he said to them.

Judas, his betrayer, was standing there with them. ⁶So when he said, "I'm the one," they went back a few paces, and fell down on the ground.

⁷Jesus repeated his question.

"Who are you looking for?" he asked.

"Jesus of Nazareth," they said.

⁸"I told you, I'm the one!" said Jesus. "So, if you're looking for me, let these people go." ⁹(He said this so as to fulfill the word he had spoken, when he said, "I haven't lost any of the people you gave me.")

¹⁰Simon Peter had a sword. He drew it and hit the high priest's servant, cutting off his right ear. The servant's name was Malchus.

¹¹"Put your sword back in its sheath!" said Jesus to Peter. "Do you imagine I'm not going to drink the cup my father has given me?"

¹²So the band of soldiers, with the officer and the Judaean attendants, arrested Jesus and tied him up. ¹³They led him off first to Annas; he was the father-in-law of Caiaphas, who was high priest that year. ¹⁴It was Caiaphas who had given advice to the Judaeans that the best thing would be for one man to die for the people.

Peter Denies Jesus

¹⁵Simon Peter and another disciple followed Jesus. That other disciple was known to the high priest; he went in to the high priest's courtyard along with Jesus, ¹⁶while Peter stood outside by the gate. So the other disciple, being known to the high priest, went out and spoke to the woman at the gate. Then he brought Peter inside.

¹⁷The woman at the gate spoke to Peter.

"You're not one of that man's disciples too, are you?" she asked.

"No, I'm not," he replied.

18It was cold. The slaves and the attendants had made a charcoal fire, and they were standing around it, warming themselves. Peter was standing there with them and warming himself.

19The high priest asked Jesus about his disciples, and about his teaching.

20"I've spoken to the world quite openly," replied Jesus. "I always taught in the synagogue and in the Temple, where all the Judaeans gather. I didn't say anything in secret. 21Why are you asking me? There were people who listened to me. Ask them what I said to them. Don't you see? They know what I said."

22When Jesus said that, one of the attendants standing there gave him a slap on the face.

"Is that how you answer the high priest?" he said.

23"If I've said something wrong," replied Jesus, "give evidence about what was wrong with it. But if what I said was true, why are you hitting me?"

24So Annas sent him off, still tied up, to Caiaphas the high priest.

25Simon Peter, meanwhile, was standing there and warming himself.

"You're not one of his disciples, are you?" they asked him.

He denied it. "No, I'm not," he said.

26Then one of the high priest's slaves, a relative of the man whose ear Peter had cut off, spoke up.

"Didn't I see you in the garden with him?" he said.

27Peter denied it once more. Instantly, the cock crowed.

28So they took Jesus from Caiaphas to the Praetorium, the governor's residence. It was early in the morning. They didn't themselves go inside the Praetorium. They were anxious not to pollute themselves, so that they would still be able to eat the Passover.

Pilate and the Judaeans

29So Pilate went outside and spoke to them.

"What's the charge, then?" he asked. "What have you got against this fellow?"

30"If he wasn't doing wicked things," they replied, "we wouldn't have handed him over to you."

31"Take him yourselves," said Pilate to them, "and judge him by your own law."

"We're not allowed to put anyone to death," replied the Judaeans. 32(This was so that the word of Jesus might come true, when he had indicated what sort of death he was going to die.)

My Kingdom Is Not from This World

33So Pilate went back into the Praetorium and spoke to Jesus.

"Are you the king of the Jews?" he asked.

34"Was it *your* idea to ask that?" asked Jesus. "Or did other people tell you about me?"

35"I'm not a Jew, am I?" retorted Pilate. "Your own people, and the chief priests, have handed you over to me! What have you done?"

36"My kingdom isn't the sort that grows in this world," replied Jesus. "If my kingdom were from this world, my supporters would have fought to stop me being handed over to the Judaeans. So, then, my kingdom is not the sort that comes from here."

37"So!" said Pilate. "You *are* a king, are you?"

"You're the one who's calling me a king," replied Jesus. "I was born for this; I've come into the world for this: to give evidence about the truth. Everyone who belongs to the truth listens to my voice."

38"Truth!" said Pilate. "What's that?"

With those words, he went back out to the Judaeans.

"I find this man not guilty!" he said to them. 39"But look here: you've got this custom that I should let someone free at Passover-time. So what about it? Would you like me to release 'the king of the Jews'?"

40"No!" they shouted. "We don't want him! Give us Barabbas!"

Now Barabbas was a brigand.

Here's the Man!

19 So Pilate then took Jesus and had him flogged. 2The soldiers wove a crown of thorns, put it on his head, and dressed him up in a purple robe. 3Then they came up to him and said, "Hail, king of the Jews!" And they slapped him.

4Pilate went out again.

"Look," he said to them, "I'm bringing him out to you, so that you'll know I find no guilt in him."

5So Jesus came out, wearing the crown of thorns and the purple cloak.

"Look!" said Pilate. "Here's the man!"

6So when the chief priests and their attendants saw him, they gave a great shout.

"Crucify him!" they yelled. "Crucify him!"

"Take him yourselves and crucify him!" said Pilate. "I find him not guilty!"

7"We've got a law," replied the Judaeans, "and according to that law he deserves to die! He made himself the son of God!"

8When Pilate heard that, he was all the more afraid. 9He went back into the Praetorium and spoke to Jesus.

No King but Caesar

"Where do you come from?" he asked.

But Jesus gave him no answer.

10So Pilate addressed him again.

"Aren't you going to speak to me?" he said. "Don't you know that I have the authority to let you go, and the authority to crucify you?"

11"You couldn't have any authority at all over me," replied Jesus, "unless it was given to you from above. That's why the person who handed me over to you is guilty of a greater sin."

12From that moment on, Pilate tried to let him go.

But the Judaeans shouted at him.

"If you let this fellow go," they said, "you are no friend of Caesar! Everyone who sets himself up as a king is speaking against Caesar!"

13So when Pilate heard them saying that, he brought Jesus out and sat down at the official judgment seat, called "the Pavement" (in Hebrew, "Gabbatha"). 14It was the Preparation day of the Passover, and it was about midday.

"Look," said Pilate, "here is your king!"

15"Take him away!" they shouted. "Take him away! Crucify him!"

"Do you want me to crucify your king?" asked Pilate.

"We have no king," the chief priests replied, "except Caesar!"

16Then he handed him over to them to be crucified.

The King
of the Jews

So they took Jesus away. [17]He carried his own cross, and went to the spot called "Skull Place" (in Hebrew, "Golgotha"). [18]That was where they crucified him. They also crucified two others, one on either side of him, with Jesus in the middle.

[19]Pilate wrote a notice and had it placed on the cross:

JESUS OF NAZARETH
THE KING OF THE JEWS

[20]Lots of the Judaeans read this notice, because the place where Jesus was crucified was close to the city. It was written in Hebrew, Latin, and Greek.

[21]So the chief priests said to Pilate, "Don't write 'The king of the Jews'! Write that he *said,* 'I am the king of the Jews'!"

[22]"What I've written," replied Pilate, "I've written."

[23]When the soldiers had crucified Jesus, they took his clothes and divided them into four parts, giving each soldier one part. When they came to his tunic, they found that it was a single piece of cloth, woven from top to bottom.

[24]"Let's not tear it," they said to each other. "Let's throw lots for it, to see who's going to have it."

This was so that the Bible would be fulfilled, when it says,

They took my clothes and divided them up,
They threw the dice to decide on my garments.

And that's what the soldiers did.

The Death
of Jesus

[25]Jesus's mother was standing beside his cross. So was her sister, Mary the wife of Clopas, with Mary Magdalene too. [26]Jesus saw his mother, and the disciple he specially loved, standing there.

"Mother," he said. "Look! there's your son."

[27]Then he spoke to the disciple.

"Look!" he said. "There's your mother."

From that time, the disciple welcomed her into his own home.

[28]After this, Jesus knew that everything had at last been completed.

"I'm thirsty," he said (fulfilling what the Bible had said).

[29]There was a jar there full of sour wine. So they put a sponge filled with the sour wine on a hyssop rod and lifted it to his mouth. [30]Jesus drank it.

"It's all done!" he said.

Then he let his head drop, and gave up his spirit.

³¹It was the day of Preparation. The coming sabbath was a very special one, and the Judaeans were anxious that the bodies should not remain on the cross during the sabbath. So they asked Pilate to have the legs of the crucified men broken, and their bodies taken away.

Blood and Water

³²So the soldiers came and broke the legs of the men who were crucified with Jesus, first the one, then the other. ³³But when they came to Jesus, they saw that he was already dead, so they didn't break his legs. ³⁴Instead, one of the soldiers thrust a spear into his side, and blood and water came out. ³⁵(The one who saw it is giving evidence, and his evidence is true. He knows he's speaking the truth, so that you too may believe.) ³⁶These things, you see, came about so that the Bible might come true: "No bone of his will be broken." ³⁷And again, another passage in the Bible says, "They shall look on the one whom they pierced."

³⁸After this, Joseph of Arimathea asked Pilate if he could take Jesus's body away. He was a disciple of Jesus, but he kept it secret because he was afraid of the Judaeans. Pilate gave him permission. So he came and took his body. ³⁹Nicodemus came too (the man who, at first, had visited Jesus by night). He brought a concoction of myrrh and aloes, about a hundred pounds in weight. ⁴⁰They took Jesus's body, and wrapped it up in cloths with the spices, according to the normal Judaean burial custom.

The Burial of Jesus

⁴¹There was a garden in the place where he was crucified. In the garden, there was a new tomb in which nobody had ever been buried. ⁴²So, because the tomb was nearby, and because of the Judaean day of Preparation, they buried Jesus there.

20 On the first day of the week, very early, Mary Magdalene came to the tomb while it was still dark. She saw that the stone had been rolled away from the tomb. ²So she ran off, and went to Simon Peter, and to the other disciple, the one Jesus loved.

The Empty Tomb

"They've taken the master out of the tomb!" she said. "We don't know where they've put him!"

³So Peter and the other disciple set off and went to the tomb. ⁴Both of them ran together. The other disciple ran faster than

Peter, and got to the tomb first. 5He stooped down and saw the linen cloths lying there, but he didn't go in. 6Then Simon Peter came up, following him, and went into the tomb. He saw the linen cloths lying there, 7and the napkin that had been around his head, not lying with the other cloths, but folded up in a place by itself.

8Then the other disciple, who had arrived first at the tomb, went into the tomb as well. He saw, and he believed. 9They did not yet know, you see, that the Bible had said he must rise again from the dead.

10Then the disciples returned to their homes.

Mary Magdalene and the Risen Jesus

11But Mary stood outside the tomb, crying. As she wept, she stooped down to look into the tomb. 12There she saw two angels, clothed in white, one at the head and one at the feet of where Jesus's body had been lying.

13"Woman," they said to her, "why are you crying?"

"They've taken away my master," she said, "and I don't know where they've put him!"

14As she said this she turned around and saw Jesus standing there. She didn't know it was Jesus.

15"Woman," Jesus said to her, "why are you crying? Who are you looking for?"

She guessed he must be the gardener.

"Sir," she said, "if you've carried him off somewhere, tell me where you've put him, and I will take him away."

16"Mary!" said Jesus.

She turned and spoke in Aramaic.

"Rabbouni!" she said (which means "Teacher").

17"Don't cling to me," said Jesus. "I haven't yet gone up to the father. But go to my brothers and say to them, 'I'm going up to my father and your father—to my God and your God.'"

18Mary Magdalene went and told the disciples, "I've seen the master!" and that he had said these things to her.

Jesus and the Disciples

19On the evening of that day, the first day of the week, the doors were shut where the disciples were, for fear of the Judaeans. Jesus came and stood in the middle of them.

"Peace be with you," he said.

20With these words, he showed them his hands and his side. Then the disciples were overjoyed when they saw the master.

21"Peace be with you," Jesus said to them again. "As the father has sent me, so I'm sending you."

22With that, he breathed on them.

"Receive the holy spirit," he said. 23"If you forgive anyone's sins, they are forgiven. If you retain anyone's sins, they are retained."

24One of the Twelve, Thomas (also known as Didymus), wasn't with them when Jesus came. 25So the other disciples spoke to him.

Jesus and Thomas

"We've seen the master!" they said.

"Unless I see the mark of the nails in his hands," replied Thomas, "and put my finger into the nail-marks, and put my hand into his side—I'm not going to believe!"

26A week later the disciples were again in the house, and Thomas was with them. The doors were shut. Jesus came and stood in the middle of them.

"Peace be with you!" he said.

27Then he addressed Thomas.

"Bring your finger here," he said, "and inspect my hands. Bring your hand here and put it into my side. Don't be faithless! Just believe!"

28"My Lord," replied Thomas, "and my God!"

29"Is it because you've seen me that you believe?" replied Jesus. "God's blessing on people who don't see, and yet believe!"

30Jesus did many other signs in the presence of his disciples, which aren't written in this book. 31But these are written so that you may believe that the Messiah, the son of God, is none other than Jesus; and that, with this faith, you may have life in his name.

21 After this, Jesus showed himself again to the disciples by the sea of Tiberias. This was how he showed himself.

Jesus on the Beach

2Simon Peter, Thomas (known as Didymus), Nathanael from Cana in Galilee, the sons of Zebedee, and two other disciples were all together.

3Simon Peter spoke up.

"I'm going fishing," he said.

"We'll go with you," they replied.

So they went off and got into the boat; but that night they caught nothing.

⁴As dawn was breaking, Jesus stood beside the seashore, but the disciples didn't know that it was Jesus.

⁵"Children," said Jesus to them, "haven't you got anything to eat?"

"No!" they replied.

⁶"Cast the net on the right side of the boat," he said, "and you'll find something."

So they cast the net; and now they couldn't draw it in because of the weight of the fish.

⁷So the disciple that Jesus loved spoke to Peter.

"It's the master!" he said.

When Simon Peter heard that it was the master, he wrapped his cloak around him (he had been naked for work), and threw himself into the sea. ⁸The other disciples brought the boat in to land, dragging the net full of fish. They weren't far from shore, about a hundred yards away.

Breakfast by the Shore

⁹When they came to land, they saw a charcoal fire laid there, with fish and bread on it.

¹⁰Jesus spoke to them.

"Bring some of the fish you've just caught," he said.

¹¹So Simon Peter went and pulled the net onto the shore. It was full of large fish, a hundred and fifty-three in all. The net wasn't torn, even though there were so many.

¹²"Come and have breakfast," said Jesus to them.

None of the disciples dared ask him, "Who are you?" They knew it was the master.

¹³Jesus came and took the bread and gave it to them, and so also with the fish. ¹⁴This was now the third time that Jesus had appeared to the disciples after he had been raised from the dead.

Jesus and Peter

¹⁵So when they had eaten breakfast, Jesus spoke to Simon Peter.

"Simon, son of John," he said, "do you love me more than these?"

"Yes, Master," he said. "You know I'm your friend."

"Well, then," he said, "feed my lambs."

¹⁶"Simon, son of John," said Jesus again, for a second time, "do you love me?"

"Yes, Master," he said. "You know I'm your friend."

"Well, then," he said, "look after my sheep."

¹⁷"Simon, son of John," said Jesus a third time, "are you my friend?"

Peter was upset that on this third time Jesus asked, "Are you my friend?"

"Master," he said, "you know everything! You know I'm your friend!"

"Well, then," said Jesus, "feed my sheep."

¹⁸"I'm telling you the solemn truth," he went on. "When you were young, you put on your own clothes and went about wherever you wanted. But when you are old, you'll stretch out your hands, and someone else will dress you up and take you where you don't want to go."

¹⁹He said this to indicate the sort of death by which Peter would bring God glory. And when he had said this, he added, "Follow me!"

²⁰Peter turned and saw, following them, the disciple that Jesus loved. This was the disciple who had leaned back against Jesus's chest at the supper, and had asked, "Master, who is it that's going to betray you?"

The Beloved Disciple

²¹"Master," said Peter to Jesus, seeing him there, "what about him?"

²²"If it's my intention," replied Jesus, "that he should remain here until I come, what's that got to do with you? You must follow me!"

²³So the rumor went around the Christian family that this disciple wouldn't die. But Jesus didn't say he wouldn't die. What he said, rather, was this: "If it's my intention that he should remain here until I come, what's that got to do with you?"

²⁴(This is the disciple who is giving evidence about these things, and who wrote them down. We know that his evidence is true.)

²⁵There are many other things which Jesus did. If they were written down one by one, I don't think the world itself would be able to contain the books that would be written.

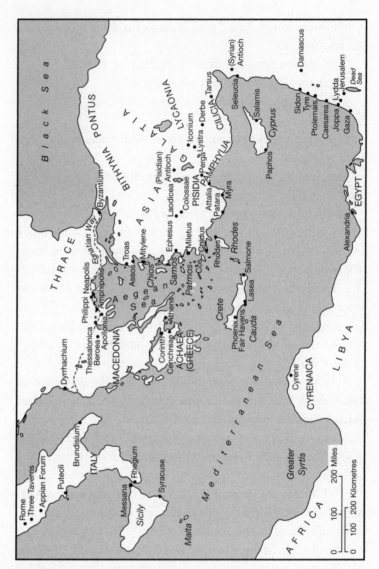

The Eastern Mediterranean in the First Century AD

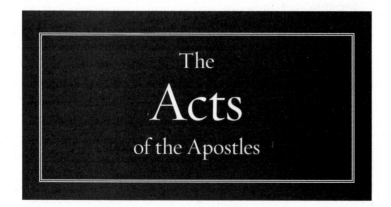

The
Acts
of the Apostles

1 Dear Theophilus,

The previous book which I wrote had to do with everything Jesus began to do and teach. [2]I took the story as far as the day when he was taken up, once he had given instructions through the holy spirit to his chosen apostles.

Here Comes the Sequel!

[3]He showed himself to them alive, after his suffering, by many proofs. He was seen by them for forty days, during which he spoke about God's kingdom. [4]As they were having a meal together, he told them not to go away from Jerusalem, but to wait, as he put it, "for the father's promise, which I was telling you about earlier. [5]John baptized with water, you see; but in a few days from now you will be baptized with the holy spirit."

[6]So when the apostles came together, they put this question to Jesus.

When, What, and How?

"Master," they said, "is this the time when you are going to restore the kingdom to Israel?"

[7]"It's not your business to know about times and dates," he replied. "The father has placed all that under his own direct authority. [8]What will happen, though, is that you will receive power when the holy spirit comes upon you. Then you will be my witnesses in Jerusalem, in all Judaea and Samaria, and to the very ends of the earth."

[9]As Jesus said this, he was lifted up while they were watching, and a cloud took him out of their sight. [10]They were gazing into heaven as he disappeared. Then, lo and behold, two men appeared, dressed in white, standing beside them.

Ascension!

[11]"Galileans," they said, "why are you standing here staring into heaven? This Jesus, who has been taken from you into heaven, will come back in the same way you saw him go into heaven."

[12]Then they went back to Jerusalem from the hill called the Mount of Olives, which is close to Jerusalem, about the distance you could travel on a sabbath. [13]They then entered the city ("they" here means Peter, John, James, Andrew, Philip, Thomas, Bartholomew, Matthew, James the son of Alphaeus, Simon the zealot, and Judas the son of James) and went to the upstairs room where they were staying. [14]They all gave themselves single-heartedly to prayer, with the women, including Mary, Jesus's mother, and his brothers.

Restoring the Twelve

[15]Around that time Peter stood up in the middle of the gathering, which by this stage numbered about a hundred and twenty.

[16]"My dear family," he said, "the holy spirit spoke long ago, through the mouth of David, about Judas, who became a guide to the people who arrested Jesus. There it is in the Bible, and it

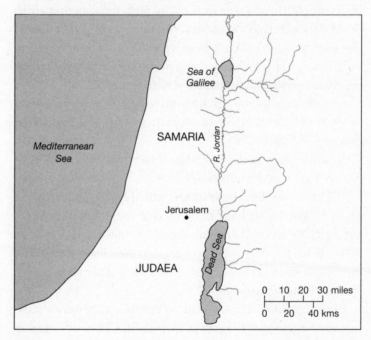

Acts 1:6–8

had to come true. ¹⁷He was counted along with us, and he had
his own share in the work we've been given."

¹⁸(Judas, you see, had bought a field with the money his
wickedness had brought him, where he fell headlong and
burst open, with all his innards gushing out. ¹⁹This became
known to everyone who lived in Jerusalem, so that the field
was called, in their local language, Akeldamach, which means
"Blood-Place.")

²⁰"For this is what it says in the book of the Psalms:

> 'Let his home become desolate
> And let nobody live in it.'

and again

> 'Let someone else receive his overseeing task.'

²¹"So this is what has to be done. There are plenty of people
who have gone about with us all the time that our master
Jesus was coming and going among us, ²²starting from John's
baptism until the day he was taken from us. Let one of them
be chosen to be alongside us as a special witness of his resurrection."

²³So they chose two: Joseph who was called Barsabbas,
with the surname Justus, and Matthias.

²⁴"Lord," they prayed, "you know the hearts of all people.
Show us which one of these two you have chosen ²⁵to receive
this particular place of service and apostleship, from which
Judas went away to go to his own place."

²⁶So they cast lots for them. The lot fell on Matthias, and he
was enrolled along with the eleven apostles.

2 When the day of Pentecost had finally arrived, they
were all together in the same place. ²Suddenly there
came from heaven a noise like the sound of a strong,
blowing wind, and it filled the whole house where they were
sitting. ³Then tongues, seemingly made of fire, appeared to
them, moving apart and coming to rest on each one of them.
⁴They were all filled with the holy spirit, and began to speak in
other languages, as the spirit gave them the words to say.

**Here Comes
the Power**

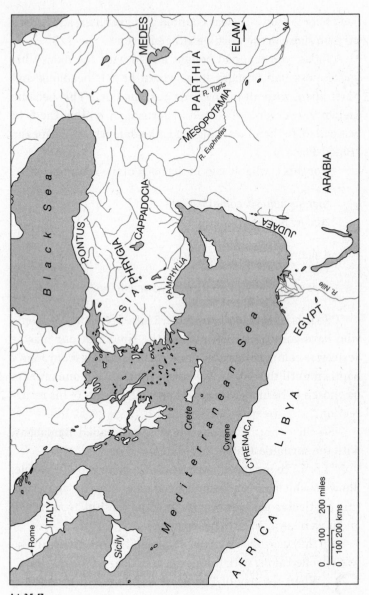

Acts 2:5–13

⁵There were devout Jews from every nation under heaven staying in Jerusalem at that time. ⁶When they heard this noise they came together in a crowd. They were deeply puzzled, because every single one of them could hear them speaking in his or her own native language. ⁷They were astonished and amazed.

"These men who are doing the speaking are all Galileans, aren't they?" they said. ⁸"So how is it that each of us can hear them in our own mother tongues? ⁹There are Parthians here, and Medians, Elamites, people from Mesopotamia, Judaea, Cappadocia, Pontus, Asia, ¹⁰Phrygia and Pamphylia, Egypt, and the parts of Libya that belong to Cyrene; there are people from Rome, ¹¹proselytes as well as Jews; there are Cretans and Arabs. We can hear them telling us about the powerful things God has done—*in our own languages*!"

¹²Everyone was astonished and perplexed.

"What does it all mean?" they were asking each other.

¹³But some sneered.

"They're full of new wine!" they said.

¹⁴Then Peter got up, with the eleven. He spoke to them in a loud voice.

"People of Judaea!" he began. "All of you staying here in Jerusalem! There's something you have to know! Listen to what I'm saying! ¹⁵These people aren't drunk, as you imagine. It's only nine o'clock in the morning! ¹⁶No, this is what the prophet Joel was talking about, when he said,

> ¹⁷*'In the last days, declares God, I will pour out my spirit*
> *   on all people.*
> *Your sons and your daughters will prophesy;*
> *Your young men will see visions, your old men will dream*
> *   dreams;*
> ¹⁸*Yes, even on slaves, men and women alike, will I pour out*
> *   my spirit in those days, and they shall prophesy.*
> ¹⁹*And I will give signs in the heavens above, and portents*
> *   on earth beneath, blood and fire and clouds of smoke.*
> ²⁰*The sun will be turned into darkness, and the moon into*
> *   blood, before the day of the Lord comes, the great and*
> *   glorious day.*

²¹*And then everyone who calls on the name of the Lord will be saved.'*

²²"You people of Israel," Peter continued, "listen to this. Jesus of Nazareth was a man marked out for you by God through the mighty works, signs, and portents which God performed through him right here among you, as you all know. ²³He was handed over in accordance with God's determined purpose and foreknowledge—and you used people outside the law to nail him up and kill him.

²⁴"But God raised him from the dead! Death had its painful grip on him; but God released him from it, because it wasn't possible for him to be mastered by it. ²⁵This, you see, is how David speaks of him:

> *'I set the Lord before me always;*
> *Because he is at my right hand, I won't be shaken.*
> ²⁶*So my heart was happy, and my tongue rejoiced,*
> *And my flesh, too, will rest in hope.*
> ²⁷*For you will not leave my soul in Hades,*
> *Nor will you allow your Holy One to see corruption.*
> ²⁸*You showed me the path of life;*
> *You filled me with gladness in your presence.'*

²⁹"My dear family, I can surely speak freely to you about the patriarch David. He died and was buried, and his tomb is here with us to this day. ³⁰He was of course a prophet, and he knew that God had sworn an oath to him to set one of his own physical offspring on his throne. ³¹He foresaw the Messiah's resurrection, and spoke about him "not being left in Hades," and about his flesh "not seeing corruption." ³²This is the Jesus we're talking about! God raised him from the dead, and all of us here are witnesses to the fact! ³³Now he's been exalted to God's right hand; and what you see and hear is the result of the fact that he is pouring out the holy spirit, which had been promised, and which he has received from the father.

³⁴"David, after all, did not ascend into the heavens. This is what he says:

> *'The Lord said to my Lord,*
> *Sit at my right hand,*

35*Until I place your enemies*
Underneath your feet.'

36"So the whole house of Israel must know this for a fact: God has made him Lord and Messiah—this Jesus, the one you crucified."

37When they heard this, the people in the crowd were cut to the heart.

God's Rescue Plan

"Brothers," they said to Peter and the other apostles, "what shall we do?"

38"Turn back!" replied Peter. "Be baptized—every single one of you—in the name of Jesus the Messiah, so that your sins can be forgiven and you will receive the gift of the holy spirit. 39The promise is for you and for your children, and for everyone who is far away, as many as the Lord our God will call."

40He carried on explaining things to them with many other words.

"Let God rescue you," he was urging them, "from this wicked generation!"

41Those who welcomed his word were baptized. About three thousand people were added to the community that day.

42They all gave full attention to the teaching of the apostles and to the common life, to the breaking of bread and the prayers. 43Great awe fell on everyone, and many remarkable deeds and signs were performed by the apostles.

The New Family

44All of those who believed came together, and held everything in common. 45They sold their possessions and belongings and divided them up to everyone in proportion to their various needs. 46Day by day they were all together attending the Temple. They broke bread in their various houses, and ate their food with glad and sincere hearts, 47praising God and standing in favor with all the people. And every day the Lord added to their number those who were being rescued.

3 One day, Peter and John were going up to the Temple at three o'clock in the afternoon, the time for prayer. 2There was a man being carried in who had been lame since birth. People used to bring him every day to the Temple gate called "Beautiful," so that he could ask for alms from folk on their way in to the Temple. 3When he saw Peter and John

More Than He Bargained For

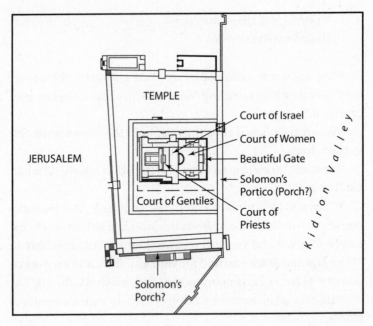

Acts 3:1–16

going in to the Temple, he asked them to give him some money. ⁴Peter, with John, looked hard at him.

"Look at us," he said.

⁵The man stared at them, expecting to get something from them.

⁶"I haven't got any silver or gold," Peter said, "but I'll give you what I have got. In the name of the Messiah, Jesus of Nazareth, get up and walk!"

⁷He grabbed the man by his right hand and lifted him up. At once his feet and ankles became strong, ⁸and he leaped to his feet and began to walk. He went in with them into the Temple, walking and jumping up and down and praising God. ⁹All the people saw him walking and praising God, ¹⁰and they recognized him as the man who had been sitting begging for alms by the Beautiful Gate of the Temple. They were filled with amazement and astonishment at what had happened to him.

An Explanation Is Called For ¹¹All the people ran together in astonishment toward Peter and John, and the man who was clinging to them. They were in the part of the Temple known as "Solomon's Porch." [12]Peter saw them all and began to speak.

"Fellow Israelites," he said, "why are you amazed at this? Why are you staring at us as though it was our own power or piety that made this man walk? [13]'The God of Abraham, the God of Isaac, the God of Jacob—the God of our ancestors'—he has glorified his child Jesus, the one you handed over and denied in the presence of Pilate, although he had decided to let him go. [14]But you denied the Holy One, the Just One, and requested instead to have a murderer given to you; [15]and so you killed the Prince of Life. But God raised him from the dead, and we are witnesses to the fact. [16]And it is his name, working through faith in his name, that has given strength to this man, whom you see and know. It is faith which comes through him that has given him this new complete wholeness in front of all of you.

[17]"Now, my dear family," Peter continued, "I know that you acted in ignorance, just as your rulers did. [18]But this is how God has fulfilled what he promised through the mouth of all the prophets, that his Messiah would suffer. [19]So now repent, and turn back, so that your sins may be blotted out, [20]so that times of refreshment may come from the presence of the Lord, and so that he will send you Jesus, the one he chose and appointed to be his Messiah. [21]He must be received in heaven, you see, until the time which God spoke about through the mouth of his holy prophets from ancient days, the time when God will restore all things. [22]Moses said, 'The Lord your God will raise up for you a prophet like me, one from among your own brothers; whatever he says to you, you must pay attention to him. [23]And everyone who does not listen to that prophet will be cut off from the people.' [24]All the prophets who have spoken, from Samuel and his successors, spoke about these days too. [25]You are the children of the prophets, the children of the covenant which God established with your ancestors when he said to Abraham, 'In your seed shall all the families of the earth be blessed.' [26]When God raised up his servant he sent him to you first, to bless you by turning each of you away from your wicked deeds."

Restoration and Refreshment

**Resurrection
Plus the Name
of Jesus Equals
Trouble**

4 As they were speaking to the people, along came the priests, the chief of the Temple police, and the Sadducees. [2]They were thoroughly annoyed that they were teaching the people and proclaiming that "the resurrection of the dead" had begun to happen in Jesus. [3]They seized them and put them under guard until the next day, since it was already evening. [4]But a large number of the people who had heard the message believed it, and the number of men grew to five thousand.

[5]On the next day their rulers, the elders, and the scribes gathered in Jerusalem, [6]along with Annas the high priest, Caiaphas, John, Alexander, and all the members of the high-priestly family. [7]They stood them in the midst.

"How did you do this?" they asked them. "What power did you use? What name did you invoke?"

[8]Peter was filled with the holy spirit. "Rulers of the people and elders," he said, [9]"if the question we're being asked today is about a good deed done for a sick man, and whose power it was that rescued him, [10]let it be known to all of you, and to all the people of Israel, that this man stands before you fit and well because of the name of the Messiah, Jesus of Nazareth, whom you crucified, but whom God raised from the dead. [11]He is the stone which you builders rejected, but which has become the head cornerstone. [12]Rescue won't come from anybody else! There is no other name given under heaven and among humans by which we must be rescued."

**The Clash of
Loyalties**

[13]When they saw how boldly Peter and John were speaking, and realized that they were untrained, ordinary men, they were astonished, and they recognized them as people who had been with Jesus. [14]And when they saw the man who had been healed standing with them, they had nothing to say in reply. [15]They ordered them to be put out of the assembly while they conferred among themselves.

[16]"What can we do to these men?" they said. "This is a spectacular sign that has happened through them. All Jerusalem knows it, and we can't deny it! [17]But we certainly don't want it to spread any further among the people. So let's threaten them with awful consequences if they speak anymore in this name to anybody."

[18]So they called them in and gave them orders not to speak at all, or to teach, in the name of Jesus.

[19]But Peter and John gave them this reply.

"You judge," they said, "whether it's right before God to listen to you rather than to God! [20]As far as we're concerned, we can't stop speaking about what we have seen and heard."

[21]Then they threatened them some more, and let them go. They couldn't find any way to punish them because of the people, since everyone was glorifying God for what had happened. [22]After all, the man to whom this sign of healing had happened was over forty years old.

[23]When they had been released, they went back to their own people, and told them everything that the chief priests and the elders had said. [24]When they heard it, they all together lifted up their voices to God.

Look upon Their Threats

"Sovereign Master," they said, "you made heaven and earth, and the sea, and everything in them. [25]And you said through the holy spirit, by the mouth of our ancestor David, your servant,

> 'Why did the nations fly into a rage,
> And why did the peoples think empty thoughts?
> [26]The kings of the earth arose
> And the rulers gathered themselves together
> Against the Lord and against his anointed Messiah.'

[27]"It's true: Herod and Pontius Pilate, together with the nations and the peoples of Israel, gathered themselves together in this very city against your holy child Jesus, the one you anointed, [28]to do whatever your hand and your plan had foreordained to take place. [29]So now, Master, look on their threats; and grant that we, your servants, may speak your word with all boldness, [30]while you stretch out your hand for healing, so that signs and wonders may come about through the name of your holy child Jesus."

[31]When they had prayed, the place where they were gathered was shaken. They were all filled with the holy spirit, and they boldly spoke the word of God.

[32]The company of those who believed had one heart and soul. Nobody said that they owned their property; instead,

Signs of the New Covenant

they had everything in common. 33The apostles gave their testimony to the resurrection of the Lord Jesus with great power, and great grace was upon all of them. 34For there was no needy person among them, since any who possessed lands or houses sold them, brought the money from the sale, 35and placed it at the feet of the apostles, who then gave to each according to their need.

36Joseph, a Levite from Cyprus, to whom the apostles gave the surname Barnabas (which means "son of encouragement"), 37sold some land which belonged to him, brought the money, and laid it at the apostles' feet.

Disaster

5There was, however, a man named Ananias, married to a woman called Sapphira. He sold some property, 2and, with his wife's knowledge, kept back part of the price. He brought the rest and laid it at the apostles' feet.

3"Ananias!" said Peter. "Why did the satan fill your heart, to make you tell a lie to the holy spirit and to keep back part of the price of the land? 4While it was still yours, it belonged to you, didn't it? And, when you sold it, it was still in your power! Why did you get such an idea in your heart? It isn't humans that you've lied to: it's God!"

5When Ananias heard these words, he fell down and died. Everyone who heard about it was scared out of their wits. 6The young men got up, took him away, wrapped up his body, and buried him.

7After an interval of about three hours, his wife came in, not knowing what had happened.

8Peter spoke to her.

"Tell me," he said, "did you sell the land for this much?"

"Yes," she replied, "that was the price."

9"So why," Peter answered, "did you agree together to put the holy spirit to the test? Look: the feet of those who have buried your husband are at the door—and they will carry you out too!"

10At once she fell down at his feet and died. The young men were just coming in, and they found her dead, so they took her out and buried her beside her husband. 11Great fear came upon the whole gathering, and on all who heard about these things.

Healed by Peter's Shadow

12Many signs and wonders were performed by the apostles among the people. They were all together in Solomon's

Porch, 13while none of the others dared to join them, though the people spoke highly of them. 14But more people, a crowd both of men and women, believed in the Lord, and were added to their number. 15They used to bring the sick into the streets, and place them on beds and mats so that at least Peter's shadow might fall on them as he went by. 16Crowds gathered from the towns around Jerusalem, bringing people who were sick, or infested with unclean spirits. All of them were cured.

17Then the high priest got up, and all who were with him, namely the group called the Sadducees. They were filled with righteous indignation, 18and seized the apostles and put them in the public jail. 19But an angel of the Lord came in the night, opened the prison doors, and brought them out.

20"Go and take your stand in the Temple," he said, "and speak all the words of this Life to the people."

21When they heard this, they went in at early morning and began to teach.

When the high priest arrived with his entourage, they called the official Assembly and all the elders of the children of Israel, and they sent to the prison to have the apostles brought in. 22But when the attendants went, they didn't find them in the prison. So they came and reported back.

23"We found the jail shut up with maximum security," they said, "and the guards were standing in front of the doors. But when we opened up we found nobody inside."

24When they heard these words, the commander of the Temple police and the chief priests were at a loss about them, with no idea what had happened. 25But then someone came with a message for them.

"Look!" he said. "The men you put in prison are standing in the Temple and teaching the people!"

26Then the commander went with his attendants and brought them. They didn't use force, though, because they were afraid that the people might stone them.

27So they brought them and stood them in the Assembly. The high priest questioned them.

28"We gave you strict orders, didn't we?" he demanded. "We told you not to teach in this name, and look what you're doing!

The Words of This Life

Human Inventions and Divine Instructions

You have filled Jerusalem with your teaching, and you're trying to bring this man's blood on us!"

29"We must obey God, not human beings!" responded Peter and the apostles. 30"The God of our ancestors raised Jesus, after you had laid violent hands on him and hanged him on a tree. 31God exalted him to his right hand as leader and savior, to give repentance to Israel and forgiveness of sins. 32We are witnesses of these things, and so is the holy spirit, which God gave to those who obey him."

33When they heard this, they were infuriated, and wanted to kill them. 34But then a Pharisee by the name of Gamaliel stood up in the Assembly. He was a law teacher, highly respected by all the people. He ordered the men to be put outside for a short while.

35"Men of Israel," he said to the gathering, "be careful what you do to these men. 36Before these times Theudas rose up, claiming to be someone special, and about four hundred men went off to join him. But he was killed, and all the people who had trusted him were dispersed. The movement came to nothing. 37After that, Judas the Galilean arose, in the days of the census, and drew a crowd after himself. But he was killed, and all those who trusted him were scattered. 38So my advice to you now is this. Leave off from these men; let them be. You see, if this plan or this work is of merely human origin, it will come to ruin. 39But if it's from God—well, you won't be able to stop them. You might even be found to be fighting against God!"

They were persuaded by him, 40and they called the apostles back in. They beat them and told them not to speak in the name of Jesus. Then they let them go. 41They, however, went out from the presence of the Assembly celebrating, because they had been reckoned worthy to suffer disgrace for the name. 42And all day, in the Temple and from house to house, they did not stop teaching and proclaiming Jesus as the Messiah.

Problems of Family Living

6 Around that time, as the number of disciples increased, the "Hellenists" raised a dispute with the "Hebrews" because their widows were being overlooked in the daily distribution of food. 2So the Twelve called the whole crowd of disciples together.

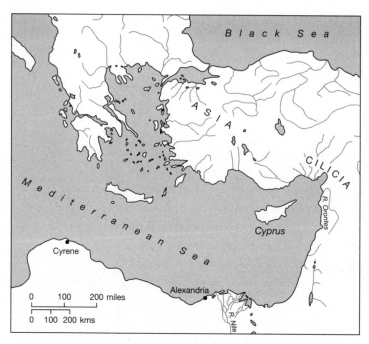

Acts 6:9

"Listen," they said. "It wouldn't be right for us to leave the word of God to wait on tables. ³So, brothers and sisters, choose seven men from among yourselves who are well spoken of and filled with the spirit and wisdom. We will put them in charge of what needs to be done in this matter. ⁴We will continue to pay attention to prayer and to the ministry of the word."

⁵The whole gathering was pleased with what they said. They chose Stephen, a man full of faith and the holy spirit, and Philip, Prochorus, Nicanor, Timon, Parmenas, and Nicolaus (a proselyte from Antioch). ⁶They presented them before the apostles, who prayed and laid their hands on them.

⁷The word of God increased, and the number of disciples in Jerusalem grew by leaps and bounds. This included a large crowd of priests who became obedient to the faith.

⁸Stephen was filled with grace and power, and performed great signs and wonders among the people. ⁹But some from the "Freemen's Synagogue," as it was named, and from Cyrene, Alexandria, Cilicia, and Asia, stood up and disputed with

Stephen Becomes a Target

Stephen. [10]They could not, however, resist the wisdom and the spirit with which he spoke.

[11]Then they put up men to say, "We heard this man speaking blasphemous words against Moses and against God!" [12]They aroused the people, the elders, and the scribes. They set upon him, seized him, and took him in front of the Assembly. [13]They set up false witnesses to say, "This man never stops speaking words against this holy place and the law! [14]We heard him say that this Jesus the Nazorean will destroy this place, and change the customs which Moses handed down to us!"

[15]Everyone who was sitting in the Assembly looked hard at Stephen. They all saw that his face was like the face of an angel.

Stephen Tells the Story

7 The high priest addressed Stephen.

"Are these things true?" he said.

[2]"My brothers and fathers," replied Stephen, "please give me a hearing.

"The God of glory appeared to our father Abraham when he was in Mesopotamia, before he moved to live in Haran. [3]'Leave your land and your family,' he said to him, 'and go to the land which I will show you.' [4]So he left the land of the Chaldeans and went to live in Haran. Then, from there, after his father's death, God moved him on to this land in which you now live. [5]God didn't give him an inheritance here, not even a place to stand up in. Instead, he promised (when Abraham still had no child) that he would give it as a possession to his seed after him. [6]This is what God said to him: that his seed would be strangers in a foreign land, that they would serve there as slaves, and that they would be afflicted for four hundred years. [7]But God said that he would judge the nation that had enslaved them, and that they would then come out and worship him 'on this mountain.' [8]And he gave them the covenant of circumcision. So Abraham became the father of Isaac, and he circumcised him on the eighth day. Isaac became the father of Jacob, and Jacob the father of the twelve patriarchs.

[9]"Now the patriarchs became angry with Joseph, and were jealous of him. They sold him into Egypt. But God was with him, [10]and rescued him from all his troubles and gave him grace and wisdom before Pharaoh, king of Egypt, making him

ruler over Egypt and over all his household. [11]But then there was a famine over the whole of Egypt and Canaan, which resulted in great hardship. Our ancestors couldn't find food to eat. [12]Jacob, however, heard that there was grain in Egypt, and sent our ancestors there on an initial visit. [13]On their second trip, Joseph made himself known to his brothers, and revealed to Pharaoh what family he was from. [14]So Joseph sent and summoned Jacob his father and all the family, seventy-five people in all. [15]Jacob came to Egypt, and he and our ancestors died there. [16]They were brought back to Shechem, and buried in the tomb which Abraham had bought with silver, at a named price, from the sons of Hamor in Shechem.

[17]"God had sworn an oath to Abraham," Stephen continued. "When the time drew near for this promise to be fulfilled, the people had increased and multiplied in Egypt, [18]until another king arose over Egypt, one who had not known Joseph. [19]He got the better of our people, and ill-treated our ancestors, forcing them to abandon their newborn children so that they would die.

Stephen and Moses

[20]"It was at that time that Moses was born, and he was a noble-looking child. He was nursed for three months in his father's house. [21]But, when they abandoned him, Pharaoh's daughter claimed him and brought him up as her own son. [22]So Moses was educated in the full teaching of Egyptian wisdom, and he was powerful in what he said and did.

[23]"When he had grown to about forty years old, it came into his heart to see how his family, the children of Israel, were doing. [24]He saw someone being wronged, and came to the man's defense; he took revenge on behalf of the man who was being oppressed, by striking down the Egyptian. [25]He thought his kinsfolk would grasp the fact that God was sending him to their rescue, but they didn't.

[26]"The next day he showed up as two Hebrews were fighting, and he tried to bring them back together again. 'Now then, you two,' he said, 'you are brothers! Why are you wronging each other?' [27]But the man who was wronging the other wasn't having it. 'Who d'you think you are?' he retorted, pushing him away. 'Who made you a ruler or judge over us? [28]Do you want

to kill me in the same way you killed the Egyptian yesterday?' 29At that word, Moses ran away, and lived as a guest in the land of Midian, where he had two sons.

30"After another forty years, an angel appeared to him in the desert at Mount Sinai, in the flame of a burning bush. 31When Moses saw it, he was amazed at the vision. But, as he came closer to see, there came the voice of the Lord: 32'I am the God of your ancestors, the God of Abraham, of Isaac, and of Jacob.' Moses was very frightened, and didn't dare to look. 33But the Lord said to him, 'Take your sandals off your feet, for the place where you are standing is holy ground. 34I have looked long and hard at the trouble my people are having in Egypt. I have heard their groaning, and I have come down to rescue them. So, come on now: I'm going to send you to Egypt.'

Handmade Shrines

35"So," Stephen continued, "this same Moses—the one they rejected, saying, 'Who made you a ruler or judge?'—this is the man God sent as ruler and redeemer, by the hand of the angel who had appeared to him in the bush. 36He did signs and wonders in the land of Egypt, and led them out, through the Red Sea and for forty years in the wilderness. 37This is the Moses who said to the children of Israel, 'God will raise up a prophet like me from among your brothers.' 38And this is the one who was in the Assembly in the desert with the angel who had spoken to him on Mount Sinai, and with our ancestors; and he received living words to give to us.

39"This is the one whom our ancestors had not wanted to obey, but instead rejected him and turned back in their hearts to Egypt, 40by saying to Aaron, 'Make us gods who will go before us; for this Moses, who brought us out of the land of Egypt—we don't know what has become of him!' 41They made a calf in those days, and offered sacrifice to an idol. They celebrated things their own hands had made.

42"Then God turned and handed them over to worship the host of heaven, as it stands written in the book of the prophets: 'Did you bring sacrifices and offerings to me in those forty years in the wilderness, O house of Israel? 43You took up the tent of Moloch, and the star of your god Rhephan, the carved images you made to worship! I will remove you beyond Babylon!'

44"Our ancestors had the 'tent of meeting' in the desert. God had commanded Moses to make it according to the pattern which he had seen. 45Our ancestors in their turn brought it in when, with Joshua, they dispossessed the nations whom God drove out before our ancestors, and it was there until the time of David. 46David found favor with God, and requested permission to establish a Tabernacle for the house of Jacob. 47But it was Solomon who built him a house.

48"The Most High, however, does not live in shrines made by human hands. The prophet put it like this:

> 49'Heaven is my throne, and earth my footstool!
> What sort of house will you build me, says the Lord,
> Or what place will you give me to rest in?
> 50My own hand made all these, did it not?'

51"You stiff-necked people! Your hearts and ears are uncircumcised! You always resist the holy spirit, just as your ancestors did before you! 52Which of the prophets did your ancestors not persecute? And you killed those who announced in advance the coming of the Righteous One—and now you have betrayed him and murdered him. 53You received the law at the command of angels, but you didn't keep it!"

54What Stephen said was a blow right to the heart. When they heard it, they gnashed their teeth against him. 55He, however, was filled with the holy spirit, and looked steadily up into heaven. There he saw the glory of God, and Jesus standing at God's right hand.

The Stoning of Stephen

56"Look!" he said. "I can see heaven opened, and the son of man standing at God's right hand!"

57But they yelled at him at the tops of their voices, blocked their ears, and made a concerted dash at him. 58They bundled him out of the city and stoned him. The witnesses laid down their cloaks at the feet of a young man named Saul.

59So they stoned Stephen.

"Lord Jesus," he cried out, "receive my spirit."

60Then he knelt down and shouted at the top of his voice, "Lord, don't let this sin stand against them."

Once he had said this, he fell asleep.

8 Now Saul was giving his consent to Stephen's death.
That very day a great persecution was started against
the church in Jerusalem. Everyone except the apostles
was scattered through the lands of Judaea and Samaria. ²Devout men buried Stephen, and made a great lamentation over
him. ³But Saul was doing great damage to the church by going
from one house to another, dragging off men and women and
throwing them into prison.

**Samaria, the
Spirit, and
Simon Magus**

⁴Those who were scattered went all over the place announcing the word. ⁵Philip went off to a town in Samaria and
announced the Messiah to them. ⁶The crowds, acting as one,
clung to what Philip was saying, as they heard him and saw the
signs he performed. ⁷For unclean spirits came out of many of
them, and several who were paralyzed or lame were cured. ⁸So
there was great joy in that town.

⁹But there was a man named Simon, who had lived in the
town for some while and who practiced magic. He used to
astonish the Samaritan people, giving out that he was some

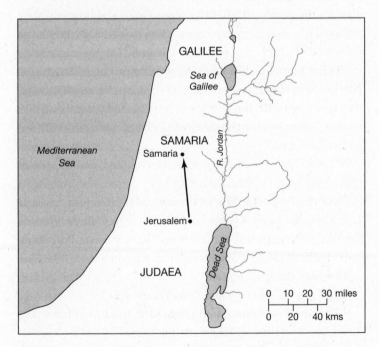

Acts 8:4–25

great personage. [10]Everyone, small and great alike, paid attention to him, and said, "This man is the one called 'God's Great Power'!" [11]They had been under his spell for some time, since they were amazed at the magic he could perform. [12]But when they believed Philip as he was announcing to them the message about God's kingdom and the name of Jesus the Messiah, they were baptized, men and women alike. [13]Simon too believed and was baptized, paying close attention to Philip. When he saw signs, and great and powerful deeds, it was his turn to be astonished.

[14]When the apostles in Jerusalem heard that Samaria had received God's word, they sent Peter and John to them. [15]When they arrived, they prayed for them, asking that they would receive the holy spirit, [16]since up to that point the spirit had come upon none of them; they had simply been baptized into the name of the Lord Jesus. [17]Then they laid their hands on them, and they received the holy spirit.

[18]When Simon saw that the spirit was given through the laying on of the apostles' hands, he offered them money.

[19]"Give me this power too," he said, "so that anyone I lay my hands on will receive the holy spirit."

[20]"You and your silver belong in hell!" retorted Peter. "Did you really think that God's gift could be bought with money? [21]You have no part or share in this word! Your heart is not straight before God. [22]So repent from this wickedness, and pray to the Lord. Perhaps he will forgive the scheme you had in your heart. [23]I can see that you are still stuck in the bitter poison and chains of unrighteousness."

[24]"Pray to the Lord for me," said Simon in reply, "that none of what you've said will happen to me."

[25]After Peter and John had finished bearing witness and speaking the word of the Lord, they returned to Jerusalem, announcing the good news to many Samaritan villages.

[26]An angel of the Lord spoke to Philip.

"Get up and go south," he said. "Go to the desert road that runs down from Jerusalem to Gaza."

[27]So he got up and went. Lo and behold, there was an Ethiopian eunuch, a court official of the Candace (the queen of

Philip and the Ethiopian

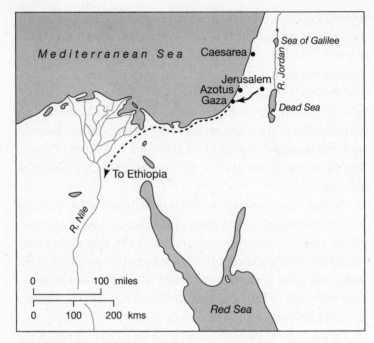

Acts 8:26–40

Ethiopia), who was in charge of her whole treasury. He had come to Jerusalem to worship, 28and was on his way back home. He was sitting in his chariot and reading the prophet Isaiah.

29"Go up and join his chariot," said the spirit to Philip. 30So Philip ran up, and heard him reading the prophet Isaiah.

"Do you understand what you're reading?" he asked.

31"How can I," he replied, "unless someone gives me some help?"

So he invited Philip to get up and sit beside him. 32The biblical passage he was reading was this one:

> He was led like a sheep to the slaughter
> And as a lamb is silent before its shearers,
> So he does not open his mouth.
> 33In his humiliation, judgment was taken away from him.
> Who can explain his generation?
> For his life was taken away from the earth.

[34]"Tell me," said the eunuch to Philip, "who is the prophet talking about? Himself or someone else?"

[35]Then Philip took a deep breath and, starting from this biblical passage, told him the good news about Jesus.

[36]As they were going along the road, they came to some water.

"Look!" said the eunuch. "Here is some water! What's to stop me being baptized?"

[38]So he gave orders for the chariot to stop, and both of them went down into the water, Philip and the eunuch together, and he baptized him. [39]When they came up out of the water, the spirit of the Lord snatched Philip away, and the eunuch didn't see him anymore, but went on his way rejoicing. [40]Philip, however, turned up at Azotus. He went through all the towns, announcing the good news, until he came to Caesarea.

9 Meanwhile, Saul was still breathing out threats and murder on the Lord's disciples. He went to the high priest [2]and requested from him official letters to the synagogues in Damascus, so that he could find people who

The Conversion of Saul

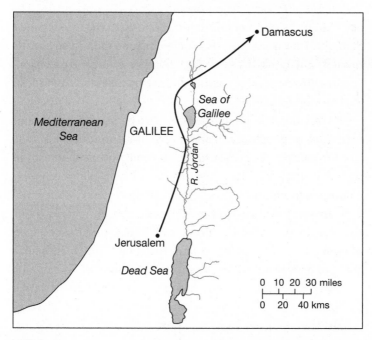

belonged to the Way, men and women alike, tie them up, and bring them back to Jerusalem.

³While he was on the journey, and was getting near to Damascus, suddenly a light from heaven shone around him. ⁴He fell on the ground and heard a voice speaking to him.

"Saul, Saul!" said the voice. "Why are you persecuting me?"

⁵"Who are you, Lord?" he asked.

"I am Jesus," he said, "and you are persecuting me. ⁶But get up and go into the city, and it will be told you what you have to do."

⁷The men who were traveling with Saul stood speechless. They heard the voice but couldn't see anybody. ⁸Saul got up from the ground, but when he opened his eyes he couldn't see anything. So they led him by the hand and took him to Damascus. ⁹He went for three days, being unable to see, and he neither ate nor drank.

Ananias and Saul   ¹⁰In Damascus there was a disciple named Ananias. The Lord spoke to him in a vision.

"Ananias!" he said.

"Here I am, Lord," he replied.

¹¹"Get up," said the Lord to him, "and go to the street called Straight. Inquire at the house of Judas for a man from Tarsus named Saul. Look—he's praying! ¹²And he has seen, in a vision, a man named Ananias coming and laying his hands on him so that he can see again."

¹³"Well, Lord," replied Ananias, "I've heard about this man from several people . . . all about how he's done wicked things to your holy people in Jerusalem . . . ¹⁴and now he's come here with authority from the chief priests to tie up everybody who calls on your name!"

¹⁵"Just go," replied the Lord. "He is a chosen vessel for me, to carry my name before nations and kings—and the children of Israel, too. ¹⁶I am going to show him how many things he is going to have to suffer for the sake of my name."

¹⁷So Ananias set off, went into the house, and laid his hands on him.

"Brother Saul," he said, "the Lord has sent me—yes, Jesus, who appeared to you on the road as you were coming here—so that you may be able to see again, and receive the holy spirit."

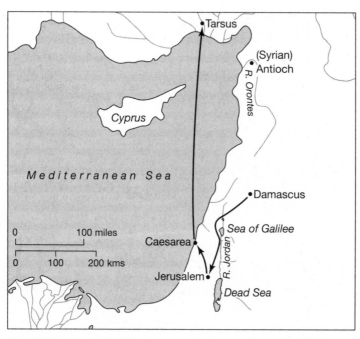

Acts 9:19–26, 30

¹⁸At once something like scales fell off his eyes, and he was able to see. He got up and was baptized. ¹⁹He had something to eat and regained his strength.

Saul stayed with the disciples in Damascus for a few days. ²⁰At once he proclaimed Jesus in the synagogues, saying, "This really is the son of God!" ²¹Everyone was astonished, and said, "Isn't this the man who caused havoc to those in Jerusalem who call on this name? And here he is, coming to tie them up and take them off to the high priests!" ²²But Saul grew all the stronger, and threw the Jews in Damascus into confusion by demonstrating that Jesus is indeed the Messiah.

²³After some days, the Jews made a plot to kill him, ²⁴but Saul got wind of their plan. They were watching the city gates day and night so that they could do away with him. ²⁵But the disciples took him by night and let him down through the wall, lowering him in a basket.

²⁶When he got back to Jerusalem he tried to join the disciples, but they were all afraid of him, not believing that he really was a disciple. ²⁷But Barnabas took him, brought him to

"He Is God's Son"

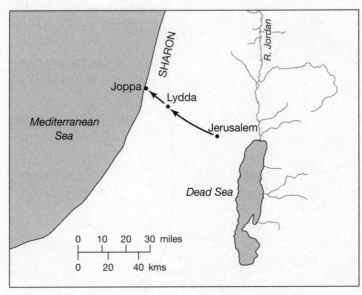

Acts 9:32, 35, 36

the apostles, and explained to them how he had seen the Lord on the road, and that he had spoken to him, and how in Damascus he had spoken boldly in the name of Jesus.

28He was with them in Jerusalem, coming and going and speaking boldly in the name of the Lord. 29He spoke, as well, to the Hellenists, who tried to kill him. 30But the family heard of it and took him down to Caesarea. There they sent him off to Tarsus.

31So the church in all Judaea, Galilee, and Samaria found itself at peace. It was built up and gained in numbers, living in the fear of the Lord and the comfort of the holy spirit.

Back to Peter   32As Peter was going through various places among all the believers, he went down to God's people who lived in Lydda. 33There he found a paralyzed man named Aeneas who had been confined to bed for eight years.

34"Aeneas," Peter said to him, "Jesus the Messiah heals you! Stand up and fold up your bed!"

And at once he stood up. 35Everyone who lived at Lydda and Sharon saw it, and they turned to the Lord.

36In Joppa there was a disciple named Tabitha, whose name translates as Dorcas. She was full of good works and generous deeds. 37Around that time she fell ill and died. They washed her and laid her in an upper room. 38Lydda is near Joppa, and the disciples, hearing that Peter was there, sent two men to him with the urgent request that he shouldn't delay, but come to them at once. 39So Peter got up and went with them. When he arrived, they took him to the upper room, where all the widows were weeping. They showed him the tunics and the other clothes that Dorcas had made while she was with them.

40Peter requested them all to leave. Then he knelt down and prayed, and turned to the body.

"Tabitha," he said, "get up!"

She opened her eyes, and when she saw Peter she sat up. 41He gave her his hand and lifted her up. Then he called God's people, including the widows, and presented her alive.

42This became known throughout the whole of Joppa, and many believed in the Lord. 43Peter stayed on in Joppa for some days, at the house of Simon the tanner.

10 In Caesarea there was a man named Cornelius, a centurion with the cohort called "the Italian." 2He was devout, and he and all his household revered God. He gave alms generously to the people, and constantly prayed to God.

Peter's Vision

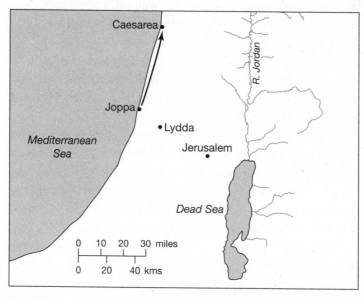

Acts 10:1–16

³He had a vision. Around three o'clock in the afternoon he saw, quite clearly, one of God's angels coming to him.

"Cornelius!" said the angel.

⁴He looked hard at him, terrified.

"What is it, Sir?" he said.

"Your prayers and your alms have come to God's notice," said the angel. ⁵"What you must do is this. Send men to Joppa, and ask for someone called Simon, surnamed Peter. ⁶He is staying with a man called Simon, a tanner, whose house is beside the sea."

⁷When the angel who had spoken with him went away, he called two of his household and a devout soldier from among his retinue. ⁸He explained everything to them, and sent them off to Joppa.

⁹The next day, as they were on their journey and getting near the town, Peter went up onto the roof of the house to pray. It was around midday; ¹⁰he was hungry, and asked for something to eat. While they were preparing it, he fell into a trance. ¹¹He saw heaven opened, and a vessel like a great sail coming down toward the earth, suspended by its four corners. ¹²In the sail there was every kind of four-footed creature, reptiles of the earth and birds of the air. ¹³Then he heard a voice: "Get up, Peter!" said the voice. "Kill and eat!"

¹⁴"Certainly not, Master!" said Peter. "I've never eaten anything common or unclean!"

¹⁵"What God has made clean," said the voice, coming now for a second time, "you must not regard as common."

¹⁶This all happened three times, and then suddenly the sail was whisked back up to heaven.

Peter Goes to Cornelius

¹⁷When Peter came to himself, he was puzzled as to what the vision he had seen was all about. Then, suddenly, the men sent by Cornelius appeared, standing by the gate. They had been asking for Simon's house, ¹⁸inquiring if someone by the name of Simon called Peter was staying there. ¹⁹Peter was still pondering the vision when the spirit spoke to him.

"Look," said the spirit. "There are three men searching for you. ²⁰It's all right; get up, go down, and go with them. Don't be prejudiced; I have sent them."

²¹So Peter went down to the men.

"Here I am," he said. "I'm the one you're looking for. Why have you come?"

22"There is a man called Cornelius," they replied. "He is a centurion, and he's a righteous and God-fearing man. The whole people of the Jews will testify to him. A holy angel told him in a vision to send for you to come to his house, so that he can hear any words you may have to say."

23So he invited them in and put them up for the night.

In the morning he got up and went with them. Some of the believers from Joppa went with him. 24They reached Caesarea the following day. Cornelius had summoned his relatives and close friends and was waiting for him.

25When Peter came in, Cornelius went to meet him. He fell down at his feet and worshipped him.

26"Get up!" said Peter, lifting him up. "I'm just a man, too."

27So they talked together, and Peter came in and found lots of people assembled.

28"You must know," he said to them, "that it is forbidden for a Jewish man to mix with or visit a Gentile. But God showed me that I should call nobody 'common' or 'unclean.' 29So I came when I was asked, and raised no objections. Do tell me, then, the reason why you sent for me."

30Cornelius gave him the answer.

"Four days ago," he said, "I was praying in my house at around this time, about three o'clock, and suddenly a man stood beside me in shining clothes. 31'Cornelius,' he said, 'your prayer has been heard, and your almsgiving has been remembered by God. 32So send someone to Joppa and call Simon, who is named Peter; he is staying in the house of Simon the tanner, beside the sea.' 33So I sent for you at once, and you have been kind enough to come. So now we are all here, in God's presence, to listen to everything which the Lord has told you to say."

34Peter took a deep breath and began.

"It's become clear to me," he said, "that God really does show no favoritism. 35No: in every race, people who fear him and do what is right are acceptable to him. 36He sent his word to the children of Israel, announcing peace through Jesus Christ—he is Lord of all! 37You know all about this, and how

Telling the Gentiles About Jesus

the word spread through all Judaea, beginning from Galilee after the baptism which John proclaimed.

38"God anointed this man, Jesus of Nazareth, with the holy spirit and with power. He went about doing good and healing all who were overpowered by the devil, since God was with him. 39We are witnesses of everything he did in the land of Judaea and in Jerusalem. They killed him by hanging him on a tree; 40but God raised him on the third day, and allowed him to be seen, 41not indeed by all the people, but by those of us whom God had appointed beforehand. We ate and drank with him after he had been raised from the dead. 42And he commanded us to announce to the people, and to bear testimony, that he is the one appointed by God to be judge of the living and the dead. 43All the prophets give their witness: he is the one! Everyone who believes in him receives forgiveness of sins through his name."

44While Peter was still speaking these words, the holy spirit fell on everyone who was listening to the word. 45The circumcised believers who had accompanied Peter were astonished, because the gift of the holy spirit had been poured out on the Gentiles too. 46They heard them speaking with tongues and praising God.

Then Peter spoke up.

47"Nobody can deny these people water to be baptized, can they?" he said. "They have received the holy spirit, just like we did!" 48So he ordered them to be baptized in the name of Jesus the Messiah.

Then they asked him to stay for a few days.

Controversy and Vindication

11 The apostles, and the brothers and sisters with them in Judaea, heard that the Gentiles had received the word of God. 2So when Peter went up to Jerusalem, those who wanted to emphasize circumcision took issue with him.

3"Why did you do it?" they asked. "Why did you go in to visit uncircumcised men and eat with them?"

4So Peter began to explain it all, step by step.

5"I was in the town of Joppa," he said, "and I was praying. I was in a trance, and I saw a vision: something like a great sail suspended by its four corners was let down from heaven, and came toward me. 6I stared at it; then I began to look in, and I saw four-footed land animals, wild beasts, reptiles, and birds of the air. 7I heard a voice saying to me, 'Get up, Peter! Kill and eat!' 8'Certainly not, Lord,' I replied. 'Nothing common or unclean has ever entered my mouth!' 9Then the voice came from heaven a second time: 'What God made clean, you must not regard as common.' 10All this happened three times, and then the whole lot was drawn back up into heaven.

11"Just then, suddenly, three men appeared at the house where I was, sent to me from Caesarea. 12The spirit told me to go with them, without raising scrupulous objections. These six brothers also came with me, and we went into the man's house. 13He told us that he had seen an angel standing in his house and saying, 'Send to Joppa and fetch Simon called Peter, 14who will speak to you words by which you and all your house will be saved.' 15As I began to speak, the holy spirit fell on them, just as the spirit did on us at the beginning. 16And I remembered the word which the Lord had spoken: 'John baptized with water, but you will be baptized with the holy spirit.'

17"So, then," Peter concluded, "if God gave them the same gift as he gave to us when we believed in the Lord Jesus the Messiah, who was I to stand in the way of God?"

18When they heard this, they had nothing more to say. They praised God.

"Well, then," they declared, "God has given the Gentiles, too, the repentance that leads to life!"

19The people who had been scattered because of the persecution that came about over Stephen went as far afield as Phoenicia, Cyprus, and Antioch, speaking the word only to Jewish people. 20But some from among them, who were from Cyprus and Cyrene in the first place, arrived in Antioch and spoke to the Hellenists as well, announcing the good news of the Lord Jesus. 21The Lord's hand was with them, and a large number of people believed and turned to the Lord.

22News of all this reached the ears of the church in Jerusalem, and they sent Barnabas to Antioch. 23When he arrived and saw the grace of God he was glad, and he urged them all to

Taking Root— and a Name!— in Antioch

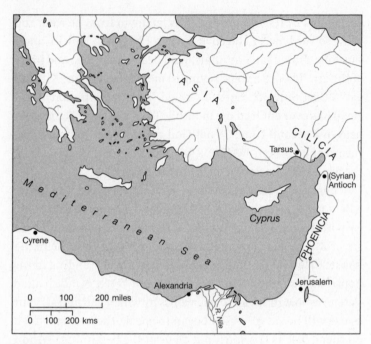

Acts 11:19–30

stay firmly loyal to the Lord from the bottom of their hearts.
²⁴He was a good man, full of the holy spirit and faith. And a
substantial crowd was added to the Lord.

²⁵Then Barnabas went to Tarsus to look for Saul ²⁶and,
when he had found him, he brought him to Antioch. They
were there a whole year, and were received hospitably in the
church, and taught a substantial crowd. And it was in Antioch
that the disciples were first called "Christians."

²⁷Around that time, prophets came from Jerusalem to
Antioch. ²⁸One of them, Agabus by name, stood up and gave
an indication through the spirit that there would be a great
famine over the whole world. (This took place in the reign of
Claudius.) ²⁹Each of the disciples determined, according to
their ability, to send what they could to help the brothers and
sisters living in Judaea. ³⁰They carried out this plan, sending
their gift to the elders by the hand of Barnabas and Saul.

Herod Kills James

12 Around that time, King Herod began to use violence toward some people in the church. ²He killed
James the brother of John with the sword. ³When

he saw that it pleased the Judaeans, he proceeded to arrest Peter, too. (This was around the time of the Festival of Unleavened Bread.) 4So, when he had seized him, he put him in prison, and gave four squads of soldiers the job of guarding him, with the intention of bringing him out to the people after Passover. 5So Peter was kept in prison. But the church prayed earnestly to God on his behalf.

6On the night when Herod was intending to bring Peter out, Peter was sleeping between two soldiers, bound with two chains. There were guards on the doors, watching the prison. 7Suddenly an angel of the Lord stood there, and a light shone in the cell.

Peter's Rescue and Rhoda's Mistake

The angel hit Peter on the side and woke him up.

"Get up quickly!" he said.

The chains fell off his hands. 8Then the angel spoke again.

"Get dressed and put on your sandals," he said. So Peter did. "Put on your cloak and follow me," said the angel.

9So he went out, following the angel. He didn't think all this business with the angel was really happening. He thought he was seeing a vision. 10They went through the first set of guards; then the second; and then they came to the iron gate that led into the city. It opened all by itself. They went out and walked along a street. Suddenly the angel left him.

11Then Peter came to his senses.

"Now I know it's true!" he said. "The Lord sent his angel and snatched me out of Herod's hands. He rescued me from all the things the Judaeans were intending to do."

12Once he had realized this, he went to the house of Mary, John Mark's mother. Lots of people were gathered there, praying. 13Peter knocked at the door in the outer gate, and a maid called Rhoda came to answer it. 14When she heard Peter's voice, she was so excited she didn't open the gate. Instead, she ran back in and told them that Peter was standing outside the gate.

15"You're crazy!" they said to her. But she insisted that it really was true.

"It must be his angel!" they said.

16Meanwhile Peter carried on knocking. They opened the door and saw him, and were astonished. 17He made a sign with

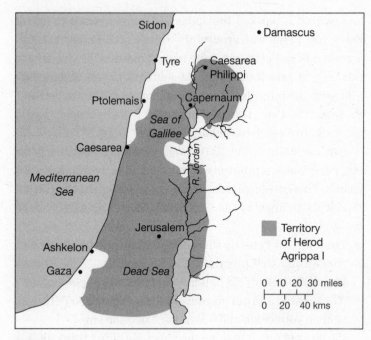

Acts 12:20–25

his hand for them to be quiet. Then he told them how the Lord had led him out of the prison.

"Tell this to James, and to the other brothers and sisters," he said.

Then he left and went somewhere else.

¹⁸When morning came, there was quite a commotion among the guards as to what had become of Peter. ¹⁹Herod looked for him but couldn't find him. He interrogated the guards and ordered them to be put to death. Then he left Judaea and went down to Caesarea, and stayed there.

Herod's Vanity and Death

²⁰Now Herod was angry with the people of Tyre and Sidon. They all came together to meet him, and they persuaded Blastus, who was in charge of the king's bedchamber, to seek a reconciliation. (They were, you see, dependent on the king's country for their food.) ²¹So a day was set, and Herod dressed himself in his royal robes and took his seat on the official platform to make a public address to them.

²²The people began to shout, "The voice of a god, not of a mortal!"

23Immediately an angel of the Lord struck him, because he didn't give God the glory. He was eaten by worms and expired.

24But God's word grew and multiplied. 25Barnabas and Saul had by now accomplished their ministry in Jerusalem, and they came back to Antioch, bringing John Mark with them.

13 In the church at Antioch there were prophets and teachers: Barnabas, Symeon called Niger, Lucius of Cyrene, Manaen from the court of Herod the tetrarch, and Saul. 2As they were worshipping the Lord and fasting, the holy spirit said, "Set apart Barnabas and Saul for the work to which I have called them." 3So they fasted and prayed; and then they laid their hands on them and sent them off.

Mission and Magic

4So off they went, sent out by the holy spirit, and arrived at Seleucia. From there they set sail to Cyprus, 5and when they arrived in Salamis they announced God's word in the Jewish synagogues. John was with them as their assistant. 6They went through the whole of the island, all the way to Paphos. There they found a magician, a Jewish false prophet named Bar-Jesus. 7He was with the governor, Sergius Paulus, who

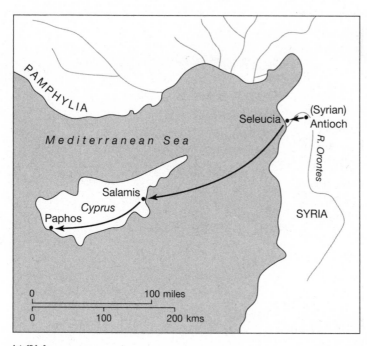

Acts 13:1–6

was an intelligent man. He called Barnabas and Saul and asked to hear the word of God. 8The magician Elymas (that's the translation of his name) was opposing them, and doing his best to turn the governor away from the faith. 9But Saul, also named Paul, looked intently at him, filled with the holy spirit.

10"You're full of trickery and every kind of villainy!" he said. "You're a son of the devil! You're an enemy of everything that's right! When are you going to stop twisting the paths that God has made straight? 11Now see here: the Lord's hand will be upon you, and you will be blind for a while; you won't even be able to see the sun!"

At once mist and darkness fell on him, and he went about looking for someone to lead him by the hand. 12When the governor saw what had happened, he believed, since he was astonished at the teaching of the Lord.

Address in Antioch 13Paul and his companions set off from Paphos and came to Perga in Pamphylia. John, however, left them and went back to Jerusalem. 14But they came through from Perga and arrived in Antioch of Pisidia, where they went into the synagogue on

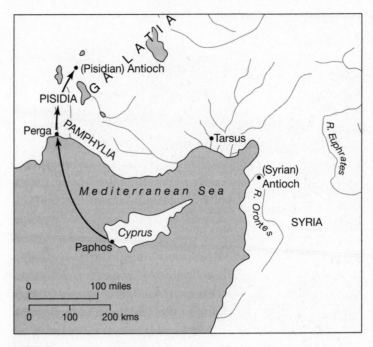

Acts 13:13–25

the sabbath day and sat down. [15]After the reading of the law and the prophets, the ruler of the synagogue sent word to them.

"My brothers," he said, "if you have any word of exhortation for the people, let us hear it."

[16]So Paul stood up and motioned with his hand for attention.

"Fellow Israelites," he said, "and the godfearers among you: listen. [17]The God of this people Israel chose our ancestors, and he raised the people up to greatness during their stay in the land of Egypt. Then he led them out from there with his hand lifted high, [18]and for about forty years he put up with them in the desert. [19]He drove out seven nations from the land of Canaan, and gave them the land as their inheritance [20]for about four hundred and fifty years. After that, he gave them judges, up until Samuel the prophet. [21]After that, they asked for a king, and God gave them Saul the son of Kish, a man from the tribe of Benjamin. He ruled for forty years, [22]and after God had removed him he raised up for them David as king. He is the one to whom God bore witness when he said, 'I have found David, son of Jesse, a man after my own heart; he will accomplish all my purpose.'

[23]"From this man's offspring, in accordance with his promise, God has produced a savior for Israel: Jesus! [24]Before he appeared, John had announced a baptism of repentance for the whole people of Israel. [25]As John was finishing his course, he said, 'What do you suppose I am? I am not the one. But look: someone is coming after me, and I am not worthy to untie the sandals on his feet.'

[26]"My brothers and sisters," Paul continued, "children of Abraham's family, and the godfearers among you: it is to us that the word of this salvation has been sent! [27]The people who live in Jerusalem, and their rulers, didn't recognize him, and they fulfilled the words of the prophets which are read to them every sabbath by condemning him. [28]Even though they found no reason to condemn him to death, they asked Pilate to have him killed. [29]When they had completed everything that had been written about him in prophecy, they took him down from the cross and put him in a tomb. [30]But God raised him from the dead, [31]and he was seen for several days by those who had

The Messianic Challenge

come with him from Galilee to Jerusalem. They are now his witnesses to the people.

32"We are here now to bring you the good news which was promised to our ancestors, 33that God has fulfilled this promise to us, their children, by raising Jesus. This corresponds, indeed, to what is written in the second psalm:

> 'You are my son; this day I have begotten you.'

34"That he raised him from the dead, never more to return to corruption, conforms to what was written:

> 'I will give you the holy and faithful mercies of David.'

35"Because, as it says in another place,

> 'You will not hand over your Holy One to see
>   corruption.'

36"Now David served his own generation, and in the purposes of God he fell asleep and was gathered to his fathers. He did experience corruption. 37But the one God raised up did not experience corruption. 38So let it be known to you, my brothers and sisters, that forgiveness of sins is announced through him, and that everything from which you were unable to be set right by the law of Moses, 39by him everyone who believes is set right.

40"Beware, then, lest what the prophets foretold comes true of you:

> 41'Look out, you scoffers—be amazed, and disappear!
> I am doing something in your days, a work which you
>   wouldn't believe
> Even if someone were to explain it to you.'"

42As Paul and Barnabas were leaving, they begged them to come back the next sabbath and tell them more about these things. 43Many of the Jews and devout proselytes followed them once the synagogue was dismissed. They spoke to them some more, and urged them to remain in God's grace.

A Light to the Gentiles
44On the next sabbath, almost the whole city came together to hear the word of the Lord. 45But when the Jews saw the

crowds, they were filled with righteous indignation, and spoke blasphemous words against what Paul was saying.

46Paul and Barnabas grew very bold.

"God's word had to be spoken to you first," they declared. "But since you are rejecting it, and judging yourselves un-worthy of the life of God's new age, look! We are turning to the Gentiles! 47This is what the Lord has commanded, you see:

> 'I have set you for a light to the nations,
> So that you can be salvation-bringers to the end
>   of the earth.'"

48When the Gentiles heard this, they were thrilled, and they praised the word of the Lord. All those who were marked out for the life of God's new age became believers. 49And the word of the Lord spread through the whole land.

50But the Jews incited the devout aristocratic women and the leading men of the city. They stirred up persecution against Paul and Barnabas, and drove them out of their dis-trict. 51They, however, shook the dust off their feet and went

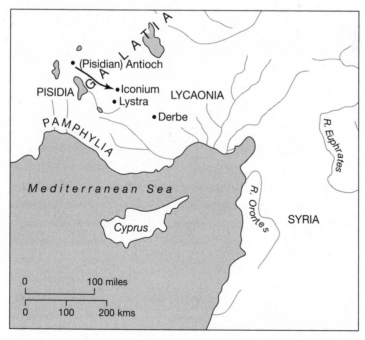

on to Iconium. ⁵²The disciples were filled with joy and with the holy spirit.

Iconium

14 What happened in Iconium was much the same. They went into the Jewish synagogue and spoke, with the result that a large crowd, both of Jews and of Greeks, came to faith. ²But the unbelieving Jews stirred up and poisoned the minds of the Gentiles against the brothers. ³They stayed there a long time, speaking boldly on behalf of the Lord, who bore them witness to the word of his grace by giving signs and wonders which were done at their hands.

⁴But the inhabitants of the city were divided. Some were with the Jews, and some with the apostles. ⁵But then the Gentiles and Jews, with their rulers, made an attempt to ill-treat them and stone them. ⁶They got wind of it, however, and fled to Lystra and Derbe, cities of Lycaonia, and to the surrounding countryside. ⁷There they went on announcing the good news.

Confusion in Lystra

⁸There was a man sitting in Lystra who was unable to use his feet. He had been lame from his mother's womb, and had never walked. ⁹He heard Paul speaking. When Paul looked

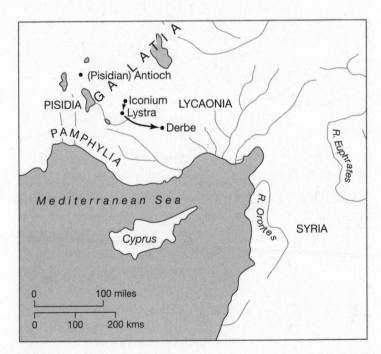

Acts 14:1–7

hard at him, and saw that he had faith to be made well, 10he said with a loud voice, "Stand up straight on your feet!"

Up he jumped, and walked about.

11When the crowds saw what Paul had done, they shouted loudly in the Lycaonian language, "The gods have come down to us in human form!"

12They called Barnabas "Zeus," and Paul, because he was the main speaker, "Hermes." 13The priest of Zeus, whose temple was just outside the city, brought oxen and garlands to the city gates. There was a crowd with him, and he was all ready to offer sacrifice.

14But when the apostles, Paul and Barnabas, heard of it, they tore their clothes and rushed into the crowd.

15"Men, men," they shouted, "what on earth are you doing? We are just ordinary humans, with the same nature as you, and we are bringing you the wonderful message that you should turn away from these foolish things to the living God, the one who made heaven and earth and the sea and everything in them. 16In earlier generations he allowed all the nations to go their own ways, 17but even then he didn't leave himself without witness. He has done you good, giving you rain from heaven and times of fruitfulness, filling your bodies with food and your hearts with gladness."

18Even by saying this, they only just restrained the crowds from offering them sacrifice. 19But some Jews arrived from Antioch and Iconium, and persuaded the crowds to stone Paul. They dragged him outside the city, thinking he was dead. 20The disciples gathered around him, however, and he got up and went into the city. The next day he and Barnabas went off to Derbe.

21They preached in Derbe, and made many disciples. Then they returned to Lystra, Iconium, and Antioch, 22strengthening the hearts of the disciples, and urging them to remain in the faith. They warned them that getting into God's kingdom would mean going through considerable suffering. 23In every church they appointed elders by laying hands on them. They fasted, prayed, and commended them to the Lord in whom they had believed.

Opening the Door of Faith

24They went through Pisidia and came to Pamphylia; 25and when they had spoken the word in Perga they went down to

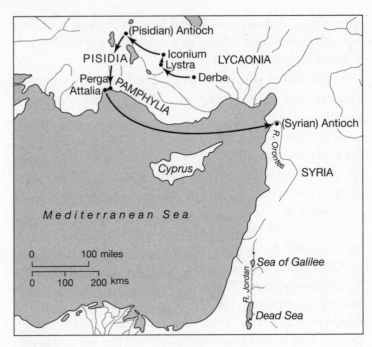

Acts 14:21-28

Attalia. 26From there they sailed to Antioch, which was where they had been commended to God's grace for the work which they had accomplished. 27Once there, they called the church together, and told them all the things which God had done with them, and how he had opened a door of faith for the Gentiles. 28They stayed there a long time with the disciples.

Is Circumcision Necessary?

15 Some people came from Judaea to Antioch and, on arrival, began to teach the Christians that they could not be saved unless they were circumcised according to the custom of Moses. 2This caused considerable uproar and dispute between them and Paul and Barnabas, and the church decided to send Paul and Barnabas, and some others from their fellowship, to the apostles and elders in Jerusalem, to try to sort out the problem. 3So they were sent off by the church. They traveled through Phoenicia and Samaria, telling people as they went about the conversion of the Gentiles. They brought great joy to the Christian communities.

4When they arrived in Jerusalem they were welcomed by

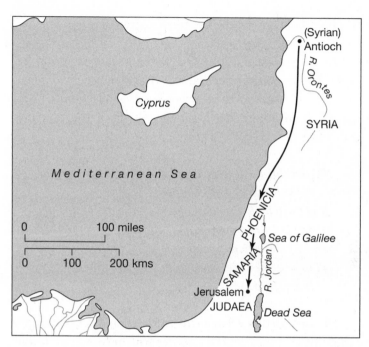

Acts 15:1–11

the church, the apostles, and the elders, and they told them all the things that God had done with them. ⁵But some believers from the party of the Pharisees stood up.

"They must be circumcised," they said, "and you must tell them to keep the law of Moses."

⁶The apostles and elders gathered together to see what to do about this matter. ⁷After considerable argument, Peter got up.

"My brothers," he said, "you know that from our early days together God chose that it should be from my mouth that the Gentiles should hear the word of the gospel and believe. ⁸And God, who knows the heart, bore them witness, by giving them the holy spirit just as he did to us. ⁹He made no distinction between us and them, but he purified their hearts through faith. ¹⁰So now, why are you putting God to the test, by placing a yoke on the disciples' neck which neither we nor our ancestors have been able to bear? ¹¹Rather, we believe that it is by the grace of the Lord Jesus that we shall be saved, just like them."

¹²The whole company was silent, listening to Barnabas and Paul describe the signs and wonders which God had done

The Judgment of James

through them among the Gentiles. ¹³After they had finished, James replied.

"My dear brothers," he said, "listen to me. ¹⁴Symeon has explained how, at the beginning, God graciously favored the Gentiles, to take from them a people for his own name. ¹⁵This, indeed, is in accordance with the words of the prophets, which say,

> ¹⁶'*After this I will return, and will rebuild the Tabernacle*
>   *of David which had collapsed,*
> *And I will build the ruins again, and set them straight,*
> ¹⁷*So that the rest of the human race may seek the Lord,*
> *And all the nations upon whom my name has been called.*
> *Thus says the Lord, who has made these things* ¹⁸*known*
>   *from of old.'*

¹⁹"Therefore this is my judgment: we should not cause extra difficulties for those of the Gentiles who have turned to God. ²⁰Rather, we should send them a message, warning them to keep away from things that have been polluted by idols, from fornication, from what has been strangled, and from blood. ²¹Moses, after all, has from ancient times had people proclaiming him from city to city, since he is read in the synagogues sabbath after sabbath."

The Letter to the Churches

²²Then the apostles and elders, with the whole assembly, decided to send people from their number, Judas Barsabbas and Silas (men well thought of by the Christian community) to Antioch with Paul and Barnabas. ²³They sent a letter with them, which read as follows.

"The apostles and elders send greetings to our Gentile brothers and sisters in Antioch, Syria, and Cilicia. ²⁴Since we have heard that some of our number (not, however, sent by us) have been saying things which have troubled you, causing you distress of heart, ²⁵we resolved unanimously that it would be best to send to you men whom we have chosen, together with our beloved Barnabas and Paul, ²⁶who have risked their lives for the name of the Messiah, the Lord Jesus. ²⁷So we have sent Judas and Silas, and they will tell you the same things face to

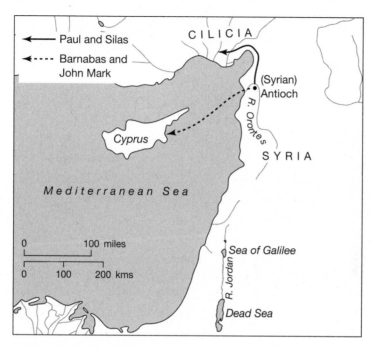

Acts 15:39–41

face. 28For it seemed good to the holy spirit and to us not to lay any burden on you beyond the following necessary things: 29that you should abstain from what has been sacrificed to idols, from blood, from what has been strangled, and from fornication. If you keep yourselves from these, you will do well. Farewell."

30So they went off and came down to Antioch, where they gathered the people together and presented the letter. 31When they read it, they were delighted with the message it contained. 32Judas and Silas, who were themselves prophets, said a good deal to encourage the brothers and sisters, and they gave them strength. 33When they had spent some time there, they left the family in peace and returned to those who had sent them. 35But Paul and Barnabas stayed on in Antioch, teaching and preaching the word of the Lord, with many others as well.

36After some days, Paul said to Barnabas, "Let's go back and visit the brothers and sisters in all the various cities where we preached the word of the Lord, and see how they are doing."

A Huge Row

Acts 16:1–10

³⁷Barnabas wanted to take John, called Mark, along with them. ³⁸But Paul reckoned that it was not a good idea to take with them someone who had left them in Pamphylia and had not gone on with them to the rest of the work. ³⁹There was a huge row, which resulted in them splitting up. Barnabas took Mark and sailed off for Cyprus. ⁴⁰Paul chose Silas and went off, having been commended by the church to the grace of the Lord. ⁴¹They went through Syria and Cilicia, strengthening the churches.

Timothy— and New Developments

16.Paul went on further, to Derbe and then Lystra. There was a disciple there by the name of Timothy, the son of a believing Jewish woman, but with a Greek father. ²The Christians in Lystra and Iconium spoke well of him. ³Paul wanted Timothy to go with them, so he took him and circumcised him because of the Jews in those regions, since they all knew that his father was Greek. ⁴When they went through the cities, they handed on to them the decisions which had been taken by the apostles and elders at Jeru-

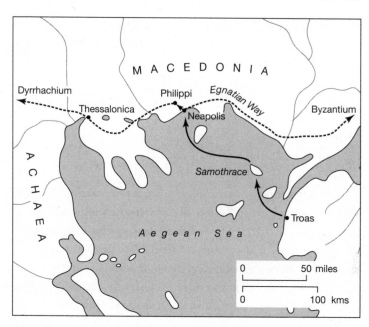

Acts 16:11–12

salem, so that they could observe them. ⁵The churches were strengthened in faith, and grew in number every day.

⁶They went through the region of Phrygia and Galatia, since the holy spirit had forbidden them to speak the word in the province of Asia. ⁷When they came to Mysia, they tried to go into Bithynia, but the spirit of Jesus didn't allow them to do so. ⁸So, passing by Mysia, they came down to Troas. ⁹Then a vision appeared to Paul in the night: a man from Macedonia was standing there, pleading with him, and saying, "Come across to Macedonia and help us!" ¹⁰When he saw the vision, at once we set about finding a way to get across to Macedonia, concluding that God had called us to preach the good news to them.

¹¹So we sailed away from Troas and made a straight course to Samothrace, and the next day to Neapolis. ¹²From there we went on to Philippi, a Roman colony that is the chief city of the district of Macedonia. We stayed in this city for some days.

¹³On the sabbath day we went outside the gate to a place by a

Preaching and Prison in Philippi

river where we reckoned there was a place of prayer, and there we sat down. Some women had gathered, and we spoke to them. ¹⁴There was a woman called Lydia, a godfearer, who was a seller of purple from Thyatira. The Lord opened her heart to pay attention to what Paul was saying. ¹⁵She was baptized, with all her household.

"If you have judged me faithful to the Lord," she begged us, "please come and stay at my home."

So she persuaded us.

¹⁶As we were going to the place of prayer we were met by a girl who had a spirit of divination. She and her oracles made a good living for her owners. ¹⁷She followed Paul and the rest of us.

"These men are servants of God Most High!" she would shout out. "They are declaring to you the way of salvation!"

¹⁸She did this for many days. Eventually, Paul got fed up with it. He turned around and addressed the spirit.

"I command you in the name of Jesus the Messiah," he said, "come out of her!"

And it came out then and there.

¹⁹When the girl's owners saw that their hope of profit had vanished, they seized Paul and Silas, dragged them into the public square before the authorities, ²⁰and presented them to the magistrates.

"These men," they said, "are throwing our city into an uproar! They are Jews, ²¹and they are teaching customs which it's illegal for us Romans to accept or practice!"

²²The crowd joined in the attack on them, and the magistrates had their clothes torn off them and gave orders for them to be beaten with rods. ²³When they had thoroughly beaten them, they threw them into prison and gave orders to the jailer to guard them securely. ²⁴With that instruction, he put them into the innermost part of the prison, and fastened their feet in the stocks.

Earthquake and Salvation

²⁵Around midnight, Paul and Silas were praying and singing hymns to God, and the prisoners were listening to them. ²⁶Suddenly there was a huge earthquake, which shook the foundations of the prison. At once all the doors flew open, and everyone's chains became loose. ²⁷When the jailer woke up and saw the prison doors open, he drew his sword and was

about to kill himself, supposing that the prisoners had escaped. 28But Paul shouted at the top of his voice, "Don't harm yourself! We're all still here!"

29The jailer called for lights and rushed in. Trembling all over, he fell down before Paul and Silas. 30Then he brought them outside.

"Gentlemen," he said, "will you please tell me how I can get out of this mess?"

31"Believe in the Lord Jesus," they replied, "and you will be rescued—you and your household."

32And they spoke the word of the Lord to him, with everyone who was in his house. 33He took them, at that very hour of the night, and washed their wounds. Then at once he was baptized, and all his household with him. 34Then he took them into his house, put food on the table, and rejoiced with his whole house that he had believed in God.

35When day broke, the magistrates sent their officers with the message, "Let those men go." 36The jailer passed on what they said to Paul.

Publicly Vindicated

"The magistrates have sent word that you should be released," he said. "So now you can leave and go in peace."

37But Paul objected.

"We are Roman citizens!" he said. "They didn't put us on trial, they beat us in public, they threw us into prison, and now they are sending us away secretly? No way! Let them come themselves and take us out."

38The officers reported these words to the magistrates. When they heard that they were Roman citizens, they were afraid. 39They went and apologized, brought them out of the prison, and requested that they leave the city. 40So when they had left the prison they went to Lydia's house. There they saw and encouraged the brothers and sisters, and then they went on their way.

17 Paul and Silas traveled through Amphipolis and Apollonia, and came to Thessalonica, where there was a Jewish synagogue. 2Paul went there, as he usually did, and for three sabbaths he spoke to them, expounding the scriptures, 3interpreting and explaining that it was necessary for the Messiah to suffer and to rise from the

Another King!

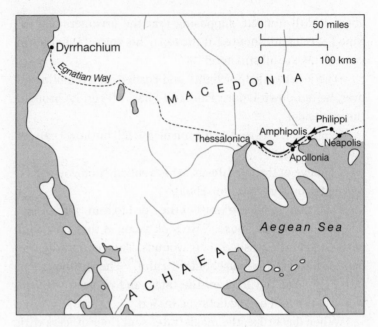

Acts 17:1

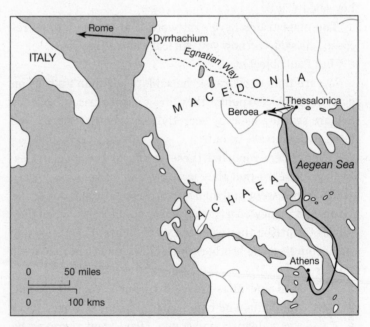

Acts 17:10-21

dead, and that "this Jesus, that I am announcing to you, is the Messiah." 4Some of them were persuaded and threw in their lot with Paul and Silas, including a large crowd of godfearing Greeks, together with quite a few of the leading women.

5But the Jews were righteously indignant. They took some villainous men from the marketplace, drew a crowd, and threw the city into an uproar. They besieged Jason's house and searched for Paul and Silas, to bring them out to the mob. 6When they couldn't find them, they dragged Jason and some of the Christians before the town authorities.

"These are the people who are turning the world upside down!" they yelled. "Now they've come here! 7Jason has had them in his house! They are all acting against the decrees of Caesar—and they're saying that there is another king, Jesus!"

8When they heard these words, the crowd and the authorities were both greatly agitated. 9They bound Jason and the others over, and then dismissed them.

10The Christians in Thessalonica quickly sent Paul and Silas on, by night, to Beroea. When they got there, they went to the Jewish synagogue. 11The people there were more generous in spirit than those in Thessalonica. They received the word with considerable eagerness, searching the scriptures day by day to see if what they were hearing was indeed the case. 12Many of them became believers, including some of the well-born Greek women, and quite a few men.

Paul Reaches Athens

13But when the Jews from Thessalonica knew that the word of God had been proclaimed by Paul in Beroea, too, they came there as well, stirring up trouble and whipping up the crowd. 14So the Christians quickly sent Paul away as far as the seacoast, while Silas and Timothy remained behind. 15Those who were conducting Paul brought him all the way to Athens, where he told them to tell Silas and Timothy to join him as soon as possible. Then they left him there.

16So Paul waited in Athens. While he was there, his spirit was stirred up as he saw the whole city simply full of idols. 17He argued in the synagogue with the Jews and the godfearers, and in the marketplace every day with those who happened to be there. 18Some of the Epicurean and Stoic philosophers were disputing with him.

"What can this word-scatterer be on about?" some were saying.

"He seems to be proclaiming foreign divinities," declared others—since he was preaching "Jesus and Anastasis." ("Anastasis" means "resurrection.") ¹⁹So they took him up to the Areopagus.

"Are we able to know," they said, "what this new teaching really is that you are talking about? ²⁰You are putting very strange ideas into our minds. We'd like to find out what it all means."

²¹All the Athenians, and the foreigners who live there, spend their time simply and solely in telling and hearing the latest novelty.

Paul Among the Philosophers

²²So Paul stood up in the midst of the Areopagus.

"Men of Athens," he said, "I see that you are in every way an extremely religious people. ²³For as I was going along and looking at your objects of worship, I saw an altar with the inscription TO AN UNKNOWN GOD. Well: I'm here to tell you about what it is that you are worshipping in ignorance. ²⁴The God who made the world and everything in it, the one who is Lord of heaven and earth, doesn't live in temples made by human hands. ²⁵Nor does he need to be looked after by human hands, as though he lacked something, since he himself gives life and breath and all things to everyone. ²⁶He made from one stock every race of humans to live on the whole face of the earth, allotting them their properly ordained times and the boundaries for their dwellings. ²⁷The aim was that they would search for God, and perhaps reach out for him and find him. Indeed, he is actually not far from each one of us, ²⁸for in him we live and move and exist; as also some of your own poets have put it, 'For we are his offspring.'

²⁹"Well, then, if we really are God's offspring, we ought not to suppose that the divinity is like gold or silver or stone, formed by human skill and ingenuity. ³⁰That was just ignorance; but the time for it has passed, and God has drawn a veil over it. Now, instead, he commands all people everywhere to repent, ³¹because he has established a day on which he intends to call the world to account with full and proper justice by a man whom he has appointed. God has given all people his pledge of this by raising this man from the dead.'

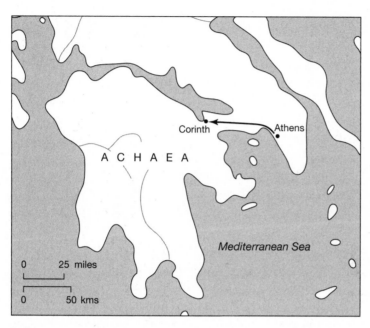

Acts 18:1

³²When they heard about the resurrection of the dead, some of them ridiculed Paul. But others said, "We will give you another hearing about this." ³³So Paul went out from their presence. ³⁴But some people joined him and believed, including Dionysius, a member of the court of the Areopagus, and a woman named Damaris, and others with them.

18 After this, Paul left Athens and went to Corinth. ²There he found a Jew named Aquila, a native of Pontus, who had recently arrived from Italy with Priscilla his wife, due to Claudius's edict banishing all Jews from Rome. Paul paid them a visit ³and, because they were in the same business, he stayed with them and worked. They were, by trade, tent-makers.

⁴Paul argued every sabbath in the synagogue, and persuaded both Jews and Greeks. ⁵When Silas and Timothy arrived from Macedonia, Paul was putting great energy into the task of bearing forthright witness to the Jews that the Messiah really was Jesus. ⁶When they opposed him, and blasphemed, he shook out his clothes.

A Year in Corinth

"Your blood be on your own heads!" he said. "I am innocent. From now on I shall go to the Gentiles."

7He moved on from the synagogue, and went into the house of a man named Titius Justus, a godfearer who lived opposite the synagogue. 8But Crispus, the ruler of the synagogue, believed in the Lord, with all his household, and many of the Corinthians heard about it, came to faith, and were baptized.

9The Lord spoke to Paul by night in a vision.

"Don't be afraid," he said. "Speak on, and don't be silent, 10because I am with you, and nobody will be able to lay a finger on you to harm you. There are many of my people in this city."

11He stayed there eighteen months, teaching the word of God among them.

Christianity Declared Legal in Achaea

12When Gallio was proconsul of Achaea, the Jews made a concerted attack on Paul, and led him to the official tribunal. 13"This man," they said, "is teaching people to worship God in illegal ways."

14Paul was getting ready to speak when Gallio intervened.

"Look here, you Jews," he said to them. "If this was a matter of serious wrongdoing or some wicked villainy, I would receive your plea in the proper way. 15But if this is a dispute about words, names, and laws within your own customs, you can sort it out among yourselves. I don't intend to be a judge in such matters."

16Then he dismissed them from the tribunal. 17But the crowd seized Sosthenes, the ruler of the synagogue, and beat him right there in front of the tribunal. Gallio, however, totally ignored this.

Apollos in Ephesus and Corinth

18Paul stayed on for several more days with the Christians, and then said his farewells and sailed away to Syria, taking Priscilla and Aquila with him. In Cenchreae he had his hair cut off, since he was under a vow. 19When they arrived at Ephesus he left them there, while he himself went into the synagogue and disputed with the Jews. 20When they asked him to stay with them for a longer time, he refused 21and took his leave.

"I will come back to you again," he said, "if that's God's will."

Then he left Ephesus 22and went to Caesarea. Then he went up to Jerusalem, greeted the church, and went back to An-

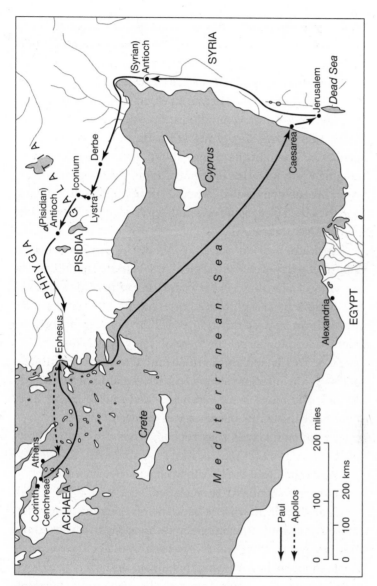

Acts 18:18–28

tioch. 23When he had spent some time there, he went off again and traveled from one place to another throughout the region of Galatia and Phrygia, encouraging all the disciples.

24Now there arrived in Ephesus a Jew named Apollos, who came from Alexandria. He was an eloquent man, and powerful when it came to expounding scripture. 25He had received instruction in the Way of the Lord. He was an enthusiastic speaker, and taught the things about Jesus accurately, even though he only knew the baptism of John. 26He began to speak boldly in the synagogue. When Priscilla and Aquila heard him, they took him to one side and expounded the Way of God to him more accurately.

27He wanted to go across to Achaea. The Christians in Ephesus, by way of encouragement, wrote letters to the church there to welcome him. On his arrival, his work made a considerable impact, through God's grace, on the believers, 28since he openly and powerfully refuted the Jews by demonstrating from the scriptures that the Messiah really was Jesus.

Paul in Ephesus

19 While Apollos was in Corinth, Paul traveled through the interior regions and arrived at Ephesus. There he found some disciples, 2and said to them, "Did you receive the holy spirit when you believed?"

"We had not heard," they replied, "that there *was* a 'holy spirit.'"

3"Well then," said Paul, "into what were you baptized?"

"Into John's baptism," they replied.

4"John baptized with a baptism of repentance for the people," said Paul, "speaking about the one who was to come after him, and saying that that person would be the one that people should believe in—and that means Jesus."

5When they heard this, they were baptized in the name of Jesus. 6Paul then laid his hands on them, and the holy spirit came upon them, and they spoke in tongues and prophesied. 7There were about twelve men in all.

8Paul went into the synagogue and spoke boldly there for three months, arguing and persuading them about the kingdom of God. 9But when some of them were hard-hearted, and wouldn't believe, and made wicked allegations about the Way in front of everybody else, Paul left them. He took the disciples

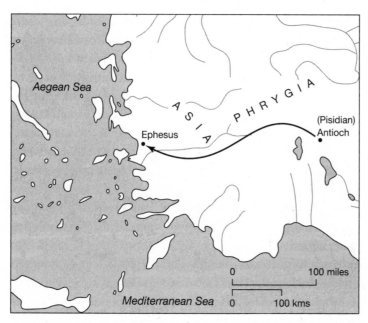

Acts 19:1–10

with him, and argued every day in the lecture-hall of Tyran-
nus. ¹⁰He did this for two years, so that all the inhabitants of
Asia, Jews and Greeks alike, heard the word of the Lord.

¹¹God performed unusual works of power through Paul's
hands. ¹²People used to take handkerchiefs or towels that had
touched his skin and put them on the sick, and then their diseases would leave them and evil spirits would depart.

The Power of God and the Powers at Ephesus

¹³There were some traveling Jewish exorcists who tried to
use the name of the Lord Jesus on people with evil spirits.

"I command you," they used to say, "in the name of Jesus,
the one Paul proclaims!"

¹⁴There were seven of them who used to do this. They were
the sons of Sceva, a Jewish high priest. ¹⁵But on one occasion
the evil spirit answered them back.

"I know Jesus," it shouted, "and I am well acquainted with
Paul; but who are you?"

¹⁶The man who had the evil spirit pounced on them and,
since he was much too strong for them, overpowered all of
them, so that they fled out of the house naked and battered.

17This became common knowledge among both Jews and Greeks living in Ephesus. Fear came on all of them, and the name of the Lord Jesus grew greatly in prestige.

18Many people who became believers came forward to make public confession, revealing what they had been up to. 19Some who had been practicing magic brought their books and burned them in front of everyone; someone calculated how much they were all worth, and it came to fifty thousand silver pieces. 20So the word grew and was strong, in accordance with the Lord's power.

21Once all this had been finished, Paul decided in his spirit to go back through Macedonia and Achaea and, from there, on to Jerusalem.

"After I've been there," he said, "I'll have to go and see Rome."

22He sent two of his helpers, Timothy and Erastus, on ahead to Macedonia, while he himself spent a little more time in Asia.

"Great Is Ephesian Artemis!" 23Around that time there was a major disturbance because of the Way. 24There was a silversmith called Demetrius who made silver statues of Artemis, which brought the workmen a tidy income. 25He got them all together, along with other workers in the same business.

"Gentlemen," he began. "You know that the reason we are doing rather well for ourselves is quite simply this business of ours. 26And now you see, and hear, that this fellow Paul is going around not only Ephesus but pretty well the whole of Asia, persuading the masses to change their way of life, telling them that gods made with hands are not gods after all! 27This not only threatens to bring our proper business into disrepute, but it looks as if it might make people disregard the temple of the great goddess Artemis. Then she—and, after all, the whole of Asia, indeed the whole world, worships her!—she might lose her great majesty."

28When they heard this, they were filled with rage.

"Great is Ephesian Artemis!" they shouted. "Great is Ephesian Artemis!"

29The whole city was filled with the uproar, and everyone rushed together into the theater, dragging along with them the

Macedonians Gaius and Aristarchus, two of Paul's companions.
30Paul wanted to go in to speak to the people, but his followers
wouldn't let him. 31Indeed, some of the local magistrates, who
were friendly toward him, sent him a message urging him not to
take the risk of going into the theater. 32Meanwhile, some people
were shouting one thing, some another. In fact, the whole assembly was thoroughly confused, and most of them had no idea
why they had come there in the first place. 33The Jews pushed
Alexander forward, and some of the crowd informed him what
was going on. He motioned with his hand and was going to
make a statement to the people to explain things. 34But when
they realized he was a Jew, they all shouted together, for about
two hours, "Great is Ephesian Artemis!"

35The town clerk quieted the crowd.

"Men of Ephesus," he said, "is there anyone who doesn't
know that our city of Ephesus is the place which has the honor
of being the home of Artemis the Great, and of the statue that
fell from heaven? 36Nobody can deny it! So you should be quiet,
and not do anything rash. 37You've brought these men here, but
they haven't stolen from the temple or blasphemed our goddess.
38If Demetrius and his colleagues have a charge they want to
bring against anyone, the courts are open and we have magistrates. People can present their cases against one another.
39But if you are wanting to know anything beyond that, it must
be sorted out in the authorized assembly. 40Let me remind you
that we ourselves are risking legal proceedings because of this
riot today, since there is no reason we could give which would
enable us to present a satisfactory explanation for this uproar."

41With these words, he dismissed the assembly.

20 After the hue and cry had died down, Paul sent for
the disciples. He encouraged them, said his farewells, and set off to go to Macedonia. 2He went
through those regions, encouraging them with many words
and, arriving in Greece, 3stayed there three months. He was
intending to set sail for Syria, but the Jews made a plot against
him, and he decided to return instead through Macedonia.

4He was accompanied on this trip by Sopater, son of Pyrrhus
of Beroea; by Aristarchus and Secundus from Thessalonica; by
Gaius from Derbe; and Timothy, and Tychicus and Trophimus

**Round the Coast
and Out of the
Window**

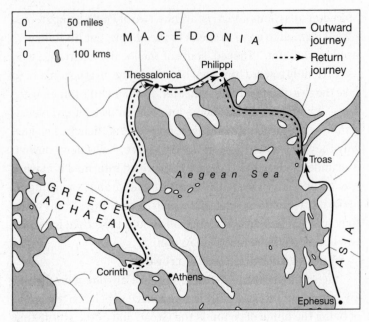

Acts 20:1–12

from Asia. ⁵They went on ahead and waited for us at Troas, ⁶while we got on board ship at Philippi, after the days of Unleavened Bread, and joined them in Troas five days later. We stayed there for a week.

⁷On the first day of the week we gathered to break bread. Paul was intending to leave the following morning. He was engaged in discussion with them, and he went on talking up to midnight. ⁸There were several lamps burning in the upper room where we were gathered. ⁹A young man named Eutychus was sitting by the window, and was overcome with a deep sleep as Paul went on and on. Once sleep had gotten the better of him, he fell down out of the third-story window, and was picked up dead.

¹⁰Paul went down, stooped over him, and picked him up.

"Don't be alarmed," he said. "There is life still in him."

¹¹He went back upstairs, broke bread and ate with them, and continued speaking until dawn. Then he left. ¹²They took up the young man alive and were very much comforted.

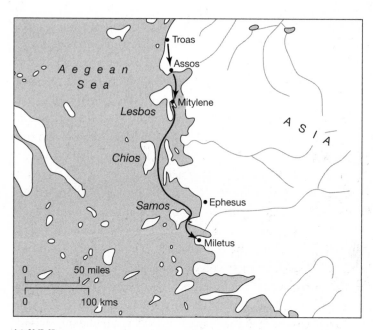

Acts 20:13–27

¹³We went on ahead to the ship and set off for Assos, with the intention of picking Paul up there. (He had decided that he would walk to that point.) ¹⁴When we arrived at Assos, we picked him up and went on to Mitylene, ¹⁵and from there we sailed on the next day and arrived opposite Chios. The following day we got near to Samos, and the day after that we came to Miletus. ¹⁶Paul had decided, you see, to pass by Ephesus, so that he wouldn't have to spend more time in Asia. He was eager to get to Jerusalem, if he could, in time for the day of Pentecost.

¹⁷From Miletus, Paul sent to Ephesus and called for the elders of the church, ¹⁸and they came to him.

"You know very well," he began, "how I have behaved with you all the time, since the first day I arrived in Asia. ¹⁹I have served the Lord with all humility, with the tears and torments that came upon me because of the plots of the Jews. ²⁰You know that I kept back nothing that would have been helpful to you, preaching to you and teaching you both in public and

Paul the Pastor Looks Back— and Looks On

from house to house. 21I bore witness both to Jews and Greeks about repentance toward God and faith in our Lord Jesus.

22"And now, look, I am going to Jerusalem, bound by the spirit. I have no idea what's going to happen to me there, 23but only that the holy spirit testifies to me in city after city that captivity and trouble are in store for me. 24But I don't reckon my life at any value, so long as I can finish my course, and the ministry which I have received from the Lord Jesus, to bear witness to the gospel of God's grace.

25"So now," he went on, "I have gone to and fro preaching the kingdom among you, but I know that none of you will ever see my face again. 26Therefore I bear witness to you this very day that I am innocent of everyone's blood, 27since I did not shrink from declaring to you God's entire plan.

Watch Out for Yourselves, the Flock, and the Wolves

28"Watch out for yourselves," Paul continued, "and for the whole flock, in which the holy spirit has appointed you as guardians, to feed the church of God, which he purchased with his very own blood. 29I know that fierce wolves will come in after I am gone, and they won't spare the flock. 30Yes, even from among yourselves people will arise, saying things which will distort the truth, and they will draw the disciples away after them. 31Therefore keep watch, and remember that for three years, night and day, I didn't stop warning each of you, with tears.

32"So now I commit you to God, and to the word of his grace, which is able to build you up and give you the inheritance among all those whom God has sanctified. 33I never coveted anyone's silver, or gold, or clothes. 34You yourselves know that these very hands worked to serve my own needs and those of the people with me. 35I showed you in all such matters that this is how we should work to help the weak, remembering the words of the Lord Jesus; as he put it, 'It is more blessed to give than to receive.'"

36When he had said this, he knelt down with them all and prayed. 37There was great lamentation among them all, and they fell on Paul's neck and kissed him. 38They were particularly sorry to hear the word he had spoken about never seeing his face again.

Then they brought him to the ship.

21 When we had left them behind and had set sail, we made a straight course to Cos, and went on the next day to Rhodes and from there to Patara. 2There we found a ship heading for Phoenicia, and we got on board and set sail. 3We came in sight of Cyprus, passed it on our left side, sailed to Syria, and arrived in Tyre, which was where the boat was going to unload its cargo. 4We found some disciples and stayed there a week—and they told Paul, by the spirit, not to go to Jerusalem. 5When our time there was up, we left and went on our way, with everyone, women and children included, coming with us out of the city. We knelt down on the seashore and prayed. 6Then we said our farewells to one another. We got on the ship and they returned home.

7The end of our voyage from Tyre saw us arrive at Ptolemais. There we greeted the Christians and stayed a day with them. 8On the next day we left and went on to Caesarea, and went into the house of Philip the evangelist, one of the Seven,

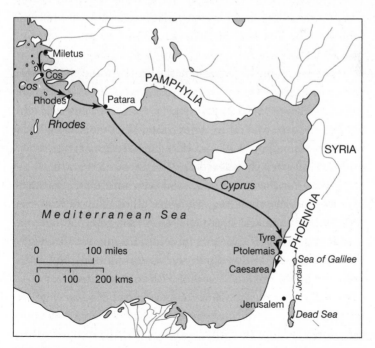

Acts 21:1–14

and stayed with him. ⁹He had four unmarried daughters who prophesied.

¹⁰After we'd been there several days, Agabus the prophet arrived from Jerusalem. ¹¹He came to us, took Paul's girdle, and tied himself up with it, hand and foot.

"This is what the holy spirit says," he declared. "The Judaeans in Jerusalem will tie up the man to whom this girdle belongs, just like this, and they will hand him over to the Gentiles."

¹²When we heard that, we and the people of that place begged Paul not to go up to Jerusalem.

¹³Then Paul responded.

"What are you doing with all this weeping," he said, "breaking my heart in pieces? I am quite prepared not only to be tied up but to die in Jerusalem for the name of the Lord Jesus."

¹⁴When we realized we couldn't dissuade him, we gave up the attempt.

"May the Lord's will be done," was all we said.

Warding Off the Inevitable ¹⁵After those days we made preparations to go up to Jerusalem. ¹⁶Some of the disciples from Caesarea went with us, and took us to the house of Mnason, an elderly disciple from Cyprus. That was where we were going to be staying.

¹⁷When we came to Jerusalem, the brothers and sisters welcomed us gladly. ¹⁸On the next day Paul went in with us to see James, with all the elders present. ¹⁹He greeted them and laid out before them everything which God had done through his ministry among the Gentiles, telling it all step by step. ²⁰They praised God when they heard it.

"You see, brother," they said, "that there are many thousands of Jews who have believed. They are all of them fiercely enthusiastic for the law. ²¹But what they have heard about you is that you teach all the Jews who live among the nations to abandon Moses, telling them not to circumcise their children and not to keep the customs. ²²Where does this leave us? They will certainly hear that you have come. ²³So do what we tell you: there are four men here who have taken a vow upon themselves. ²⁴Join in with these men. Purify yourself along with them, and pay the expenses for them as they have their heads shaved. That way everyone will know that there is no

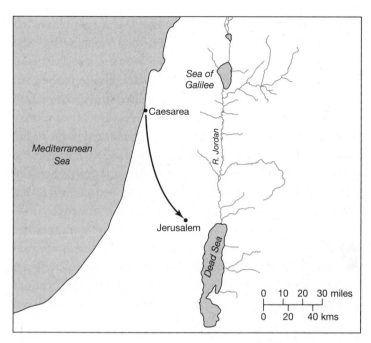

Acts 21:15–17

truth in the accusations against you, but rather that you too are behaving as a law-observant Jew should. 25As for the Gentiles who have believed, we have written to them with our decision that they should keep themselves from what has been sacrificed to idols, from blood, from what is strangled, and from fornication."

26So Paul took the men and, the next day, underwent the ritual of purification alongside them. He went into the Temple and made the declaration, stating when the days of purification would be completed and when the time would come for sacrifice to be offered for each of them.

27When the seven days were completed, some Jews from Asia spotted Paul in the Temple. They gathered a crowd and grabbed him.

Riot in the Temple

28"Men of Israel," they yelled, "come and help us! This is the man who's been teaching everybody everywhere against our people, our law, and this place! And now, what's more, he's brought some Greeks into the Temple, and he's defiled this holy place!" ²⁹(They had previously seen Trophimus the Ephesian with Paul in the city, and they thought Paul had taken him into the Temple.)

³⁰The whole city was stirred up, and people rushed together from all around. They seized Paul and dragged him outside the Temple, and the gates were shut at once. ³¹As they were trying to kill him, word reached the tribune of the guard that all Jerusalem was in an uproar. ³²At once he took soldiers and centurions and ran down to them. When the crowd saw the tribune and the soldiers, they stopped beating Paul. ³³Then the tribune came up, arrested him, ordered him to be bound with two chains, and asked who he was and what he had done. ³⁴Some in the crowd said one thing; some said another. Since he couldn't find out what was really going on because of the uproar, he gave orders for Paul to be brought into the barracks. ³⁵When they got to the steps, the pressure of the crowd was so strong that the soldiers had to carry Paul. ³⁶The great mob of people was following and shouting, "Kill him! Kill him!"

Why Not Hear My Story?

³⁷As they were about to go into the barracks, Paul turned to the tribune.

"Am I allowed to say something to you?" he asked.

"Well!" replied the tribune. "So you know some Greek, do you? ³⁸Aren't you the Egyptian who raised a revolt some while back and led those four thousand 'assassins' into the desert?"

³⁹"Actually," replied Paul, "I'm a Jew! I'm from Tarsus in Cilicia. That's not an insignificant place to be a citizen of. Please, please, let me speak to the people."

⁴⁰So he gave him permission. Paul stood on the steps and motioned with his hand to the people. When, eventually, there was silence, he spoke to them in Aramaic.

22 "My brothers and fathers," he began, "hear me as I explain myself to you." ²When they heard him speaking in Aramaic they became even quieter.

³"I am a Jew," he continued, "and I was born in Tarsus in Cilicia. I received my education here, in this city, and I studied

at the feet of Gamaliel. I was trained in the strictest interpretations of our ancestral laws and became zealous for God,
just as all of you are today. ⁴I persecuted this Way, right to the
point of killing people, and I bound and handed over to prison
both men and women—⁵as the high priest and all the elders
can testify. I received letters from them to the Jews of Damascus, where I was going in order to find the heretics who were
there, tie them up, and bring them to Jerusalem to face their
just deserts.

⁶"Just as I was on the way, and getting near to Damascus,
suddenly a bright light shone from heaven all around me. It
was about midday. ⁷I fell down on the ground and I heard a
voice saying, 'Saul, Saul, why are you persecuting me?' ⁸I answered, 'Who are you, Master?' And he said to me, 'I am Jesus
of Nazareth, and you are persecuting me!'

⁹"The people who were with me saw the light, but they
didn't hear the voice of the person speaking to me. ¹⁰So I said,
'What shall I do, Master?' And the Lord said to me, 'Get up and
go into Damascus, and there you will be informed of all the
things that have been arranged for you to do.'

¹¹"So, as I couldn't see because of the brightness of that
light, the people with me led me by the hand, and I came to
Damascus.

¹²"There was a man named Ananias," Paul continued. "He **Out of His**
was a devout, law-keeping Jew, and all the Jews living in Da- **Own Mouth**
mascus would testify to the fact. ¹³He came and stood beside
me and said, 'Brother Saul, receive your sight.' In that very
moment I could see, and I looked at him. ¹⁴This is what he said.
'The God of our ancestors chose you to know his will, to see the
Righteous One, and to hear the word from his mouth. ¹⁵This
is because you are going to bear witness for him to all people,
telling them what you have seen and heard. ¹⁶Now, then, what
are you going to do? Get up, be baptized, and wash away your
sins by calling on his name.'"

¹⁷"After I came back to Jerusalem, and was praying in the
Temple, I fell into a trance, ¹⁸and I saw him speaking to me.
'Hurry up!' he said. 'Leave Jerusalem as quickly as possible!
They won't accept your testimony about me.' ¹⁹'But, Lord,'

I replied, 'they themselves know that in all the synagogues I used to imprison and beat those who believe in you. 20And when they shed the blood of Stephen, your witness, I was myself standing there and giving my approval. I was looking after the cloaks of those who were killing him.'

21"'No,' he said to me. 'Go away from here! I'm sending you far away—to the Gentiles!'"

22Up to this point the crowd listened to Paul. But now they began to shout.

"Away with him from the face of the earth!" they yelled. "Someone like that has no right to live!"

Roman Citizenship Comes in Useful

23The crowd was shouting, tearing their clothes, and throwing dust in the air. 24The tribune gave orders for Paul to be brought into the barracks, and he told the guards to examine him by flogging, so that he could find out just what was the reason for all the uproar against him.

25As they were tying Paul up ready for the whips, Paul spoke to the centurion who was standing beside him.

"Is it lawful," he said, "to flog a Roman citizen without first finding him guilty?"

26When the centurion heard that, he went off to the tribune and spoke to him.

"What d'you think you're doing?" he said. "This fellow's a Roman citizen!"

27The tribune came and spoke to Paul.

"Tell me," he said. "Are you a Roman citizen?"

"Yes," replied Paul.

28"It cost me a lot of money to buy this citizenship," said the tribune.

"Ah," said Paul, "but it came to me by birth."

29The people who were about to torture Paul stepped back quickly from him. As for the tribune, he was afraid, discovering that he was a Roman citizen and that he had had him tied up.

30On the next day, still wanting to get to the bottom of it all, and to find out what was being alleged by the Jews, he released Paul, and ordered the chief priests to come together, with the whole Sanhedrin. He brought Paul in and presented him to them.

23

Paul looked hard at the Sanhedrin.

"My brothers," he said. "I have conducted myself before God in a completely good conscience all my life up to this day."

²Ananias, the high priest, ordered the bystanders to strike Paul on the mouth.

³"God will strike you, you whitewashed wall!" said Paul to Ananias. "You are sitting to judge me according to the law, and yet you order me to be struck in violation of the law?"

⁴"You are insulting the high priest?" asked the bystanders.

⁵"My brothers," replied Paul, "I didn't know he was the high priest. Scripture says, of course, 'You mustn't speak evil of the ruler of your people.'"

⁶Paul knew that one part of the gathering were Sadducees, and the other part Pharisees.

"My brothers," he shouted to the Sanhedrin, "I am a Pharisee, the son of Pharisees. This trial is about the hope, about the resurrection of the dead!"

⁷At these words, an argument broke out between the Pharisees and Sadducees, and they were split among themselves. ⁸(The Sadducees deny that there is any resurrection, or any intermediate state of "angel" or "spirit," but the Pharisees affirm them both.) ⁹There was quite an uproar, with some of the scribes from the Pharisees' party standing up and arguing angrily, "We find nothing wrong in this man! What if a spirit spoke to him, or an angel for that matter?"

¹⁰Faced with another great riot, the tribune was worried that Paul was going to be pulled in pieces between them. He ordered the guard to go down and snatch him out of the midst of them and bring him back up into the barracks.

¹¹On the next night, the Lord stood by him.

"Cheer up!" he said. "You have given your testimony about me in Jerusalem. Now you have to do it in Rome."

¹²The next morning, the Jews made a plot together. They swore an oath, binding themselves not to eat or drink until they had killed Paul. ¹³There were more than forty of them who made this solemn vow with one another. ¹⁴They went to the high priest and the elders.

"We have sworn a solemn and binding oath," they said, "not to taste anything until we have killed Paul. ¹⁵What you need to do is this: tell the tribune, with the Sanhedrin, to bring him down to you, as if you wanted to make a more careful examination of his case. And then, before he arrives, we'll be ready to dispatch him."

¹⁶Paul's nephew (his sister's son) heard of the plot. He went off, entered the barracks, and told Paul about it. ¹⁷Paul called one of the centurions.

"Take this young man to the tribune," he said. "He's got something to tell him."

¹⁸So he took him off and brought him to the tribune.

"Paul the prisoner called me and asked me to bring this young man to you," he said. "Apparently he's got something to tell you."

¹⁹So the tribune took the young man by the hand and led him off into a private room.

"What is it you have to tell me?" he asked.

²⁰"The Judaeans have agreed to ask you to bring Paul down to the Sanhedrin tomorrow," he said. "It will look as if they're wanting to make a more thorough investigation about him. ²¹But don't do what they want! There are more than forty men who are setting an ambush for him, and they've sworn a solemn oath not to eat or drink until they've killed him. They are ready right now, waiting for the word from you!"

²²So the tribune dismissed the lad.

"Don't tell anyone at all that you've told me about this," he said.

We Have Ways of Keeping You Safe

²³So the tribune summoned two of the centurions.

"Get ready a squad of two hundred," he said. "They're going to Caesarea. Also take seventy horsemen and two hundred light-armed guards. They leave at nine o'clock tonight. ²⁴Get horses ready for Paul to ride, and take him safely to Felix the governor."

²⁵He wrote a letter which went like this:

²⁶"Claudius Lysias, to the most excellent governor Felix, greeting. ²⁷This man was seized by the Jews, who were going to kill him. When I learned that he was a Roman citizen I

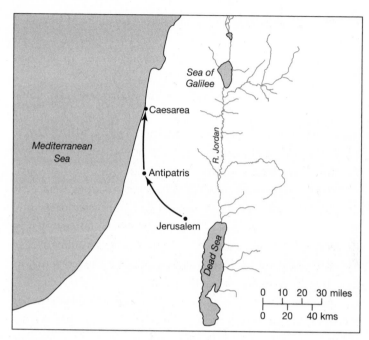

Acts 23:23–35

went with the guard and rescued him. ²⁸I wanted to know the charge on which they were accusing him, so I took him into their Sanhedrin. ²⁹There I discovered that he was being accused in relation to disputes about their law, but that he was not being charged with anything for which he would deserve to die or to be imprisoned. ³⁰I then received information that there was to be a plot against him. So I am sending him to you at once. I have told his accusers that they must inform you of their charges against him."

³¹So the soldiers did what they were told. They took Paul and brought him by night to Antipatris, ³²and the next day they allowed the horsemen to go on with him while they returned to the barracks. ³³The company arrived at Caesarea and handed over the letter to the governor, presenting Paul at the same time. ³⁴Felix read the letter, and asked which jurisdiction Paul was from. He found out that he was from Cilicia.

35"I will hear your case," he said, "when your accusers arrive."

He ordered that he be kept under guard in Herod's Praetorium.

Bring on the
Barristers

24 After five days, Ananias the high priest came down to Caesarea with some of the elders, and with a barrister named Tertullus. They told the governor what they had against Paul. 2Paul was summoned, and Tertullus began his speech of accusation.

"Most excellent Felix! We are enjoying great peace because of you! Through your wise foresight and planning things have greatly improved for this people. 3We welcome it in every way, in every place, and with every feeling of gratitude. 4But, so as not to keep you waiting any longer, I beg you, of your forbearance, to listen to us briefly.

5"We find this fellow to be a public nuisance. He stirs up civil strife among all the Jews, all over the world. He is a ringleader in the sect of the Nazoreans. 6He even tried to defile the Temple! But we caught him. 8If you examine him yourself you will be able to find out about all these things of which we're accusing him."

9The Jews added their voices to this speech, agreeing that it was just as had been said.

A Defense
of the Hope

10The governor motioned to Paul to speak.

"I understand that you have been governor of this nation for several years," he began, "and therefore I am all the more pleased to make my defense before you. 11You will be able to discover that it is not more than twelve days since I came up to worship at Jerusalem. 12They didn't find me disputing with anybody in the Temple; nor was I stirring up a crowd, either in the synagogues or elsewhere in the city. 13They can provide no proof of any of the charges they are now bringing against me.

14"But this much I will confess to you: that it is true that I do worship the God of my ancestors according to the Way which they call a 'sect.' I believe everything which is written in the law and the prophets, 15and I hold to the hope in God, for which they also long, that there will be a resurrection of the righteous and the unrighteous. ¹⁶For that reason I make it my settled aim always to have a clear conscience before God and all people.

¹⁷"For several years I have been collecting alms and offerings to bring to my nation. ¹⁸That was the business I was engaged in when they found me purified in the Temple, without any crowds and without any riot. ¹⁹There were some Jews from Asia there; they are the ones who should appear before you and bring any accusations against me that they may have. ²⁰Or let these people themselves say what wrong they found in me when I stood before the Sanhedrin—²¹unless it is about this one thing, which I shouted out as I was standing among them: 'It's because of the resurrection of the dead that I am being judged before you today.'"

²²Felix was quite well informed about the Way. He adjourned the hearing.

"When Lysias the tribune comes down," he said, "then I will make my decision about your business."

²³He told the centurion to keep Paul under guard, to allow him some freedom, and not to stop any of his companions from looking after him.

²⁴After some days, Felix came with Drusilla his wife, who was Jewish. They sent for Paul and listened to him speaking about faith in the Messiah Jesus. ²⁵As he talked about justice, self-control, and the judgment to come, Felix became afraid.

"That's quite enough for now," he said. "You can go. When I get a good opportunity I'll call for you again another time."

²⁶At the same time he was hoping that Paul would give him money, and so he sent for him frequently and talked with him. ²⁷After two years Felix handed over the reins of office to Porcius Festus. He wanted to do the Jews a favor, and so he left Paul in prison.

25 So Festus arrived in the province, and after three days he went up from Caesarea to Jerusalem. ²The high priests and the leading men of the Jews appeared before him, laying charges against Paul, and putting a request to him. ³They wanted him to do a special favor for them and against Paul, by sending for him to

Felix Calms (and Slows) Things Down

To Caesar You Shall Go

be brought up to Jerusalem. They were making a plan to kill him on the way. 4But Festus answered that he was keeping Paul at Caesarea, and that he himself would shortly be going back there.

5"So," he said, "your officials should come down with me. They can put any accusations of wrongdoing they may have against the man."

6He stayed with them for a few days (about eight or ten) and then went down to Caesarea. On the next day he took his seat on the tribunal and ordered Paul to be brought to him. 7When he appeared, the Jews who had come down from Jerusalem surrounded him and hurled many serious accusations at him, which they were not able to substantiate. 8Paul made his response: "I have offended neither against the Jews' law, nor against the Temple, nor against Caesar."

9Festus, however, wanted to do a favor to the Jews. "Tell me," he said to Paul in reply, "how would you like to go up to Jerusalem and be tried by me there about these things?"

10"I am standing before Caesar's tribunal," said Paul, "which is where I ought to be tried. I have done no wrong to the Jews, as you well know. 11If I have committed any wrong, or if I have done something which means I deserve to die, I'm not trying to escape death. But if I have done none of the things they are accusing me of, nobody can hand me over to them. I appeal to Caesar."

12Festus consulted with his advisers.

"You have appealed to Caesar," he said, "and to Caesar you shall go."

Agrippa and Bernice 13After some days King Agrippa came to Caesarea, with Bernice, to greet Festus. 14They spent several days there, and during that time Festus put to the king the whole matter of Paul and the case against him.

"I have a man here," he said, "who was left by Felix as a prisoner. 15When I was up in Jerusalem, the chief priests and the Jewish elders came before me and asked me to pass sentence on him. 16My response was that it is not our Roman custom to hand anyone over until the accused has had a chance to look his accusers in the face and make a defense against the charges. ¹⁷So they came down here, and I didn't postpone the business, but sat in court the next day and commanded the man to be brought. ¹⁸His accusers stood there and brought charges—but not of the sort of wrongdoing I had been expecting. ¹⁹It turned out to have to do with various wranglings concerning their own religion, and about some dead man called Jesus whom Paul asserted was alive. ²⁰I simply didn't know what to do about all this dispute, and so I asked him if he would like to go up to Jerusalem and be judged there about these things. ²¹But Paul then appealed for his case to be sent up to His Majesty! So I gave the order that he should be kept under guard until I can send him to Caesar."

²²"I should like to hear this man for myself," said Agrippa to Festus.

"Very well," said Festus. "You shall do so tomorrow."

²³On the next day, Agrippa and Bernice came with great ceremony, and entered the audience chamber. With them came the tribunes and the leading men of the city. Festus gave the order, and Paul was brought in.

²⁴"King Agrippa," said Festus, "and all of you assembled here, you see this man. The whole multitude of the Jews appealed to me about him, both in Jerusalem and here. They shouted that it wasn't right to let him live. ²⁵But I found that he had done nothing to deserve death, and since he then himself appealed to His Majesty I decided to send him. ²⁶I don't have anything definite to write to our Lord and Master about him, and so I've brought him here to you, and particularly before you, King Agrippa, so that I may know what to write once we have had a judicial hearing. ²⁷There seems no sense to me in sending a prisoner without giving some indication of the charges against him."

26

Agrippa addressed Paul.

"You are permitted," he said, "to speak for yourself."

Paul stretched out his hand and began his defense.

²"I consider myself blessed, King Agrippa," he said, "to have the chance to speak before you today in my defense

Paul Before Agrippa

concerning all the things of which the Jews have charged me, ³in particular because I know you are an expert on all matters of Jewish customs and disputes. I beg you, therefore, to give me a generous hearing.

⁴"All the Jews know my manner of life. I lived from my earliest days among my own people and in Jerusalem. ⁵They have known already for a long time (if they are willing to testify!) that I lived as a Pharisee, according to the strictest sect of our religion. ⁶And now I stand accused because of the hope of the promise made by God to our ancestors, ⁷the hope for which our twelve tribes wait with earnest longing in their worship night and day. And it is this hope, O King, for which I am now accused by the Jews! ⁸Why should any of you judge it unbelievable that God would raise the dead?

⁹"I thought I was under obligation to do many things against the name of Jesus of Nazareth, ¹⁰and that is what I did in Jerusalem. I received authority from the chief priests to shut up many of God's people in prison, and when they were condemned to death I cast my vote against them. ¹¹I punished them many times in all the synagogues and forced many of them to blaspheme. I became more and more furious against them, and even pursued them to cities in other lands.

Paul's Conversion (One More Time)

¹²"While I was busy on this work," Paul continued, "I was traveling to Damascus with authority and commission from the chief priests. ¹³Around midday, while I was on the road, O King, I saw a light from heaven, brighter than the light of the sun, and shining all around me and my companions on the road. ¹⁴We all fell to the ground, and I heard a voice speaking to me in Aramaic.

"'Saul, Saul,' he said, 'why are you persecuting me? It's hard for you, this kicking against the goads.'

¹⁵"'Who are you, Lord?' I said.

"'I am Jesus,' said the Lord, 'and you are persecuting me. ¹⁶But get up and stand on your feet. I'm going to tell you why I have appeared to you. I am going to establish you as a servant, as a witness both of the things you have already seen and of the occasions I will appear to you in the future. ¹⁷I will rescue you from the people, and from the nations to whom I am going to send you [18]so that you can open their eyes to enable them to turn from darkness to light, and from the power of the satan to God—so that they can have forgiveness of sins, and an inheritance among those who are made holy by their faith in me.'

[19]"So then, King Agrippa, I didn't disobey this vision from heaven. [20]I preached that people should repent, and turn to God, and do the works that demonstrate repentance. I preached it first to those in Damascus, then also in Jerusalem, in the whole countryside of Judaea, and among the nations. [21]That is the reason the Jews seized me in the Temple and tried to slaughter me. [22]But I have had help from God, right up to this very day. And so I stand here to bear witness, to small and great alike, of nothing except what the prophets, and Moses too, said would happen: [23]namely, that the Messiah would suffer, that he would be the first to rise from the dead, and that he would proclaim light to the people and to the nations."

[24]As Paul was making his defense in this way, Festus roared out at the top of his voice, "Paul, you're mad! All this learning of yours has driven you crazy!"

"Paul, You're Mad!"

[25]"I'm not mad, most excellent Festus," responded Paul. "On the contrary, I am speaking words full of truth and good sense. [26]The king knows about these things, and it is to him that I am speaking so boldly. I cannot believe that any of this has escaped his notice. After all, these things didn't happen in a corner. [27]Do you believe the prophets, King Agrippa? I know you believe them."

[28]"You reckon you're going to make *me* a Christian, then," said Agrippa to Paul, "and pretty quick, too, by the sound of it!"

[29]"Whether quick or slow," replied Paul, "I pray to God that not only you but also all who hear me today will become just as I am—apart, of course, from these chains."

[30]The king, the governor, and Bernice, and those sitting with them, got up. [31]As they were going away, they talked to one another about it.

"This man," they were saying, "has done nothing to deserve death or chains."

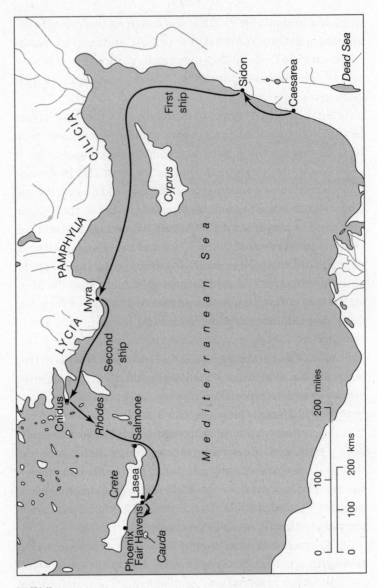

Acts 27:1–12

³²And Agrippa commented to Festus, "This man could have been set free, if only he hadn't gone and appealed to Caesar."

27 When it was decided that we should sail to Italy, they handed Paul over, along with some other prisoners, to a centurion named Julius, who belonged to the Imperial Cohort. ²They got into a ship from Adramyttium that was intending to sail to various places along the coast of Asia. So off we set. Aristarchus, a Macedonian from Thessalonica, came too.

³Next day we put in at Sidon. Julius was kind to Paul, and allowed him to go to his friends to be cared for. ⁴When we left Sidon, we sailed under the lee of Cyprus, because the winds were against us, ⁵and then crossed the sea off the coast of Cilicia and Pamphylia, arriving at Myra in Lycia. ⁶There the centurion found a ship going from Alexandria to Italy, and we got on board.

⁷After a few days we were making very heavy weather of it, and only got to the shore at Cnidus. Since the wind was not helping us, we sailed under the lee of Crete, off the coast from Salmone. ⁸Getting past that point with some difficulty, we came to a place which is called Fair Havens, not far from the town of Lasea.

⁹Quite a bit of time had now elapsed, and sailing was becoming dangerous. The Fast had already come and gone. Paul gave his advice.

¹⁰"Men," he said, "I can see we're going to have trouble on this voyage. It's going to be dangerous. We may well sustain heavy losses both to the cargo and to the ship, not to mention to human life."

¹¹But the centurion put his faith in the helmsman and the ship-owner rather than in what Paul had said. ¹²Unfortunately, the harbor was not suitable for wintering in, so most people were in favor of going on from there to see if they could get to Phoenix, a harbor on Crete which faces both southwest and northwest. They would then be able to spend the winter there.

¹³Well, a moderate southerly breeze sprang up, and they thought they had the result they wanted. So they lifted the

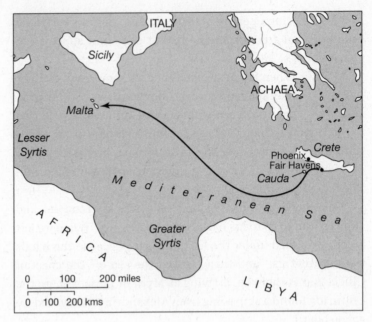

Acts 27:13–32

anchor and sailed along, hugging the shore of Crete. ¹⁴But before long a great typhoon—they call it "Eurakylon," the North-
easter—swept down from Crete, ¹⁵and the ship was caught up
by it. Since the ship couldn't turn and face into the wind, it had
to give way and we were carried along.

¹⁶When we came in behind an island called Cauda, we were
just able to get the ship's boat under control. ¹⁷They pulled it
up, and did what was necessary to undergird the ship. Then,
because they were afraid that we would crash into the Syrtis
sandbanks, they lowered the sea-anchor and allowed the ship
to be driven along. ¹⁸The storm was so severe that on the next
day they began to throw cargo overboard, ¹⁹and on the third
day they threw the ship's tackle overboard as well, with their
own hands. ²⁰We then went for a good many days without
seeing either the sun or the stars, with a major storm raging.
All hope of safety was finally abandoned.

²¹We had gone without food a long time. Then Paul stood up
in the middle of them all.

"It does seem to me, my good people," he said, "that you should have taken my advice not to leave Crete. We could have managed without this damage and loss. 22But now I want to tell you: take heart! No lives will be lost—only the ship. 23This last night, you see, an angel of the God to whom I belong, and whom I worship, stood beside me. 24'Don't be afraid, Paul,' he said. 'You must appear before Caesar, and let me tell you this: God has granted you all your traveling companions.' 25So take heart, my friends. I believe God, that it will be as he said to me. 26We must, however, be cast up on some island or other."

27On the fourteenth night we were being carried across the sea of Adria when, around the middle of the night, the sailors reckoned that we were getting near some land. 28They took soundings and found twenty fathoms; then, a little bit further, they took soundings again and found fifteen fathoms. 29They were afraid that we might crash into a rocky place, so they let down four anchors from the stern and prayed for day to come. 30The sailors wanted to escape from the ship, and let down the boat into the sea under the pretense of going to put out anchors from the bow. 31But Paul spoke to the centurion and the soldiers.

"If these men don't stay in the ship," he said, "there is no chance of safety."

32Then the soldiers cut the ropes of the boat, and let it fall away.

33When it was nearly daytime, Paul urged all of them to eat something. **Shipwreck**

"It's now all of fourteen days," he said, "that you've been hanging on without food, not eating a thing. 34So let me encourage you to have something to eat. This will help you get rescued. No hair of any of your heads will be lost."

35So saying, he took some bread, gave thanks to God in front of them all, broke the bread, and ate it. 36Then all of them cheered up and took some food. 37The whole company on board was two hundred and seventy-six. 38When we had eaten enough food, they threw the grain overboard to lighten the ship.

39When day came, they didn't recognize the land. It appeared to have a bay with a sandy shore, and that was where they hoped, if possible, to beach the ship. 40They let the anchors drop away into the sea, and at the same time slackened the ropes on the rudders, hoisted the foresail, and headed for the beach. 41But they crashed into a reef and ran the ship aground. The prow stuck fast and wouldn't budge, while the strong waves were smashing the stern to bits. 42The soldiers planned to kill the prisoners so that none of them would swim away and escape. 43But the centurion wanted to rescue Paul, and refused permission for them to carry out their intention. Instead, he ordered all who were able to swim to leap overboard first and head for land, 44while the rest were to come after, some on boards and some on bits and pieces of the ship. And so everyone ended up safely on land.

The Snake on Malta

28 When we reached safety, we discovered that the island was called Malta. 2The local inhabitants treated us with unusual kindness: they set to and built a fire for us all, since it was cold and had started to rain. 3Paul had collected quite a bundle of brushwood and was putting it on the fire, when a viper, escaping the heat, fastened onto his hand. 4The natives saw the animal clinging to his hand.

"Aha!" they said to one another. "This man must be a murderer! He's been rescued from the sea, but Justice hasn't allowed him to live."

5Paul, however, shook off the snake into the fire and suffered no harm. 6They kept watching him to see if he would swell up or suddenly fall down dead. But when they had waited and watched for quite some time, and nothing untoward had happened to him, they changed their minds.

"He must be a god," they said.

7Publius, the leading man of the island, owned lands in the region where we were. He welcomed us, and entertained us in a most friendly fashion for three days. 8Publius's father was lying sick in bed with a fever and with dysentery. Paul went in to see him and prayed; then he laid his hands on him and cured him. 9At this, everyone else on the island who was sick came and was cured. 10They gave us many honors, and when

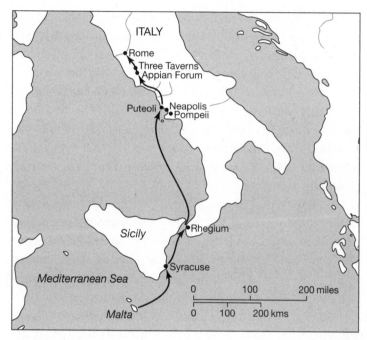

Acts 28:11–22

we were getting ready to sail away they gave us everything we needed.

[11]After three months we set sail on a ship that had been spending the winter on the island. It was from Alexandria, and had the insignia of the Heavenly Twins. [12]We arrived at Syracuse and stayed three days. [13]From there we raised anchor and sailed across to Rhegium. After one day there, a south wind arose, and on the second day we arrived at Puteoli, [14]where we found Christians, who encouraged us to stay with them for seven days.

And so we came to Rome. [15]Christians from there, hearing about us, came to meet us as far as Appian Forum and Three Taverns. When Paul saw them, he thanked God and took heart.

[16]When we arrived in Rome, Paul was allowed to lodge privately. He had a soldier to guard him.

[17]After three days, Paul called together the leading men of the Jews. When they arrived, he began to speak.

To Rome at Last

"My brothers," he said, "I have done nothing against our people or our ancestral customs. Yet I was made a prisoner in Jerusalem and handed over to the Romans. 18The Romans put me on trial and wanted to let me go, because they couldn't find me guilty of any capital crime. 19But the Judaeans opposed this, and forced me to appeal to Caesar. This had nothing to do with my bringing any charges against my nation! 20So that's why I have asked to see you and talk with you. It is because of the hope of Israel, you see, that I am wearing this chain."

21"For our part," they responded, "we haven't received any letters about you from Judaea. Nor has anyone of our nation come here to tell us anything, or to say anything bad about you. 22We want to hear from your own lips what you have in mind. However, as for this new sect, the one thing we know is that people everywhere are speaking out against it."

The End Is Where We Start From

23So they fixed a day and came in large numbers to Paul's lodgings. He spoke to them and gave his testimony about the kingdom of God. From morning to night, he explained to them the things about Jesus, from the law of Moses and the prophets.

24Some were persuaded by what he said, and others did not believe. 25They disagreed among themselves. So, as they were getting ready to leave, Paul said one last thing.

"The holy spirit," he said, "spoke truly through the prophet Isaiah to your ancestors, 26when he said,

> 'Go to this people and say to them:
> Listen and listen, but never hear;
> Look and look, but never see!
> 27For this people's heart has grown dull,
> And their ears are dim with hearing,
> And they have closed their eyes—
> So that they might not see with their eyes,
> And hear with their ears,
> And understand with their heart,
> And turn, and I would heal them.'

28"Let it then be known to you that this salvation from God has been sent to the Gentiles. They will listen."

[30]Paul lived there for two whole years at his own expense, and welcomed everyone who came to see him. [31]He announced the kingdom of God and taught the things about the Lord Jesus the Messiah with all boldness, and with no one stopping him.

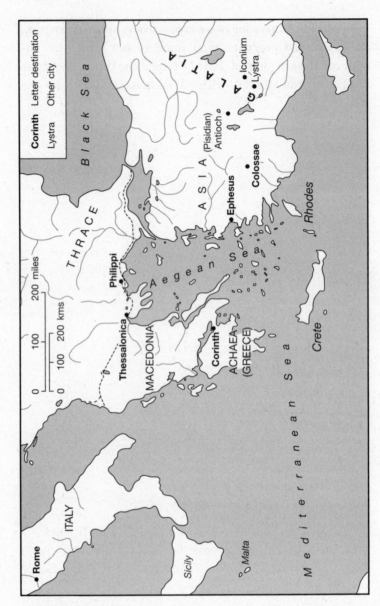

The Destinations of Paul's Letters

The Letter of Paul to the
Romans

1 Paul, a slave of King Jesus, called to be an apostle, set apart for God's good news, ²which he promised beforehand through his prophets in the sacred writings—³the good news about his son, who was descended from David's seed in terms of flesh, ⁴and who was marked out powerfully as God's son in terms of the spirit of holiness by the resurrection of the dead: Jesus, the king, our Lord!

Good News About the New King

⁵Through him we have received grace and apostleship to bring about believing obedience among all the nations for the sake of his name. ⁶That includes you, too, who are called by Jesus the king.

⁷This letter comes to all in Rome who love God, all who are called to be his holy people. Grace and peace to you from God our father, and King Jesus, the Lord.

Paul Longs to See the Roman Christians

⁸Let me say first that I thank my God for all of you, through Jesus the king, because all the world has heard the news of your faith. ⁹God is my witness—the God I worship in my spirit in the good news of his son—that I never stop remembering you ¹⁰in my prayers. I ask God again and again that somehow at last I may now be able, in his good purposes, to come to you. ¹¹I'm longing to see you! I want to share with you some spiritual blessing to give you strength; ¹²that is, I want to encourage you, and be encouraged by you, in the faith you and I share. ¹³I don't want you to be unaware, my dear family, that I've often made plans to come to you; it's just that up to now something has always gotten in the way. I want to bear some fruit among you, as I have been doing among the other nations.

**Good News,
Salvation, and
the Justice
of God**

¹⁴I am under obligation to barbarians as well as to Greeks, you see; both to the wise and to the foolish. ¹⁵That's why I'm eager to announce the good news to you, too, in Rome. ¹⁶I'm not ashamed of the good news; it's God's power, bringing salvation to everyone who believes—to the Jew first, and also, equally, to the Greek. ¹⁷This is because God's covenant justice is unveiled in it, from faithfulness to faithfulness. As it says in the Bible, "the just shall live by faith."

**Humans
Reject God
and Embrace
Corruption**

¹⁸For the anger of God is unveiled from heaven against all the ungodliness and injustice performed by people who use injustice to suppress the truth. ¹⁹What can be known of God, you see, is plain to them, since God has made it plain to them. ²⁰Ever since the world was made, his eternal power and deity have been seen and known in the things he made. As a result, they have no excuse: ²¹they knew God, but didn't honor him as God or thank him. Instead, they learned to think in useless ways, and their unwise heart grew dark. ²²They declared themselves to be wise, but in fact they became foolish. ²³They swapped the glory of the immortal God for the likeness of the image of mortal humans—and of birds, animals, and reptiles.

**Unclean Desires,
Dishonored
Bodies**

²⁴So God gave them up to uncleanness in the desires of their hearts, with the result that they dishonored their bodies among themselves. ²⁵They swapped God's truth for a lie, and worshipped and served the creature rather than the creator, who is blessed forever, Amen.

²⁶So God gave them up to shameful desires. Even the women, you see, swapped natural sexual practice for unnatural; ²⁷and the men, too, abandoned natural sexual relations with women, and were inflamed with their lust for one another. Men performed shameless acts with men, and received in themselves the appropriate repayment for their mistaken ways.

**Darkened Mind,
Darkened
Behavior**

²⁸Moreover, just as they did not see fit to hold on to knowledge of God, God gave them up to an unfit mind, so that they would behave inappropriately. ²⁹They were filled with all kinds of injustice, wickedness, greed, and evil; they were full of envy, murder, enmity, deceit, and cunning. They became gossips, ³⁰slanderers, God-haters, arrogant, self-important, boastful, inventors of evil, disobedient to parents, ³¹unwise,

unfaithful, unfeeling, uncaring. 32They know that God has rightly decreed that people who do things like that deserve death. But not only do they do them; they give their approval to people who practice them.

2 So you have no excuse—anyone, whoever you are, who sit in judgment! When you judge someone else, you condemn yourself, because you, who are behaving as a judge, are doing the same things. 2God's judgment falls, we know, in accordance with the truth, on those who do such things. 3But if you judge those who do them and yet do them yourself, do you really suppose that you will escape God's judgment?

God's Coming Judgment Will Be Impartial, the Same for All

4Or do you despise the riches of God's kindness, forbearance and patience? Don't you know that God's kindness is meant to bring you to repentance? 5But by your hard, unrepentant heart you are building up a store of anger for yourself on the day of anger, the day when God's just judgment will be unveiled—6the God who will "repay everyone according to their works."

7When people patiently do what is good, and so pursue the quest for glory and honor and immortality, God will give them the life of the age to come. 8But when people act out of selfish desire, and do not obey the truth, but instead obey injustice, there will be anger and fury. 9There will be trouble and distress for every single person who does what is wicked, the Jew first and also, equally, the Greek—10and there will be glory, honor, and peace for everyone who does what is good, the Jew first and also, equally, the Greek. 11God, you see, shows no partiality.

12Everyone who sinned outside the law, you see, will be judged outside the law—and those who sinned from within the law will be judged by means of the law. 13After all, it isn't those who *hear* the law who are in the right before God. It's those who *do* the law who will be declared to be in the right!

How God's Impartial Judgment Will Work

14This is how it works out. Gentiles don't possess the law as their birthright; but whenever they do what the law says, they are a law for themselves, despite not possessing the law. 15They show that the work of the law is written on their hearts. Their conscience bears witness as well, and their thoughts will run this way and that, sometimes accusing them and sometimes excusing, ¹⁶on the day when (according to the gospel I proclaim) God judges all human secrets through King Jesus.

The Claim of the Jew—and Its Problems

¹⁷But supposing you call yourself a "Jew." Supposing you rest your hope in the law. Supposing you celebrate the fact that God is your God, ¹⁸and that you know what he wants, and that by the law's instruction you can make appropriate moral distinctions. ¹⁹Supposing you believe yourself to be a guide to the blind, a light to people in darkness, ²⁰a teacher of the foolish, an instructor for children—all because, in the law, you possess the outline of knowledge and truth.

²¹Well then: if you're going to teach someone else, aren't you going to teach yourself? If you say people shouldn't steal, do you steal? ²²If you say people shouldn't commit adultery, do you commit adultery? If you loathe idols, do you rob temples? ²³If you boast in the law, do you dishonor God by breaking the law? ²⁴This is what the Bible says: "Because of you, God's name is blasphemed among the nations!"

The Badge, the Name, and the Meaning

²⁵Circumcision, you see, has real value for people who keep the law. If, however, you break the law, your circumcision becomes uncircumcision. ²⁶Meanwhile, if uncircumcised people keep the law's requirements, their uncircumcision will be regarded as circumcision, won't it? ²⁷So people who are by nature uncircumcised, but who fulfill the law, will pass judgment on people like you who possess the letter of the law and circumcision but who break the law.

²⁸The "Jew" isn't the person who appears to be one, you see. Nor is "circumcision" what it appears to be, a matter of physical flesh. ²⁹The "Jew" is the one in secret; and "circumcision" is a matter of the heart, in the spirit rather than the letter. Such a person gets "praise," not from humans, but from God.

God's Determined Faithfulness

3 What advantage, then, does the Jew possess? What, indeed, is the point of circumcision? ²A great deal, in every way. To begin with, the Jews were entrusted with God's oracles. ³What follows from that? If some of them were unfaithful to their commission, does their unfaithfulness nullify God's faithfulness? ⁴Certainly not! Let God be true, and every human being false! As the Bible says,

So that you may be found in the right in what you say,
And may win the victory when you come to court.

⁵But if our being in the wrong proves that God is in the right, what are we going to say? That God is unjust to inflict anger on people? (I'm reducing things to a human scale!) ⁶Certainly not! How then could God judge the world? ⁷But if God's truthfulness grows all the greater and brings him glory in and through my falsehood, why am I still being condemned as a sinner? ⁸And why not "do evil so that good may come"—as some people blasphemously say about us, and as some allege that we say? People like that, at least, deserve the judgment they get!

⁹What then? Are we in fact better off? No, certainly not. I have already laid down this charge, you see: Jews as well as Greeks are all under the power of sin. ¹⁰This is what the Bible says:

Jews as Well as Gentiles Are Guilty of Sin

No one is in the right—nobody at all!
¹¹No one understands, or goes looking for God;
¹²All of them alike have wandered astray,
Together they have all become futile;
None of them behaves kindly, no, not one.
¹³Their throat is an open grave,
They use their tongues to deceive,
The poison of vipers is under their lips.
¹⁴Their mouth is full of cursing and bitterness,
¹⁵Their feet are quick when there's blood to be shed,
¹⁶Disaster and wretchedness are in their paths,
¹⁷And they did not know the way of peace.
¹⁸They have no fear of God before their eyes.

¹⁹Now we know that whatever the law says, it is speaking to those who are "in the law." The purpose of this is that every mouth may be stopped, and the whole world may be brought to the bar of God's judgment. ²⁰No mere mortal, you see, can be declared to be in the right before God on the basis of the works of the law. What you get through the law is the knowledge of sin.

The Unveiling of God's Covenant Justice

21But now, quite apart from the law (though the law and the prophets bore witness to it), God's covenant justice has been displayed. 22God's covenant justice comes into operation through the faithfulness of Jesus the Messiah, for the benefit of all who have faith. For there is no distinction: 23all sinned, and fell short of God's glory—24and by God's grace they are freely declared to be in the right, to be members of the covenant, through the redemption which is found in the Messiah, Jesus.

Jesus's Death Reveals God's Covenant Justice

25God put Jesus forth as the place of mercy, through faithfulness, by means of his blood. He did this to demonstrate his covenant justice, because of the passing over (in divine forbearance) of sins committed beforehand. 26This was to demonstrate his covenant justice in the present time: that is, that he himself is in the right, and that he declares to be in the right everyone who trusts in the faithfulness of Jesus.

The God of Both Jew and Gentile

27So what happens to boasting? It is ruled out! Through what sort of law? The law of works? No: through the law of faith! 28We calculate, you see, that a person is declared to be in the right on the basis of faith, apart from works of the law. 29Or does God only belong to Jews? Doesn't he belong to the nations as well? Yes, of course, to the nations as well, 30since God is one. He will make the declaration "in the right" over the circumcised on the basis of faith, and over the uncircumcised through faith.

31Do we then abolish the law through faith? Certainly not! Rather, we establish the law.

God's Covenant with Abraham

4 What shall we say, then? Have we found Abraham to be our ancestor in a human, fleshly sense? 2After all, if Abraham was reckoned "in the right" on the basis of works, he has grounds to boast—but not in God's presence!

3So what does the Bible say? "Abraham believed God, and it was calculated in his favor, putting him in the right." 4Now when someone "works," the "reward" they get is not calculated on the basis of generosity, but on the basis of what they are owed. 5But if someone doesn't "work," but simply believes in the one who declares the ungodly to be in the right, that person's faith is calculated in their favor, putting them in the right.

⁶We see the same thing when David speaks of the blessing that comes to someone whom God calculates to be in the right apart from works:

⁷*Blessed are those whose lawbreaking is forgiven
And whose sins have been covered over;*
⁸*Blessed is the man to whom the Lord will not
    calculate sin.*

⁹So, then, does this blessing come on circumcised people or on uncircumcised? This is the passage we quoted: "His faith was calculated to Abraham as indicating that he was in the right." ¹⁰How was it calculated? When he was circumcised or when he was uncircumcised? It wasn't when he was circumcised; it was when he was uncircumcised! ¹¹He received circumcision as a sign and seal of the status of covenant membership, on the basis of faith, which he had when he was still uncircumcised. This was so that he could be the father of all who believe even when uncircumcised, so that the status of covenant membership can be calculated to their account as well. ¹²He is also, of course, the father of the circumcised who are not merely circumcised but who follow the steps of the faith which Abraham possessed while still uncircumcised.

Abraham, the Father of Both Uncircumcised and Circumcised

¹³The promise, you see, didn't come to Abraham or to his family through the law—the promise, that is, that he would inherit the world. It came through the covenant justice of faith. ¹⁴For if those who belong to the law are going to inherit, then faith is empty, and the promise has been abolished. ¹⁵For the law stirs up God's anger; but where there is no law, there is no lawbreaking.

Abraham, the Father of All Believers

¹⁶That's why it's "by faith": so that it can be in accordance with grace, and so that the promise can thereby be validated for the entire family—not simply those who are from the law, but those who share the faith of Abraham. He is the father of us all, ¹⁷just as the Bible says, "I have made you the father of many nations." This happened in the presence of the God in whom he believed, the God who gives life to the dead and calls into existence things that do not exist.

¹⁸Against all hope, but still in hope, Abraham believed that he would become the father of many nations, in line with what

Abraham's Faith—and Ours

had been said to him: "That's what your family will be like." 19He didn't become weak in faith as he considered his own body (which was already as good as dead, since he was about a hundred years old), and the lifelessness of Sarah's womb. 20He didn't waver in unbelief when faced with God's promise. Instead, he grew strong in faith and gave glory to God, 21being fully convinced that God had the power to accomplish what he had promised. 22That is why "it was calculated to him in terms of covenant justice."

23But it wasn't written for him alone that "it was calculated to him." 24It was written for us as well! It will be calculated to us, too, since we believe in the one who raised from the dead Jesus our Lord, 25who was handed over because of our trespasses and raised because of our justification.

Peace and Hope

5 The result is this: since we have been declared "in the right" on the basis of faith, we have peace with God through our Lord Jesus the Messiah. 2Through him we have been allowed to approach, by faith, into this grace in which we stand; and we celebrate the hope of the glory of God.

3That's not all. We also celebrate in our sufferings, because we know that suffering produces patience, 4patience produces a well-formed character, and a character like that produces hope. 5Hope, in its turn, does not make us ashamed, because the love of God has been poured out in our hearts through the holy spirit who has been given to us.

Jesus's Death Reveals God's Love and Guarantees Final Salvation

6This is all based on what the Messiah did: while we were still weak, at that very moment he died on behalf of the ungodly. 7It's a rare thing to find someone who will die on behalf of an upright person—though I suppose someone might be brave enough to die for a good person. 8But this is how God demonstrates his own love for us: the Messiah died for us while we were still sinners.

9How much more, in that case—since we have been declared to be in the right by his blood—are we going to be saved by him from God's coming anger! 10When we were enemies, you see, we were reconciled to God through the death of his son; if that's so, how much more, having already been reconciled, shall we be saved by his life. 11And that's not all. We even celebrate in God, through our Lord Jesus the Messiah, through whom we have now received this reconciliation.

¹²Therefore, just as sin came into the world through one human being, and death through sin, and in that way death spread to all humans, in that all sinned . . . ¹³Sin was in the world, you see, even in the absence of the law, though sin is not calculated when there is no law. ¹⁴But death reigned from Adam to Moses, even over the people who did not sin by breaking a command, as Adam had done—Adam, who was the imprint of the one who would come.

¹⁵But it isn't "as the trespass, so also the gift." For if many died by one person's trespass, how much more has God's grace, and the gift in grace through the one person Jesus the Messiah, abounded to the many. ¹⁶And nor is it "as through the sin of the one, so also the gift." For the judgment which followed the one trespass resulted in a negative verdict, but the free gift which followed many trespasses resulted in a positive verdict. ¹⁷For if, by the trespass of the one, death reigned through that one, how much more will those who receive the abundance of grace, and of the gift of covenant membership, of "being in the right," reign in life through the one man Jesus the Messiah.

¹⁸So, then, just as, through the trespass of one person, the result was condemnation for all people, even so, through the upright act of one person, the result is justification—life for all people. ¹⁹For just as through the disobedience of one person many received the status of "sinner," so through the obedience of one person many will receive the status of "in the right."

²⁰The law came in alongside, so that the trespass might be filled out to its full extent. But where sin increased, grace increased all the more; ²¹so that, just as sin reigned in death, even so, through God's faithful covenant justice, grace might reign to the life of the age to come, through Jesus the Messiah, our Lord.

6 What are we to say, then? Shall we continue in the state of sin, so that grace may increase? ²Certainly not! We died to sin; how can we still live in it? ³Don't you know that all of us who were baptized into the Messiah, Jesus, were

The Big Picture in Shorthand: Adam and the Messiah

The Triumphant Reign of Grace

Leaving the State of Sin Through Baptism

baptized into his death? [4]That means that we were buried with him, through baptism, into death, so that, just as the Messiah was raised from the dead through the father's glory, we too might behave with a new quality of life. [5]For if we have been planted together in the likeness of his death, we shall also be in the likeness of his resurrection.

Dead to Sin, Alive to God

[6]This is what we know: our old humanity was crucified with the Messiah, so that the bodily solidarity of sin might be abolished, and that we should no longer be enslaved to sin. [7]A person who has died, you see, has been declared free from all charges of sin.

[8]But if we died with the Messiah, we believe that we shall live with him. [9]We know that the Messiah, having been raised from the dead, will never die again. Death no longer has any authority over him. [10]The death he died, you see, he died to sin, once and only once. But the life he lives, he lives to God. [11]In the same way you, too, must calculate yourselves as being dead to sin, and alive to God in the Messiah, Jesus.

The Call to Holy Living

[12]So don't allow sin to rule in your mortal body, to make you obey its desires. [13]Nor should you present your limbs and organs to sin to be used for its wicked purposes. Rather, present yourselves to God, as people alive from the dead, and your limbs and organs to God, to be used for the righteous purposes of his covenant. [14]Sin won't actually rule over you, you see, since you are not under law but under grace.

The Two Types of Slavery

[15]What then? Shall we sin, because we are not under law but under grace? Certainly not! [16]Don't you know that if you present yourselves to someone as obedient slaves, you really are slaves of the one you obey, whether that happens to be sin, which leads to death, or obedience, which leads to final vindication? [17]Thank God that, though you once were slaves to sin, you have become obedient from the heart to the pattern of teaching to which you were committed. [18]You were freed from sin, and now you have been enslaved to God's covenant justice. [19](I'm using a human picture because of your natural human weakness!) For just as you presented your limbs and organs as slaves to uncleanness, and to one degree of lawlessness after another, so now present your limbs and organs as slaves to covenant justice, which leads to holiness.

²⁰When you were slaves of sin, you see, you were free with respect to covenant justice. ²¹What fruit did you ever have from the things of which you are now ashamed? Their destination is death. ²²But now that you have been set free from sin and enslaved to God, you have fruit for holiness. Its destination is the life of the age to come. ²³The wages paid by sin, you see, are death; but God's free gift is the life of the age to come, in the Messiah, Jesus our Lord.

Where the Two Roads Lead

7 Surely you know, my dear family—I am, after all, talking to people who know the law!—that the law rules a person as long as that person is alive? ²The law binds a married woman to her husband during his lifetime; but if he dies, she is free from the law as regards her husband. ³So, then, she will be called an adulteress if she goes with another man while her husband is alive; but if the husband dies, she is free from the law, so that she is not an adulteress if she goes with another man.

Dying to the Law

⁴In the same way, my dear family, you too died to the law through the body of the Messiah, so that you could belong to someone else—to the one who was raised from the dead, in fact—so that we could bear fruit for God. ⁵For when we were living a mortal human life, the passions of sins which were through the law were at work in our limbs and organs, causing us to bear fruit for death. ⁶But now we have been cut loose from the law; we have died to the thing in which we were held tightly. The aim is that we should now be enslaved in the new life of the spirit, not in the old life of the letter.

⁷What then shall we say? That the law is sin? Certainly not. But I would not have known sin except through the law. I would not have known covetousness if the law had not said, "You shall not covet." ⁸But sin grabbed its opportunity through the commandment, and produced all kinds of covetousness within me.

When the Law Arrived: Sinai Looks Back to the Fall

Apart from the law, sin is dead. ⁹I was once alive apart from the law; but when the commandment came, sin sprang to life ¹⁰and I died. The commandment which pointed to life turned out, in my case, to bring death. ¹¹For sin grabbed its opportunity through the commandment. It deceived me and, through it, killed me.

¹²So, then, the law is holy; and the commandment is holy, upright, and good.

Looking Back on Life Under the Law

¹³Was it that good thing, then, that brought death to me? Certainly not! On the contrary; it was sin, in order that it might appear as sin, working through the good thing and producing death in me. This was in order that sin might become very sinful indeed, through the commandment.

¹⁴We know, you see, that the law is spiritual. I, however, am made of flesh, sold as a slave under sin's authority. ¹⁵I don't understand what I do. I don't do what I want, you see, but I do what I hate. ¹⁶So if I do what I don't want to do, I am agreeing that the law is good.

¹⁷But now it is no longer I that do it; it's sin, living within me. ¹⁸I know, you see, that no good thing lives in me, that is, in my human flesh. For I can will the good, but I can't perform it. ¹⁹For I don't do the good thing I want to do, but I end up doing the evil thing I don't want to do. ²⁰So if I do what I don't want to do, it's no longer "I" doing it; it's sin, living inside me.

The Double "Law" and the Miserable "I"

²¹This, then, is what I find about the law: when I want to do what is right, evil lies close at hand! ²²I delight in God's law, you see, according to my inmost self; ²³but I see another "law" in my limbs and organs, fighting a battle against the law of my mind, and taking me as a prisoner in the law of sin which is in my limbs and organs.

²⁴What a miserable person I am! Who is going to rescue me from the body of this death? ²⁵Thank God—through Jesus our king and Lord! So, then, left to my own self I am enslaved to God's law with my mind, but to sin's law with my human flesh.

God's Action in Messiah and Spirit

8 So, therefore, there is no condemnation for those in the Messiah, Jesus! ²Why not? Because the law of the spirit of life in the Messiah, Jesus, released you from the law of sin and death.

³For God has done what the law (being weak because of human flesh) was incapable of doing. God sent his own son in the likeness of sinful flesh, and as a sin-offering; and, right there in the flesh, he condemned sin. ⁴This was in order that the right and proper verdict of the law could be fulfilled in us, as we live not according to the flesh but according to the spirit.

⁵Look at it like this. People whose lives are determined by human flesh focus their minds on matters to do with the flesh, but people whose lives are determined by the spirit focus their minds on matters to do with the spirit. ⁶Focus the mind on the flesh, and you'll die; but focus it on the spirit, and you'll have life, and peace. ⁷The mind focused on the flesh, you see, is hostile to God. It doesn't submit to God's law; in fact, it can't. ⁸Those who are determined by the flesh can't please God.

⁹But you're not people of flesh; you're people of the spirit (if indeed God's spirit lives within you; note that anyone who doesn't have the spirit of the Messiah doesn't belong to him). ¹⁰But if the Messiah is in you, the body is indeed dead because of sin, but the spirit is life because of covenant justice. ¹¹So, then, if the spirit of the one who raised Jesus from the dead lives within you, the one who raised the Messiah from the dead will give life to your mortal bodies, too, through his spirit who lives within you.

¹²So then, my dear family, we are in debt—but not to human flesh, to live our life in that way. ¹³If you live in accordance with the flesh, you will die; but if, by the spirit, you put to death the deeds of the body, you will live.

¹⁴All who are led by the spirit of God, you see, are God's children. ¹⁵You didn't receive a spirit of slavery, did you, to go back again into a state of fear? But you received the spirit of sonship, in whom we call out "Abba, Father!" ¹⁶When that happens, it is the spirit itself giving supporting witness to what our own spirit is saying, that we are God's children. ¹⁷And if we're children, we are also heirs: heirs of God, and fellow heirs with the Messiah, as long as we suffer with him so that we may also be glorified with him.

¹⁸This is how I work it out. The sufferings we go through in the present time are not worth putting in the scale alongside the glory that is going to be unveiled for us. ¹⁹Yes: creation itself is on tiptoe with expectation, eagerly awaiting the moment when God's children will be revealed. ²⁰Creation, you see, was subjected to pointless futility, not of its own volition, but because of the one who placed it in this subjection, in the hope ²¹that creation itself would be freed from its slavery to

The Work of the Spirit

Children of God, Led by the Spirit

Creation Renewed and Patient Hope

decay, to enjoy the freedom that comes when God's children are glorified.

²²Let me explain. We know that the entire creation is groaning together, and going through labor pains together, up until the present time. ²³Not only so: we too, we who have the first fruits of the spirit's life within us, are groaning within ourselves, as we eagerly await our adoption, the redemption of our body. ²⁴We were saved, you see, in hope. But hope isn't hope if you can see it! Who hopes for what they can see? ²⁵But if we hope for what we don't see, we wait for it eagerly—but also patiently.

Prayer, Sonship, and the Sovereignty of God

²⁶In the same way, too, the spirit comes alongside and helps us in our weakness. We don't know what to pray for as we ought to; but that same spirit pleads on our behalf, with groanings too deep for words. ²⁷And the Searcher of Hearts knows what the spirit is thinking, because the spirit pleads for God's people according to God's will.

²⁸We know, in fact, that God works all things together for good to those who love him, who are called according to his purpose. ²⁹Those he foreknew, you see, he also marked out in advance to be shaped according to the model of the image of his son, so that he might be the firstborn of a large family. ³⁰And those he marked out in advance, he also called; those he called, he also justified; those he justified, he also glorified.

Nothing Shall Separate Us from God's Love

³¹What then shall we say to all this?

If God is for us, who is against us?

³²God, after all, did not spare his own son; he gave him up for us all!

How then will he not, with him, freely give all things to us?

³³Who will bring a charge against God's chosen ones?

It is God who declares them in the right.

³⁴Who is going to condemn?

It is the Messiah, Jesus, who has died, or rather has been raised;

who is at God's right hand, and who also prays on our behalf!

³⁵Who shall separate us from the Messiah's love?

Suffering, or hardship, or persecution, or famine, or nakedness, or danger, or sword? ³⁶As the Bible says,

Because of you we are being killed all day long;
We are regarded as sheep destined for slaughter.

³⁷No: in all these things we are completely victorious through the one who loved us. ³⁸I am persuaded, you see, that neither death nor life, nor angels nor rulers, nor the present, nor the future, nor powers, ³⁹nor height, nor depth, nor any other creature will be able to separate us from the love of God in King Jesus our Lord.

9 I'm speaking the truth in the Messiah; I'm not lying. I call my conscience as witness, in the holy spirit, ²that I have great sorrow and endless pain in my heart. ³Left to my own self, I am half-inclined to pray that I would be accursed, cut off from the Messiah, on behalf of my own family, my own flesh-and-blood relatives. ⁴They are Israelites; the sonship, the glory, the covenants, the giving of the law, the worship and the promises all belong to them. ⁵The patriarchs are their ancestors; and it is from them, according to the flesh, that the Messiah has come—who is God over all, blessed forever. Amen!

The Privileges and Tragedy of Israel

⁶But it can't be the case that God's word has failed! Not all who are from Israel, you see, are in fact Israel. ⁷Nor is it the case that all the children count as "seed of Abraham." No: "in Isaac shall your seed be named." ⁸That means that it isn't the flesh-and-blood children who are God's children; rather, it is the children of the promise who will be calculated as "seed." ⁹This was what the promise said, you see: "Around this time I shall return, and Sarah shall have a son."

Abraham's Two Families

¹⁰And that's not all. The same thing happened when Rebecca conceived children by one man, our ancestor Isaac. ¹¹When they had not yet been born, and had done nothing either good or bad—so that what God had in mind in making his choice might come to pass, ¹²not because of works but because of the one who calls—it was said to her, "The elder shall serve the younger." ¹³As the Bible says, "I loved Jacob, but I hated Esau."

¹⁴So what are we going to say? Is God unjust? Certainly not! ¹⁵He says to Moses, you see, "I will have mercy on those on whom I will have mercy, and I will pity those I will pity."

God's Purpose and Justice

¹⁶So, then, it doesn't depend on human willing, or on human effort; it depends on God who shows mercy. ¹⁷For the Bible says to Pharaoh: "This is why I have raised you up, to show my power in you, and so that my name may be proclaimed in all the earth." ¹⁸So, then, he has mercy on the one he wants, and he hardens the one he wants.

¹⁹You will say to me, then, "So why does he still blame people? Who can stand against his purpose?" ²⁰Are you, a mere human being, going to answer God back? "Surely the clay won't say to the potter, 'Why did you make me like this?'" ²¹Doesn't the potter have authority over the clay, so that he can make from the same lump one vessel for honor, and another for dishonor? ²²Supposing God wanted to demonstrate his anger and make known his power, and for that reason put up very patiently with the vessels of anger created for destruction, ²³in order to make known the riches of his glory on the vessels of mercy, the ones he prepared in advance for glory—²⁴including us, whom he called not only from among the Jews but also from among the Gentiles?

God Calls a Remnant

²⁵This is what he says in Hosea,

> *I will call "not my people" "my people";*
> *And "not beloved" I will call "beloved."*
> *²⁶And in the place where it was said to them,*
> *"You are not my people,"*
> *There they will be called "sons of the living God."*

²⁷Isaiah cries out, concerning Israel,

> *Even if the number of Israel's sons are like the sand by*
> *   the sea,*
> *Only a remnant shall be saved;*
> *²⁸For the Lord will bring judgment on the earth,*
> *Complete and decisive.*

²⁹As Isaiah said in an earlier passage,

> *If the Lord of hosts had not left us seed,*
> *We would have become like Sodom, and been made like*
> *   Gomorrah.*

³⁰What then shall we say? That the nations, who were not aspiring toward covenant membership, have obtained covenant membership, but it is a covenant membership based on faith. ³¹Israel, meanwhile, though eager for the law which defined the covenant, did not attain to the law. ³²Why not? Because they did not pursue it on the basis of faith, but as though it was on the basis of works. They have stumbled over the stumbling stone, ³³as the Bible says:

> Look: I am placing in Zion
> A stone that will make people stumble,
> A rock that will trip people up;
> And the one who believes in him
> Will never be put to shame.

10 My dear family, the longing of my heart, and my prayer to God on their behalf, is for their salvation. ²I can testify on their behalf that they have a zeal for God; but it is not based on knowledge. ³They were ignorant, you see, of God's covenant faithfulness, and they were trying to establish a covenant status of their own; so they didn't submit to God's faithfulness. ⁴The Messiah, you see, is the goal of the law, so that covenant membership may be available for all who believe.

⁵Moses writes, you see, about the covenant membership defined by the law, that "the person who performs the law's commands shall live in them." ⁶But the *faith*-based covenant membership puts it like this: "Don't say in your heart, Who shall go up to heaven?" (in other words, to bring the Messiah down), ⁷"or, Who shall go down into the depths?" (in other words, to bring the Messiah up from the dead). ⁸But what does it say? "The word is near you, in your mouth and in your heart" (that is, the word of faith which we proclaim); ⁹because if you profess with your mouth that Jesus is Lord, and believe in your heart that God raised him from the dead, you will be saved. ¹⁰Why? Because the way to covenant membership is by believing with the heart, and the way to salvation is by professing with the mouth. ¹¹The Bible says, you see, "Everyone who believes in him will not be put to shame." ¹²For there is

no distinction between Jew and Greek, since the same Lord is Lord of all, and is rich toward all who call upon him. [13]"All who call upon the name of the Lord," you see, "will be saved."

The Call to the World, and the Failure of Israel

[14]So how are they to call on someone when they haven't believed in him? And how are they to believe if they don't hear? And how will they hear without someone announcing it to them? [15]And how will people make that announcement unless they are sent? As the Bible says, "How beautiful are the feet of the ones who bring good news of good things."

[16]But not all obeyed the good news. Isaiah asks, you see, "Lord, who has believed our report?" [17]So faith comes from hearing, and hearing comes from the word of the Messiah.

[18]This might make us ask, Did they not hear? But they certainly did:

> Their sound went out into all the world,
> And their words to the ends of the earth.

[19]But I ask, did Israel not know? To begin with, Moses says,

> I will make you jealous with a non-nation;
> And stir you to anger with a foolish people.

[20]Then Isaiah, greatly daring, puts it like this:

> I was found by those who were not looking for me;
> I became visible to those who were not asking for me.

[21]But in respect of Israel he says,

> All day long I have stretched out my hands
> To a disbelieving and disagreeable people.

The Remnant of Grace

11 So I ask, has God abandoned his people? Certainly not! I myself am an Israelite, from the seed of Abraham and the tribe of Benjamin. [2]"God has not abandoned his people," the ones he chose in advance.

Don't you know what the Bible says in the passage about Elijah, describing how he pleads with God against Israel? [3]"Lord," he says, "they have killed your prophets, they have thrown down your altars; I'm the only one left, and they are trying to kill me!" [4]But what is the reply from the divine word?

"I have left for myself seven thousand men who have not bowed the knee to Baal."

5In the same way, at the present time there is a remnant, chosen by grace. 6But if it is by grace, it is no longer by works; otherwise grace would no longer be grace.

7What then? Did Israel not obtain what it was looking for? Well, the chosen ones obtained it—but the rest were hardened, 8as the Bible says:

> God gave them a spirit of stupor,
> Eyes that wouldn't see, and ears that wouldn't hear,
> Right down to this present day.

9And David says,

> Let their table become a snare and a trap,
> And a stumbling block and a punishment for them;
> 10Let their eyes be darkened so that they can't see,
> And make their backs bend low forever.

11So I ask, then: Have they tripped up in such a way as to fall completely? Certainly not! Rather, by their trespass, salvation has come to the nations, in order to make them jealous. 12If their trespass means riches for the world, and their impoverishment means riches for the nations, how much more will their fullness mean!

13Now I am speaking to you Gentiles. Insofar as I am the apostle of the Gentiles, I celebrate my particular ministry, 14so that, if possible, I can make my "flesh" jealous, and save some of them. 15If their casting away, you see, means reconciliation for the world, what will their acceptance mean but life from the dead?

16Take another illustration: if the first fruits are holy, so is the whole lump.

And another: if the root is holy, so are the branches.

17But if some of the branches were broken off, and you—a *wild* olive tree!—were grafted in among them, and came to share in the root of the olive with its rich sap, 18don't boast over the branches. If you do boast, remember this: it isn't you that supports the root, but the root that supports you.

A Stumble with a Purpose

The Two Olive Trees

¹⁹I know what you'll say next: "Branches were broken off so that I could be grafted in." ²⁰That's all very well. They were broken off because of unbelief—but you stand firm by faith. Don't get big ideas about it; instead, be afraid. ²¹After all, if God didn't spare the natural branches, there's a strong possibility he won't spare you.

²²Note carefully, then, that God is both kind and severe. He is severe to those who have fallen, but he is kind to you, provided you continue in his kindness—otherwise you too will be cut off. ²³And they, too, if they do not remain in unbelief, will be grafted back in. God is able, you see, to graft them back in. ²⁴For if you were cut out of what is by nature a wild olive tree, and grafted, contrary to nature, into a cultivated olive tree, how much more will they, the natural branches, be grafted back into their own olive tree.

Mercy upon All   ²⁵My dear brothers and sisters, you mustn't get the wrong idea and think too much of yourselves. That is why I don't want you to remain in ignorance of this mystery: a hardening has come for a time upon Israel, until the fullness of the nations comes in. ²⁶That is how "all Israel shall be saved," as the Bible says:

> The Deliverer will come from Zion,
> And will turn away ungodliness from Jacob.
> ²⁷And this will be my covenant with them,
> Whenever I take away their sins.

²⁸As regards the good news, they are enemies—for your sake! But as regards God's choice they are beloved because of the patriarchs. ²⁹God's gifts and God's call, you see, cannot be undone. ³⁰For just as *you* were once disobedient to God, but now have received mercy through *their* disobedience, ³¹so *they* have now disbelieved as well, in order that, through the mercy which has come *your* way, they too may now receive mercy. ³²For God has shut up all people in disobedience, so that he may have mercy upon all.

To God Be   ³³O, the depth of the riches
the Glory   And the wisdom and knowledge of God!
            We cannot search his judgments;

We cannot fathom his ways.
³⁴*For "Who has known the mind of the Lord?*
Or who has given him counsel?
³⁵*Who has given a gift to him*
Which needs to be repaid?"
³⁶*For from him, through him, and to him are all things.*
Glory to him forever! Amen.

12 So, my dear family, this is my appeal to you by the mercies of God: offer your bodies as a living sacrifice, holy and pleasing to God. Worship like this brings your mind into line with God's. ²What's more, don't let yourselves be squeezed into the shape dictated by the present age. Instead, be transformed by the renewing of your minds, so that you can work out what God's will is—what is good, acceptable, and complete.

The Living Sacrifice

³Through the grace which was given to me, I have this to say to each one of you: don't think of yourselves more highly than you ought to think. Rather, think soberly, in line with faith, the true standard which God has marked out for each of you. ⁴As in one body we have many limbs and organs, you see, and all the parts have different functions, ⁵so we, many as we are, are one body in the Messiah, and individually we belong to one another.

⁶Well then, we have gifts that differ in accordance with the grace that has been given to us, and we must use them appropriately. If it is prophecy, we must prophesy according to the pattern of the faith. ⁷If it is serving, we must work at our serving; if teaching, at our teaching; ⁸if exhortation, at our exhortation; if giving, with generosity; if leading, with energy; if doing acts of kindness, with cheerfulness.

Living Together in the Messiah

⁹Love must be real. Hate what is evil; stick fast to what is good. ¹⁰Be truly affectionate in showing love for one another; compete with each other in giving mutual respect. ¹¹Don't get tired of working hard. Be on fire with the spirit. Work as slaves for the Lord. ¹²Celebrate your hope; be patient in suffering; give constant energy to prayer; ¹³contribute to the needs of God's people; make sure you are hospitable to strangers.

¹⁴Bless those who persecute you; bless them, don't curse them. ¹⁵Celebrate with those who are celebrating; mourn with the mourners. ¹⁶Come to the same mind with one another. Don't give yourselves airs, but associate with the humble. Don't get too clever for yourselves.

¹⁷Never repay anyone evil for evil; think through what will seem good to everyone who is watching. ¹⁸If it's possible, as far as you can, live at peace with all people. ¹⁹Don't take revenge, my dear people, but allow God's anger room to work. The Bible says, after all, "Vengeance is mine; I will repay, says the Lord." ²⁰No: "If your enemy is hungry, feed him; if he is thirsty, give him a drink. If you do this, you will pile up burning coals on his head." ²¹Don't let evil conquer you. Rather, conquer evil with good.

13 Every person must be subject to the ruling authorities. There is no authority, you see, except from God, and those that exist have been put in place by God. ²As a result, anyone who rebels against authority is resisting what God has set up, and those who resist will bring judgment on themselves. ³For rulers hold no terrors for people who do good, but only for people who do evil.

If you want to have no fear of the ruling power, do what is good, and it will praise you. ⁴It is God's servant, you see, for you and your good. But if you do evil, be afraid; the sword it carries is no empty gesture. It is God's servant, you see: an agent of justice to bring his anger on evildoers. ⁵That is why it is necessary to submit, not only to avoid punishment but because of conscience.

⁶That, too, is why you pay taxes. The officials in question are God's ministers, attending to this very thing. ⁷So pay each of them what is owed: tribute to those who collect it, revenue to those who collect it. Respect those who should be respected. Honor the people one ought to honor.

⁸Don't owe anything to anyone, except the debt of mutual love. If you love your neighbor, you see, you have fulfilled the law. ⁹Commandments like "don't commit adultery, don't kill, don't steal, don't covet"—and any other commandment—are summed up in this: "Love your neighbor as yourself." ¹⁰Love

does no wrong to its neighbor; so love is the fulfillment of the law.

¹⁷This is all the more important because you know what time it is. The hour has come for you to wake up from sleep. Our salvation, you see, is nearer now than it was when first we came to faith. ¹²The night is nearly over; the day is almost here. So let's put off the works of darkness and put on the armor of light. ¹³Let's behave appropriately, as in the daytime: not in wild parties and drunkenness, not in orgies and shameless immorality, not in bad temper and jealousy. ¹⁴Instead, put on the Lord Jesus, the Messiah, and don't make any allowance for the flesh and its lusts.

14 Welcome someone who is weak in faith, but not in order to have disputes on difficult points. ²One person believes it is all right to eat anything, while the weak person eats only vegetables. ³The one who eats should not despise the one who does not, and the one who does not should not condemn the one who does—because God has welcomed them.

The Weak and the Strong

⁴Who do you think you are to judge someone else's servants? They stand or fall before their own master. And stand they will, because the master can make them stand.

⁵One person reckons one day more important than another. Someone else regards all days as equally important. Each person must make up their own mind. ⁶The one who celebrates the day does so in honor of the Lord. The one who eats does so in honor of the Lord, and gives thanks to God; the one who does not eat abstains in honor of the Lord, and gives thanks to God.

⁷None of us lives to ourselves; none of us dies to ourselves. ⁸If we live, we live to the Lord, and if we die, we die to the Lord. So, then, whether we live or whether we die, we belong to the Lord. ⁹That is why the Messiah died and came back to life, so that he might be Lord both of the dead and of the living.

The Final Judgment Is the Only One That Counts

¹⁰You, then: why do you condemn your fellow Christian? Or you: why do you despise a fellow Christian? We must all appear before the judgment seat of God, ¹¹as the Bible says:

As I live, says the Lord, to me every knee shall bow,
And every tongue shall give praise to God.

[12]So, then, we must each give an account of ourselves to God.

The Way of Love and Peace

[13]Do not, then, pass judgment on one another any longer. If you want to exercise your judgment, do so on this question: how to avoid placing obstacles or stumbling blocks in front of a fellow family member.

[14]I know, and am persuaded in the Lord Jesus, that nothing is unclean in itself, except that some things do become unclean for the person who regards them as such. [15]For if your brother or sister is being harmed by what you eat, you are no longer behaving in accordance with love. Don't let your food destroy someone for whom the Messiah died!

[16]So don't let something that is good for you make other people blaspheme. [17]God's kingdom, you see, isn't about food and drink, but about justice, peace, and joy in the holy spirit. [18]Anyone who serves the Messiah like this pleases God and deserves respect from other people. [19]So, then, let's find and follow the way of peace, and discover how to build each other up. [20]Don't pull down God's work on account of food. Everything is pure, but it becomes evil for anyone who causes offense when they eat. [21]It is good not to eat meat, or drink wine, or anything else which makes your fellow Christian stumble.

[22]Hold firmly to the faith which you have as a matter between yourself and God. When you've thought something through, and can go ahead without passing judgment on yourself, God's blessing on you! [23]But anyone who doubts is condemned even in the act of eating, because it doesn't spring from faith. Whatever is not of faith is sin.

Unity: Modeled by the Messiah, Encouraged by Scripture

15 We, the "strong" ones, should bear with the frailty of the "weak," and not please ourselves. [2]Each one of us should please our neighbor for his or her good, to build them up.

[3]The Messiah, you see, did not please himself. Instead, as the Bible says, "The reproaches of those who reproached you are fallen on me." [4]Whatever was written ahead of time, you see, was written for us to learn from, so that through patience,

and through the encouragement of the Bible, we might have hope. [5]May the God of patience and encouragement grant you to come to a common mind among yourselves, in accordance with the Messiah, Jesus, [6]so that, with one mind and one mouth, you may glorify the God and father of our Lord Jesus the Messiah.

[7]Welcome one another, therefore, as the Messiah has welcomed you, to God's glory. [8]Let me tell you why: the Messiah became a servant of the circumcised people in order to demonstrate the truthfulness of God—that is, to confirm the promises to the patriarchs, [9]and to bring the nations to praise God for his mercy. As the Bible says:

United Praise Under the Messiah's Universal Rule

> *That is why I will praise you among the nations,*
> *And will sing to your name.*

[10]And again it says,

> *Rejoice, you nations, with his people.*

[11]And again,

> *Praise the Lord, all nations,*
> *And let all the peoples sing his praise.*

[12]And Isaiah says once more:

> *There shall be the root of Jesse,*
> *The one who rises up to rule the nations;*
> *The nations shall hope in him.*

[13]May the God of hope fill you with all joy and peace in believing, so that you may overflow with hope by the power of the holy spirit.

[14]When I think of you, my dear family, I myself am thoroughly convinced that you are full of goodness, filled with all knowledge, and well able to give one another instruction. [15]But I have written to you very boldly at some points, calling things to your mind through the grace which God has given me [16]to enable me to be a minister of King Jesus for the nations, working in the priestly service of God's good news, so that the offering of the nations may be acceptable, sanctified in the holy spirit.

Coming to Rome at Last

¹⁷This is the glad confidence I have in King Jesus, and in God's own presence. ¹⁸Far be it from me, you see, to speak about anything except what the Messiah has accomplished through me for the obedience of the nations, in word and deed, ¹⁹in the power of signs and wonders, in the power of God's spirit. I have completed announcing the good news of the Messiah from Jerusalem around as far as Illyricum. ²⁰My driving ambition has been to announce the good news in places where the Messiah has not been named, so that I can avoid building on anyone else's foundation. ²¹Instead, as the Bible says,

> *People who hadn't been told about him will see;*
> *People who hadn't heard will understand.*

²²That's why I have faced so many obstacles to stop me coming to you. ²³But now, finding myself with no more room in these regions, I have a great longing to come to you now at last after so many years, ²⁴and so to make my way to Spain. You see, I'm hoping to see you as I pass through, and to be sent on my way there by you, once I have been refreshed by you for a while.

Aid for Jerusalem
²⁵Now, though, I am going to Jerusalem to render service to God's people there. ²⁶Macedonia and Achaea, you see, have happily decided to enter into partnership with the poor believers in Jerusalem. ²⁷They were eager to do this, and indeed they owe them a debt. If the nations have shared in the Jews' spiritual blessings, it is right and proper that they should minister to their earthly needs. ²⁸So when I have completed this, and tied up all the loose ends, I will come via you to Spain. ²⁹And I know that when I come to you I shall come with the full blessing of the Messiah.

³⁰I urge you, my dear family, through our Lord Jesus the Messiah and through the love of the spirit: fight the battle for me in your prayers to God on my behalf, ³¹so that I may be rescued from the unbelievers in Judaea, and so that my service for Jerusalem may be welcomed gladly by God's people. ³²If this happens, I will come to you in joy, through the will of God, and be refreshed by being with you. ³³May the God of peace be with you all. Amen.

16

Let me introduce to you our sister Phoebe. She is a deacon in the church at Cenchreae. ²I want you to welcome her in the Lord, as is proper for one of God's people. Please give her whatever practical assistance she may need from you. She has been a benefactor to many people, myself included.

³Greet Prisca and Aquila, my fellow workers in King Jesus. ⁴They put their lives on the line for me. It isn't only me, but all the Gentile churches, that owe them a debt of gratitude. ⁵Greet the church in their house as well.

Greet my dear Epainetus; he was the first fruits of the Messiah's harvest in Asia. ⁶Greet Mary, who has worked hard for you. ⁷Greet Andronicus and Junia, my relatives and fellow prisoners, who are well known among the apostles, and who were in the Messiah before I was. ⁸Greet Ampliatus, my dear friend in the Lord. ⁹Greet Urbanus, our fellow worker in the Messiah, and my dear Stachys. ¹⁰Greet Apelles, who has proved his worth in the Messiah. Greet the people from the Aristobulus household.

¹¹Greet my relative Herodion. Greet those in the Lord who belong to the household of Narcissus. ¹²Greet Tryphaena and Tryphosa, who have worked hard in the Lord. Greet dear Persis, who has done a great deal of work in the Lord. ¹³Greet Rufus, one of the Lord's chosen, and also his mother—my mother too, in effect! ¹⁴Greet Asyncritus, Phlegon, Hermes, Patrobas, Hermas, and the family with them.

¹⁵Greet Philologus and Julia, Nereus and his sister, Olympas too, and all God's people who are with them. ¹⁶Greet one another with a holy kiss. All the Messiah's churches send you greetings.

Commending Phoebe, Greeting Friends

¹⁷I urge you, my dear family, to watch out for those who cause divisions and problems, contrary to the teaching you learned. Avoid them. ¹⁸People like that are serving their own appetites instead of our Lord the Messiah. They deceive the hearts of simple-minded people with their smooth and flattering speech. ¹⁹Your obedience, you see, is well known to all, and so I am rejoicing over you. But I want you to be wise when it comes to good, and innocent when it comes to evil. ²⁰The God

Warnings and Greetings

of peace will quickly crush the satan under your feet. May the grace of our Lord Jesus be with you.

²ᵀTimothy, my fellow worker, sends you greetings, as do Lucius, Jason, and Sosipater, my relatives. ²²I, Tertius, the scribe for this letter, greet you in the Lord. ²³Gaius, who is host to me and the whole church, sends you greetings. Erastus the city treasurer sends you greetings, as does another brother, Quartus.

Final Blessing   ²⁵Now to him who is able to strengthen you according to my gospel, the proclamation of Jesus the Messiah, in accordance with the unveiling of the mystery kept hidden for long ages ²⁶but now revealed and made known through the prophetic writings, according to the command of the eternal God, for the obedience of faith among all the nations—²⁷to the only wise God, through Jesus the Messiah, to whom be glory to the coming ages! Amen.

The First Letter of Paul to the
Corinthians

1 Paul, called by God's will to be an apostle of King Jesus, and Sosthenes our brother; ²to God's assembly at Corinth, made holy in King Jesus, called to be holy, with everyone who calls on the name of our Lord, King Jesus, in every place—their Lord, indeed, as well as ours! ³Grace to you and peace from God our father and King Jesus the Lord.

⁴I always thank my God for you, for the grace of God that was given to you in King Jesus. ⁵You were enriched in him in everything, in every kind of speech and knowledge, ⁶just as the messianic message was established among you, ⁷so that you aren't missing out on any spiritual gift as you wait eagerly for our Lord, King Jesus, to be revealed. ⁸He will establish you right through to the end, so that you are blameless on the day of our Lord, King Jesus. ⁹God is faithful! And it is through God that you have been called into the fellowship of his son, King Jesus, our Lord.

¹⁰Now I must appeal to you, my brothers and sisters, through the name of King Jesus our Lord, that you should all be in agreement, and that there should be no divisions among you. Instead, you should be fully equipped with the same mind and the same opinion.

¹¹You see, my dear family, Chloe's people have put me in the picture about you—about the fact that you are having quarrels. ¹²What I'm talking about is this. Each one of you is saying, "I'm with Paul!" "I'm with Apollos!" "I'm with Cephas!" "I'm with the Messiah!"

¹³Well! Has the Messiah been cut up into pieces? Was Paul crucified for you? Or were you baptized into Paul's name?! ¹⁴I'm grateful to God that I didn't baptize any of you except Crispus and Gaius, ¹⁵so that none of you could say that you were baptized into *my* name. ¹⁶(All right, I did baptize Stephanas and his household as well. Apart from that, I don't know if I baptized anybody else.) ¹⁷This is the point, you see: the Messiah didn't send me to baptize; he sent me to announce the gospel! Not with words of wisdom, either; otherwise the Messiah's cross would lose its power.

God's Folly   ¹⁸The word of the cross, you see, is madness to people who are being destroyed. But to us—those who are being saved—it is God's power. ¹⁹This is what the Bible says, after all:

> *I will destroy the wisdom of the wise;*
> *The shrewdness of the clever I'll abolish.*

²⁰Where is the wise person? Where is the educated person? Where is the debater of this present age? Don't you see that God has turned the world's wisdom into folly? ²¹This is how it's happened: in God's wisdom, the world didn't know God through wisdom, so it gave God pleasure, through the folly of our proclamation, to save those who believe. ²²Jews look for signs, you see, and Greeks search for wisdom; ²³but we announce the crucified Messiah, a scandal to Jews and folly to Gentiles, ²⁴but to those who are called, Jews and Greeks alike, the Messiah—God's power and God's wisdom. ²⁵God's folly is wiser than humans, you see, and God's weakness is stronger than humans.

Boasting in the Lord   ²⁶Think back to your own call, my brothers and sisters. Not many of you were wise in human terms. Not many of you were powerful. Not many were nobly born. ²⁷But God chose the foolish things of the world to shame the wise; God chose the weak things of the world to shame the strong; ²⁸God chose the insignificant and despised things of the world—yes, even things that don't exist!—to abolish the power of the things that do exist, ²⁹so that no creature could boast in God's presence. ³⁰Who and what you now are is a gift from God in King Jesus, who has become for us God's wisdom—and righteousness, sanctification, and redemption as well;

³¹so that, as the Bible puts it, "Anyone who boasts should boast in the Lord."

2 This is how it was for me, too, my dear family. When I came to you, I didn't come and proclaim God's mystery to you by means of a superior style of speaking or wisdom. ²No: I decided to know nothing in my dealings with you except Jesus the Messiah, especially his crucifixion. ³I came to you in weakness, in great fear and trembling. ⁴My speech and my proclamation were not in persuasive words of wisdom, but in transparent proof brought home powerfully by the spirit, ⁵so that your faith might not be in human wisdom but in God's power.

The Powerful Message of the Cross

⁶We do, however, speak wisdom among the mature. But this isn't a wisdom of this present world, or of the rulers of this present world—those same rulers who are being done away with. ⁷No: we speak God's hidden wisdom in a mystery. This is the wisdom God prepared ahead of time, before the world began, for our glory.

God's Strange Wisdom

⁸None of the rulers of this present age knew about this wisdom. If they had, you see, they wouldn't have crucified the Lord of glory. ⁹But, as the Bible says,

> *Human eyes have never seen,*
> *Human ears have never heard,*
> *It's never entered human hearts:*
> *All that God has now prepared*
> *For those who truly love him.*

¹⁰—and that's what God has revealed to us through the spirit! The spirit, you see, searches everything, yes, even the depths of God. ¹¹Think of it this way: who knows what is really going on inside a person, except the spirit of the person which is inside them? Well, it's like that with God. Nobody knows what is going on inside God except God's spirit. ¹²And we haven't received the spirit of the world, but the spirit that comes from God, so that we can know the things that have been given to us by God.

¹³That, then, is what we speak. We don't use words we've been taught by human wisdom, but words we've been taught by the spirit, interpreting spiritual things to spiritual people.

Spiritual or
Merely Human? ¹⁴Someone living at the merely human level doesn't accept the things of God's spirit. They are foolishness to such people, you see, and they can't understand them because they need to be discerned spiritually. ¹⁵But spiritual people discern everything, while nobody else can discern the truth about them! ¹⁶For "Who has known the mind of the Lord, so as to instruct him?" But we have the mind of the Messiah.

3 In my own case, my dear family, I couldn't speak to you as spiritual people, but as people who were all too obviously merely human, little babies in the Messiah. ²I fed you with milk, not solid food, because you weren't able to take it—and you still can't, even now! ³You're still determined to live in the old way! Yes, wherever there is jealousy and quarreling, doesn't that mean you're living in the old way, behaving as any merely human being might do? ⁴When someone says "I'm with Paul!" and someone else says "I'm with Apollos!" are you not mere humans?

God's Farm,
God's Building ⁵So what d'you suppose Apollos actually is? What d'you think Paul is? I'll tell you: servants, through whom you came to faith, each one as the Lord gave. ⁶I planted and Apollos watered, but it was God who gave the growth. ⁷It follows that the person who plants isn't anything special, and the person who waters isn't anything special; what matters is God who gives the growth. ⁸The person who plants and the person who waters are just the same, and each will receive his own reward according to his own work. ⁹We are God's fellow workers, you see: you are God's farm, God's building.

¹⁰According to God's grace, I laid the foundation like a wise master builder, and someone else is building on it. Everyone should take care how they build on it. ¹¹Nobody can lay any foundation, you see, except the one which is laid, which is Jesus the Messiah!

The Coming Day,
the Coming Fire ¹²If anyone builds on the foundation with gold, silver, precious stones, wood, grass, or straw—¹³well, everyone's work will become visible, because the Day will show it up, since it will be revealed in fire. Then the fire will test what sort of work everyone has done. ¹⁴If the building work that someone has done stands the test, they will receive a reward. ¹⁵If someone's work is burned up, they will be punished by bearing

the loss; they themselves will be saved, however, but only as though through a fire.

16Don't you see? You are God's Temple! God's spirit lives in you! 17If anyone destroys God's Temple, God will destroy them. God's Temple is holy, you see, and that is precisely what you are.

18Don't let anyone deceive themselves. If anyone among you supposes they are wise in the present age, let them become foolish, so that they can become wise. 19The wisdom of this world, you see, is folly with God. This is what the Bible says: "He catches the wise in their trickery." 20And again, "The Lord knows the thinking of the wise—and he knows that it's all a sham!"

Everything Belongs to You

21So don't let anyone boast about mere human beings. For everything belongs to you, 22whether it's Paul or Apollos or Cephas, whether it's the world or life or death, whether it's the present or the future—everything belongs to you! 23And you belong to the Messiah; and the Messiah belongs to God.

4 This is how we should be thought of: as servants of the Messiah, and household managers for God's mysteries. 2And this is what follows: the main requirement for a manager is to be trustworthy. 3Having said that, I regard it as a matter of minimal concern to think that I should be interrogated by you, or indeed by any human court. I don't even interrogate myself. 4I don't actually know of anything that stands against me, but that isn't what vindicates me; it's the Lord who interrogates me.

Judgment Then Rather Than Now

5So don't pass judgment on anything before the time when the Lord comes! He will bring to light the secrets of darkness, and will lay bare the intentions of the heart. Then everyone will receive praise—from God.

6I have applied all this to myself and Apollos because of you, my dear family, so that you may learn from us, as the saying goes, not to go beyond what the Bible says—so that nobody gets puffed up in favor of one person and against another.

Apostles on Display

7Who is going to concede that you are special, after all? What have you got that you didn't receive? Well then, if you received it, why boast as if you didn't? 8Do you really suppose you've already had all the food you need? Do you think you've already become rich? Do you think you've already been crowned as royalty, leaving us behind? I wish you really were already reigning, so that we could reign alongside you!

9This is how I look at it, you see: God has put us apostles on display at the end of the procession, like people sentenced to death. We have become a public show for the world, for angels and humans alike. 10We are fools because of the Messiah, but you are wise in the Messiah! We are weak, but you are strong! You are celebrated; we are nobodies! 11Yes, right up to the present moment we go hungry and thirsty; we are badly clothed, roughly treated, with no home to call our own. 12What's more, we work hard, doing manual labor. When we are insulted, we give back blessings. When we are persecuted, we put up with it. 13When we are slandered, we speak gently in return. To this day we have become like the rubbish of the world, fit only to be scraped off the plate and thrown away with everything else.

Puffed Up or Powerful?

14I'm not writing this to make you ashamed! I am simply treating you as dear children, and putting you straight. 15You've got a thousand babysitters in Christ, I know, but you haven't got many fathers—because I became your father in the Messiah, Jesus, through the gospel.

16So let me appeal to you: copy me! 17That's why I have sent Timothy to you; he's my child in the Lord, and I love him and trust him. He will remind you how I conduct myself in the Messiah Jesus, just as I teach everywhere, in each assembly.

18Some people are getting puffed up, as though I wasn't going to come to you. 19But I will come to you quickly, if the Lord wants it that way; and then I'll find out not what these puffed-up people are saying but how powerful they are. 20The kingdom of God, you see, isn't about talk—it's about power. 21What d'you want, then? Shall I come to you with a big stick, or with love, and in a gentle spirit?

Scandal and Judgment

5 Everybody's talking about the sex scandal that's going on in your community, not least because it's a kind of immorality that even the pagans don't practice! Well I never—a man taking his father's wife! 2And you're puffed up! Why aren't you in mourning? Why aren't you getting rid of the person who's done such a thing?

³Let me tell you what I've already done. I may be away from you physically, but I'm present in the spirit; and I've already passed judgment, as though I was there with you, on the person who has behaved in this way. ⁴When you are assembled together in the name of our Lord Jesus, and my spirit is there too with the power of our Lord Jesus, ⁵you must hand over such a person to the satan for the destruction of the flesh, so that his spirit may be saved on the day of the Lord Jesus.

⁶Your boasting is no good. Don't you know that a little yeast works its way through the whole lump of dough? ⁷Cleanse out the old yeast, so that you can be a new lump, the yeast-free lump you really are. It's Passover-time, you see, and the Passover lamb—the Messiah, I mean—has already been sacrificed! ⁸What we now have to do is to keep the festival properly: none of the yeast of the old life, and none of the yeast of depravity and wickedness, either. What we need is yeast-free bread, and that means sincerity and truth.

Get Rid of the "Leaven"!

⁹I wrote to you in the previous letter not to become associated with immoral people. ¹⁰I didn't (of course) mean immoral people in the world at large, or greedy people, or thieves, or idolaters. To avoid them, you'd have to remove yourselves from the world altogether! ¹¹No: I was referring to people who call themselves Christians but who are immoral, or greedy, or idolaters, or blasphemers, or drunkards, or robbers. You shouldn't associate with them; you shouldn't even eat with a person like that. ¹²Why should I worry about judging people outside? It's the people *in*side you should judge, isn't it? ¹³God judges the people outside. "Drive out the wicked person from your company."

6 Can it really be the case that one of you dares to go to law against a neighbor, to be tried before unjust people, and not before God's people? ²Don't you know that God's people will judge the world? And if the world is to be judged by you, are you really incompetent to try smaller matters? ³Don't you know that we shall be judging angels? Why not then also matters to do with ordinary life? ⁴So if you have lawsuits about ordinary matters, are you actually going to appoint as judges people whom the church despises? ⁵I'm say-

Lawsuits in the Church?

ing this to bring shame on you. Is it really true that there is no wise person among you who is able to decide between one Christian and another? 6But one Christian is being taken to court by another, and before unbelievers at that!

7Actually, to have lawsuits with one another at all represents a major setback for you. Why not rather let yourselves be wronged? Why not rather put up with loss? 8But you yourselves are wronging and defrauding people, and fellow Christians at that!

Inheriting God's Kingdom— or Not

9Don't you know that the unjust will not inherit God's kingdom? Don't be deceived! Neither immoral people, nor idolaters, nor adulterers, nor practicing homosexuals of whichever sort, 10nor thieves, nor greedy people, nor drunkards, nor abusive talkers, nor robbers will inherit God's kingdom. 11That, of course, is what some of you were! But you were washed clean; you were made holy; you were put back to rights—in the name of the Lord, King Jesus, and in the spirit of our God.

What Is the Body For?

12"Everything is lawful for me"—but not everything is helpful! "Everything is lawful for me"—but I'm not going to let anything give me orders! 13"Food for the stomach, and the stomach for food, and God will destroy the one and the other"—but the body is not meant for immorality, but for the Lord, and the Lord for the body. 14What's more, God raised the Lord; and he will raise us, too, through his power.

15Don't you know that your bodies are members of the Messiah? Shall I then take the members of the Messiah and make them members of a prostitute? Of course not! 16Or don't you know that anyone who joins himself to a prostitute is one body with her? "The two shall become one flesh"—that's what it says. 17But the one who joins himself to the Lord becomes one spirit with him.

18Run away from immorality. Every sin that it's possible for someone to commit happens outside the body; but immorality involves sinning against your own body. 19Or don't you know that your body is a temple of the holy spirit within you, the spirit God gave you, so that you don't belong to yourselves? 20You were quite an expensive purchase! So glorify God in your body.

7 Let me now turn to the matters you wrote about. "It is good for a man to have no sexual contact with a woman." [2]Well, yes; but the temptation to immorality means that every man should maintain sexual relations with his own wife, and every woman with her own husband. [3]The man should give his wife her marital rights, and the woman should do the same for her husband. [4]The woman isn't in charge of her own body; her husband is. In the same way, the man isn't in charge of his own body; his wife is. [5]Don't deny one another, except perhaps by agreement for a period of time, so that you may have more space for prayer. But then come together again, in case the satan might tempt you because of your weakness of will.

[6]I'm not saying this as a command, but as a concession. [7]I would be happy to see everyone be in the same situation as myself. But each person has his or her own gift from God, one this way, another that way.

[8]To unmarried people, and to widows, I have this to say: it's perfectly all right for you to remain like me. [9]But if you don't have power over your passions, then get married. Much better to marry than to have desire smoldering away inside you!

[10]I have a command, too, for married people—actually, it's not just from me, it's from the Lord: that a woman should not separate from her husband. [11]If she does, she should remain unmarried or return to her husband. So, too, a man should not divorce his wife.

[12]To everyone else I have this to say (this is just me, not the Lord). If a Christian has an unbelieving wife, and she is happy to live with him, he shouldn't divorce her. [13]If a woman has an unbelieving husband, and he is happy to live with her, she shouldn't divorce him. [14]The unbelieving husband, you see, is made holy by his wife, and the unbelieving wife is made holy by her husband; otherwise your children would be impure, whereas in fact they are holy. [15]But if the unbelieving partner wants to separate, let them separate; a brother or sister is not bound in a case like that. God has called you in peace. [16]If you're a wife, how d'you know whether or not you will save your husband? If you're a husband, how d'you know whether or not you will save your wife?

Life Within Marriage

Marriage and Divorce

**Stay the Way
You Were Called**

¹⁷This is the overriding rule: everyone should conduct their lives as the Lord appointed, as God has called them. This is what I lay down in all the churches. ¹⁸If someone was circumcised when he was called, he shouldn't try to remove the marks. If someone was uncircumcised when he was called, he shouldn't get circumcised. ¹⁹Circumcision is nothing; uncircumcision is nothing; what matters is keeping God's commandments!

²⁰Everyone should stay within the calling they had when they were called. ²¹Were you a slave when you were called? Don't worry about it (but if you get the chance of freedom, seize it!). ²²The one who is in the Lord and called as a slave is the Lord's freedman, just as the one who is called as a free person is the Messiah's slave. ²³You were bought at a high price; don't become the slaves of human beings. ²⁴So, brothers and sisters, let each person remain before God in the state in which they were called.

**On Remaining
Unmarried**

²⁵Now when it comes to unmarried people, I have no command from the Lord, but I give my opinion as (thanks to the Lord's mercy!) a trustworthy person. ²⁶This, then, is what I think is for the best: just at the moment we are in the middle of a very difficult time, and it's best for people to remain as they are. ²⁷Are you bound to a wife? Don't try to dissolve the marriage. Have you had your marriage dissolved? Don't look for another wife. ²⁸But if you do marry, you are not sinning, and if an unmarried woman marries, she is not sinning. But people who go that way will have trouble at a human level, and I would prefer to spare you that.

²⁹This is what I mean, my brothers and sisters. The present situation won't last long; for the moment, let those who have wives live as though they weren't married, ³⁰those who weep as though they were not weeping, those who celebrate as though they were not celebrating, those who buy as though they had no possessions, ³¹those who use the world as though they were not making use of it. The pattern of this world, you see, is passing away.

Divided Loyalties

³²I want you to be free from worries. The unmarried man worries about the things of the Lord, how to please the Lord; ³³but the married man worries about the things of the world,

in other words, how to please his wife—[34]and he is pulled in both directions. So too the unmarried woman or girl worries about the things of the Lord, how to be holy both in body and spirit; but the married woman worries about the things of the world, in other words, how to please her husband.

[35]I'm saying this for your own benefit. I'm not placing restrictions on you; my aim is that nothing will get in the way of your appropriate behavior and steady devotion to the Lord.

[36]If anyone thinks he is behaving improperly toward his fiancée—if he finds the situation overly stressful, and matters reach a point of necessity—then let him do as he wishes; he won't be sinning: let them marry. [37]But the man who settles it firmly in his heart and is not under necessity, but in control of his own will, and has made his judgment in his own heart to keep her as his fiancée, will do well. [38]So the one who marries his fiancée will do well; and the one who holds back from marrying will do better.

[39]A woman is bound in marriage as long as her husband lives. But if the husband dies she is free to marry anyone she likes, only in the Lord. [40]But in my opinion she is happier if she remains as she is. And I think I too have the spirit of God.

8 Now when it comes to meat offered to idols, we know that "we all have knowledge." Knowledge puffs you up, but love builds you up! [2]If anybody thinks they "know" something, they don't yet "know" in the way they ought to know. [3]But if anybody loves God, they are "known"—by him.

Meat Offered to Idols

[4]So when it comes to food that has been offered to idols, we know that "idols are nothing in the world," and that "there is no God but one." [5]Yes, indeed: there may be many so-called "gods," whether in heaven or on earth, just as there are many "gods" and many "lords." [6]But for us

> There is one God, the father,
> From whom are all things, and we live to him and for him;
> And one Lord, Jesus the Messiah,
> Through whom are all things, and we live through him.

[7]The problem is that not everybody has this "knowledge." Some have been accustomed up to now to eating idol-food with the assumption that it really does belong to the idol. This

Respecting Weak Consciences

has left them with a weak conscience, and now that conscience will be polluted. 8But the food we eat won't recommend us to God. We won't be any worse off if we don't eat, and we won't be any better off if we do.

9But you must take care in case this official right of yours becomes a danger to the weak. 10Look at it like this: if someone with a weak conscience sees you, a person with "knowledge," sitting down to eat in an idol-house, that conscience of theirs is likely to make up its mind actually to eat idol-food, isn't it? 11And so, you see, the weak person—a brother or sister for whom the Messiah died!—is then destroyed by your "knowledge." 12That means you'll be sinning against your brother or sister, and attacking their weak conscience; and in doing this you'll be sinning against the Messiah. 13So, for this reason, if food causes my brother or sister to stumble, I will never, ever eat meat, so that I won't make my brother or sister trip up.

The "Rights" of an Apostle

9 I'm a free man, aren't I? I'm an apostle, aren't I? I've seen Jesus our Lord, haven't I? You are my work in the Lord, aren't you? 2I may not be an apostle to other people, but I certainly am to you; in fact, you are the authorized stamp of my apostleship in the Lord.

3This is the defense I make to anyone who wants to bring a charge against me. 4Do we not have the right to eat and drink? 5Do we not have the right to take a Christian wife with us on our travels, as the other apostles do, as the Lord's brothers do, as Cephas does? 6Or are Barnabas and I the only ones who don't have the right to be set free from the need to work? 7Who serves in the army at their own expense? Who plants a vineyard and doesn't eat its fruit? Who looks after animals and doesn't drink the milk?

8I'm not just using human illustrations to make the point; the law says the same thing, doesn't it? 9This is what is written in Moses's law: "You must not muzzle a threshing ox." God isn't concerned for oxen, is he? 10Doesn't it refer completely to us? Yes, it does—because it's written that the one who plows should do so in hope of the produce, and the thresher should thresh in hope of a share in the crop. 11So if we have sown spiritual things among you, is it such a big thing that we should reap worldly things? 12If others have that kind of right over you, don't we have it even more?

But we haven't made use of this right. Instead, we put up with everything, so as to place no obstacle in the way of the Messiah's gospel.

13Don't you know that those who work in the Temple eat the Temple food, and those who serve at the altar share in the food from the altar? 14In the same way the Lord has laid it down that those who announce the gospel should get their living from the gospel.

15But I haven't made use of any of this. I'm not writing this in order to make it happen like this for me. It would be better for me to die than . . . Nobody's going to deprive me of my boast! 16If I announce the gospel, you see, that's no reason for me to be proud. I'm under compulsion! Woe betide me if I *don't* announce the gospel! 17If I do it willingly, I have a reward; if I do it unwillingly—well, this is the commission that's been entrusted to me! 18So what is my reward? Just this: that when I announce the gospel I should give it away free of charge; that I shouldn't make use of my rights in the gospel.

19The reason for all this is as follows. I am indeed free from everyone; but I have enslaved myself to everyone, so that I can win all the more. 20I became like a Jew to the Jews, to win Jews. I became like someone under the law to the people who are under the law, even though I'm not myself under the law, so that I could win those under the law. 21To the lawless I became like someone lawless (even though I'm not lawless before God, but under the Messiah's law), so that I could win the lawless. 22I became weak to the weak, to win the weak. I have become all things to all people, so that in all ways I might save some. 23I do it all because of the gospel, so that I can be a partner in its benefits.

24Don't you know that when people run on the racetrack everybody runs, but only one person gets the prize? Run in such a way that you'll win it. 25Everyone who goes in for athletics exercises self-discipline in everything. They do it to gain a crown that perishes; we do it for an imperishable one. 26Well then: I don't run in an aimless fashion! I don't box like

someone punching the air! 27No: I give my body rough treatment, and make it my slave, in case, after announcing the message to others, I myself should end up being disqualified.

The First Exodus

10 I don't want you to be ignorant, my brothers and
sisters, that our fathers were all under the cloud
and all went through the sea. 2They were all baptized into Moses in the cloud and in the sea. 3They all ate the
same spiritual food 4and drank the same spiritual drink. They
drank, you see, from the spiritual rock that followed them,
and the rock was the Messiah. 5But God wasn't pleased with
most of them, as you can tell by the fact that he laid them low
in the desert.

**Don't Make the
Same Mistake
Again!**

6Now these things were patterns for us, so that we should
not start to crave for wicked things as they did. 7Nor should
we commit idolatry, as some of them did—as the Bible says,
"The people sat down to eat and drink, and got up to play."
8Nor should we become immoral, like some of them became
immoral, and twenty-three thousand fell on a single day. 9Nor
should we put the Messiah to the test, as some of them put him
to the test and were destroyed by serpents. 10Nor should we
grumble, as some of them grumbled and were destroyed by
the destroyer.

11Now these things happened to them as a pattern, and
they were written for our instruction, since it's upon us that
the ends of the ages have now come. 12As a result, anyone who
reckons they are standing upright should watch out in case
they fall over. 13Every test that comes upon you is normal for
human beings. But God is faithful: he won't let you be tested
beyond your ability. Along with the testing, he will provide the
way of escape, so that you can bear it.

**The Table of the
Lord and the
Table of Demons**

14Therefore, my dear people, run away from idolatry. 15I'm
speaking as to intelligent people: you yourselves must weigh
my words. 16The cup of blessing which we bless is a sharing in
the Messiah's blood, isn't it? The bread we break is a sharing
in the Messiah's body, isn't it? 17There is one loaf; well, then,
there may be several of us, but we are one body, because we all
share the one loaf.

18Consider ethnic Israel. Those who eat from the sacrifices
share in the altar, don't they? 19So what am I saying? That

idol-food is real, or that an idol is a real being? 20No: but when they offer sacrifices, they offer them to demons, not to God. And *I don't want you to be table-partners with demons.* 21You can't drink the cup of the Lord and the cup of demons. You can't share in the table of the Lord and the table of demons. 22Surely you don't want to provoke the Lord to jealousy? We aren't stronger than he is, are we?

23"Everything is lawful," but not everything is helpful. "Everything is lawful," but not everything builds you up. 24Nobody should seek their own advantage, but the other person's instead.

Do Everything to God's Glory

25Eat whatever is sold in the market without making any judgments on the basis of conscience. 26"The earth and its fullness," after all, "belong to the Lord." 27If one of the unbelievers invites you to dinner, and you want to go, eat whatever is put in front of you without making any judgments on the basis of conscience. 28But if someone says, "This was offered in sacrifice," then don't eat it—because of the person who told you about it, and because of conscience, 29by which I don't mean your own conscience, but your neighbor's. For why should my freedom be condemned by someone else's conscience? 30If I eat my share gratefully, why should someone else speak evil of me because of something I've given thanks for?

31So, then, whether you eat or drink or whatever you do, do everything to God's glory. 32Be blameless before Jews and Greeks and the church of God, 33just as I try to please everybody in everything, not pursuing my own advantage, but that of the great majority, so that they may be saved.

11 Copy me, just as I'm copying the Messiah.

2I congratulate you that you are remembering me in everything, and you are keeping the traditions as I handed them on to you. 3But I want you to know this: that the Messiah is the "head" of every man, and the husband is the "head" of every wife, and God is the "head" of the Messiah. 4Every man who prays or prophesies while wearing something on his head brings shame on his "head"; 5and every woman who prays or prophesies with her head uncovered brings shame on her "head." It would be just the same if she had her head shaved. 6For if a woman isn't covered, then she

Male and Female in the Worshipping Church

should be shaved; but if it's shameful for a woman to have her hair cut off or her head shaved, then let her be covered.

7A man ought not to cover his head, you see; he is the image and glory of God. But a wife is the glory of her husband. 8For man was not made from woman, but woman from man. 9And man was not created for the sake of woman, but woman for the sake of man. 10That's why the wife must have authority on her head, because of the angels. 11However, woman is not apart from man, nor man apart from woman, in the Lord; 12for just as woman came from man, so now man comes into the world by means of woman. And everything is from God.

13Judge the matter for yourselves. Is it really appropriate for a woman to pray to God with her head uncovered? 14Doesn't nature itself teach you that if a man has long hair, it is shameful to him, 15but if a woman has long hair, it's her glory? Her hair is given her, you see, instead of a covering. 16If anyone wants to dispute this, we have no other custom, nor do the churches of God.

Rich and Poor at the Table of the Lord

17What I have to talk about now isn't a matter for praise. When you meet together, you make things worse, not better! 18What I mean is this: to begin with, I hear that when you come together in the assembly there are divisions among you. Well, I believe it—at least partly. 19There are bound to be groupings among you; that's how the genuine ones among you will stand out, I suppose! 20So when you gather together into one meeting, it isn't the Lord's Supper that you eat. 21Everyone brings their own food to eat, and one person goes hungry while another gets drunk. 22Haven't you got houses to eat and drink in? Or do you despise God's assembly, and shame those who have nothing? What shall I say to you? Shall I praise you? No, in this matter I shan't!

Recognizing the Body

23This, you see, is what I received from the Lord, and handed on to you. On the night when the Lord Jesus was betrayed, he took bread, 24gave thanks, broke it, and said, "This is my body; it's for you! Do this as a memorial of me." 25He did the same with the cup after supper, and said, "This cup is the new covenant in my blood. Whenever you drink it, do this as a memorial of me." 26For whenever you eat this bread and drink the cup, you are announcing the Lord's death until he comes.

27It follows from this that anyone who eats the bread or drinks the cup of the Lord in an unworthy manner will be guilty of the body and blood of the Lord. 28Everyone should test themselves; that's how you should eat the bread and drink the cup. 29You see, if you eat and drink without recognizing the body, you eat and drink judgment on yourself. 30That's why several of you are weak and sick, and some have died. 31But if we learned how to judge ourselves, we would not incur judgment. 32But when we are judged by the Lord, we are punished, so that we won't be condemned along with the world.

33So, my brothers and sisters, when you come together to eat, treat one another as honored guests by waiting for each other. 34If anyone is hungry, they should eat at home, so that you don't come together and find yourselves facing judgment. I will put the other matters in order when I come.

12 Now: about things relating to the spirit's work, my brothers and sisters, I don't want you to remain ignorant. 2You know that when you were still pagans you were led off, carried away again and again, after speechless idols. 3So I want to make it clear to you that nobody who is speaking by God's spirit ever says, "Jesus be cursed!"; and nobody can say "Jesus is Lord!" except by the holy spirit.

The Same Spirit at Work

4There are different types of spiritual gifts, but the same spirit; 5there are different types of service, but the same Lord; 6and there are different types of activity, but it is the same God who operates all of them in everyone. 7The point of the spirit being revealed in each one is so that all may benefit. 8One person is given a word of wisdom through the spirit; another, a word of knowledge by the same spirit; 9another, faith through the same spirit; another, gifts of healing by the one spirit; 10another, the working of mighty deeds; another, prophecy; another, the ability to distinguish spirits; another, various kinds of languages; another, the interpretation of languages. 11It is the one spirit, the same one, whose work produces all these things, and the spirit gives different gifts to each one in accordance with the spirit's own wishes.

**Many Members,
One Body**

12Let me explain. Just as the body is one, and has many members, and all the members of the body, though they are many, are one body, so also is the Messiah. 13For we all were baptized into one body, by one spirit—whether Jews or Greeks, whether slaves or free—and we were all given one spirit to drink.

14For the body, indeed, is not one member, but many. 15If the foot were to say, "Because I'm not a hand, I'm not part of the body," that wouldn't make it any less a part of the body, would it? 16And if the ear were to say, "Because I'm not an eye, I'm not part of the body," that wouldn't make it any less a part of the body, would it? 17If the whole body were an eye, where would the hearing be? If the whole body were the sense of hearing, what would happen to the sense of smell? 18But as it is, God has organized the members, placing each one individually in the body according to his wishes. 19If all the parts were one member, where would the body be? 20So the result is this: there are many members, but one body.

**The
Responsibilities
of Each Member**

21The eye can't say to the hand, "I don't need you"; and again, the head can't say to the feet, "I don't need you." 22No: the parts of the body which seem to be weaker are all the more necessary, 23and we give much greater honor to the parts of the body we reckon more dishonorable, so that the parts we hide in shame have a far greater dignity 24which our more presentable parts don't need. In fact, God has made the body a single, organized whole; he has given greater honor to the lesser part, 25so that there won't be any division in the body, but that all the members may have the same concern for one another. 26If one member suffers, all the members suffer with it. If one member is exalted, all the members celebrate along with it.

**Gifts and
Ministries**

27Now you together are the Messiah's body, and individually you are members of it. 28In the church, God has placed apostles first, then prophets, then teachers, then powerful deeds, then gifts of healing, helpful deeds, organizational gifts, different types of languages. 29Not everyone is an apostle, are they? Not everyone is a prophet! Not everyone is a teacher! Not everyone does powerful deeds! 30Not everyone has gifts of healing! Not everyone speaks with tongues! Not everyone interprets!

31You should be eager for the better kinds of gifts.

Now I'm going to show you a better way, a much better way.

13

If I speak in human languages, or even
in those of angels, but do not have love,
Then I've become a clanging gong or else
A clashing cymbal. ²*And if I should have*
Prophetic gifts, and know all mysteries,
All knowledge, too; have faith, to move the mountains,
But have no love—I'm nothing. ³*If I give*
All my possessions to the poor, and, for pride's sake,
My very body, but do not have love,
It's useless to me.

⁴*Love's great-hearted; love is kind,*
Knows no jealousy, makes no fuss,
Is not puffed up, ⁵*no shameless ways,*
Doesn't force its rightful claim,
Doesn't rage or bear a grudge,
⁶*Doesn't cheer at others' harm,*
Rejoices, rather, in the truth.
⁷*Love bears all things, believes all things;*
Love hopes all things, endures all things.

⁸*Love never fails. But prophecies will be*
Abolished; tongues will stop; and knowledge, too,
Be done away. ⁹*We know, you see, in part;*
We prophesy in part; ¹⁰*but, with perfection,*
The partial is abolished. ¹¹*As a child*
I spoke, and thought, and reasoned like a child;
When I grew up, I threw off childish ways.
¹²*For at the moment all that we can see*
Are puzzling reflections in a mirror;
Then, face to face. I know in part, for now;
But then I'll know completely, through and through,
Even as I'm completely known. ¹³*So, now,*
Faith, hope, and love remain, these three; and, of them,
Love is the greatest.

The Need for Love and the Character of Love

Love: The Bridge to God's Future

14

Pursue love; and long for the spiritual gifts, especially that you may prophesy. ²Someone who speaks
in a tongue, you see, isn't speaking to human beings

Priorities in Worship

but to God. Nobody can understand such speakers, because they speak mysteries in the spirit. ³But the one who prophesies speaks to other people, to build them up, to strengthen them, and to console them. ⁴The one who speaks in a tongue builds up himself or herself; but the one who prophesies builds up the church.

⁵I would be delighted for all of you to speak in tongues, but I would be even more delighted to have you all prophesying. The one who prophesies is greater than the one who speaks in a tongue, unless they also give an interpretation so that the church may be built up.

Speaking Clearly in Church

⁶Well then, my brothers and sisters, if I come to you speaking in tongues, how am I going to bring you any benefit unless I speak to you either in a revelation or in a word of knowledge or in a prophecy or in teaching? ⁷It's the same with lifeless objects that make a sound, like a flute or a lyre. If they don't give a distinct note, how will anyone know what tune is being blown or plucked? ⁸Think about it: if the trumpet doesn't make a clear sound, who will get ready to fight?

⁹It's the same with you. Unless your tongue gives a distinct message, how will anyone be able to tell what you're talking about? You will be like someone speaking into thin air. ¹⁰To be sure, there are all kinds and types of languages in the world, and none of them is meaningless. ¹¹But if I don't know the force of the words, I will remain a foreigner to the speaker, and the speaker will be a foreigner to me. ¹²It's the same with you. Since you are so eager for spiritual matters, try to specialize in doing things that will build up the church.

Praying with Mind as Well as Spirit

¹³So the one who speaks in a tongue should pray to be able to say the same thing in clear speech. ¹⁴If I pray in a tongue, you see, my spirit prays, but my mind remains fruitless. ¹⁵Why is that important? I will pray with the spirit, and I will pray with the mind as well. I will sing with the spirit, and I will sing with the mind as well. ¹⁶You see, if you say a blessing in the spirit, how can someone who isn't one of the inner circle say the "Amen" to your prayer? They won't know what you're talking about! ¹⁷You may well be giving thanks in fine style, but the other person isn't being built up. ¹⁸I thank God that I speak in tongues more than all of you. ¹⁹But in the assembly I would

rather speak five words with my mind, to teach other people, than a thousand words in a tongue.

20Brothers and sisters, don't be children in your thinking. Be babies when it comes to evil, but in your thinking be grown-ups. 21This is what it says in the law: "I will speak to this people in foreign languages and with the lips of strangers, and even so they won't listen to me, says the Lord." 22So tongues are not meant for believers, but are a warning for unbelievers; while prophecy is not designed for unbelievers, but for those who come to faith. 23What I mean is this: if the whole assembly comes together and everybody speaks in tongues, and outsiders or unbelievers come in, they'll say you're crazy, won't they? 24But if everyone prophesies, and outsiders or unbelievers come in, they will be called to account by everyone, judged by everyone, 25the secrets of their hearts will be laid bare, and so they will fall down on their faces and worship God, declaring that "God is truly among you."

26So where does this leave us, my brothers and sisters? When you come together, one person has a psalm, another some teaching, another a revelation, another a tongue, and another some interpretation. Let everything be done for the general upbuilding. 27If anyone speaks in a tongue, there should be two or at most three, each taking their turn, and one of them should put it into plain speech. 28But if none of them can do that, let them be silent in the assembly, and speak to themselves and to God.

29As for prophets, let two or three speak, and the others evaluate what is said. 30If fresh revelation comes to someone sitting there, the first person should be silent. 31You can all prophesy one by one, so that everyone can learn, and everyone can be encouraged. 32The spirits of prophets are under the control of prophets, 33since God is the God, not of chaos, but of peace.

As in all the assemblies of God's people, 34the women should keep silence in the assemblies. They are not permitted to speak; they should remain in submission, just as the law declares. 35If they want to understand something more, they should ask their own husbands when they get home. It's shameful, you see, for a woman to speak in the assembly. 36Do you suppose God's word began with you? Are you the only ones it has reached?

37If anyone thinks they are a prophet, or spiritual, they should acknowledge that what I write to you is the Lord's command. 38If anyone disregards this, that person can be disregarded.

39So, my brothers and sisters, be eager to prophesy, and don't forbid speaking in tongues. 40But everything should be done in a seemly fashion, and in proper order.

The Gospel of the Messiah, Crucified, Buried, and Risen

15 Let me remind you, brothers and sisters, about the good news which I announced to you. You received this good news, and you're standing firm on it, 2and you are saved through it, if you hold fast the message I announced to you—unless it was for nothing that you believed!

3What I handed on to you at the beginning, you see, was what I received, namely this: "The Messiah died for our sins in accordance with the Bible; 4he was buried; he was raised on the third day in accordance with the Bible; 5he was seen by Cephas, then by the Twelve; 6then he was seen by over five hundred brothers and sisters at once, most of whom are still with us, though some fell asleep; 7then he was seen by James, then by all the apostles; 8and, last of all, as to one ripped from the womb, he appeared even to me."

9I'm the least of the apostles, you see. In fact, I don't really deserve to be called "apostle" at all, because I persecuted God's church! 10But I am what I am because of God's grace, and his grace to me wasn't wasted. On the contrary. I worked harder than all of them—though it wasn't me, but God's grace which was with me. 11So whether it was me or them, that was the way we announced it, and that was the way you believed.

What If the Messiah Wasn't Raised?

12Well, then: if the royal proclamation of the Messiah is made on the basis that he's been raised from the dead, how can some of you say that there is no such thing as resurrection of the dead? 13If there is no such thing as resurrection of the dead, the Messiah hasn't been raised, either; 14and if the Messiah hasn't been raised, our royal proclamation is empty, and so is your faith. 15We even turn out to have been misrepresenting God, because we gave it as our evidence about God that he raised the Messiah, and he didn't!—if, that is, the dead are not raised. 16For if the dead aren't raised, the Messiah wasn't raised either; 17and if the Messiah wasn't raised, your faith is pointless, and you are still in your sins. 18What's more, people who have fallen asleep in the Messiah have perished for good. 19If it's only for this present life that we have put our hope in the Messiah, we are the most pitiable members of the human race.

20But in fact the Messiah has been raised from the dead, as the first fruits of those who have fallen asleep. 21For since it was through a human that death arrived, it's through a human that the resurrection from the dead has arrived. 22All die in Adam, you see, and all will be made alive in the Messiah.

The Reign of the Messiah

23Each, however, in proper order. The Messiah rises as the first fruits; then those who belong to the Messiah will rise at the time of his royal arrival. 24Then comes the end, the goal, when he hands over the kingly rule to God the father, when he has destroyed all rule and all authority and power. 25He has to go on ruling, you see, until "he has put all his enemies under his feet." 26Death is the last enemy to be destroyed, 27because "he has put all things in order under his feet." But when it says that everything is put in order under him, it's obvious that this doesn't include the one who put everything in order under him. 28No: when everything is put in order under him, then the son himself will be placed in proper order under the one who placed everything in order under him, so that God may be all in all.

29Otherwise, what are people doing when they get baptized on behalf of the dead? If the dead simply aren't raised, why should people get baptized on their behalf?

Resurrection Gives Meaning to Present Christian Living

30And why should we face danger every hour? 31I die every day—yes, that's something for you to boast about, my dear family, and that's the boast I have in the Messiah, Jesus our Lord! 32If, in human terms, I fought with wild animals at Ephesus, what use is that to me? If the dead are not raised, "let's eat and drink, because tomorrow we're going to die"!

33Don't be deceived: "bad company kills off good habits"! 34Sober up; straighten up; stop sinning. Yes, some of you simply don't know God! I'm saying this to bring shame on you.

The Transformed Resurrection Body

35But someone is now going to say, "How are the dead raised? What sort of body will they have when they come back?" 36Stupid! What you sow doesn't come to life unless it dies. 37The thing you sow isn't the body that is going to come later; it's just a naked seed of, let's say, wheat, or some other plant. 38God then gives it a body of the sort he wants, with each of the seeds having its own particular body.

39Not all physical objects have the same kind of physicality. There is one kind of physicality for humans, another kind for animals, another for birds, and another for fish. 40Some bodies belong in the heavens, and some on the earth; and the kind of glory appropriate for the ones in the heavens is different from the kind of glory appropriate for the ones on the earth. 41There is one kind of glory for the sun, another for the moon, and another for the stars, since the stars themselves vary, with different degrees of glory.

42That's what it's like with the resurrection of the dead. It is sown decaying, and raised undecaying. 43It is sown in shame, and raised in glory. It is sown in weakness, and raised in power. 44It is sown as the embodiment of ordinary nature, and raised as the embodiment of the spirit. If ordinary nature has its embodiment, then the spirit too has its embodiment. 45That's what it means when the Bible says, "The first man, Adam, became a living natural being"; the last Adam became a life-giving spirit.

46But you don't get the spirit-animated body first; you get the nature-animated one, and you get the spirit-animated one later. 47The first man is from the ground, and is made of earth; the second man is from heaven. 48Earthly people are like the man of earth; heavenly people are like the man from heaven. 49We have borne the image of the man made of earth; we shall also bear the image of the man from heaven.

The Mystery and the Victory

50This is what I'm saying, my dear family. Flesh and blood can't inherit God's kingdom; decay can't inherit undecaying life. 51Look! I'm telling you a mystery. We won't all sleep; we're all going to be changed—52in a flash, at the blink of an eye, at the last trumpet. This is how it will be, you see: the trumpet's going to sound, the dead will be raised undecaying, and we're going to be changed. 53This decaying body must put on the undecaying one; this dying body must put on deathlessness. ⁵⁴When the decaying puts on the undecaying, and the dying puts on the undying, then the saying that has been written will come true:

> Death is swallowed up in victory!
> ⁵⁵Death, where's your victory gone?
> Death, where's your sting gone?

⁵⁶The "sting" of death is sin, and the power of sin is the law. ⁵⁷But thank God! He gives us the victory, through our Lord Jesus the Messiah.

⁵⁸So, my dear family, be firmly fixed, unshakable, always full to overflowing with the Lord's work. In the Lord, as you know, the work you're doing will not be worthless.

16

Now when it comes to the collection for God's people, you should do the same as I laid down for the churches in Galatia. ²On the first day of each week, every one of you should set aside and store up whatever surplus you have gained, so that when I come I won't have to take an actual collection. ³Then, when I get to you, I will write formal letters to send the people you approve, whoever they are, to Jerusalem with your gift. ⁴If it's appropriate for me to go as well, we can travel together.

The Collection and Paul's Plans

⁵I shall come to you when I've been through Macedonia. I intend to pass through Macedonia, you see, ⁶and I may well end up staying with you, perhaps even through the winter. Then you will be able to send me on to wherever I shall be going next. ⁷I don't want just to see you for a short time; I'm hoping to stay with you for a while, if the Lord allows me to. ⁸I shall be staying on in Ephesus until Pentecost. ⁹A huge and important door has opened for me here, and there is plenty of opposition.

¹⁰If Timothy comes, take care that he isn't fearful when he's with you. He's doing the Lord's work, after all, just as I am. ¹¹Nobody should look down on him. Send him on in peace, so that he can come to me. I'm expecting him, and so is the family here.

Timothy and Apollos

¹²As for our brother Apollos, I did my best to persuade him to go to you with the other family members, but it simply

wasn't for the best that he should come just now. He will come when the right moment appears.

[13] Keep alert, stand firm in the faith, be brave, be strong! [14] Whatever you do, do it with love.

The Love That Stitches It All Together

[15] One more word of exhortation for you, my dear family. You know the household of Stephanas: they were the first fruits of Achaea, and they have set themselves to serve God's people. [16] You should submit to people like that, and to everyone who is working with them and laboring hard. [17] I have thoroughly enjoyed the visit of Stephanas, Fortunatus, and Achaicus; they have made up for the fact that I haven't been able to see you. [18] They have refreshed my spirit and yours. Give proper recognition to such people.

[19] The churches in Asia send you greetings. Aquila and Prisca send you many greetings in the Lord, together with the church in their house. [20] All the family send you greetings. Greet one another with the holy kiss.

[21] I, Paul, add my greetings in my own hand.

[22] If anyone doesn't love the Lord, let them be accursed! Come, Lord, come! [23] The grace of the Lord Jesus be with you. [24] My love be with you all in the Messiah, Jesus.

The Second Letter of Paul to the
Corinthians

1 Paul, an apostle of King Jesus through God's will, and Timothy our brother; to God's assembly in Corinth, with all God's people in the whole of Achaea: ²grace and peace to you from God our father and the Lord, King Jesus!

³Let us bless God, the father of our Lord, King Jesus; he is the father of mercies and the God of all comfort. ⁴He comforts us in all our trouble, so that we can then comfort people in every kind of trouble, through the comfort with which God comforts us. ⁵Just as we have an overflowing share of the Messiah's sufferings, you see, so we have an overflowing share in comfort through the Messiah. ⁶If we are troubled, it's for the sake of your comfort and salvation; if we are comforted, it's because of your comfort, which comes about as you bear patiently with the same sufferings that we are going through. ⁷And our hope about you remains firm, because we know that, just as you've shared in our sufferings, so you will also share in our comfort.

⁸You see, my dear family, we don't want to keep you in the dark about the suffering we went through in Asia. The load we had to carry was far too heavy for us; it got to the point where we gave up on life itself. ⁹Yes: deep inside ourselves we received the death sentence. This was to stop us relying on ourselves, and to make us rely on the God who raises the dead. ¹⁰He rescued us from such a great and deadly peril, and he'll do it again; we have placed our hope in him, that he'll do it again! ¹¹But you must cooperate with us through prayer for us, so that

when God gives us this gift, answering the prayers of so many, all the more will give thanks because of what's happened to us.

¹²This is what we boast of, you see; this is what our conscience is telling us: that our conduct in the world, and in particular in relation to you, has been marked by holiness and godly sincerity, not in merely human wisdom but in God's grace. ¹³We are not writing anything to you, after all, except what you can read and understand. And I hope you will go on understanding right through to the end, ¹⁴just as you have understood us already—well, partly, at least! We are your pride and joy, just as you are ours, on the day of our Lord Jesus.

Paul's Plans and God's Yes

¹⁵I was quite sure of this. That's why I wanted to come to you again, so that you could have a double blessing. ¹⁶I intended to go on to Macedonia by way of you, and to come back to you from Macedonia and have you send me on to Judaea.

¹⁷Was I just fooling around when I was making plans like this? Was I concocting schemes in a merely human way, prepared to say "Yes, yes," and "No, no," at the same moment? ¹⁸God can bear me faithful witness that our word to you was not a mixture of yes and no. ¹⁹The son of God, Jesus the Messiah, who was proclaimed among you by Silvanus, Timothy, and myself, wasn't a yes-and-no person; in him it's always yes! ²⁰All God's promises, you see, find their yes in him; and that's why we say the yes, the "Amen," through him when we pray to God and give him glory. ²¹It's God who strengthens us with you into the Messiah, the anointed one; and he has anointed us, too. ²²God has stamped his seal on us, by giving us the spirit in our hearts as a first payment and guarantee of what is to come.

Painful Visit, Painful Letter

²³For my own part, I call on God as witness, against my own life, that the reason I haven't yet come back to Corinth is because I wanted to spare you. ²⁴This isn't because I am making myself the lord and master over your faith; your faith is the reason you stand fast! Rather, it's because we are cooperating with you for your joy.

2 You see, I settled it in my mind that I wouldn't make you another sad visit. ²After all, if I make you sad, who is there to cheer me up except the one who is sad because of me? ³And I wrote what I did so that I wouldn't come and find

sadness where I should have found joy. I have this confidence about all of you, that my joy belongs to all of you. ⁴No: I wrote to you in floods of tears, out of great trouble and anguish in my heart, not so that I could make you sad but so that you would know just how much overflowing love I have toward you.

⁵But if anyone has caused sadness, it isn't me that he has saddened, but, in a measure (I don't want to emphasize this too much), all of you. ⁶The punishment that the majority has imposed is quite enough; ⁷what's needed now is rather that you should forgive and console him, in case someone like that might be swallowed up by such abundant sorrow. ⁸Let me urge you, then, to reaffirm your love for him.

Time to Forgive

⁹The reason I wrote to you, you see, was in order to know whether you would pass the test and be obedient in every-thing. ¹⁰If you forgive anyone anything, so do I; and whatever I have forgiven—if indeed I have forgiven anyone anything!—it's all happened under the eyes of the Messiah, and for your own sake. ¹¹The point is that we shouldn't be outsmarted by the satan. We know what he's up to!

¹²However, when I came to Troas to announce the Messiah's gospel, and found an open door waiting for me in the Lord, ¹³I couldn't get any quietness in my spirit because I didn't find my brother Titus there. So I left them and went off to Macedonia.

The Smell of Life, the Smell of Death

¹⁴But thanks be to God—the God who always leads us in his triumphal procession in the Messiah, and through us re-veals everywhere the sweet smell of knowing him. ¹⁵We are the Messiah's fragrance before God, you see, to those who are being saved and to those who are being lost. ¹⁶To the latter, it's a smell which comes from death and leads to death; but to the former it's the smell of life which leads to life.

Who can rise to this challenge? ¹⁷We aren't mere peddlers of God's word, as so many people are. We speak with sincerity; we speak from God; we speak in God's presence; we speak in the Messiah.

3 So: we're starting to "recommend ourselves" again, are we? Or perhaps we need—as some do—official refer-ences to give to you? Or perhaps even to get from you? ²You are our official reference! It's written on our hearts! Everybody can know it and read it! ³It's quite plain that you

The Letter and the Spirit

are a letter from the Messiah, with us as the messengers—a letter not written with ink but with the spirit of the living God, not on tablets of stone but on the tablets of beating hearts.

⁴That's the kind of confidence we have toward God, through the Messiah. ⁵It isn't as though we are qualified in ourselves to reckon that we have anything to offer on our own account. Our qualification comes from God: ⁶God has qualified us to be stewards of a new covenant, not of the letter but of the spirit. The letter kills, you see, but the spirit gives life.

Death and Glory

⁷But just think about it: when death was being distributed, carved in letters of stone, it was a glorious thing, so glorious in fact that the children of Israel couldn't look at Moses's face because of the glory of his face—a glory that was to be abolished. ⁸But in that case, when the spirit is being distributed, won't that be glorious too? ⁹If distributing condemnation is glorious, you see, how much more glorious is it to distribute vindication! ¹⁰In fact, what used to be glorious has come in this respect to have no glory at all, because of the new glory which goes so far beyond it. ¹¹For if the thing which was to be abolished came with glory, how much more glory will there be for the thing that lasts.

The Veil and the Glory

¹²So, because that's the kind of hope we have, we speak with great freedom. ¹³We aren't like Moses: he put a veil over his face, to stop the children of Israel from gazing at the end of what was being abolished. ¹⁴The difference is that their minds were hardened. You see, the same veil lies over the reading of the old covenant right up to this very day. It isn't taken away, because it's in the Messiah that it is abolished.

¹⁵Yes, even to this day, whenever Moses is read, the veil lies upon their hearts; ¹⁶but "whenever he turns back to the Lord, the veil is removed." ¹⁷Now "the Lord" here means the spirit; and where the spirit of the Lord is, there is freedom. ¹⁸And all of us, without any veil on our faces, gaze at the glory of the Lord as in a mirror, and so are being changed into the same image, from glory to glory, just as you'd expect from the Lord, the spirit.

Light Out of Darkness

4 For this reason, since we have this work entrusted to us in accordance with the mercy we have received, we don't lose heart. ²On the contrary, we have renounced the secret things that make people ashamed. We don't use

tricks; we don't falsify God's word. Rather, we speak the truth openly, and recommend ourselves to everybody's conscience in the presence of God.

3However, if our gospel still remains "veiled," it is veiled for people who are perishing. 4What's happening there is that the god of this world has blinded the minds of unbelievers, so that they won't see the light of the gospel of the glory of the Messiah, who is God's image. 5We don't proclaim ourselves, you see, but Jesus the Messiah as Lord, and ourselves as your servants because of Jesus; 6because the God who said, "Let light shine out of darkness," has shone in our hearts, to produce the light of the knowledge of the glory of God in the face of Jesus the Messiah.

7But we have this treasure in earthenware pots, so that the extraordinary quality of the power may belong to God, not to us. 8We are under all kinds of pressure, but we are not crushed completely; we are at a loss, but not at our wits' end; 9we are persecuted, but not abandoned; we are cast down, but not destroyed. 10We always carry the deadness of Jesus about in the body, so that the life of Jesus may be revealed in our body. 11Although we are still alive, you see, we are always being given over to death because of Jesus, so that the life of Jesus may be revealed in our mortal humanity. 12So this is how it is: death is at work in us—but life in you!

Treasure in Earthenware Pots

13We have the same spirit of faith as you see in what is written: "I believed, and so I spoke." We too believe, and so we speak, 14because we know that the God who raised the Lord Jesus will raise us with Jesus and present us with you. 15It's all because of you, you see! The aim is that, as grace abounds through the thanksgiving of more and more people, it will overflow to God's glory.

The God of All Comfort

16For this reason we don't lose heart. Even if our outer humanity is decaying, our inner humanity is being renewed day by day. 17This slight momentary trouble of ours is working to produce a weight of glory, passing and surpassing everything, lasting forever; 18for we don't look at the things that can be seen, but at the things that can't be seen. After all, the things you can see are here today and gone tomorrow; but the things you can't see are everlasting.

**A House Waiting
in the Heavens**

5 For we know that if our earthly house, our present "tent," is destroyed, we have a building from God, a house no human hands have built: it is everlasting, in the heavenly places. 2At the present moment, you see, we are groaning, as we long to put on our heavenly building, 3in the belief that by putting it on we won't turn out to be naked. 4Yes: in the present "tent," we groan under a great weight. But we don't want to put it off; we want to put on something else on top, so that what is doomed to die may be swallowed up with life. 5It is God who has been at work in us to do this, the God who has given us the spirit as the first installment and guarantee.

**The Judgment
Seat of the
Messiah**

6So we are always confident: we know that while we are at home in the body we are away from the Lord. 7We live our lives by faith, you see, not by sight. 8We are confident, and we would much prefer to be away from the body and at home with the Lord. 9So we work hard, as a point of honor, to please him, whether we are at home or away. 10For we must all appear before the judgment seat of the Messiah, so that each may receive what has been done through the body, whether good or bad.

**The Messiah's
Love Makes Us
Press On**

11So we know the fear of the Lord; and that's why we are persuading people—but we are open to God, and open as well, I hope, to your consciences. 12We aren't trying to recommend ourselves again! We are giving you a chance to be proud of us, to have something to say to those who take pride in appearances rather than in people's hearts.

13If we are beside ourselves, you see, it's for God; and if we are in our right mind, it's for you. 14For the Messiah's love makes us press on. We have come to the conviction that one died for all, and therefore all died. 15And he died for all in order that those who live should live no longer for themselves, but for him who died and was raised on their behalf.

**New Creation,
New Ministry**

16From this moment on, therefore, we don't regard anybody from a merely human point of view. Even if we once regarded the Messiah that way, we don't do so any longer. 17Thus, if anyone is in the Messiah, there is a new creation! Old things have gone, and look—everything has become new!

18It all comes from God. He reconciled us to himself through the Messiah, and he gave us the ministry of reconciliation. 19This is how it came about: God was reconciling the world to himself in the Messiah, not counting their transgressions against them, and entrusting us with the message of reconciliation. 20So we are ambassadors, speaking on behalf of the Messiah, as though God were making his appeal through us. We implore people on the Messiah's behalf to be reconciled to God. 21The Messiah did not know sin, but God made him to be sin on our behalf, so that in him we might embody God's faithfulness to the covenant.

6 So, as we work together with God, we appeal to you in particular: when you accept God's grace, don't let it go to waste! 2This is what he says:

I listened to you when the time was right;
I came to your aid on the day of salvation.

Look! The right time is now! Look! The day of salvation is here!

3We put no obstacles in anybody's way, so that nobody will say abusive things about our ministry. 4Instead, we recommend ourselves as God's servants: with much patience, with sufferings, difficulties, hardships, 5beatings, imprisonments, riots, hard work, sleepless nights, going without food, 6with purity, knowledge, great-heartedness, kindness, the holy spirit, genuine love, 7by speaking the truth, by God's power, with weapons for God's faithful work in left and right hand alike, 8through glory and shame, through slander and praise; as deceivers, and yet true; 9as unknown, yet very well known; as dying, and look—we are alive; as punished, yet not killed; 10as sad, yet always celebrating; as poor, yet bringing riches to many; as having nothing, yet possessing everything.

God's Servants at Work

11We have been wide open in our speaking to you, my dear Corinthians! Our heart has been opened wide! 12There are no restrictions at our end; the only restrictions are in your affection! 13I'm speaking as though to children: you should open your hearts wide as well in return. That's fair enough, isn't it?

14Don't be drawn into partnership with unbelievers. What kind of sharing can there be, after all, between justice and lawlessness? What partnership can there be between light and darkness? 15What kind of harmony can the Messiah have with Beliar? What has a believer in common with an unbeliever?

Don't Be Mismatched

¹⁶What kind of agreement can there be between God's temple and idols? We are the temple of the living God, you see, just as God said:

> I will live among them and walk about with them;
> I will be their God, and they will be my people.
> ¹⁷So come out from the midst of them,
> And separate yourselves, says the Lord;
> No unclean thing must you touch.
> Then I will receive you gladly,
> ¹⁸And I will be to you as a father,
> And you will be to me as sons and daughters,
> Says the Lord, the Almighty.

7 So, my beloved people, with promises like these, let's make ourselves clean from everything that defiles us, outside and inside, and let's become completely holy in the fear of God.

The God Who Comforts the Downcast

²Make room for us! We haven't wronged anybody; we haven't ruined anybody; we haven't taken advantage of anybody. ³I'm not saying this to pass judgment against you; I've already said that you are in our hearts, to die together and to live together. ⁴I speak to you freely and openly; I regularly boast about you; I am full of comfort, and fuller still of joy, over and above all our trouble.

⁵You see, even when we arrived in Macedonia, we couldn't relax or rest. We were troubled in every way; there were battles outside and fears inside. ⁶But the God who comforts the downcast comforted us by the arrival of Titus, ⁷and not only by his arrival but in the comfort he had received from you, as he told us about your longing for us, your lamenting, and your enthusiasm for me personally.

As a result, I was more inclined to celebrate; ⁸because, if I did make you sad by my letter, I don't regret it; and, if I did regret it, it was because I saw that I made you sad for a while by what I had written. ⁹Anyway, I'm celebrating now, not because you were saddened, but because your sadness brought you to repentance. It was a sadness from God, you see, and it did you no harm at all on our account; ¹⁰because God's way of sadness is designed to produce a repentance which leads to salvation,

and there's nothing to regret there! But the world's way of sadness produces death.

[11]Just look and see what effect God's way of sadness has
had among you! It's produced eagerness, explanations, indignation, fear, longing, keenness, and punishment. You have
shown yourselves faultless in the whole business. [12]So if I'm
writing to you, it's not because of the person who's done the
wrong, nor because of the people who were wronged, but so
that you can recognize for yourselves, in God's presence, just
how eager you really have been for us. [13]We have been comforted by all of this.

The real celebration, though, on top of all our comfort,
came because Titus was so overjoyed. You really did cheer
him up and set his mind at rest. [14]I wasn't ashamed of the various boasts I had made to him about you. Just as I had always
spoken the truth to you, so our boast to Titus turned out to be
true as well. [15]He is constantly yearning for you deeply as he
remembers the obedience you showed, all of you, and how you
welcomed him with fear and trembling. [16]I am celebrating the
fact that I have confidence in you in everything.

Our Boasting Proved True!

8 Let me tell you, my dear family, about the grace which
God has given to the Macedonian churches. [2]They have
been sorely tested by suffering. But the abundance of
grace which was given to them, and the depths of poverty they
have endured, have overflowed in a wealth of sincere generosity on their part. [3]I bear them witness that of their own accord,
up to their ability and even beyond their ability, [4]they begged
us eagerly to let them have the privilege of sharing in the work
of service for God's people. [5]They didn't just do what we had
hoped; they gave themselves, first to the Lord, and then to us
as God willed it. [6]This put us in a position where we could encourage Titus that he should complete this work of grace that
he had begun among you. [7]You have plenty of everything, after
all—plenty of faith, and speech, and knowledge, and all kinds
of eagerness, and plenty of love coming from us to you; so why
not have plenty of this grace too?

The Generosity of the Macedonian Churches

[8]I'm not saying this as though I was issuing an order. It's
a matter of putting their enthusiasm and your own love side
by side, and making sure you genuinely pass the test. [9]For you

Copying the Generosity of the Lord Jesus

know the grace of our Lord, King Jesus: he was rich, but because of you he became poor, so that by his poverty you might become rich. ¹⁰Let me give you my serious advice on this: you began to be keen on this idea, and to start putting it into practice, a whole year ago; it will now be greatly to your advantage ¹¹to complete your performance of it. If you do so, your finishing the job as far as you are able will be on the same scale as your eagerness in wanting to do it. ¹²If the eagerness is there, you see, the deed is acceptable, according to what you have, not according to what you don't have. ¹³The point is not, after all, that others should get off lightly and you be made to suffer, but rather that there should be equality. ¹⁴At the present time your abundance can contribute to their lack, so that their abundance can contribute to your lack. That's what makes for equality, ¹⁵just as the Bible says: "The one who had much had nothing to spare, and the one who had little didn't go short."

Paul's Companions Are on Their Way

¹⁶But God be thanked, since he put the same eagerness for you into Titus's heart. ¹⁷He welcomed the appeal we made, and of his own accord he was all the more eager to come to you. ¹⁸We have sent along with him the brother who is famous through all the churches because of his work for the gospel. ¹⁹Not only so, but he was formally chosen by the churches to be our traveling companion as we engage in this work of grace, both for the Lord's own glory and to show our own good faith. ²⁰We are trying to avoid the possibility that anyone would make unpleasant accusations about this splendid gift which we are administering. ²¹We are thinking ahead, you see, about what will look best, not only to the Lord, but to everybody else as well.

²²Anyway, along with the two of them we are sending our brother, who has proved to us how eager and enthusiastic he is in many situations and on many occasions; he now seems all the more eager because he is convinced about you. ²³If there's any question about Titus, he is my partner, and a fellow worker for you. As for our brothers, they are messengers of the churches, the Messiah's glory. ²⁴So please give them a fine demonstration of your love, and of our boasting about you! Show all the churches that you mean business!

Please Have
the Gift Ready!

9 When it comes to the service you are doing for God's people, you see, I don't need to write to you. ²For I know your eagerness, and indeed I boasted about it to the Macedonians, saying that Achaea had been ready since last year. Your enthusiasm has stimulated most of them into action. ³I have sent the brothers so that our boasting about you in this respect may turn out to be true—so that you may be ready, just as I said you were. ⁴Otherwise, imagine what it would be like if people from Macedonia came with me and found you weren't ready! That would bring shame on us in this business, not to say on you. ⁵So I thought it necessary to exhort the brothers that they should go on to you in advance, and get everything about your gracious gift in order ahead of time. You've already promised it, after all. Then it really will appear as a gift of grace, not something that has had to be extorted from you.

God Loves a
Cheerful Giver

⁶This is what I mean: someone who sows sparingly will reap sparingly as well. Someone who sows generously will reap generously. ⁷Everyone should do as they have determined in their heart, not in a gloomy spirit or simply because they have to, since "God loves a cheerful giver." ⁸And God is well able to lavish all his grace upon you, so that in every matter and in every way you will have enough of everything, and may be lavish in all your own good works, ⁹just as the Bible says:

They spread their favors wide, they gave to the poor;
Their righteousness endures forever.

¹⁰The one who supplies "seed to be sown and bread to eat" will supply and increase your seed and multiply the yield of your righteousness. ¹¹You will be enriched in every way in all single-hearted goodness, which is working through us to produce thanksgiving to God. ¹²The service of this ministry will not only supply what God's people so badly need, but it will also overflow with many thanksgivings to God. ¹³Through meeting the test of this service you will glorify God in two ways: first, because your confession of faith in the Messiah's gospel has brought you into proper order, and second, because you have entered into genuine and sincere partnership with

them and with everyone. ¹⁴What's more, they will then pray for you and long for you because of the surpassing grace God has given to you. ¹⁵Thanks be to God for his gift, the gift we can never fully describe!

The Battle for the Mind

10 Think of the Messiah, meek and gentle; then think of me, Paul—yes, Paul himself!—making his appeal to you. You know what I'm like: I'm humble when I'm face to face with you, but I'm bold when I'm away from you! ²Please, please don't put me in the position of having to be bold when I'm with you, of having to show how confident I dare to be when I'm standing up to people who think we are behaving in a merely human way. ³Yes, we are mere humans, but we don't fight the war in a merely human way. ⁴The weapons we use for the fight, you see, are not merely human; they carry a power from God that can tear down fortresses! We tear down clever arguments ⁵and every proud notion that sets itself up against the knowledge of God. We take every thought prisoner and make it obey the Messiah. ⁶We are holding ourselves in readiness to punish every disobedience, when your obedience is complete.

⁷Look at what's in front of your face. If anyone trusts that they belong to the Messiah, let them calculate it once more: just as they belong to the Messiah, so also do we! ⁸For if I do indeed boast a bit too enthusiastically about the authority which the Lord has given me—which is for building you up, not for pulling you down!—I shan't be ashamed. ⁹I wouldn't want to look as if I were trying to frighten you with my letters. ¹⁰I know what they say: "His letters are serious and powerful, but when he arrives in person he is weak, and his words aren't worth bothering about." ¹¹Anyone like that should reckon on this: the way we talk in letters, when we're absent, will be how we behave when we're present.

Boasting in the Lord

¹²We wouldn't dare, you see, to figure out where we belong on some scale or other, or compare ourselves with people who commend themselves. They measure themselves by one another, and compare themselves with one another. That just shows how silly they are! ¹³But when we boast, we don't go off into flights of fancy; we boast according to the measure of the rule God has given us to measure ourselves by, and that rule

includes our work with you! 14We weren't going beyond our assigned limits when we reached you; we were the first to get as far as you with the gospel of the Messiah. 15We don't boast without a measuring rule in the work someone else has done. This is what we hope for: that, as your faith increases, we will be given a much larger space for work, according to our rule, 16which is to announce the gospel in the lands beyond you, not to boast in what has already been accomplished through the rule someone else has been given. 17"Anyone who boasts should boast in the Lord!" 18Who is it, after all, who gains approval? It isn't the person who commends himself. It's the person whom the Lord commends.

11 I'd be glad if you would bear with me in a little bit of foolishness. Yes: bear with me, please! 2I'm jealous over you, and it's God's own jealousy: I arranged to marry you off, like a pure virgin, to the one man I presented you to, namely the Messiah. 3But the serpent tricked Eve with its cunning, and in the same way I'm afraid that your minds may be corrupted from the single-mindedness and purity which the Messiah's people should have. 4For if someone comes and announces a different Jesus from the one we announced to you, or if you receive a different spirit, one you hadn't received before, or a different gospel, one you hadn't accepted before, you put up with that all right. 5According to my calculations, you see, I am every bit as good as these super-apostles. 6I may be untutored in speaking, but that certainly doesn't apply to my knowledge. Surely that's been made quite clear to you, in every way and on every point!

Super-Apostles?

7Did I then commit a sin when I humbled myself in order to exalt you? When I announced the gospel of God to you without charging you for it? 8I robbed other churches by accepting payment from them in order to serve you; 9and when I was with you, and was in need of anything, I didn't lay a burden on anybody, because my needs were more than met by the brothers who came from Macedonia. That's how I stopped myself from being a burden to you—and I intend to carry on in the same way. 10As the Messiah's truthfulness is in me, this boast of mine will not be silenced in the regions of Achaea. 11Why? Because I don't love you? God knows . . . !

No, They Are False Apostles!

¹²I'm going to continue to do what I've always done, so as to cut off any opportunity (for those who want such an opportunity!) for anyone to look as if they can match us in the things they boast about. ¹³Such people are false apostles! The only work they do is to deceive! They transform themselves so that they look like apostles of the Messiah—¹⁴and no wonder. The satan himself transforms himself to look like an angel of light, ¹⁵so it isn't surprising if his servants transform themselves to look like servants of righteousness. They will end up where their deeds are taking them.

The Boasting of a Reluctant Fool

¹⁶I'll say it again: don't let anyone think I'm a fool! But if they do—well, all right then, welcome me as a fool, so that I can do a little bit of boasting! ¹⁷What I'm going to say now, I'm not saying as if it came from the Lord, but as if I was a fool, as if I really did want to indulge myself in this kind of boasting. ¹⁸Plenty of people are boasting in human terms, after all, so why shouldn't I boast as well? ¹⁹After all, you put up with fools readily enough, since you are so wise yourselves. ²⁰You put up with it if someone makes you their slave, or if they eat up your property, or overpower you, or give themselves airs, or slap you in the face. ²¹Well, I'm ashamed to say it: we weren't strong enough for that!

Boasting of Weaknesses

Whatever anyone else dares to boast about (I'm talking nonsense, remember), I'll boast as well. ²²Are they Hebrews? So am I. Are they Israelites? So am I. Are they the seed of Abraham? So am I. ²³Are they servants of the Messiah?—I'm talking like a raving madman—I'm a better one. I've worked harder, been in prison more often, been beaten more times than I can count, and I've often been close to death. ²⁴Five times I've had the Jewish beating, forty lashes less one. ²⁵Three times I was beaten with rods; once I was stoned; three times I was shipwrecked; I was adrift in the sea for a night and a day. ²⁶I've been constantly traveling, facing dangers from rivers, dangers from brigands, dangers from my own people, dangers from foreigners, dangers in the town, dangers in the countryside, dangers at sea, dangers from false believers. ²⁷I've toiled and labored; I've burned the candle at both ends; I've been hungry and thirsty; I've often gone without food altogether; I've been cold and naked.

28Quite apart from all that, I have this daily pressure on me, my care for all the churches. 29Who is weak and I'm not weak? Who is offended without me burning with shame?

30If I must boast, I will boast of my weaknesses. 31The God and father of the Lord Jesus, who is blessed forever, knows that I'm not lying: 32in Damascus, King Aretas, the local ruler, was guarding the city of Damascus so that he could capture me, 33but I was let down in a basket through a window and over the wall, and I escaped his clutches.

12 I just have to boast—not that there's anything to be gained by it; but I'll go on to visions and revelations of the Lord. 2Someone I know in the Messiah, fourteen years ago (whether in the body or out of the body I don't know, though God knows), was snatched up to the third heaven. 3I know that this particular Someone (whether in the body or apart from the body I don't know, God knows)—4this person was snatched up to paradise, and heard . . . words you can't pronounce, which humans aren't allowed to repeat. 5I will boast of Someone like that, but I won't boast of myself, except of my weaknesses. 6If I did want to boast, you see, I wouldn't be mad; I'd be speaking the truth. But I'm holding back, so that nobody will think anything of me except what they can see in me or hear from me, 7even considering how remarkable the revelations were.

As a result, so that I wouldn't become too exalted, a thorn was given to me in my flesh, a messenger from the satan, to keep stabbing away at me. 8I prayed to the Lord three times about this, asking that it would be taken away from me, 9and this is what he said to me: "My grace is enough for you; my power comes to perfection in weakness." So I will be all the more pleased to boast of my weaknesses, so that the Messiah's power may rest upon me. 10So I'm delighted when I'm weak, insulted, in difficulties, persecuted, and facing disasters, for the Messiah's sake. When I'm weak, you see, then I am strong.

11I've been a fool! You forced me into it. If I *was* to have received an official commendation, it ought actually to have come from you! After all, I'm not inferior to the super-apostles, even though I am nothing. 12The signs of a true apostle, you see, were performed among you in all patience, with signs and

The Vision and the Thorn

The Signs of a True Apostle

wonders and powers. ¹³In what way have you been worse off than all the other churches, except in the fact that I myself didn't become a burden to you? Forgive me this injustice!

¹⁴Now look: this is the third time I'm ready to come to you. And I'm not going to be a burden, because I'm not looking for what belongs to you, but you yourselves. Children, after all, shouldn't be saving up for their parents, but parents for their children! ¹⁵For my part, I will gladly spend and be spent on your behalf. If I love you all the more, am I going to be loved any the less?

¹⁶Grant me this, that I didn't lay any burden on you. But— maybe I was a trickster, and I took you by deceit! ¹⁷Did I cheat you by any of the people I sent to you? ¹⁸I urged Titus to go to you, and I sent the brother with him. Did Titus cheat you? He behaved in the same spirit as me, didn't he? He conducted himself in the same manner, didn't he?

What Will Happen When Paul Arrives?

¹⁹You will imagine we are explaining ourselves again. Well, we're speaking in God's presence, in the Messiah! My beloved ones, it has all been intended to build you up. ²⁰I'm afraid, you see, that when I come I may find you rather different from what I would wish—and *I* may turn out to be rather different from what *you* would wish! I'm afraid there may still be fighting, jealousy, anger, selfishness, slander, gossip, arrogance, and disorder. ²¹I'm afraid that perhaps, when I come once more, my God may humble me again in front of you, and I will have to go into mourning over many who sinned before and have not repented of the uncleanness and fornication and shameless immorality that they have practiced.

13 This is the third time I'm coming to you. "Every charge must be substantiated at the mouth of two or three witnesses." ²I said it before when I was with you the second time, and I say it now in advance while I'm away from you, to all those who had sinned previously, and all the others, that when I come back again I won't spare them— ³since you are looking for proof of the Messiah who speaks in me, the Messiah who is not weak toward you but powerful in your midst! ⁴He was crucified in weakness, you see, but he lives by God's power. For we too are weak in him, but we shall live with him, for your benefit, by God's power.

⁵Test yourselves to see if you really are in the faith! Put yourselves through the examination. Or don't you realize that Jesus the Messiah is in you?—unless, that is, you've failed the test. ⁶I hope you will discover that we didn't fail the test. ⁷But we pray to God that you will never, ever do anything wrong; not so that we can be shown up as having passed the test, but so that you will do what is right, even if that means that we appear like people who've failed. ⁸For we cannot do anything against the truth, but only for the truth. ⁹We celebrate, you see, when we are weak but you are strong.

This is what we pray for, that you may become complete and get everything in order. ¹⁰That's why I'm writing this to you while I'm away, so that when I come I won't have to use my authority to be severe with you. The Lord has given me this authority, after all, not to pull down but to build up.

¹¹All that remains, my dear family, is this: celebrate, put everything in order, strengthen one another, think in the same way, be at peace; and the God of love and peace will be with you. ¹²Greet one another with the holy kiss. All God's people send you their greetings.

¹³The grace of King Jesus the Lord, the love of God, and the fellowship of the holy spirit be with you all.

Test Yourselves!

Grace, Love, and Fellowship

The Letter of Paul to the
Galatians

Paul's Distress
over the
Galatians

1 Paul, an apostle . . . (my apostleship doesn't derive from human sources, nor did it come through a human being; it came through Jesus the Messiah, and God the father who raised him from the dead) . . . ²and the family who are with me; to the churches of Galatia. ³Grace to you and peace from God our father and Jesus the Messiah, our Lord, ⁴who gave himself for our sins, to rescue us from the present evil age, according to the will of God our father, ⁵to whom be glory to the ages of ages. Amen.

⁶I'm astonished that you are turning away so quickly from the one who called you by grace, and going after another gospel—⁷not that it is another gospel, it's just that there are some people stirring up trouble for you and wanting to pervert the gospel of the Messiah. ⁸But even if we—or an angel from heaven!—should announce a gospel other than the one we announced to you, let such a person be accursed. ⁹I said it before and I now say it again: if anyone offers you a gospel other than the one you received, let that person be accursed.

Paul's
Conversion
and Call

¹⁰Well now . . . does *that* sound as though I'm trying to make up to people—or to God? Or that I'm trying to curry favor with people? If I were still pleasing people, I wouldn't be a slave of the Messiah.

¹¹You see, brothers and sisters, let me make it clear to you: the gospel announced by me is not a mere human invention. ¹²I didn't receive it from human beings, nor was I taught it; it came through an unveiling of Jesus the Messiah.

13You heard, didn't you, the way I behaved when I was still within "Judaism." I persecuted the church of God violently, and ravaged it. 14I advanced in Judaism beyond many of my own age and people; I was extremely zealous for my ancestral traditions. 15But when God, who set me apart from my mother's womb, and called me by his grace, was pleased 16to unveil his son in me, so that I might announce the good news about him among the nations—immediately I did not confer with flesh and blood. 17Nor did I go up to Jerusalem to those who were apostles before me. No, I went away to Arabia, and afterward returned to Damascus.

18Then, after three years, I went up to Jerusalem to speak with Cephas. I stayed with him for two weeks. 19I didn't see any other of the apostles except James, the Lord's brother. 20(Look, I'm not lying! The things I'm writing to you are written in God's presence.) 21Then I went to the regions of Syria and Cilicia. 22I remained unknown by sight to the messianic assemblies in Judaea. 23They simply heard that the one who had been persecuting them was now announcing the good news of the faith which he once tried to destroy. 24And they glorified God because of me.

Paul's First Visit to Peter

2 Then, after fourteen years, I went up again to Jerusalem. I took Barnabas with me, and Titus. 2I went up because of a revelation. I laid before them the gospel which I announce among the Gentiles (I did this privately, in the presence of the key people), in case somehow I might be running, or might have run, to no good effect. 3But even the Greek, Titus, who was with me, was not forced to get circumcised . . . 4but because of some pseudo–family members who had been secretly smuggled in, who came in on the side to spy on the freedom which we have in the Messiah, Jesus, so that they might bring us into slavery . . . 5I didn't yield authority to them, no, not for a moment, so that the truth of the gospel might be maintained for you.

Standing Firm Against Opposition

6However, those who appeared to be Something—what sort of "thing" they were makes no difference to me; God shows no partiality—those of reputation added nothing extra to me. 7On the contrary, they saw that I had been entrusted with the

Paul's Agreement with Peter and James

gospel for the uncircumcision, just as Peter had been with
the gospel for the circumcision 8(for the one who gave Peter
the power to be an apostle to the circumcision gave me the
power to go to the Gentiles). They knew, moreover, the grace
that had been given to me. 9So James, Cephas, and John, who
were reputed to be "pillars," gave to Barnabas and me the right
hand of fellowship, that we should go to the Gentiles, and they
to the circumcision. 10The only extra thing they asked was that
we should continue to remember the poor—the very thing I
was eager to do.

**Paul Confronts
Peter in Antioch**

11But when Cephas came to Antioch, I stood up to him face
to face. He was in the wrong. 12Before certain persons came
from James, Peter was eating with the Gentiles. But when
they came, he drew back and separated himself, because he
was afraid of the circumcision-people. 13The rest of the Jews
did the same, joining him in this play-acting. Even Barnabas
was carried along by their sham. 14But when I saw that they
weren't walking straight down the line of gospel truth, I said
to Cephas in front of them all: "Look here: you're a Jew, but
you've been living like a Gentile. How can you force Gentiles
to become Jews?"

**Justified by
Faith, Not
Works of Law**

15We are Jews by birth, not "Gentile sinners." 16But we
know that a person is not declared "righteous" by works of the
Jewish law, but through the faithfulness of Jesus the Messiah.

That is why we too believed in the Messiah, Jesus: so that
we might be declared "righteous" on the basis of the Messiah's
faithfulness, and not on the basis of works of the Jewish law.
On that basis, you see, no creature will be declared "righteous."

17Well, then; if, in seeking to be declared "righteous" in the
Messiah, we ourselves are found to be "sinners," does that
make the Messiah an agent of "sin"? Certainly not! 18If I build
up once more the things which I tore down, I demonstrate
that I am a lawbreaker.

19Let me explain it like this. Through the law I died to the
law, so that I might live to God. I have been crucified with the
Messiah. 20I am, however, alive—but it isn't me any longer;
it's the Messiah who lives in me. And the life I do still live in
the flesh, I live within the faithfulness of the son of God, who
loved me and gave himself for me.

²¹I don't set aside God's grace. If "righteousness" comes through the law, then the Messiah died for nothing.

3 You witless Galatians! Who has bewitched you? King Jesus was portrayed on the cross before your very eyes! ²There's just one thing I want to know from you. Did you receive the spirit by doing the works of Torah, or by hearing and believing? ³You are so witless: you began with the spirit, and now you're ending with the flesh? ⁴Did you really suffer so much for nothing—if indeed it is going to be for nothing? ⁵The one who gives you the spirit and performs powerful deeds among you—does he do this through your performance of Torah, or through hearing and believing?

God's Promise and Abraham's Faith

⁶It's like Abraham. "He believed God, and it was counted to him for righteousness." ⁷So you know that it's people of faith who are children of Abraham. ⁸The Bible foresaw that God would justify the nations by faith, so it announced the gospel to Abraham in advance, when it declared that "the nations will be blessed in you." ⁹So you see: the people of faith are blessed along with faithful Abraham.

¹⁰Because, you see, those who belong to the "works-of-the-law" camp are under a curse! Yes, that's what the Bible says: "Cursed is everyone who doesn't stick fast by everything written in the book of the law, to perform it." ¹¹But, because nobody is justified before God in the law, it's clear that "the righteous shall live by faith." ¹²The law, however, is not by faith: rather, "the one who does them shall live in them."

Redeemed from the Law's Curse

¹³The Messiah redeemed us from the curse of the law, by becoming a curse on our behalf, as the Bible says: "Cursed is everyone who hangs on a tree." ¹⁴This was so that the blessing of Abraham could flow through to the nations in King Jesus—and so that we might receive the promise of the spirit, through faith.

¹⁵My brothers and sisters, let me use a human illustration. When someone makes a covenanted will, nobody sets it aside or adds to it. ¹⁶Well, the promises were made "to Abraham and his seed"—that is, his family. It doesn't say "his seeds," as though referring to several families, but indicates a single family by saying "and to your seed," meaning the Messiah.

Christ the Seed, Christ the Mediator

¹⁷This is what I mean. God made this covenanted will; the law, which came four hundred and thirty years later, can't

undermine it and make the promise null and void. ¹⁸If the inheritance came through the law, it would no longer be by promise; but God gave it to Abraham by promise.

¹⁹Why then the law? It was added because of transgressions, until the family should come to whom it had been promised. It was laid down by angels, at the hand of a mediator. ²⁰He, however, is not the mediator of the "one"—but God is one!

²¹Is the law then against God's promises? Of course not! No, if a law had been given that could have given life, then covenant membership really would have been by the law. ²²But the Bible shut up everything together under the power of sin, so that the promise—which comes by the faithfulness of Jesus the Messiah—might be given to those who believe.

The Coming of Faith

²³Before this faithfulness arrived, we were kept under guard by the law, in close confinement until the coming faithfulness should be revealed. ²⁴Thus the law was like a babysitter for us, looking after us until the coming of the Messiah, so that we might be given covenant membership on the basis of faithfulness.

²⁵But now that faithfulness has come, we are no longer under the rule of the babysitter. ²⁶For you are all children of God, through faith, in the Messiah, Jesus.

²⁷You see, every one of you who has been baptized into the Messiah has put on the Messiah. ²⁸There is no longer Jew or Greek; there is no longer slave or free; there is no "male and female"; you are all one in the Messiah, Jesus.

²⁹And, if you belong to the Messiah, you are Abraham's family. You stand to inherit the promise.

The Son and the Spirit

4 Let me put it like this. As long as the heir is a child, he is no different from a slave—even if, in fact, he is master of everything! ²He is kept under guardians and stewards until the time set by his father.

³Well, it's like that with us. When we were children, we were kept in "slavery" under the "elements of the world." ⁴But when the fullness of time arrived, God sent out his son, born of a woman, born under the law, ⁵so that he might redeem those under the law, so that we might receive adoption as sons.

⁶And, because you are sons, God sent out the spirit of his son into our hearts, calling out "Abba, Father!" ⁷So you are no

longer a slave, but a son! And, if you're a son, you are an heir, through God.

8However, at that stage you didn't know God, and so you were enslaved to beings that, in their proper nature, are not gods. 9But now that you've come to know God—or, better, to be known *by* God—how can you turn back again to that weak and poverty-stricken lineup of elements that you want to serve all over again? 10You are observing days, and months, and seasons, and years! 11I am afraid for you; perhaps my hard work with you is all going to be wasted.

The True God and the False Gods

12Become like me!—because I became like you, my dear family. This is my plea to you. You didn't wrong me: 13no, you know that it was through bodily weakness that I announced the gospel to you in the first place. 14You didn't despise or scorn me, even though my condition was quite a test for you, but you welcomed me as if I were God's angel, as if I were the Messiah, Jesus! 15What's happened to the blessing you had then? Yes, I can testify that you would have torn out your eyes, if you'd been able to, and given them to me. 16So have I become your enemy by telling you the truth?

Paul's Appeal to His Children

17The other lot are eager for you, but it's not in a good cause. They want to shut you out, so that you will then be eager for them. 18Well, it's always good to be eager in a good cause, and not only when I'm there with you. 19My children—I seem to be in labor with you all over again, until the Messiah is fully formed in you! 20I wish I were there with you right now, and could change my tone of voice. I really am at a loss about you.

21So, you want to live under the law, do you? All right, tell me this: are you prepared to hear what the law says? 22For the Bible says that Abraham had two sons, one by the slave-girl and one by the free woman. 23Now the child of the slave-girl was born according to the flesh, while the child of the free woman was born according to promise.

Abraham's Two Sons

24Treat this as picture-language. These two women stand for two covenants: one comes from Mount Sinai and gives birth to slave-children; that is Hagar. 25(Sinai, you see, is a mountain in Arabia, and it corresponds, in the picture, to the present Jerusalem, since she is in slavery with her children.) 26But the Jerusalem which is above is free—and she is our mother.

27For the Bible says,

> *Celebrate, childless one, who never gave birth!*
> *Go wild and shout, girl that never had pains!*
> *The barren woman has many more children*
> *Than the one who has a husband!*

28Now you, my family, are children of promise, in the line of Isaac. 29But things now are like they were then: the one who was born according to the flesh persecuted the one born according to the spirit. 30But what does the Bible say? "Throw out the slave-girl and her son! For the son of the slave-girl will not inherit with the son of the free." 31So, my family, we are not children of the slave-girl, but of the free.

Freedom in Christ

5 The Messiah set us free so that we could enjoy freedom! So stand firm, and don't get yourselves tied down by the chains of slavery.

2Look here: I, Paul, am telling you that if you get circumcised, the Messiah will be of no use to you. 3I testify once more, against every person who gets circumcised, that he is thereby under obligation to perform the entire law. 4You are split off from the Messiah, you people who want to be justified by the law! You have dropped out of grace. 5For we are waiting eagerly, by the spirit and by faith, for the hope of righteousness. 6For in the Messiah, Jesus, neither circumcision nor uncircumcision has any power. What matters is faith, working through love.

Warnings Against Compromise

7You were running well. Who got in your way and stopped you being persuaded by the truth? 8This persuasion didn't come from the one who called you! 9A little yeast works its way through the whole lump. 10I am persuaded in the Lord that you won't differ from me on this. But the one who is troubling you will bear the blame, whoever he may be. 11As for me, my dear family, if I am still announcing circumcision, why are people still persecuting me? If I were, the scandal of the cross would have been neutralized. 12If only those who are making trouble for you would cut the whole lot off!

The Law and the Spirit

13When God called you, my dear family, he called you to make you free. But you mustn't use that freedom as an opportunity for the flesh. Rather, you must become each other's servants, through love. 14For the whole law is summed up in one word, namely this: "Love your neighbor as yourself." 15But if you bite each other and devour each other, watch out! You may end up being destroyed by each other.

16Let me say this to you: live by the spirit, and you won't do what the flesh wants you to. 17For the flesh wants to go against the spirit, and the spirit against the flesh. They are opposed to each other, so that you can't do what you want. 18But if you are led by the spirit, you are not under the law.

19Now the works of the flesh are obvious. They are such things as fornication, uncleanness, licentiousness, 20idolatry, sorcery, hostilities, strife, jealousy, bursts of rage, selfish ambition, factiousness, divisions, 21moods of envy, drunkenness, wild partying, and similar things. I told you before, and I tell you again: people who do such things will not inherit God's kingdom.

22But the fruit of the spirit is love, joy, peace, greatheartedness, kindness, generosity, faithfulness, 23gentleness, self-control. There is no law that opposes things like that! 24And those who belong to the Messiah, Jesus, crucified the flesh with its passions and desires. 25If we live by the spirit, let's line up with the spirit. 26We shouldn't be conceited, vying with one another and jealous of each other.

Fruit of the Spirit

My dear family, if someone is found out in some trespass, then you—the "spiritual" ones!—should set such a person right, in a spirit of gentleness. Watch out for yourselves: you too may be tested. 2Carry each other's burdens; that's the way to fulfill the Messiah's law. 3If you think you're something when you are not, you deceive yourself. 4Every one of you should test your own work, and then you will have a reason to boast of yourself, not of somebody else. 5Each of you, you see, will have to carry your own load.

Bearing One Another's Burdens

6If someone is being taught the word, they should share with the teacher all the good things they have. 7Don't be misled; God won't have people turning their noses up at him. What you sow is what you'll reap. 8Yes: if you sow in the field of your flesh you will harvest decay from your flesh, but if you sow in the field of the spirit you will harvest eternal life from the spirit. 9Don't lose your enthusiasm for behaving properly.

Practical Support in the Church

You'll bring in the harvest at the proper time, if you don't become weary. [10]So, then, while we have the chance, let's do good to everyone, and particularly to the household of the faith.

Boasting in the Cross

[11]Look at the large-size letters I'm writing to you in my own hand. [12]It's the people who want to make a fine showing in the flesh who are trying to force you into getting circumcised—for this purpose only, that they may avoid persecution for the Messiah's cross. [13]You see, even the circumcised ones don't keep the law; rather, they want you to be circumcised, so that they may boast about your flesh.

[14]As for me, God forbid that I should boast—except in the cross of our Lord Jesus the Messiah, through whom the world has been crucified to me and I to the world. [15]Circumcision, you see, is nothing; neither is uncircumcision! What matters is new creation. [16]Peace and mercy on everyone who lines up by that standard—yes, on God's Israel.

[17]For the rest, let nobody make trouble for me. You see, I carry the marks of Jesus on my body.

[18]The grace of our Lord Jesus the Messiah be with your spirit, my dear family. Amen.

The Letter of Paul to the
Ephesians

1 From Paul, one of King Jesus's apostles through God's purpose, to the holy ones in Ephesus who are also loyal believers in King Jesus: ²may God our father and the Lord Jesus, the king, give you grace and peace!

³Let us bless God, the father of our Lord Jesus, the king! He has blessed us in the king with every spirit-inspired blessing in the heavenly realm.

⁴He chose us in him before the world was made, so as to be holy and irreproachable before him in love. ⁵He foreordained us for himself, to be adopted as sons and daughters through Jesus the king. That's how he wanted it, and that's what gave him delight, ⁶so that the glory of his grace, the grace he poured on us in his beloved one, might receive its due praise.

⁷In the king, and through his blood, we have deliverance—that is, our sins have been forgiven—through the wealth of his grace ⁸which he lavished on us. Yes, with all wisdom and insight ⁹he has made known to us the secret of his purpose, just as he wanted it to be and set it forward in him ¹⁰as a blueprint for when the time was ripe. His plan was to sum up the whole cosmos in the king—yes, everything in heaven and on earth, in him.

¹¹In him we have received the inheritance! We were foreordained to this, according to the intention of the one who does all things in accordance with the counsel of his purpose. ¹²This was so that we, we who first hoped in the king, might live for the praise of his glory. ¹³In him you too, who heard the word of truth, the gospel of your salvation, and believed it—in him

you were marked out with the spirit of promise, the Holy One.
¹⁴The spirit is the guarantee of our inheritance, until the time
when the people who are God's special possession are finally re-
claimed and freed. This, too, is for the praise of his glory.

Knowing the Power of the King

¹⁵Because of all this, and because I'd heard that you are
loyal and faithful to Jesus the master, and that you show love
to all God's holy people, ¹⁶I never stop giving thanks for you as
I remember you in my prayers. ¹⁷I pray that the God of King
Jesus our Lord, the father of glory, would give you, in your
spirit, the gift of being wise, of seeing things people can't normally see, because you are coming to know him ¹⁸and to have
the eyes of your inmost self opened to God's light. Then you
will know exactly what the hope is that goes with God's call;
you will know the wealth of the glory of his inheritance in his
holy people; ¹⁹and you will know the outstanding greatness of
his power toward us who are loyal to him in faith, according to
the working of his strength and power.

²⁰This was the power at work in the king when God raised
him from the dead and sat him at his right hand in the heavenly
places, ²¹above all rule and authority and power and lordship,
and above every name that is invoked, both in the present
age and also in the age to come. ²²Yes: God has "put all things
under his feet," and has given him to the church as the head
over all. ²³The church is his body; it is the fullness of the one
who fills all in all.

Warning Signs on the Wrong Road

2 So where do you come into it all? Well, you were dead
because of your offenses and sins! ²That was the road
you used to travel, keeping in step with this world's
"present age"; in step, too, with the ruler of the power of the
air, the spirit that is, even now, at work among people whose
whole lives consist of disobeying God. ³Actually, that's how all
of us used to behave, conditioned by physical desires. We used
to do what our flesh and our minds were urging us to do. What
was the result? We too were subject to wrath in our natural
state, just like everyone else.

⁴But when it comes to mercy, God is rich! He had such great
love for us that ⁵he took us at the very point where we were
dead through our offenses, and made us alive together with
the king. (Yes, you are saved by sheer grace!) ⁶He raised us up

with him, and made us sit with him—in the heavenly places, in King Jesus! 7This was so that in the ages to come he could show just how unbelievably rich his grace is, the kindness he has shown us in King Jesus.

8How has this all come about? You have been saved by grace, through faith! This doesn't happen on your own initiative; it's God's gift. 9It isn't on the basis of works, so no one is able to boast. 10This is the explanation: God has made us what we are. God has created us in King Jesus for the good works that he prepared, ahead of time, as the road we must travel.

Grace, Not Works

11So, then, remember this! In human terms—that is, in your "flesh"—you are "Gentiles." You are the people whom the so-called circumcision refer to as the so-called uncircumcision—circumcision, of course, being something done by human hands to human flesh. 12Well, once upon a time you were separated from the king. You were detached from the community of Israel. You were foreigners to the covenants which contained the promise. There you were, in the world with no hope and no god!

Two into One Will Go

13But now, in King Jesus, you have been brought near in the king's blood—yes, you, who used to be a long way away! 14He is our peace, you see. He has made the two to be one. He has pulled down the barrier, the dividing wall, that turns us into enemies of each other. He has done this in his flesh, 15by abolishing the law with its commands and instructions.

The point of doing all this was to create, in him, one new human being out of the two, so making peace. 16God was reconciling both of us to himself in a single body, through the cross, by killing the enmity in him.

17So the Messiah came and gave the good news. Peace had come! Peace, that is, for those of you who were a long way away, and peace, too, for those who were close at hand. 18Through him, you see, we both have access to the father in the one spirit.

Unveiling the New Temple

19This is the result. You are no longer foreigners or strangers. No: you are fellow citizens with God's holy people. You are members of God's household. 20You are built on the foundation of the apostles and prophets, with King Jesus himself as the cornerstone. 21In him the whole building is fitted together, and grows into a holy temple in the Lord. 22You, too, are being built up together, in him, into a place where God will live by the spirit.

God's Secret Plan Unveiled at Last

3 It's because of all this that I, Paul, the prisoner of King Jesus on behalf of you Gentiles...

²I'm assuming, by the way, that you've heard about the plan of God's grace that was given to me to pass on to you? ³You know—the secret purpose that God revealed to me, as I wrote briefly just now? ⁴Anyway...

When you read this you'll be able to understand the special insight I have into the king's secret. ⁵This wasn't made known to human beings in previous generations, but now it's been revealed by the spirit to God's holy apostles and prophets. ⁶The secret is this: that, through the gospel, the Gentiles are to share Israel's inheritance. They are to become fellow members of the body, along with them, and fellow sharers of the promise in King Jesus.

⁷This is the gospel that I was appointed to serve, in line with the free gift of God's grace that was given to me. It was backed up with the power through which God accomplishes his work.

Wisdom for the Rulers

⁸I am the very least of all God's people. However, he gave me this task as a gift: that I should be the one to tell the Gentiles the good news of the king's wealth, wealth no one could begin to count. ⁹My job is to make clear to everyone just what the secret plan is, the purpose that's been hidden from the very beginning of the world in God who created all things. ¹⁰This is it: that God's wisdom, in all its rich variety, was to be made known to the rulers and authorities in the heavenly places—through the church!

¹¹This was God's eternal purpose, and he's accomplished it in King Jesus our Lord. ¹²We have confidence, and access to God, in him, in full assurance, through his faithfulness. ¹³So I beg you: don't lose heart because of my sufferings on your behalf! That's your glory!

God's Love, God's Power— in Us

¹⁴Because of this, I am kneeling down before the father, ¹⁵the one who gives the name of "family" to every family that there is, in heaven and on earth. ¹⁶My prayer is this: that he will lay out all the riches of his glory to give you strength and power, through his spirit, in your inner being; ¹⁷that the king

may make his home in your hearts, through faith; that love may be your root, your firm foundation; ¹⁸and that you may be strong enough (with all God's holy ones) to grasp the breadth and length and height and depth, ¹⁹and to know the king's love—though actually it's so deep that nobody can really know it! So may God fill you with all his fullness.

²⁰So: to the one who is capable of doing far, far more than we can ask or imagine, granted the power which is working in us—²¹to him be glory, in the church, and in King Jesus, to all generations, and to the ages of ages! Amen!

4 So, then, this is my appeal to you—yes, it's me, the prisoner in the Lord! You must live up to the calling you received. ²Bear with one another in love; be humble, meek, and patient in every way with one another. ³Make every effort to guard the unity that the spirit gives, with your lives bound together in peace.

Live Up to Your Calling!

⁴There is one body and one spirit; you were, after all, called to one hope which goes with your call. ⁵There is one Lord, one faith, one baptism; ⁶one God and father of all, who is over all, through all, and in all.

⁷But grace was given to each one of us, according to the measure the king used when he was distributing gifts. ⁸That's why it says,

> *When he went up on high*
> *He led bondage itself into bondage*
> *And he gave gifts to people.*

⁹When it says here that "he went up," what this means is that he also came down into the lower place—that is, the earth. ¹⁰The one who came down is the one who also "went up"—yes, above all the heavens!—so that he might fill all things.

¹¹So these were the gifts that he gave. Some were to be apostles, others prophets, others evangelists, and others pastors and teachers. ¹²Their job is to give God's people the equipment they need for their work of service, and so to build up the king's body. ¹³The purpose of this is that we should all reach unity in our belief and loyalty, and in knowing God's son. Then we shall reach the stature of the mature Man measured by the standards of the king's fullness.

Grown-Up Christianity

¹⁴As a result, we won't be babies any longer! We won't be thrown this way and that on a stormy sea, blown about by every gust of teaching, by human tricksters, by their cunning and deceitful scheming. ¹⁵Instead, we must speak the truth in love, and so grow up in everything into him—that is, into the king, who is the head. ¹⁶He supplies the growth that the whole body needs, linked as it is and held together by every joint which supports it, with each member doing its own proper work. Then the body builds itself up in love.

Off with the Old, On with the New

¹⁷So this is what I want to say; I am bearing witness to it in the Lord. You must no longer behave like the Gentiles, foolish-minded as they are. ¹⁸Their understanding is darkened; they are cut off from God's life because of their deep-seated ignorance, which springs from the fact that their hearts are hard. ¹⁹They have lost all moral sensitivity, and have given themselves over to whatever takes their fancy. They go off greedily after every kind of uncleanness.

²⁰But that's not how you learned the king!—²¹if indeed you did hear about him, and were taught in him, in accordance with the truth about Jesus himself. ²²That teaching stressed that you should take off your former lifestyle, the old humanity. That way of life is decaying, as a result of deceitful lusts. ²³Instead, you must be renewed in the spirit of your mind, ²⁴and you must put on the new humanity, which is being created the way God intended it, displaying justice and genuine holiness.

The Kindness That Imitates God Himself

²⁵Put away lies, then. "Each of you, speak the truth with your neighbor," because we are members of one another. ²⁶"Be angry, but don't sin"; don't let the sun go down on you while you're angry, ²⁷and don't leave any loophole for the devil. ²⁸The thief shouldn't steal any longer, but should rather get on with some honest manual work, so as to be able to share with people in need.

²⁹Don't let any unwholesome words escape your lips. Instead, say whatever is good and will be useful in building people up, so that you will give grace to those who listen.

³⁰And don't disappoint God's holy spirit—the spirit who put God's mark on you to identify you on the day of freedom. ³¹All bitterness and rage, all anger and yelling, and all blasphemy—

put it all away from you, with all wickedness. ³²Instead, be kind to one another, cherish tender feelings for each other, forgive one another, just as God forgave you in the king.

5 So you should be imitators of God, like dear children. ²Conduct yourselves in love, just as the Messiah loved us, and gave himself for us, as a sweet-smelling offering and sacrifice to God.

³As for fornication, uncleanness of any kind, or greed: you shouldn't even mention them! You are, after all, God's holy people. ⁴Shameful, stupid, or coarse conversations are quite out of place. Instead, there should be thanksgiving.

⁵You should know this, you see: no fornicator, nobody who practices uncleanness, no greedy person (in other words, an idolator) has any inheritance in the Messiah's kingdom, or in God's. ⁶Don't let anyone fool you with empty words. It's because of these things, you see, that God's wrath is coming on people who are disobedient.

⁷So don't share in their practices. ⁸After all, at one time you were darkness, but now, in the Lord, you are light! So behave as children of light. ⁹Light has its fruit—doesn't it?—in everything that's good, and just, and true. ¹⁰Think through what's going to be pleasing to the Lord. Work it out.

¹¹So don't get involved in the works of darkness, which all come to nothing. Instead, expose them! ¹²The things they do in secret, you see, are shameful even to talk about. ¹³But everything becomes visible when it's exposed to the light, ¹⁴since everything that is visible is light. That's why it says:

Wake up, you sleeper!
Rise up from the dead!
The Messiah will shine on you!

¹⁵So take special care how you conduct yourselves. Don't be unwise, but be wise. ¹⁶Make use of any opportunity you have, because these are wicked times we live in. ¹⁷So don't be foolish; rather, understand what the Lord's will is. ¹⁸And don't get drunk with wine; that way lies dissipation. Rather, be filled with the spirit! ¹⁹Speak to each other in psalms and hymns and spiritual songs, singing and chanting in your heart to the

Darkness and Light in Matters of Sex

Light and Darkness

Lord, ²⁰always giving thanks for everything to God the father in the name of our Lord Jesus the Messiah.

Wives and Husbands

²¹Be subject to one another out of reverence for the Messiah.

²²Wives, be subject to your own husbands, as to the Lord. ²³The man, you see, is the head of the woman, just as the Messiah, too, is head of the church. He is himself the savior of the body. ²⁴But, just as the church is subject to the Messiah, in the same way women should be subject in everything to their husbands.

²⁵Husbands, love your wives, as the Messiah loved the church, and gave himself for it, ²⁶so that he could make it holy, cleansing it by washing it with water through the word. ²⁷He did this in order to present the church to himself in brilliant splendor, without a single spot or blemish or anything of the kind—that it might be holy and without blame. ²⁸That's how husbands ought to love their own wives, just as they love their own bodies.

Someone who loves his wife loves himself. ²⁹After all, nobody ever hates his own flesh: he feeds it and takes care of it, just as the Messiah does with the church, ³⁰because we are parts of his body. ³¹"That's why a man leaves his father and mother and is joined to his wife, and the two become one flesh."

³²The hidden meaning in this saying is very deep; but I am reading it as referring to the Messiah and the church. ³³Anyway, each one of you must love your wife as you love yourself; and the wife must see that she respects her husband.

Children, Parents, Slaves, and Masters

6 Children, obey your parents in the Lord. This is right and proper. ²"Honor your father and your mother"—this is the first commandment that comes with a promise attached!—³"so that things may go well with you and that you may live a long life on earth."

⁴Fathers, don't make your children angry. Bring them up in the training and instruction of the Lord.

⁵Slaves, obey your human masters, with respect and devotion, with the same single-mindedness that you have toward the Messiah. ⁶You must get on with your work, not only when

someone is watching you, as if you were just trying to please another human being, but as slaves of the Messiah. Do God's will from your heart. ⁷Get on with your tasks with a kind and ready spirit as if you were serving the master himself and not human beings. ⁸After all, you know that if anyone, slave or free, does something good, they will receive it back from the master.

⁹Masters, do the same to them! Give up using threats. You know, after all, that the master in heaven is their master and yours, and he is no respecter of persons.

¹⁰What else is there to say? Just this: be strong in the Lord, and in the strength of his power. ¹¹Put on God's complete armor. Then you'll be able to stand firm against the devil's trickery. ¹²The warfare we're engaged in, you see, isn't against flesh and blood. It's against the leaders, against the authorities, against the powers that rule the world in this dark age, against the wicked spiritual elements in the heavenly places.

God's Complete Armor

¹³For this reason, you must take up God's complete armor. Then, when wickedness grabs its moment, you'll be able to withstand, to do what needs to be done, and still to be on your feet when it's all over. ¹⁴So stand firm! Put the belt of truth around your waist; put on justice as your breastplate; ¹⁵for shoes on your feet, ready for battle, take the good news of peace. ¹⁶With it all, take the shield of faith; if you've got that, you'll be able to quench all the flaming arrows of the evil one. ¹⁷Take the helmet of salvation, and the sword of the spirit, which is God's word.

¹⁸Pray on every occasion in the spirit, with every type of prayer and intercession. You'll need to keep awake and alert for this, with all perseverance and intercession for all God's holy ones—¹⁹and also for me! Please pray that God will give me his words to speak when I open my mouth, so that I can make known, loud and clear, the secret truth of the gospel. ²⁰That, after all, is why I'm a chained-up ambassador! Pray that I may announce it boldly; that's what I'm duty-bound to do.

Prayer and Peace

²¹It's important that you should know how things are with me, and what I'm up to; so our dear brother Tychicus will tell you about it. He is a loyal servant in the Lord. ²²I've sent him

to you with this in mind, so that you may know how things are with us, and so that he may encourage your hearts.

23Peace be to the whole family, and love with faith, from God the father and the Lord Jesus, the Messiah. 24Grace be with all who love our Lord, King Jesus, with a love that never dies!

The Letter of Paul to the
Philippians

1 From Paul and Timothy, slaves of King Jesus, to all God's holy ones in King Jesus who are in Philippi, together with the overseers and ministers: ²grace to you and peace, from God our father and King Jesus the Lord.

Paul's Reasons for Thanks

³I thank my God every time I think of you! ⁴I always pray with joy, whenever I pray for you all, ⁵because of your partnership in the gospel from the first day until now. ⁶Of this I'm convinced: the one who began a good work in you will thoroughly complete it by the day of King Jesus.

⁷It's right for me to think this way about all of you. You have me in your hearts, here in prison as I am, working to defend and bolster up the gospel. You are my partners in grace, all of you! ⁸Yes: God can bear witness how much I'm longing for all of you with the deep love of King Jesus.

⁹And this is what I'm praying: that your love may overflow still more and more, in knowledge and in all astute wisdom. ¹⁰Then you will be able to tell the difference between good and evil, and be sincere and faultless on the day of the Messiah, ¹¹filled to overflowing with the fruit of right living, fruit that comes through King Jesus to God's glory and praise.

¹²Now, my dear family, I want you to know that the things I've been through have actually helped the gospel on its way. ¹³You see, everybody in the Imperial Guard, and all the rest for that matter, have heard that I am here, chained up, because of the Messiah, the king. ¹⁴My imprisonment has given new confidence to most of the Lord's family; they are now much more prepared to speak the word boldly and fearlessly.

The King Is Proclaimed

¹⁵There are some, I should say, who are proclaiming the king because of envy and rivalry; but there are others who are doing it out of good will. ¹⁶These last are acting from love, since they know that I'm in prison because of defending the gospel; ¹⁷but the others are announcing the king out of selfishness and jealousy. They are not acting from pure motives; they imagine that they will make more trouble for me in my captivity.

¹⁸So what? Only this: the king is being announced, whether people mean it or not! I'm happy to celebrate that!

To Live or to Die?

Yes, and I really am going to celebrate: ¹⁹because I know that this will result in my rescue, through your prayer and the support of the spirit of King Jesus. ²⁰I'm waiting eagerly and full of hope, because nothing is going to put me to shame. I am going to be bold and outspoken, now as always, and the king is going to gain a great reputation through my body, whether in life or in death.

²¹You see, for me to live means the Messiah; to die means to make a profit. ²²If it's to be living on in the flesh, that means fruitful work for me.

Actually, I don't know which I would choose. ²³I'm pulled both ways at once: I would really love to leave all this and be with the king, because that would be far better. ²⁴But staying on here in the flesh is more vital for your sake. ²⁵Since I've become convinced of this, I know that I will remain here, and stay alongside all of you, to help you to advance and rejoice in your faith, ²⁶so that the pride you take in King Jesus may overflow because of me, when I come to visit you once again.

The Gospel in Public

²⁷The one thing I would stress is this: your public behavior must match up to the gospel of the king. That way, whether I do come and see you or whether I remain elsewhere, the news that I get about you will indicate that you are standing firm with a single spirit, struggling side by side with one united intent for the faith of the gospel, ²⁸and not letting your opponents intimidate you in any way. This is a sign from God: one that signifies their destruction, but your salvation.

²⁹Yes: God has granted you that, on behalf of the king, you should not only believe in him, but also suffer for his sake. ³⁰You are engaged in the same struggle which you once watched me go through; and, as you now hear, I'm still going through it.

2 So if our shared life in the king brings you any comfort; if love still has the power to make you cheerful; if we really do have a partnership in the spirit; if your hearts are at all moved with affection and sympathy—²then make my joy complete! Bring your thinking into line with one another.

Here's how to do it. Hold on to the same love; bring your innermost lives into harmony; fix your minds on the same object. ³Never act out of selfish ambition or vanity; instead, regard everybody else as your superior. ⁴Look after each other's best interests, not your own.

⁵This is how you should think among yourselves—with the mind that you have because you belong to the Messiah, Jesus:

Unity in Everything

The Mind of the Messiah

> ⁶*Who, though in God's form, did not*
> *Regard his equality with God*
> *As something he ought to exploit.*
>
> ⁷*Instead, he emptied himself,*
> *And received the form of a slave,*
> *Being born in the likeness of humans.*
>
> *And then, having human appearance,*
> ⁸*He humbled himself, and became*
> *Obedient even to death,*
>
> *Yes, even the death of the cross.*
> ⁹*And so God has greatly exalted him,*
> *And to him in his favor has given*
>
> *The name which is over all names:*
> ¹⁰*That now at the name of Jesus*
> *Every knee within heaven shall bow—*
>
> *On earth, too, and under the earth;*
> ¹¹*And every tongue shall confess*
> *That Jesus, Messiah, is Lord,*
> *To the glory of God, the father.*

¹²So, my dear people: you always did what I said, so please now carry on in the same way, not just as though I was there with you, but much more because I'm not! Your task now is to work at bringing about your own salvation; and naturally

How Salvation Is Worked Out

you'll be taking this with utter seriousness. 13After all, God himself is the one who's at work among you, who provides both the will and the energy to enable you to do what pleases him.

14There must be no grumbling and disputing in anything you do. 15That way, nobody will be able to fault you, and you'll be pure and spotless children of God in the middle of a twisted and depraved generation. You are to shine among them like lights in the world, 16clinging to the word of life. That's what I will be proud of on the day of the Messiah. It will prove that I didn't run a useless race, or work to no purpose.

17Yes: even if I am to be poured out like a drink-offering on the sacrifice and service of your faith, I shall celebrate, and celebrate jointly with you all. 18In the same way, you should celebrate, yes, and celebrate with me.

On Timothy   19I hope in the Lord Jesus to send Timothy to you soon, so that I in turn may be encouraged by getting news about you. 20I have nobody else of his quality: he will care quite genuinely about how you are. 21Everybody else, you see, looks after their own interests, not those of Jesus the Messiah. 22But you know how Timothy has proved himself. Like a child with a father he has worked as a slave alongside me for the sake of the gospel. 23So I'm hoping to send him just as soon as I see how it will turn out with me. 24And I am confident in the Lord that I myself will come very soon as well.

On Epaphroditus   25But I did think it was necessary to send Epaphroditus to you. He is my brother; he has worked alongside me and fought alongside me; and he's served as your agent in tending to my needs. 26He was longing for you all, you see, and he was upset because you heard that he was sick. 27And he really was sick, too; he nearly died. But God took pity on him—yes, and on me too as well, so that I wouldn't have one sorrow piled on top of another.

28This has made me all the more eager to send him, so that you'll see him again and be glad, and my own anxieties will be laid to rest. 29So give him a wonderfully happy welcome in the Lord, and hold people like him in special respect. 30He came close to death through risking his life for the king's work, so that he could complete the service to me that you hadn't been able to perform.

3 So then, my dear family, it comes down to this: celebrate in the Lord! It's no trouble for me to write the same things to you, and it's safe for you.

²Watch out for the dogs! Watch out for the "bad works" people! Watch out for the "incision" party—that is, the mutilators! ³We are the "circumcision," you see—we who worship God by the spirit, and boast in King Jesus, and refuse to trust in the flesh.

⁴Mind you, I've got good reason to trust in the flesh. If anyone else thinks they have reason to trust in the flesh, I've got more. ⁵Circumcised? On the eighth day. Race? Israelite. Tribe? Benjamin. Descent? Hebrew through and through. Torah-observance? A Pharisee. ⁶Zealous? I persecuted the church! Official status under the law? Blameless.

⁷Does that sound as though my account was well in credit? Well, maybe; but whatever I had written in on the profit side, I calculated it instead as a loss—because of the Messiah. ⁸Yes, I know that's weird, but there's more: I calculate everything as a loss, because knowing King Jesus as my Lord is worth far more than everything else put together! In fact, because of the Messiah I've suffered the loss of everything, and I now calculate it as trash, so that my profit may be the Messiah, ⁹and that I may be discovered in him, not having my own covenant status defined by Torah, but the status which comes through the Messiah's faithfulness: the covenant status from God which is given to faith. ¹⁰This means knowing him, knowing the power of his resurrection, and knowing the partnership of his sufferings. It means sharing the form and pattern of his death, ¹¹so that somehow I may arrive at the final resurrection from the dead.

¹²I'm not implying that I've already received "resurrection," or that I've already become complete and mature! No: I'm hurrying on, eager to overtake it, because King Jesus has overtaken me. ¹³My dear family, I don't reckon that I have yet overtaken it. But this is my one aim: to forget everything that's behind, and to strain every nerve to go after what's ahead. ¹⁴I mean to chase on toward the finishing post, where the prize waiting for me is the upward call of God in King Jesus.

¹⁵Those of us who are mature should think like this! If you think differently about it, God will reveal this to you as well.

¹⁶Only let's be sure to keep in line with the position we have reached.

Citizens of
Heaven

¹⁷So, my dear family, I want you, all together, to watch what I do and copy me. You've got us as a pattern of behavior; pay careful attention to people who follow it.

¹⁸You see, there are several people who behave as enemies of the cross of the Messiah. I told you about them often enough, and now I'm weeping as I say it again. ¹⁹They are on the road to destruction; their stomach is their god, and they find glory in their own shame. All they ever think about is what's on the earth.

²⁰We are citizens of heaven, you see, and we're eagerly waiting for the savior, the Lord, King Jesus, who is going to come from there. ²¹Our present body is a shabby old thing, but he's going to transform it so that it's just like his glorious body. And he's going to do this by the power which makes him able to bring everything into line under his authority.

Celebrate in
the Lord!

4 Well then, my dear family—I miss you so much, you're my joy and crown!—this is how you must stand firm in the Lord, my beloved people.

²I have a special appeal which goes jointly to Euodia and Syntyche: please, please, come to a common mind in the Lord. ³(And here's a request for you too, my loyal comrade: please help these women. They have struggled hard in the gospel alongside me, as have Clement and my other fellow workers, whose names are in the book of life.)

⁴Celebrate joyfully in the Lord, all the time. I'll say it again: celebrate! ⁵Let everybody know how gentle and gracious you are. The Lord is near.

⁶Don't worry about anything. Rather, in every area of life let God know what you want, as you pray and make requests, and give thanks as well. ⁷And God's peace, which is greater than we can ever understand, will keep guard over your hearts and minds in King Jesus.

⁸For the rest, my dear family, these are the things you should think through: whatever is true, whatever is holy, whatever is upright, whatever is pure, whatever is attractive, whatever has a good reputation; anything virtuous, anything praiseworthy. ⁹And these are the things you should do: what

you learned, received, heard, and saw in and through me. And the God of peace will be with you.

[10]I've been having a great celebration in the Lord because your concern for me has once again burst into flower. (You were of course concerned for me before, but you didn't have an opportunity to show it.)

The Hidden Secret

[11]I'm not talking about lacking anything. I've learned to be content with what I have. [12]I know how to do without, and I know how to cope with plenty. In every possible situation I've learned the hidden secret of being full and hungry, of having plenty and going without, and it's this: [13]I have strength for everything in the one who gives me power.

[14]But you did the right thing by entering into partnership with me in my suffering. [15]Indeed, as you people in Philippi know well, when the gospel was getting under way and I was moving on from Macedonia, there wasn't a single other church, except yourselves, that entered into a two-way partnership with me, giving and receiving. [16]Yes: when I was in Thessalonica you sent help to me, not just once but twice.

Closing Thanks and Greetings

[17]I stress that it isn't the gift I'm interested in. My concern is that you should have a healthy profit balance showing up on your account. [18]For myself, I've received full payment, and I'm well stocked up. In fact, I'm full to overflowing, now that I have received from Epaphroditus what you sent. It's like a sacrifice with a beautiful smell, a worthy offering, giving pleasure to God. [19]What's more, my God will meet all your needs, too, out of his store of glorious riches in King Jesus. [20]Glory be to our God and father forever and ever! Amen!

[21]Give my greetings to all God's people in King Jesus. The family with me here send their greetings. [22]All God's people send you greetings, especially those from Caesar's household.

[23]The grace of the Lord Jesus, the Messiah, be with your spirit.

The Letter of Paul to the
Colossians

Thanksgiving for the Gospel's Work

1 Paul, an apostle of King Jesus by God's purpose and Timothy my brother; 2to God's holy people in Colossae, the king's faithful family; grace to you and peace, from God our father.

3We always thank God, the father of our Lord, King Jesus, when we pray for you, 4because we've heard of your faith in King Jesus and the love you have for all God's holy people, 5because of the hope which is kept safe for you in the heavenly places. You heard about this before in the word of truth, the gospel 6which has arrived on your doorstep—just as, in fact, it's producing fruit and growing in all the world, as it has been among you, from the day you heard it and came to know the grace of God in truth. 7That's how you learned it from Epaphras our beloved fellow slave. He's a loyal and faithful servant of the king on your behalf. 8He it was who gave us the news about your love in the spirit.

Prayer for Wisdom and Gratitude

9For this reason, from the day we heard it, we haven't stopped praying for you. We're asking God to fill you with the knowledge of what he wants in all wisdom and spiritual understanding. 10This will mean that you'll be able to conduct yourselves in a manner worthy of the Lord, and so give him real delight, as you bear fruit in every good work and grow up in the knowledge of God. 11I pray that you'll be given all possible strength, according to the power of his glory, so that you'll have complete patience and become truly steadfast and joyful.

12And I pray that you will learn to give thanks to the father, who has made you fit to share the inheritance of God's holy ones in the light. [13]He has delivered us from the power of darkness, and transferred us into the kingdom of his beloved son. [14]He is the one in whom we have redemption, the forgiveness of sins.

> [15]*He is the image of God, the invisible one,*
> *The firstborn of all creation.*
> [16]*For in him all things were created,*
> *In the heavens and here on the earth.*
> *Things we can see and things we cannot—*
> *Thrones and lordships and rulers and powers—*
> *All things were created both through him and for him.*
>
> [17]*And he is ahead, prior to all else,*
> *And in him all things hold together;*
> [18]*And he himself is supreme, the head*
> *Over the body, the church.*
>
> *He is the start of it all,*
> *Firstborn from realms of the dead;*
> *So in all things he might be the chief.*
> [19]*For in him all the Fullness was glad to dwell*
>   [20]*And through him to reconcile all to himself,*
>   *Making peace through the blood of his cross,*
> *Through him—yes, things on the earth,*
>   *And also the things in the heavens.*

In Praise of Jesus Christ

[21]So what about you? Well, there was a time when you were excluded! You were enemies in your thinking, and in wicked behavior. [22]But now he has reconciled you in the body of his flesh, through death, in order to bring you into his presence holy, blameless and without any accusation.

[23]This assumes, of course, that you keep firmly on in the faith—by which I mean, solid on your foundations, and not shifting from the hope of the gospel which you heard. This gospel, after all, has been announced in all creation under heaven! And this is the gospel of which I, Paul, became a servant.

Reconciled and Firm in Faith

[24]Right now I'm having a celebration—a celebration of my sufferings, which are for your benefit! And I'm steadily completing, in my own flesh, what is presently lacking in the king's

The King, Living Within You

afflictions on behalf of his body, which is the church. 25I became the church's servant, according to the terms laid down
by God when he gave me my commission on your behalf, the
commission to fulfill God's word.

26This word declares the mystery that was kept secret from
past ages and generations, but now has been revealed to God's
holy people. 27God's intention was to make known to them
just what rich glory this mystery contains, out there among
the nations. And this is the key: the king, living within you as
the hope of glory!

28He is the one we are proclaiming. We are instructing
everybody and teaching everybody in every kind of wisdom,
so that we can present everybody grown up, complete, in the
king. 29That's what I am working for, struggling with all his
energy which is powerfully at work within me.

God's Hidden Treasure— King Jesus!

2 You see, I'd like you to know just what a struggle I am
having on behalf of you, and the family in Laodicea, and
all the people who don't know me by sight. 2I want their
hearts to be encouraged as they're brought together in love.
I want them to experience all the wealth of definite understanding, and to come to the knowledge of God's mystery—the
Messiah, the king! 3He is the place where you'll find all the
hidden treasures of wisdom and knowledge.

4I'm saying this so that nobody will deceive you with
plausible words. 5Though I'm away from you in person, you
see, I am present with you in the spirit, and I'm celebrating as
I keep an eye on your good order, and the solidity of your faith
in the king.

6So, then, just as you received King Jesus the Lord, you
must continue your journey in him. 7You must put down
healthy roots in him, being built up brick by brick in him, and
established strongly in the faith, just as you were taught, with
overflowing thankfulness.

Beware of Deceivers

8Watch out that nobody uses philosophy and hollow trickery to take you captive! These are in line with human tradition, and with the "elements of the world"—not the king. 9In
him, you see, all the full measure of divinity has taken up
bodily residence. 10What's more, you are fulfilled in him, since
he's the head of all rule and authority.

¹¹In him, indeed, you were circumcised with a special, new type of circumcision. It isn't something that human hands can do. It is the king's version of circumcision, and it happens when you put off the "body of flesh": ¹²when you're buried with him in baptism, and indeed also raised with him, through faith in the power of the God who raised him from the dead.

¹³In the same way, though you were dead in legal offenses, and in the uncircumcision of your flesh, God made you alive together with Jesus, forgiving us all our offenses. ¹⁴He blotted out the handwriting that was against us, opposing us with its legal demands. He took it right out of the way, by nailing it to the cross. ¹⁵He stripped the rulers and authorities of their armor, and displayed them contemptuously to public view, celebrating his triumph over them in him.

The Law and the Cross

¹⁶So don't let anyone pass judgment on you in a question of food or drink, or in the matter of festivals, new moons, or sabbaths. ¹⁷These things are a shadow cast by the coming reality—and the body that casts the shadow belongs to the king! ¹⁸Don't let anyone rule you out of order by trying to force you into a kind of fake humility, or into worshipping angels. Such people will go on and on about visions they've had; they get puffed up without good reason by merely human thinking, ¹⁹and they don't keep hold of the Head. It's from him that the whole body grows with the growth God gives it, as it's nourished and held together by its various ligaments and joints.

²⁰If you died with the king, coming out from the rule of the "worldly elements," what's the point of laying down laws as though your life was still merely worldly? ²¹"Don't handle! Don't taste! Don't touch!" ²²Rules like that all have to do with things that disappear as you use them. They are the sort of regulations and teachings that mere humans invent. ²³They may give an appearance of wisdom, since they promote a do-it-yourself religion, a kind of humility, and severe treatment of the body. But they are of no use when it comes to dealing with physical self-indulgence.

Dying and Rising with Christ

3 So if you were raised to life with the king, search for the things that are above, where the king is seated at God's right hand! ²Think about the things that are above, not the things that belong on the earth. ³Don't you see: you died,

and your life has been hidden with the king, in God! ⁴When the king is revealed (and he is your life, remember), then you too will be revealed with him in glory.

Old Clothes, New Clothes

⁵So, then, you must kill off the parts of you that belong on the earth: illicit sexual behavior, uncleanness, passion, evil desire, and greed (which is a form of idolatry). ⁶It's because of these things that God's wrath comes on the children of disobedience. ⁷You too used to behave like that once, when your life consisted of that sort of thing.

⁸But now you must put away the lot of them: anger, rage, wickedness, blasphemy, dirty talk coming out of your mouth. ⁹Don't tell lies to each other! You have stripped off the old human nature, complete with its patterns of behavior, ¹⁰and you have put on the new one—which is being renewed in the image of the creator, bringing you into possession of new knowledge. ¹¹In this new humanity there is no question of "Greek and Jew," or "circumcised and uncircumcised," of "barbarian, Scythian," or "slave and free." The king is everything and in everything!

Love, Peace, and Thanksgiving

¹²These are the clothes you must put on, then, since God has chosen you, made you holy, and lavished his love upon you. You must be tender-hearted, kind, humble, meek, and ready to put up with anything. ¹³You must bear with one another and, if anyone has a complaint against someone else, you must forgive each other. Just as the master forgave you, you must do the same. ¹⁴On top of all this you must put on love, which ties everything together and makes it complete. ¹⁵Let the king's peace be the deciding factor in your hearts; that's what you were called to, within the one body. And be thankful.

¹⁶Let the king's word dwell richly among you, as you teach and exhort one another in all wisdom, singing psalms, hymns, and spiritual songs to God with grateful hearts. ¹⁷And whatever you do, in word or action, do everything in the name of the master, Jesus, giving thanks through him to God the father.

The Christian Household

¹⁸Now a word for wives: you should be subject to your husbands. This is appropriate in the Lord. ¹⁹And for husbands: you should treat your wives with love, and not be bitter with them. ²⁰And for children: obey your parents in everything;

this pleases the Lord. ²¹And for fathers: don't provoke your children to anger; otherwise they might lose heart.

²²A word, too, for slaves: obey your earthly masters in everything. Don't do it simply out of show, to curry favor with human beings, but wholeheartedly, because you fear the master. ²³Whatever you do, give it your very best, as if you were working for the master and not for human beings. ²⁴After all, you know that you're going to receive the true inheritance from the master as your reward! It is the master, the king, that you are serving. ²⁵Anyone who does wrong will be paid back for wrongdoing, and there will be no favorites.

4 And a word for masters: do what is just and fair for your slaves. Remember that you too have a Master—in heaven.

The Fellowship of Prayer

²Devote yourselves to prayer; keep alert in it, with thanksgiving. ³While you're about it, pray for us, too, that God will open in front of us a door for the word, so that we may speak of the mystery of the king—which is why I'm here in chains. ⁴Pray that I may speak clearly about it. That's what I am duty-bound to do.

⁵Behave wisely toward outsiders; buy up every opportunity. ⁶When you speak, make sure it's always full of grace, and well flavored with salt! That way you'll know how to give each person an appropriate answer.

⁷Our dear brother Tychicus will tell you all my news. He is a faithful servant, indeed a fellow slave in the Lord. ⁸This is why I'm sending him to you—to let you know how things are with us, and to encourage your hearts. ⁹I'm also sending Onesimus, who is a dear and faithful brother. He is one of your own number. They will tell you everything that's going on here.

Greetings from Others

¹⁰Aristarchus (who's in jail with me here) sends you greetings. So does Mark, Barnabas's nephew. You've received instructions about him; if he comes to you, do make him welcome. ¹¹Jesus Justus sends greetings as well. These three are the only fellow Jews I have among my colleagues working for God's kingdom, and they have been an encouragement to me.

¹²Epaphras, one of your own folk and also one of King Jesus's slaves, sends you greetings. He's always struggling in

prayer on your behalf, praying that you will stand firm and mature, and have your minds fully settled on everything that God wants you to do. [13]I can bear him witness that he's gone to a lot of trouble on your behalf, and also on behalf of the family in Laodicea and in Hierapolis. [14]Luke, the beloved doctor, sends greetings; so too does Demas.

[15]Pass my greetings on to the family in Laodicea, and to Nympha and the church in her house. [16]When this letter has been read to you, make sure it's read in Laodicea as well; and you, too, should read the letter that will come on to you from Laodicea. [17]And say to Archippus: "Take care to complete the service that you have received in the Lord."

[18]I'm signing off in my own hand: PAUL.

Remember the chains I'm wearing.

Grace be with you.

The First Letter of Paul to the
Thessalonians

1 Paul, Silvanus, and Timothy, to the assembly of Thessalonians in God the father and the Lord Jesus, the Messiah. Grace to you and peace.

²We always give thanks to God for all of you, as we make mention of you in our prayers. ³We constantly remember the accomplishment of your faith, the hard work of your love, and the patience of your hope in our Lord Jesus the Messiah, in the presence of God our father.

⁴Dear family, beloved by God, we know that God has chosen you, ⁵because our gospel didn't come to you in word only, but in power, and in the holy spirit, and in great assurance. You know what sort of people we became for your sake, when we were among you.

⁶And you learned how to copy us—and the Lord! When you received the word, you had a lot to suffer, but you also had the holy spirit's joy. ⁷As a result, you became a model for all the believers in both Macedonia and Achaea. ⁸For the word of the Lord has resonated out from you, not only in Macedonia and Achaea; your faith in God has gone out to people everywhere. This means that we haven't had to say anything. ⁹They themselves tell the story of the kind of welcome we had from you, and how you turned to God from idols, to serve a living and true God, ¹⁰and to wait for his son from heaven, whom he raised from the dead—Jesus, who delivers us from the coming fury.

2 For you yourselves know, my dear family, that our visit to you didn't turn out to be empty. ²On the contrary. We had already undergone awful things and been

shamefully treated in Philippi, as you know; but we were open and exuberant in our God in declaring to you the gospel of God, despite a good deal of opposition.

³When we make our appeal, you see, we are not deceiving people. We don't have any impure motives; we aren't playing some kind of trick. ⁴Rather, we speak as people whom God has validated to be entrusted with the gospel; not with a view to pleasing people, but in order to please God, who validates our hearts.

⁵For we never used flattering words, as you know. Nor were we saying things insincerely, as a cover-up for greed, as God is our witness. ⁶We weren't looking for recognition from anybody, either you or anyone else—⁷though we could have imposed on you, as the Messiah's emissaries. But we were gentle among you, like a nurse taking care of her own children. ⁸We were so devoted to you that we gladly intended to share with you not only the gospel of God but our own lives, because you became so dear to us.

Paul's Fatherly Concern ⁹My dear family, you will recall our hard toil, our labor. We worked night and day so as not to be a burden to any of you while we announced to you the gospel of God. ¹⁰You are witnesses, and so is God, of our holy, upright, and blameless behavior toward you believers. ¹¹You know how, like a father to his own children, ¹²we encouraged each of you, and strengthened you, and made it clear to you that you should behave in a manner worthy of the God who calls you into his own kingdom and glory.

The Persecuted Church ¹³So, therefore, we thank God constantly that when you received the word of God which you heard from us, you accepted it, not as the word of a mere human being but—as it really is!—the word of God which is at work in you believers. ¹⁴For, my dear family, you came to copy God's assemblies in Judaea in the Messiah, Jesus. You suffered the same things from your own people as they did from those of the Judaeans ¹⁵who killed the Lord Jesus and the prophets, and who expelled us. They displease God; they oppose all people; ¹⁶they forbid us to speak to the Gentiles so that they may be saved. This has had the effect, all along, of completing the full total of their sins. But the fury has come upon them for good.

Paul's Joy and Crown

[17]As for us, my dear family, we were snatched away from you for a short time, in person though not in heart. We longed eagerly, with a great desire, to see you face to face. [18]That's why we wanted to come to you—I, Paul, again and again—but the satan got in our way.

[19]Don't you see? When our Lord Jesus is present once more, what is our hope, our joy, the crown of our boasting before him? It's you! [20]Yes: you are our glory and our joy.

The Sending of Timothy

3 So, when it got to the point that we couldn't bear it any longer, Silvanus and I decided to remain in Athens by ourselves, [2]and we sent Timothy—our brother, and God's fellow worker in the gospel of the Messiah—so that he could strengthen you and bring comfort to your faith, [3]so that you wouldn't be pulled off course by these sufferings. You yourselves know, don't you, that this is what we are bound to face. [4]For when we were with you, we told you ahead of time that we would undergo suffering; that's how it has turned out, and you know about it. [5]That's why, when I too couldn't bear it any longer, I sent Timothy, so that I could find out about your faithfulness, in case somehow the tempter had put you to the test and our work would be in ruins.

Timothy's Report

[6]But now Timothy has returned to us from you. He has brought us the good news of your faith—and your love; he has told us that you always have good memories of us, and that you are longing to see us, just as we are to see you. [7]So, my dear family, we are comforted about you, in all our difficulties and troubles, because of your faithfulness. [8]Now, you see, we are really alive, if you are standing firmly in the Lord. [9]For what thanks can we give back to God about you, for all the joy which we celebrate because of you in the presence of our God, [10]praying with even more fervor than you can imagine, night and day, that we may see you face to face and may put into proper order anything that is lacking in your faith?

Paul's Words of Blessing

[11]Now may God himself, our father, and our Lord Jesus, steer us on our way to you. [12]And may the Lord make your love for one another, and for everybody, abound and overflow, just as ours does for you. [13]That way, your hearts will be strengthened and kept blameless in holiness before God our father when our Lord Jesus is present again with all his holy ones. Amen.

Instructions on Holy Living

4 What remains, my dear family, is for us to ask you, and indeed to urge you in the Lord Jesus, that you should continue more and more to behave in the manner that you received from us as the appropriate way of behaving and of pleasing God. ²You know, of course, what instructions we gave you through the Lord Jesus. ³This is God's will, you see: he wants you to be holy, to keep well away from fornication. ⁴Each of you should know how to control your own body in holiness and honor, ⁵not in the madness of lust like Gentiles who don't know God. ⁶Nobody should break this rule, or cheat a fellow Christian in this area; the Lord is the avenger in all such matters, just as we told you before and testified most solemnly. ⁷For God did not call us to a dirty life, but in holiness. ⁸Anyone who rejects this, then, is not rejecting a human command, but the God who gives his holy spirit to you.

A Life of Love

⁹Now, about charitable concern for the whole family: I don't really need to write to you, because you yourselves have been taught by God to show loving care for one another. ¹⁰Indeed, you are doing this for all the Christian family in the whole of Macedonia. But we urge you, my dear family, to make this an even more prominent part of your lives. ¹¹You should make it your ambition to live peacefully, to mind your own business, and to work with your own hands, just as we commanded you, ¹²so that you may behave in a way which outsiders will respect, and so that none of you may be in financial difficulties.

The Lord's Coming

¹³Now concerning those who have fallen asleep: we don't want you to remain in ignorance about them, my dear family. We don't want you to have the kind of grief that other people do, people who don't have any hope. ¹⁴For, you see, if we believe that Jesus died and rose, that's the way God will also, through Jesus, bring with him those who have fallen asleep.

¹⁵Let me explain. (This is the word of the Lord I'm speaking to you!) We who are alive, who remain until the Lord is present, will not find ourselves ahead of those who fell asleep. ¹⁶The Lord himself will come down from heaven with a shouted order, with the voice of an archangel and the sound of God's trumpet. The Messiah's dead will rise first; ¹⁷then we who are alive, who are left, will be snatched up with them among the clouds, to meet the Lord in the air. And in this way

we shall always be with the Lord. ¹⁸So comfort each other with these words.

5 Now when it comes to specific times and dates, my dear family, you don't need to have anyone write to you. ²You yourselves know very well that the day of the Lord will come like a midnight robber. ³When people say, "Peace and security!" then swift ruin will arrive at their doorstep, like the pains that come over a woman in labor, and they won't have a chance of escape.

Children of Light

⁴But as for you, my dear family—you are not in darkness. That day won't surprise you like a robber. ⁵You are all children of light, children of the day! We don't belong to the night, or to darkness. ⁶So, then, let's not go to sleep, like the others, but let's keep awake and stay sober.

⁷People who sleep, you see, sleep at night. People who get drunk get drunk at night. ⁸But we daytime people should be self-controlled, clothing ourselves with the breastplate of faith and love, and with the helmet of the hope of salvation; ⁹because God has not placed us on the road to fury, but to gaining salvation, through our Lord Jesus the Messiah. ¹⁰He died for us, so that whether we stay awake or go to sleep we should live together with him. ¹¹So strengthen one another, and build each other up, just as you are doing.

¹²This, my dear family, is the request we make of you. Take note of those who work among you and exercise leadership over you in the Lord, those who give you instruction. ¹³Give them the highest possible rank of love because of their work. Live at peace among yourselves.

Final Exhortations

¹⁴And, my dear family, we beg you to warn those who step out of line. Console the downcast; help the weak; be warm-hearted and patient toward everybody. ¹⁵Make sure nobody pays anyone back evil for evil. Instead, always find the way to do good to one another, and to everybody.

¹⁶*Always celebrate,*
¹⁷*Never stop praying;*
¹⁸*In everything be thankful*
(This is God's will for you in the Messiah Jesus);
¹⁹*Don't quench the spirit,*

20Don't look down on prophecies,
21Test everything.
If something is good, hold it fast;
22If something looks evil, keep well away.

Final Blessings and Charge

23Now may the God of peace himself make you completely holy. May your complete spirit, soul, and body be kept blameless at the coming of our Lord Jesus the Messiah. 24The one who calls you is faithful; he will do it.

25My dear family, pray for us.

26Greet the whole family with a holy kiss. 27I charge you by the Lord to have this letter read to the whole family.

28The grace of our Lord Jesus the Messiah be with you.

The Second Letter of Paul to the
Thessalonians

1 Paul, Silvanus, and Timothy, to the assembly of Thessalonians in God our father and the Lord Jesus, the Messiah: ²grace to you and peace from God our father and the Lord Jesus, the Messiah.

³We owe God a constant debt of gratitude concerning you, my dear family. It is only right and proper. Your faith is growing marvelously, and the love which every single one of you has for each other is multiplying. ⁴As a result, we ourselves can tell all the churches of God how proud we are of you—of your patience and loyalty in all your troubles, and in all the sufferings you are going through.

⁵All this is a clear sign of the just judgment of God, to make you thoroughly worthy of the kingdom of God, for which you are suffering—⁶since it is just, on God's part, to pay back with suffering those who inflict suffering on you, ⁷and to give you, with us, respite from your sufferings.

This will come about when the Lord Jesus is revealed from heaven with his powerful angels, ⁸in a flaming fire, meting out punishment to those who don't know God and those who don't obey the gospel of our Lord Jesus. ⁹They will pay the penalty of eternal destruction from the face of the Lord and from the glory of his power, ¹⁰when he comes to be glorified in all his holy ones, and to be marveled at by all who believe in him, because our testimony to you was met with faith, on that day.

¹¹To that end we always pray for you, that our God may make you worthy of his call, and may complete every plan he

has to do you good, and every work of faith in power, [12]so that
the name of our Lord Jesus may be glorified in you, and you in
him, according to the grace of our God and of the Lord Jesus,
the Messiah.

2 Now concerning the royal presence of our Lord Jesus
the Messiah, and our gathering together around him,
this is our request, my dear family. [2]Please don't be suddenly blown off course in your thinking, or be unsettled, either
through spiritual influence, or through a word, or through a
letter supposedly from us, telling you that the day of the Lord
has already arrived.

[3]Don't let anyone deceive you in any way. You see, it can't
happen unless first the rebellion takes place, and the man of
lawlessness, the son of destruction, is revealed. [4]He is the one
who sets himself against every so-called god or cult object,
and usurps their role, so that he installs himself in God's temple, and makes himself out to be a god.

[5]Don't you remember that I told you this while I was with
you? [6]And now you know what is restraining him so that he
will be revealed at his proper time. [7]For the mystery of lawlessness is already at work, but the restrainer is in place—until
he is taken away; [8]and then the lawless one will be revealed.
The Lord Jesus will destroy him with the breath of his mouth,
and will wipe him out with the unveiling of his presence.

[9]The presence of the lawless one will be accompanied by
the activity of the satan, with full power, with signs, and spu-
rious wonders, [10]with every kind of wicked deceit over those
on the way to ruin, because they did not receive the love of the
truth so as to be saved. [11]For that reason God sends upon them
a strong delusion, leading them to believe the lie, [12]so that
judgment may come upon all who did not believe the truth but
took pleasure in wickedness.

[13]But we always owe God a debt of gratitude for you, my
family beloved by the Lord, because God chose you as the first
fruits of his work of salvation, through sanctification by the
spirit and belief of the truth. [14]To this he called you through
our gospel, so that you might obtain the glory of our Lord
Jesus the Messiah.

15So then, my dear family, stand firm, and hold on tight to the traditions which you were taught, whether through what we said or through our letter. 16And may our Lord Jesus the Messiah himself, and God our father who loved us and gave us eternal comfort and good hope by grace, 17comfort your hearts and strengthen you in every good work and word.

3 Finally, my dear family, pray for us, that the word of the Lord will go forward quickly and be glorified, as it has among you; 2and that we may be rescued from evil and wicked people. Not all, you see, have faith! 3But the Lord is faithful, and he will strengthen you and guard you from the evil one.

Requests for Prayer

4We are confident in the Lord about you, that you are doing, and will continue to do, what we instructed you. 5May the Lord direct your hearts toward the love of God and the patience of the Messiah.

6Here is a command we have for you, my dear family, in the name of our Lord Jesus the Messiah. Keep away from any member of the family who is stepping out of line, and not behaving according to the tradition that you received from us.

The Dangers of Idleness

7You yourselves know, after all, how you should copy us. We didn't step out of line, 8nor did we eat anyone's food without paying for it. We worked night and day, with labor and struggle, so as not to place a burden on any of you. 9It wasn't that we don't have the right; it was so that we could give you an example, for you to copy us. 10And, indeed, when we were with you, we gave you this command: those who won't work shouldn't eat!

11You see, we hear that there are some among you who are stepping out of line, behaving in an unruly fashion, not being busy with real work, but just busybodies. 12To people like that we give this commandment and exhortation in the Lord Jesus the Messiah: do your own work in peace, and eat your own bread. 13As for you, my dear family, don't get tired of doing what is right!

14If anyone doesn't obey our word in this letter, take note of them. Don't have any dealings with such a person, so that they may be ashamed. 15Don't consider a person like this an enemy:

Final Remarks

rebuke them as a member of the family. ¹⁶Now may the Lord of peace give you peace always in every way. The Lord be with you all.

¹⁷I, Paul, am sending you this greeting in my own hand. This is the sign in each letter of mine; this is how I write. ¹⁸The grace of our Lord Jesus the Messiah be with you all.

The First Letter of Paul to
Timothy

1 Paul, an apostle of King Jesus according to the command of God our savior and King Jesus our hope, 2to Timothy, my true child in faith: grace, mercy, and peace from God the father and King Jesus our Lord.

3This is my charge to you, just as it was when I went to Macedonia: stay in Ephesus, so that you can tell the relevant people not to teach anything different, 4or to cling to myths and endless genealogies. That sort of thing breeds disputes rather than the instruction in faith that comes from God. 5The goal of such instruction is love—the love that comes from a pure heart, a good conscience, and sincere faith. 6Some people have wandered off from these things and turned aside to foolish talk. 7They want to be teachers of the law; but they don't understand either what they're talking about or the things about which they pronounce so confidently.

8We know, after all, that the law is good—if someone uses it lawfully! 9We recognize that the law is laid down not for people who are in the right, but for the lawless and disobedient, for the godless and sinners, the unholy and worldly, for people who kill their father or mother, for murderers, 10fornicators, practicing homosexuals, slave traders, liars, perjurers, and those who practice any other behavior contrary to healthy teaching, 11in accordance with the gospel of the glory of God, the blessed one, that was entrusted to me.

12I thank King Jesus our Lord, who gave me strength. He regarded me as trustworthy by appointing me to his service—13even though I used to say blasphemous things against him,

True Teaching About the Truth

The Purpose of the Law

Paul as an Example of God's Saving Grace

and persecuted his people violently! But I received mercy, because in my unbelief I didn't know what I was doing. ¹⁴And the grace of our Lord was more than enough for me, with the faith and love that are in King Jesus. ¹⁵Here is a word you can trust, which deserves total approval: "King Jesus came into the world to save sinners"—and I'm the worst of them! ¹⁶But this was why I received mercy: so that in me, precisely as the worst, King Jesus could demonstrate the full scale of his patience, and make me a pattern for those who were going to believe in him and so attain the life of the age to come. ¹⁷To the king of the ages, the one and only God, immortal and invisible, be honor and glory to the ages of ages. Amen!

The Battle of Faith

¹⁸I am giving you this command, Timothy my child, in accordance with the prophecies which were made about you before, so that, as they said, you may fight the glorious battle, ¹⁹holding on to faith and a good conscience. Some have rejected conscience, and their faith has been shipwrecked. ²⁰I include Hymenaeus and Alexander in that category. Indeed, I have handed them over to the satan, so that they may be taught not to blaspheme.

The First Rule: Prayer for the World

2 So, then, this is my very first command: God's people should make petitions, prayers, intercessions, and thanksgivings on behalf of all people—²on behalf of kings, and all who hold high office, so that we may lead a tranquil and peaceful life, in all godliness and holiness. ³This is good; it is acceptable with God our savior, ⁴who wants all people to be saved and to come to know the truth. ⁵For, you see,

> There is one God,
> And also one mediator between God and humans,
> King Jesus, himself a human being.
> ⁶He gave himself as a ransom for all,
> And this was testified when the time was right.

⁷This is why I was appointed a herald and an apostle (I'm speaking the truth, I'm not lying!), a teacher of the Gentiles in faith and truth.

Women Must Be Allowed to Be Learners

⁸So this is what I want: the men should pray in every place, lifting up holy hands, with no anger or disputing. ⁹In the same way the women, too, should clothe themselves decently, being

modest and sensible about it. They should not go in for elaborate hairstyles, or gold, or pearls, or expensive clothes. ¹⁰Instead, as is appropriate for women who profess to be godly, they should adorn themselves with good works. ¹¹They must study undisturbed, in full submission to God. ¹²I'm not saying that women should teach men, or try to dictate to them; rather, that they should be left undisturbed. ¹³Adam was created first, you see, and then Eve; ¹⁴and Adam was not deceived, but the woman was deceived, and fell into trespass. ¹⁵She will, however, be kept safe through the process of childbirth, if she continues in faith, love, and holiness with prudence.

3 Here is a trustworthy saying: if someone is eager for the work of overseeing God's people, the task they seek is a fine one. ²The bishop must be beyond reproach. He must not have more than one wife. He must be temperate, sensible, respectable, hospitable, a good teacher. ³He must not be a heavy drinker, or violent, but must be gentle, not quarrelsome, and not in love with money. ⁴He must be good at managing his own household, with his children being subject to him with all godliness. ⁵(After all, if a man doesn't know how to run his own household, how can he take care of God's church?) ⁶He must not be a recent convert, in case he gets puffed up and falls into the devil's condemnation. ⁷In addition, he must have a good reputation with outsiders, so that he may not incur reproach and fall into the devil's snare.

The Character of a Bishop

⁸In the same way, deacons must be serious-minded, not the sort of people who say one thing today and another tomorrow, not heavy drinkers, not eager for shameful gain. ⁹They must hold on to the mystery of the faith with a pure conscience. ¹⁰They must first be tested; then, when they have been found without reproach, they may serve as deacons. ¹¹The womenfolk, too, should be serious-minded, not slanderers, but temperate and faithful in all things. ¹²Deacons should have only one wife, and should be well in charge of their children and their own households. ¹³Those who serve well as deacons, you see, gain a good platform for themselves to speak out boldly in the faith which is in King Jesus.

The Character of Deacons

¹⁴I'm writing this to you in the hope that I'll be able to come to you in the near future. ¹⁵But, if I'm delayed, this will help

The Mystery of Godliness

you to know how people should behave in God's household, which is the assembly of the living God, the pillar and firm foundation of the truth. ¹⁶Indeed, the mystery of godliness is certainly great:

> He was revealed in the flesh,
> And vindicated in the spirit;
> He appeared to angels,
> And was announced to Gentiles;
> He was believed in the world,
> And taken up in glory.

Beware of False Teaching!

4 Now the spirit specifically declares that in the last times some people will abandon the faith, and will cling to deceitful spirits and demonic teachings ²perpetrated by hypocritical false teachers whose consciences are branded with a hot iron. ³They will forbid marriage, and teach people to abstain from foods which God created to be received with thanksgiving by people who believe and know the truth. ⁴Every creation of God, you see, is good; nothing is to be rejected if it is received with thanksgiving, ⁵for then it is made holy by God's word and prayer.

Get into Training!

⁶Set these instructions before the family. If you do this, you will be a good servant of King Jesus; you will be nourished by the words of faith and the good teaching which you have been following. ⁷Keep well away from worthless myths, the sort of things some old women mumble on about.

Go into training in godliness! ⁸Physical exercise, you see, has a limited usefulness, but godliness is useful in every way. It carries the promise of life both now and in the future. ⁹That saying is trustworthy; it deserves to be accepted totally! ¹⁰This is what we are working and struggling for, you see, because we have set our hope on the living God, who is the savior of all people—especially of believers.

Pay Attention to Yourself and Your Teaching

¹¹You must urge and teach these things. ¹²Don't let anyone look down on you because you are young, but be an example to the believers in what you say, how you behave, in love, faith, and holiness. ¹³Until I come, give attention to reading, to exhortation, and to teaching. ¹⁴Don't neglect the gift that is in you, which was given to you through prophecy when the elders

laid hands on you. [15]Work hard at these things; give yourself to them, so that everyone may see your progress. [16]Pay attention to yourself and your teaching, and keep steadily on with them. If you do that, you see, you will save yourself, and those who hear you as well.

5 Don't rebuke a senior man in the church, but exhort him as you might do with your father—or, in the case of younger ones, with your brothers. [2]Treat the older women as mothers, and the younger ones as sisters, with all purity.

Human Families and God's Family

[3]Pay respect to widows who really are widows. [4]If a widow has children or grandchildren, let them first learn to respect their own family and to make some repayment to those who brought them up. This, you see, pleases God. [5]A real widow is one who, left by herself, has set her hope on God, and continues in prayer and supplication night and day; [6]but a self-indulgent woman is dead even while she's alive. [7]Give these commands so that they may be beyond blame. [8]If anyone doesn't take care of their own relatives, especially their own household, they have denied the faith; they are worse than unbelievers.

[9]Let a woman be registered as a widow if she is at least sixty years old, the wife of one husband, [10]with a reputation for good works, having brought up children, shown hospitality, washed the feet of God's people, helped those who were suffering, and been steadfast in doing good wherever she can. [11]Refuse to register younger widows. When their desires become strong against the King, you see, they will want to marry, [12]and they will receive condemnation because they have abandoned their earlier faith. [13]In addition, they learn the habit of idleness, going around from one house to another, not only doing nothing but gossiping and meddling, saying things they shouldn't.

Widows

[14]So this is my wish: the younger ones should marry, have children, run their households, and give the enemy no opportunity to slander us. [15](Some, you see, have already gone off after the satan!) [16]If any believing woman has relatives who are widowed, let her help them, so that the church won't be burdened. That way, it can help widows who really are widows.

[17]Elders who are good leaders ought to be paid double, particularly those who work hard in speaking and teaching. [18]The

Elders

Bible says, you see, "Don't muzzle an ox when it's threshing," and "the worker deserves his pay."

¹⁹Don't accept an accusation against an elder, unless it is supported "by two or three witnesses." ²⁰When people persist in sin, rebuke them openly, so that the rest may be afraid.

²¹Before God, King Jesus, and the chosen angels, I give you solemn warning to keep these commands without discrimination. Never act out of favoritism. ²²Don't be too quick to lay hands on anyone; don't share in other people's sins. Keep yourself pure.

²³You should stop confining yourself to drinking water. Use wine (in moderation!). That will be good for your digestion, and for the physical problems you often have.

²⁴Some people's sins are obvious, and walk ahead of them into the courtroom. Other people's follow them there. ²⁵In the same way, good works are obvious; but, even when they aren't, they can't stay hidden forever.

Slaves, Masters, and Sound Teaching

6 All who live as slaves, "under the yoke" so to speak, should consider their own masters as worthy of all respect, so that people may not say wicked things against the name of God and the teaching. ²Those who have masters who are also believers should not look down on them because they are brothers, but rather give them service, since those who receive the benefit of their work are beloved fellow believers.

Teach these things, and exhort people to do them. ³Some people teach other things and don't hold firmly to the healthy words of our Lord King Jesus, and the teaching which goes with piety; ⁴people like that are conceited and have no understanding. They have a diseased craving for disputes and arguments about words. That just leads to envy, jealousy, evil speaking, wicked suspicions, ⁵and irritating arguments among people with depraved minds who have lost their grip on the truth and imagine that godliness is a means of gain.

Godliness and Contentment

⁶If it's gain you want, though, there is plenty to be had in godliness—if it's combined with contentment. ⁷We brought nothing into the world, after all, and we certainly can't take anything out. ⁸If we have food and clothing, we should be satisfied with it. ⁹People who want to be rich, by contrast, fall into

temptation and a trap, and into many foolish and dangerous lusts which drown people in devastation and destruction. [10]The love of money, you see, is the root of all evil. Some people have been so eager to get rich that they have wandered away from the faith and have impaled themselves painfully in several ways.

[11]But you, man of God—you must run away from all this. Instead, chase after justice, godliness, faith, love, patience, and gentleness. [12]Fight the noble fight of the faith; get a firm grasp on the life of the coming age, the life you were called to when you made the noble public profession before many witnesses. [13]I give you this charge before God, who gives life to all things, and King Jesus, who made the noble profession before Pontius Pilate: [14]be undefiled and blameless as you keep the commandment, until the royal appearing of our Lord King Jesus, [15]which the blessed and only Sovereign One, the King of kings and Lord of lords, will reveal at its proper time. [16]He is the only one who possesses immortality; he lives in unapproachable light; no human being has seen him, or can see him. To him be eternal honor and power. Amen!

The King's Royal Appearing

[17]What about people who are rich in this present world? Tell them not to think of themselves too highly, and to set their hopes, not on something so uncertain as riches, but on the God who richly provides us with everything to enjoy. [18]They are to do good, to be rich in good works, generous and eager to share. [19]That way, they will treasure up for themselves a good foundation for the future, and thereby come to possess the life which really is life.

What to Do with Money

[20]Well then, Timothy: keep guard over what has been entrusted to you. Turn away from the pointless and empty talk and contradictions of what is wrongly called "knowledge." [21]Some have claimed to be experts in it, but have missed the target when it comes to the faith.

Grace be with you all.

The Second Letter of Paul to
Timothy

Rekindle
the Gift!

1 Paul, an apostle of King Jesus by God's will, according to the promise of life in King Jesus; ²to Timothy, my dear child. Grace, mercy, and peace from God the father and King Jesus our Lord.

³I serve God with a clear conscience, as my forebears did, and I am grateful to him that I remember you all the time, as I pray for you night and day. ⁴I remember how you cried when I left, and I'm longing to see you and be filled with joy. ⁵I have in my mind a clear picture of your sincere faith—the faith which first came to live in Lois your grandmother and Eunice your mother, and which, I am confident, lives in you as well.

⁶That's why I now want to remind you that God gave you a gift when I laid my hands on you, and that you must bring it back into a blazing fire! ⁷After all, the spirit given to us by God isn't a fearful spirit; it's a spirit of power, love, and prudence.

Don't Be
Ashamed!

⁸So don't be ashamed of the testimony of our Lord, nor of me as his prisoner. Rather, suffer for the gospel along with us, in accordance with God's power. ⁹God saved us, and called us with a holy calling, not according to our works, but according to his own purpose and grace. He gave us this grace in King Jesus before all time and ages, ¹⁰but has now made it visible through the appearing of our savior King Jesus, who abolished death and, through the gospel, shone a bright light on life and immortality.

¹¹I was made a herald, apostle, and teacher for this gospel; ¹²that's why I suffer these things. But I am not ashamed, because I know the one I have trusted, and I'm convinced that he

has the power to keep safe until that day what I have entrusted to him.

[13]Keep a firm hold on the pattern of healthy teaching which you heard from me, in the faith and love which are in King Jesus. [14]You have had something very important entrusted to you, too; make sure you look after it, through the holy spirit who dwells in us.

[15]You will know that everyone in Asia has turned away from me, including Phygelus and Hermogenes. [16]May the Lord give mercy to the household of Onesiphorus; he has often refreshed me. He wasn't ashamed of my chains, [17]but when he was in Rome he eagerly hunted for me and found me. [18]May the Lord grant him to find mercy from the Lord on that day. And you know very well all the things he did for me in Ephesus.

Foes and Friends

2 So then, my child: you must be strong in the grace which is in King Jesus. [2]You heard the teaching I gave in public; pass it on to faithful people who will be capable of instructing others as well. [3]Take your share of suffering as one of King Jesus's good soldiers. [4]No one who serves in the army gets embroiled in civilian activities, since they want to please the officer who enlisted them. [5]If you take part in athletic events, you don't win the crown unless you compete according to the rules. [6]The farmer who does the work deserves the first share of the crops. [7]Think about what I say; the Lord will give you understanding in everything.

Conditions of Service

[8]Remember Jesus the king, risen from the dead, from the seed of David, according to my gospel—[9]for which I suffer like a criminal, even being chained up! But God's word is not tied up. [10]That's why I put up with everything for the sake of God's chosen ones, so that they too may obtain, with glory that lasts forever, the salvation which is in King Jesus. [11]You can rely on this saying:

God's Word Is Not Tied Up

If we die with him, we shall live with him;
[12]*If we endure patiently, we shall reign with him;*
If we deny him, he will deny us;
[13]*If we are faithless, he remains faithful,*
For he cannot deny his own self.

**Foolish Words
and the Word
of Truth**

¹⁴Remind them about these things; and warn them, in God's presence, not to quarrel about words. This doesn't do any good; instead, it threatens to ruin people who listen to it. ¹⁵Do your very best to present yourself before God as one who has passed the test—a workman who has no need to be ashamed, who can carve out a straight path for the word of truth. ¹⁶Avoid pointless and empty chatter. It will push people further and further toward ungodliness, ¹⁷and their talk will spread like a cancer. I'm thinking in particular of Hymenaeus and Philetus; ¹⁸they have turned aside from the truth by saying that the resurrection has already happened. They are upsetting some people's faith. ¹⁹But God's firm foundation stands, and it has this as its seal: "The Lord knows those who belong to him," and "Everyone who uses the name of the Lord must leave wickedness behind."

**Vessels for
God's Use**

²⁰In a great house there are vessels not only of gold and silver, but also of wood and pottery. Some of them are given special honor in the way they're used; others are for menial purposes. ²¹So if people purify themselves from dishonorable things, they will become vessels for honor, made holy, pleasing to the master of the house, fit for every good work.

²²Run away from the passions of youth. Instead, chase after justice, faith, love, and peace; you'll be in the company of all who call on the Lord from a pure heart. ²³Avoid silly and unprofitable disputes, because you know that they produce fights; ²⁴and the Lord's servant mustn't be a fighter, but must be gentle to all people, able to teach, able to bear evil without resentment, ²⁵able to correct opponents with a meek spirit. It may be that God will give them repentance so that they can arrive at a knowledge of the truth ²⁶and, in coming to their senses, escape the devil's snare, after having been held captive by him and made to do his will.

**Opponents of
the Truth**

3 You need to know this: bad times are coming in the last days. ²People will be in love with themselves, you see, and with money too. They will be boastful, arrogant, abusive, haters of parents, ungrateful, unholy, ³unfeeling, implacable, accusing, dissolute, savage, haters of the good, ⁴traitors, reckless, puffed up, lovers of pleasure rather than lovers of God, ⁵holding on to a pattern of godliness but

denying its power. Avoid people like that! 6This group, you see, includes those who worm their way into people's houses and ensnare foolish women who are overwhelmed with their sins and are pulled and pushed by all kinds of desires, 7always learning but never able to arrive at the truth. 8Just as Jannes and Jambres stood up against Moses, so people like this oppose the truth. In their minds they are corrupt; in their faith they are of no account. 9They won't get very far, though, because their foolishness will become obvious to everyone, as it was with those two.

10So what about you? You have followed my teaching faithfully, and also my way of life, my aims and goals, my faith, longsuffering, love, and patience, 11my persecutions, my sufferings, the things I went through in Antioch, in Iconium, in Lystra, the persecutions I endured—and the Lord rescued me from all of them. 12Yes, everyone who wants to live a godly life in King Jesus will be persecuted, 13while evil people and impostors will go on to even worse things, deceiving others and being themselves deceived. 14But you, on the other hand, must stand firm in the things you learned and believed. You know who it was you received them from, 15and how from childhood you have known the holy writings which have the power to make you wise for salvation through faith in King Jesus. 16All scripture is breathed by God, and it is useful for teaching, for rebuke, for improvement, for training in righteousness, 17so that people who belong to God may be complete, fitted out and ready for every good work.

Continue in the Scriptures!

4 This is my solemn charge to you, in the presence of God and King Jesus, who will judge the living and the dead, and by his appearance and his kingdom: 2announce the word; keep going whether the time is right or wrong; rebuke, warn, and encourage with all patience and explanation. 3The time is coming, you see, when people won't tolerate healthy teaching. Their ears will start to itch, and they will collect for themselves teachers who will tell them what they want to hear. 4They will turn away from listening to the truth and will go after myths instead. 5But as for you, keep your balance in everything! Put up with suffering; do the work of an evangelist; complete the particular task assigned to you.

Judgment Is Coming— So Get On with Your Work

Waiting for the Crown

6For I am already being poured out as a drink-offering; my departure time has arrived. 7I have fought the good fight; I have completed the course; I have kept the faith. 8What do I still have to look for? The crown of righteousness! The Lord, the righteous judge, will give it to me as my reward on that day—and not only to me, but also to all who have loved his appearing.

Come to Me Soon

9Make every effort to come to me soon. 10Demas, you see, has left me and gone to Thessalonica; he's in love with this present world! Crescens has gone to Galatia, and Titus to Dalmatia. 11Luke is the only one with me. Get Mark and bring him with you; he's very helpful in looking after me. 12I sent Tychicus to Ephesus. 13I left a cloak at Carpus's house in Troas; please bring it with you when you come—and also the scrolls, and especially the books.

14Alexander the coppersmith did me a lot of damage. The Lord will pay him back according to what he's done! 15Watch out for him yourself. He stood out strongly against our message.

16The first time my case came to court nobody showed up to support me; they all left me alone. May it not be reckoned against them! 17But the Lord stood there beside me and gave me strength to enable me to complete my work as his royal herald, and to make sure all the Gentiles heard the proclamation; and I was snatched clear of the lion's mouth. 18The Lord will snatch me clear from every wicked deed and will save me for his heavenly kingdom. Glory to him for the ages of ages. Amen!

19Greet Prisca and Aquila, and the household of Onesiphorus.

20Erastus stayed in Corinth. I left Trophimus behind in Miletus, where he was sick.

21Do your best to come before winter.

Eubulus sends his greetings; so do Pudens, Linus, Claudia, and all the family.

22The Lord be with your spirit. Grace be with you all.

The Letter of Paul to
Titus

1 From Paul, a slave of God and an apostle of Jesus the king, in accordance with the faith of God's chosen people, and the knowledge of the truth that goes with godliness, ²in the hope of the life of the coming age. God, who never lies, promised this before the ages began, ³and has now, at the right time, unveiled his word through the proclamation entrusted to me, according to the command of our divine savior.

⁴To Titus, my true child, according to the faith which we share.

Grace and peace from God the father and King Jesus our savior.

⁵This is why I left you in Crete: you are to set straight all the remaining matters, and appoint elders for every town, as I charged you to do. ⁶Elders must be blameless, the husband of only one wife. Their children must be believers, and must not be open to the accusation of loose living or being rebellious. ⁷This is because an overseer, as one of God's household managers, must be blameless. He must not be stubborn, or hotheaded, or a heavy drinker, or a bully, or eager for shameful gain. ⁸He must be hospitable, a lover of goodness, sensible, just, holy, and self-controlled. ⁹He must hold firmly to the reliable word which goes with the teaching, so that he may have the power both to exhort people with healthy instruction and to give a proper rebuttal to those who oppose it.

¹⁰There are many, you see, who refuse to come into line—people who speak foolishness and deceive others. This is true in particular of the circumcision party. ¹¹It's important that

they should be silenced, because they are overturning whole households by teaching things that shouldn't be taught—and trying to make a shameful living out of it! 12One of their own, a native prophet, said, "Cretans are always liars, evil animals, idle guzzlers." 13This testimony is true! That's why you must rebuke them sternly, so that they may become healthy in the faith, 14paying no attention to Jewish myths and the commandments of people who reject the truth. 15Everything is pure to people who are pure. But if people are defiled or faithless, nothing is pure for them; even their mind and conscience are defiled. 16They declare that they know God, but they deny him by what they do. They are detestable and disobedient, and useless for any good work.

Commands to Households

2 So what must you do? Just this: you must instruct people how to conduct themselves in accordance with healthy teaching.

2The older men are to be sober, dignified, sensible, and healthy in faith, love, and patience. 3In the same way, older women are to be reverent in their behavior, not slanderers or enslaved to heavy drinking, able to teach what is good. 4That way, they can give sensible instructions to the younger women on how to love their husbands and their children, 5and how to be sensible, holy, good at looking after the household, and submissive to their own husbands, so that people won't have bad things to say about the word of God. 6You must urge the younger men, in the same way, to be sensible 7in all things.

Make sure you present yourself as a pattern of good works. Your teaching must be consistent and serious, 8in healthy speech that is beyond reproach. That way, our opponents will be ashamed, since they won't have anything bad to say about us.

9Slaves must be submissive in everything to their masters. They must do what is wanted and not answer back 10or help themselves to their masters' property. They are to show good faith in everything, so that in every way they may be a good advertisement for the teaching of God our savior.

Grace, Hope, and Holiness

11God's saving grace, you see, appeared for all people. 12It teaches us that we should turn our backs on ungodliness and the passions of the world, and should live sober, just, and devout lives in the present age, 13while we wait eagerly for the blessed hope and royal appearing of the glory of our great God and savior, Jesus the king. ¹⁴He gave himself for us so that he could ransom us from all lawless actions and purify for himself a people as his very own who would be eager for good works.

¹⁵This is what you must say. Exhort people and rebuke them. Use full authority. Don't let anyone look down on you.

3 Remind them to submit to rulers and authorities, to be obedient, to be ready for every good work. ²They are not to speak evil of anyone, nor to be quarrelsome, but to be kindly. They must be completely gentle with everyone.

God's Kindness and Generosity— and Ours

³We ourselves, you see, used at one time to be foolish, disobedient, deceived, and enslaved to various kinds of passions and pleasures. We spent our time in wickedness and jealousy. We were despicable in ourselves, and we hated each other. ⁴But when the kindness and generous love of God our savior appeared, ⁵he saved us, not by works that we did in righteousness, but in accordance with his own mercy, through the washing of the new birth and the renewal of the holy spirit, ⁶which was poured out richly upon us through Jesus, our king and savior, ⁷so that we might be justified by his grace and be made his heirs, in accordance with the hope of the life of the age to come. ⁸The saying is sure.

I want you to insist on these things, so that those who have put their faith in God may take care to be energetic in good works. Such things are good and profitable for people. ⁹But stay well clear of foolish disputes, genealogies, quarrels, and squabbles about the law; they serve no purpose and are worthless. ¹⁰If someone is causing divisions, give them a first warning, then a second, and then avoid them. ¹¹You know that a person like that is twisted, sinful, and self-condemned.

Watch Out for Disputes and Divisions

¹²When I send Artemas to you, or maybe Tychicus, do your best to come to me at Nicopolis. That's where I've decided to spend the winter. ¹³Give a really good send-off to Zenas the lawyer and Apollos; make sure they don't go short of anything. ¹⁴All our people must learn to busy themselves with good works, so that they may meet any urgent needs that arise, and not be unfruitful.

¹⁵All the people with me send you their greetings. Greet those who love us in faith. Grace be with you all.

The Letter of Paul to
Philemon

¹Paul, a prisoner of King Jesus, and Timothy our brother: to our beloved Philemon, our colleague and partner, ²to Apphia our sister, and to Archippus our comrade-in-arms, and to God's people who meet in their house. ³May grace and peace be upon you, from God our father and King Jesus the Lord.

⁴I always thank my God when your name comes up in my prayers, ⁵because I've heard of your love and faithful loyalty toward the Lord Jesus and to all God's people. ⁶My prayer is this: that the partnership which goes with your faith may have its powerful effect, in realizing every good thing that is at work in us to lead us into the king. ⁷You see, my dear brother, your love gives me so much joy and comfort! You have refreshed the hearts of God's people.

⁸Because of all this I could be very bold in the king, and order you to do the right thing. ⁹But, because of love, I'd much rather appeal to you—yes, it's me, Paul, speaking, an old man as I am and now a prisoner of King Jesus! ¹⁰I am appealing to you about my child, the one I have fathered here in prison: Onesimus, "Mr. Useful." ¹¹There was a time when he was use*less* to you; but now he's very useful, to you and to me.

¹²I'm sending him to you for your decision—yes, sending the man himself; and this means sending my own heart. ¹³I would have liked to keep him here with me, so that he could have been your representative in serving me in the chains of the gospel. ¹⁴But I didn't want to do anything without you knowing about it. That way, when you did the splendid thing that

the situation requires, it wouldn't be under compulsion, but of your own free will.

¹⁵Look at it like this. Maybe this is the reason he was separated from you for a while, so that you could have him back forever—¹⁶no longer as a slave, but much more than a slave, as a beloved brother, beloved especially to me, but how much more to you, both as part of your household and in the Lord. ¹⁷So, anyway, if you reckon me a partner in your work, receive him as though he was me. ¹⁸And if he's wronged you in any way, or owes you anything, put that down on my account. ¹⁹This is me, Paul, writing with my own hand: I'll pay you back (and far be it from me to remind you that you owe me your own very self!). ²⁰Yes, my brother, I want some benefit from you in the Lord! Refresh my heart in the king.

Paul's Perspective

²¹As I write this I'm confident that you'll do what I say. In fact, I know you'll do more than I say. ²²But, at the same time, get a guest room ready for me. I'm hoping, you see, that through your prayers I will be granted to you.

²³Epaphras, my fellow prisoner in King Jesus, sends you greetings. ²⁴So do Mark, Aristarchus, Demas, and Luke, my colleagues here.

²⁵The grace of the Lord, King Jesus, be with your spirit.

The Letter to the
Hebrews

God's One and Only Son

1 In many ways and by many means God spoke in ancient times to our ancestors in the prophets; 2but at the end of these days he spoke to us in a son.

> He appointed this son to be heir of all things;
> Through him, in addition, he created the worlds.
> 3He is the shining reflection of God's own glory,
> The precise expression of his own very being;
> He sustains all things through his powerful word.
> He accomplished the cleansing needed for sins,
> And sat down at the right of the Majesty Supreme.
> 4See how much greater he is than the angels:
> The name he was granted is finer than theirs.

5For to which angel did God ever say, "You are my son; today I became your father"? Or, again, "I will be his father, and he will be my son"?

The Messiah Is Superior to Angels

6Again, when God brings the firstborn son into the world, he says,

> Let all God's angels worship him.

7In relation to the angels, this is what it says:

> God makes his angels spirits, and his servants flames
> of fire.

8In relation to the son, however, it says,

> Your throne, O God, is forever and ever;
> The scepter of uprightness is the scepter of your kingdom.

9*You loved justice and hated lawlessness;*
Therefore God, your God, anointed you with the oil
    of gladness,
As superior to your comrades.

10And again:

You established the earth, O Lord, from the beginning;
And the heavens are the works of your hands;
11*They will be destroyed, but you will remain;*
All of them will grow old like clothing;
12*You will roll them up like a cloak,*
And they will be changed like clothing.
But you are the same, and your years will never give out.

13But to which of the angels did God ever say,

Sit at my right hand,
Until I make your enemies a stool for your feet?

14Must we not say, then, that the angels are all servant spirits, sent to act on behalf of those who are to inherit salvation?

2 So, then, we must pay all the closer attention to what we heard, in case we drift away from it. 2You see, if the word which was spoken through angels was reliable, with appropriate and just punishment every time anyone broke it or disobeyed it, 3how shall we escape if we ignore a rescue as great as this? It started by being declared through the Lord, and it was confirmed to us by those who heard him; 4and God bore witness as well, along with them, in signs and wonders and many different types of powerful deeds, and by the holy spirit, distributed in accordance with his will.

Don't Neglect God's Salvation!

5You see, God didn't place the world to come (which is what I'm writing about) under the control of angels. 6Someone has spoken of it somewhere in these terms:

Jesus as the Truly Human Being

What are humans, that you should remember them?
What is the son of man, that you should take thought
    for him?
7*You made him a little lower than the angels,*
You crowned him with glory and honor,
8*And you placed everything under his feet.*

When it speaks of everything being subjected to him, it leaves nothing that is not subjected to him. As things are at present, we don't see everything subjected to him. ⁹What we do see is the one who was, for a little while, made lower than the angels—that is, Jesus—crowned with glory and honor because of the suffering of death, so that by God's grace he might taste death on behalf of everyone.

The Messiah and His Brothers and Sisters

¹⁰This is how it works out. Everything exists for the sake of God and because of him; and it was appropriate that, in bringing many children to glory, he should make perfect, through suffering, the one who leads the way to salvation. ¹¹For the one who makes others holy, and the ones who are made holy, all belong to a single family.

This is why he isn't ashamed to call them his brothers and sisters, ¹²when he says,

> *I will announce your name to my brothers and sisters;*
> *I will sing your praise in the middle of the assembly,*

¹³and again,

> *I will place my trust in him,*

and again,

> *Look, here I am, with the children God has given me.*

¹⁴Since the children share in blood and flesh, he too shared in them, in just the same way, so that through death he might destroy the one who has the power of death—that is, the devil—¹⁵and set free the people who all their lives long were under the power of slavery because of the fear of death. ¹⁶It's obvious, you see, that he isn't taking special thought for angels; he's taking special thought for Abraham's family. ¹⁷That's why he had to be like his brothers and sisters in every way, so that he might become a merciful and trustworthy high priest in God's presence, to make atonement for the sins of the people. ¹⁸He himself has suffered, you see, through being put to the test, and that's why he is able to help those who are being tested right now.

3 Well then, my brothers and sisters: you are God's holy ones, and you share the call from heaven. So think carefully about Jesus, the apostle and high priest of our confession of faith. ²He was faithful to the one who appointed him, just as Moses was faithful in all God's house. ³He deserves much more glory than Moses, you see, just as the one who builds a house deserves more glory than the house. ⁴For every house is built by someone, but the one who builds all things is God. ⁵And "Moses was faithful, as a servant, in all his house," thereby bearing witness to the things that were yet to be spoken of; ⁶but the Messiah is over God's house as a son. What is that house? It's us—those of us who hold on tightly to the free delight and confidence of our hope.

⁷So listen to what the holy spirit says:

Today's the Time to Listen!

Today, if you hear his voice,
⁸*Don't harden your hearts, as in the great bitterness,*
Like the day in the desert when they faced the test,
⁹*When your fathers put me to the test, and challenged me,*
And saw my works ¹⁰*for forty years.*
And so I was angry with that generation,
And said, "They are always straying in their hearts;
They do not know my ways." ¹¹*As I swore*
In my anger, "They'll never enter my rest."

¹²Take care, my dear family, that none of you should possess an evil and unbelieving heart, leading you to withdraw from the living God. ¹³But encourage one another every day, as long as it's called "Today," so that none of you may become hardened by the deceitfulness of sin.

Hold on Tight!

¹⁴We share the life of the Messiah, you see, only if we keep a firm, tight grip on our original confidence, right through to the end. ¹⁵That's what it means when it says, "Today, if you hear his voice, don't make your hearts hard, as in the great bitterness."

¹⁶Who was it, after all, who heard and then became bitter? It was all those who went out of Egypt under Moses, wasn't it? ¹⁷And who was it that God was angry with for forty years? It was those who sinned, wasn't it—those whose bodies fell in the desert? ¹⁸And to whom did God swear that they would

never enter his rest? Wasn't it the people who didn't believe? [19]So we can see that it was their unbelief that prevented them from entering.

Getting Through
to the Sabbath
Rest

4 So we are bound to worry that some of you might seem to have missed out on God's promise of entering his rest, the promise which is still open before us. [2]For we certainly had the good news announced to us, just as they did; but the word which they heard didn't do them any good, because they were not united in faith with those who heard it. [3]For it is we who believe who enter into the rest; as it has been said,

> As I swore in my anger,
> They will never enter my rest

—even though God's works had been complete since the foundation of the world. [4]For it says this somewhere about the seventh day,

> And God rested on the seventh day from all his works,

[5]and again, in the present passage,

> They will never enter my rest.

[6]Therefore, since some failed to enter into it, and those who received the good news earlier on didn't enter because of unbelief, [7]he once again appoints a day, "Today," saying through David—after such a long interval of time!—in the words already quoted,

> Today, if you hear his voice,
> Don't harden your hearts.

[8]If Joshua had given them rest, you see, he wouldn't be speaking about another subsequent "rest." [9]Thus we conclude: there is still a future sabbath "rest" for God's people. [10]Anyone who enters that "rest" will take a rest from their works, as God did from his.

Danger! God's
Word at Work

[11]So, then, let's make every effort to enter that "rest," so that nobody should trip and fall through the same pattern of unbelief. [12]God's word is alive, you see! It's powerful, and it's sharper than any double-edged sword. It can pierce right

in between soul and spirit, or joints and marrow; it can go straight to the point of what the human heart is thinking or intends to do. ¹³No creature remains hidden before God. All are naked, laid bare before the eyes of the one to whom we must present an account.

¹⁴Well, then, since we have a great high priest who has gone right through the heavens, Jesus, God's son, let us hold on firmly to our confession of faith. ¹⁵For we don't have a high priest who is unable to sympathize with our weaknesses, but one who has been tempted in every way just as we are, yet without sin. ¹⁶Let us then come boldly to the throne of grace, so that we may receive mercy, and may find grace to help us at the moment when we need it.

The Sympathetic High Priest

5 Every high priest, you see, is chosen from among human beings, and is placed before God on their behalf, so that he can offer gifts and sacrifices for sins. ²He is able to sympathize with people who don't know very much, or who wander off in different directions, since he too has his own share of weakness. ³That's why he has to offer sacrifices in relation to his own sins as well as those of the people.

⁴Nobody takes the office of priesthood on himself; you have to be called by God, just as Aaron was. ⁵In the same way, the Messiah didn't exalt himself so that he might become a high priest. It came about through the one who said to him,

The Son Becomes the Priest

You are my son; today I have become your father.

⁶As he says in another passage,

You are a priest forever, according to the order of Melchizedek.

⁷During the time of Jesus's earthly life, he offered up prayers and supplications, with loud shouts and tears, to the one who was able to save him from death. He was heard because of his devotion. ⁸Although he was a son, he learned obedience through what he suffered. ⁹When he had been made complete and perfect, he became the source of eternal salvation for all who obey him, ¹⁰since he has been designated by God as a high priest according to the order of Melchizedek.

Are You Ready for Solid Food?

¹¹We have plenty to say about all this; but it may be hard to make it clear, because your capacity to take things in has become sluggish. ¹²Yes: by now you really should have become teachers, but you need someone to teach *you* the basic elementary beginnings of God's oracles. You need milk, not solid food! ¹³Everyone who drinks milk, you see, is unskilled in the word of God's justice; such people are just babies. ¹⁴Mature people need solid food—and by "mature" I mean people whose faculties have been trained, by practice, to distinguish good from evil.

No Way Back

6 So let's leave the basic level of teaching about the Messiah, and go on toward maturity! (Let's not repeat the performance of laying a foundation of repentance from dead works and faith toward God, ²teaching about baptisms, laying on of hands, the resurrection of the dead, and eternal judgment.) ³We shall do this, if God allows us to.

⁴For once people have been enlightened—when they've tasted the heavenly gift and have had a share in the holy spirit, ⁵and have tasted the good word of God and the powers of the coming age—⁶it's impossible to restore them again to repentance if they fall away, since they are crucifying God's son all over again, on their own account, and holding him up to contempt. ⁷You see, when rain falls frequently on the earth, and the land drinks it up and produces a crop useful to the people for whom it's being cultivated, it shares in God's blessing. ⁸But if it produces thorns and thistles, it's useless, and not far off from being cursed. What happens in the end is that it will be burned up.

Keep Up the Good Work

⁹Even though we speak in this way, my dear people, we are confident that there are better things to be said about you, things that point to salvation. ¹⁰God is not unjust, after all—and he'd have to be if he forgot your work, and the love you showed for his name, and all the service you have rendered and are still rendering to his holy people. ¹¹I want to encourage each one of you to show the same energetic enthusiasm for the task of bringing your hope to its full, assured goal. ¹²You mustn't become lazy. There are people who are inheriting the promises through faith and patience, and you should copy them!

13When God was making his promise to Abraham, you see, he had nobody else greater than himself by whom he could swear, and so he swore by himself, 14with the words, "I will most surely bless you, and multiply you very greatly." 15And so in this way Abraham, after much patience, obtained the promise. 16People regularly swear by someone greater than themselves, and in all their disputes the oath confirms the matter and brings it to closure. 17So when God wanted to show all the more clearly to the heirs of the promise just how unchangeable his will was, he guaranteed it with an oath, 18so that through two unchangeable things, in which it is impossible that God should tell a lie, those of us who have come for refuge should have solid encouragement to take hold of the hope which lies before us. 19We have this hope like an anchor, secure, solid, and penetrating into the inner place behind the curtain, 20where Jesus has gone in ahead of us and on our behalf, having become a high priest forever according to the order of Melchizedek.

God's Unchangeable Promise

7 For this Melchizedek, "king of Salem, priest of the Most High God, met Abraham as he was coming back after defeating the kings, and blessed him; 2and Abraham portioned out to him a tenth of everything."

Melchizedek, the Great Priest-King

To begin with, if you translate Melchizedek's name, it means "king of righteousness"; then he is also "king of Salem," which means "king of peace." 3No mention is made of his father or mother or genealogy, nor of the beginning or end of his earthly life. He is described in a similar way to the son of God; and he continues as a priest forever.

4Look and see what an exalted status he has. Abraham the patriarch gave him a tenth of the spoils! 5Those of Levi's sons who receive the priesthood have a command to take tithes from the people according to the law—from, that is, their own brothers and sisters, although they, too, are physical descendants of Abraham. 6But this man, who doesn't share their genealogy at all, received tithes from Abraham, and blessed the man who possessed the promises. 7It is beyond all question that the lesser is blessed by the greater. 8In the former case, mortal humans receive tithes; in the latter case, the one who received them was one of whom scripture declares that he is alive. 9And, if I can put it like this, even Levi paid tithes through Abraham—Levi, the one who receives tithes! 10He was still in his ancestor's loins, you see, when Melchizedek met him.

A New Order of Priesthood

11So, you see, if it had been possible to arrive at complete perfection through the Levitical priesthood (for the people received the law by that means), what further need would there have been to speak of another priesthood being established "according to the order of Melchizedek," rather than "according to the order of Aaron"? 12Change the priesthood, after all, and you're bound to change the law—13especially when you consider that the one of whom these things are spoken comes from another tribe altogether, one from which nobody is recruited to serve at the altar. 14It's obvious, isn't it, that our Lord was descended from Judah, and Moses never made any connection between that tribe and the priesthood.

15This is even clearer when another priest arises "according to the order of Melchizedek," 16who attains this rank not because of a law concerning physical descent but through the power of a life that cannot be destroyed. 17What scripture says about him, after all, is, "You are a priest forever, according to the order of Melchizedek." 18What is happening here is that the previous commandment is being set aside. It was, after all, weak and useless; 19the law brought nothing to perfection, did it? Instead, what appears is a better hope, through which we draw near to God.

The Permanent Priesthood of Jesus

20This is all the more so when you consider that an oath was sworn. The Levitical priests, you see, become priests without an oath, 21but the Messiah attains his priesthood with an oath, through what was said to him:

The Lord has sworn and will not repent;
You are a priest forever.

22Jesus has thus, additionally, become the guarantee of a better covenant.

23There needed to be a large number of Levitical priests, since they stop holding office at death. 24But since he continues as a priest forever, his priesthood is permanent. 25That's why he is able to save those who come to God through him, completely and forever—since he always lives to make intercession for them.

26It was appropriate that we should have a high priest like this. He is holy, without blame or stain, separated from sinners, and elevated high above the heavens. 27He doesn't need (like the ordinary high priests do) to offer sacrifices every day, first for his own sins and then for those of the people. He did this once for all, you see, when he offered himself. 28For the law appoints ordinary, weak, mortal men as high priests; but the word of the oath, which comes after the law, appoints the son, who has been made perfect forever.

8 The point of all this now appears. We have just such a high priest, who sat down at the right hand of the throne of the heavenly Majesty, 2as a minister of the holy things and of the true Tabernacle, the one set up by God rather than by humans.

Better Ministry, Better Covenant

3Every high priest, you see, is appointed in order to offer gifts and sacrifices, which is why this one, too, must have something to offer. 4If he were on earth, he wouldn't even be a priest, since there already are priests who make offerings in accordance with the law. 5They serve a copy and shadow of the heavenly realities, in line with what Moses was told, when he was getting ready to construct the Tabernacle: "Take care that you make everything according to the pattern that was shown you on the mountain." 6Now, you see, Jesus has obtained a vastly superior ministry. In the same way, he is the mediator of a better covenant, which is established on better promises.

7If the first covenant had been faultless, you see, there wouldn't have been any reason to look for a second one. 8God finds fault with them when he says:

The Promise of a New Covenant

> See, says the Lord, the days are coming,
> When I will complete, with the house of Israel,
> With Judah's house also, a covenant that's new:
> 9Not like the one which I made with their ancestors
> On the day when I reached out and took them by the hand
> To lead them away from the land of Egypt.
> They didn't remain, after all, in my covenant,
> And (says the Lord) I ceased to care for them.

¹⁰*This is the covenant I will establish,*
After those days with the house of Israel:
My laws will I place in their minds, says the Lord,
And write on their hearts; thus I shall be God ·
For all of them; they'll be my people indeed.
¹¹*No more will they need to teach their own neighbors,*
Or their brothers and sisters, to know me, the Lord,
For from least unto greatest, each one shall know me,
¹²*For I shall be merciful to their injustices,*
And as for their sins, I'll forget them forever.

¹³Thus, when it speaks of a new covenant, it puts the first one out of date. And something that is out of date, and growing old, is about to disappear.

The Old Tabernacle Points Forward to the New

9 The first Tabernacle had, of course, its own regulations for worship, and it contained the earthly sanctuary. ²A double tent was constructed. In the outer one was the lampstand, the table, and the "bread of the presence." This is called "the holy place." ³After the second curtain came the inner tent, called "the holy of holies." ⁴This contained the golden altar, and the ark of the covenant, which was covered completely in gold. In the ark were the golden urn containing the manna, Aaron's rod that budded, and the tablets of the covenant. ⁵Above it were the cherubim of glory, which overshadowed the mercy seat. There is much we could say about all this, but now is not the time.

⁶With all these things in place, the priests continually go into the first Tabernacle in the ordinary course of their duties. ⁷But only the high priest goes into the second Tabernacle, once every year, and he always takes blood, which he offers for himself and for the unintentional sins of the people. ⁸The holy spirit indicates by this that, as long as the original Tabernacle is still standing, the way is not yet open into the sanctuary.

⁹This is a picture, so to speak, of the present age. During this period, gifts and sacrifices are offered which have no power to perfect the conscience of those who come to worship. ¹⁰They only deal with foods and drinks and various kinds of washings. These are regulations for the ordering of bodily life

until the appointed time, the moment when everything will be put into proper order.

[11]But when the Messiah arrived as high priest of the good things that were coming, he entered through the greater and much superior Tabernacle, not made with hands (that is, not of the present creation), [12]and not with the blood of goats and calves, but with his own blood. He entered, once and for all, into the holy place, accomplishing a redemption that lasts forever.

The Sacrifice of the Messiah

[13]If the blood of bulls and goats, you see, and the sprinkled ashes of a heifer, make people holy (in the sense of purifying their bodies) when they had been unclean, [14]how much more will the blood of the Messiah, who offered himself to God through the eternal spirit as a spotless sacrifice, cleanse our conscience from dead works to serve the living God!

[15]For this reason, Jesus is the mediator of the new covenant. The purpose was that those who are called should receive the promised inheritance of the age to come, since a death has occurred which provides redemption from transgressions committed under the first covenant.

The Purpose of the Blood

[16]Where there is a covenant, you see, it is vital to establish the death of the one who made it. [17]A will laid down in covenant only takes effect after death; it has no validity during the lifetime of the one who made it. [18]That's why even the first covenant was not inaugurated without blood. [19]For when every commandment had been read out to the people by Moses, he took the blood of calves and goats, with water and scarlet wool and hyssop, and sprinkled the book itself and all the people, [20]saying, "This is the blood of the covenant which God has made with you." [21]Then, in the same way, he sprinkled the Tabernacle, and all the vessels used in worship, with blood. [22]In fact, more or less everything is purified with blood according to the law; there's no pardon without bloodshed!

[23]That's why it was necessary for the copies of the heavenly objects to be purified in this way, while the heavenly things themselves require better sacrifices than these. [24]For the Messiah did not enter into a sanctuary made by human hands, the copy and pattern of the heavenly one, but into the

The Messiah's Work in the Heavenly Sanctuary

heavenly one itself, where he now appears in God's presence on our behalf.

²⁵Nor did he intend to offer himself over and over again, in the same way that the high priest goes into the sanctuary year after year with blood that isn't his own. ²⁶Had that been the case, he would have had to suffer repeatedly since the foundation of the world. Instead, he has appeared once, at the close of the ages, to put away sin by the sacrifice of his own self.

²⁷Furthermore, just as it is laid down that humans have to die once, and after that comes judgment, ²⁸so the Messiah, having been offered once and for all to take away the sins of many, will appear a second time. This will no longer have anything to do with sin. It will be in order to save those who are eagerly awaiting him.

The Stopping of the Sacrifices

10 The law, you see, possesses a shadow of the good things that are coming, not the actual form of the things themselves. Thus it is unable to make worshippers perfect through the annual round of the same sacrifices which are continually being offered. ²If the worshippers really had been purified once and for all, they would no longer have sin on their consciences—so they would have stopped offering sacrifices, wouldn't they? ³But, as it is, the sacrifices serve as a regular annual reminder of sins, ⁴since it's impossible for the blood of bulls and goats to take sins away.

⁵That's why, when the Messiah comes into the world, this is what he says:

> You didn't want sacrifices and offerings;
> Instead, you've given me a body.
> ⁶You didn't like burnt offerings and sin-offerings;
> ⁷Then I said, "Look! Here I am!
> This is what it says about me in the scroll, the book:
> I've come, O God, to do your will."

⁸When he says, earlier, "You didn't want, and you didn't like, sacrifices, offerings, burnt offerings, and sin-offerings" (all of which are offered in accordance with the law), ⁹then he says, "Look! I've come to do your will!" He takes away the first so that he can establish the second. ¹⁰And it's by that "will"

that we have been sanctified through the offering of the body of Jesus the Messiah, once for all.

¹¹Thus it comes about that every priest stands daily at his duty, offering over and over the same sacrifices, which can never take away sins. ¹²But Jesus offered a single sacrifice on behalf of sins, for all time, and then "sat down at the right hand of God." ¹³From that moment on he is waiting "until his enemies are made a stool for his feet." ¹⁴By a single sacrifice, you see, he has made perfect forever those who are sanctified.

The Finished Achievement of the Messiah

¹⁵The holy spirit bears witness to this too. For, after it is said,

> ¹⁶*This is the covenant I will establish with them*
> *After those days, says the Lord;*
> *I will give them my laws in their hearts, and*
>   *will write them*
> *Upon their minds,*

then he adds:

> ¹⁷*And I shan't ever remember*
> *Their sins and all their lawlessness.*

¹⁸Where these are put away, there is no longer a sacrifice for sin.

¹⁹So then, my brothers and sisters, we have boldness to go into the sanctuary through the blood of Jesus. ²⁰He has inaugurated a brand-new, living path through the curtain (that is, his earthly body). ²¹We have a high priest who is over God's house. ²²Let us therefore come to worship, with a true heart, in complete assurance of faith, with our hearts sprinkled clean from an evil conscience and our bodies washed with pure water.

So—Come to Worship!

²³Let us hold on tightly to our confession of hope, without being diverted; the one who announced the message to us is trustworthy! ²⁴Let us, as well, stir up one another's minds to energetic effort in love and good works. ²⁵We mustn't do what some people have gotten into the habit of doing: neglecting to meet together. Instead, we must encourage one another, and all the more as you can see the great day coming closer.

**Warning of
Judgment**

26For if we sin deliberately and knowingly after having received the knowledge of the truth, there is no further sacrifice for sin. 27Instead, there is a fearful prospect of judgment, and a hungry fire which will consume the opponents. 28If someone sets aside the law of Moses, they are to be "put to death on the testimony of two or three witnesses," with no pity. 29How much worse punishment, do you think, will be appropriate for people who trample the son of God underfoot, and profane the blood of the covenant by which they were sanctified, and scorn the spirit of grace? 30We know the one who said, "Vengeance belongs to me; I will pay everyone back," and again, "The Lord will judge his people." 31It's a terrifying thing to fall into the hands of the living God.

**Suffering
in Hope**

32But remember the earlier times! When you were first enlightened, you went through great struggles and suffering. 33Sometimes you were exposed to public reproach and physical abuse. Sometimes you stood alongside people who were being treated in that way. 34You even shared the sufferings of those who were imprisoned. When people looted your property, you actually welcomed it joyfully, because you knew that you had a better possession, a lasting one.

35So don't throw away your confidence. It carries a great reward. 36What you need is patience, you see; then, when you've done what God wants, you will receive the promise.

> 37*For in just a little while from now*
> *The Coming One will come, and won't delay;*
> 38*But my righteous one will live by faith;*
> *And if he hesitates, my soul will not delight in him.*

39We are not among the hesitators, who are destroyed! We are people of faith, and our lives will be kept safe.

**What Faith
Really Means**

11 What then is faith? It is what gives assurance to our hopes; it is what gives us conviction about things we can't see. 2It is what the men and women of old were famous for. 3It is by faith that we understand that the worlds were formed by God's word; in other words, that the visible world was not made from things that can be seen.

4It was by faith that Abel offered a better sacrifice to God than Cain. That earned him the testimony that he was in the right, since God himself bore witness in relation to his gifts. Through faith, he still speaks, even though he's dead. 5It was by faith that Enoch was taken up so that he wouldn't see death; nobody could find him, because God took him up. Before he was taken up, you see, it had been said of him that "he had pleased God." 6And without faith it's impossible to please God; for those who come to worship God must believe that he really does exist, and that he rewards those who seek him.

7It was by faith that Noah, who had been warned by God about things that were not yet seen, took the warning seriously and built an ark to save his household. He thus put the rest of the world in the wrong, and became heir to the righteous standing which accords with faith.

Faith and the Future: Noah, Abraham, Sarah

8It was by faith that Abraham, when God called him, obeyed and went out to a place where he was to receive an inheritance. Off he went, not knowing where he was going. 9It was by faith that he stayed in the promised land as a stranger, living in tents with Isaac and Jacob, who were joint heirs of the same promise. 10He was looking ahead, you see, to the city which has foundations, the city of which God is the designer and builder.

11It was by faith that Sarah herself, who was barren, received the ability to conceive a child even when long past the right age, since she considered that God, who had promised, was trustworthy. 12Thus it came about that from one man, and him more or less dead, there was born a family as many as the stars of heaven in number, as uncountable as the sand on the seashore.

13All these people died in faith. They hadn't received the promise, but they had seen it from far off, and had greeted it, and had recognized that they were strangers and wanderers in the land. 14People who say that sort of thing, you see, make it clear that they are looking for a homeland. 15Had they been thinking of the place from which they had set out, they would have had plenty of opportunity to go back to it. 16But as it was they were longing for a better place, a heavenly one. That's why God is not ashamed to be called "their God," since he has prepared a city for them.

Faith That Looks Beyond Death

17It was by faith that Abraham, when he was put to the test, offered up Isaac; yes, Abraham, who had received the promise, was in the very act of offering up his only son, 18the one about whom it had been said, "in Isaac shall your family be named." 19He reckoned that God was capable of raising him even from the dead; and, in one sense, he did indeed receive him back from there.

20It was by faith in the things that were to come that Isaac blessed Jacob and Esau. 21It was by faith that, when Jacob was dying, he blessed the two sons of Joseph, and "worshipped, leaning on the top of his staff." 22It was by faith that, when Joseph was coming to the end, he spoke about the Exodus of the children of Israel and gave instructions concerning his own bones.

Faith and the Future: Moses and the Exodus

23It was by faith that, when Moses was born, he was hidden for three months by his parents. They saw that the child was beautiful, and they weren't afraid of the king's orders. 24It was by faith that Moses, when he grew up, refused to be called the son of Pharaoh's daughter, 25preferring to suffer hardship along with God's people than to enjoy the short-term pleasures of sin. 26He reckoned that reproach suffered for the Messiah was worth more than all the treasures of Egypt; he was looking ahead to the reward.

27It was by faith that he left Egypt, without fear of Pharaoh's anger; he kept the invisible one constantly before his eyes. 28It was by faith that he kept the Passover and the sprinkling of blood, so that the Destroyer of the firstborn wouldn't touch them. 29It was by faith that they crossed the Red Sea as though they were on dry ground, while the Egyptians, when they tried to do the same, were drowned. 30It was by faith that the walls of Jericho fell down after they had been encircled for seven days. 31It was by faith that the prostitute Rahab was not destroyed along with those who didn't believe; she had welcomed the spies in peace.

Faith and the Future: The Great Crowd

32What more can I say, then? I've run out of time to tell you about Gideon, Barak, Samson, Jephthah, David, Samuel, and the prophets. 33It was through faith that they overcame kingdoms, put justice into practice, received promises, shut the mouths of lions, 34quenched the power of fire, escaped the edge of the sword, were strong where they had been weak, became powerful in battle, and sent foreign armies packing. 35Women received their dead by resurrection; others were tortured, not accepting release, so that they might receive a better resurrection. 36Others again experienced painful derision and flogging, and even chains and imprisonment; 37they were stoned, they were sawn in two, they were put to the sword, they went about in sheepskins or goat-hides, they were destitute, they were persecuted, they were ill-treated—38the world didn't deserve them!—and they wandered in deserts and mountains, in caves and holes in the ground.

39All these people gained a reputation for their faith; but they didn't receive the promise. 40God was providing something better for us, so that they wouldn't reach perfection without our doing so as well.

12 What about us, then? We have such a great cloud of witnesses all around us! What we must do is this: we must put aside each heavy weight, and the sin which gets in the way so easily. We must run the race that lies in front of us, and we must run it patiently. 2We must look ahead, to Jesus. He is the one who carved out the path for faith, and he's the one who brought it to completion. **Looking to Jesus**

He knew that there was joy spread out and waiting for him. That's why he endured the cross, making light of its shame, and has now taken his seat at the right hand of God's throne. 3He put up with enormous opposition from sinners. Weigh up in your minds just how severe it was; then you won't find yourselves getting weary and worn out.

4You have been struggling against sin, but your resistance hasn't yet cost you any blood. 5And perhaps you have forgotten the word of exhortation which speaks to you as God's children: **Christian Suffering Is God's Discipline**

> *My child, don't make light of the Lord's rebuke,*
> *Or grow weary when he takes issue with you;*
> *6For the Lord disciplines those whom he loves,*
> *And chastises every child he welcomes.*

7You must be patient with discipline. God is dealing with you as his sons and daughters. What child is there that the parent doesn't discipline? 8If you are left without discipline (we've all had our fair share of it!), you are illegitimate, and not true children. 9After all, we had earthly parents who disciplined us, and we respected them; shouldn't we much rather submit ourselves to the father of spirits, and live? 10Our earthly parents disciplined us for a little while, as they judged best; but when he disciplines us it's for our advantage. It is so that we may share his holiness. 11No discipline seems to bring joy at the time, but only sorrow. Later, though, it produces fruit, the peaceful fruit of righteousness, for those who are trained by it.

Watch Out for Dangers!

12So stop letting your hands go slack, and get some energy into your sagging knees! 13Make straight paths for your feet. If you're lame, make sure you get healed instead of being put out of joint. 14Follow after peace with everyone, and the holiness which is necessary before you can see the Lord. 15Take good care that nobody lacks God's grace; don't let any "root of bitterness spring up to cause trouble," defiling many people. 16No one must be immoral or worldly-minded, like Esau: he sold his birthright for a single meal! 17You know—don't you?—that later on, when he wanted to inherit the blessing, he was rejected. There was no way he could change either his mind or Isaac's, even though he wept bitterly in trying to do so.

From Mount Sinai to Mount Zion

18You haven't come, after all, to something that can be touched—a blazing fire, darkness, gloom and whirlwind, 19the sound of a trumpet and a voice speaking words which the hearers begged not to have to listen to anymore. 20(They couldn't bear the command that "if even a beast touches the mountain, it must be stoned.") 21The sight was so terrifying that even Moses said, "I'm trembling with fear."

22No: you have come to Mount Zion—to the city of the living God, the heavenly Jerusalem. You have come to where thousands and thousands of angels are gathered for a festival; 23to the assembly of the firstborn, whose names are written in heaven. You have come to God the judge of all, to the spirits of righteous people who have been made perfect, 24and to Jesus the mediator of the new covenant, and to the sprinkled blood which has better words to say than the blood of Abel.

The Kingdom That Cannot Be Shaken

25Take care that you don't refuse the one who is speaking. For if people didn't escape when they rejected the one who gave them earthly warnings, how much more if we turn away from the one who speaks from heaven! 26At that point, his voice shook the earth; but now he has issued a promise in the following words: "One more time I will shake not only the earth but heaven as well." 27The phrase "one more time" shows that the things that are to be shaken (that is, the created things) will be taken away, so that the things that cannot be shaken will remain.

28Well, then: we are to receive a kingdom which cannot be shaken! This calls for gratitude! That's how to offer God true and acceptable worship, reverently and with fear. 29Our God, you see, is a devouring fire.

13 Let the family continue to care for one another. 2Don't forget to be hospitable; by that means, some people have entertained angels without realizing it. 3Remember people in prison, as though you were in prison with them. When you think of people who are having a difficult time, remember that you too live in a frail body.

The Practical Life of God's People

4Let marriage be honored by everyone; let the marriage bed remain undefiled. God will judge those who misbehave sexually or commit adultery.

5Keep your life free from love of money; be content with what you have. He himself has said, after all, "I will never, ever, leave you or forsake you." 6That's why we can be cheerfully confident and say, "The Lord is helping me; I'm not going to be afraid; what can anyone do to me?"

7Remember your leaders, who spoke God's word to you. Look carefully at how their lives came to complete fruition, and imitate their faith. 8Jesus the Messiah is the same, yesterday, today, and forever.

9Don't let yourselves be carried off by strange teachings of whatever sort. The heart needs to be strengthened by grace, you see, not by rules about what to eat, which don't do any good to those who observe them.

Outside the Old City, Seeking the New

10We have an altar from which those who minister in the Tabernacle are not allowed to eat. 11For the bodies of the animals whose blood is taken into the sanctuary by the high priest as a sin-offering are burned outside the camp. 12That's why Jesus too suffered outside the gate, so that he might make the people holy with his own blood. 13So, then, let's go out to him, outside the camp, bearing his shame. ¹⁴Here, you see, we have no city that lasts; we are looking for the one that is still to come.

¹⁵Our part, then, is this: to bring, through him, a continual sacrifice of praise to God—that is, mouths that confess his name, and do so fruitfully. ¹⁶Don't neglect to do good, and to let "fellowship" mean what it says. God really enjoys sacrifices of that kind!

The God of Peace Be with You

¹⁷Obey your leaders; submit to them. They are keeping watch over your lives, you see, as people who will have to give account. Make sure they can do this with joy, not with a groan as a burden. That would be of no value to you.

¹⁸Pray for us! Our conscience is clear; we are quite sure of it. We wish to act appropriately in everything. ¹⁹I beg you especially to do this, so that I may quickly be restored to you.

²⁰May the God of peace, who led up from the dead our Lord Jesus, the great shepherd of the sheep, through the blood of the eternal covenant, ²¹make you complete in every good work so that you may do his will. May he perform, in you, whatever will be pleasing in his sight, through Jesus the Messiah. Glory be to him forever and ever. Amen!

²²I beg you, my dear family, bear with this word of exhortation; I've written to you quite briefly, after all. ²³You should know that our brother Timothy has been released. If he comes soon, I will see you and him at the same time.

²⁴Greet all your leaders, and all God's people. Those from Italy send you greetings. ²⁵Grace be with you all.

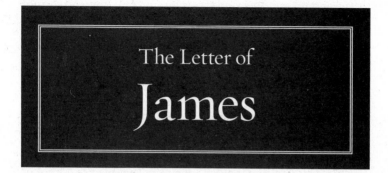

The Letter of
James

1 James, a slave of God and of the Lord Jesus the Messiah, to the twelve dispersed tribes: greetings.

²My dear family, when you find yourselves tumbling into various trials and tribulations, learn to look at it with complete joy, ³because you know that, when your faith is put to the test, what comes out is patience. ⁴What's more, you must let patience have its complete effect, so that you may be complete and whole, not falling short in anything.

⁵If any one of you falls short in wisdom, they should ask God for it, and it will be given them. God, after all, gives generously and ungrudgingly to all people. ⁶But they should ask in faith, with no doubts. A person who doubts is like a wave of the sea which the wind blows and tosses about. ⁷Someone like that should not suppose they will receive anything from the Lord, ⁸since they are double-minded and unstable in everything they do.

⁹Brothers and sisters who find themselves impoverished should celebrate the fact that they have risen to this height— ¹⁰and those who are rich that they are brought down low, since the rich will disappear like a wildflower. ¹¹You see, the rich will be like the grass: when the sun rises with its scorching heat, it withers the grass so that its flower droops and all its fine appearance comes to nothing. That's what it will be like when the rich wither away in the midst of their busy lives.

¹²God's blessing on the man who endures testing! When he has passed the test, he will receive the crown of life, which God has promised to those who love him. ¹³Nobody being

tested should say, "It's God that's testing me," for God cannot be tested by evil, and he himself tests nobody. [14]Rather, each person is tested when they are dragged off and enticed by their own desires. [15]Then desire, when it has conceived, gives birth to sin; and when sin reaches maturity it gives birth to death.

[16]Don't be deceived, my dear family. [17]Every good gift, every perfect gift, comes down from above, from the father of lights. His steady light doesn't vary. It doesn't change and produce shadows. [18]He became our father by the word of truth; that was his firm decision, and the result is that we are a kind of first fruits of his creatures.

The Word That Goes to Work

[19]So, my dear brothers and sisters, get this straight. Every person should be quick to hear, slow to speak, slow to anger. [20]Human anger, you see, doesn't produce God's justice! [21]So put away everything that is sordid, all that overflowing malice, and humbly receive the word which has been planted within you and which has the power to rescue your lives.

[22]But be people who do the word, not merely people who hear it and deceive themselves. [23]Someone who hears the word but doesn't do it, you see, is like a man who looks at his natural face in a mirror. [24]He notices himself, but then he goes away and quickly forgets what he looked like. [25]But the person who looks into the perfect law of freedom, and goes on with it, not being a hearer who forgets but a doer who does the deed—such a person is blessed in their doing.

[26]If anyone supposes that they are devout, and does not control their tongue, but rather deceives their heart—such a person's devotion is futile. [27]As far as God the father is concerned, pure, unsullied devotion works like this: you should visit orphans and widows in their sorrow, and prevent the world leaving its dirty smudge on you.

No Favorites!

2 My brothers and sisters, as you practice the faith of our Lord Jesus, the anointed king of glory, you must do so without favoritism. [2]What I mean is this: if someone comes into your assembly wearing gold rings, all dressed up, and a poor person comes in wearing shabby clothes, [3]you cast your eyes over the person wearing fine clothes and say, "Please! Have a seat up here!" but then you turn to the poor person and say, "Stand there!" or, "Get down there by my

footstool!" 4When you do this, are you not discriminating among yourselves? Are you not turning into judges with evil thoughts? 5Listen, my dear brothers and sisters. Isn't it the case that God has chosen the poor (as the world sees it) to be rich in faith, and to inherit the kingdom which he has promised to those who love him? 6But you have dishonored the poor man. After all, who are the rich? The rich are the ones who lord it over you and drag you into court, aren't they? 7The rich are the ones who blaspheme the wonderful name which has been pronounced over you, aren't they?

8Supposing, however, you keep the royal law, as it is written, "You shall love your neighbor as yourself"; if you do this, you will do well. 9But if you show favoritism, you are committing sin, and you will be convicted by the law as a lawbreaker. 10Anyone who keeps the whole law, you see, but fails in one point, has become guilty of all of it. 11For the one who said, "Do not commit adultery," also said, "Do not murder." So if you do not commit adultery, but do murder, you have become a lawbreaker. 12Speak and act in such a way as people who are going to be judged by the law of freedom. 13Judgment is without mercy, you see, for those who have shown no mercy. But mercy triumphs over judgment.

14What use is it, my dear family, if someone says they have faith when they don't have works? Can faith save such a person? 15Supposing a brother or sister is without clothing, and is short even of daily food, 16and one of you says to them, "Go in peace; be warm, be full!"—but doesn't give them what their bodies need—what use is that? 17In the same way, faith, all by itself and without works, is dead.

Faith and Works

18But supposing someone says, "Well: you have faith, and I have works." All right: show me your faith—but without doing any works; and then I will show you *my* faith, and I'll do it by my works! 19You believe that "God is one"? Well and good! The demons believe that, too, and they tremble! 20Do you want to know, you stupid person, that faith without works is lifeless? 21Wasn't Abraham our father justified by his works when he offered up his son Isaac on the altar? 22You can see from this that faith was cooperating along with the works, and the faith reached its fulfillment through the works. 23That is how the scripture was fulfilled which says, "Abraham believed God, and it was reckoned to him as righteousness," and he was called "God's friend." 24So you see that a person is justified by works and not by faith alone. 25In the same way, wasn't Rahab the prostitute justified by works when she gave shelter to the spies and sent them off by another road? 26Just as the body without the spirit is dead, you see, so faith without works is dead.

Taming the Tongue

3 Not many of you should become teachers, my brothers and sisters; you know that we will be judged more severely. 2All of us make many mistakes, after all. If anyone makes no mistakes in what they say, such a person is a fully complete human being, capable of keeping firm control over the whole body as well. 3We put bits into the mouths of horses to make them obey us, and then we can direct their whole bodies. 4Consider, too, the case of large ships; it takes strong winds to blow them along, but one small rudder will turn them whichever way the helmsman desires and decides. 5In the same way, the tongue is a little member but boasts great things. See how small a fire it takes to set a large forest ablaze! 6And the tongue is a fire. The tongue is a world of injustice, with its place established right there among our members. It defiles the whole body; it sets the wheel of nature ablaze, and is itself set ablaze by hell. 7Every species of beast and bird, of reptile and sea creature, you see, can be tamed, and has been tamed, by humans. 8But no single human is able to tame the tongue. It is an irrepressible evil, full of deadly poison. 9By it we bless the Lord and father; and by it we curse humans who are made in God's likeness! 10Blessing and curses come out of the same mouth! My dear family, it isn't right that it should be like that. 11Does a spring put out both sweet and bitter water from the same source? 12Dear friends, can a fig tree bear olives, or a vine bear figs? Nor can salt water yield fresh.

True and False Wisdom

13Who is wise and discerning among you? Such a person should, by their upright behavior, display their works in the humility of wisdom. 14But if you have bitter jealousy and contention in your hearts, don't boast and tell lies against the truth. 15This isn't the wisdom that comes from above. It is earthly, merely human, coming from the world of demons.

[16]For where there is jealousy and contention, there you will get unruly behavior and every kind of evil practice. [17]But the wisdom that comes from above is first holy, then peaceful, gentle, compliant, filled with mercy and good fruits, unbiased, sincere. [18]And the fruit of righteousness is sown in peace by those who make peace.

4 Where do wars come from? Why do people among you fight? It all comes from within, doesn't it—from your desires for pleasure which make war in your members. [2]You want something and you haven't got it, so you murder someone. You long to possess something but you can't get it, so you fight and wage war. The reason you don't have it is because you don't ask for it! [3]And when you do ask, you don't get it, because you ask wrongly, intending to spend it on your pleasures. [4]Adulterers! Don't you know that to be friends with the world means being enemies with God? So anyone who wants to be friends with the world is setting themselves up as God's enemy. [5]Or do you suppose that when the Bible says, "He yearns jealously over the spirit he has made to dwell in us," it doesn't mean what it says?

Humility and Faith

[6]But God gives more grace; so it says, "God opposes the proud, but gives grace to the humble." [7]Submit to God, then; resist the devil and he will run away from you. [8]Draw near to God, and he will draw near to you. Make your hands clean, you sinners; and make your hearts pure, you double-minded lot. [9]Make yourselves wretched; mourn and weep. Let your laughter turn to mourning, and your joy to sorrow. [10]Humble yourselves before the Lord, and he will exalt you.

[11]Do not speak evil against one another, my dear family. Anyone who speaks evil against another family member, or passes judgment against them, speaks evil against the law and judges the law. But if you judge the law, you are not a doer of the law but a judge! [12]There is one lawgiver, one judge who can rescue or destroy. But who are you to judge your neighbor?

Living by Trust in God

[13]Now look here, you people who say, "Today, or tomorrow, we will go to such and such a town and spend a year there, and trade, and make some money." [14]You have no idea what the next day will bring. What is your life? You are a mist which appears for a little while and then disappears again. [15]Instead,

you ought to say, "If the Lord wills, we shall live, and we shall do this, or that." ¹⁶But, as it is, you boast in your pride. All such boasting is evil. ¹⁷So, then, if anyone knows the right thing to do, but doesn't do it, it becomes sin for them.

Warnings to the Rich

5 Now look here, you rich! Weep and wail for the horrible things that are going to happen to you! ²Your riches have rotted, and your clothes have become moth-eaten, ³your gold and your silver have rusted, and their rust will bear witness against you and will eat up your flesh like fire. You have stored up riches in the last days! ⁴Look: you cheated the workers who mowed your fields by keeping back their wages, and those wages are crying out! The cries of the farmworkers have reached the ears of the Lord of hosts. ⁵You have lived off the fat of the land, in the lap of luxury. You have fattened your own hearts on a day of slaughter. ⁶You have condemned the Righteous One and killed him, and he doesn't resist you.

Patience and Trust

⁷So be patient, my brothers and sisters, for the appearing of the Lord. You know how the farmer waits for the valuable crop to come up from the ground. He is patient over it, waiting for it to receive the early rain and then the late rain. ⁸In the same way, you must be patient, and make your hearts strong, because the appearing of the Lord is near at hand. ⁹Don't grumble against one another, my brothers and sisters, so that you may not be judged. Look—the judge is standing at the gates! ¹⁰Consider the prophets, my brothers and sisters, who spoke in the name of the Lord. Take them as an example of longsuffering and patience. ¹¹When people endure, we call them "blessed by God." Well, you have heard of the endurance of Job; and you saw the Lord's ultimate purpose. The Lord is deeply compassionate and kindly.

¹²Above all, my brothers and sisters, do not swear. Don't swear by heaven; don't swear by earth; don't use any other oaths. Let your yes be yes and your no be no. That way, you will not fall under judgment.

Praying in Faith

¹³Are any among you suffering? Let them pray. Are any cheerful? Let them sing psalms. ¹⁴Are any among you sick? They should call for the elders of the church, and they should pray over the sick person, anointing them with oil in the name of the Lord. ¹⁵Faithful prayer will rescue the sick person, and

the Lord will raise them up. If they have committed any sin, it will be forgiven them. [16]So confess your sins to one another, and pray for one another, that you may be healed.

When a righteous person prays, that prayer carries great power. [17]Elijah was a man with passions like ours, and he prayed and prayed that it might not rain—and it did not rain on the earth for three years and six months. [18]Then he prayed again, the sky gave rain, and the earth produced its fruit.

[19]My dear family, if someone in your company has wandered from the truth, and someone turns them back, [20]know this: the one who turns back a sinner from wandering off into error will rescue that person's life from death, and cover a multitude of sins.

The First Letter of
Peter

Genuine Faith and Sure Hope

1 Peter, an apostle of Jesus the Messiah, to God's chosen ones who live as foreigners among the Dispersion in Pontus, Galatia, Cappadocia, Asia, and Bithynia, ²who have been set aside in advance by God the father, through the sanctification of the spirit, for obedience and for sprinkling with the blood of Jesus the Messiah. May grace and peace be poured out lavishly on you!

³May God be blessed, God the father of our Lord Jesus the Messiah! His mercy is abundant, and so he has become our father in a second birth into a living hope through the resurrection from the dead of Jesus the Messiah. ⁴This has brought us into an incorruptible inheritance, which nothing can stain or diminish. At the moment it is kept safe for you in the heavens, ⁵while you are being kept safe by God's power, through faith, for a rescue that is all ready and waiting to be revealed in the final time.

⁶That is why you celebrate! Yes, it may well be necessary that, for a while, you may have to suffer trials and tests of all sorts. ⁷But this is so that the true value of your faith may be discovered. It is worth more than gold, which is tested by fire even though it can be destroyed. The result will be praise, glory, and honor when Jesus the Messiah is revealed. ⁸You love him, even though you've never seen him. And even though you don't see him, you believe in him, and celebrate with a glorified joy that goes beyond anything words can say, ⁹since you are receiving the proper goal of your faith—namely, the rescue of your lives.

1 Peter 1:1

Ransomed by Grace

¹⁰The prophets who prophesied about the grace that was to be given to you searched and inquired about this rescue. ¹¹They asked what sort of time it would be, the time that the Messiah's spirit within them was indicating when speaking of the Messiah's sufferings and subsequent glory. ¹²It was revealed to them that they were not serving themselves, but you, when they were ministering these things—things which have now been announced to you by the holy spirit who was sent from heaven, through those who preached the good news to you. The angels long to gaze on these things!

¹³So fasten your belts—the belts of your minds! Keep yourselves under control. Set your hope completely on the grace that will be given you when Jesus the Messiah is revealed. ¹⁴As children of obedience, don't be squashed into the shape of the passions you used to indulge when you were still in ignorance. ¹⁵Rather, just as the one who called you is holy, so be holy yourselves, in every aspect of behavior. ¹⁶It is written, you see, "Be holy, for I am holy." ¹⁷If you call on God as "father"—the God,

that is, who judges everyone impartially according to their work—behave with holy fear throughout the time in which you are resident here.

18You know, after all, that you were ransomed from the futile practices inherited from your ancestors, and that this ransom came not through perishable things like gold or silver, 19but through the precious blood of the Messiah, like a lamb without spot or blemish. 20He was destined for this from before the foundation of the world, and appeared at the end of the times for your sake, 21for you (that is) who through him believe in the God who raised him from the dead and gave him glory, so that your faith and hope are in God.

Newborn Babies

22Once your lives have been purified by obeying the truth, resulting in a sincere love for all your fellow believers, love one another eagerly, from a pure heart. 23You have been born again, not from seed which decays but from seed which does not—through the living and abiding word of God. 24Because, you see—

> All flesh is like grass
> And all its glory is like the flower of the field.
> The grass withers, and the flower falls,
> 25But the word of the Lord lasts forever.

That is the word that was announced to you.

The Living Stone

2 So put away all evil, all deceitful, hateful malice, and all ill-speaking. 2As newborn babies, long for the spiritual milk, the real stuff, not watered down. That is what will make you grow up to salvation—3if indeed you have tasted that the Lord is gracious.

4Come to him, to that living stone. Humans rejected him, but God chose him and values him very highly! 5Like living stones yourselves, you are being built up into a spiritual house, to be a holy priesthood, to offer spiritual sacrifices that will be well pleasing to God through Jesus the Messiah.

6That's why it stands in scripture:

> Look! I'm setting up in Zion
> A chosen, precious cornerstone;
> Believe in him! You'll not be ashamed.

[7]He is indeed precious for you believers. But when people don't believe, "the stone which the builders rejected has become the head cornerstone," [8]and "a stone of stumbling and a rock of offense." They stumble as they disobey the word, which indeed was their destiny. [9]But you are a "chosen race; a royal priesthood"; a holy nation; a people for God's possession. Your purpose is to announce the virtuous deeds of the one who called you out of darkness into his amazing light. [10]Once you were "no people"; now you are "God's people." Once you had not received mercy; now you have received mercy.

[11]My beloved ones, I beg you—strangers and resident aliens as you are—to hold back from the fleshly desires that wage war against your true lives. [12]Keep up good conduct among the pagans, so that when they speak against you as evildoers they will observe your good deeds and praise God on the day of his royal arrival.

Living in a Pagan World

[13]Be subject to every human institution, for the sake of the Lord: whether to the emperor as supreme, [14]or to governors as sent by him to punish evildoers and praise those who do good. [15]This, you see, is God's will. He wants you to behave well and so to silence foolish and ignorant people. [16]Live as free people (though don't use your freedom as a veil to hide evil!), but as slaves of God. [17]Do honor to all people; love the family; reverence God; honor the emperor.

[18]Let slaves obey their masters with all respect, not only the good and kind ones but also the unkind ones. [19]It is to your credit, you see, if because of a godly conscience you put up with unjust and painful suffering. [20]After all, what credit is it if you do something wrong, are beaten for it, and take it patiently? But if you do what is right, suffer for it, and bear it patiently, this is to your credit before God.

Suffering as the Messiah Did

[21]This, after all, is what came with the terms of your call; because:

> The Messiah, too, suffered on your behalf,
> Leaving behind a pattern for you
> So that you should follow the way he walked.
> [22]He committed no sin,
> Nor was there any deceit in his mouth.

23*When he was insulted, he didn't insult in return,*
When he suffered, he didn't threaten,
But he gave himself up to the one who judges justly.
24*He himself bore our sins*
In his body on the cross,
So that we might be free from sins
And live for righteousness.
It is by his wound that you are healed.
25*For you were going astray like sheep,*
But now you have returned to the shepherd
And guardian of your true lives.

Marriage and Its Challenges

3 In the same way, let me say a word to the women. You should be subject to your husbands, so that if there should be some who disobey the word, they may be won, without a word, through the behavior of their wives, 2as they notice you conducting yourselves with reverence and purity. 3The beauty you should strive for ought not to be the external sort—elaborate hairdressing, gold trinkets, fine clothes! 4Rather, true beauty is the secret beauty of the heart, of a sincere, gentle, and quiet spirit. That is very precious to God. 5That is how the holy women of old, who hoped in God, used to make themselves beautiful in submission to their husbands. 6Take Sarah, for instance, who obeyed Abraham and called him "master." You are her children if you do good and have no fear of intimidation.

7You men, in the same way, think out how to live with your wives. Yes, they are physically weaker than you, but they deserve full respect. They are heirs of the grace of life, just the same as you. That way nothing will obstruct your prayers.

The New Way of Life

8The aim of this is for you all to be like-minded, sympathetic and loving to one another, tender-hearted and humble. 9Don't repay evil for evil, or slander for slander, but rather say a blessing. This is what you were called to, so that you may inherit a blessing.

10*For the one who wants to love life and see good days*
Should guard the tongue from evil, and the lips from
speaking deceit;

¹¹Should turn away from evil and do good;
Should seek peace, and follow after it.
¹²For the Lord's eyes are upon the righteous, and his ears
*   are open to their prayer,*
But the face of the Lord is against those who do evil.

¹³Who is there, then, to harm you if you are eager to do what is right? ¹⁴But if you do suffer because of your righteous behavior, God's blessing is upon you! "Don't fear what they fear; don't be disturbed." ¹⁵Sanctify the Messiah as Lord in your hearts, and always be ready to make a reply to anyone who asks you to explain the hope that is in you. ¹⁶Do it, though, with gentleness and respect. Hold on to a good conscience, so that when people revile your good behavior in the Messiah they may be ashamed.

¹⁷It's better to suffer for good conduct (if God so wills it) than for bad. ¹⁸For the Messiah, too, suffered once for sins, the just for the unjust, so that he might bring you to God. He was put to death in the flesh, but made alive by the spirit. ¹⁹In the spirit, too, he went and made the proclamation to the spirits in prison ²⁰who had earlier on been disobedient during the days of Noah, when God waited in patience. Noah built the ark, in which a few people, eight in fact, were rescued through water. ²¹That functions as a signpost for you, pointing to baptism, which now rescues you—not by washing away fleshly pollution, but by the appeal to God of a good conscience, through the resurrection of Jesus the Messiah. ²²He has gone into heaven and is at God's right hand, with angels, authorities, and powers subject to him.

Suffering for Doing Right

4 So, then, just as the Messiah suffered in the flesh, you too must equip yourselves with the same mental armor. Someone who suffers in the flesh has ceased from sin, ²so as to live the rest of their mortal life no longer according to human desires but according to God's will. ³Pagan ways of life have had quite enough of your time already, and you should put all that behind you for good—all that uncleanness, passion, drunkenness, excessive feasting, drinking-parties, and lawless idolatry. ⁴People are shocked that you don't now join in with the same wild and reckless behavior, and so they

Transformed Living

call down curses on you. ⁵But they will have to account for it before the one who is ready to judge the living and the dead. ⁶That is why, you see, the gospel was preached even to the dead, so that, being judged in human fashion, in the flesh, they might live in God's fashion, in the spirit.

⁷The end of all things is upon us. You must keep sober, then, and self-disciplined for your prayers. ⁸Above all, keep absolutely firm in your love for one another, because "love covers a multitude of sins." ⁹Be hospitable to one another without complaining. ¹⁰Just as each of you has received a gift, so you should use it for ministry one to another, as good stewards of God's many-sided grace. ¹¹If anyone speaks, they should do so as speaking God's oracles. If anyone ministers, they should do it as in the strength which God grants, so that God may be glorified in all things through Jesus the Messiah, to whom be glory and power forever and ever. Amen.

Sharing the Messiah's Sufferings

¹²Beloved, don't be surprised at the fiery ordeal which is coming upon you to test you, as though this were some strange thing that was happening to you. ¹³Rather, celebrate! You are sharing the sufferings of the Messiah. Then, when his glory is revealed, you will celebrate with real, exuberant joy. ¹⁴If you are abused because of the name of the Messiah, you are blessed by God, because the spirit of glory and of God is resting upon you. ¹⁵None of you, of course, should suffer as a murderer or thief or evildoer, or even as a busybody. ¹⁶But if you suffer as a Christian, don't be ashamed; rather, give God the glory for that name! ¹⁷The time has come, you see, for judgment to begin at God's own household. And if it begins with us, what will be the end of those who do not obey the gospel? ¹⁸And if the righteous person is scarcely saved, where will the ungodly and the sinner appear? ¹⁹So also those who suffer according to God's will should entrust their whole lives to the faithful creator by doing what is good.

Humble Shepherds

5 So, then, I appeal to the elders among you, as a fellow elder and a witness of the sufferings of the Messiah, and as one who will share in the glory that is to be revealed. ²Do the proper work of a shepherd as you look after God's flock which has been entrusted to you, not under compulsion, but gladly, as in God's presence; not for shameful profit, but

eagerly. ³You should not lord it over those for whom you are responsible, but rather be an example to the flock. ⁴And when the chief shepherd appears, you will receive the crown of glory that won't wither away. ⁵In the same way, too, the younger men should submit to the elders. But let all of you clothe yourselves with humility toward one another. You see, "God resists the proud, but gives grace to the lowly." ⁶Humble yourselves, then, under God's powerful hand, so that he may lift you up at the right time. ⁷Throw all your care upon him, because he cares about you.

⁸Stay in control of yourselves; stay awake. Your enemy, the devil, is stalking around like a roaring lion, looking for someone to devour. ⁹Resist him, staying resolute in your faith, and knowing that other family members in the rest of the world are facing identical sufferings. ¹⁰Then, after you have suffered a little while, the God of all grace, who called you in the Messiah Jesus to the glory of his new age, will himself put you in good order, and will establish and strengthen you and set you on firm foundations. ¹¹To him be the power forever. Amen.

Standing Firm by God's Power

¹²I have written this briefly, and am sending it to you with Silvanus, whom I regard as a faithful brother. My main point is to urge and bear witness to you that this grace, in which you stand, is the true grace of God. ¹³Your chosen sister in Babylon sends you greetings; so does my son Mark. ¹⁴Greet one another with a holy kiss.

Peace to you all in the Messiah.

The Second Letter of

Peter

1 Simon Peter, a slave and apostle of Jesus the Messiah, to those who have obtained a share of faith equal to ours in the righteousness of our God and savior Jesus the Messiah: ²may grace and peace be multiplied to you, in the knowledge of God and of Jesus our Lord.

³God has bestowed upon us, through his divine power, everything that we need for life and godliness, through the knowledge of him who called us by his own glory and virtue. ⁴The result is that he has given us, through these things, his precious and wonderful promises; and the purpose of all this is so that you may run away from the corruption of lust that is in the world, and may become partakers of the divine nature. ⁵So, because of this, you should strain every nerve to supplement your faith with virtue, and your virtue with knowledge, ⁶and your knowledge with self-control, and your self-control with patience, and your patience with piety, ⁷and your piety with family affection, and your family affection with love. ⁸If you have these things in plentiful supply, you see, you will not be wasting your time, or failing to bear fruit, in relation to your knowledge of our Lord Jesus the Messiah. ⁹Someone who doesn't have these things, in fact, is so shortsighted as to be actually blind, and has forgotten what it means to be cleansed from earlier sins. ¹⁰So, my dear family, you must make the effort all the more to confirm that God has called you and chosen you. If you do this, you will never trip up. ¹¹That is how you will have, richly laid out before you, an entrance into the kingdom

of God's coming age, the kingdom of our Lord and savior Jesus the Messiah.

Prophecy
Made Sure

12So I intend to go on and on reminding you about all this— even though you know it, and have been firmly established in the truth which has come to you. 13But it seems right to me, as long as I am living in this present tent, to stir you up with a reminder, 14since I know that I shall shortly be putting off this tent, as our Lord Jesus the Messiah showed me. 15So I shall also be making every effort to ensure that, once I am gone, you may be able to call these things to mind at any time.

16When we made known to you the power and appearing of our Lord Jesus the Messiah, you see, we were not following cleverly devised myths. Rather, we were eyewitnesses of his grandeur. 17For when he received honor and glory from God the father, a voice spoke to him from the Wonderful Glory, "This is my son, my beloved one, in whom I am well pleased." 18We heard this voice, spoken from heaven, when we were with him on the holy mountain. 19And we have the prophetic word made more certain. You will do well to hold on to this, as to a lamp shining in a dark place, until the day dawns and the morning star shines in your hearts. 20You must know this first of all, that no scriptural prophecy is a matter of one's own interpretation. 21No prophecy, you see, ever came by human will. Rather, people were moved by the holy spirit, and spoke from God.

False Prophets

2 There were, however, false prophets among the people, just as there will be false teachers among yourselves, who will sneak in with their destructive false teachings, even denying the master who paid the price for them. They will earn swift destruction for themselves, 2and many will follow after their disgusting practices. The way of truth will be blasphemed because of them, 3and in their greed they will exploit you with fake prophecies. Their condemnation has not been idle for a long time now, and their destruction has not fallen asleep.

4God didn't spare the angels who sinned, you see, but he threw them into the Pit, into dark caverns, handing them over to be guarded until the time of judgment. 5Similarly, he didn't spare the ancient world, but brought a flood on the

world of the ungodly and rescued Noah, a herald of righteousness, with seven others. ⁶Similarly, he condemned the cities of
Sodom and Gomorrah, reducing them to ashes and ruin, thus
setting up an example of what would happen to the ungodly.
⁷He snatched righteous Lot out of the disaster, a man who
had been deeply troubled by their shameful and unprincipled
behavior. ⁸That righteous man, you see, living in their midst,
could see and hear day after day lawless deeds which tortured
his righteous soul. ⁹The Lord knows how to rescue the godly
from testing, and also how to keep the unrighteous ready for
the day of judgment and punishment, ¹⁰ᵃ especially those who
follow after the pollution of fleshly lust and despise authority.

**From Bad
to Worse**

¹⁰ᵇSuch people are arrogant and self-willed! They are not
afraid to blaspheme the glorious ones, ¹¹whereas the angels,
stronger and more powerful though they are, do not bring a
charge of blasphemy against them before the Lord.

¹²These people are like unreasoning beasts, by nature born
to be caught and destroyed. They curse at things of which
they have no knowledge; they are destroyed by their own self-
destructive tendencies. ¹³They commit injustice, and receive
injustice as their reward. They count it pleasure to hold wild
revels in the daytime. If they join you for a meal, they pollute
and stain the whole thing as they wallow in their disgusting pleasures. ¹⁴Their eyes are full of adultery; they can't get
enough of sin; when they find unsteady souls, they lead them
astray; their hearts have been trained in greed; they are children of the curse. ¹⁵They have left the straight path and have
wandered off in pursuit of Balaam son of Bosor, who loved the
reward of unrighteousness, ¹⁶and was rebuked for his disobedience when a normally speechless donkey spoke in a human
voice to stop the prophet's madness in its tracks.

¹⁷These people are springs without water. They are patches
of fog driven along by a storm. The depth of darkness has been
reserved for them! ¹⁸They utter bombastic words of folly as
they entice, with licentious fleshly desires, those who have
only just escaped from the company of people who behave
improperly. ¹⁹They promise them freedom, but they themselves are slaves to corruption. (A person who is defeated by
something, you see, is enslaved to it.) ²⁰For if they have fled

the pollutions of the world through the knowledge of our Lord and savior Jesus the Messiah, but again become entangled in them and are defeated, they have ended up in a worse state than they were before. 21It would have been better for them never to have known the way of righteousness than, having known it, to turn away from the holy commandment which had been given to them. 22There is a true proverb which now applies to them: the dog returns to its own vomit, and the sow gets washed only to wallow once more in the mud.

3 My dear family, this is now the second time I am writing you a letter. Your motives are pure, and what I'm trying to do in reminding you is to stir them into action, 2so that you'll remember the words spoken earlier by the holy prophets, and by the command of the Lord and savior which you received from your apostles. 3But you must first know this. Deceivers will come in the last days, with deceitful ways, behaving according to their own desires. 4This is what they will say: "Where is the promise of his royal arrival? Ever since the previous generation died, everything has continued just as it has from the beginning of creation." 5They willingly overlook this one thing, you see: the ancient heavens and earth were formed out of water and through water, by God's word—6and it was by flooding the world of that time with water that it was destroyed. 7The heavens and earth that we now have are being preserved for fire by the same word, being kept for the day of judgment and the destruction of the wicked. 8So, beloved, don't forget this one thing, that a single day with the Lord is like a thousand years, and a thousand years like a single day. 9The Lord is not delaying his promise, in the way that some reckon delay, but he is very patient toward you. He does not want anyone to be destroyed. Rather, he wants everyone to arrive at repentance.

The Day of the Lord

10But the Lord's day will come like a thief. On that day the heavens will pass away with a great rushing sound, the elements will be dissolved in fire, and the earth and all the works on it will be disclosed.

11Since everything is going to dissolve in this way, what sort of people should you be? You should live lives that are holy and godly, 12as you look for God's day to appear, and indeed hurry it

God's Patience

on its way—the day because of which the heavens will be set on fire and dissolved, and the elements will melt with heat. [13]But we are waiting for new heavens and a new earth, in which justice will be at home. That is what he has promised.

[14]So, my dear family, as you wait for these things, be eager to be found without spot or blemish before him, in peace. [15]And when our Lord waits patiently to act, see that for what it is—salvation! Our beloved brother Paul has written to you about all this, according to the wisdom that has been given him, [16]speaking about these things as he does in all his letters. There are some things in them which are difficult to understand. Untaught and unstable people twist his words to their own destruction, as they do with the other scriptures.

[17]But as for you, my dear family, be on your guard, since you have been warned in advance. That way you won't be led astray through the error of lawless people and fall away from your own solid grounding. [18]Instead, grow in grace and in the knowledge of our Lord and savior Jesus the Messiah. To him be glory both now and in the day when God's new age dawns. Amen.

The First Letter of

John

1 That which was from the beginning, which we have heard, which we have seen with our eyes, which we have gazed at, and our hands have handled—concerning the Word of Life! ²That life was displayed, and we have seen it, and bear witness, and we announce to you the life of God's coming age, which was with the father and was displayed to us. ³That which we have seen and heard we announce to you too, so that you also may have fellowship with us. And our fellowship is with the father, and with his son Jesus the Messiah. ⁴We are writing these things so that our joy may be complete.

The Word of Life

⁵This is the message which we have heard from him, and announce to you: God is light, and there is no darkness at all in him. ⁶If we say that we have fellowship with him and walk in the dark, we are telling lies, and not doing what is true. ⁷But if we walk in the light, just as he is in the light, we have fellowship with one another, and the blood of Jesus his son makes us pure and clean from all sin. ⁸If we say that we have no sin, we deceive ourselves and the truth is not in us. ⁹If we confess our sins, he is faithful and just, and will forgive us our sins, and cleanse us from all unrighteousness. ¹⁰If we say that we have not sinned, we make him out to be a liar, and his word is not in us.

God's Light and Our Darkness

2 My children, I am writing these things to you so that you may not sin. If anyone does sin, we have one who pleads our cause before the father—namely, the Righteous One, Jesus the Messiah! ²He is the sacrifice which atones for our sins—and not ours only, either, but those of the whole world.

God's New Commandment

³This is how we are sure that we have known him, if we keep his commandments. ⁴Anyone who says, "I know him," but doesn't keep his commandments, is a liar. People like that have no truth in them. ⁵But if anyone keeps his word, God's love is truly made complete in such a person. This is how we are sure that we are in him: ⁶anyone who says, "I abide in him," ought to behave in the same way that he behaved.

⁷My beloved ones, I am not writing a new command to you, but an old command which you have had from the very beginning. The old command is the word which you heard. ⁸Again, however, I am writing a new command to you: it is true in him and in you, because the darkness is passing away and the true light is already shining. ⁹Anyone who says, "I am in the light," while hating another family member, is still in darkness up to this very moment. ¹⁰Anyone who loves another family member abides in the light, and there is no cause of offense in such a person. ¹¹Anyone who hates another family member is in the darkness, and walks about in the darkness. Such people have no idea where they are going, because the darkness has blinded their eyes.

> ¹²*I am writing to you, children,*
> *Because your sins are forgiven through his name.*
> ¹³*I am writing to you, fathers,*
> *Because you have known the one who is*
>   *from the beginning.*
> *I am writing to you, young people,*
> *Because you have conquered the evil one.*
> ¹⁴*I have written to you, children,*
> *Because you have known the father.*
> *I have written to you, fathers,*
> *Because you have known the one who is*
>   *from the beginning.*
> *I have written to you, young people,*
> *Because you are strong,*
> *And the word of God abides in you,*
> *And you have conquered the evil one.*

People of the Lie

¹⁵Do not love the world, or the things that are in the world. If anyone loves the world, the father's love is not in them.

¹⁶Everything in the world, you see—the greedy desire of the flesh, the greedy desire of the eyes, the pride of life—none of this is from the father. It is from the world. ¹⁷The world is passing away, with all its greedy desires. But anyone who does God's will abides forever.

¹⁸Children, it is the last hour. You have heard that "Antimessiah" is coming—and now many Antimessiahs have appeared! That's how we know that it is the last hour. ¹⁹They went out from among us, but they were not really of our number. If they had been of our number, you see, they would have remained with us. This happened so that it would be made crystal-clear that none of them belonged to us. ²⁰You, however, have the anointing from the Holy One, and you all have knowledge. ²¹I am not writing to you because you don't know the truth, but because you do know it, and you know that no liar is of the truth.

²²Who is the liar? Is it not the one who denies that Jesus is the Messiah? Such a one is the Antimessiah—who denies the father and the son. ²³Nobody who denies the son has the father. One who acknowledges the son has the father too. ²⁴As for you: let what you heard from the beginning abide in you. If what you heard from the beginning abides in you, you too will abide in the son and in the father. ²⁵And this is the promise which he himself promised us: the life of the age to come.

²⁶I am writing to you about the people who are deceiving you. ²⁷You have received the anointing from him; it abides in you, and you do not need to have anyone teach you. That anointing from him teaches you about everything; it is true, it isn't a lie. So, just as he taught you, abide in him.

²⁸And now, children, abide in him, so that when he is revealed we may have boldness and may not be put to shame before him at his royal appearing. ²⁹If you know that he is righteous, you know that everyone who does what is right has been fathered by him.

3 Look at the remarkable love the father has given us— that we should be called God's children! That indeed is what we are. That's why the world doesn't know us, because it didn't know him. ²Beloved ones, we are now, already, God's children; it hasn't yet been revealed what we are going

Born of God

to be. We know that when he is revealed we shall be like him, because we shall see him as he is. ³All who have this hope in him make themselves pure, just as he is pure.

⁴Everyone who goes on sinning is breaking the law; sin, in fact, is lawlessness. ⁵And you know that he was revealed so that he might take away sins, and there is no sin in him. ⁶Everyone who abides in him does not go on sinning. Everyone who goes on sinning has not seen him, or known him.

⁷Children, don't let anyone deceive you. The person who does righteousness is righteous, just as he is righteous. ⁸The person who goes on sinning is from the devil, because the devil is a sinner from the very start. The son of God was revealed for this purpose, to destroy the works of the devil. ⁹Everyone who is fathered by God does not go on sinning, because God's off-spring remain in him; they cannot go on sinning, because they have been fathered by God. ¹⁰That is how it is clear who are the children of God and who are the children of the devil: every-one who does not do what is right is not of God, particularly those who do not love their brother or sister.

The Challenge of Love

¹¹This is the message which you heard right from the start, you see—that we should love one another. ¹²We should not be like Cain, who was of the evil one, and murdered his brother. Why did he murder him? Because his deeds were evil, while his brother's were right.

¹³Don't be surprised, my brothers and sisters, if the world hates you. ¹⁴We know that we have passed from death to life, because we love the family. Anyone who doesn't love abides in death. ¹⁵Everyone who hates their brother or sister is a mur-derer, and you know that no murderer has the life of the com-ing age abiding in them. ¹⁶This is how we know love: he laid down his life for us. And we too ought to lay down our lives for our brothers and sisters. ¹⁷Anyone who has the means of life in this world, and sees a brother or sister in need, and closes their heart against them—how can God's love be abiding in them? ¹⁸Children, let us not love in word, or in speech, but in deed and in truth.

¹⁹Because of this, we know we are of the truth, and we will persuade our hearts of this fact before him, ²⁰because if our

hearts condemn us, God is greater than our hearts. He knows everything. 21Beloved, if our hearts do not condemn us, we have boldness before God, 22and we receive from him whatever we ask, because we keep his commands and give him pleasure when he sees what we are doing. 23And this is his command, that we should believe in the name of his son Jesus the Messiah, and should love one another, just as he gave us the commandment. 24Anyone who keeps his commandments abides in him, and he in them. This is how we know that he abides in us, by his spirit that he has given us.

4 Beloved, do not believe every spirit. Rather, test the spirits to see whether they are from God. Many false prophets, you see, have gone out into the world. 2This is how we know God's spirit: every spirit that agrees that Jesus the Messiah has come in the flesh is from God, 3and every spirit that does not confess Jesus is not from God. This spirit is actually the spirit of the Antimessiah. You have heard that it was coming, and now it is already in the world.

False Prophets

4But you, children, are from God, and you have overcome them, because the one who is in you is greater than the one who is in the world. 5They are from the world, and that is why they speak from the world, and why the world listens to them. 6We are from God; people who know God listen to us, but people who are not from God do not listen to us. That is how we can tell the spirit of truth from the spirit of error.

7Beloved, let us love one another, because love is from God, and all who love are fathered by God and know God. 8The one who does not love has not known God, because God is love. 9This is how God's love has appeared among us: God sent his only son into the world, so that we should live through him. 10Love consists in this: not that we loved God, but that he loved us and sent his son to be the sacrifice that would atone for our sins. 11Beloved, if that's how God loved us, we ought to love one another in the same way. 12Nobody has ever seen God. If we love one another, God abides in us and his love is completed in us. 13That is how we know that we abide in him, and he in us, because he has given us a portion of his spirit. 14And we have seen and bear witness that the father sent the son to be

God's Love

the world's savior. [15]Anyone who confesses that Jesus is God's son—God abides in them and they abide in God. [16]And we have known and have believed the love which God has for us.

God is love; those who abide in love abide in God, and God abides in them. [17]This is what makes love complete for us, so that we may have boldness and confidence on the day of judgment, because just as he is, so are we within this world. [18]There is no fear in love; complete love drives out fear. Fear has to do with punishment, and anyone who is afraid has not been completed in love. [19]We love because he first loved us. [20]If someone says, "I love God," but hates their brother or sister, that person is a liar. Someone who doesn't love a brother or sister whom they have seen, how can they love God, whom they haven't seen? [21]This is the command we have from him: anyone who loves God should love their brother or sister too.

Faith Wins the Victory

5 Everyone who believes that the Messiah is Jesus has been fathered by God. Everyone who loves the parent loves the child as well. [2]That is how we know that we love the children of God, because we love God and do what he commands. [3]This is what loving God means: it means keeping his commandments. His commandments, what's more, are no trouble, [4]because everything that is fathered by God conquers the world. This is the victory that conquers the world: our faith.

[5]Who is the one who conquers the world? Surely the one who believes that Jesus is God's son! [6]It was he who came by means of water and blood, Jesus the Messiah, not by water only but by the water and the blood. The spirit is the one who bears witness, because the spirit is the truth. [7]There are three that bear witness, you see—[8]the spirit, the water, and the blood—and these three agree together. [9]If we have received human witness, God's witness is greater. This is the witness of God, the testimony he has borne to his son. [10]All those who believe in the son of God have the witness in themselves, but anyone who does not believe in God has made a liar of him, because they have not believed in the witness which God bore concerning his son. [11]This is the witness: God has given us the life of the age to come, and this life is in his son. [12]Anyone who

has the son has life. Anyone who does not have the son of God does not have life.

13I am writing these things to you so that you may know that you, who believe in the name of the son of God, do indeed have the life of the age to come. 14This is the bold confidence we have before him: if we ask for something according to his will, he hears us. 15And if we know that he hears us in whatever we ask, we know that we already possess the requests we have asked from him.

The True God

16If anyone sees a brother or sister committing a sin which is not deadly, they should ask, and God will give life to the people who are sinning in a way which is not deadly. There is such a thing as deadly sin; I do not say that one should pray about that. 17All sin is unrighteousness, and there is a sin which is not deadly.

18We know that everyone fathered by God does not go on sinning. The one who was fathered by God keeps them, and the evil one does not touch them. 19We know that we are from God, and the whole world is under the power of the evil one. 20We know that the son of God has come and has given us understanding so that we should know the truth. And we are in the truth, in his son Jesus the Messiah.

This is the true God; this is the life of the age to come. 21Children, guard yourselves against idols.

The Second Letter of
John

The Sign of Life

[1]From the Elder to the Chosen Lady and her children, whom I love in truth—as indeed, in addition to myself, do all those who know the truth, [2]because of the truth that abides in us and is with us forever. [3]Grace, mercy, and peace from God the father and from Jesus the Messiah, the son of the father, be with us in truth and love.

[4]I was delighted when I found some of your children walking in the truth, just as we received the commandment from the father. [5]And now, dear Lady, I ask you, not as though I were writing you a new commandment, but the one we had from the very beginning, that we should love one another. [6]This is love: that we should behave in accordance with his commandments. And this is the commandment, just as you heard it from the very start, that we should behave in accordance with it.

Don't Be Deceived!

[7]Many deceivers, you see, have gone out into the world. These are people who do not admit that Jesus the Messiah has come in the flesh. Such a person is the Deceiver—the Antimessiah! [8]Watch out for yourselves, so that you won't lose what we have worked for, but may receive the full reward.

[9]Anyone who goes out on their own, and does not abide in the teaching of the Messiah, does not have God. One who abides in the teaching—such a one has the father and the son. [10]If anyone comes to you and does not bring this teaching, don't receive them into the house; don't even give them

a greeting. [11]Anyone who utters a greeting to such a person shares in their wicked deeds.

[12]I have many things to write to you, but I did not wish to write with pen and ink. I am hoping instead to come to you, and to speak face to face. That will complete our joy.

[13]The children of your Chosen Sister send you greetings.

The Third Letter of
John

⁷The Elder to beloved Gaius, whom I love in truth.

²Beloved, I pray that all is going well with you, and that you are every bit as healthy physically as you are spiritually. ³I was absolutely delighted, you see, when some of the family arrived and bore witness to your truthfulness, since clearly you are walking in the truth. ⁴Nothing gives me greater joy than this, to hear that my children are walking in the truth.

⁵Beloved, when you are doing all that you do for family members, even when they are strangers, you are doing a faithful work. ⁶These people have borne witness to your love in the presence of the assembly, and you will do well to send them on their way in a manner worthy of God. ⁷They went out for the sake of the name, not accepting help from outsiders. ⁸We ought to support people like that, so that we may become fellow workers with the truth.

⁹I have written something to the assembly. But Diotrephes, who wants to be the most important person there, refuses to acknowledge us. ¹⁰So, then, if I come, I will refer back to what he has done, and the slanderous words he has spoken against us. Not being satisfied with that, he doesn't welcome family members himself; and, when others want to do so, he forbids them and throws them out of the assembly.

¹¹Beloved, don't imitate evil; imitate good! Someone who does good is from God; someone who does evil has not seen God. ¹²Demetrius has been well attested by everybody, and by

the truth itself. We join in this testimony, and you know that our testimony is true.

[13]I have much to write to you, but I don't want to do it with pen and ink. [14]I am hoping instead to see you very soon, so that we can talk face to face.

[15]Peace be with you. All the friends greet you. Greet all the friends by name.

The Letter of
Judah

Contend for the Faith

¹Judah, slave of Jesus the Messiah, brother of James, to those who are called, the people whom God loves and whom Jesus, the Messiah, keeps safe! ²May mercy, peace, and love be multiplied to you.

³Beloved, I was doing my best to write to you about the rescue in which we share, but I found it necessary to write to you to urge you to struggle hard for the faith which was once and for all given to God's people. ⁴Some people have sneaked in among you, it seems, who long ago were marked out for this condemnation—ungodly people, who are transforming God's grace into licentiousness, and denying the one and only master, our Lord Jesus the Messiah.

False Teachers

⁵I do want to remind you, even though you know it all well, that when the Lord once and for all delivered his people out of the land of Egypt, he subsequently destroyed those who did not believe. ⁶In the same way, when some of the angels did not keep to their rightful place of authority, but abandoned their own home, he kept them under conditions of darkness and in eternal chains to await the judgment of the great day. ⁷In similar fashion, Sodom, Gomorrah, and the cities round about, which had lived in gross immorality and lusted after unnatural flesh, are set before us as a pattern, undergoing the punishment of endless fire.

⁸However, these people are behaving in the same way! They are dreaming their way into defiling the flesh, rejecting authority, and cursing the glorious ones. ⁹Even Michael

the archangel, when disputing with the devil about the body of Moses, did not presume to lay against him a charge of blasphemy, but simply said, "The Lord rebuke you." 10These people, however, curse anything they don't know. They are like dumb animals; there are some things they understand instinctively—but it is these very things that destroy them. 11A curse on them! They go off in the way of Cain; they give themselves over for money into Balaam's deceitful ways; they are destroyed in Korah's rebellion. 12These are the ones who pollute your love-feasts; they share your table without fear while simply looking after their own needs. They are water-less clouds blown along by the winds. They are fruitless autumn trees, doubly dead and uprooted. 13They are stormy waves out at sea, splashing up their own shameful ways. They are wandering stars, and the deepest everlasting darkness has been kept for them in particular.

14Enoch, the seventh in line from Adam, prophesied about these people. "Look!" he said. "The Lord comes with ten thousand of his holy ones, 15to perform judgment against all, and to charge every human being with all the ungodly ways in which they have done ungodly things, and with every harsh word which ungodly sinners have spoken against him." 16These people are always grumbling and complaining, chasing off after their own desires. From their mouths come arrogant words, buttering people up for the sake of gain.

17But you, my beloved ones, remember the words that were spoken before by the apostles of our Lord Jesus the Messiah. 18"In the last time," they said to you, "there will be scornful people who follow their own ungodly desires. 19These are the people who cause divisions. They are living on the merely human level; they do not have the spirit. 20But you, beloved ones, build yourselves up in your most holy faith. Pray in the holy spirit. 21Keep yourselves in the love of God, as you wait for our Lord Jesus the Messiah to show you the mercy which leads to the life of the age to come.

22With some people who are wavering, you must show mercy. 23Some you must rescue, snatching them from the fire. To others you must show mercy, but with fear, hating even the clothes that have been defiled by the flesh.

Rescued by God's Power

[24]Now to the one who is able to keep you standing upright, and to present you before his glory, undefiled and joyful—[25]to the one and only God, our savior through Jesus the Messiah our Lord, be glory, majesty, power, and authority before all the ages, and now, and to all the ages to come. Amen.

The Revelation of John

1 Revelation of Jesus the Messiah! God gave it to him to show his servants what must soon take place. He signified it by sending a message through his angel to his servant John, ²who, by reporting all he saw, bore witness to the word of God and to the testimony of Jesus the Messiah. ³God's blessing on the one who reads the words of this prophecy, and on those who hear them and keep what is written in it. The time, you see, is near!

⁴John, to the seven churches in Asia: grace to you and peace from He Who Is and Who Was and Who Is to Come, and from the seven spirits that are before his throne, ⁵and from Jesus the Messiah, the faithful witness, the firstborn from the dead, and the ruler of the kings of the earth. Glory to the one who loved us, and freed us from our sins by his blood, ⁶and made us a kingdom, priests to his God and father—glory and power be to him forever and ever. Amen.

⁷Look! He is coming with the clouds, and every eye shall see him; yes, even those who pierced him. All the tribes of the earth shall mourn because of him. Yes! Amen.

⁸"I am the Alpha and the Omega," says the Lord God, Who Is and Who Was and Who Is to Come, the Almighty.

⁹I, John, your brother and your partner in the suffering, the kingdom, and the patient endurance in Jesus, was on the island called Patmos because of the word of God and the testimony of Jesus. ¹⁰I was in the spirit on the Lord's day, and I heard behind me a loud voice like a trumpet. ¹¹"Write down

Look! He Is Coming!

Jesus Revealed

what you see in a book," it said, "and send it to the seven churches: to Ephesus, Smyrna, Pergamum, Thyatira, Sardis, Philadelphia, and Laodicea."

12So I turned to see the voice that was speaking with me. As I turned, I saw seven golden lampstands, 13and in the middle of the lampstands "one like a son of man," wearing a full-length robe and with a golden belt across his chest. 14His head and his hair were white—white like wool, white like snow. His eyes were like a flame of fire, 15his feet were like exquisite brass, refined in a furnace, and his voice was like the sound of many waters. 16He was holding seven stars in his right hand, and a sharp two-edged sword was coming out of his mouth. The sight of him was like the sun when it shines with full power. 17When I saw him, I fell at his feet as though I were dead.

He touched me with his right hand. "Don't be afraid," he said. "I am the first and the last 18and the living one. I was dead, and look! I am alive forever and ever. I have the keys of death and Hades. 19Now write what you see, both the things that already are, and also the things that are going to happen afterward. 20The secret meaning of the seven stars which you saw in my right hand, by the way, and the seven golden lampstands, is this. The seven stars are the angels of the seven churches, and the seven lampstands are the seven churches themselves."

The Letter to Ephesus

2 "Write this to the angel of the church in Ephesus. 'These are the words of the one who holds the seven stars in his right hand, and who walks in among the seven golden lampstands. 2I know what you have done, your hard labor and patience. I know that you cannot tolerate evil people, and that you have tested those who pass themselves off as apostles, but are not, and you have demonstrated them to be frauds. 3You have patience, and you have put up with a great deal because of my name, and you haven't grown weary. 4I do, however, have one thing against you: you have abandoned the love you showed at the beginning. 5So remember the place from which you have fallen. Repent, and do the works you did at the beginning. If not—if you don't repent—I will come and remove your lampstand out of its place. 6You do, though, have this in your favor: you hate what the Nicolaitans are doing, and I hate it

The Seven Churches of Asia

too. ⁷Let anyone who has an ear listen to what the spirit is saying to the churches. The tree of life stands in God's paradise, and I will give to anyone who conquers the right to eat from it.'

⁸"Write this to the angel of the church in Smyrna. 'These are the words of the First and the Last, the one who was dead and came to life. ⁹I know your suffering and poverty (but you are rich!). I know the blasphemy of those self-styled Jews. They are nothing of the kind. They are a satan-synagogue. ¹⁰Don't be afraid of what you are going to suffer. Look: the devil is going to throw some of you into prison so that you may be put to the test. You will have ten days of affliction. Be faithful all the way to death, and I will give you the crown of life. ¹¹Let anyone who has an ear listen to what the spirit is saying to the churches. The second death will not harm the one who conquers.'

¹²"Write this to the angel of the church in Pergamum. 'These are the words of the one who has the sharp two-edged

The Letter to Smyrna

The Letter to Pergamum

sword. ¹³I know where you live—right there where the satan
has his throne! You have clung to my name, and have not denied my faith, even in the days of Antipas, my faithful witness,
who was killed in your midst, in the dwelling-place of the
satan. ¹⁴But I do have a few things against you: you have some
people there who hold the teaching of Balaam, who instructed
Balak to cause the children of Israel to stumble, making them
eat idol-food and indulge in sexual immorality. ¹⁵So, too, you
have some among you who hold the teaching of the Nicolaitans. ¹⁶So: repent! If you don't, I will come to you quickly
and will fight against them with the sword of my mouth. ¹⁷Let
anyone who has an ear listen to what the spirit is saying to the
churches. To anyone who conquers I will give secret manna,
and a white stone, with a new name written on that stone
which nobody knows except the one who receives it.'

**The Letter to
Thyatira**

¹⁸"Write this to the angel of the church in Thyatira. 'These
are the words of the son of God, whose eyes are like flaming
fire and whose feet are like exquisite brass. ¹⁹I know what you
have done: I know your love, your faith, your service, and your
patience. I know that your works have been more impres-
sive recently than they were before. ²⁰But I have something
against you: you tolerate the woman Jezebel, who calls herself
a prophet and teaches my servants (in fact, deceives my servants!) to practice fornication and to eat idol-food. ²¹I gave her
time to repent, but she had no wish to repent of her immorality. ²²Look! I am going to throw her on a bed, and those who
have committed fornication with her will have great distress,
unless they repent of the works into which she has led them.
²³I will utterly slaughter her children, and all the churches
will know that I am the one who searches minds and hearts.
I will give to each of you what your deeds deserve. ²⁴For the
rest of you in Thyatira, those who have not held this teaching,
who haven't discovered the so-called "satanic depths": I'm not
going to put any other pressure on you. ²⁵Just hold on tightly
to what you have until I come. ²⁶To anyone who conquers, who
keeps my works right through to the end, I will give authority
over the nations, ²⁷to rule them with a rod of iron, as when clay
pots get smashed! ²⁸That is the authority I myself received

from my father. What's more, I will give them the morning star. ²⁹Let anyone who has an ear listen to what the spirit says to the churches.'

3 "Write this to the angel of the church in Sardis. 'These are the words of the one who has the seven spirits of God, and the seven stars. I know what you have done. You have the reputation of being alive, but you are dead. ²Wake up! Strengthen the things that remain—the things that are about to die—because I haven't found your works to be complete in the sight of my God. ³So remember how you received the message, how you heard it and kept it—and repent! So if you don't keep awake, I will come like a thief, and you won't know what time I'm coming to you. ⁴You do, however, have a few people in Sardis who haven't allowed their clothes to become dirty and polluted. They will be clothed in white and will walk with me, as they deserve. ⁵Anyone who conquers will be clothed like this in white robes, and I won't blot their name out of the book of life. I will acknowledge their name in the presence of my father and in the presence of his angels. ⁶Let anyone who has an ear listen to what the spirit is saying to the churches.'

The Letter to Sardis

⁷"Write this to the angel of the church in Philadelphia. 'These are the words of the Holy One, the True One, the one who has the key of David, who opens and nobody shuts, who shuts and nobody opens. ⁸I know your works. Look! I have given you an open door, right in front of you, and nobody can shut it, since you have a little power; you have kept my word, and you haven't denied my name. ⁹Look: this is what I will do to the satan-synagogue, who call themselves Jews but who are frauds, nothing of the kind. Take note: this is what I will grant you—that I will make them come and worship before your feet, and they will know that I have loved you. ¹⁰You have kept my word about patience, and so I will keep you from the time of trial that is going to come upon the whole world, to test out all the inhabitants of the earth. ¹¹I am coming quickly! Hold on to what you have, so that nobody takes away your crown. ¹²Anyone who conquers, I will make them a pillar in the temple of my God. They will never go out of it again. I will write on that person the name of my God and the name of the city of

The Letter to Philadelphia

my God, the new Jerusalem, which comes down out of heaven from my God, and my own new name. [13]Let anyone who has an ear listen to what the spirit is saying to the churches.'

[14]"Write this to the angel of the church in Laodicea. 'These are the words of the Amen, the faithful and true witness, the beginning of God's creation. [15]I know your works: you are neither cold nor hot. I wish you were either cold or hot! [16]So, because you are lukewarm, neither cold nor hot, I am going to vomit you out of my mouth. [17]You say, "I'm rich! I've done well! I don't need anything!"—but you don't know that you are miserable, pitiful, poor, blind, and naked. [18]This is my advice to you: buy from me gold refined in the fire—that'll make you rich!—and white clothes to cover yourselves and prevent your shameful nakedness being seen; and also healing ointment to put on your eyes, so that you will be able to see. [19]When people are my friends, I tell them when they're in the wrong, and I punish them for it; so stir up your spirits and repent! [20]Look! I'm standing here, knocking at the door. If anyone hears my voice and opens the door, I will come in to them and eat with them, and they with me. [21]This will be my gift to the one who conquers: I will sit them beside me on my throne, just as I conquered and sat with my father on his throne. [22]Let the one who has an ear listen to what the spirit is saying to the churches.'"

4 After this I looked—and there was a door in heaven, standing open! The voice like a trumpet, which I had heard speaking with me at the beginning, spoke again. "Come up here," it said, "and I will show you what must take place after these things."

[2]At once I was in the spirit. There in heaven stood a throne, and someone was sitting on it. [3]The seated figure had the appearance of a jasper stone or a carnelian, and there was a rainbow around the throne, looking like an emerald. [4]Around the throne were twenty-four thrones, and sitting on the thrones were twenty-four elders, clothed in white robes, and with golden crowns on their heads. [5]Flashes of lightning, rumblings, and thunderclaps were coming from the throne, and in front of the throne seven lampstands, which are the seven spirits of God, were burning with fire. [6a] In front of the throne there was something like a sea of glass, like crystal.

6bIn the middle of the throne, and all around the throne, **Praise to**
were four living creatures, full of eyes in front and behind. **the Creator**
7The first creature was like a lion, the second creature was
like an ox, the third creature had a human face, and the fourth
creature was like a flying eagle. 8Each of the four creatures
had six wings, and they were full of eyes all around and inside.
Day and night they take no rest, as they say,

> "Holy, holy, holy,
> Lord God Almighty,
> Who Was and Who Is and Who Is to Come."

9When the creatures give glory and honor and thanksgiving
to the one who is sitting on the throne, the one who lives forever and ever, 10the twenty-four elders fall down in front of the
one who is sitting on the throne and worship the one who lives
forever and ever. They throw down their crowns in front of the
throne, saying, 11"O Lord our God, you deserve to receive glory
and honor and power, because you created all things; because
of your will they existed and were created."

5 I saw that there was a scroll in the right hand of the one   **The Lion,**
sitting on the throne. The scroll was written on the in-   **the Lamb**
side and the outside, and it was sealed with seven seals.
2I saw a strong angel announcing in a loud voice, "Does anybody deserve to open the scroll, to undo its seals?" 3And nobody in heaven or on the earth or under the earth could open
the scroll or look at it. 4I burst into tears because it seemed
that there was nobody who was worthy to open the scroll or
look inside it. 5One of the elders, however, spoke to me. "Don't
cry," he said. "Look! The lion from the tribe of Judah, the Root
of David, has won the victory! He can open the scroll and its
seven seals."

6Then I saw in the midst of the throne and of the four living
creatures, and in the midst of the elders, a lamb. It was standing there as though it had been slaughtered; it had seven horns
and seven eyes, which are the seven spirits of God sent out into
all the earth. 7The lamb came up and took the scroll from the
right hand of the one who was sitting on the throne.

8When he took the scroll, the four living creatures and the   **Worthy Is**
twenty-four elders fell down in front of the lamb. They each   **the Lamb!**

had a harp, and they each had golden bowls full of incense,
which are the prayers of God's holy people. ⁹They sing a new
song, which goes like this:

> *"You are worthy to take the scroll;*
> *You are worthy to open its seals;*
> *For you were slaughtered and with your own blood*
> *You purchased a people for God,*
> *From every tribe and tongue,*
> *From every people and nation,*
> *¹⁰And made them a kingdom and priests to our God*
> *And they will reign on the earth."*

¹¹As I watched, I heard the voice of many angels around the
throne, the living creatures, and the elders. Their number was
ten thousand times ten thousand, thousands upon thousands,
¹²and they were saying in full voice,

> *"The slaughtered lamb has now deserved*
> *To take the riches and the power,*
> *To take the wisdom, strength, and honor,*
> *To take the glory and the blessing."*

¹³Then I heard every creature in heaven, on the earth,
under the earth, and in the sea, and everything that is in them,
saying,

> *"To the One on the throne and the lamb*
> *Be blessing and honor and glory*
> *And power forever and ever!"*

¹⁴"Amen!" cried the four living creatures. As for the elders,
they fell down and worshipped.

Four Horsemen

6 The next thing I saw was this. When the lamb had
opened one of the seven seals, I heard one of the four
living creatures say in a voice like thunder, "Come!"
²And, as I watched, there was a white horse. Its rider was holding a bow. He was given a crown, and he went off winning vic-
tories, and to win more of them.

³When the lamb opened the second seal, I heard the second
living creature say, "Come!" ⁴And another horse went out,

fiery red this time. Its rider was given permission to take peace away from the earth, so that people would kill one another. He was given a great sword.

5When the lamb opened the third seal, I heard the third living creature say, "Come!" As I watched, there was a black horse. Its rider held a pair of scales in his hand. 6I heard something like a voice coming from the midst of the four living creatures. "A quart of wheat for a denarius!" said the voice. "And three quarts of barley for a denarius! But don't ruin the oil and the wine!"

7When the lamb opened the fourth seal, I heard the voice of the fourth living creature say, "Come!" 8As I looked, there was a pale horse, and its rider's name was Death. Hades followed along behind him. They were given authority over a quarter of the earth, to kill with the sword, and with famine, and with death, and by means of earth's wild animals.

9When the lamb opened the fifth seal, I saw under the altar the souls of those who had been killed because of the word of God and because of the witness which they had borne. 10They shouted at the tops of their voices. "Holy and true Master!" they called. "How much longer are you going to put off giving judgment, and avenging our blood on the earth-dwellers?" 11Each of them was given a white robe, and they were told to rest for a little while yet, until the full number of those to be killed, as they had been, was reached—including both their fellow servants and their kinsfolk.

The Day Is Coming!

12As I looked, he opened the sixth seal. There was a great earthquake, the sun turned black like sackcloth, the whole moon became like blood, 13and the stars were falling from heaven onto the earth as when a fig tree, shaken by a strong wind, drops its late fruit. 14The heaven disappeared like a scroll being rolled up, and every mountain and island was moved out of its place. 15The kings of the earth, the leading courtiers, the generals, the rich, the power brokers, and everyone, slave and free, all hid themselves among the caves and rocks of the mountains. 16"Fall upon us!" they were saying to the mountains and the rocks. "Hide us from the face of the One who sits on the throne, and from the anger of the lamb! 17The great day of their anger has come, and who can stand upright?"

**Sealing God's
People**

7 After this I saw four angels, standing at the four corners of the earth, holding back the four winds of the earth to stop any wind from blowing on earth, or on the sea, or on any tree. ²And I saw another angel coming up from the east, holding the seal of the living God. He shouted out in a loud voice to the four angels who had responsibility for harming the earth and the sea. ³"Don't harm the earth just yet," he shouted, "or the sea, or the trees. Don't do it until we have sealed the servants of our God on their foreheads."

⁴I heard the number of the people who were sealed: it was one hundred and forty-four thousand who were sealed from all the tribes of the children of Israel. ⁵Twelve thousand were sealed from the tribe of Judah, twelve thousand from the tribe of Reuben, twelve thousand from the tribe of Gad, ⁶twelve thousand from the tribe of Asher, twelve thousand from the tribe of Naphtali, twelve thousand from the tribe of Manasseh, ⁷twelve thousand from the tribe of Simeon, twelve thousand from the tribe of Levi, twelve thousand from the tribe of Issachar, ⁸twelve thousand from the tribe of Zebulun, twelve thousand from the tribe of Joseph, and twelve thousand from the tribe of Benjamin. That is the number that were sealed.

**The Great
Rescue**

⁹After this I looked, and lo and behold a huge gathering which nobody could possibly count, from every nation and tribe and people and language. They were standing in front of the throne, and in front of the lamb. They were dressed in white robes, holding palm branches in their hands. ¹⁰They were shouting out at the tops of their voices, "Salvation belongs to our God, to the one who sits on the throne, and to the lamb!" ¹¹All the angels who were standing around the throne and the elders and the four creatures fell down on their faces before the throne and worshipped God. ¹²"Yes! Amen!" they were saying. "Blessing and glory and wisdom and thanks and honor and power and strength be to our God forever and ever! Amen!"

¹³One of the elders spoke to me. "Who are these people dressed all in white?" he asked. "Where have they come from?"

¹⁴"Sir," I replied, "you know!"

"These are the ones," he said, "who have come out of the great suffering. They have washed their clothes and made them white in the blood of the lamb. [15]That is why they are there in front of God's throne, serving him day and night in his temple. The one who sits on the throne will shelter them with his presence. [16]They will never be hungry again, or thirsty again. The sun will not scorch them, nor will any fierce heat. [17]The lamb, who is in the midst of the throne, will be their shepherd. He will lead them to springs of running water, and God will wipe away every tear from their eyes."

8 When the lamb opened the seventh seal, there was silence in heaven, lasting about half an hour. [2]I saw the seven angels who were standing in front of God; they were given seven trumpets. [3]Another angel came and stood before the altar. He was holding a golden censer, and he was given a large quantity of incense so that he could offer it, along with the prayers of all God's holy people, on the golden altar in front of the throne. [4]The smoke of incense, with the prayers of the saints, rose up from the hand of the angel in front of God. [5]Then the angel took the censer, filled it with fire from the altar, and threw it on the earth. There were crashes of thunder, loud rumblings, lightning, and an earthquake.

The Golden Censer

[6]Then the seven angels who had the seven trumpets got ready to blow them. [7]The first angel blew his trumpet, and hail and fire, mixed with blood, were thrown down on the earth. A third of the earth was burned up, a third of the trees were burned up, and so was every blade of green grass. [8]Then the second angel blew his trumpet, and something like a huge mountain, flaming with fire, was thrown into the sea. A third of the sea turned into blood, [9]a third of all living sea creatures died, and a third of the ships were destroyed. [10]Then the third angel blew his trumpet, and a huge star, burning like a torch, fell from the sky, falling on a third of the rivers and on the springs of water. [11]The name of the star is Poisonwood: a third of the waters turned to poison, and many people died because of the waters that had become bitter. [12]Then the fourth angel blew his trumpet, and a third of the sun was struck, and a third of the moon, and a third of the stars, so that a third of their light would be darkened, with a third of the day losing its light and a third of the night as well. [13]Then I looked, and I heard a lone eagle flying in mid-heaven, and

The Plagues Begin

calling out loudly. "Woe, woe, woe to the earth-dwellers," it called, "because of the sound of the other trumpets that the last three angels are going to blow!"

Locust Attack Then the fifth angel blew his trumpet. I saw a star falling from heaven to earth, and it was given the key to the shaft which leads down to the Abyss. ²The shaft of the Abyss was opened, and smoke came out of the pit like the smoke from a great furnace. The sun and the air became dark with the smoke from the pit. ³Then, out of that smoke, there appeared locusts on the earth, and they were given authority like the authority of scorpions on the earth. ⁴They were told not to harm the grass on the earth, nor any plant or tree, but only those people who did not have the seal of God on their foreheads. ⁵They were given instructions not to kill them, but to torture them for five months, and their torture was like the torture inflicted when a scorpion stings someone. ⁶In those days people will look for death, and won't find it. They will long to die, and death will run away from them.

⁷In appearance, the locusts looked like horses prepared for battle. They had what seemed to be crowns of gold on their heads, and their faces were like human faces. ⁸They had hair like women's hair, and their teeth were like lions' teeth. ⁹They had breastplates like iron breastplates, and the sound of their wings was like the noise of many horse-drawn chariots charging into battle. ¹⁰They have tails like scorpions' tails, and stings as well, and their tails have the power to harm people for five months. ¹¹They have as their king the angel of the Abyss, whose name in Hebrew is Abaddon, and whose name in Greek is Apollyon.

¹²The first Woe has come and gone. The next two Woes are on the way after this.

The Fiery Riders ¹³Then the sixth angel blew his trumpet. I heard a lone voice from the four horns of the golden altar in front of God ¹⁴addressing the sixth angel, who had the trumpet.

"Release the four angels," said the voice, "the ones who are tied up by the Great River, the Euphrates." ¹⁵So the four angels were released. They had been prepared for this hour, day, month, and year, so that they would kill a third of the human race. ¹⁶The number of the troops and horsemen was two hundred million. (I heard the number.) ¹⁷As I looked, this is how the horses and their riders appeared. They had breast-plates made of fire, sapphire, and sulphur. Their heads were like lions' heads, and fire, smoke, and brimstone came out of their mouths. ¹⁸One-third of the human race was killed by these three plagues, by the fire, smoke, and sulphur that came out of their mouths. ¹⁹The power of the horses, you see, is in their mouths and their tails, since their tails are like serpents with heads. That is how they do their damage.

²⁰All the other people, the ones who had not been killed in these plagues, did not repent of the things they had made. They did not stop worshipping demons—idols made of gold, silver, bronze, stone, and wood, which cannot see, hear, or walk. ²¹Nor did they repent of their murders, or their magic, or their fornication, or their stealing.

10 Then I saw another strong angel coming down from heaven, dressed in a cloud. Over his head was a rainbow; his face was like the sun, and his feet were like fiery pillars. ²He was holding a small scroll, open, in his hand. Placing his right foot on the sea, and his left on the land, ³he shouted in a loud voice like a lion roaring. When he shouted, the seven thunders answered with their own voices. ⁴When the seven thunders spoke, I was about to write, but I heard a voice from heaven. "Seal up what the seven thunders said," instructed the voice. "Don't write it down."

A Little Scroll

⁵Then the angel whom I had seen standing on the sea and the land raised his right hand toward heaven ⁶and swore an oath by the One who lives forever and ever, who made heaven and what it contains, the earth and what it contains, and the sea and what it contains. This was the oath: that there would be no more time, ⁷but that God's mystery would be completed in the days of the voice of the seventh angel, who was going to blow his trumpet. That is what he had announced to his servants the prophets.

⁸The voice I had heard from heaven spoke to me again. "Go," it said, "and take the open scroll from the hand of the angel who is standing on the sea and on the land." ⁹So I went up to the angel.

"Give me the little scroll," I said.

"Take it," he said to me, "and eat it. It will be bitter in your stomach, but sweet as honey in your mouth." 10So I took the little scroll from the angel's hand, and I ate it. It tasted like sweet honey in my mouth, but when I had eaten it my stomach felt bitter. 11"You must prophesy again," he said to me, "about many peoples, nations, languages, and kingdoms."

Two Witnesses 11 Then a measuring rod like a staff was given to me. "Get up," said a voice, "and measure God's Temple, and the altar, and those who are worshipping in it. 2But leave out the outer court of the temple. Don't measure it. It is given to the nations, and they will trample the holy city for forty-two months. 3I will give my two witnesses the task of prophesying, clothed in sackcloth, for those one thousand two hundred and sixty days. 4These two are the two olive trees, the two lampstands, which stand before the Lord of the earth. 5If anyone wants to harm them, fire comes out of their mouths and devours their enemies. So if anyone wants to harm them, that is how such a person must be killed. 6These two have authority to shut up the sky, so that it will not rain during the days of their prophecy. They have authority over the waters, to turn them into blood, and to strike the earth with any plague, as often as they see fit. 7When they have completed their testimony, the monster that comes up from the Abyss will make war on them, and will defeat and kill them. 8Their bodies will lie in the street of the great city, which is spiritually called Sodom and Egypt, where their Lord was crucified. 9Their bodies will be seen by the peoples, tribes, languages, and nations for three and a half days. They will not allow their bodies to be buried in a tomb. 10The inhabitants of the earth will celebrate over them, and make merry, and send presents to one another, because these two prophets tormented those who live on earth."

11After the three and a half days the spirit of life from God came in to them, and they stood up on their feet, and great fear fell on all who saw them. 12Then they heard a loud voice from heaven. "Come up here!" it said. And they went up to heaven on a cloud, with their enemies looking on. 13At that moment there was a huge earthquake, and a tenth of the city fell, and seven thousand of the people were killed by the earthquake. The rest were very much afraid, and glorified the God of heaven.

¹⁴The second Woe has passed. The third Woe is coming very soon.

¹⁵The seventh angel blew his trumpet, and loud voices were heard from heaven. "Now the kingdom of the world has passed to our Lord and his Messiah," said the voices, "and he will reign forever and ever." ¹⁶The twenty-four elders sitting on their thrones in God's presence fell on their faces and worshipped God.

¹⁷This is what they said:

> "Almighty Lord God, we give you our thanks,
> Who Is and Who Was,
> Because you have taken your power, your great power,
> And begun to reign.
> ¹⁸The nations were raging; your anger came down
> And with it the time for judging the dead
> To give the reward to your servants the prophets,
> The holy ones, too, and the small and the great—
> Those who fear your name.
> It is time to destroy the destroyers of earth."

¹⁹God's temple in heaven was opened, and the ark of his covenant appeared inside his temple. There were flashes of lightning, rumblings, thunderclaps, an earthquake, and heavy hail.

12 Then a great sign appeared in heaven: a woman clothed with the sun, with the moon under her feet, and a crown of twelve stars on her head. ²She was expecting a child, and she cried out in pain, in the agony of giving birth. ³Then another sign appeared in heaven: a great fiery-red dragon with seven heads and ten horns. On its heads were seven coronets, ⁴and its tail swept a third of the stars out of heaven and threw them down to the earth. The dragon stood opposite the woman who was about to give birth, so that he could devour her child when it was born. ⁵She gave birth to a male child, who is going to rule all the nations with a rod of iron. And the child was snatched away to God and to his throne. ⁶The woman, meanwhile, fled into the desert,

where a place has been prepared for her by God, so that she could be looked after there for one thousand two hundred and sixty days.

The Dragon Is Angry

7Then war broke out in heaven, with Michael and his angels fighting against the dragon, and the dragon and his angels fighting back. 8But they could not win, and there was no longer any place for them in heaven. 9So the great dragon was thrown down to the earth—the ancient serpent who is called the devil and the satan, who deceives the whole world. His angels were thrown down with him. 10Then I heard a loud voice in heaven saying, "Now at last has come salvation and power: the kingdom of our God and the authority of his Messiah! The accuser of our family has been thrown down, the one who accuses them before God day and night. 11They conquered him by the blood of the lamb and by the word of their testimony, because they did not love their lives unto death. 12So rejoice, you heavens and all who live there! But woe to the earth and the sea, because the devil has come down to you in great anger, knowing that he only has a short time."

13When the dragon saw that he had been cast down to the earth, he set off in pursuit of the woman who had borne the baby boy. 14The woman, however, was given a pair of wings from a great eagle so that she could fly away from the presence of the serpent into the desert, to the place where she is looked after for a time, two times and half a time. 15The serpent, for its part, spat out of its mouth a jet of water like a river after the woman, to carry her off with the force of the water. 16But the earth helped the woman by opening its mouth and swallowing up the river which the dragon had spat out of his mouth. 17Then the dragon was angry with the woman, and went off to wage war against the rest of her children, those who keep God's commands and the testimony of Jesus. 18And he stood on the sand beside the sea.

A First Monster

13 Then I saw a monster coming up out of the sea. It had ten horns and seven heads. Each of the ten horns was wearing a coronet, and blasphemous names were written on the heads. 2The monster I saw was like a leopard, with a bear's feet and a lion's mouth. And the dragon gave the monster its power and its throne and great authority.

³One of the heads appeared to have been slaughtered and killed, but its fatal wound had been healed. The whole earth was awed and astonished by the monster, ⁴and worshipped the dragon because it had given the monster its authority. They worshipped the monster too. "Who is like the monster?" they were saying. "Who can fight against it?" ⁵And the monster was given a mouth that speaks great, blasphemous words, and was given authority for forty-two months. ⁶It opened its mouth to utter blasphemies against God, to curse his name and his dwelling-place—that is, those who dwell in heaven. ⁷It was granted the right to make war against God's holy people and to defeat them, and it was given authority over every tribe and people and language and nation. ⁸So everyone who lived on earth worshipped it—everyone, that is, whose name has not been written from the foundation of the world in the book of life belonging to the lamb who was slaughtered.

⁹If anyone has ears, let them hear!

¹⁰If anyone is to be taken captive, into captivity they will go. If anyone is to be killed with the sword, with the sword they will be killed. This is a summons for God's holy people to be patient and have faith.

¹¹Then I saw another monster coming up from the earth. It had two horns like those of a lamb, and it spoke like a dragon.

A Second Monster

¹²It acts in the presence of the first monster and with its full authority, and it makes the earth and those who live on it worship the first monster, whose fatal wound had been healed. ¹³It performs great signs, so that it even makes fire come down from heaven on the earth in the sight of people, ¹⁴and it deceives the people who live on earth by the signs which it has been allowed to perform in front of the monster, instructing the earth's inhabitants to make an image of the monster who had the sword-wound but was alive. ¹⁵It was allowed to give breath to the monster's image, so that the monster's image could speak, and it could kill anyone who didn't worship the monster's image. ¹⁶It makes everyone, small and great, rich and poor, free and slaves, receive a sign from it, marked on their right hands and on their foreheads, ¹⁷so that nobody can buy or sell unless they have the mark of the name of the monster or the number of its name.

18This calls for wisdom. Anyone with a good head on their shoulders should work out the monster's number, because it's the number of a human being. Its number is Six Hundred and Sixty-Six.

The Lamb's Elite Warriors

14 As I watched, there was the lamb standing on Mount Zion, and with him were a hundred and forty-four thousand who had his name, and the name of his father, written on their foreheads. 2I heard a voice from heaven, like the sound of many waters, and like the sound of mighty thunder, and the voice I heard was like harpists playing on their harps. 3And they are singing a new song before the throne, and before the four creatures and the elders. Nobody can learn that song except for the hundred and forty-four thousand who have been redeemed from the earth. 4These are the ones who have never polluted themselves with women; they are celibate. They follow the lamb wherever he goes. They have been redeemed from the human race as first fruits for God and the lamb, 5and no lie has been found in their mouths. They are without blemish.

A Call for Endurance

6Then I saw another angel flying in mid-heaven, carrying an eternal gospel to announce to those who live on earth, to every nation and tribe and language and people. 7He spoke with a loud voice, and this is what he said: "Fear God! Give him glory! The time has come for his judgment! Worship the one who made heaven and earth and the sea and the springs of water!"

8He was followed by another angel, and this is what he said: "Babylon the Great has fallen! She has fallen! She is the one who made all the nations drink the wine of the anger that comes upon her fornication."

9They were followed by a third angel, who also spoke in a loud voice: "If anyone worships the monster and its image, or receives its mark on their forehead or their hand, 10that person will drink the wine of God's anger, poured neat into the cup of his anger, and they will be tortured in fire and sulphur before the holy angels and before the lamb. 11The smoke of their torture goes up forever and ever. Those who worship the monster and its image, and those who receive the mark of its name, will have no respite, day or night."

¹²This demands patience from God's holy people, who keep God's commands and the faith of Jesus.

¹³Then I heard a loud voice from heaven saying, "Write this: God's blessing on the dead who from this time onward die in the Lord."

"Yes," says the spirit, "so that they may rest from their works, for the deeds they have done follow after them."

¹⁴Then I looked, and there was a white cloud, and sitting on the cloud one like a son of man. He had a gold crown on his head, and a sharp sickle in his hand. ¹⁵And another angel came out of the temple, shouting in a loud voice to the one who was sitting on the cloud, "It's harvest time! Put in your sickle and reap: the harvest of the earth is ripe!" ¹⁶So the one sitting on the cloud applied his sickle to the earth, and reaped the harvest of the earth.

Reaping the Harvest

¹⁷Then another angel came out of the temple in heaven. He, too, had a sharp sickle. ¹⁸Yet another angel came from the altar; he had authority over fire, and he spoke with a loud voice to the one who had the sharp sickle. "Go to work with your sharp sickle," he said, "and gather the clusters of fruit from the vine of the earth; the grapes are there in ripe bunches!" ¹⁹So the angel went to work with his sickle on the earth, and gathered the fruit from the vine of the earth, and threw it into the great winepress of God's anger. ²⁰The winepress was trodden outside the city, and blood came out of the winepress, as high as a horse's bridle, for about two hundred miles.

15 Then I saw another sign—a great, amazing sight in heaven: seven angels who were bringing the seven last plagues. With them God's anger is completed. ²And I saw what looked like a sea of glass, mixed with fire. There, by that glassy sea, stood the people who had won the victory over the monster and over its image, and over the number of its name. They were holding harps of God, ³and they were singing the song of Moses the servant of God, and the song of the lamb. This is how it went:

Preparing the Final Plagues

> Great and amazing are your works,
> O Lord God, the Almighty One.
> Just and true are your ways,

O king of the nations.
⁴Who will not fear you, Lord,
And glorify your name?
For you alone are holy.
For all nations shall come
And worship before you,
Because your judgments have been revealed.

⁵After this I looked, and the temple of the "tabernacle of witness" was opened in heaven. ⁶The seven angels who had the seven plagues came out of the temple, clothed in clean, shining linen, wearing golden belts across their chests. ⁷Then one of the four living creatures gave the seven angels seven golden bowls filled with the anger of the God who lives forever and ever. ⁸The temple was filled with smoke from the glory of God and his power. Nobody was able to go into the temple until the seven plagues of the seven angels had been completed.

The First Four Plagues

16 Then I heard a loud voice coming from the temple, addressing the seven angels. "Off you go," said the voice, "and pour out on the earth the seven bowls of God's anger." ²So the first one went off and poured out his bowl on the earth, and foul, painful sores came on the people who had the mark of the monster, and those who worshipped its image. ³The second one poured his bowl on the sea, and it turned into blood like that from a corpse. Every living thing in the sea died. ⁴The third one poured his bowl on the rivers and the springs of water, and they turned into blood. ⁵Then I heard the angel of the waters saying,

"You are the One Who Is and Who Was,
You are the Holy One, and you are just!
You have passed the righteous sentence:
⁶They spilled the blood of saints and prophets
And you have given them blood to drink.
They deserve it."

⁷And I heard the altar respond, "Yes, Lord God Almighty, your judgments are true and just."

⁸Then the fourth angel poured his bowl upon the sun, and it was allowed to burn people with its fire. ⁹People were burned

up by its great heat, and they cursed the name of the God who had authority over these plagues. They did not repent or give him glory.

Then the fifth angel poured his bowl upon the throne of the monster. Its kingdom was plunged into darkness, and people chewed their tongues because of the pain [11]and cursed the God of heaven because of their agonies and their terrible sores. They did not repent of what they had been doing.

The Last Three Plagues

[12]Then the sixth angel poured his bowl on the great river Euphrates, and its water was dried up in order to prepare the way for the kings from the rising sun. [13]Then I saw three unclean spirits coming out of the mouth of the dragon, out of the mouth of the monster, and out of the mouth of the false prophet. They were like frogs. [14]These are the spirits of demons, who perform signs and go off to the kings of the whole earth, to gather them together for war on the great day of Almighty God. [15](Look— I am coming like a thief! God's blessing on the one who stays awake, and on those who keep their robes about them, so as not to go around naked and have their shame exposed!) [16]And they gathered the kings together at the place which in Hebrew is called Mount Megiddo.

[17]Then the seventh angel poured his bowl on the air, and a loud voice came out of the temple from the throne. "It is done!" said the voice. [18]And there were lightnings and rumblings, and thunderclaps and a great earthquake, such as there had never been before—no, not such a great earthquake since the time that humans came on the earth. [19]The great city was split into three parts, and the cities of the nations collapsed. Then Babylon the Great was recalled in the presence of God, so that he could give her the cup of the wine of his anger. [20]Every island fled away, and the mountains disappeared. [21]Enormous hailstones, each weighing a hundred pounds, fell from the sky on people. They cursed God because of the plague of the hail, because its plague was terrible.

17 Then one of the seven angels who had the seven bowls came over and spoke to me. "Come with me," he said, "and I will show you the judgment of the great whore who sits on many waters. [2]She is the one with whom the kings of the earth committed fornication; she is the

Babylon the Great

one whose fornication has been the wine that has made all the earth-dwellers drunk."

³So he took me away, in the spirit, to the desert. There I saw a woman sitting on a scarlet monster. It was full of blasphemous names and had seven heads and ten horns. ⁴The woman was wearing purple and scarlet, and was decked out with gold, precious stones, and pearls. In her hand she was holding a golden goblet, full of abominations and the impurities of her fornications. ⁵On her forehead was written a name: "Mystery! Babylon the Great, Mother of Whores and of Earth's Abominations!" ⁶I saw that the woman was drunk with the blood of God's holy people, and with the blood of the witnesses of Jesus. When I saw her, I was very greatly astonished.

⁷"Why are you so astonished?" asked the angel. "I will explain to you the secret of the woman, and of the monster that is carrying her, the one which has the seven heads and the ten horns. ⁸The monster you saw was, and is not, and is due to come up from the Abyss and go to destruction. All the inhabitants of the earth will be amazed—all, that is, whose names are not written in the book of life from the foundation of the world—when they see the monster that was and is not and is to come.

The Monster and the Whore

⁹"This is a moment for a wise and discerning mind. The seven heads are seven hills, on which the woman sits. And there are seven kings; ¹⁰five have fallen, one is still there, and the other has not yet arrived, and when he does come he is destined to remain for only a short time. ¹¹And the monster, which was and is not, he is the eighth king. He is also one of the seven, and he goes to destruction. ¹²The ten horns that you saw are ten kings who have not yet received their kingdom, but will receive their authority as kings with the monster for a single hour. ¹³All of these are of one mind: they give their power and authority to the monster. ¹⁴They will make war with the lamb, and the lamb will conquer them, because he is Lord of lords and King of kings. Those with him are called and chosen and faithful.

¹⁵"As for the waters you saw," he continued, "where the whore was sitting, these are peoples and multitudes and nations and languages. ¹⁶The ten horns you saw, and the monster,

will hate the whore and will make her desolate and naked, and will eat her flesh and then burn her in the fire. [17]God has put it into their hearts to do his will and, with a single purpose, to give their kingdom to the monster, until God's words are completed. [18]The woman which you saw is the great city that has royal dominion over the kings of the earth."

18 After this I saw another angel coming down from heaven with great authority; the earth was flooded with the light of his glory. [2]He shouted out in a strong voice, and this is what he said: "Babylon the Great has fallen! She has fallen! She has become a place for demons to live, a refuge for every unclean spirit, a refuge for every unclean bird, a refuge for every unclean, hateful monster. [3]All the nations drank from the wine of the wrath of her fornication; the kings of the earth committed fornication with her, and the traders of the earth became rich from the power of her luxury."

Babylon's Plagues

[4]Then I heard another voice from heaven, and this is what it said: "Come out of her, my people, so that you don't become embroiled in her sins, and so that you don't receive any of her plagues. [5]Her sins are piled up to the sky, and God has remembered her wickedness. [6]Pay her back as she has paid others; give her double again for all her deeds. Mix her a double dose in her own cup—the cup in which she mixed her poisons. [7]She made herself glorious and lived in luxury; balance that by giving her torture and sorrow! She said in her heart, 'I'm the queen! I'm on the throne! I'm not a widow! I'm never going to be a mourner!' [8]Therefore her plagues will come in a single day—death, mourning, and famine—and she will be burned with fire, because God the Lord, who judges her, is strong."

[9]The kings of the earth who committed fornication with her and shared her luxury will weep and lament over her when they see the smoke from her fire. [10]They will stand far off, fearful of her tortures. "Alas, alas," they will say, "the great city! Babylon the powerful city! Your judgment has come in a single hour." [11]The merchants of the earth will weep and mourn over her, because nobody will buy their cargo anymore, [12]their cargo of gold and silver, of precious stones and pearls, fine linen and purple, silk and scarlet, all the sweet-smelling wood,

Babylon's Judgment

 b

carved ivory, vessels of expensive wood, brass, iron, marble, [13]cinnamon, Oriental spice, incense, myrrh, frankincense, wine, olive oil, fine flour, wheat, cattle, sheep, horses, chariots, and bodies . . . yes, human lives.

[14]All the fruit for which you longed has gone from you; all your luxuries and sparkling objects have been destroyed; you won't find them anymore. [15]The merchants who sold these things, and who made themselves rich from her, will stand a long way off for fear of her tortures. They will weep and mourn [16]and say, "Alas, alas! The great city! It was clothed in fine linen, purple and scarlet, decked out in gold, precious stones, and pearls—[17]but in a single hour such great wealth has been destroyed!"

All the master mariners, all those who ply their ships to and fro, all sailors, and all who do business on the sea, stood a long way off [18]and shouted out when they saw the smoke of her fire. "Who is like the great city?" they said. [19]They threw dust on their heads and shouted out, weeping and mourning. "Alas, alas," they said, "the great city! Everyone who had ships on the sea could get rich from her wealth, but in a single hour she has become a desert."

[20]Celebrate over her, heaven, and you holy ones, apostles and prophets, because God has passed against her the sentence she passed against you.

[21]Then a strong angel picked up a rock like a huge millstone and hurled it into the sea, with these words: "Babylon the great city will be thrown down like that with a splash, and will never be seen again! [22]Never again will people hear the sound of harps, musicians, flute players and trumpeters in you. Never again will there be any skilled workmen plying their trade in you. Never again will people hear the sound of the mill in you. [23]Never again will anyone see the light of a lamp in you. Never again will anyone hear the voice of bridegroom and bride in you. Your merchants were the mighty ones of the earth; all the nations were deceived by your magic."

[24]In her has been found the blood of prophets and God's holy ones, and all those who have been slaughtered on the earth.

19

After this I heard something like a loud voice coming from a huge crowd in heaven. "Alleluia!" they were saying. "Salvation and glory and power belong to our God! 2His judgments are true and just! He has judged the great whore who corrupted the earth with her fornication, and he has avenged the blood of his servants for which she was responsible." 3Once more they said, "Alleluia! The smoke from her goes up forever and ever."

4Then the twenty-four elders and the four creatures fell down and worshipped God who is seated on the throne. "Amen!" they said. "Alleluia!" 5And a voice came from the throne: "Give praise to our God, all you his servants, and you who fear him, both small and great." 6Then I heard something like the sound of a great crowd, like the sound of many waters, and like the sound of strong thunder, saying, "Alleluia! The Lord our God, the Almighty, has become king! 7Let us celebrate and rejoice and give him the glory, because the marriage of the lamb has come, and his bride has prepared herself. 8She has been given shining, pure linen to wear." (The linen is the righteous deeds of God's holy people.)

9"Write this," he said to me. "God's blessing on those who are called to the marriage supper of the lamb." And he added, "These words are the true words of God." 10I fell down at his feet to worship him, but he said to me, "Look! Don't do that! I am a fellow servant with you, and with your brothers and sisters who hold on to the testimony of Jesus. Worship God!" (The testimony of Jesus, you see, is the spirit of prophecy.)

11Then I saw heaven opened, and there was a white horse. The one who was sitting on it is called Faithful and True, and he judges and makes war justly. 12His eyes are like a flaming fire, and there are many coronets on his head. He has a name written there which nobody knows except himself. 13He is clothed in a robe dipped in blood, and he is called by the name God's Word. 14The armies of heaven follow him on white horses, all wearing shining, pure linen. 15A sharp two-edged sword is coming out of his mouth, so that with it he can strike down the nations. He will rule them with a rod of iron, and he will tread the winepress of the wine of the anger of the wrath of Almighty God. ¹⁶On his robe, and on his thigh, is written a name: King of kings, and Lord of lords.

¹⁷Then I saw a single angel standing in the sun, and shouting in a loud voice, calling to all the birds that fly in mid-heaven: "Come here! Gather round! This is God's great feast! ¹⁸Come and eat the flesh of kings, and the flesh of generals, the flesh of the strong, the flesh of horses and their riders, the flesh of all people, free and slave, small and great!" ¹⁹And I saw the monster and the kings of the earth and their armies gathered for war with the one who sits on the horse and with his army. ²⁰And the monster was captured, and with it the false prophet who had performed the signs in its presence, with which it had deceived those who received the monster's mark and those who worshipped its image. The two of them were thrown alive into the lake of fire which burns with sulphur. ²¹All the rest were killed by the sword which came out of the mouth of the one who was sitting on the horse. All the birds feasted on their flesh.

Reigning for a Thousand Years

20 Then I saw an angel coming down from heaven. In his hand he held the key to the Abyss, and a large chain. ²He grabbed hold of the dragon, the ancient serpent, who is the devil and the satan. He tied him up for a thousand years, ³threw him into the Abyss, and locked and sealed it over him, so that he wouldn't be able to deceive the nations anymore, until the thousand years were complete. After that he must be let out for a short time.

⁴Then I saw thrones, with people sitting on them, who were given authority to judge. And I saw the souls of those who had had their heads cut off because they had borne witness to Jesus, and because of the word of God; and also those who had not worshipped the monster or its image, and had not received the mark on their foreheads or their hands. They came to life, and reigned with the Messiah for a thousand years. ⁵The rest of the dead did not come back to life until the thousand years were complete. This is the first resurrection. ⁶Blessed and holy is the one who has a share in the first resurrection! The second death has no power over them. They will be priests to God and the Messiah, and they will reign with him for a thousand years.

7When the thousand years are complete, the satan will be released from his prison. 8Out he will come to deceive the nations at the four corners of the earth, Gog and Magog. He will summon them for battle, a throng like the sand of the sea in number. 9They came up over the full width of the earth, and closed in on the place where God's holy people are encamped, and the beloved city. Then fire came down from heaven and burned them up. 10And the devil who had deceived them was thrown into the lake of fire and sulphur where the monster and the false prophet had already been thrown. They will be tortured day and night forever and ever.

11Then I saw a large white throne, and the one who was sitting on it. Earth and heaven fled away from his presence, and there was no room left for them. 12Then I saw the dead, great and small, standing in front of the throne. Books were opened; and another book was opened, which is the book of life. The dead were judged on the basis of what was written in the books, in accordance with what they had done. 13The sea gave back the dead that were in it; Death and Hades gave back the dead that were in them; and each was judged in accordance with what they had done. 14Then Death and Hades were thrown into the lake of fire. This is the second death, the lake of fire. 15And if anyone was not found written in the book of life, they were thrown into the lake of fire.

Final Judgment

21 Then I saw a new heaven and a new earth. The first heaven and the first earth had passed away, and there was no longer any sea. 2And I saw the holy city, the new Jerusalem, coming down out of heaven, from God, prepared like a bride dressed up for her husband. 3I heard a loud voice from the throne, and this is what it said: "Look! God has come to dwell with humans! He will dwell with them, and they will be his people, and God himself will be with them and will be their God. 4He will wipe away every tear from their eyes. There will be no more death or mourning or weeping or pain anymore, since the first things have passed away."

New Heaven, New Earth

5The one who sat on the throne said, "Look, I am making all things new." And he said, "Write, because these words are faithful and true."

⁶Then he said to me, "It is done! I am the Alpha and the Omega, the beginning and the end. I will freely give water to the thirsty, water from the spring of the water of life. ⁷The one who conquers will inherit these things. I will be his God and he shall be my son. ⁸But as for cowards, faithless people, the unclean, murderers, fornicators, sorcerers, idolaters, and all liars—their destiny will be in the lake that burns with fire and sulphur, which is the second death."

⁹Then one of the seven angels who had the seven bowls filled with the seven last plagues came over and spoke to me. "Come with me," he said, "and I will show you the bride, the wife of the lamb." ¹⁰Then he took me in the spirit up a great high mountain, and he showed me the holy city, Jerusalem, coming down out of heaven from God. ¹¹It has the glory of God; it is radiant, like the radiance of a rare and precious jewel, like a jasper stone, crystal-clear. ¹²It has a great high wall with twelve gates, and twelve angels at the gates, and names inscribed on the gates, which are the names of the twelve tribes of the children of Israel. ¹³There are three gates coming in from the east, three gates from the north, three gates from the south, and three gates from the west. ¹⁴And the wall of the city has twelve foundation-stones, and on them are written the twelve names of the twelve apostles of the lamb.

¹⁵The one who was talking with me had a golden measuring-rod, so that he could measure the city, its gates, and its wall. ¹⁶The city stands foursquare, with the same length and breadth. He measured the city with his rod: it was twelve thousand stadia (that is, fifteen hundred miles), with the length, the breadth, and the height being equal. ¹⁷Then he measured its wall, and it was one hundred and forty-four cubits in terms of human measurement (which was what the angel was using). ¹⁸The material of which the wall is built is jasper, and the city itself is pure gold, like pure glass. ¹⁹The foundations of the city wall are decorated with every kind of precious stone: the first foundation is jasper, the second sapphire, the third agate, the fourth emerald, ²⁰the fifth onyx, the sixth carnelian, the seventh chrysolite, the eighth beryl, the ninth topaz, the tenth chrysoprase, the eleventh jacinth, the twelfth amethyst. ²¹The twelve gates are twelve pearls, with

each gate consisting of a single pearl. The street of the city is pure gold, clear as glass.

²²I saw no temple in the city, because the Lord God the Almighty is its temple, together with the lamb. ²³And the city has no need of sun or moon to shine on it, for the glory of God gives it light, and its lamp is the lamb. ²⁴The nations will walk in its light, and the kings of the earth will bring their glory into it. ²⁵Its gates will never be shut by day, for there will be no night there. ²⁶They will bring the glory and the honor of the nations into it. ²⁷Nothing that has not been made holy will ever come into it, nor will anyone who practices abomination or who tells lies, but only those who are written in the lamb's book of life.

God and the Lamb Are There

22 Then he showed me the river of the water of life. It was sparkling like crystal, and flowing from the throne of God and of the lamb ²through the middle of the street of the city. On either bank of the river was growing the tree of life. It produces twelve kinds of fruit, bearing this fruit every month; and the leaves of the tree are for the healing of the nations. ³Nothing accursed is there anymore. Rather, the throne of God and of the lamb are in the city, and his servants will worship him; ⁴they will see his face, and his name will be on their foreheads. ⁵There will be no more night, and they will not need the light of a lamp or the light of the sun, because the Lord God will shine on them; and they will reign forever and ever.

⁶"These words," he said to me, "are trustworthy and true. The Lord, the God of the spirits of the prophets, has sent his angel to show his servants what must soon take place. ⁷Look, I am coming soon. God's blessing on the one who keeps the words of the prophecy of this book."

"I Am Coming Soon!"

⁸I, John, am the one who heard and saw these things. And when I heard them and saw them, I fell down to worship before the feet of the angel who showed them to me. ⁹"Look! Don't do that!" he said to me. "I am a fellow servant with you, and with the other members of your prophetic family, and with those who keep the words of this book. Worship God!

¹⁰"Don't seal up the words of the prophecy of this book," he added. "The time is near, you see. ¹¹Let the unjust go on being

unjust, and the filthy go on being filthy—and let the just go on doing justice, and let the holy still be holy.

¹²"Look! I am coming soon. I will bring my reward with me, and I will pay everyone back according to what they have done. ¹³I am the Alpha and the Omega, the first and the last, the beginning and the end."

¹⁴God's blessing on those who wash their clothes, so that they may have the right to eat from the tree of life and may enter the city by its gates. ¹⁵But the dogs, the sorcerers, the fornicators, the murderers, the idolaters, and everyone who loves to invent lies—they will all be outside.

¹⁶"I, Jesus, have sent my angel to give you this testimony for the churches. I am David's root and offspring; I am the bright morning star."

¹⁷The spirit and the bride say, "Come!" And let anyone who hears say, "Come!" Let the thirsty come; let anyone who wants the water of life take it freely.

¹⁸I testify to everyone who hears the words of the prophecy of this book: if anyone adds to them, God will add to that person the plagues that are written in this book. ¹⁹And if anyone takes away from the words of the book of this prophecy, God will take away that person's share in the tree of life, and in the holy city, which are described in this book.

²⁰The one who gives this testimony says, "Yes, I am coming soon!"

Amen! Come, Lord Jesus.

²¹The grace of the Lord Jesus be with you all.